edited by ROBERT L. PFALTZGRAFF, JR.
University of Pennsylvania

Politics and the International System

J. B. Lippincott Company
Philadelphia   New York   Toronto

Preface

M ANY WRITERS, classical and contemporary, have contributed both to the development of International Relations as a discipline and the study of international phenomena. In the belief that access to a multiplicity of writings is essential to an appreciation of International Relations as a field of study and an understanding of international phenomena, the editor has prepared this volume, which brings together selections from some of the most important writings on International Relations and closely related fields.

Included are selections on the nature and scope of international relations, as well as major theory-building efforts from utopianism and realism to systems frameworks and theories of integration at the international level. Moreover, the volume contains selections on nationalism in both its Western and non-Western settings, the nature of power and demand—response relationships, theories of conflict and contemporary military strategy, transnational images and national character, diplomacy, disarmament and arms control, balance of power and world government.

The editor has attempted to ensure that selections are sufficiently concise to enable the reader to be exposed to the principal themes of many authors, and long enough to give the student more than a cursory treatment of the ideas under consideration. In introductions to each section, the editor makes an effort to relate major themes contained in readings, to show relationships between materials presented in separate sections, and to place the readings in an overall framework for the study of the international system. Wherever possible, the editor has sought to include readings which contain alternative, or opposing, points of view. This volume is designed to be used either as a companion to textual materials or as the principal source of assigned readings.

The editor is indebted to the Work-Study Program of the University of Pennsylvania for financial support to Mr. James L. Deghand, a graduate student, who assisted in the collection of materials for inclusion in this volume. The editor expresses gratitude to those authors whose writings are included for permission to reprint selections in this volume.

Finally, he is indebted to students who have provided the opportunity for fruitful intellectual exchange and a classroom learning experience for which many selections in this volume have been selected, and from which others have emerged. To them this book is dedicated.

September 16, 1968   ROBERT L. PFALTZGRAFF, JR.
Philadelphia, Pennsylvania

Contents

Politics and the International System

Part I

International Relations as a Discipline

WHY, IT may appropriately be asked, should International Relations be studied as a separate field? It is, in fact, a relatively new field of study, for not until the period between the two world wars did American universities and colleges offer courses in International Relations. Today far greater emphasis is placed upon the study of International Relations in the United States than elsewhere in the world, even in western Europe.

To focus upon the study of International Relations is to assume the existence of a distinctive series of relationships or processes. At the very least, international relations differ from other relations because they take place across the frontiers of the national political units into which the world is divided. According to Quincy Wright, International Relations designates the "relations between groups of major importance in the life of the world at any period of history, in particular those of territorially organized nation-states." According to Stanley Hoffmann, International Relations is "concerned with the factors and the activities which affect the external policies and the power of the basic units into which the world is divided." Broadly conceived, International Relations includes all types of transactions between governments and between peoples, from the sending of letters to a recipient in another country to the exchange of gunfire between the military forces of two countries.

Thus defined, the study of International Relations presents formidable problems for the would-be student. He would need first to have acquired extensive training in a variety of other disciplines, including political science, history, and economics, as well as psychology, anthropology, and sociology.

1

Although the term, International Relations, remains in vogue, the focus of international studies generally is narrower than that set forth above. In fact, students of politics have usually bracketed for study only a part of this vast field, and have termed it International Politics. Largely, but not exclusively, the focus of International Politics is upon relations between the governments of the individual national units of the world. The student of International Politics is primarily concerned with interaction between governments. He is interested in relations between peoples living in different countries only to the extent that they affect interaction between their governments. Moreover, he has as a central concern the study of demand-response relationships, or influence relationships. Nation-state "A" makes a demand upon nation-state "B," which in turn may respond with another demand, this time on nation-state "A." According to Wright, International Politics is the "art of influencing, manipulating, or controlling major groups in the world so as to advance the purpose of some against the opposition of others." Demand-response or influence relationships may take many forms. They include the efforts of a nation to mold the behavior of a long-term trusted ally. They include the attempts of one nation to prevent an opponent from taking undesirable action. In short, demand-response or influence relationships, which are the object of study, may exhibit conflict or collaboration.

In the aftermath of World War I, International Relations emerged as a distinctive field of study in response to a perceived need to develop a greater understanding of the causes of conflict and to create institutions and norms to ensure a more peaceful world. In this period, E. H. Carr suggests, International Relations was ". . . in that initial stage in which wishing prevails over thinking, generalization over observation, and in which little attempt is made at a critical analysis of existing facts or available means." Carr notes that students in the field then devoted themselves essentially to the development of schemes for world order and to the study of international law and organization.

Initially, the study of International Relations was dominated by a school of thought called utopianism. According to utopian thought, man was improvable through education; enlightened peoples ruled by representative governments would choose peace rather than war. Utopianism contained the proposition that, with the growth of nationalism, the prospects for a more peaceful world might be enhanced. If peoples were given the right to national self-determination, they might cast off oppressive regimes in favor of representative governments. Erroneously, it was believed that nationalism would produce democracy. Utopianism established norms, or standards of conduct, to which political practice was expected to conform. Among students of International Relations after World War II there was a feeling of great optimism about the potential for changing the behavior of man from conflict to collaboration at the international level.

Events of the 1930's contributed to the growth of dissatisfaction with the essentially normative utopian approach to the study of International Relations. Contrary to earlier expectations, nationalism did not always lead to political systems in which both leaders and population had an abiding interest in peace. Certain powers had foreign policy objectives which were incompatible with, and took precedence over, the preservation of international peace. Men were slow to alter their behavior to conform to the standards set forth in such documents as the League of Nations Covenant.

General dissatisfaction with the utopian approach, together with the emigration to the United States of central European students of International Relations, led to the emergence of realism as an approach to the field. In several ways, the realist differed fundamentally from the utopian. Realism emphasized that man was not only evil, but essentially unchanging and unchangeable in nature. Therefore, international relations were characterized more by a clash, rather than a harmony, of interests among leading members of the international system. Nations strove to maximize national power and to achieve and preserve the national interest. Not unlike Machiavelli, realist writings in International Relations contained the idea that the statesman *qua* statesman has standards of conduct different from those of the private citizen. The statesman does what he must to preserve the national interest, to ensure the survival of the nation.

If man is essentially evil, unchanging, and unchangeable, it is not possible to expect world order to be derived from the establishment of standards of international conduct which do not conform to existing behavioral patterns. Through the study of history, the realist purported to have ascertained the prevalent patterns of behavior of the international system. In contrast to utopianism, realists held that theory derived from political practice. The observation of political practice led the realist to believe that the prospects for a peaceful world based upon international organization were slim indeed. At best, nations could be restrained by balancing them with other nations. For the realist, the balance of power became the principal device for the management of power.

In the study of International Relations the utopian-realist controversy has been superseded by what is known as the traditional-behavioralist controversy. Especially within the past decade in the United States, as Hedley Bull notes with disapproval, "the scientific approach, founded on the idea that propositions are based either upon logical or mathematical proof, or upon strict, empirical procedures of verification, has progressed from being a fringe activity in the academic study of International Relations to almost becoming the orthodox methodology of the subject."

As the proponent of a more scientific approach, Morton Kaplan stresses the need for conceptual precision and the building of empirically based theories of international relations. Rather than emphasizing the accumulation of facts about seemingly unique events, the advocate of a more scientific study of politics is preoccupied with the development of generalizations derived from the comparative analysis of data about many events, such as wars, revolutions, alliances, and political integration. In general, the student who espouses the scientific study of politics holds that much of the phenomena under observation can be quantified and, furthermore, that it is possible to discern patterns of similarity in the phenomena under examination, and conceivably even to develop theories of political behavior with predictive power. The proponent of the scientific study of politics, as in the case of Kaplan, develops models which consist of hypotheses about relationships among variables. As Kaplan suggests, models provide criteria on the basis of which the student "can pick and choose from among the infinite reservoir of facts available to him. These initial hypotheses indicate the areas of facts which have the greatest importance for this type of investigation, presumably if the hypotheses are wrong, this will become reasonably evident in the course of attempting to use them." Thus to Kaplan, models in international relations provide a guide to research.

Surveying not only his own work but also the writings of other proponents of a scientific study of International Relations, Kaplan suggests that traditionalists, although they have sometimes criticized "those using the scientific method of neglecting Aristotle's dictum to use those methods appropriate to the subject matter," have themselves been *insensitive* to such problems. For example, "traditional balance of power theory is asserted to apply regardless of the number and kinds of states, variations in motivations, and so forth." Moreover, traditional literature about international relations contains many implicit assumptions about *motivation* and the relationship among variables—important assumptions which have often been neither clearly stated nor subjected to rigorous examination. Although traditionalists have faulted the proponents of a scientific approach for their alleged neglect of history, traditional writers, Kaplan contends, have largely confined themselves either to "problems of diplomatic history that are unrelated to their generalizations about international politics" or to "more specialized problems that are idiosyncratic." In short, traditionalists are said to have lacked either an articulated theoretical structure, or model, or the methodologies appropriate to finding answers to the questions of importance to international relations.

In contrast to Kaplan's sanguine view about the potential inherent in a scientific study of International Relations, Hedley Bull believes that the behavioral approach has contributed little to international relations theory, and since it is encroaching upon and displacing the classical approach, it is "positively harmful." Bull contends that the practitioners of a scientific approach are not likely to advance greatly the state of knowledge because of the nature of the data with which they deal. It is asserted that the emphasis upon quantification will exclude from study many important problems for which quantifiable data are either not available or irrelevant. In contrast to the proponents of a scientific approach, the traditionalist often argues that political events are unique; therefore, it is not possible, as the behavioralist would like, to find patterns of similarity between discrete events and situations.

Whatever the respective merits of the contending factions within the discipline, International Relations is becoming more empirically based. The disputes which divide students of International Relations are not likely to subside until one approach or another clearly demonstrates its worth in advancing dramatically the frontier of knowledge. Even before that time, however, if the history of the development of International Relations is instructive, other disputes will arise among scholars whose objective is to advance knowledge about the international activity of nation-states.

SECTION ONE: Origins and Scope

1. THE MEANING OF INTERNATIONAL RELATIONS

Quincy Wright

THE WORD *international* appears to have been first used by Jeremy Bentham in the latter part of the eighteenth century, although its Latin equivalent *intergentes* was used by Richard Zouche a century earlier. These men used the word to define the branch of law which had been called the law of nations or *jus gentium*, a term of Roman law referring to the principles applied by a Roman official—the *praetor peregrinus*—in cases involving aliens. The concept, therefore, was that of a universal law applicable to persons irrespective of nationality, discovered, however, by observing similarities of practice rather than by reasoning from generally accepted principles, as was the case with the *jus naturale* or natural law. As the concept of sovereignty developed in the sixteenth century and came to be applied to geographically defined societies known as nations in the seventeenth century, it was seen that the Roman law concept of *jus gentium* did not adequately express the developing law between sovereign nations. Consequently, the term *international* served a genuine need in defining the official relations between sovereigns. Perhaps the word *interstate* would have been more accurate because in political science the state came to be the term applied to such societies.

There were relations between nations other than official, legal, and

---

From *The Study of International Relations* by Quincy Wright, pp. 3–8. Copyright 1955, by Appleton-Century-Crofts, Inc. Reprinted by permission of Appleton-Century-Crofts, Division of Meredith Corporation.

QUINCY WRIGHT (1890–   ) Formerly Professor of International Law, University of Virginia; Professor Emeritus of International Law, University of Chicago. His other books include *The Study of War*, (Chicago: University of Chicago Press, 1965); *The Role of International Law in the Elimination of War*, (New York: Oceana Publications, 1961); *International Law and the United Nations*, (New York: Asia Publishing House, 1960).

diplomatic relations. Trade and finance developed international economic relations sometimes official and sometimes unofficial. Activities of missionaries; travel of students, teachers, and tourists; migrations of peoples; and the development of the press, radio, and films developed international cultural relations mostly unofficial, but sometimes supervised or even conducted by governments. Private and public organizations representing groups within, or governments of, many nations were formed, especially since the mid-nineteenth century. Their activities in all aspects of human interest—communication, transportation, commerce, finance, agriculture, labor, health, sports, science, philosophy, education, arbitration, disarmament, peace—established innumerable international social relations and gave birth to the word *internationalism* to suggest both the fact of the increase of international relations of all kinds and the interest of many people in such an increase. The word *internationalism* has been preferred by modern writers because, without denying the existence and autonomy of nations, it recognizes them as parts of a larger whole. It excludes both the excessive standardization and integration of mankind implied by the words *imperialism* and *cosmopolitanism* and the militant insistence upon sovereignty implied by the words *nationalism* and *isolationism*.

The development of internationalism, however, gives rise to two questions: (1) Is it only the nations that are related? (2) Is there a universal community of which numerous groups or even individuals are members?

The words *nation, state, government,* and *people* are sometimes used interchangeably, but each has a distinct connotation. The word *nation* suggests a considerable group of people, united by common culture, values, standards, and political aspirations, usually occupying a definite territory, but not always, as witness the Jewish nation during the Diaspora, and usually enjoying legal sovereignty, but not always, as witness the Scotch nation within Great Britain or the Bohemian nation within the Habsburg Empire.

The word *state* has a legal flavor. It is a term of art in political science referring to political groups that enjoy legal sovereignty, but it is also commonly applied to nonsovereign political groups as the states of the United States or the states of India before independence. A state in the modern sense implies a population occupying a definite territory, subject to a government which other states recognize as having some legal status. The population may be a nation, but not necessarily so, as in the case of such multinational states as the Habsburg, British, and Russian Empires before World War I.

The word *government* refers to the organization which makes and enforces the law of the state, decides and carries out its policy, and conducts its official relations. In absolutisms, the government and the state merge in one man, but in democracies, the state is the entire people legally organized while the government is only that small portion of the people for the time being constituting and operating its organization.

The word *people* has biological and geographical implications with cultural and social overtones making it similar to the word *nation,* but without the element of self-consciousness. Anthropologists use the word *people* as a term of art to designate primitive groups that exhibit a considerable degree of biological, cultural, and often linguistic uniformity and occupy a defined territory even though not politically or socially organized as a group. Use of the word *people* suggests some type of similarity—racial, geographic, cultural, linguistic, political, or social— among the individuals who compose it, but without definite specification of a particular type of similarity. The United States Constitution was said to have been made by "we the people of the United States" while the United Nations Charter was said to have been made by "we the peoples of the United Nations," thus suggesting that it was easier to think of all the individuals of the United States as a "people" than to think of all the individuals of the world as a single "people." There was, however, a vigorous debate during the San Francisco Conference in which some urged that the word *people* be used in the singular in the Preamble of the Charter.

It is clear that international relations is intended to include not only relations between nations, but also relations between states, governments, and peoples. It does, however, ordinarily refer only to relations between nations, states, governments, and peoples which are *sovereign.* That term, however, presents new difficulties. The word is not static. There are entities like Massachusetts, Geneva, Bavaria, Hyderabad, the six nations of the Iroquois, Tunis, Algeria, and Scotland, which once were, but are no longer, entirely sovereign. And there are entities like Israel, Egypt, Ukraine, Iceland, Ireland, Pakistan, Jordan, Burma, Philippine Islands, Canada, Indochina, and Korea, which have recently become, or are in process of becoming, sovereign, or have certain aspects of sovereignty. Clearly international relations includes relations between many entities of uncertain sovereignty. As a subject of study it is not limited by the legal formalism which alone could at any moment precisely define what entities are sovereign and what are not.

It may be suggested that international relations, even if it abandoned the qualification of *sovereign* for the entities which it relates, must insist on the qualifications *political* and *territorial.* It is said to be concerned only with the relations among *political* communities occupying definite *territories.* The relations of Virginia and Pennsylvania may be international relations (certainly they were during the Battle of Gettysburg), but the relations of the United Mine Workers of America and coal mining companies seem not to be, even though both are large groups exercising considerable power imperfectly controlled by the laws of the United States to which both are nominally subject. But doubt arises whether even this limitation is always applicable. The United Nations makes agreements with the Specialized Agencies. The International Labor Organization has dealt with the World Federation of Trade Unions. UNESCO deals with numerous international, cultural, educational, and scientific organizations which are unofficial. Many *nongovernmental organizations* have a recognized status in relation to the United Nations. To the sociologist the difference between the co-operation, competition, bargaining, and fighting of industrial groups is in the same class as the co-operation, competition, bargaining, and fighting of states. Thus, for purposes of scientific treatment, it seems that international relations includes the relations of all groups exercising some degree of independent power or initiative. While it may be that the central interest in international relations today is the relation between sovereign nations, in the Middle Ages the central interest was in the relations of Pope and Emperor and in antiquity in the relations between cities.

Of the future one speaks with diffidence. Relations between great regions—the Atlantic community, the Soviet bloc, the Commonwealth—each composed of many nations, many states, many governments, and many peoples may be important. Perhaps the relations between universal parties—Communists, Democrats, Catholics, Moslems, Zionists—will be of increasing importance, or relations between universal organizations of labor, of agriculture, and of commerce. As once, in the United States, relations of North, South, and West were of major significance, so today relations of agriculture, labor, and capital are of equal or of greater importance. It has been said that the growth of national parties crossing sectional lines and the development of rivalries among them, superseding in importance sectional rivalries, accounts for the survival of the United States.

We must, therefore, answer our first question negatively. It is not only the nations which *international relations* seeks to relate. Varied types of groups—nations, states, governments, peoples, regions, alliances, confederations, international organizations, even industrial organizations, cultural organizations, religious organizations—must be dealt with in the study of international relations, if the treatment is to be realistic.

With this wide concept of the subject, we come to our second question. Should not our subject be renamed *world affairs,* or perhaps *cosmopolitanism,* with such divisions as *world economy, world politics, world culture, world organization,* and *world law?* Is not the subject matter of *international relations* really the history, organization, law, economy, culture, and processes of the world community? Should we not conceive of the human race as a community which, while divided into numerous geographic, functional, cultural, racial, political, economic, and other subgroups, is becoming integrated into a society with the progress of technology and the growth of population bringing the members of all subgroups into closer and closer contact with one another?

The adjective *world* certainly rivals the adjective *international* in textbooks and treatises on the subject. It suffers, however, from the objection that there are *international relations* which are not *world relations* as for instance Anglo-American relations, Latin American relations, relations among the Arab countries, and so forth. Until recently *international relations* generally concerned diplomatic or military relations between two states. The word *world* also fails to indicate the dominant problems dealt with in the subject, that is, the relations between the major groups. The phenomena of national, regional, functional, and political groups in rivalry with one another is likely to dominate the life of mankind even if the world shrinks much more than it has today, and even if the national sovereign state becomes less important. The divergencies of interest and policy inherent in climatic and geographical differences, varied resources, differences of culture and political tradition, assure that mankind will not in any foreseeable future be reduced to a uniform mass.

Cosmopolitanism, envisaged as an ideal by the Stoics of Rome and the Deists of the Enlightenment, failed to take adequate account of the factors making for a differentiation of mankind into groups with different objectives and often in opposition to one another. For this reason, as has been noted, modern writers like Jeremy Bentham, Nicholas Murray Butler, Sir Alfred Zimmern, and Inazo Nitobe have preferred the word *international*.

While recognizing that the term *international relations* is too narrow—perhaps *relations between powerful groups* would be technically better—it seems advisable to accept predominant usage. The term *international relations* will therefore be used as the subject of study, dividing it into such special studies as *international politics, international law, international organization, international economics, international education, international ethics*, and the *psychology and sociology of international relations*. The term will, however, also be used to include such studies as world history, political geography, political demography and technology which have a *world* rather than an *international* orientation. These studies are clearly fundamental to the understanding of *international relations*.

Before leaving the subject of terminology, reference should be made to the frequent use of the adjective *foreign* in preference to either *world* or *international* relations. Foreign relations, foreign affairs, foreign policy, foreign trade, are words of common discourse. Clearly the adjective *foreign* implies the point of view of one nation and thus is hardly suitable for use in a discipline or study designed to be of universal validity and understanding. The use of the word, however, raises the question whether a discipline of *international relations* is possible. It has been suggested that the conditions, material and ideological, of each nation are so peculiar that the *foreign relations* of each country must be studied as a unique discipline. As the American lawyer studies American law and can learn little useful to his professional activity from the study of French or Japanese law, so it is said that the American statesman or citizen should confine his study to *American foreign relations*. However, there are general disciplines of *jurisprudence, comparative law,* and *sociology of law,* useful to lawyers of all countries. The thesis is accepted in this book, as it has been in general practice, that general disciplines exist in the field of *international relations*. These disciplines have proved useful to statesmen and citizens of all countries and their synthesis is at least conceivable.

We will, therefore, accept the term *international relations* to designate the relations between groups of major importance in the life of the world at any period of history, and particularly relations among territorially organized nation states which today are of such importance. We will also use the term to designate the studies or disciplines describing, explaining, evaluating, or assisting in the conduct of those relations.

2. INTERNATIONAL RELATIONS AS A DISCIPLINE

Stanley Hoffmann

A. COMMENTARY

IN HIS BOOK, *The Study of International Relations,* Quincy Wright remarks that "at the least a discipline implies consciousness by the writers that there is a subject with some sort of unity," [1] even though

From *Contemporary Theory in International Relations,* edited by Stanley Hoffmann, pp. 1–7, © 1960. Reprinted by permission of Prentice-Hall, Inc., Englewood Cliffs, New Jersey.

STANLEY HOFFMANN (1928–   ) Professor of Government, Research Associate, Center of International Affairs, Harvard University. His other books include *The State of War: Essays on the Theory and Practice of International Politics,* (New York: Praeger, 1965); *In Search of France,* (Cambridge: Harvard University Press, 1963), co-author.

[1] Quincy Wright, *The Study of International Relations,* New York 1957, p. 23.

disagreement and uncertainty might exist about the criterion, the limits, and the methods of the discipline. I think that it is possible to consider international relations as a largely autonomous field within the sprawling and loose science of politics. This is precisely the reason why there is a great need for theory.

THE CASE FOR AN AUTONOMOUS DISCIPLINE

Arguments about the degree of autonomy of international relations, both as an area of human activity and as an intellectual discipline, can go on forever. No one will argue that the field can be isolated, or that the problems asked by political science and political philosophy in general are not relevant here too. However, for those who are interested in trying to develop the discipline in the same way in which political science has been growing for two thousand years, and sociology during the last century, the two following points should be decisive.

First, the field *can* be sufficiently distinguished for analytical purposes. International relations owe their character to the fact that the milieu in which they take place is a decentralized one. It may be easy to exaggerate the degree to which, within a nation, the supreme political authority effectively controls the lesser centers of power; nevertheless such an authority exists. This is not the case in the international sphere: international relations owe their distinctive character to the fact that power has been fragmented into competing or independent groups throughout the world's history. The nature of the basic units has changed; what has not disappeared is the coexistence of multiple units; no empire has ever stretched across the whole world. Also, past and present empires, which do indeed possess at their center a supreme authority, are nevertheless no exception to the rule, since their establishment normally proceeds from one community's drive to subjugate others, and their structure generally reflects this origin. An empire is "a creation of force artificially superimposed upon a multiplicity of unwilling national societies," [2] not the realization of a community which transcends such societies.

It is the very lack of a supreme and generally accepted authority which explains why the rules of the game in world politics differ so sharply from the rules of domestic politics: the overriding loyalty of each of the groups into which the world has been divided belongs to the group rather than to the world as a whole. Even in the period when those groups had a common ideal transcending their boundaries, such as "the majestic conception of the unity of the Christian community," [3] political authority

---

[2] Hans J. Morgenthau, *Politics Among Nations*, 2nd ed., New York, 1955, p. 482.
[3] Charles de Visscher, *Theory and Reality in Public International Law*, Princeton, 1957, p. 3.

remained fragmented; the common ideal, at best, was no more than a restraint on the actions of the groups—not the expression of a supreme temporal power. Hence, in particular, the striking differences between domestic law and international law, whose elaboration, interpretation and enforcement continue to depend on the will and consent of its very subjects. Hence also the difference in perspective between the disciplines of world politics and "domestic" political science. As one writer has put it, the former begins with the context and is then led to consider the content: its interest is in the environment and in the interralatedness of everything within; the latter begins within the basic unit and is then led to consider the setting: its interest is in the individual organism and in its relationships with everything without.[4] Certainly the contrast should not be exaggerated; there are twilight periods, and even in times of sharply distinguished multiple sovereignties, there are twilight zones, such as the areas in which a federalizing process goes on. Nevertheless the basic distinction remains normatively valid.

Second, since the prerequisite can be met, *i.e.*, since it is intellectually possible to distinguish the field, I would argue that the field *should* be treated as an autonomous discipline. This does not mean that it should necessarily be taught in separate departments. Indeed, the fragmentation of the social sciences into sovereign units has begun to resemble the present state of world affairs. Paradoxically enough, this trend comes at a time when the specialists in each field realize that their own subjects— political science, sociology, or even economics, the most autonomous of all—really require both a separate set of theories and techniques *and* a considerable dose of interdisciplinary cooperation. Certainly the autonomy of any field within the social sciences, in so far as it arbitrarily isolates and elevates one sector of social activity, performs a kind of vivisection.

However, the difference in perspective which I have mentioned justifies a separate treatment. The great historian Marc Bloch quoted an economist's remark to the effect that an epidemic would be interpreted differently by a doctor and by a sociologist; the former would see the spreading of microbes as the cause, and the country's poverty as a condition, the latter would find exactly the reverse.[5] A similar contrast can be obtained when the same event, for instance a country's decision to attack its neighbor, is studied both from the viewpoint of domestic affairs and from the perspective of international politics: internal tensions (such as the pressure of social conflicts and the need to find a diversion from

---

[4] C. A. W. Manning, *The University Teaching of Social Sciences: International Relations,* Paris, 1954, p. 74.
[5] Marc Bloch, *The Historian's Craft,* New York, 1953, p. 193.

them) could be seen as the cause and external insecurity as the condition in the first case, and the reverse might be found in the second.

There is a much more important reason for advocating autonomy. No social scientist can work without having in mind at least an implicit model of his field. If we look at the two social sciences whose contributions have been most vital for the development of international relations —political science and sociology—we see that disciplines use as a model the image of the integrated community. The norm for scientific analysis, and also, usually, for implicit evaluation, is the society which agrees on a certain notion (more or less extensive) of the common good. The norm is the society in which political power is institutionalized and law made for the realization of this common good, and in which the conflicts of ideas and interests are both dampened by the underlying agreement on fundamentals and ultimately resolved in a way which confirms this consensus and the equilibrium of the system. In this society, social functions are differentiated and carried out in such a way that the unity, harmony, or internal consistency of the society is achieved and maintained. Now, whatever else the nature of international relations may be, it is not an integrated system. It would be very dangerous in the long run to continue to work in our field with a model that does not fit. Many of the mistakes of contemporary theoretical attempts in international relations and international law come from the systematic misapplication of the model of the integrated *Rechtsstaat*—the modern state characterized by a sense of common purpose, a rational organization of power, a bureacracy and the rule of law—to the decentralized international milieu, either as a norm for analysis or as a goal. The most extreme and revealing example is provided by Hans Kelsen's theory of international law, which assumes that the international legal order is already supreme. In order to explain the obvious differences between such a legal order (which is backed neither by a sense of community nor by any central system of power) and domestic legal orders, he is obliged to resort to an impressive gamut of fictions and to reason "as if" there existed a superpower over and above the units of the world. The gap between theory and practice becomes so great that the former ceases to have any value as an interpretation of the latter. For he did not ask the indispensable previous question, "whether an international community exists capable of supporting a legal order."[6]

There is a last and, I think, decisive reason for advocating an autonomous treatment of international relations. Without wanting to sound like an imperialist for a relatively green science, I would add that the architectonic role Aristotle attributed to the science of the Polis might well

---

[6] Julius Stone, *Legal Controls of International Conflicts*, New York, 1954, p. 34.

belong today to international relations, for these have become in the twentieth century the very condition of our daily life. To philosophize about the ideal State in isolation, or to theorize about political systems in the abstract, has become almost meaningless. If, in the study of politics, we were to put the primary emphasis on world affairs, and to treat domestic politics in the light of world affairs, we might produce a Copernican revolution even bigger than the change that transformed economics when macroanalysis replaced microanalysis. This should not be taken as a plea to treat domestic affairs as a by-product of world politics, for to do so would be just as mistaken as to study domestic political systems in isolation. The relations between internal and world affairs are highly complicated. One of the crucial features and paradoxes of politics today is that whereas internal politics are conditioned and affected by world problems more than ever before, the foreign policies of nations remain largely dictated by the domestic experience and by the nation's image of itself. World problems become domestic issues, but the nation's reaction to these issues and the nation's conduct on the world stage can often be explained only by internal history and by the values developed in those happier days when the outside world did not press so heavily on each country. The impossibility of unscrambling domestic and world affairs is not an argument against an autonomous discipline of international relations; it merely shows that we do indeed need an architectonic conception of our discipline.

PROBLEMS OF SCOPE, METHOD, AND PURPOSE

As a discipline, international relations is not in very fine shape. There is, first of all, broad disagreement on a definition of the field. I confess that this does not worry me very much, for debates which try to determine the scope of a social science are rather pointless. Writers argue for their respective definitions as if there were an immutable essence of world politics, or sociology, and so on. Recent arguments concerning the criterion of political science, in particular, cannot be said to have led anywhere; for such arguments normally end with formulas even more ambiguous than the absence of any definition. If one calls political science the study of the state, one runs into the objection that there are one hundred and forty-five discernible definitions of the state, and that furthermore political science deals with phenomena which no such definition of the state can embrace.[7] If one sees in political science the science of power, or of the phenomena of control, one is left with the burden of distinguishing this discipline from the other social sciences, in which power and control are also important concepts. To speak of the "au-

---

[7] David Easton, *The Political System,* New York, 1953, p. 107.

thoritative allocation of values in a society" as the proper criterion raises the further question of a definition of the society which one selects as the focus of analysis.[8]

Similar problems arise in connection with current definitions of the domain of international relations. Some say that the discipline is concerned with the relations among states. But this glosses over the fact that states are not monolithic blocs and that within them and often side by side with them, individuals and ideological or interest groups are the real decision-makers. Some see in power the criterion of international politics and thus define international relations as the discipline concerned with those relations among nations (i.e. between their governments or between individuals or groups belonging to different nations) which involve the power of states. Such a definition does not quite conceal the fact that it is not always obvious whether a certain activity involves the power of states or not. It is pretty clear that international postal communications do not, and it is clear today that international trade does, but in the nineteenth century, international politics and law operated largely under the assumption that the commercial activities of the nations' citizens did not concern, at least directly, the power of the states, except in the case of incidents of which these citizens were the victims in a foreign country. If we try to avoid all these difficulties by defining international relations as "relations between powerful groups,"[9] we are then faced with a discipline so broad that the need would soon arise to distinguish the relations that are political from the others, and to give more precision to the concept of powerful groups. Should we, finally, try to answer those two questions by saying that the discipline of international politics is concerned with the relations between *all* groups in so far as they affect international society, but *only* with those relations among groups which are indeed important for world society[10]—we would then be back exactly where we started, and the quest of a definition of world society would decamp us into a new and formidable jungle.

A nominalist approach to the problem makes more sense: the best definition is the statement which, without violating common sense notions about the substance and purpose of the discipline, leads to the most perceptive investigations. The function of a definition is to indicate proper areas of inquiry, not to reveal the essence of the subject. How could one agree once and for all upon the definition of a field whose scope is in constant flux, indeed a field whose fluctuation is one of its principal characteristics? The basic units—city-state, empire, nation-state, et

---

[8] *Ibid.*, pp. 129 ff.

[9] Wright, *The Study of International Relations*, p. 7.

[10] Georg Schwarzenberger, *Power Politics*, New York, 1951, p. 4.

cetera—have changed frequently; the range of problems with which these units have been concerned in their external affairs, and the intensity and the geographical scope of the relations among them have also known great variations. Today, Sweden and Indonesia are likely to join in a multilateral convention for the regulation of labor conditions within their respective territories; a century ago, world affairs did not cover such a subject matter, and Indonesia was part of the Dutch empire.

Thus for practical purposes here is what I would suggest as a purely operational definition: The discipline of international relations is concerned with the factors and the activities which affect the external policies and the power of the basic units into which the world is divided. Such a formula (which solves nothing and *cannot* solve anything) indicates only what I think we should investigate. It shows that we should deal, for instance, with the United Nations, but not *necessarily* with the World Meteorological Organization; or that we should deal with private groups such as the United Fruit Company or the Socialist International, but not *necessarily* with a group such as the International Political Science Association—at least until political scientists begin to play the role of grey eminences and social engineers to which some of them aspire.

Next to the problem of definition, there is a second and much larger area of confusion: the confusion that concerns the proper method and purposes of the discipline. We find in our field a bewildering multitude of contributions from all kinds of disciplines. A chart drafted by Quincy Wright makes room for twenty-three "disciplines concerned with international relations"; at the four corners of the chart, we have technical aid, international propaganda, the art of war, and the control of foreign relations.[11] Another recent survey gives "specific examples of possible approaches" and after a cautionary note which denies any claim to providing a definitive list, enumerates no less than twenty-seven approaches—alphabetically ranged from "action analysis" and "analytical field" to "structural-functional requisite analysis" and "war and peace." [12] Such a conglomeration of partial approaches makes little sense. No one will deny that most fields have something to offer, but a flea market is not a discipline. Interdisciplinary cooperation is not good under all conditions.

On the one hand, unless there is a discipline which supervises all those "approaches," each one of them will consider international relations from a perspective that is parochial. There is no point at all in wondering

---

11 Q. Wright, *op. cit.*, p. 506.
12 Charles O. Lerche and Burton M. Sapin (eds.), "Some Problems in the Study and Teaching of International Politics" (mimeographed), Emory University, 1958, pp. 10–12.

why, for instance, studies in international communication or in international trade answer so few of the questions which political scientists have in mind with respect to international relations: such studies normally do not *try* to answer these questions, and the juxtaposition of the answers which such studies give to their own questions does not necessarily amount even to a partial answer to our questions. If no effort at harmony is ever made, the mixture of notes can hardly fail to produce cacophony. On the other hand, the purposes which the various approaches try to achieve are very different and sometimes conflicting. Some of these approaches are purely descriptive. Others represent attempts at explaining scientifically the role of certain factors, or certain types of behavior, in international affairs. Others try to define what such behavior ought to be, from the viewpoint of morality or of law. Others still are oriented toward practical action and manipulation. It is not surprising that many of these attempts should never really intersect, like planes flying in different directions, and that the contributions of other such attempts should be somewhat contradictory, like planes colliding in the air.

3. THE UTOPIAN BACKGROUND

E. H. Carr

THE FOUNDATIONS OF UTOPIANISM

THE MODERN SCHOOL of utopian political thought must be traced back to the break-up of the mediaeval system, which presupposed a universal ethic and a universal political system based on divine authority. The realists of the Renaissance made the first determined onslaught on the primacy of ethics and propounded a view of politics which made ethics an instrument of politics, the authority of the state being thus

From *The Twenty Years' Crisis 1919–1939* by E. H. Carr (New York: 1958) pp. 22–31; 36–38; 41–46; 51–53; 60–62. Reprinted by permission of St. Martin's Press, Inc., Macmillan & Company, Ltd., and the Macmillan Company of Canada, Ltd. Footnotes have been renumbered to appear in consecutive order.

EDWARD HALLETT CARR (1892–   ) Fellow, Trinity College, Cambridge. His other books include *International Relations Between the Wars, 1919–1939,* (New York: St. Martin's Press, 1963); *What is History?* (New York: Alfred A. Knopf, 1962); *The Bolshevik Revolution, 1917–1923* (3 vols.), (London: Macmillan, 1950–1953).

substituted for the authority of the church as the arbiter of morality. The answer of the utopian school to this challenge was not an easy one. An ethical standard was required which would be independent of any external authority, ecclesiastical or civil; and the solution was found in the doctrine of a secular "law of nature" whose ultimate source was the individual human reason. Natural law, as first propounded by the Greeks, had been an intuition of the human heart about what is morally right. "It is eternal," said Sophocles' Antigone, "and no man knows whence it came." The Stoics and the mediaeval schoolmen identified natural law with reason; and in the seventeenth and eighteenth centuries this identification was revived in a new and special form. In science, the laws of nature were deduced by a process of reasoning from observed facts about the nature of matter. By an easy analogy, the Newtonian principles were now applied to the ethical problems. The moral law of nature could be scientifically established; and rational deduction from the supposed facts of human nature took the place of revelation or intuition as the source of morality. Reason could determine what were the universally valid moral laws; and the assumption was made that, once these laws were determined, human beings would conform to them just as matter conformed to the physical laws of nature. Enlightenment was the royal road to the millennium.

By the eighteenth century, the main lines of modern utopian thought were firmly established. It was essentially individualist in that it made the human conscience the final court of appeal in moral questions; in France it became associated with a secular, in England with an evangelical tradition. It was essentially rationalist in that it identified the human conscience with the voice of reason.[1] But it had still to undergo important developments; and it was Jeremy Bentham who, when the industrial revolution had transferred the leadership of thought from France to England, gave to nineteenth-century utopianism its characteristic shape. Starting from the postulate that the fundamental characteristic of human nature is to seek pleasure and avoid pain, Bentham deduced from this postulate a rational ethic which defined the good in the famous formula "the greatest happiness of the greatest number." As has often been pointed out, "the greatest happiness of the greatest number" performed the function, which natural law had performed for a previous generation,

---

[1] While this is the form of utopianism which has been predominant for the past three centuries, and which still prevails (though perhaps with diminishing force) in English-speaking countries, it would be rash to assert that individualism and rationalism are necessary attributes to utopian thought. Fascism contained elements of a utopianism which was anti-individualist and irrational. These qualities were already latent in the utopian aspects of Leninism—and perhaps even of Marxism.

of an absolute ethical standard. Bentham firmly believed in this absolute standard, and rejected as "anarchical" the view that there are "as many standards of right and wrong as there are men." [2] In effect, "the greatest happiness of the greatest number" was the nineteenth-century definition of the content of natural law.

The importance of Bentham's contribution was twofold. In the first place, by identifying the good with happiness, he provided a plausible confirmation of the "scientific" assumption of the eighteenth-century rationalists that man would infallibly conform to the moral law of nature once its content had been rationally determined. Secondly, while preserving the rationalist and individualist aspect of the doctrine, he succeeded in giving it a broader basis. The doctrine of reason in its eighteenth-century guise was pre-eminently intellectual and aristocratic. Its political corollary was an enlightened despotism of philosophers, who alone could be expected to have the necessary reasoning power to discover the good. But now that happiness was the criterion, the one thing needful was that the individual should understand where his happiness lay. Not only was the good ascertainable—as the eighteenth century had held—by a rational process, but this process—added the nineteenth century—was not a matter of abstruse philosophical speculation, but of simple common sense. Bentham was the first thinker to elaborate the doctrine of salvation by public opinion. The members of the community "may, in their aggregate capacity, he considered as constituting a sort of judicatory or tribunal—call it . . . *The Public-Opinion Tribunal.*" [3] It was James Mill, Bentham's pupil, who produced the most complete argument yet framed for the infallibility of public opinion:

> Every man possessed of reason is accustomed to weigh evidence and to be guided and determined by its preponderance. When various conclusions are, with their evidence, presented with equal care and with equal skill, there is a moral certainty, though some few may be misguided, that the greatest number will judge right, and that the greatest force of evidence, whatever it is, will produce the greatest impression.[4]

This is not the only argument by which democracy as a political institution can be defended. But this argument was, in fact, explicitly or implicitly accepted by most nineteenth-century liberals. The belief that public opinion can be relied on to judge rightly on any question rationally presented to it, combined with the assumption that it will act in

---

2 Bentham, *Works,* ed. Bowring, i. p. 31.
3 Bentham, *Works,* ed. Bowring, viii. p. 561.
4 James Mill, *The Liberty of the Press,* pp. 22–3.

accordance with this right judgment, is an essential foundation of the liberal creed. In Great Britain, the later eighteenth and the nineteenth centuries were pre-eminently the age of popular preaching and of political oratory. By the voice of reason men could be persuaded both to save their own immoral souls and to move along the path of political enlightenment and progress. The optimism of the nineteenth century was based on the triple conviction that the pursuit of the good was a matter of right reasoning, that the spread of knowledge would soon make it possible for everyone to reason rightly on this important subject, and that anyone who reasoned rightly on it would necessarily act rightly.

The application of these principles to international affairs followed, in the main, the same pattern. The Abbé Saint-Pierre, who propounded one of the earliest schemes for a League of Nations, "was so confident in the reasonableness of his projects that he always believed that, if they were fairly considered, the ruling powers could not fail to adopt them." [5] Both Rousseau and Kant argued that, since wars were waged by princes in their own interest and not in that of their peoples, there would be no wars under a republican form of government. In this sense, they anticipated the view that *public opinion,* if allowed to make itself effective, would suffice to prevent war. In the nineteenth century, this view won widespread approval in Western Europe, and took on the specifically rationalist colour proper to the doctrine that the holding of the right moral beliefs and the performance of the right actions can be assured by process of reasoning. Never was there an age which so unreservedly proclaimed the supremacy of the intellect. "It is intellectual evolution," averred Comte, "which essentially determines the main course of social phenomena." [6] Buckle, whose famous *History of Civilisation* was published between 1857 and 1861, boldly declared that dislike of war is "a cultivated taste peculiar to an intellectual people". He chose a cogent example, based on the assumption, natural to a British thinker, of the ingrained bellicosity of Great Britain's most recent enemy. "Russia is a warlike country," he wrote, "not because the inhabitants are immoral, but because they are unintellectual. The fault is in the head, not in the heart." [7] The view that the spread of education would lead to international peace was shared by many of Buckle's contemporaries and successors. Its last serious exponent was Sir Norman Angell, who sought, by *The Great Illusion* and other books, to convince the world that war never brought profit to anyone. If he could establish this point by irrefutable argument, thought Sir Norman, then war could not occur. War was

---

[5] J. S. Bury, *The Idea of Progress,* p. 131.
[6] Comte, *Cours de Philosophie Positive,* Lecture LXI.
[7] Buckle, *History of Civilisation* (World's Classics ed.), i. pp. 151-2.

simply a "failure of understanding." Once the head was purged of the
illusion that war was profitable, the heart could look after itself. "The
world of the Crusades and of heretic burning," ran the opening manifesto of a monthly journal called *War and Peace* which started publication in October 1913, ". . . was not a badly-meaning, but a
badly-thinking world. . . . We emerged from it by correcting a defect in
understanding; we shall emerge from the world of political warfare or
armed peace in the same way." [8] Reason could demonstrate the absurdity
of the international anarchy; and with increasing knowledge, enough
people would be rationally convinced of its absurdity to put an end to it.

BENTHAMISM TRANSPLANTED

Before the end of the nineteenth century, serious doubts had been
thrown from more than one quarter on the assumptions of Benthamite
rationalism. The belief in the sufficiency of reason to promote right conduct was challenged by psychologists. The identification of virtue with
enlightened self-interest began to shock philosophers. The belief in the
infallibility of public opinion had been attractive on the hypothesis of the
earlier utilitarians that public opinion was the opinion of the masses; and
as early as 1859, in his essay *On Liberty*, J. S. Mill had been preoccupied
with the dangers of "the tyranny of the majority." After 1900, it
would have been difficult to find, either in Great Britain or in any other
European country, any serious political thinker who accepted the Benthamite assumptions without qualification. Yet, by one of the ironies of
history, these half-discarded nineteenth-century assumptions reappeared,
in the second and third decades of the twentieth century, in the special
field of international politics, and there became the foundation-stones of a
new utopian edifice. The explanation may be in part that, after 1914,
men's minds naturally fumbled their way back, in search of a new
utopia, to those apparently firm foundations of nineteenth-century peace
and security. But a more decisive factor was the influence of the United
States, still in the heyday of Victorian prosperity and of Victorian belief
in the comfortable Benthamite creed. Just as Bentham, a century earlier,
had taken the eighteenth-century doctrine of reason and refashioned it to
the needs of the coming age, so now Woodrow Wilson, the impassioned
admirer of Bright and Gladstone, transplanted the nineteenth-century
rationalist faith to the almost virgin soil of international politics, and,
bringing it back with him to Europe, gave it a new lease of life. Nearly all
popular theories of international politics between the two world wars

---

[8] Quoted in Angell, *Foundations of International Polity*, p.224. Internal evidence
suggests that the passage was written by Sir Norman Angell himself.

were reflexions, seen in an American mirror, of nineteenth-century liberal thought.

In a limited number of countries, nineteenth-century liberal democracy had been a brilliant success. It was a success because its presuppositions coincided with the stage of development reached by the countries concerned. Out of the mass of current speculation, the leading spirits of the age took precisely that body of theory which corresponded to their needs, consciously and unconsciously fitting their practice to it, and it to their practice. Utilitarianism and *laissez-faire* served, and in turn directed, the course of industrial and commercial expansion. But the view that nineteenth-century liberal democracy was based, not on a balance of forces peculiar to the economic development of the period and the countries concerned, but on certain *a priori* rational principles which had only to be applied in other contexts to produce similar results, was essentially utopian; and it was this view which, under Wilson's inspiration, dominated the world after the first world war. When the theories of liberal democracy were transplanted, by a purely intellectual process, to a period and to countries whose stage of development and whose practical needs were utterly different from those of Western Europe in the nineteenth century, sterility and disillusionment were the inevitable sequel. Rationalism can create a utopia, but cannot make it real. The liberal democracies scattered throughout the world by the peace settlement of 1919 were the product of abstract theory, stuck no roots in the soil, and quickly shrivelled away.

RATIONALISM AND THE LEAGUE OF NATIONS

The most important of all the institutions affected by this one-sided intellectualism of international politics was the League of Nations, which was an attempt "to apply the principles of Lockeian liberalism to the building of a machinery of international order."[9] "The Covenant," observed General Smuts, ". . . simply carries into world affairs that outlook of a liberal democratic society which is one of the great achievements of our human advance."[10] But this transplantation of democratic rationalism from the national to the international sphere was full of unforeseen difficulties. The empiricist treats the concrete case on its individual merits. The rationalist refers it to an abstract general principle. Any social order implies a large measure of standardisation, and therefore of abstraction; there cannot be a different rule for every member of the community. Such standardisation is comparatively easy in a community

---

[9] R. H. S. Crossman in J. P. Mayer, *Political Thought*, p. 202.
[10] New Year's Eve broadcast from Radio-Nations, Geneva: *The Times*, January 1, 1938.

of several million anonymous individuals conforming more or less closely to recognised types. But it presents infinite complications when applied to sixty known states differing widely in size, in power, and in political, economic and cultural development. The League of Nations, being the first large-scale attempt to standardise international political problems on a rational basis, was particularly liable to these embarrassments.

The founders of the League, some of whom were men of political experience and political understanding, had indeed recognised the dangers of abstract perfection. "Acceptance of the political facts of the present", remarked the official British Commentary on the Covenant issued in 1919, "has been one of the principles on which the Commission has worked" [11] and this attempt to take account of political realities distinguished the Covenant not only from previous paper schemes of world organisation, but also from such purely utopian projects as the International Police Force, the Briand-Kellogg Pact and the United States of Europe. The Covenant possessed the virtue of several theoretical imperfections. Purporting to treat all members as equal, it assured to the Great Powers a permanent majority on the Council of the League.[12] It did not purport to prohibit war altogether, but only to limit the occasions on which it might legitimately be resorted to. The obligation imposed on members of the League to apply sanctions to the Covenant-breaker was not free from vagueness; and this vagueness had been discreetly enhanced by a set of "interpretative" resolutions passed by the Assembly of 1921. The starkness of the territorial guarantee provided by Article 10 of the Covenant was smoothed away in a resolution which secured an almost unanimous vote at the Assembly of 1923. It seemed for the moment as if the League might reach a working compromise between utopia and reality and become an effective instrument of international politics.

Unhappily, the most influential European politicians neglected the League during its critical formative years. Abstract rationalism gained

---

[11] *The Covenant of the League of Nations and a Commentary Thereon*, Cmd. 151 (1919), p. 12. "The great strength of the Covenant," said the British Government some years later, "lies in the measure of discretion which it allows to the Council and Assembly dealing with future contingencies which may have no parallel in history and which therefore cannot all of them be forseen in advance" (*League of Nations: Official Journal*, May 1928, p. 703).

[12] The defection of the United States upset this balance, and left four major confronted with four minor Powers. Subsequent increases in membership, which have taken place at frequent intervals since 1923, gave a permanent preponderance to the minor Powers. The Council, in becoming more "representative," lost much of its effectiveness as a political instrument. Reality was sacrificed to an abstract principle. It should be added that the prudent Swiss Delegate foresaw this result when the first increase was mooted in 1922 (*League of Nations: Third Assembly*, First Committee, pp. 37–8).

the upper hand, and from about 1922 onwards the current at Geneva set strongly in the utopian direction.[13] It came to be believed, in the words of an acute critic, "that there can exist, either at Geneva or in foreign offices, a sort of carefully classified card-index of events or, better still, 'situation', and that, when the event happens or the situation presents itself, a member of the Council or Foreign Minister can easily recognise that event or situation and turn up the index to be directed to the files where the appropriate action is prescribed."[14] There were determined efforts to perfect the machinery, to standardise the procedure, to close the "gaps" in the Covenant by an absolute veto on all war, and to make the application of sanctions "automatic". The Draft Treaty of Mutual Assistance, the Geneva Protocol, the General Act, the plan to incorporate the Briand-Kellogg Pact in the Covenant and "the definition of the aggressor", were all milestones on the dangerous path of rationalisation. The fact that the utopian dishes prepared during these years at Geneva proved unpalatable to most of the principal governments concerned was a symptom of the growing divorce between theory and practice.

Even the language current in League circles betrayed the growing eagerness to avoid the concrete in favour of the abstract generalisations. When it was desired to arrange that the Draft Treaty of Mutual Assistance could be brought into force in Europe without waiting for the rest of the world, a stipulation was inserted that it might come into force "by continents"—a proviso with farcical implications for every continent except Europe. A conventional phraseology came into use, which served as the current coin of delegates at Geneva and of League enthusiasts elsewhere and which, through constant repetition, soon lost all contact with reality. "I cannot recall any time", said Mr. Churchill in 1932, "when the gap between the kind of words which statesmen used and what was actually happening in many countries was so great as it is now."[15] The Franco-Soviet Pact, which was a defensive alliance against Germany, was so drafted as to make it appear an instrument of general application, and was described as a shining example of the principle of "collective security". A member of the House of Commons, when asked in the debate on sanctions in June 1936 whether he would run the risk of war with Italy, replied that he was prepared to face "all the

---

[13] By a curious irony, this development was strongly encouraged by a group of American intellectuals; and some European enthusiasts imagined that, by following this course, they would propitiate American opinion. The rift between the theory of the intellectuals and the practice of the government, which develop in Great Britain from 1932 onwards, began in the United States in 1919.

[14] J. Fischer-Williams, *Some Aspects of the Covenant of the League of Nations*, p. 238.

[15] Winston Churchill, *Arms and the Covenant*, p. 43.

consequences naturally flowing from the enforcement of the Covenant against an aggressor nation." [16] These linguistic contortions encouraged the frequent failure to distinguish between the world of abstract reason and the world of political reality. "Metaphysicians, like savages", remarks Mr. Bertrand Russell, "are apt to imagine a magical connexion between words and things." [17] The metaphysicians of Geneva found it difficult to believe that an accumulation of ingenious texts prohibiting war was not a barrier against war itself. "Our purpose", said M. Benes in introducing the Geneva Protocol to the 1924 Assembly, "was to make war impossible, to kill it, to annihilate it. To do this we had to create a system." [18] The Protocol was the "system." Such presumption could only provoke nemesis. Once it came to be believed in League circles that salvation could be found in a perfect card-index, and that the unruly flow of international politics could be canalised into a set of logically impregnable abstract formulae inspired by the doctrines of nineteenth-century liberal democracy, the end of the League as an effective political instrument was in sight.

· · ·

THE NEMESIS OF UTOPIANISM

The nemesis of utopianism in international politics came rather suddenly. In September 1930, the President of Columbia University, Dr. Nicholas Murray Butler, ventured on the "reasonably safe prediction that the next generation will see a constantly increasing respect for Cobden's principles and point of view and a steadily growing endeavour more largely to give them practical effect in public policy." [19] On September 10, 1931, Lord Cecil told the Assembly of the League of Nations that "there has scarcely ever been a period in the world's history when war seems less likely than it does at present." [20] On September 18, 1931, Japan opened her campaign in Manchuria; and in the following month, the last important country which had continued to adhere to the principle of free trade took the first steps towards the introduction of a general tariff.

From this point onwards, a rapid succession of events forced upon all serious thinkers a reconsideration of premises which were becoming more and more flagrantly divorced from reality. The Manchurian crisis had

---

[16] Quoted in Toynbee, *Survey of International Affairs, 1935,* ii. p. 448.
[17] B. Russell in *Atlantic Monthly,* clix. (February 1937), p. 155.
[18] *League of Nations: Fifth Assembly,* p. 497.
[19] N. M. Butler, *The Path to Peace,* p. xii.
[20] *League of Nations: Twelfth Assembly,* p. 59.

demonstrated that the "condemnation of international public opinion", invoked by Taft and by so many after him, was a broken reed. In the United States, this conclusion was drawn with extreme reluctance. In 1932, an American Secretary of State still cautiously maintained that "the sanction of public opinion can be made one of the most potent sanctions of the world." [21] In September 1938, President Roosevelt based his intervention in the Czecho-Slovak crisis on the belief of the United States Government in "the moral force of public opinion;" [22] and in April 1939, Mr. Cordell Hull once again announced the conviction that "a public opinion, the most potent of all forces for peace, is more strongly developing throughout the world." [23] But in countries more directly menaced by international crisis, this consoling view no longer found many adherents; and the continued addition to it of American statesmen was regarded as an index of American unwillingness to resort to more potent weapons. Already in 1932, Mr. Churchill taunted the League of Nations Union with "long-suffering and inexhaustible gullibility" for continuing to preach this outworn creed.[24] Before long the group of intellectuals who had once stressed the relative unimportance of the "material" weapons of the League began to insist loudly on economic and military sanctions as the necessary cornerstones of an international order. When Germany annexed Austria, Lord Cecil indignantly enquired whether the Prime Minister "holds that the use of material force is impracticable and that the League should cease to attempt 'sanctions' and confine its efforts to moral force." [25] The answer might well have been that, if Neville Chamberlain did in fact hold this view, he could have learned it from Lord Cecil's own earlier utterances.

Moreover, scepticism attacked not only the premise that public opinion is certain to prevail, but also the premise that public opinion is certain to be right. At the Peace Conference, it had been observed that statesmen were sometimes more reasonable and moderate in their demands than the public opinion which they were supposed to represent. Even Wilson himself once used—no doubt, in perfect sincerity—an argument which directly contradicted his customary thesis that reason can be made to prevail by appealing to "the plain people everywhere throughout the world." In the League of Nations Commission of the Conference, the

---

[21] Mr. Stimson to the Council of Foreign Relations on August 8, 1932 (*New York Times*, August 9, 1932).

[22] "Believing, as this government does, in the moral force of public opinion . . ." (Sumner Welles in *State Department Press Releases*, October 8, 1938, p. 237).

[23] *The Times*, April 18, 1939.

[24] Winston Churchill, *Arms and the Covenant*, p. 36.

[25] *Daily Telegraph*, March 24, 1938.

Japanese had raised the issue of race equality. "How can you treat on its merits in this quiet room," enquired the President, "a question which will not be treated on its merits when it gets out of this room?" [26] Later history provided many examples of this phenomenon. It became a commonplace for statesmen at Geneva and elsewhere to explain that they themselves had every desire to be reasonable, but that public opinion in their countries was inexorable; and though this plea was sometimes a pretext or a tactical manœuvre, there was often a solid substratum of reality beneath it. The prestige of public opinion correspondingy declined. "It does not help the conciliator, the arbitrator, the policeman or the judge," wrote a well-known supporter of the League of Nations Union recently, "to be surrounded by a crowd emitting either angry or exulting cheers." [27] Woodrow Wilson's "plain men throughout the world," the spokesmen of "the common purpose of enlightened mankind," had somehow transformed themselves into a disorderly mob emitting incoherent and unhelpful noises. It seemed undeniable that, in international affairs, public opinion was almost as often wrong-headed as it was impotent. But where so many of the presuppositions of 1919 were crumbling, the intellectual leaders of the utopian school stuck to their guns; and in Great Britain and the United States—and to a lesser degree in France—the rift between theory and practice assumed alarming dimensions. Armchair students of international affairs were unanimous about the kind of policy which ought to be followed, both in the political and in the economic field. Governments of many countries acted in a sense precisely contrary to this advice, and received the endorsement of public opinion at the polls.

.   .   .

THE UTOPIAN SYNTHESIS

No political society, national or international, can exist unless people submit to certain rules of conduct. The problem why people should submit to such rules is the fundamental problem of political philosophy. The problem presents itself just as insistently in a democracy as under other forms of government and in international as in national politics; for such a formula as "the greatest good of the greatest number" provides no answer to the question why the minority, whose greatest good is *ex hypothesi* not pursued, should submit to rules made in the interest of the greatest number. Broadly speaking, the answers given to the question fall into two categories, corresponding to the antithesis, discussed in a pre-

---

[26] Miller, *The Drafting of the Covenant*, ii. p. 701.
[27] Lord Allen of Hurtwood, *The Times*, May 30, 1938.

vious chapter, between those who regard politics as a function of ethics and those who regard ethics as a function of politics.

Those who assert the primacy of ethics over politics will hold that it is the duty of the individual to submit for the sake of the community as a whole, sacrificing his own interest to the interest of others who are more numerous, or in some other way more deserving. The "good" which consists in self-interest should be subordinated to the "good" which consists in loyalty and self-sacrifice for an end higher than self-interest. The obligation rests on some kind of intuition of what is right and cannot be demonstrated by rational argument. Those, on the other hand, who assert the primacy of politics over ethics, will argue that the ruler rules because he is the stronger, and the ruled submit because they are the weaker. This principle is just as easily applicable to democracy as to any other form of government. The majority rules because it is stronger, the minority submits because it is weaker. Democracy, it has often been said, substitutes the counting of heads for the breaking of heads. But the substitution is merely a convenience, and the principle of the two methods is the same. The realist, therefore, unlike the intuitionist, has a perfectly rational answer to the question why the individual should submit. He should submit because otherwise the stronger will compel him; and the results of compulsion are more disagreeable than those of voluntary submission. Obligation is thus derived from a sort of spurious ethic based on the reasonableness of recognising that might is right.

Both these answers are open to objection. Modern man, who has witnessed so many magnificent achievements of human reason, is reluctant to believe that reason and obligation sometimes conflict. On the other hand, men of all ages have failed to find satisfaction in the view that the rational basis of obligation is merely the right of the stronger. One of the strongest points of eighteenth- and nineteenth-century utopianism was its apparent success in meeting both these objections at once. The utopian, starting from the primacy of ethics, necessarily believes in an obligation which is ethical in character and independent of the right of the stronger. But he has also been able to convince himself, on grounds other than those of the realist, that the duty of the individual to submit to rules made in the interest of the community can be justified in terms of reason, and that the greatest good of the greatest number is a rational end even for those who are not included in the greatest number. He achieves this synthesis by maintaining that the highest interest of the individual and the highest interest of the community naturally coincide. In pursuing his own interest, the individual pursues that of the community, and in promoting the interest of the community he promotes his own. This is the famous doctrine of the harmony of interests. It is a necessary corollary of the postulate that moral laws can be established by right reasoning. The admission of any ultimate divergence of interests would be fatal to this postulate; and any apparent clash of interests must therefore be explained as the result of wrong calculation. Burke tacitly accepted the doctrine of identity when he defined expediency as "that which is good for the community and for every individual in it." [28] It was handed on from the eighteenth-century rationalists to Bentham, and from Bentham to the Victorian moralists. The utilitarian philosophers could justify morality by the argument that, in promoting the good of others, one automatically promotes one's own. Honesty is the best policy. If people or nations behave badly, it must be, as Buckle and Sir Norman Angell and Professor Zimmern think, because they are unintellectual and short-sighted and muddle-headed.

THE PARADISE OF LAISSEZ-FAIRE

It was the *laissez-faire* school of political economy created by Adam Smith which was in the main responsible for popularising the doctrine of the harmony of interests. The purpose of the school was to promote the removal of state control in economic matters; and in order to justify this policy, it set out to demonstrate that the individual could be relied on, without external control, to promote the interests of the community for the very reason that those interests were identical with his own. This proof was the burden of *The Wealth of Nations*. The community is divided into those who live by rent, those who live by wages and those who live by profit; and the interests of "those three great orders" are "strictly and inseparably connected with the general interest of the society." [29] The harmony is none the less real if those concerned are unconscious of it. The individual "neither intends to promote the public interest, nor knows how much he is promoting it. . . . He intends only his own gain, and he is in this, as in many other cases, led by an invisible hand to promote an end which was no part of his intention." [30] The invisible hand, which Adam Smith would perhaps have regarded as a metaphor, presented no difficulty to Victorian piety. "It is curious to observe", remarks a tract issued by the Society for the Propagation of Christian Knowledge towards the middle of the nineteenth century, "how, through the wise and beneficent arrangement of Providence, men thus do the greatest service to the public when they are thinking of nothing but their own gain." [31] About the same time an English clergyman wrote a work entitled *The Temporal Benefits of Christianity Explained*. The harmony of interests provided a solid ra-

---

[28] Burke, *Works*, v. 407.
[29] Adam Smith, *The Wealth of Nations*, Book I. ch. xi. conclusion.
[30] *Ibid.* Book IV. ch. ii.
[31] Quoted in J. M. Keynes, *A Tract on Monetary Reform*, p. 7.

tional basis for morality. To love one's neighbour turned out to be a
thoroughly enlightened way of loving oneself. "We now know", wrote
Mr. Henry Ford as recently as 1930, "that anything which is economically right is also morally right. There can be no conflict between good
economics and good morals." [32]

The assumption of a general and fundamental harmony of interests is
prima facie so paradoxical that it requires careful scrutiny. In the form
which Adam Smith gave to it, it had a definite application to the economic structure of the eighteenth century. It presupposed a society of
small producers and merchants, interested in the maximisation of production and exchange, infinitely mobile and adaptable, and unconcerned with
the problem of the distribution of wealth. Those conditions were substantially fulfilled in an age when production involved no high degree of
specialisation and no sinking of capital in fixed equipment, and when the
class which might be more interested in the equitable distribution of
wealth than in its maximum production was insignificant and without
influence. But by a curious coincidence, the year which saw the publication of *The Wealth of Nations* was also the year in which Watt invented
his steam-engine. Thus, at the very moment when *laissez-faire* theory was
receiving its classical exposition, its premises were undermined by an
invention which was destined to call into being immobile, highly specialised, mammoth industries and a large and powerful proletariat more interested in distribution than in production. Once industrial capitalism
and the class system had become the recognised structure of society, the
doctrine of the harmony of interests acquired a new significance, and
became, as we shall presently see, the ideology of a dominant group
concerned to maintain its predominance by asserting the identity of its
interests with those of the community as a whole.

But this transformation could not have been effected, and the doctrine
could not have survived at all, but for one circumstance. The survival of
the belief in a harmony of interests was rendered possible by the unparalleled expansion of production, population and prosperity, which marked
the hundred years following the publication of *The Wealth of Nations*
and the invention of the steam-engine. Expanding prosperity contributed
to the popularity of the doctrine in three different ways. It attenuated
competition for markets among producers, since fresh markets were constantly becoming available; it postponed the class issue, with its insistence on the primary importance of equitable distribution, by extending
to members of the less prosperous classes some share in the general
prosperity; and by creating a sense of confidence in present and future

---

[32] Quoted in J. Truslow Adams, *The Epic of America*, p. 400. I have failed to
trace the original.

well-being, it encouraged men to believe that the world was ordered on so rational a plan as the natural harmony of interests. "It was the continual widening of the field of demand which, for half a century, made capitalism operate as if it were a liberal utopia." [33] The tacit presupposition of infinitely expanding markets was the foundation on which the supposed harmony of interests rested. As Dr. Mannheim points out, traffic control is unnecessary so long as the number of cars does not exceed the comfortable capacity of the road.[34] Until that moment arrives, it is easy to believe in a natural harmony of interests between road-users.

What was true of individuals was assumed to be also true of nations. Just as individuals, by pursuing their own good, unconsciously compass the good of the whole community, so nations in serving themselves serve humanity. Universal free trade was justified on the ground that the maximum economic interest of each nation was identified with the maximum economic interest of the whole world. Adam Smith, who was a practical reformer rather than a pure theorist, did indeed admit that governments might have to protect certain industries in the interests of national defence. But such derogations seemed to him and to his followers trivial exceptions to the rule. "Laissez-faire," as J. S. Mill puts it, ". . . should be the general rule: every departure from it, unless required by some great good, a certain evil." [35] Other thinkers gave the doctrine of the harmony of national interests a still wider application. "The true interests of a nation," observes a late eighteenth-century writer, "never yet stood in opposition to the general interest of mankind; and it can never happen that philanthropy and patriotism can impose on any man inconsistent duties." [36] T. H. Green, the English Hegelian who tempered the doctrines of his master with concessions to British nineteenth-century *liberalism*, held that "no action in its own interest of a state which fulfilled its idea could conflict with any true interest or right of general society," [37] though it is interesting to note that the question-begging epithet "true", which in the eighteenth-century quotation is attached to the interests of the nation, has been transferred by the nineteenth century to the interest of the general society. Mazzini, who embodied the liberal nineteenth-century philosophy of nationalism, believed in a sort of division of labour between nations. Each nation had its own special task for which its special apti-

---

[33] *Nationalism: A Study by a Group of Members of the Royal Institute of International Affairs*, p. 229.

[34] K. Mannheim, *Mensch und Gesellschaft im Zeitalter des Umbaus*, p. 104.

[35] J. S. Mill, *Principles of Political Economy*, II. Book V. ch. xi.

[36] Romilly, *Thoughts on the Influence of the French Revolution*, p. 5.

[37] T. H. Green, *Principles of Political Obligation*, § 166.

tudes fitted it, and the performance of this task was its contribution to the welfare of humanity. If all nations acted in this spirit, international harmony would prevail. The same condition of apparently infinite expansibility which encouraged belief in the economic harmony of interests made possible the belief in the political harmony of rival national movements. One reason why contemporaries of Mazzini thought nationalism a good thing was that there were few recognised nations, and plenty of room for them. In an age when Germans, Czechs, Poles, Ukrainians, Magyars and half a dozen more national groups were not yet visibly jostling one another over an area of a few hundred square miles, it was comparatively easy to believe that each nation, by developing its own nationalism, could make its own special contribution to the international harmony of interests. Most liberal writers continued to believe, right down to 1918, that nations, by developing their own nationalism, promoted the cause of internationalism; and Wilson and many other makers of the peace treaties saw in national self-determination the key to world peace. More recently still, responsible Anglo-Saxon statesmen have been from time to time content to echo, probably without much reflexion, the old Mazzinian formulae.[38]

. . .

THE COMMON INTEREST IN PEACE

Politically, the doctrine of the identity of interests has commonly taken the form of an assumption that every nation has an identical interest in peace, and that any nation which desires to disturb the peace is therefore both irrational and immoral. This view bears clear marks of its Anglo-Saxon origin. It was easy after 1918 to convince that part of mankind which lives in English-speaking countries that war profits nobody. The argument did not seem particularly convincing to Germans, who had profited largely from the wars of 1866 and 1870, and attributed their more recent sufferings, not to the war of 1914, but to the fact that they had lost it; or to Italians, who blamed not the war, but the treachery of allies who defrauded them in the peace settlement; or to Poles or Czecho-Slovaks who, far from deploring the war, owed their national existence to it; or to Frenchmen, who could not unreservedly regret a war which had restored Alsace-Lorraine to France; or to people of other nationalities who remembered profitable wars waged by Great Britain and the United States in the past. But these people had fortunately little

---

[38] Mr. Eden, for example, in 1938 advocated "a comity of nations in which each can develop and flourish and give to their uttermost their own special contribution to the diversity of life" (Anthony Eden, *Foreign Affairs*, p. 277).

influence over the formation of current theories of international relations, which emanated almost exclusively from the English-speaking countries. British and American writers continued to assume that the uselessness of war had been irrefutably demonstrated by the experience of 1914–18, and that an intellectual grasp of this fact was all that was necessary to induce the nations to keep the peace in the future; and they were sincerely puzzled as well as disappointed at the failure of other countries to share this view.

The confusion was increased by the ostentatious readiness of other countries to flatter the Anglo-Saxon world by repeating its slogans. In the fifteen years after the first world war, every Great Power (except, perhaps, Italy) repeatedly did lip-service to the doctrine by declaring peace to be one of the main objects of its policy.[39] But as Lenin observed long ago, peace in itself is a meaningless aim. "Absolutely everybody is in favour of peace in general", he wrote in 1915, "including Kitchener, Joffre, Hindenburg and Nicholas the Bloody, for everyone of them wishes to end the war." [40] The common interest in peace masks the fact that some nations desire to maintain the *status quo* without having to fight for it, and others to change the *status quo* without having to fight in order to do so.[41] The statement that it is in the interest of the world as a whole either that the *status quo* should be maintained, or that it should be changed, would be contrary to the facts. The statement that it is in the interest of the world as a whole that the conclusion eventually reached,

---

[39] "Peace must prevail, must come before all" (Briand, *League of Nations: Ninth Assembly*, p. 83). "The maintenance of peace is the first objective of British foreign policy" (Eden, *League of Nations: Sixteenth Assembly*, p. 106). "Peace is our dearest treasure" (Hitler, in a speech in the German Reichstag on January 30, 1937, reported in *The Times*, February 1, 1937). "The principal aim of the international policy of the Soviet Union is the preservation of peace" (Chicherin in The Soviet Union and Peace (1929), p. 249). "The object of Japan, despite propaganda to the contrary, is peace" (Matsuoka, *League of Nations: Special Assembly 1932–33*, iii. p. 73). The paucity of Italian pronouncements in favour of peace was probably explained by the poor reputation of Italian troops as fighters: Mussolini feared that any emphatic expression of preference for peace would be construed as an admission that Italy had no stomach for war.

[40] Lenin, *Collected Works* (Engl. transl.), xviii. p. 264. Compare Spenser Wilkinson's dictum: "It is not peace but preponderance that is in each case the real object. The truth cannot be too often repeated that peace is never the object of policy: you cannot define peace except by reference to war, which is a means and never an end" (*Government and the War*, p. 121).

[41] "When a saint complains that people do not know the things belonging to their peace, what he really means is that they do not sufficiently care about the things belonging to his peace" (*The Note-Books of Samuel Butler*, ed. Festing-Jones, pp. 211–12). This would seem to be true of those latter-day saints, the satisfied Powers.

whether maintenance or change, should be reached by peaceful means, would command general assent, but seems a rather meaningless platitude. The utopian assumption that there is a world interest in peace which is identifiable with the interest of each individual nation helped politicians and political writers everywhere to evade the unpalatable fact of a fundamental divergence of interest between nations desirous of maintaining the *status quo* and nations desirous of changing it.[42] A peculiar combination of platitude and falseness thus became endemic in the pronouncements of statesmen about international affairs. "In this whole Danubian area", said a Prime Minister of Czecho-Slovakia, "no one really wants conflicts and jealousies. The various countries want to maintain their independence, but otherwise they are ready for any co-operative measures. I am thinking specially of the Little Entente, Hungary and Bulgaria."[43] Literally the words may pass as true. Yet the conflicts and jealousies which nobody wanted were a notorious feature of Danubian politics after 1919, and the co-operation for which all were ready was unobtainable. The fact of divergent interests was disguised and falsified by the platitude of a general desire to avoid conflict.

. . .

THE HARMONY BROKEN

We must therefore reject as inadequate and misleading the attempt to base international morality on an alleged harmony of interests which identifies the interest of the whole community of nations with the interest of each individual member of it. In the nineteenth century, this attempt met with widespread success, thanks to the continuously expanding economy in which it was made. The period was one of progressive prosperity, punctuated only by minor set-backs. The international economic structure bore considerable resemblance to the domestic economic structure of the United States. Pressure could at once be relieved by expansion to hitherto unoccupied and unexploited territories; and there was a plentiful supply of cheap labour, and of backward countries, which had not yet reached the level of political consciousness. Enterprising indi-

---

[42] It is sometimes maintained not merely that all nations have an equal interest in preferring peace to war (which is, in a sense, true), but that war can never in any circumstances bring to the victor advantages comparable with its cost. The latter view does not appear to be true of the past, though it is possible to argue (as does Bertrand Russell, *Which Way Peace?*) that it is true of modern warfare. If accepted, this view leads, of course, to absolute pacifism; for there is no reason to suppose that it is any truer of "defensive" than of "offensive" war (assuming the distinction between them to be valid).

[43] *Daily Telegraph*, August 26, 1938.

viduals could solve the economic problem by migration, enterprising
nations by colonisation. Expanding markets produced an expanding
population, and population in turn reacted on markets. Those who were
left behind in the race could plausibly be regarded as the unfit. A
harmony of interests among the fit, based on individual enterprise and
free competition, was sufficiently near to reality to form a sound basis for
the current theory. With some difficulty the illusion was kept alive till
1914. Even British prosperity, though its foundations were menaced by
German and American competition, continued to expand. The year 1913
was a record year for British trade.

The transition from the apparent harmony to the transparent clash of
interests may be placed about the turn of the century. Appropriately
enough, it found its first expression in colonial policies. In the British
mind, it was primarily associated with events in South Africa. Mr.
Churchill dates the beginning of "these violent times" from the Jameson
Raid.[44] In North Africa and the Far East, there was a hasty scramble
by the European Powers to secure the few eligible sites which were
still vacant. Emigration of individuals from Europe, the point of
principal tension, to America assumed unparalleled dimensions. In Europe itself, anti-Semitism—the recurrent symptom of economic stress—
reappeared after a long interval in Russia, Germany and France.[45] In
Great Britain, agitation against unrestricted alien immigration began in
the 1890's; and the first act controlling immigration was passed in 1905.

The first world war, which proceeded from this growing tension, aggravated it tenfold by intensifying its fundamental causes. In belligerent
and neutral countries in Europe, Asia and America, industrial and agricultural production were everywhere artificially stimulated. After the war
every country struggled to maintain its expanded production; and an
enhanced and inflamed national consciousness was invoked to justify the
struggle. One reason for the unprecedented vindictiveness of the peace
treaties, and in particular of their economic clauses, was that practical
men no longer believed—as they had done fifty or a hundred years earlier
—in an underlying harmony of interests between victors and defeated.
The object was now to eliminate a competitor, a revival of whose prosperity might menace your own. In Europe, the struggle was intensified by
the creation of new states and new economic frontiers. In Asia, India and
China built up large-scale manufactures to make themselves independent
of imports from Europe. Japan became an exporter of textiles and other

---

[44] Winston Churchill, *World Crisis*, p. 26.

[45] The same conditions encouraged the growth of Zionism; for Zionism, as the
Palestine Royal Commission of 1937 remarked, "on its negative side is a creed of
escape" Cmd. 5479, p. 13).

cheap goods which undercut European manufactures on the world market. Most important of all, there were no more open spaces anywhere awaiting cheap and profitable development and exploitation. The ample avenues of migration which had relieved the economic pressures of the pre-war period were closed; and in place of the natural flow of migration came the problem of forcibly evicted refugees.[46] The complex phenomenon known as economic nationalism swept over the world. The fundamental character of this clash of interests became obvious to all except those confirmed utopians who dominated economic thought in the English-speaking countries. The hollowness of the glib nineteenth-century platitude that nobody can benefit from what harms another was revealed. The basic presupposition of utopianism had broken down.

What confronts us in international politics to-day is, therefore, nothing less than the complete bankruptcy of the conception of morality which has dominated political and economic thought for a century and a half. Internationally, it is no longer possible to deduce virtue from right reasoning, because it is no longer seriously possible to believe that every state, by pursuing the greatest good of the whole world, is pursuing the greatest good of its own citizens, and *vice versa*. The synthesis of morality and reason, at any rate in the crude form in which it was achieved by nineteenth-century liberalism, is untenable. The inner meaning of the modern international crisis is the collapse of the whole structure of utopianism based on the concept of the harmony of interests. The present generation will have to rebuild from the foundations. But before we can do this, before we can ascertain what can be salved from the ruins, we must examine the flaws in the structure which led to its collapse; and we can best do this by analysing the realist critique of the utopian assumptions.

---

[46] "The existence of refugees is a symptom of the disappearance of economic and political liberalism. Refugees are the by-product of an economic isolationism which has practically stopped free migration" (J. Hope Simpson, *Refugees: Preliminary Report of a Survey,* p. 193).

SECTION TWO: Approaches to the Study of International Relations

4. SIX PRINCIPLES OF POLITICAL REALISM

Hans J. Morgenthau

1. POLITICAL REALISM believes that politics, like society in general, is governed by objective laws that have their roots in human nature. In order to improve society it is first necessary to understand the laws by which society lives. The operation of these laws being impervious to our preferences, men will challenge them only at the risk of failure.

Realism, believing as it does in the objectivity of the laws of politics, must also believe in the possibility of developing a rational theory that reflects, however imperfectly and one-sidedly, these objective laws. It believes also, then, in the possibility of distinguishing in politics between truth and opinion—between what is true objectively and rationally, supported by evidence and illuminated by reason, and what is only a subjec-

From *Politics Among Nations* by Hans J. Morgenthau (New York: 1967) pp. 4–14. Copyright 1948, 1954 by Alfred A. Knopf, Inc. Reprinted by permission. Footnotes have been renumbered to appear in consecutive order.

HANS MORGENTHAU (1904–   ) Alfred A. Michelson Distinguished Service Professor of Political Science and Modern History, and Director of the Center for the Study of American Foreign Policy, University of Chicago. His other books include *Politics in the Twentieth Century,* (Chicago: University of Chicago Press, 1962); *Dilemmas of Politics,* (Chicago: University of Chicago Press, 1958); *In Defense of the National Interest,* (New York: Alfred A. Knopf, 1951).

tive judgment, divorced from the facts as they are and informed by prejudice and wishful thinking.

Human nature, in which the laws of politics have their roots, has not changed since the classical philosophies of China, India, and Greece endeavored to discover these laws. Hence, novelty is not necessarily a virtue in political theory, nor is old age a defect. The fact that a theory of politics, if there be such a theory, has never been heard of before tends to create a presumption against, rather than in favor of, its soundness. Conversely, the fact that a theory of politics was developed hundreds or even thousands of years ago—as was the theory of the balance of power—does not create a presumption that it must be outmoded and obsolete. A theory of politics must be subjected to the dual test of reason and experience. To dismiss such a theory because it had its flowering in centuries past is to present not a rational argument but a modernistic prejudice that takes for granted the superiority of the present over the past. To dispose of the revival of such a theory as a "fashion" or "fad" is tantamount to assuming that in matters political we can have opinions but no truths.

For realism, theory consists in ascertaining facts and giving them meaning through reason. It assumes that the character of a foreign policy can be ascertained only through the examination of the political acts performed and of the foreseeable consequences of these acts. Thus, we can find out what statesmen have actually done, and from the foreseeable consequences of their acts we can surmise what their objectives might have been.

Yet examination of the facts is not enough. To give meaning to the factual raw material of foreign policy, we must approach political reality with a kind of rational outline, a map that suggests to us the possible meanings of foreign policy. In other words, we put ourselves in the position of a statesman who must meet a certain problem of foreign policy under certain circumstances, and we ask ourselves what the rational alternatives are from which a statesman may choose who must meet this problem under these circumstances (presuming always that he acts in a rational manner), and which of these rational alternatives this particular statesman, acting under these circumstances, is likely to choose. It is the testing of this rational hypothesis against the actual facts and their consequences that gives meaning to the facts of international politics and makes a theory of politics possible.

2. The main signpost that helps political realism to find its way through the landscape of international politics is the concept of interest defined in terms of power. This concept provides the link between reason trying to understand international politics and the facts to be understood. It sets politics as an autonomous sphere of action and understanding apart from

other spheres, such as economics (understood in terms of interest defined as wealth), ethics, aesthetics, or religion. Without such a concept a theory of politics, international or domestic, would be altogether impossible, for without it we could not distinguish between political and nonpolitical facts, nor could we bring at least a measure of systematic order to the political sphere.

We assume that statesmen think and act in terms of interest defined as power, and the evidence of history bears that assumption out. That assumption allows us to retrace and anticipate, as it were, the steps a statesman—past, present, or future—has taken or will take on the political scene. We look over his shoulder when he writes his dispatches; we listen in on his conversation with other statesmen; we read and anticipate his very thoughts. Thinking in terms of interest defined as power, we think as he does, and as disinterested observers we understand his thoughts and actions perhaps better than he, the actor on the political scene, does himself.

The concept of interest defined as power imposes intellectual discipline upon the observer, infuses rational order into the subject matter of politics, and thus makes the theoretical understanding of politics possible. On the side of the actor, it provides for rational discipline in action and creates that astounding continuity in foreign policy which makes American, British, or Russian foreign policy appear as an intelligible, rational continuum, by and large consistent within itself, regardless of the different motives, preferences, and intellectual and moral qualities of successive statesmen. A realist theory of international politics, then, will guard against two popular fallacies: the concern with motives and the concern with ideological preferences.

To search for the clue to foreign policy exclusively in the motives of statesmen is both futile and deceptive. It is futile because motives are the most illusive of psychological data, distorted as they are, frequently beyond recognition, by the interests and emotions of actor and observer alike. Do we really know what our own motives are? And what do we know of the motives of others?

Yet even if we had access to the real motives of statesmen, that knowledge would help us little in understanding foreign policies, and might well lead us astray. It is true that the knowledge of the statesman's motives may give us one among many clues as to what the direction of his foreign policy might be. It cannot give us, however, the one clue by which to predict his foreign policies. History shows no exact and necessary correlation between the quality of motives and the quality of foreign policy. This is true in both moral and political terms.

We cannot conclude from the good intentions of a statesman that his foreign policies will be either morally praiseworthy or politically successful. Judging his motives, we can say that he will not intentionally pursue policies that are morally wrong, but we can say nothing about the probability of their success. If we want to know the moral and political qualities of his actions, we must know them, not his motives. How often have statesmen been motivated by the desire to improve the world, and ended by making it worse? And how often have they sought one goal, and ended by achieving something they neither expected nor desired?

Neville Chamberlain's policies of appeasement were, as far as we can judge, inspired by good motives; he was probably less motivated by considerations of personal power than were many other British prime ministers, and he sought to preserve peace and to assure the happiness of all concerned. Yet his policies helped to make the Second World War inevitable, and to bring untold miseries to millions of men. Sir Winston Churchill's motives, on the other hand, have been much less universal in scope and much more narrowly directed toward personal and national power, yet the foreign policies that sprang from these inferior motives were certainly superior in moral and political quality to those pursued by his predecessor. Judged by his motives, Robespierre was one of the most virtuous men who ever lived. Yet it was the utopian radicalism of that very virtue that made him kill those less virtuous than himself, brought him to the scaffold, and destroyed the revolution of which he was a leader.

Good motives give assurance against deliberately bad policies; they do not guarantee the moral goodness and political success of the policies they inspire. What it is important to know, if one wants to understand foreign policy, is not primarily the motives of a statesman, but his intellectual ability to comprehend the essentials of foreign policy, as well as his political ability to translate what he has comprehended into successful political action. It follows that while ethics in the abstract judges the moral qualities of motives, political theory must judge the political qualities of intellect, will, and action.

A realist theory of international politics will also avoid the other popular fallacy of equating the foreign policies of a statesman with his philosophic or political sympathies, and of deducing the former from the latter. Statesmen, especially under contemporary conditions, may well make a habit of presenting their foreign policies in terms of their philosophic and political sympathies in order to gain popular support for them. Yet they will distinguish with Lincoln between their "*official* duty," which is to think and act in terms of the national interest, and their "*personal* wish," which is to see their own moral values and political principles realized throughout the world. Political realism does not require, nor does it condone, indifference to political ideals and moral principles, but it requires indeed a sharp distinction between the desirable and the possible—between what is desirable everywhere and at all times and what is possible under the concrete circumstances of time and place.

It stands to reason that not all foreign policies have always followed so rational, objective, and unemotional a course. The contingent elements of personality, prejudice, and subjective preference, and of all the weaknesses of intellect and will which flesh is heir to, are bound to deflect foreign policies from their rational course. Especially where foreign policy is conducted under the conditions of democratic control, the need to marshal popular emotions to the support of foreign policy cannot fail to impair the rationality of foreign policy itself. Yet a theory of foreign policy which aims at rationality must for the time being, as it were, abstract from these irrational elements and seek to paint a picture of foreign policy which presents the rational essence to be found in experience, without the contingent deviations from rationality which are also found in experience.

The difference between international politics as it actually is and a rational theory derived from it is like the difference between a photograph and a painted portrait. The photograph shows everything that can be seen by the naked eye; the painted portrait does not show everything that can be seen by the naked eye, but it shows, or at least seeks to show, one thing that the naked eye cannot see: the human essence of the person portrayed.

Political realism contains not only a theoretical but also a normative element. It knows that political reality is replete with contingencies and points to the typical influences they exert upon foreign policy. Yet it shares with all social theory the need, for the sake of theoretical understanding, to stress the rational elements of political reality; for it is these rational elements that make reality intelligible for theory. Political realism presents the theoretical construct of a rational foreign policy which experience can never completely achieve.

At the same time political realism considers a rational foreign policy to be good foreign policy; for only a rational foreign policy minimizes risks and maximizes benefits and, hence, complies both with the moral precept of prudence and the political requirement of success. Political realism wants the photographic picture of the political world to resemble as much as possible its painted portrait. Aware of the inevitable gap between good—that is, rational—foreign policy and foreign policy as it actually is, political realism maintains not only that theory must focus upon the rational elements of political reality, but also that foreign policy ought to be rational in view of its own moral and practical purposes.

Hence, it is no argument against the theory here presented that actual foreign policy does not or cannot live up to it. That argument misunderstands the intention of this book, which is to present not an indiscriminate description of political reality, but a rational theory of international politics. Far from being invalidated by the fact that, for instance, a perfect balance of power policy will scarcely be found in reality, it assumes that reality, being deficient in this respect, must be understood and evaluated as an approximation to an ideal system of balance of power.

3. Realism does not endow its key concept of interest defined as power with a meaning that is fixed once and for all. The idea of interest is indeed of the essence of politics and is unaffected by the circumstances of time and place. Thucydides' statement, born of the experiences of ancient Greece, that "identity of interest is the surest of bonds whether between states or individuals" was taken up in the nineteenth century by Lord Salisbury's remark that "the only bond of union that endures" among nations is "the absence of all clashing interests." It was erected into a general principle of government by George Washington:

> A small knowledge of human nature will convince us, that, with far the greatest part of mankind, interest is the governing principle; and that almost every man is more or less, under its influence. Motives of public virtue may for a time, or in particular instances, actuate men to the observance of a conduct purely disinterested; but they are not of themselves sufficient to produce a persevering conformity to the refined dictates and obligations of social duty. Few men are capable of making a continual sacrifice of all views of private interest, or advantage, to the common good. It is vain to exclaim against the depravity of human nature on this account; the fact is so, the experience of every age and nation has proved it and we must in a great measure, change the constitution of man, before we can make it otherwise. No institution, not built on the presumptive truth of these maxims can succeed.[1]

It was echoed and enlarged upon in our century by Max Weber's observation:

> Interests (material and ideal), not ideas, dominate directly the actions of men. Yet the "images of the world" created by these ideas have very often served as switches determining the tracks on which the dynamism of interests kept actions moving.[2]

Yet the kind of interest determining political action in a particular period of history depends upon the political and cultural context within which foreign policy is formulated. The goals that might be pursued by nations in their foreign policy can run the whole gamut of objectives any nation has ever pursued or might possibly pursue.

The same observations apply to the concept of power. Its content and the manner of its use are determined by the political and cultural en-

---

[1] *The Writings of George Washington*, edited by John C. Fitzpatrick (Washington: United States Printing Office, 1931–44), Vol. X, p. 363.

[2] Marianne Weber, *Max Weber* (Tuebingen: J. C. B. Mohr, 1926), pp. 347–8.

vironment. Power may comprise anything that establishes and maintains the control of man over man. Thus power covers all social relationships which serve that end, from physical violence to the most subtle psychological ties by which one mind controls another. Power covers the domination of man by man, both when it is disciplined by moral ends and controlled by constitutional safeguards, as in Western democracies, and when it is that untamed and barbaric force which finds its laws in nothing but its own strength and its sole justification in its aggrandizement.

Political realism does not assume that the contemporary conditions under which foreign policy operates, with their extreme instability and the ever present threat of large-scale violence, cannot be changed. The balance of power, for instance, is indeed a perennial element of all pluralistic societies, as the authors of *The Federalist* papers well knew; yet it is capable of operating, as it does in the United States, under the conditions of relative stability and peaceful conflict. If the factors that have given rise to these conditions can be duplicated on the international scene, similar conditions of stability and peace will then prevail there, as they have over long stretches of history among certain nations.

What is true of the general character of international relations is also true of the nation state as the ultimate point of reference of contemporary foreign policy. While the realist indeed believes that interest is the perennial standard by which political action must be judged and directed, the contemporary connection between interest and the national state is a product of history, and is therefore bound to disappear in the course of history. Nothing in the realist position militates against the assumption that the present division of the political world into nation states will be replaced by larger units of a quite different character, more in keeping with the technical potentialities and the moral requirements of the contemporary world.

The realist parts company with other schools of thought before the all-important question of how the contemporary world is to be transformed. The realist is persuaded that this transformation can be achieved only through the workmanlike manipulation of the perennial forces that have shaped the past as they will the future. The realist cannot be persuaded that we can bring about that transformation by confronting a political reality that has its own laws with an abstract ideal that refuses to take those laws into account.

4. Political realism is aware of the moral significance of political action. It is also aware of the ineluctable tension between the moral command and the requirements of successful political action. And it is unwilling to gloss over and obliterate that tension and thus to obfuscate both the moral and the political issue by making it appear as though the

stark facts of politics were morally more satisfying than they actually are, and the moral law less exacting than it actually is.

Realism maintains that universal moral principles cannot be applied to the actions of states in their abstract universal formulation, but that they must be filtered through the concrete circumstances of time and place. The individual may say for himself: *"Fiat justitia, pereat mundus* (Let justice be done, even if the world perish)," but the state has no right to say so in the name of those who are in its care. Both individual and state must judge political action by universal moral principles, such as that of liberty. Yet while the individual has a moral right to sacrifice himself in defense of such a moral principle, the state has no right to let its moral disapprobation of the infringement of liberty get in the way of successful political action, itself inspired by the moral principle of national survival. There can be no political morality without prudence; that is, without consideration of the political consequences of seemingly moral action. Realism, then, considers prudence—the weighing of the consequences of alternative political actions—to be the supreme virtue in politics. Ethics in the abstract judges action by its conformity with the moral law; political ethics judges action by its political consequences. Classical and medieval philosophy knew this, and so did Lincoln when he said:

> I do the very best I know how, the very best I can, and I mean to keep doing so until the end. If the end brings me out all right, what is said against me won't amount to anything. If the end brings me out wrong, ten angels swearing I was right would make no difference.

5. Political realism refuses to identify the moral aspirations of a particular nation with the moral laws that govern the universe. As it distinguishes between truth and opinion, so it distinguishes between truth and idolatry. All nations are tempted—and few have been able to resist the temptation for long—to clothe their own particular aspirations and actions in the moral purposes of the universe. To know the nations are subject to the moral law is one thing, while to pretend to know with certainty what is good and evil in the relations among nations is quite another. There is a world of difference between the belief that all nations stand under the judgment of God, inscrutable to the human mind, and the blasphemous conviction that God is always on one's side and that what one wills oneself cannot fail to be willed by God also.

The lighthearted equation between a particular nationalism and the counsels of Providence is morally indefensible, for it is that very sin of pride against which the Greek tragedians and the Biblical prophets have warned rulers and ruled. That equation is also politically pernicious, for it is liable to engender the distortion in judgment which, in the blindness of crusading frenzy, destroys nations and civilizations—in the name of moral principle, ideal, or God himself.

On the other hand, it is exactly the concept of interest defined in terms of power that saves us from both that moral excess and that political folly. For if we look at all nations, our own included, as political entities pursuing their respective interests defined in terms of power, we are able to do justice to all of them. And we are able to do justice to all of them in a dual sense: We are able to judge other nations as we judge our own and, having judged them in this fashion, we are then capable of pursuing policies that respect the interests of other nations, while protecting and promoting those of our own. Moderation in policy cannot fail to reflect the moderation of moral judgment.

6. The difference, then, between political realism and other schools of thought is real and it is profound. However much the theory of political realism may have been misunderstood and misinterpreted, there is no gainsaying its distinctive intellectual and moral attitude to matters political.

Intellectually, the political realist maintains the autonomy of the political sphere, as the economist, the lawyer, the moralist maintain theirs. He thinks in terms of interest defined as power, as the economist thinks in terms of interest defined as wealth; the lawyer, of the conformity of action with legal rules; the moralist, of the conformity of action with moral principles. The economist asks: "How does this policy affect the wealth of society, or a segment of it?" The lawyer asks: "Is this policy in accord with the rules of law?" The moralist asks: "Is this policy in accord with moral principles?" And the political realist asks: "How does this policy affect the power of the nation?" (Or of the federal government, of Congress, of the party, of agriculture, as the case may be.)

The political realist is not unaware of the existence and relevance of standards of thought other than political ones. As political realist, he cannot but subordinate these other standards to those of politics. And he parts company with other schools when they impose standards of thought appropriate to other spheres upon the political sphere. It is here that political realism takes issue with the "legalistic-moralistic approach" to international politics. That this issue is not, as has been contended, a mere figment of the imagination, but goes to the very core of the controversy, can be shown from many historical examples. Three will suffice to make the point.[3]

---

[3] See the other examples discussed in Hans J. Morgenthau, "Another 'Great Debate': The National Interest of the United States," *The American Political Science Review,* XLVI (December 1952), pp. 979 ff. See also Hans J. Morgenthau, *Dilemmas of Politics* (Chicago: University of Chicago Press, 1958), pp. 54 ff.

In 1939 the Soviet Union attacked Finland. This action confronted France and Great Britain with two issues, one legal, the other political. Did that action violate the Covenant of the League of Nations and, if it did, what countermeasures should France and Great Britain take? The legal question could easily be answered in the affirmative, for obviously the Soviet Union had done what was prohibited by the Covenant. The answer to the political question depended, first, upon the manner in which the Russian action affected the interests of France and Great Britain; second, upon the existing distribution of power between France and Great Britain, on the one hand, and the Soviet Union and other potentially hostile nations, especially Germany, on the other; and, third, upon the influence that the countermeasures were likely to have upon the interests of France and Great Britain and the future distribution of power. France and Great Britain, as the leading members of the League of Nations, saw to it that the Soviet Union was expelled from the League, and they were prevented from joining Finland in the war against the Soviet Union only by Sweden's refusal to allow their troops to pass through Swedish territory on their way to Finland. If this refusal by Sweden had not saved them, France and Great Britain would shortly have found themselves at war with the Soviet Union and Germany at the same time.

The policy of France and Great Britain was a classic example of legalism in that they allowed the answer to the legal question, legitimate within its sphere, to determine their political actions. Instead of asking both questions, that of law and that of power, they asked only the question of law; and the answer they received could have no bearing on the issue that their very existence might have depended upon.

The second example illustrates the "moralistic approach" to international politics. It concerns the international status of the Communist government of China. The rise of that government confronted the Western world with two issues, one moral, the other political. Were the nature and policies of that government in accord with the moral principles of the Western world? Should the Western world deal with such a government? The answer to the first question could not fail to be in the negative. Yet it did not follow with necessity that the answer to the second question should also be in the negative. The standard of thought applied to the first—the moral—question was simply to test the nature and the policies of the Communist government of China by the principles of Western morality. On the other hand, the second—the political—question had to be subjected to the complicated test of the interests involved and the power available on either side, and of the bearing of one or the other course of action upon these interests and power. The application of this test could well have led to the conclusion that it would be wiser not to deal with the Communist government of China. To arrive at this conclusion by neglecting this test altogether and answering the political question in terms of the moral issue was indeed a classic example of the "moralistic approach" to international politics.

The third case illustrates strikingly the contrast between realism and the legalistic-moralistic approach to foreign policy. Great Britain, as one of the guarantors of the neutrality of Belgium, went to war with Germany in August 1914 because Germany had violated the neutrality of Belgium. The British action could be justified either in realistic or legalistic-moralistic terms. That is to say, one could argue realistically that for centuries it had been axiomatic for British foreign policy to prevent the control of the Low Countries by a hostile power. It was then not so much the violation of Belgium's neutrality per se as the hostile intentions of the violator which provided the rationale for British intervention. If the violator had been another nation but Germany, Great Britain might well have refrained from intervening. This is the position taken by Sir Edward Grey, British Foreign Secretary during that period. Under Secretary for Foreign Affairs Hardinge remarked to him in 1908: "If France violated Belgian neutrality in a war against Germany, it is doubtful whether England or Russia would move a finger to maintain Belgian neutrality, while if the neutrality of Belgium was violated by Germany, it is probable that the converse would be the case." Whereupon Sir Edward Grey replied: "This is to the point." Yet one could also take the legalistic and moralistic position that the violation of Belgium's neutrality per se, because of its legal and moral defects and regardless of the interests at stake and of the identity of the violator, justified British and, for that matter, American intervention. This was the position which Theodore Roosevelt took in his letter to Sir Edward Grey of January 22, 1915:

> To me the crux of the situation has been Belgium. If England or France had acted toward Belgium as Germany has acted I should have opposed them, exactly as I now oppose Germany. I have emphatically approved your action as a model for what should be done by those who believe that treaties should be observed in good faith and that there is such a thing as international morality. I take this position as an American who is no more an Englishman than he is a German, who endeavors loyally to serve the interests of his own country, but who also endeavors to do what he can for justice and decency as regards mankind at large, and who therefore feels obliged to judge all other nations by their conduct on any given occasion.

This realist defense of the autonomy of the political sphere against its subversion by other modes of thought does not imply disregard for the existence and importance of these other modes of thought. It rather implies that each should be assigned its proper sphere and function. Political realism is based upon a pluralistic conception of human nature. Real man is a composite of "economic man," "political man," "moral man," "religious man," etc. A man who was nothing but "political man" would be a beast, for he would be completely lacking in moral restraints. A man who was nothing but "moral man" would be a fool, for he would be completely lacking in prudence. A man who was nothing but "religious man" would be a saint, for he would be completely lacking in worldly desires.

Recognizing that these different facets of human nature exist, political realism also recognizes that in order to understand one of them one has to deal with it on its own terms. That is to say, if I want to understand "religious man," I must for the time being abstract from the other aspects of human nature and deal with its religious aspect as if it were the only one. Furthermore, I must apply to the religious sphere the standards of thought appropriate to it, always remaining aware of the existence of other standards and their actual influence upon the religious qualities of man. What is true of this facet of human nature is true of all the others. No modern economist, for instance, would conceive of his science and its relations to other sciences of man in any other way. It is exactly through such a process of emancipation from other standards of thought, and the development of one appropriate to its subject matter, that economics has developed as an autonomous theory of the economic activities of man. To contribute to a similar development in the field of politics is indeed the purpose of political realism.

5. INTERNATIONAL THEORY: THE CASE FOR A CLASSICAL APPROACH

Hedley Bull

TWO APPROACHES to the theory of international relations at present compete for our attention. The first of these I shall call the classical approach. By this I do not mean the study and criticism of the "classics" of international relations, the writings of Hobbes, Grotius, Kant,

From *World Politics*, XVIII, No. 3 (April 1966), 361–362; 363–364; 366–376. Reprinted by permission of the author and publisher.

HEDLEY BULL (1932–   ) Professor of International Relations, Australian National University. Former Director of the Arms Control and Disarmament Research Unit, Her Majesty's Foreign Office, United Kingdom. Author of *Strategy and the Atlantic Alliance; A Critique of United States Doctrine*, (Princeton: Center of International Studies, 1964); *The Control of the Arms Race*, (New York: Praeger, 1965).

and other great thinkers of the past who have turned their attention to international affairs. Such study does indeed exemplify the classical approach, and it provides a method that is particularly fruitful and important. What I have in mind, however, is something much wider than this: the approach to theorizing that derives from philosophy, history, and law, and that is characterized above all by explicit reliance upon the exercise of judgment and by the assumptions that if we confine ourselves to strict standards of verification and proof there is very little of significance that can be said about international relations, that general propositions about this subject must therefore derive from a scientifically imperfect process of perception or intuition, and that these general propositions cannot be accorded anything more than the tentative and inconclusive status appropriate to their doubtful origin.

Until very recently virtually all attempts at theorizing about international relations have been founded upon the approach I have just described. We can certainly recognize it in the various twentieth-century systematizations of international theory—in works like those of Alfred Zimmern, E. H. Carr, Hans Morgenthau, Georg Schwarzenberger, Raymond Aron, and Martin Wight. And it is clearly also the method of their various precursors, whose scattered thoughts and partial treatments they have sought to draw together: political philosophers like Machiavelli and Burke, international lawyers like Vattel and Oppenheim, pamphleteers like Gentz and Cobden, historians like Heeren and Ranke. It is because this approach has so long been the standard one that we may call it classical.

The second approach I shall call the scientific one. I have chosen to call it scientific rather than scientistic so as not to prejudge the issue I wish to discuss by resort to a term of opprobrium. In using this name for the second approach, however, it is the aspirations of those who adopt it that I have in mind rather than their performance. They aspire to a theory of international relations whose propositions are based either upon logical or mathematical proof, or upon strict, empirical procedures of verification. Some of them dismiss the classical theories of international relations as worthless, and clearly conceive themselves to be the founders of a wholly new science. Others concede that the products of the classical approach were better than nothing, and perhaps even regard them with a certain affection, as the owner of a 1965 model might look at a vintage motor car. But in either case they hope and believe that their own sort of theory will come wholly to supersede the older type; like the logical positivists when they sought to appropriate English philosophy in the 1930's, or like Mr. McNamara's Whiz Kids when they moved into the Pentagon, they see themselves as tough-minded and expert new men, taking over an effete and woolly discipline, or pseudo-discipline, which has so far managed by some strange quirk to evade the scientific method but has always been bound to succumb to it in the end.

.   .   .

In the British academic community, by contrast, the scientific approach to the theory of international relations has had virtually no impact at all. The only Englishman to have made a major contribution in the new genre—Lewis F. Richardson—worked alone and unrecognized in his lifetime, and when a few years ago his work was exhumed and hailed as that of a great pioneer, it was by American editors addressing themselves to a predominantly American audience. Not only have British students of international relations not sought to contribute to theory in this vein, but, with one or two exceptions, the work of the American and other writers who have ploughed this field has failed to command their respect or even their attention.

If it were clear that this disdain has been founded upon an understanding of the scientific approach and a considered rejection of it there might be no cause for us to revise our attitude. We might even see in our imperviousness to this fashion the proof of the fundamental soundness and solidity of our own approach. The actual position, however, is that we are largely ignorant of what the new literature contains and that our rejection of it stems much less from any reasoned critique than it does from feelings of aesthetic revulsion against its language and methods, irritation at its sometimes arrogant and preposterous claims, frustration at our inability to grasp its meaning or employ its tools, *a priori* confidence that as an intellectual enterprise it is bound to fail, and professional insecurity induced by the awful gnawing thought that it might perhaps succeed.

There is no doubt that the writing that has emerged from the scientific approach should be taken seriously. Judged by its own standards of logical precision and scientific rigor its quality is sometimes high. Moreover, however adverse a view we take of this literature, it is impossible to examine it with any degree of care and sympathy and yet to conclude that its contribution to the understanding of international relations is nil. Indeed, given the great concentration of energy and talent that has gone into producing it in recent years, it would be extraordinary if this were otherwise.

.   .   .

However, the scientific approach has contributed and is likely to contribute very little to the theory of international relations, and in so far as it is intended to encroach upon and ultimately displace the classical approach, it is positively harmful. In support of this conclusion I wish to put forward seven propositions.

The first proposition is that by confining themselves to what can be logically or mathematically proved or verified according to strict procedures, the practitioners of the scientific approach are denying themselves the only instruments that are at present available for coming to grips with the substance of the subject. In abstaining from what Morton Kaplan calls "intuitive guesses" or what William Riker calls "wisdom literature" they are committing themselves to a course of intellectual puritanism that keeps them (or would keep them if they really adhered to it) as remote from the substance of international politics as the inmates of a Victorian nunnery were from the study of sex.

To appreciate our reliance upon the capacity for judgment in the theory of international relations we have only to rehearse some of the central questions to which that theory is addressed. Some of these are at least in part moral questions, which cannot by their very nature be given any sort of objective answer, and which can only be probed, clarified, reformulated, and tentatively answered from some arbitrary standpoint, according to the method of philosophy. Others of them are empirical questions, but of so elusive a nature that any answer we provide to them will leave some things unsaid, will be no more than an item in conversation that has yet to be concluded. It is not merely that in *framing* hypotheses in answer to these empirical questions we are dependent upon intuition or judgment (as has often been pointed out, this is as true in the natural as in the social sciences); it is that in the *testing* of them we are utterly dependent upon judgment also, upon a rough and ready observation, of a sort for which there is no room in logic or strict science, that things are this way and not that.

For example, does the collectivity of sovereign states constitute a political society or system, or does it not? If we can speak of a society of sovereign states, does it presuppose a common culture or civilization? And if it does, does such a common culture underlie the worldwide diplomatic framework in which we are attempting to operate now? What is the place of war in international society? Is all private use of force anathema to society's working, or are there just wars which it may tolerate and even require? Does a member state of international society enjoy a right of intervention in the internal affairs of another, and if so in what circumstances? Are sovereign states the sole members of international society, or does it ultimately consist of individual human beings, whose rights and duties override those of the entities who act in their name? To what extent is the course of diplomatic events at any one time determined or circumscribed by the general shape or structure of the international system; by the number, relative weight, and conservative or radical disposition of its constituent states, and by the instruments for getting their way that military technology or the distribution of wealth has put into their hands; by the particular set of rules of the game underlying diplomatic practice at that time? And so on.

These are typical of the questions of which the theory of international relations essentially consists. But the scientific theorists have forsworn the means of coming directly to grips with them. When confronted with them they do one of two things. Either they shy away and devote themselves to peripheral subjects—methodologies for dealing with the subject, logical extrapolations of conceptual frameworks for thinking about it, marginalia of the subject that are susceptible of measurement or direct observation—or they break free of their own code and resort suddenly and without acknowledging that this is what they are doing to the methods of the classical approach—methods that in some cases they employ very badly, their preoccupations and training having left them still strangers to the substance of the subject.

This congenital inability of the scientific approach to deal with the crux of the subject while yet remaining true to its own terms leads me to an observation about the teaching of the subject in universities. Whatever virtues one might discern in the scientific approach, it is a wholly retrograde development that it should now form the basis of undergraduate courses of instruction in international politics, as in some universities in the United States it now does. The student whose study of international politics consists solely of an introduction to the techniques of systems theory, game theory, simulation, or content analysis is simply shut off from contact with the subject, and is unable to develop any feeling either for the play of international politics or for the moral dilemmas to which it gives rise.

The second proposition I wish to put forward arises out of the first: It is that where practitioners of the scientific approach have succeeded in casting light upon the substance of the subject it has been by stepping beyond the bounds of that approach and employing the classical method. What there is of value in their work consists essentially of judgments that are not established by the mathematical or scientific methods they employ, and which may be arrived at quite independently of them.

. . .

My third proposition is that the practitioners of the scientific approach are unlikely to make progress of the sort to which they aspire. Some of the writers I have been discussing would be ready enough to admit that so far only peripheral topics have been dealt with in a rigidly scientific way. But their claim would be that it is not by its performance so far that their approach should be judged, but by the promise it contains of ultimate advance. They may even say that the modesty of their beginnings show how faithful they are to the example of natural science: Modern physics too, Morton Kaplan tells us, "has reared its present lofty edifice by setting itself problems that it has the tools or techniques to solve."[4]

The hope is essentially that our knowledge of international relations will reach the point at which it becomes genuinely cumulative: that from the present welter of competing terminologies and conceptual frameworks there will eventually emerge a common language, that the various insignificant subjects that have now been scientifically charted will eventually join together and become significant, and that there will then exist a foundation of firm theory on which newcomers to the enterprise will build.

No one can say with certainty that this will not happen, but the prospects are very bleak indeed. The difficulties that the scientific theory has encountered do not appear to arise from the quality that international relations is supposed to have of a "backward" or neglected science, but from characteristics inherent in the subject matter which have been catalogued often enough: the unmanageable number of variables of which any generalization about state behavior must take account; the resistance of the material to controlled experiment: the quality it has of changing before our eyes and slipping between our fingers even as we try to categorize it; the fact that the theories we produce and the affairs that are theorized about are related not only as subject and object but also as cause and effect, thus ensuring that even our most innocent ideas contribute to their own verification or falsification.

A more likely future for the theory of international politics is that it will remain indefinitely in the philosophical stage of constant debate about fundamentals; that the works of the new scientific theorists will not prove to be solid substructure on which the next generation will build, but rather that those of them that survive at all will take their place alongside earlier works as partial and uncertain guides to an essentially intractable subject; and that successive thinkers, while learning what they can from what has gone before, will continue to feel impelled to build their own houses of theory from the foundations up.

A fourth proposition that may be advanced against many who belong to the scientific school is that they have done a great disservice to theory in this field by conceiving of it as the construction and manipulation of so-called "models." Theoretical inquiry into an empirical subject normally proceeds by way of the assertion of general connections and distinctions between events in the real world. But it is the practice of many of these writers to cast their theories in the form of a deliberately

---

[4] "Problems of Theory Building and Theory Confirmation in International Politics," *World Politics*, XIV (October 1961), 7.

simplified abstraction from reality, which they then turn over and examine this way and that before considering what modifications must be effected if it is to be applied to the real world. A model in the strict sense is a deductive system of axioms and theorems; so fashionable has the term become, however, that it is commonly used also to refer to what is simply a metaphor or an analogy. It is only the technique of constructing models in the strict sense that is at issue here. However valuable this technique may have proved in economics and other subjects, its use in international politics is to be deplored.

The virtue that is supposed to lie in models is that by liberating us from the restraint of constant reference to reality, they leave us free to set up simple axioms based on a few variables and thenceforward to confine ourselves to rigorous deductive logic, thereby generating wide theoretical insights that will provide broad signposts to guide us in the real world even if they do not fill in the details.

I know of no model that has assisted our understanding of international relations that could not just as well have been expressed as an empirical generalization. This, however, is not the reason why we should abstain from them. The freedom of the model-builder from the discipline of looking at the world is what makes him dangerous; he slips easily into a dogmatism that empirical generalization does not allow, attributing to the model a connection with reality it does not have, and as often as not distorting the model itself by importing additional assumptions about the world in the guise of logical axioms. The very intellectual completeness and logical tidiness of the model-building operation lends it an air of authority which is often quite misleading as to its standing as a statement about the real world.

I shall take as an example the most ambitious of all the model-builders, Morton Kaplan. He provides us with models of two historical and four possible international systems, each with its "essential rules" or characteristic behavior. He claims that the models enable him to make predictions only, it is true, of a high level of generality—about characteristic or modal behavior within the present international system, about whether or not transformations of this system into some other are likely and what form they might take.

The six systems that Kaplan identifies, and the "essential rules" or characteristic behavior of each, are in fact quite commonplace ideas, drawn from the everyday discussion of international affairs, about the general political structure that the world has had or might have. They are the international political system of the eighteenth and nineteenth centuries, the present so-called bipolar system, the structure that might exist if the present polarization of power were not moderated by the United Nations and by powerful third parties, the system we might have if the

United Nations were to become the predominant political force in a world of still sovereign states, a world state, and a world of many nuclear powers.

In discussing the conditions under which equilibrium is maintained in each of these systems, and in predicting the likelihood and direction of their transformation into different systems, Kaplan appears to resort to a kind of guesswork a good deal more arbitrary than any involved in the style of international theory he wishes to displace. In discussing the two historical systems he uses some pertinent examples from recent history, but there is no reason to assume that behavior in future international systems of this sort is bound to be the same. In discussing the nonhistorical systems, his remarks are either tautological extensions of the definitions he employs, or are quite arbitrarily formulated empirical judgments that do not properly belong to the model at all.

Kaplan's six systems are of course not the only ones possible. He admits, for example, that they do not cover the cases of Greek antiquity or of the Middle Ages, and they do not embrace the infinite variety the future might unveil. What reason, therefore, is there to suppose that transformation of any one of the systems must be into one of the others? The whole enterprise of attempting to predict transformations on the basis of these models requires at every stage that we go outside the models themselves and introduce further considerations.

One objection to Kaplan's models, therefore, is that they are not models; they are lacking in internal rigor and consistency. But even if they possessed such qualities, they would not provide the illumination of reality that Kaplan claims for them. We have no means of knowing that the variables excluded from the models will not prove to be crucial. He has provided an intellectual exercise and no more. I should not wish to contend that someone exploring the question of what changes might take place in the present international system, or the question of what might be the shape and structure of a world of many nuclear powers, is unable to quarry some nuggets of value from Kaplan's work. But how much more fruitfully can these questions be explored, how much better indeed might so gifted a person as Kaplan himself have explored them, by paying attention to the actual variety of events in the real world, by taking note of the many elements that are pushing the present international system this way and that, and the large number of political and technical factors that might contrive to mold a world of many nuclear powers in any one of a dozen shapes different from those that can be confined within the bounds of Kaplan's model.

The fashion for constructing models exemplifies a much wider and more long-standing trend in the study of social affairs: the substitution of methodological tools and the question "Are they useful or not?" for the assertion of propositions about the world and the question "Are they true or not?" Endemic though it has become in recent thinking, I believe this change to have been for the worse. The "usefulness" of a tool has in the end to be translated as the truth of a proposition, or a series of propositions, advanced about the world, and the effect of the substitution is simply to obscure the issue of an empirical test and to pave the way for shoddy thinking and the subordination of inquiry to practical utility. However, this is a theme that requires more amplification than it can be given here, and in introducing it I am perhaps taking on more antagonists than I need do for my present purpose.

A fifth proposition is that the work of the scientific school is in some cases distorted and impoverished by a fetish for measurement. For anyone dedicated to scientific precision, quantification of the subject must appear as the supreme ideal, whether it takes the form of the expression of theories themselves in the form of mathematical quations or simply that of the presentation of evidence amassed in quantitative form. Like the Anglican bishop a year or so ago who began his sermon on morals by saying that he did not think all sexual intercourse is necessarily wrong, I wish to take a liberal view of this matter. There is nothing inherently objectionable, just as there is nothing logically peculiar, in a theoretical statement about international politics cast in mathematical form. Nor is there any objection·to the counting of phenomena that do not differ from one another in any relevant respect, and presenting this as evidence in support of a theory. The difficulty arises where the pursuit of the measurable leads us to ignore relevant differences between the phenomena that are being counted, to impute to what has been counted a significance it does not have, or to be so distracted by the possibilities that do abound in our subject for counting as to be diverted from the qualitative inquiries that are in most cases more fruitful.

I should like to take as an example the work of Karl Deutsch and his pupil Bruce Russett. These writers have sought to investigate the bonds of community that link different nations, and in explaining the cohesiveness or mutual responsiveness that exists between different peoples or different groups within a single people they have especially focused their attention upon social communication, that is to say, upon the flow of persons, goods, and ideas, or of the "messages" they carry. Karl Deutsch, together with a number of collaborators, has provided a study of the extent to which the various peoples of the North Atlantic area are linked by such bonds of community, and he is concerned particularly with the question of the measure in which these peoples form what he calls a "security-community"—that is to say, a group of people who agree that their common problems will in fact be resolved in this way.[5]

---

[5] Deutsch has, of course, been author or part-author of a number of other works besides *Political Community and the North Atlantic Area,* but apart from his *Political Community at the International Level* (Princeton 1953), this is the one that most comes to grips with the theory of international relations.

Bruce Russett has tackled the more manageable subject of community simply in the relationship between Britain and America, and has sought in particular to determine whether these two peoples have become more or less "responsive" to one another as the twentieth century has progressed.[6]

A feature of the work of both these writers is their presentation of quantitative material as an index of the degree of community that exists between one people and another. They produce figures, for example, on resources devoted to trade as a proportion of total resources; mail sent abroad, or to a particular destination, as a proportion of total mail; number of diplomatic agreements arrived at with another country as a proportion of total agreements arrived at; student exchanges; "content analysis" of newspapers and learned journals; and so on.

The work of Karl Deutsch and Bruce Russett in this field is certainly original and suggestive. Moreover, these two writers are not uncritical in their use of quantitative analysis. But the prominence they give to it is a source of weakness rather than strength in their arguments. Their counting often ignores (or, if it does not ignore, skates over) the most relevant differences between the units counted: differences between the content of one item of mail and another, the diplomatic importance of one treaty and another, the significance of one inch of newspaper column and another. Differences in these other relevant respects may cancel themselves out, but they also may not; and in practice we are likely to respect these statistics only in cases where they confirm some intuitive impression we already have, as, e.g., where Russett's figures confirm, as many of them do, the very confident judgment we may make that as this century has progressed America has become relatively more important to Britain than Britain is to America. Even so, such a judgment is quite external to the statistics that are provided, and does not establish that they measure anything relevant.

Deutsch and Russett, furthermore, are inclined to attribute to their statistics a place in the total chain of the argument that they do not have. They often seem to assume that there is something so irrefutable and final about a piece of evidence that can be put into figures that they are absolved of the necessity of showing in detail how it supports the general thesis they are seeking to demonstrate. Foreign trade is foreign trade, and a precise measurement of foreign trade is not a precise measurement of anything else unless an explanation is advanced as to why this is so. A number of the crucial but missing links in Deutsch's chain of argument seem to have been lost to sight because of this tendency of those who have succeeded in producing figures to be blinded by the illumination

---

[6] *Community and Contention: Britain and America in the Twentieth Century* (Cambridge, Mass., 1963).

they cast. Are the figures of "communication flow" an index of political community at the international level, or a cause of it? Does the "communication flow" contribute to producing the vital element, in Deutsch's scheme, of "mutual identification," or does the latter arise in some quite different way?

Finally, even if one may concede that statistics have some place in an inquiry into political community and social communication, it appears to me that Deutsch and Russett have been distracted by them from the more fruitful parts of the subject. By far the most interesting things that these two writers have to say lie in their attempts to think out the distinguishing features of a community, the different sorts of communities that obtain, the elements that make up the cohesion of a community, the determinants of mutual responsiveness between one people and another. And by far the most pertinent evidence they bring forward lies in the qualitative judgments they are able to bring to bear on history and contemporary affairs.

My sixth proposition is that there is a need for rigor and precision in the theory of international politics, but that the sort of rigor and precision of which the subject admits can be accommodated readily enough within the classical approach. Some of the targets at which the scientific theorists aim their barbs are quite legitimate ones. The classical theory of international relations has often been marked by failure to define terms, to observe logical canons of procedure, or to make assumptions explicit. It has sometimes also, especially when associated with the philosophy of history, sought to pursue into international politics implications of a fundamentally scientific view of the world. The theory of international relations should undoubtedly attempt to be scientific in the sense of being a coherent, precise, and orderly body of knowledge, and in the sense of being consistent with the philosophical foundations of modern science. Insofar as the scientific approach is a protest against slipshod thinking and dogmatism, or against a residual providentialism, there is everything to be said for it. But much theorizing in the classical mold is not open to this sort of objection. The writings of the great international lawyers from Victoria to Oppenheim (which, it may be argued, form the basis of the traditional literature of the subject) are rigorous and critical. There are plenty of contemporary writers who are logical and rigorous in their approach and yet do not belong to the school I have called the scientific one: Raymond Aron, Stanley Hoffmann, and Kenneth Waltz are examples. Moreoever, it is not difficult to find cases where writers in the scientific vein have failed to be rigorous and critical in this sense.

My seventh and final proposition is that the practitioners of the scientific approach, by cutting themselves off from history and philosophy, have deprived themselves of the means of self-criticism, and in consequence have a view of their subject and its possibilities that is callow and brash. I hasten to add that this is not true, or not equally true, of them all. But their thinking is certainly characterized by a lack of any sense of inquiry into international politics as a continuing tradition to which they are the latest recruits; by an insensitivity to the conditions of recent history that have produced them, provided them with the preoccupations and perspectives they have, and colored these in ways of which they might not be aware; by an absence of any disposition to wonder why, if the fruits their researches promise are so great and the prospects of translating them into action so favorable, this has not been accomplished by anyone before; by an uncritical attitude toward their own assumptions, and especially toward the moral and political attitudes that have a central but unacknowledged position in much of what they say.

6. THE GREAT DEBATE: TRADITIONALISM VERSUS SCIENCE IN INTERNATIONAL RELATIONS

Morton A. Kaplan

THE TRADITIONALIST asserts that those who aspire to a "science" of politics insist upon precision, rigor, quantification, and general theory. The traditionalist further claims that the complexity of international politics is such that these goals cannot be attained nor the important questions of international politics be investigated by these means. Whether the charge is correct cannot be answered in general. The appropriate degree of theory and of precision depends both on the state of the discipline and on the subject matter.[1] Since I am most familiar with my

From *World Politics*, XVIII, No. 9 (October 1966), 7–20. Reprinted by permission of the author and publisher. Footnotes have been renumbered to appear in consecutive order.

MORTON A. KAPLAN (1921–   ) Professor of Political Science, University of Chicago. Author of *The Revolution in World Politics*, (New York: Wiley, 1962); *System and Process in International Politics*, (New York: Wiley, 1957); *United States Foreign Policy, 1945–1955*, (Washington: Brookings, 1956). Co-author of *Political Foundations of International Law*, (New York: Wiley, 1961).

[1] The assertion that my *System and Process in International Politics* (New York 1957) attempts a completely deductive theory has been made both by Hedley Bull and by Stanley Hoffmann. Hoffmann apparently quotes *System and Process* to this

own work, I should like to consider it first in some detail and then to examine a number of other scientific approaches criticized by traditionalists. I shall try to show that fundamentally different enterprises are involved and that blanket analyses obscure more than they clarify.

The conception that underlies *System and Process* is fairly simple. If the number, type, and behavior of nations differ over time, and if their military capabilities, their economic assets, and their information also vary over time, then there is some likely interconnection between these elements such that different structural and behavioral systems can be discerned to operate in different periods of history. This conception may turn out to be incorrect, but it does not seem an unreasonable basis for an investigation of the subject matter. To conduct such an investigation requires systematic hypotheses concerning the nature of the connections of the variables. Only after these are made can past history be examined in a way that illuminates the hypotheses. Otherwise the investigator has no criteria on the basis of which he can pick and choose from among the infinite reservoir of facts available to him. These initial hypotheses indicate the areas of facts which have the greatest importance for this type of investigation; presumably if the hypotheses are wrong, this will become reasonably evident in the course of attempting to use them.

The models of *System and Process* provide a theoretical framework within which seemingly unconnected kinds of events can be related. A few examples of these can be given. For instance, it is asserted in the

---

effect ("The Long Road to Theory," *World Politics*, xi [April 1959], 357). And Bull, apparently relying upon Hoffmann, then uses the admitted fact that not all assertions of the models are rigorously deduced as a disproof of the claims made for the models ("International Theory: The Case for a Classical Approach," *World Politics*, xviii [April 1966], 366–67, 371–72). Yet the first page of the preface—the page from which Hoffmann takes his quotations—which contains the paragraph describing what an ideal deductive theory would look like, includes as the last line of that paragraph the following sentence: "If 'theory' is interpreted in this strict sense, this book does not contain a theory." It then goes on to say, "If some of the requirements for a theory are loosened; if systematic completeness is not required; if proof of logical consistency is not required; if unambiguous interpretation of terms and laboratory methods of confirmation are not required; then this book is, or at least contains, a theory. This theory may be viewed as an initial or introductory theory of international politics." This qualification is repeated in the conclusion (pp. 245–46): "A complete and systematic statement of these assumptions has not been offered. One reason for this gap lies in the belief of the author that international politics, and social science generally, is so poorly developed that the construction of a precise deductive system would be more constrictive and misleading than enlightening, that, at this stage of development, some ambiguity is a good thing." I did believe, however, that the ambiguity could be reduced and that more disciplined reasoning and scientific method could be introduced into the study of international politics. *That* was what *System and Process* tried to do.

traditional literature that the framework of European international law is the product of a common civilization, culture, set of values, and personal ties. Our hypotheses indicate that the "balance of power" type of system is likely to motivate and reinforce the kinds of norms that were observed during the modern European "balance of power" period. If the traditionalist hypothesis is correct, then one would expect that international law would have been strongest in the earliest part of the modern European "balance of power" period, when, as a consequence of a common Catholicism and interrelated dynasticism, the cultural factors making for uniformity of norms would have been strongest. If the systems model is correct, then one would instead expect the norms to develop over time as the actors learned how these norms reinforced their common interests. One would also expect on the basis of the systems model that a number of these norms would receive less reinforcement in a loose bipolar system. No systematic study of these hypotheses has yet been carried out. Peripheral results from comparative studies directed to other aspects of "balance of power" behavior, however, indicate the likelihood that the systems explanation will account for the historic evidence better than the traditionalist one. The early evidence indicates that the norms were weaker in the earlier phases of the period. Such results are not conclusive. We may find still other "balance of power" systems in which our initial expectations are falsified. This would then create a new problem for investigation. However, the systematic nature of the systems hypotheses would make this kind of comparative analysis easier by providing a framework within which questions could be generated and research carried on. It is perhaps no accident that the first set of comparative theories of international relations was developed within a systems framework and not within a traditionalistic framework.

An illustration of the way in which systems models may be used to connect or to explain seemingly discordant facts may also be offered. According to the systems model of the "balance of power" system, alliances will be short in duration, shifting as to membership, and wars will be limited in objectives. The reason offered for this is that the need to maintain the availability of potential alliance partners is greater than the need for the additional assets that would result from the destruction of the defeated foe. If one looks at Europe after 1870, however, one finds a set of relatively permanent alliances centered on France and Germany which produced a war that, according to the standards of the time, was relatively unlimited. The models, however, are closed in such a way that public opinion does not interfere with the rationality of external decision-making. The seizure of Alsace-Lorraine by Germany after the war of 1870, as Bismarck foresaw, produced in France a desire for revenge that, despite German attempts to buy France off, made it impossible for France and Germany to be alliance partners in any serious sense. For this reason,

Germany considered a preventive war against France. That Germany and France became the hubs of opposing alliances therefore is consistent with the model if the parameter change is taken into account. Since neither France nor Germany viewed the other as a potential alliance partner, the motivation that served to limit war would not have been operative with respect to these two nations. Although this is surely not a complete—nor even a "proved"—explanation of the events leading to the First World War, it does establish a consistency between the predictions of the model suitably adjusted for a changed parameter and the actual course of events. Thus the systems model has some additional explanatory power even for some nonconforming events.[2] It may be possible to offer similar explanations for other parameter changes. One would not expect that this could be done with respect to problems of system change involving the transformation rules of the system. If this were possible, we should have a general theory of the system rather than a set of comparative theories. Although it cannot be demonstrated that a general theory is impossible, the reasons for its lack of likelihood have been stated by me elsewhere." [3]

In addition to empirical investigations, the systems theory of international politics calls for the use of models. The reason for this is quite simple. Even statesmen make statements about the relationship of states. From what assumptions are such statements derived? This is often unclear. Are they correctly derived? Only a much more systematic statement of the assumptions and of the conditions under which they are proposed to apply permits any kind of answer. Under what conditions do the generalizations apply, if at all? How much difference does it make to add one state or two states to a five-state system and under what conditions? Is Arthur Burns correct in asserting that five is the optimal number for security, with declining security both below and above that number,[4] or is Kaplan correct in believing that five is the minimal lower bound for security but that security increases as the number of states is increased up to some as-yet-undiscovered upper bound? How many deviant states can a system tolerate? What degree of deviance is tolerable? Can devi-

---

[2] It was long known that certain poisons produced death. It was not known, however, how they did so. Eventually chemists learned that when certain poisons entered the blood stream, they combined with the oxygen in the blood and thereby deprived vital organs of the oxygen necessary for life. Although the end result of the poisoning was long known, the chemical explanation contributes to knowledge. Under some circumstances it has important utility. For instance, if one knows the mechanism involved, it may be easier to find the antidote.

[3] *System and Process,* xvii–xviii.

[4] Arthur Lee Burns, "From Balance to Deterrence: A Theoretical Analysis," *World Politics,* IX (July 1957), 494–529.

ance be accommodated so that deviant states are forced to behave as if they were merely security-oriented? How will changes in weapons systems affect the problem of stability? What of geographic constraints? To what extent do internal decision-making organs, either by facilitating or impeding concentration on problems of external concern or by influencing the speed of reaction time, affect the stability of the system?

Some of these questions can be explored at a theoretical level in terms of the consistency and implications of the basic assumptions. Computer realizations are helpful to this end. The relevance of the questions for the real world can be explored by means of historical comparative studies. If the theoretical model is stable and the historical system is not, this is an indication that some factor not taken account of in the theory is operating. If both systems are stable, it is possible that this may be so for reasons other than those contained in the assumptions. Possible responses to this proposition may be obtained either through more thorough research into particular systems or by means of additional comparative studies that may permit discrimination of the cases. Elucidation of the constraining parameters would likely require a large series of comparative studies. The degree of confidence we place in our studies will never approach that which the physicist has in the study of mechanics (although other areas of physics may present problems as bad as those of politics); but without theoretical models we are unable even to make the discriminations open to us and to explore these questions to the same degree of depth.[5]

International systems theory is designed to investigate problems of macrosystem structure. It is not, for instance, easily adaptable to the investigation of microstructural problems of foreign policy. Techniques in this area would involve closer analogies with histology than with macrosystem analysis. This is an area in which extensive knowledge of a specific course of events, immense accumulations of detail, sensitivity and judgment in the selection of relevant factors, and intuitive ability of a high order are extremely important. We cannot easily use comparative evaluation, for the large number of variables involved in such events would not be even closely paralleled in other cases. In this sense, histology has an advantage over political science, for the histologist can at least examine generically similar material time and time again. Although elements of these problems can be subjected to scientific analysis, in many cases the use of intuitive judgment outweighs that of demonstrable knowledge. In these last cases, the conclusions can often be communi-

---

[5] The problem of confirmation of systems models is explored in greater depth in Kaplan, "Some Problems of International Systems Research," in *International Political Communities* (New York 1966), 497–502.

cated, though usually in poorly articulated form, but the means by which they were reached can be only badly misrepresented.

International systems theory, however, is only one of the scientific approaches to the subject matter of international politics. I hesitate to speak of the research of other scholars because I have not examined their work with the care required of a serious critic. Yet even superficial analysis would seem to indicate that the scientific approaches discussed together by Hedley Bull, for instance, have little in common.[6] They address themselves to different questions and use different methods. I shall try to indicate what some of these differences are—and my own attitude toward these other approaches—with the understanding that I do not consider myself an entirely competent judge.

Hedley Bull discusses Kaplan, Deutsch, Russett, Schelling, and various others as if they represented a sufficiently common position that similar criticisms would apply to all of them. Whereas I begin with a macrosystem analysis, however, Karl Deutsch proceeds with an inductive analysis based upon the quantification of the parameters of systems.[7] Whereas I study general system behavior, Deutsch studies the growth of community. Hedley Bull criticizes Karl Deutsch for counting all communications as if they were equal in some respect. Yet surely that is a most economical initial hypothesis. Unless Deutsch makes that assumption or a similar one, he can not discover whether such an item count will provide him with meaningful indicators for the growth of community.

In any event, it is rather discouraging to find Deutsch attacked because he does not differentiate messages according to criteria of importance. Deutsch developed his indices on the basis of a sophisticated set of hypotheses and after elaborate historical studies. If the indices prove not to be exceptionally useful, this will likely be uncovered by further empirical work. If further categorizations prove necessary—as they have, for instance, in assessing group differences in intelligence—empirical scientific work will no doubt establish this fact. If Haas is right that elite activity that produces institutions is more important than an increased flow of communications in establishing a pluralistic security community, the empirical evidence will likely indicate this also.[8] If differentiation of flows according to the kinds of systems they develop within

---

[6] Pp. 361–77.

[7] "Toward an Inventory of Basic Trends and Patterns in Comparative and International Politics," *American Political Science Review,* LIV (March 1960), 34–57. See also Deutsch and others, *Political Community and the North Atlantic Area* (Princeton 1957); Deutsch, *Nationalism and Social Communication* (New York 1953); and Deutsch, *Political Community at the International Level* (Garden City 1954).

[8] Ernst Haas, "The Challenge of Regionalism," *International Organization,* XII (Autumn 1958), 440–58.

—a systems orientation—is likely to make for finer discrimination, it is again the empirical scientific evidence and not abstract literary considerations that will establish this point.[9]

Russett uses still a different technique.[10] I believe that his fitting curves to data by means of quadratic equations is not suited to the data he uses. This, however, is true, if true at all, not on the basis of some general philosophical principle, but on the basis of a specific evaluation of the use of the technique in terms of the subject matter to which it is applied. I am also, for instance, skeptical of the techniques employed by Zaninovich in his *Empirical Theory of State Response*, with respect to the Sino-Soviet case.[11] Although I find his conclusions unexceptional—for instance, the conclusion that when two states are involved in a critical relationship, each will misperceive the intentions of the other—I do not find them particularly useful in the form in which they are applied. The phenomenon of mistaken perception is well known. As a mere phenomenon, it does not require further documentation. Nor in this abstract form does it add much to our understanding of the political process. It is not very useful for policy-makers either. It does not tell them what the misperceptions will be or the particular kinds of responses they will produce. Moreover, since most of the analysis is based upon the coding of public statements and editorials in the party newspapers, there is the additional danger that the public stance of the state will be misperceived by the investigator as its private one. Whether my judgment of the procedure is right or wrong, however, depends not upon the crude general propositions enunciated by the traditionalists but upon a specific analysis of the application of the methodology to a specific subject matter.

One may desire to raise questions about some of the simulations of international politics that are being carried on. Whether small group simulations reveal more about small groups simulating international relations than about the more complex pattern of international politics is, at the minimum, an open question. If simulation is a quite useful tool for generating hypotheses, it is likely much less useful for confirming them. Here the reader must be warned: I am not here offering an analysis of whether this is the case or not, and may merely be asserting my own prejudice.

Much of the criticism of the work of Thomas Schelling seems mis-

---

[9] For a responsible discussion of Deutsch's categories and techniques, see Ralph H. Retzlaff, "The Use of Aggregate Data in Comparative Political Analysis," *Journal of Politics*, XXVII (November 1965), 797–817.

[10] Bruce M. Russett, *Trends in World Politics* (New York 1965).

[11] Martin George Zaninovich, *An Empirical Theory of State Response: The Sino-Soviet Case* (Stanford 1964), mimeographed.

guided. It is generally agreed that there are many interesting insights in Schelling's work; [12] but the traditionalists, e.g., Hedley Bull, sometimes object that the insights are not derived from game-theoretic methods. This argument is misleading; Schelling rarely uses mathematical game-theoretic methods. Most of his analysis is sociological; that is the root of his assertion that he desires to reorient game theory. On the other hand, although his insights in the usual case are not rigorously derived from game theory, it must be admitted that insights of this kind did not seriously begin to enter the literature until the questions posed by game-theoretic analysis directed attention to them.

Schelling is so identified with game theory by the traditionalists that he is credited with contributions he has not claimed. According to Hoffman, "Until now game theory has . . . weaknesses that Schelling reviews. The main flaw is that game theory has dealt *only* [italics added] with zero-sum games. . . ." [13] It is not entirely unexpected that a political scientist would commit a technical error in the area of game theory. It is surprising, however, that one who presumes to evaluate the utility of that theory would make this elementary mistake. The point is covered in every treatise on the subject (and by Schelling), and there is a large literature on the subject. The mixed-motive game is one of the basic classifications of mathematical game theory. However, Hoffmann does not rest there. He continues, "Therefore, game theory applies only to a marginal and paradoxical case: pure conflict with limited stakes, i.e., the characteristic conflicts of moderate, balance-of-power, international systems." [14] Unfortunately, the "balance of power" case is neither paradoxical nor zero-sum. Moreover, although there are many mixed-motive games for which there are appropriate game-theoretic models, the "balance of power" case is not one of them. Game theory has only limited applicability to most problems of international politics, but we are hardly likely to learn from the traditionalists what these limits are and why they exist.

Although traditionalists quite often have accused those using scientific method of neglecting Aristotle's dictum to use those methods appropriate to the subject matter, I would contend that it is the user of scientific method who has more often observed the dictum. This is illustrated by the fact that so intelligent a student of politics as Hedley Bull, who openly recognizes the danger that he might be talking about discordant things, nonetheless falls into what I would call the trap of

---

12 Thomas C. Schelling, *The Strategy of Conflict* (Cambridge, Mass., 1960).

13 Stanley Hoffmann, *The State of War* (New York 1965), 205.

14 *Ibid.*, 206.

traditionalism: the use of overparticularization and unrelated generalization. Thus Bull lists highly disparate methods and subjects with minimal
discussion and inadequate or nonexistent classification and applies to
them extremely general criticisms. Such broad and universal generalizations are extremely difficult, if not impossible, to falsify. Who would
deny that the complexity of the subject matter places constraints on
what can be said? But different subject matters and different degrees of
complexity require different tools of analysis and different procedures.
The traditionalist, however, as in the case of Bull, does not discuss how
or why the complexity of a specific subject impedes what kind of generalization, or how and in what ways generalizations should be limited.
The traditional literature in international relations, even when it is directly concerned with the subject matter, is of much the same order: a
great mass of detail to which absurdly broad and often unfalsifiable
generalizations are applied. Thus traditional "balance of power" theory
is asserted to apply regardless of the number and kinds of states, variations in motivation, kinds of weapons systems, and so forth. Remarkably
the same generalizations are asserted to apply not merely to the macro-
structure of international politics but to the individual decisions of
foreign policy. The generalizations are applied indiscriminately over
enormous stretches of time and space. They are sufficiently loosely stated
so that almost no event can be inconsistent with them.

And the vaunted sensitivity to history that the traditionalists claim—
and that they deny to the modern scientific approaches—is difficult to
find. Those traditionalists who have done a significant amount of historical research—and they are the exceptions—confine themselves largely
to problems of diplomatic history that are unrelated to their generalizations about international politics, as in the case of Martin Wight, or
to more specialized problems that are idiosyncratic. This is not an accident but is a direct product of the lack of articulated theoretical structure in the traditionalist approach. It is ironic that the traditionalists are
so sure that they alone are concerned with subject matter that they are
unaware of the extent to which those applying the newer approaches
are using history as a laboratory for their researches. This development
is unprecedented in the discipline and is a direct product of the concern
of those using scientific approaches for developing disciplined and articulated theories and propositions that can be investigated empirically.

If those writers of the newer persuasion sometimes seem to ignore the
traditional literature, it may not be entirely without good reason. Yet
ignoring it is a mistake. There are honorable exceptions among the
traditionalists, such as Raymond Aron, whose remarkable writings are
surely useful to political scientists and whose methodology may not be
quite so far removed from the newer scientific approaches as some traditionalists like to believe. Hedley Bull, one of the more vociferous critics

of the newer approaches, has himself contributed a solid study of arms control to the literature.

The traditionalist seems to feel that scientific models are inapt for a political world in which surprises may occur. He seems to feel that scientific theories must achieve generality and completeness or lack rigor. This seems more like a seventeenth-century view of science than like a modern view.

Physical science presents analogies to the surprises that stem from parameter changes in social or political systems. One of these is the phenomenon of superconductivity under conditions of extreme temperature and pressure. The phenomena associated with superconductivity had not been predicted by the then current physical theories. Only after experimentation with extreme temperatures and pressures were the phenomena noticed. And only then did it become necessary to explain them. Whether a highly general theory comprehending all novel phenomena, of which superconductivity is merely an example, can be developed by physical theory is still open to question. For reasons already evident, such a general theory would be even more questionable in the area of international politics. Were someone to suggest to a physicist that the discovery of *novel phenomena* such as superconductivity which had not been predicted by previous theory established either the lack of rigor of previous theory or the inappropriateness of the methodology employed, the argument would be dismissed.

Another major charge made by the traditionalist against the newer methods is that since they use models, their practitioners are likely to mistake the models for reality. If the causal connection were not insisted on, I would not lightly deny the charge. There is a human tendency to reification. Surely the psychologists, sociologists, and anthropologists— and even the physicists, who know very little about politics—have a tendency to apply very simplified assumptions to very complex events. If, however, the traditionalist were to examine the propositions of the psychologists, for instance, he would find them no different from empirical generalizations—a category he likes. When a psychologist talks of projection or of a mirror image he is not, in the usual case, deriving these generalizations from an integrated theory, but is simply asserting an empirical generalization explicitly. The trouble with a generalization of this kind, apart from its general inapplicability, is that no context for its application is specified. Thus, as in the case of traditionalist arguments, it can be applied safely, for, in the form offered, it can never really be falsified.

On the other hand, it is natural to expect sophistication with respect to models from one who explicitly uses them. Only someone who has worked with models and the methodology of models knows how sensitive at least some models are to parameter adjustments. Thus a builder of models does not think of them as generally applicable. They are applicable only within a specified context; and it is extremely important to determine whether that context in fact exists. Moreover, the person who has worked with models usually has gone through the difficult task of trying to associate the parameters of the model with the real world. No one who has attempted this is likely to take it lightly.

I would argue that it is rather the traditionalist, whose assumptions are implicit rather than explicit and whose statements are made usually without reference to context, who is more likely to mistake his model for reality. Of course, even traditionalists are not likely to be as incautious as the historian Webster, who asserted that Castlereagh inherited his phlegmatic disposition from his mother who died when he was one year old. Yet the traditional literature of diplomatic history and international politics is filled with implicit assumptions as to motivation, interrelationships between variables, and so forth, that are implicit rather than specified, and the limits of application of which are never asserted. Even so careful and intelligent a traditionalist as George Kennan has made assertions about the likely effectiveness of United States aid in encouraging diversity and pluralism within the Soviet block which hardly seem to be sustained by the evidence.[15] Kennan did not explicitly articulate his model. He no doubt assumed that the provision of American aid provided the Polish government with an alternative to Soviet pressure. I would argue that had Kennan explicitly articulated his model, he might more likely have considered variables not included in his implicit model. Had he done so, he might have considered the possibility that the Polish government could argue to the Polish citizens that if the United States gave aid to Poland it must be a sign that the Polish regime was an acceptable regime. Therefore it would be unwise for the Polish citizen to oppose that regime or to expect even psychological aid from the United States in opposition. He also might have considered the hypothesis that the Polish leaders, as good Communists, and as a consequence of accepting American aid, might find it important to reassert at least some elements of Communist doctrine more strongly either to reassure themselves or to assure elements within the Polish Communist party whose support they needed that the leadership was not becoming a stooge for United States imperialism.

The probability that traditionalists will mistake their models for reality is further exemplified by Hedley Bull's criticisms of the new scientific approaches. Bull is so confident, on the basis of his premises, that those following the scientific method will engage largely in methodology both

---

[15] "Polycentrism and Western Policy," *Foreign Affairs,* XLII (January 1964), 178.

in their research and in their teaching, graduate and undergraduate, that he ignores the abundant evidence to the contrary. He himself admits that the other traditionalist critics of the new methods do not have adequate knowledge of these methods; yet he somehow fails to draw the inference from his own evidence that these critics have mistaken their implicit models for reality.

The traditional techniques with their inarticulated suppositions, their lack of specification of boundaries, and their almost necessary shifting of premises create a much greater danger that their implicit assumptions will automatically be applied to reality and a much greater sense of complacency than do scientific methods. I have no desire to be invidious, but, just as the traditionalists find it legitimate to characterize what they believe to be the inadequacies of the newer approaches, so it is equally legitimate to relate the defects of traditionalism to their sources. Bull, for instance, points out that English political science, as contrasted with American political science, remains committed to traditionalism. It is surely no secret that English political science is somewhat less than distinguished.

The traditionalists talk as if the newer methods have excluded philosophy as a tool for the analysis of international politics. Unfortunately few of them—again Raymond Aron is a conspicuous exception—have demonstrated any disciplined knowledge of philosophy; and many of them use the word as if it were a synonym for undisciplined speculation. There are many profound questions that in some senses are genuinely philosophical; the systems approach, among others, is related to a number of philosophical assumptions. The relationship between these philosophical assumptions and the validity of empirical theories is more complicated. It is entirely possible for an erroneous philosophy to furnish the ideas from which a valid empirical theory is derived. And it is dubious that the relationship between philosophical position and empirical theory is so direct—in either traditional or scientific approaches—that the arguments between or within competing approaches or theories can be settled by philosophical argument. There are, moreover, some important mistakes that ought to be avoided. Political theory ought not to be called philosophy merely because it is formulated by a man who is otherwise a philosopher unless the ideas have a genuine philosophical grounding. If the ideas are merely empirical propositions, as in the case of most philosophical statements used by traditionalists, they stand on the same footing as other empirical propositions. There is hardly much point in quoting one of the philosophers unless one understands him and can apply him correctly. I remember listening to a lecture by a well-known scholar, one cited by Bull as a good example of the traditionalist approach, who attempted to disprove Hegel's philosophy of history by showing that there were accidents in history. He was obviously unaware that for Hegel history was the realm of accident, that a major element of the Hegelian system involves the working out of necessity (often contrary to the wills of the actors) in a realm characterized by accident, and that, in any event, the whole matter was irrelevant to the point he thought he was making. Even if some matters of concern to international politics are profoundly philosophical, not all are. It is essential, if I may use that philosophical term inappropriately, to address the proper methods to the proper questions and not to make global statements about international politics, as do the traditionalists, which assume the relevance of the same melange of methods regardless of the type of question.

I have no doubt that the early attempts at a scientific approach to international politics are guilty of crudities and errors. It would be amazing—and I do not expect to be amazed—if the earliest hypotheses and models designed as tools for the orderly and comparative investigation of the history of international politics survive in their original form in the face of sustained empirical and methodological investigations. The self-corrective techniques of science will, however, likely sustain orderly progress in the discipline. The traditionalists are unlikely to be helpful in this task.

Having read the criticisms of the traditionalists, I am convinced that they understand neither the simpler assertions nor the more sophisticated techniques employed by the advocates of the newer methods. They have not helped to clarify the important issues in methodology; they have confused them. The traditionalists have accused those writers who advocate modern scientific approaches of using deterministic models despite explicit statements by those writers to the contrary. The traditionalists mistake explicitly heuristic models for dogmatic assertions. They mistake assertions about deductions within the framework of a model for statements about the open world of history. They call for historical research and do not recognize either that they have not heeded their own call or that they are merely repeating the words of the advocates of the newer approaches.

The traditionalists are often quite intelligent and witty people. Why then do they make such gross mistakes? Surely there must be something seriously wrong with an approach that devotes so much effort to such ill-informed criticism. One suspects that this sorry product is the consequence of the traditionalist view of philosophy as elegant but undisciplined speculation—speculation devoid of serious substantive or methodological concerns. Thus traditionalists repeat the same refrain like a gramophone endlessly playing a single record; that refrain is beautifully orchestrated, wittily produced, and sensitive only to the wear of the needle in the groove.

SELECTED BIBLIOGRAPHY

PART I

International Relations as a Discipline

Angell, Sir Norman, *The Political Conditions of Allied Success.* New York: G. P. Putnam's Sons, 1918.

Butterfield, Herbert, "The Scientific versus the 'Moralistic' Approach in International Relations," *International Affairs* (London). Volume 27, 1951.

Cook, Thomas J., and Malcolm Moos, *Power through Purpose:* The Realism of Idealism as a Basis for Foreign Policy. Baltimore: Johns Hopkins Press, 1954.

Cowen, L. Gray, "Theory and Practice in the Teaching of International Relations in the United States." In Geoffrey L. Goodwin (ed.), *The University Teaching of International Relations.* Oxford: Blackwell, 1951.

Fox, William T. R., "Interwar International Relations Research." *World Politics.* October 1949.

Herz, John, *Political Realism and Political Idealism.* Chicago: University of Chicago Press, 1951.

Hoffmann, Stanley (ed.), *Contemporary Theory in International Relations.* Englewood Cliffs: Prentice-Hall, 1960.

————, *The State of War: Essays on the Theory and Practice of International Politics.* New York: Praeger, 1965.

Rosenau, James H. (ed.), *International Politics and Foreign Policy: A Reader in Research and Theory.* Glencoe: The Free Press, 1961.

Kennan, George F., *Realities of American Foreign Policy.* Princeton: Princeton University Press, 1954.

Kirk, Grayson, *The Study of International Relations.* New York: Council on Foreign Relations, 1947.

Link, Arthur S., *Wilson the Diplomatist.* Baltimore: John Hopkins University Press, 1957.

Liska, George, "The Heroic Decade and After: International Relations as Events, Discipline and Profession." *SAIS Review.* Summer 1966.

Meinecke, Friedrich, *Machiavellism: The Doctrine of Raison d'Etat and its Place in Modern History.* New York: Praeger, 1965.

Morgenthau, Hans J., "Another 'Great Debate': The National Interest of the U.S." *American Political Science Review.* December 1952.

———, *In Defense of the National Interest*. New York: Knopf, 1951.

Pfaltzgraff, Robert L., Jr. "Utopianism and Realism in International Relations Theory." *Intercollegiate Review*. May–June 1966.

Rommen, Heinrich, "Realism and Utopianism in World Affairs." *Review of Politics*. April 1944.

Singer, J. David (ed.), *Quantitative International Politics: Insights and Evidence*. New York: The Free Press, 1967.

———, "The Behavioral Science Approach to International Relations: Payoff and Prospect." *SAIS Review*. Summer 1966.

Snyder, Richard C., "Some Recent Trends in International Relations Theory and Research." In Austin Ranney, *Essays on the Behavioral Study of Politics*. Urbana: University of Illinois Press, 1962.

Spykman, Nicholas J., *America's Strategy in World Politics*. New York: Harcourt, Brace, and Company, 1942.

Tannenbaum, Frank, *The American Tradition in Foreign Policy*. Norman: University of Oklahoma Press, 1955.

Thompson, Kenneth W., "American Approaches to International Politics," *Yearbook of World Affairs*. London: Stevens and Sons, 1959.

———, *Political Realism and the Crisis of World Politics: An American Approach to Foreign Policy*. Princeton: Princeton University Press, 1960.

Waldo, Dwight, *Political Science in the United States*. Paris: UNESCO, 1956.

Wolfers, Arnold, *Discord and Collaboration: Essays on International Politics*. Baltimore: Johns Hopkins Press, 1962.

Zawodny, J. K. (ed.), *Man and International Relations*. Two volumes. San Francisco: Chandler Publishing Company, 1966.

Part II

The Nature of the
International System

HISTORICALLY, the international system has consisted of great powers and small powers. Great powers were those countries which were parties to a general settlement of international affairs; small powers not only had no claim to such participation, but more often than great powers, were the object of revisions in the inter-national·status quo. Before 1914, the international system, which was essentially Europe-based, contained several great powers. In the post–World War II period, the term, "superpower," came into vogue to describe the two vast continental countries who possessed nuclear weapons. In national capabilities, the disparity between the United States and the Soviet Union, on the one hand, and the remaining members of the international system, on the other, was far greater than had been the case in preceding periods.

It is possible to speak of several kinds of international systems in which there are regular patterns of interaction and interdepend-ence. Some are composed of many great powers, others, of a few superpowers. One can envisage systems in which there are many nation-states, or one world government. According to Robert Strausz-Hupé, the world at various stages in its history has been engulfed in a systemic revolution. In Selection 9 he describes the process of system transformation. In the second Selection Stanley Hoffmann suggests that the case for the study of International Relations as an "autonomous discipline" rests upon the notion that the international system is characterized by decentralization of de-cision-making authority to a far greater extent than most national political systems. It is interesting to speculate upon the implications of Hoffmann's justification in an international system in which decision-making had become more highly centralized than it is in the contemporary international system. In another selection, Roger Masters compares the international system with a "primitive" political system. To what extent, he asks, are there similarities in structure and behavior between the contemporary international system and primitive systems? Conceivably, such an understanding may contribute to our knowledge about the international system.

Writers on the international system have discussed in exhaustive detail the notion of the state. It is an abstraction. No one has ever seen a state, which is simply a shorthand expression for designating a political unit which contains a population, a government, a territory, and an economy. Historically, a state has obtained membership in the international system when many, or all, of the great powers have extended recognition to it. In general, the act of recognition takes the form of a policy declaration or an announcement of the opening of diplomatic relations.

According to Charles McClelland, International Relations consist of the study of "interactions between certain kinds of social entities, including the study of relevant circumstances surrounding the interactions." He views the task of the student as the isolation, examination, and analysis of patterns of interaction among the national political units, which are the principal actors of the international system. McClelland suggests a systems framework for the study of International Relations. Although there are many other possible frameworks, McClelland's suggestion is illustrative of contemporary efforts to gain a greater understanding of behavioral regularities among nation-states by the analysis of data about a variety of forms of inter-nation interaction.

The principal components of the contemporary international system are the nation-states, or national units, as they are sometimes called. A pervasive influence on their behavior is the phenomenon of nationalism. According to Hans Kohn, nationalism is a "will to nationhood," and the "integration of the masses into a common political form." With the advent of nationalism, larger numbers of people, and in many cases the entire population of a territory, feel themselves a part of a political system. In the age of nationalism the historic gap between the central government and the hinterland is narrowed.

In England, nationalism was linked to the extension of liberty and the increase in popular political representation. By the twentieth century, nationalism was often identified with the integration of the masses of the population into totalitarian political systems. In Selection 3 E. H. Carr wrote that utopian thought about international relations contained the proposition that nationalism would lead to the emergence of peace-loving governments. Essentially, the nationalist "model" implicit in such thought was more akin to the nationalism of the twentieth century.

In Europe, nationalism was often based upon common language and culture, as well as a belief in common descent and a return to some imagined past. In the non-Western world, John Kautsky suggests, nationalism was identified with the anti-colonial movements. Initially, its supporters were Western educated elites as well as other persons who felt disadvantaged in the colonial system. Unlike Europe, there were few, if any, linguistic bonds. In the nationalisms of Africa and Asia, the process of the "integration of the masses into a common political form" is far from complete. In many cases, cultural, economic, and political gaps separate the leadership of new states from the masses of the population. In such countries the process of nation-building is that of narrowing the gap between the central government and population.

For several reasons the study of nationalism is vital to the study of the international system. As a process whereby the masses are integrated into a common political form, nationalism has enhanced the capabilities of national units in the international system. Before the age of nationalism it was not possible to mobilize the masses of the population to make sacrifices of life and treasure in the attainment of a major foreign policy objective. Conversely, it was not possible for the masses to help to shape foreign policy. In non-Western areas, the coming of nationalism contributed to the demise of European empires and the emergence of many new national units in the international system. Those countries where the masses of the population have not yet been integrated into a common political form—where localistic, tribalistic loyalties still predominate—are susceptible to insurgency warfare, either by indigenous groups or forces infiltrated from abroad to overthrow the central government. Thus nationalism, where it has produced a political system with which the masses of people have identified themselves, has rendered such countries less vulnerable to insurgency activity from outside. Those countries where the masses have

yet to be integrated into a common political form are subject to
pressures which may have a destabilizing effect upon the international system.

Power is one of the most frequently used words in the study of
International Relations, and especially among Realist writers has
become a focal point for study. According to K. J. Holsti, power as a
concept contains several elements: influence and the use of influence; the capabilities—military and non-military—available to
a national unit. Holsti views power as a process in which one national unit attempts, by means of a variety of capabilities, to influence another national unit to behave in some desired fashion.
Power may be studied as a demand-response relationship in which
one member of the international system, in turn, responds in some
way. Thus, using McClelland's model, and incorporating into it
Holsti's conception of power, we may view the international system
as consisting of national units in interaction, making demands upon
each other and eliciting responses. In turn, these responses give rise
to new demands and responses. Because there are fewer institutions
for the resolution of conflict in the international system than in the
domestic, the power element is more obvious.

SECTION ONE: Its Structure

7. THEORY AND THE INTERNATIONAL SYSTEM
Charles A. McClelland

INTERNATIONAL RELATIONS is the study of interactions between certain
kinds of social entities, including the study of relevant circumstances
surrounding the interactions. In interaction between any two parties, the
sources of the action are the parties. At any given instant, we should be
required to admit that the only possible sources are within the involved
parties or actors. Two complexities are involved, however, if interaction
occurs over a period of time. Each actor may be influenced by the past
experience of interacting, and on this basis it can be said that the interaction itself is a source of behavior. In the second place, from past experience with interaction, the actors may anticipate what will happen next
and each may act according to the anticipation. Almost any example of
human relations illustrates these matters concretely.

On meeting Actor B, Actor A may make an insulting remark; if Actor
A does, B may respond with an equally insulting remark; if B does, A
may be irritated enough to strike B; if A does, B may retaliate in kind;
however, A may anticipate that B will strike back and therefore A does
not strike B. The point is clear: in this case only the two parties are
interacting and they are the only real sources of behavior. Nevertheless,
the character of the interaction—in the instance cited, insult returning
insult—is a distinctive phenomenon. The interplay feeds back, so to

From *Theory and the International System* by Charles A. McClelland (New
York: 1966), pp. 18–27; 99–106. Reprinted by permission of the author and the
Macmillian Company. Footnotes have been renumbered to appear in consecutive
order.
CHARLES A. MCCLELLAND (1917–   ) Professor of Political Science, University of
Michigan. His other books include *The United Nations: The Continuing Debate,
Nuclear Weapons, Missiles and the Future of War* (San Francisco: Chandler, 1960),
editor.

speak, and affects the behavior of the involved actors, and it may be viewed as a source in itself. A block diagram (Fig. 1) symbolizes international relationships of whatever variety, once the relationships are broken down to their most elementary form:

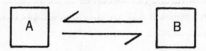

FIGURE 1   Basic pattern of interaction.

It follows that the facts of international relations can be selected and organized according to the two references of actor and interaction. This is a basic statement of theory. It would be futile, however, to undertake to organize all possible information about all actors. Only some small portion of "all the facts" about given actors would be expected to be important in accounting for some particular interactions. To include more than the relevant facts would be inefficient, distracting, or even confusing in an explanation of how and why a sequence of interacting events has occurred. A conception of the nature of a given stream of interaction gains substance only to the extent that the idea matches *some* of the behavior of the involved parties.

When we are presented with such problems of explanation, we immediately go about the task of establishing relevance by putting facts in appropriate categories. Commonly, we build a map of the situation by asking a few questions: Who is involved? Where did the action occur? When did it happen and in what order? What happened? This is the historical method of investigation; everybody uses it; and it is, indeed, a powerful tool for ordering reports of events. Due to the complexity and multiplicity of the events of international relations, however, additional means of locating and ordering data are needed.

A conventional procedure is to superimpose a second category system on the first system of the *who, where, when,* and *what* variety. This is to separate and label groups of data under headings of political, economic, social, cultural, psychological, legal, military, and ideological factors (or aspects). These analytical categories are sometimes of help in organizing facts. For example, the assumption that the data falling in the political category are more significant than any other in explaining international relations—the *primacy of politics* idea mentioned earlier—leads to the subordination of the materials in the other categories to the class of *contributing influences*. This strategic conception is open to challenge, however. As we have already noted, a psychologist may argue that the political facts are not fundamental but reflect only partially a more deeply rooted set of psychological facts. There is no fixed hierarchy for arranging the analytical categories in the order of importance.

The analytical categories give some trouble in other ways. They sometimes are used as if they were qualities inhering in events—as if there were political acts, psychological acts, economic acts, and so forth, in Nature. On other occasions, the analytical categories appear to be regarded simply as different perspectives to be focused in turn on a body of facts. There is no consistency in the usage, and confusion arises from the lack of agreement among the special cultures of the social sciences on the matter.

In the theory of international relations, the recent tendency is to view the analytical categories as different perspectives (rather than as qualities inhering in events) and to call upon them for assistance in organizing data according to the particular intellectual needs and problems of international relations research. Thus it is said frequently that the field is interdisciplinary and that it borrows materials freely from political science, economics, sociology, history, psychology, and many other studies.

Although the historical and analytical category systems are indispensable for identifying, locating, and organizing data, the ordering idea of "the international system" appears increasingly to be a concept of great usefulness in giving the study of international relations the shape of a discipline.

The conception of *the international system* is an expanded version of the notion of two-actors-in-interaction. A view of a whole phenomenon is involved. The outermost boundaries of international relations are suggested if we imagine *all* of the exchanges, transactions, contacts, flows of information, and actions of every kind going on at this moment of time between and among the separately constituted societies of the world. To this picture in the mind we should add the effects created within societies from all such interflowing events in earlier times, both of the immediate and the more remote past. Finally, the stream of these actions and responses should be conceived as moving on to the future of tomorrow and beyond, accompanied by the expectations, plans, and proposals of all observers of the phenomena. This total picture is the reference intended in the term *the international system*.

The details of the transmitting and receiving of impulses through the international system cannot be made out from the lofty vantage point where the whole system is envisaged. From the knowledge of other complex systems, we can expect to find a number of characteristics in the structure and the operations of the international system.

COMPLEX SYSTEMS

A system of whatever kind is an ensemble of parts or subsystems capable of changing from one state to another state. It is the ability to change that is interesting to the observer and that allows the ensemble to be considered a system. Any system is a structure that is perceived by its observers to have elements in interaction or relationships and some identifiable boundaries that separate it from its environment. A complex system is one that is found to have much variety in the process of changing from one state to another. Usually, it is discovered that the parts of a complex system are not simple in *their* activities but have, instead, their own subparts capable of varying their combinations and otherwise carrying on changes of state. Thus, a part or subsystem is not always in the same condition as it operates over time in the ensemble of the whole system. As the observer shifts his gaze from the system to one of the constituting parts, he discovers that the part itself is internally a system. This progression of revealing the inner makeup of a complex system reminds one of the taking apart of a Chinese puzzle box. Inside each box is another that appears as soon as the preceding one is removed.

In considering the international system, we must be prepared for its complexity in the first place by realizing that it will show much variety in its change-of-state processes, and in the second place by recognizing immediately that its main operating parts have the Chinese box characteristic. For a rough approximation, reference is made to the largest and most external box as the national society or nation. The working together of all such entities in attaining one state of affairs and then another *is* the international system. It is to be held firmly in mind that the participation of each national society in the system will not be fixed and simple, but instead will be directed in part by what has been going on in the way of shift and change in the several smaller, more internal of its boxes. The nesting effect of interactions of subsystems, of subsystems of subsystems, and of sub-sub-systems, all traced as far as significant pattern of change will carry, gives rise to complexity. It is the main task of empirical theory and research to identify, portray, measure, and relate the characteristics of the performances of the system down through the tiers or levels of the subsystems.

A vocabulary describing the parts, aspects, and operations of the international system has begun to develop. *The* international system is meant to take in and encompass all interactions, in full scope. An *international subsystem* is a portion of the whole international system. The international relations of Southeast Asia might well be described as one of the international subsystems. The United Nations might be taken to be another. The parts or components of the international system are *national systems*. The term national actor is also in common use as a description of a national system and it has been employed earlier in this discussion. *National subsystems* are components that contribute to the behavior of the national system in the latter's participation in the activity of the international system. Public opinion, for example, might be regarded as a national subsystem. So also, conceivably, would be the actions of a decision-making group, of a political party, of an organization, of a group, or of an individual person belonging in the structure of the national system.

An input is any discrete action that enters a system or subsystem and contributes thereby to a change of state within a system or subsystem. An output is the impulse emitted by a subsystem to a system, contributing to a change. Feedback is a kind of input; it is one that returns a report to the locus of the previous output and carries information about the resulting state of affairs in the system. A positive feedback is a report that causes a subsystem to continue or to increase its particular previous action sent into the system. A negative feedback is a report that causes a subsystem to change its previous line of action and to correct the behavior of that subsystem by changing its condition and its subsequent output. A system is said to be in a steady state when disturbances affecting the system and/or its subsystems are compensated for through feedbacks. The corrections prevent the changing of the basic arrangements of the structures and processes of the system. A steady state need not be an equilibrium struck among the components of a system and it is not a description of a *no change* situation. A complex system in a steady state will usually oscillate around a point with many variations in its conditions, often because of overcorrections and undercorrections by subsystems. A stable system is merely one in which the steady state is usually maintained and that has achieved a reputation among observers for doing so.

How, in general terms, do complex systems work? Generalizing statements for any complex system have been set forth in many different forms. Here are a few examples (they may or may not match the facts of the historical, existing international system):

(1) Complex systems tend to be self-organizing, due primarily to adjustments made to disturbing conditions according to negative feedback effects.

(2) Positive feedback effects lead to the filling in, over time, of a complex system with additional special purpose subsystems, to the extent of available space and energy resources.

(3) Leading characteristics in the performance of a complex system arise from the arrangement of its subsystems and of the relationships among these. Behavior depends on structure, in other words.

(4) Complex systems and their subsystems have normal operating ranges; the performance in these ranges usually is less than the maximum capacity for systems and subsystems.

(5) The loading or stressing of a system is the effect of extending a system and/or subsystem toward the maximum capacity. Several effects occur under stressing, including:

a. The tendency of the system to demand progressively larger contributions from subsystems with increases in stress.

b. The reorganization or the destruction of subsystems, from overloading to preserve the system under extreme stress.

c. The tendency of the system to require increasing amounts of information with increasing stress.

d. The tendency under severe stress on the system for subsystems to underrespond at first and subsequently to overrespond.

e. The tendency under severe stress on subsystems for the overall system to underrespond at first and subsequently to overrespond.

(6) The larger the population of subsystems in a system, the greater is the tendency to organize specialized subsystems for the purposes of guidance, control, coordination, and information-processing.

(7) Subsystems establish boundaries of exchange with other subsystems and with the system; thus a given subsystem restricts some part of its activities to its own maintenance within its boundary. How much autonomy subsystems have in allocating their activities at the boundary—inwardly for self-maintenance and development and across the boundary in exchange with other subsystems and with the whole system —is an important element in the performance of the system.

(8) A complex system is not restricted in its performance to single relationship patterns among its subsystems. For example, a task that is frustrated by the blocking of a given network of subsystem functions may still be carried out by the utilization of different combinations of subsystem actions. The ability of a complex system to establish multiple, alternative routes for its operations constitutes a characteristic that is called equifinality.

(9) A basic change in either the structure or the processes of a system will tend to bring about changes in the structures, processes, and relationships of subsystems.

(10) A basic change in a subsystem may bring about changes in other subsystems and/or in the whole system.

To some readers, the preceding propositions may suggest interesting questions to be asked about the historical, existing international system, or they may lead to insights into how it works. To others, the propositions may be lacking entirely in such suggestions. Being extremely abstract, these ideas invite reformulations at lower levels of abstraction and generality.

The lowering of the level of abstraction is easily illustrated with the third proposition given above: that the structure of a complex system gives rise to its performance traits. Professor Morton A. Kaplan has produced models of six different types of international systems and has enunciated essential rules to describe the characteristic, maintaining behavior of each of the six types. The six are called the balance of power system, the loose bipolar system, the tight bipolar system, the universal system, the hierarchical system, and the unit veto system. The names refer to structural attributes of the systems. Only a few rules of behavior of two of the systems will be cited, since our objective is only to illustrate how the level of abstraction can be lowered.

The balance of power system contains, among others, two interesting behavioral traits:

(1) National actors will act in opposition to any actor or coalition of actors seen as rising to predominance in the international system.

(2) Defeated or subordinated national actors of the system will not be held to that status by the others; they will be allowed to resume a position roughly coordinate with other members of the system.

The unit veto system has not existed in history, but it is a model that, as Kaplan states, "exhibits features of genuine peculiarity." Kaplan notes also, however, that it might come into existence if all national actors in the system had "weapons of such a character that any actor is capable of destroying any other actor that attacks it even though it cannot prevent its own destruction." [1] Two of its rules are:

(1) Each national actor in the system will act to stand off every other member to preserve the existing steady state of the unit veto international system.

(2) The unit veto system can maintain a steady state only if its actors will, without exception, resist threats of destruction and be willing to retaliate if attacked. The unit veto system is, obviously, an unstable system, since it will be transformed into a system with a different structure if an actor starts a chain reaction by attacking or if blackmail by threats of destruction should prove to be too powerful to resist.

Kaplan's systems are at too general a level to assist greatly the ordering of facts, as theories are supposed to do. The shortcoming can be remedied, however, by reformulations until a level of reduced abstraction and generalization is reached where the ordering of time-place-topic identified facts will dovetail readily with the theory. No examples of step-by-step descent of the ladder of abstraction-generality will be given at this stage of the discussion. Instead, one other proposed device for bringing theory and facts together will be mentioned.

The idea of treating some portions of the whole international system separately, according to geographical characteristics or other criteria, has been advanced by several scholars. One plan is to consider two groups of national actors and their interactions as an international subsystem.

---

[1] Morton A. Kaplan, *System and Process in International Politics* (New York: John Wiley & Sons, Inc., 1957), p. 50.

These two subsystems are viewed as interacting—or exchanging inputs and outputs. Theory and research are then to be addressed to the problems of how and why they interact. In one formulation, the East-West international subsystem, which has been operating since World War II in patterns called the Cold War, is conceived to be intersected by a North-South international subsystem. The latter is preoccupied by interests and problems of economic development, by disparities in wealth and power, and by a number of other considerations stimulating both conflict and cooperation. Another formulation for dividing the international system in two parts has already become popularized in the dichotomized concept of the Communist World and the Free World. More and more, the students of Soviet affairs have been turning to a theoretical outlook that portrays the Communist World as a dynamic, changing, interacting international system.[2] In the terminology used here, they are studying the structure and process of an international subsystem.

Yet another scheme for reducing complexity, generality, and abstraction is being championed by some students of international relations.[3] They suggest that the knowledge of international relations will advance through theory-directed research and a focusing of attention on partially self-contained international subsystems in geographical areas such as the Middle East, Southeast Asia, Latin America, and others. Their argument is that the problems of understanding the actors and the interactions in such international subsystems are not as great as in the study of the whole international system. The linking of subsystems to the whole can accompany the analysis of how and why the particular international subsystems are organized and oriented in their actions.

All the foregoing ideas and plans about international subsystems spring from the general conception of *the* international system. Eventually, it can be anticipated that interesting developments will appear from the leads to lower-level theory and research according to the international subsystem approach. There are a few more observations that should be made about the overall characteristics of the international system.

We should assume that the system is open and adaptive. That is to say, we shall not anticipate that its activities are running in foreordained cycles. Instead, it is better to assume that the total stream of interaction sometimes will flow in novel directions, according to influences brought to

---

2 Jan F. Triska, "Stanford Studies of the Communist System: The Sino-Soviet Split," *Background,* 8 (November 1964), pp. 143–159.

3 Leonard Binder, "The Middle East as a Subordinate International System," *World Politics,* 10 (April 1958), pp. 408–429; Michael Brecher, "International Relations and Asian Studies: The Subordinate State System of Southern Asia," *World Politics,* 15 (January 1963), pp. 214–215; George Modelski, "International Relations and Area Studies: The Case of Southeast Asia," *International Relations,* 2 (April 1961), pp. 143–155.

bear upon it from the environment. Because men operate it, we expect the international system to be somewhat changeable and to be adaptable to new conditions. Further, specialization of functions appears within the system and within its component parts. Societies will be observed to provide special organizations for coping with incoming and outgoing events. Again, because it is a human system, we should be surprised if it were not subjected to manipulation by its member-nations and therefore exposed to varied perturbations. Behind the disturbances and upheavals we expect to discover, however, much interacting that is of a highly regular and even routine character. Although it may not seem, at first, a helpful point to emphasize, we assume that the conditions and events produced in the international system will have but two possible sources— a source generated *within* nations and controlled by conditions, impulses, and decisions stemming from domestic national life, and a second source created by the interplay of activity *between* nations.

If every nation participating in the international system emitted a single stream of simple, slightly varying, and highly patterned behavior into the system, the problem of knowing how the system works would still be formidable. By making a false assumption of simple, single stream interaction, we can gain an idea of how much knowledge would need to be organized to understand the international system as a whole. Between two actors under this assumption there could be but a single stream of interaction. Among three actors there could be three streams. Among four and five actors, there could be, as the diagrams of Figure 2 show, respectively, six and ten streams. In the international system with about 130 recognizable national actors, there would be 8,385 streams to be taken into account for full knowledge of the flows of the system. It is hardly necessary to demonstrate how much more extensive and complicated the international system really is to discourage the hope of anyone to know all the relevant facts about the international system.

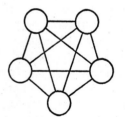 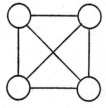

FIGURE 2   Interaction channels for 4- and 5-component systems.

·   ·   ·

THE DATA PROBLEM AND SYSTEM SOLUTIONS

It should be possible in any well-organized area of knowledge to place facts and findings in appropriate locations on the map of the field. A trained student or researcher should be able to look up all the relevant information on any subject of the field without the expenditure of a great amount of time and effort. Coherence in the specialized literature should prevail to the extent that experienced students would know where further work is needed and where fresh contributions are being made. In a word, scholarly and scientific fields require good information storage and retrieval facilities. In the case of international relations, a recent survey of the state of bibliography and bibliographical services resulted in the evaluation that conditions are chaotic.

The primary facts of international relations are historical. That is, they are reports of public events and happenings; they make up the cumulative record of the facts in the daily news, the reports, inquiries, and compilations, both public and secret, in governmental files and archives, the content in the letters and papers of public figures and public offices, the substance of what gets written down about events by participants and eyewitnesses, and the information that is compiled by special means such as interviews and the examinations of witnesses. Every day sees additions to this total record of primary facts. Depending on the use made of them in research, the reactions, the interpretations, and the repetitions that arise in many quarters in response to the reports of public events are either primary or secondary material. Thus, the records of public opinion expressions on "the two Chinas" question would be primary data in analytic studies of international opinion and attitude. Especially on international relations issues that achieve great public attention there is a vast amount of repetition of facts, of popularization, and of unsystematic interpretation. Rumors, distortion, deceptions, misconceptions and the most varied kinds of secondary processings of the record are mixed in with the primary data in the sources used in international relations research.

Two great needs are outstanding in the context of the requirements for development in the field toward a scientific footing. The first is the need for data quality control—the separation of primary data and research findings from the vast quantity of false, degraded, popularized, and secondary material. This is a problem that will not be explored here. The second need is for a comprehensive framework of categories and subclasses into which can be fitted the masses of primary data. It has become evident that the progress of the field is being held up substantially by the information storage and retrieval problem. Until students can be taught an inventory plan for the basic knowledge of international relations and until theorists and researchers agree on a system for finding out quickly and accurately what work has and has not been done, progress will be retarded by duplication of efforts, confusion of meanings, and a general tendency toward incoherence. At present, the system for locating information is a disordered complex of the classification alternatives that were enumerated in Chapter 1: (1) classification by geographical place and by historical time, (2) classification by analytic category—political, economic, psychological, legal, military, and so forth, and (3) classification by topical headings derived from diverse abstractions and mixed terminologies. Responses to the need for an improved framework of categories that will be functional for the study of international relations are already making an appearance. Several starts have been made toward providing new bibliographical services. Further efforts are to be anticipated in the period immediately ahead. The system structure is very likely to become the basis for attempts to arrive at solutions of the data problem.

Let us see, in brief outline, how system analysis applied in the general system orientation might direct the design of a functioning data management system for all the branches of international relations. Anyone who has read thoughtfully the preceding chapters of this book will see at once how to go about setting the fundamental parts of such a system in place and also how to label the general categories. At the base, one would place the most comprehensive category—the international system—with two major divisions for structure and process. Since we know that it is possible to decompose the whole of the international system by the procedures of system analysis in three main shifts of level and perspective, this decomposition will yield three further classes for data at decreasing levels of generality:

(1) International subsystems
(2) National systems
(3) National subsystems

The resulting three-part superstructure constructed on the base of the international system would be subcategorized in each part by the addition of structure and function divisions. Many additional subclassifications would need to be worked into the scheme; this requirement to elaborate would be particularly great at the national subsystem level. Time, place, and topical designations would be incorporated, not as prime classifiers as in the current practice, but rather as subgroupings within the subsystem framework.

An important innovation would be the addition of connectors between the arrays of data stored in the various categories and subclasses of the system. These connectors would be matrices of relationships of exactly the type described above in the passage on the change of level technique. These relationship matrices would encompass at least two classes of pertinent data. One class would hold facts that describe the *status* or condition of relationships between subsystems, and the other classification would contain the actual *performance* data (the detailed record of who has done what to whom, where, when, and so on). The development of the right kind of computer storage and retrieval system and a functional teaching and research information facility would make instructional procedures and approaches, research activities, and library uses closely comparable and compatibile.

The fundamental quest in the study of international relations is the search for the understanding of relationships. As we have seen earlier, it is the interplay of activities across the boundaries of national systems that is the basic preoccupation of the field. Much must be investigated within the boundaries of national systems, but the principle of selection is that the domestic or internal phenomena that are relevant must have direct linkages with external activity, effects, and relationships. The concept of system and related subsystems and the procedure of the shift and redefinition of system levels appear to provide just the intellectual equipment that is required for the building of the right kind of information structure.

Once the framework is invented and put into operation, the user would simply follow from matrix to matrix, tracing out a route of links and relationships in ascending, descending, or lateral directions in pursuit of the problem or topic at hand. At various points along the route the student or researcher would come to clusters of stored facts and ideas and the researcher would have the function of redirecting the course of the inquiry. What is being suggested speculatively is the possibility of greatly reducing the gap between the hidden riches of books on library shelves and the active but relatively uninformed interests of persons who make inquiries. In the information system that is envisaged, one could almost literally travel through the simulated spaces of the international system and make charted voyages from place to place by following level shifts of the system analysis variety. The first comprehensive test of the viability of the system approach and the system method is likely to take place in the coming struggle with the data management problem. Limited testing is already under way in applications of the system idea and technique in interaction analysis.

INTERACTION ANALYSIS

A basis in theory for several types of analysis of international transactions is found in the proposition that when the actions of one national system become disturbing to other national systems and cause the latter to change the pattern of their responses to the disturbance, a change in the state of the international system is *likely* to occur. Involved in this statement is the idea of a spreading and ramifying effect of great enough magnitude to cause an appreciable reordering of the structure of action of the international system. The citing of many historical examples will not make entirely clear what types of acts and situations are required to make the system change its structure. In the late 1920's, the failure of banking institutions in several European countries is known to have had the ramifying effect of spreading the world depression and of speeding the collapse of the structure of world trade and finance. It is obvious that the Nazi attack on Poland in 1939 was a culminating event of interwar history but it was also an initiating act that changed the international system from the state of peace to the state of war. The upsetting of the balance of power as it has usually been described at various junctures in diplomatic history represents a further example of what is meant by a change of system state.

The conception that the international system (or an international subsystem) has an observable performance record in history and that this record is changeable does not create difficulties. It is plausible to think that the system often reflects normalized relations between countries and achieves an overall behavior that remains within expected bounds. It even seems to be a correct insight that the movement away from normalized relations involves the crossing of some behavioral boundary and is accelerated typically by the act of one country that sets off something like a chain reaction in the responses of other countries. The difficulties arise from several observations of what has happened commonly in history.

First, it is clear that there is no one type of act committed that will always bring forth a related set of responses. At one time an assassination will bring about a world war and at another time it results in a flood of messages of regret and condolence. At one time a crisis results from the shooting down of an airplane and at other times only protests and denials are exchanged. In international politics there is much marching up the hill and marching down again. Sometimes, such increasing pressure at the boundary of the system is not relieved, however, and a change of state results. A further complication appears in the plain historical fact that intolerable conditions and problems that demand solutions can prevail for long periods in international relations. Normalized relations for abnormalities are, in fact, achieved and maintained for much longer periods than anyone would think possible. All of these manifestations are more or less puzzling and they call for systematic investigation. Steady state, boundary maintenance, transactional balance or symmetry, and transformations are all useful explanatory devices on the level of generalities, but it is obvious that fruitful research on the details of how the international system performs will be required to refashion and sharpen these tools of theory.

There are at least three major approaches to research on the details of actual system performance. One approach is to delve inside the subsystems of the national states for the roots of the actions transmitted abroad and contributing the elements of the resultant, which we call the international system. Another approach is to concentrate on the evidence of the perceptions and motivations of actors in the search for answers to why historical events achieve one result at one time and other results at other times. Decision-making analysis, which is discussed later in this chapter, is one of the strategies for synthesizing these two research orientations. A third approach is interaction analysis, which may also be described as demand-response pattern analysis.

Interaction analysis focuses on the outputs of national systems. The national systems, themselves, are blackboxed. Deliberately, the interaction analyst sets aside all concerns related to subsystem complexities and motivations. He tells himself that, for whatever reasons and under whatever conditions, each of the national systems contributes outputs that enter into combinations and configurations of international behavior. His preoccupation is with the tracing of the resulting patterns and trajectories of actions. Interaction studies have produced a few propositions to guide the way to further research:

(1) A dense network of transactions at the base of the international system is made up of administered and routinized activities and is substantially self-organizing and self-directing.

(2) A second network of transactions in the international system is created and perpetuated by out of the ordinary, nonroutine sequences of occurrences that require active intervention and guidance by national governments. The phenomenon of system disturbance is the leading characteristic of this network.

(3) Some coupling between the two networks exists and some exchange of materials takes place, but the nature of the coupling and exchange is not established and requires further investigation.

(4) National systems have access to only a limited inventory of demand and response actions in coping with the situations produced in the second network of nonroutine transactions.

(5) How the government of a national system tends to select types of actions from the inventory to meet different kinds of nonroutine international situations provides evidence of its operational code in international politics.

(6) Changes of state in the international system are observable and appear to be measurable in particular sequences of nonroutine occurrences. The amounts, types, and combinations of demands and responses appear to characterize such specific system conditions as acute international crises.

There is so much work waiting to be undertaken in analyses of the content and patterns of international transactions that it is very difficult to foresee what results can be obtained. Many impressions arise from the news reporting of international events. For example, some people believe that the Soviet Union will make concessions and give up claims in international disputes only in response to strong demands and threats. Others have thought that if the United States would make more proposals to negotiate differences and offer more inducements to cooperation, the communist countries would have no alternative but to respond in kind. Terrible arguments have arisen on these topics and have usually invoked appeals to evidence that is not available, such as the true motivations of the Soviet leadership elite. Interaction analysis approaches problems of this type by the accumulation of specific data to fit the form: If A does x in situation h, what is the probability that B will respond by doing y according to past performances? The acute crises of the post-World War II period have attracted much attention. Such episodes as the Berlin Wall, the Congo, the Suez, and the Cuban Missile crises have been examined in detail from several different research angles. The interaction analysis approach is to collect and analyze the data of the reported demands and responses of these crises—of the threats, warnings, acts of force and violence, complaints, protests, accusations, denials, requests, proposals, appeals, refusals, and other acts committed. How much of what kinds of action is studied carefully and evaluated in findings. It is probably a common-sense conclusion to think that during crises such as Berlin or Suez there would occur a large and spectacular increase of some types of response (threats and acts of violence, for example) and a tendency to narrow the inventory of employed actions. Several interaction studies of crises by the writer and his associates have resulted in contrary findings: that only modest increases occur in certain types of actions when these are compared with noncrisis behavior, and that the inventory of acts tends to broaden instead of narrow.

A pressing need in the development of better interaction studies is the collection in a continuing worldwide survey of a full record of what nations do in public to each other. We need to know what is normal in the short run in the relations of all pairs of nations. Some of the aggregated data for the routinized and administered transactions—the figures on the amount of trade and tourist travel between countries, for example—are easy to assemble. Other facts are more difficult—for instance, how much of what kinds of news from one country is printed *and* read widely in other countries. The data of the nonroutine network of transactions must be gathered laboriously from scattered sources, separated from comments and interpretations, coded by type, and assembled in compilations that can be used readily in research, before it will be possible to begin to determine what is normal in the relations of pairs of countries for a week, a month, or a year in time periods such as the decade of the fifties and the decade of the sixties.

8. WORLD POLITICS AS A PRIMITIVE POLITICAL SYSTEM

Roger D. Masters

REASONS FOR COMPARING PRIMITIVE AND INTERNATIONAL POLITICS

TO BE SURE, politics among the [African] Nuer—or any other primitive people—is not identical to world politics, but however important the differences may be, a number of writers have suggested the possibility of comparing the two kinds of political systems.[1] Curiously enough, however, there has been virtually no effort to elaborate these similarities comprehensively from a theoretical point of view.[2]

It should be noted in passing that there are three more general reasons for comparing primitive and international political systems. An attempt to bridge the gap between political science and anthropology has merits because such cross-disciplinary endeavors may free one from unnecessarily narrow assumptions which often dominate research in a given field. This is particularly true with respect to political anthropology, since the political aspects of primitive society have often been only imperfectly analyzed.[3]

From *World Politics* XVI, No. 4 (July 1964), 595–598; 599–602; 608–615. Reprinted by permission of the author and the publisher. Footnotes have been renumbered to appear in consecutive order.

ROGER D. MASTERS (1933–   ) Associate Professor of Political Science, Dartmouth College. Author of *The Political Philosophy of Rousseau*, (Princeton: Princeton University Press, 1968); *The Nation is Burdened; American Foreign Policy in a Changing World*, (New York: Knopf, 1967).

[1] E.g., Hans Morgenthau, *Politics Among Nations* (1st edn., New York 1953), 221; George Modelski, "Agraria and Industria: Two Models of the International System," in Klaus Knorr and Sidney Verba, eds., *The International System* (Princeton 1961), 125–26; and David Easton, "Political Anthropology," in Bernard J. Siegel, ed., *Biennial Review of Anthropology 1959* (Stanford 1959), 235–36. At least one anthropologist was aware of the analogy: see R. F. Barton, *The Half-Way Sun* (New York 1930), 109–10; *idem, The Kalingas* (Chicago 1949), 101; and *idem,* "Ifugao Law," 100, 103. In his introduction to *The Kalingas*, E. A. Hoebel wrote: "International law is primitive law on a world scale" (p. 5). Cf. Hoebel's *The Law of Primitive Man* (Cambridge, Mass., 1954), 125–26, 318, 321, 330–33.

[2] Since this study was undertaken, an article has been published that marks a first step in this direction. See Chadwick F. Alger, "Comparison of Intranational and International Politics," *American Political Science Review*, LVII (June 1963), 414–19.

[3] In 1940, A. R. Radcliffe-Brown said: "The comparative study of political institutions, with special reference to the simpler societies, is an important branch of social anthropology which has not yet received the attention it deserves" (Preface, in Fortes

Secondly, it may not be amiss to point out that long before anthropology was established as a discipline, political philosophers analyzed the social and political antecedents of existing states and governments.[4] The idea of a "state of nature," in which men lived before the establishment of governments, plays an important role in the history of political philosophy. Although recent students of primitive society have argued that "the theories of political philosophers" are "of little scientific value,"[5] the existence of a tradition which considered the "state of nature" as relevant to any political theory may indicate that political scientists should consider primitive politics more fully than they now do.

This general point is of specific importance for the theory of international politics because it can be said that the modern theory of international relations took the notion of a "state of nature" as its model.[6] Since anthropologists have asserted that such a "state of nature" never existed, consideration of the empirical and theoretical relevance of the concept may well be in order; not the least of the advantages of a comparison between primitive and international politics would be a fuller understanding of the relevance of modern political philosophy to a theory of world politics.[7]

Finally, as Ragnar Numelin has shown, "international relations" (or its analog) exists among uncivilized peoples; the "discovery" of diplomacy cannot be attributed, as it customarily is, to the "historical" cultures of the Mediterranean or Orient.[8] Thus any exhaustive theory of world politics would have to comprehend the rivalry, warfare, and diplomacy of primitive peoples as genuine examples of "international politics."

---

and Evans-Pritchard, eds., *African Political Systems,* xi). More recently, David Easton has written: "Such a subfield [as political anthropology] does not yet exist" ("Political Anthropology," 210).

[4] E.g., Montaigne, *Essays,* I, xxiii ("Of Custom, and that We Should Not Easily Change a Law Received"), and I, xxxi ("Of Cannibals"); Rousseau, *Second Discourse,* esp. First Part and notes c-q; and Locke, *Second Treatise of Civil Government,* esp. chaps. 2 and 3.

[5] Fortes and Evans-Pritchard, *African Political Systems,* 4. See also Henry Sumner Maine's sharp criticism of Rousseau's conception of the "state of nature" in *Ancient Law* (New York 1874), 84–88, 299.

[6] On the relations between the concept of a "state of nature" and the prevailing theory of politics among sovereign states, see Kenneth N. Waltz, *Man, the State and War* (New York 1959), esp. chaps. 6–8; and Richard H. Cox, *Locke on War and Peace* (Oxford 1960), esp. chap. 4.

[7] Cf. Kenneth N. Waltz, "Political Philosophy and the Study of International Relations," in William T. R. Fox, ed., *Theoretical Aspects of International Relations* (Notre Dame, Ind., 1959), 51–68; and Arnold Wolfers, "Political Theory and International Relations," in Arnold Wolfers and Laurence W. Martin, eds., *The Anglo-American Tradition in Foreign Affairs* (New Haven 1956), esp. xi-xiii.

[8] Ragnar Numelin, *The Beginnings of Diplomacy* (New York 1950), 125 *et passim.*

SIMILARITIES BETWEEN PRIMITIVE AND INTERNATIONAL POLITICS

At the outset, four elements common to politics within a number of primitive societies and international relations deserve mention: first, the absence of a formal government with power to judge and punish violations of law; second, the use of violence and "self-help" by the members of the system to achieve their objectives and enforce obligations; third, the derivation of law and moral obligations either from custom or from explicit, particular bargaining relationships (i.e., the absence of a formal legislative body operating on the basis of—and making—general rules); and fourth, a predominant organizational principle which establishes political units serving many functions in the overall social system.

The first three of these similarities between primitive and international politics are relatively self-evident when one considers those primitive societies which lack fully developed governments. The fourth, however, may not be as clear. In certain primitive societies, territorial political units are largely defined, especially in the eyes of their members, in terms of kinship groups, which are reckoned either "unilaterally" (i.e., groups such as the "lineage," in which descent is in either the male or female line from a common ancestor), or "bilaterally" (i.e., the family group includes relatives of both mother and father, as in modern, "Western" society).[9] Different combinations or divisions of these groups, on a territorial basis, often provide the basic structure of the entire political system.

Although it is not normally noted, the international system of sovereign states is also organized largely on the basis of a single principle. In this case the principle is that of "territorial sovereignty"—i.e., the conception that sovereignty "is always associated with the proprietorship of a limited portion of the earth's surface, and that 'sovereigns' *inter se* are to be deemed not *paramount*, but *absolute* owners of the state's territory." [10] This ultimate authority can, of course, be divided, as it is in federal states; but so, too, with the lineage principle in some primitive systems which are divided into different levels of units.[11]

---

[9] See Fortes and Evans-Pritchard, *African Political Systems*, 11; and Barton, "Ifugao Law," 92–94, 110. Carl Landé, in a stimulating unpublished paper entitled "Kinship and Politics in Pre-Modern and Non-Western Societies," has emphasized the different effects of these two types of kinship groups.

[10] Maine, *Ancient Law*, 99 (original italics).

[11] The foregoing comparison may appear to come strikingly close to the formulations of Maine (*ibid.*, 124–25) and Lewis H. Morgan (*Ancient Society* [New York 1877], 6–7)—formulations which have been criticized in recent years by anthropologists. See I. Schapera, *Government and Politics in Tribal Societies* (London 1956), 2–5. Despite the inadequacies of the concepts of Maine and Morgan, especially with

. . .

Up to this point we have tried to show two things: first, that there is a striking similarity between some primitive political systems and the modern international system; and second, that one element of this similarity is the "functional diffuseness" of political units in both types of system. If this is so, one cannot employ the polar opposites of "functionally specific" as the basis of a comparative analysis of primitive political systems. Because primitive political systems vary enormously, one must explicitly distinguish the particular *kind* of primitive society which is supposed to present the greatest similarity to world politics.

In order to compare primitive and international politics, therefore, one needs a classification which distinguishes primitive societies in terms of their political structure. Although the typologies of primitive political systems hitherto developed by anthropologists have been imperfect, it will be useful to accept provisionally the distinction between primitive peoples which have developed some form of governmental institutions and those which have generally been called "stateless societies." [12]

The following comparison will focus on primitive societies that lack formal governments. Such systems may be described as having "diffuse leadership," since individuals or groups have influence without formally institutionalized coercive authority. There may be a "titular chief" in these societies, but such an individual, even together with other influential men, does not act as a ruler. Since the modern world, as a political system, shares this structural characteristic of "statelessness," a résumé of political life in primitive stateless societies will show the utility of comparing them to the international political system.

---

reference to their presumption of progress in human development, some distinction between primitive or traditional society, in which kinship and personal "status" play a predominant role, and modern territorial states, based on citizenship and contract, is today accepted by many social scientists. Indeed, it is paradoxical that while anthropologists have been attacking the Maine-Morgan dichotomy (by showing that all societies have a territorial element), sociologists and political scientists have been adopting the distinction from the works of Tönnies, Weber, Parsons, or Levy. E.g., see Fred W. Riggs, "Agraria and Industria—Toward a Typology of Comparative Administration," in William J. Siffin. ed., *Toward the Comparative Study of Public Administration* (Bloomington 1959), 28–30, 111.

[12] See Fortes and Evans-Pritchard. *African Political Systems*, 5–23; John Middleton and David Tait, eds., *Tribes Without Rulers* (London 1958), 1–3; Lucy Mair, *Primitive Government* (Baltimore 1962), Part 1; Schapera, *Government and Politics*, 63–64, 208–14; and Robert Lowie, *Social Organization* (New York 1948), chap. 14. For a critique of the categories used by anthropologists, see Easton, "Political Anthropology," 210–26.

"SELF-HELP" AND VIOLENCE IN PRIMITIVE
STATELESS SOCIETIES

In stateless systems, disputes cannot be referred to an impartial government backed by a police force. The characteristic pattern of responding to criminal or civil wrongs is "self-help": the individual or group which feels injured considers himself or itself legitimately responsible for punishing a crime or penalizing a tort. Self-help in these circumstances involves two stages which appear to be directly comparable to the functions of adjudication and enforcement in modern legal systems. In either system, first it is necessary to determine that a wrong has occurred and that a particular individual or group will be punished in a particular way; second, the punishment or penalty for that wrong must be enforced or implemented.

In the simplest primitive societies, both stages are accomplished by the individual or family that has been wronged. For example, when a kinship group discovers that one of its members has been murdered, the guilty individual and his kinship group will be identified and a retaliatory killing (or other punishment) will be inflicted by the wronged group. As Barton indicated in his study of Philippine headhunters, such self-enforcement of legal penalties[13] raises a crucial problem among stateless primitive peoples. The kinship group which enforces the *lex talionis* by killing a murderer or one of his kin sees this act as not only necessary, but also legitimate. Although unrelated bystanders may accept this interpretation, since retaliatory killing is customary, the kinship group which is penalized may not consider the retaliation to be legitimate punishment.[14] When this occurs, there is often a tendency for crime and punishment to "escalate" into a more or less permanent relation of "feud" between the kinship groups involved.[15]

In feuds, violence usually takes the form of sporadic surprise attacks

---

[13] It must be emphasized that the retaliation is *legal*, being sanctioned by customary law (or, in Weber's terms, "traditional legitimacy") Cf. Mair, *Primitive Government*, 16–19; and A. R. Radcliffe-Brown, *Structure and Function in Primitive Society* (Glencoe, Ill., 1952), chap. 12.

[14] See Barton, *The Kalingas*, 231. Note the parallel tendency in world politics; "One state's aggression is always another state's 'legitimate use of force to defend vital national interests' " (Inis L. Claude, Jr., "United Nations Use of Military Force," *Journal of Conflict Resolution*, vii [June 1963], 119).

[15] Cf. Barton, *The Half-Way Sun*, chaps. 5 and 6. In some situations, however, a group may refrain from counterretaliation, either because the kinsman who was punished was offensive to his own kin or because the group lacks the power to react. As Carl Landé has pointed out to me, the principles of "an eye for an eye" and "might makes right" may, and often do, conflict in the operation of both primitive and international political systems.

by individuals or small groups. Hence a condition of feud should not be equated too completely with what we call "war";[16] rather, it is a condition of rivalry in which intermittent violence and aggression (e.g., seizure of property or person as well as retaliatory killing) appear legitimate to those who attack, and illegitimate to the victims. The similarity of this "state of feud" and a Hobbesian "state of nature" is obvious, with the important difference that kinship groups are often involved, instead of isolated individuals.

Although the notion of modern warfare cannot be accurately applied to all primitive intergroup fighting, primitive violence sometimes approximates a civilized war. The gradations of conflict arising out of self-help have been clarified by Tait and Middleton, who suggest that primitive feuds and wars be distinguished because only in the latter is there no obligation to attempt to settle the dispute.[17] They argue that within a restricted range (which varies from one primitive society to another) the more or less permanent condition of feud rivalry is rendered unlikely, if not impossible, by the existence of close kinship ties and relationships of "administrative organization."

. . .

INTERNATIONAL POLITICS AS A PRIMITIVE, STATELESS SYSTEM

The foregoing analysis has attempted to show how self-help, retaliation, and deterrence can be viewed as a characteristically primitive approach to law and order. Through this focus on stateless primitive peoples, the reliance upon self-help and deterrence in international rela-

---

[16] Numelin argues that organized, continuous warfare of the type known to civilized man is practically unknown among primitive peoples (*The Beginnings of Diplomacy*, chap. 2). Cf. Schapera, *Government and Politics*, 215, 219; and Melville J. Herskovits, *Cultural Anthropology* (New York 1955), 207-8.

[17] "Introduction," *Tribes Without Rulers*, 20-22. Cf. Radcliffe-Brown, *African Political Systems*, xx. A similar though not identical distinction is made by Barton, "Ifugao Law," 77-78. Kinds of violence in primitive society could also be distinguished in terms of the extent to which groups act as corporate units and the degree to which violence is continuous. In this sense, a true "war" would consist of more or less continuous hostilities between corporate groups, whereas "feuds," in the purest case, would be intermittent conflicts between individuals (albeit with the support of kinship groups). Although such an approach would take into consideration the fundamental issue raised by Rousseau's criticism of Hobbes's concept of a "state of war" (see *L'État de guerre*, in C. E. Vaughan, d., *The Political Writings of Rousseau* [2 vols., Cambridge, Eng., 1915], 1, 293-307), it raises theoretical questions which require a more exhaustive analysis than is here possible. For the present, therefore, it is useful to accept provisionally the distinction between feud and war as elaborated by anthropologists.

tions appears to be evidence that the world forms a political system that is in many respects similar to primitive systems. Although it is often argued that international law and politics are *sui generis*,[18] the utility of a comparison between international affairs and stateless primitive societies is shown by two characteristic similarities: first, the relation of law to violence as a means of organizing a coherent social system; and second, the relationship of custom to rivalry and bargaining as means of making and applying known rules.[19]

Although it is fashionable to describe international relations as a lawless anarchy,[20] and to admit that international law exists only on condition that it be called "weak" law,[21] these habitual opinions must be questioned. It is true that the international system permits and even sanctions a considerable amount of violence and bloodshed; but, as has been seen, there is a class of stateless political systems which have this characteristic because they depend upon self-help for the enforcement of law. In such systems law and violence are related in a way that is quite different from the internal political order under which civilized man is accustomed to live; if we speak of international "anarchy," it would be well to bear in mind that it is an "ordered anarchy."

To prove that international law is not necessarily "weak," one need only consider the functions of law in a political system. Hoffmann has suggested that any legal order has three functions: it should produce "security," "satisfaction," and "flexibility."[22] According to these criteria, a legal system dependent upon the self-enforcement of rights by autonomous groups (be they families or nation-states) is "strong" in all three respects.

Most obviously, "flexibility" is assured in a system which recognizes

---

[18] E.g., Stanley Hoffmann, "International Systems and International Law," in Knorr and Verba, eds., *The International System*, 205.

[19] The second of these characteristics is concerned, speaking crudely, with the relationship between what Almond has called the "political functions" of rule-making, rule application, and interest articulation, while the first corresponds roughly to his functions of interest aggregation and rule adjudication. The last of these functions, in a stateless system, should really be spoken of as rule enforcement, for obvious reasons. Cf. "Introduction," in Almond and Coleman, eds., *The Politics of the Developing Areas*, 17; . . .

[20] Cf. Waltz, *Man, the State, and War,* chaps. 6 and 7. While the present essay is in complete agreement with Waltz's major theme (i.e., that war is a necessary consequence of the state system, since "in anarchy there is no automatic harmony"), his emphasis on the problem of war tends to understate the elements of legality and order in world politics.

[21] E.g., Hoffmann, "International Systems and International Law," 206–7.

[22] *Ibid.*, 212.

any change in power; to the extent that might makes right, changes in might produce changes in right. It may be somewhat less evident that international law produces a "satisfactory" solution for disputes, yet this is on the whole true because of the admitted impossibility of reversing the verdict of brute force.[23] And, finally, the stateless international system even produces a modicum of security, most especially through deterrence based upon a mutual recognition that rival nations will both be harmed (if not destroyed) by the use of their legitimate right to self-help. In this respect it is worth emphasizing that the nuclear age, with its awesome potentialities for destruction, has also seen a corresponding increase in the unwillingness of powerful nation-states to resort to overt war.[24]

To reveal more clearly the orderly (if violent) aspects of a stateless international system, several elements of the relationship between force and law need to be spelled out in greater detail. As in primitive stateless societies, not only does violence erupt intermittently from a continuing condition of potential feud or war between autonomous groups; co-operation also occurs sporadically. While such cooperation is sometimes limited to actions which prepare for or prosecute warfare (as in most alliances), the members of the interstate system have also been capable of making mutually binding cooperative decisions in *ad hoc* multilateral conferences.[25] The Concert of Europe provides a more institutionalized example of such intermittent structures, which act as a kind of temporary "government" while preserving the sovereignty of the major states in the international system.[26]

---

[23] Although the "satisfaction" with defeat in war may be of short duration, this is not a necessary consequence of military defeat (as the pro-Western attitude of West Germany and Japan after World War II indicates). The limited durability of "satisfactory" settlements will be discussed below.

[24] Since World War II there have been numerous international incidents which, under prenuclear conditions, would probably have resulted in open warfare. Cf. Herman Kahn, "The Arms Race and Some of Its Hazards," in Donald G. Brennan, ed., *Arms Control, Disarmament, and National Security* (New York 1961), 93ff. On the security offered by the "impermeable" nation-state before the development of nuclear weapons, see John H. Herz, *International Politics in the Atomic Age* (New York 1959), Part 1.

[25] Most notably, of course, in peace conferences terminating major wars.

[26] On the Concert of Europe, see Richard N. Rosecrance, *Action and Reaction in World Politics* (Boston 1963), chap. 4, and the references there cited. Compare the specialized, intermittent political agencies in many stateless primitive societies: Robert H. Lowie, "Some Aspects of Political Organization Among American Aborigines," *Journal of the Royal Anthropological Institute,* LXXVII (1948), 17–18; and Radcliffe-Brown, *African Political Systems,* xix.

This type of cooperative decision-making, subject to veto by a participating state, must be seen as a feasible—if obviously limited—method of procedure; it is present not only in *ad hoc* bilateral or multilateral meetings, but also in the continuously functioning international organizations (the League of Nations and the UN) which have been developed in this century.[27] It should also be noted that the emergence of so-called "functional" organizations represents a trend toward continuously functioning institutions capable of limited but very real cooperation in the internal political system.[28]

The limitations as well as the importance of both violence and cooperation in world politics must therefore be equally emphasized in any total assessment of the international system. In so doing, the comparison with stateless primitive peoples serves the useful purpose of identifying the characteristic properties of a political system in which law is sanctioned by self-help. As among the primitives, retaliation is an acceptable means of righting a wrong, though it is true that civilized nations regard strict retaliation—"an eye for an eye"—as a more extreme recourse than do savage peoples.[29] As among stateless primitives, neutrality is possible, and non-involved groups often attempt to mediate conflict and induce rivals to cease fighting. As among stateless primitives, finally, the very possibility that conflict may escalate serves to deter violence on some occasions.[30] Hence the relation of law to force in the multistate system, like the "ordered anarchy" of primitive societies without governments, is derived from the lack of authoritative political institutions.

When we turn more directly to the decision-making process—the

---

[27] Note the similarity between the Iroquois Confederacy, which could act as a unit only if a decision was unanimous, and the UN Security Council. See Morgan, *League of the Iroquois,* 111–14; and Inis L. Claude, Jr., *Swords into Plowshares* (2nd edn., New York 1959), chap. 8.

[28] Cf. the limited but continuous role of the *pangats* and "pact-holders" among the Kalinga, which Barton contrasts with the intermittent action of the Ifugao "go-betweens" and "trading partners" (The Kalingas, 144–46). On the question of the "continuity" or "contingency" of political structures, see Easton, "Political Anthropology," 235–46.

[29] Henry S. Maine, *International Law* (New York 1888), 174–75. Primitive peoples do not always exact strict retaliation, however; the institution of a "weregild" or payment in lieu of retaliation is paralleled in international politics by reparations and other penalties exacted in the negotiation of peace treaties. Also, compare Morton A. Kaplan, "The Strategy of Limited Retaliation," Policy Memorandum No. 19 (Princeton, Center of International Studies, 1959), and, more generally, recent strategic discussions of "graduated deterrence"—e.g., Henry A. Kissinger, *The Necessity for Choice* (New York 1961), 65–70.

[30] Cf. Schelling, *The Strategy of Conflict,* chap. 8.

second characteristic mentioned above—it may be recalled that in many primitive political systems, especially those lacking governmental institutions, custom and bargaining are related in a crucial way, since they are the only methods for establishing enforceable rules. The same can be said of the international political system, for it to lacks an authoritative legislature or an all-powerful executive. International law can be said to be created in two major ways: a practice or rule either becomes a custom, having been followed for a considerable time, or it is adopted by mutual consent, as binding specific groups under particular circumstances. While the second of these legislative methods is relatively unambiguous to the extent that it produces formal treaties and agreements, the first produces customary law slowly and imperceptibly, so that in periods of rapid change one may wonder if any such law really exists. Over time, nonetheless, specific legal rules have been adopted and accepted as valid by the nation-states composing the modern international system.[31]

At any moment of time, international law seems to be chaotic and uncertain; "double standards" often appear to bind weak or law-abiding states, while permitting the ruthless or strong to satisfy their demands with impunity.[32] But when a longer-range view is taken and the world is considered as a stateless political system in which self-help is a legitimate means of legal procedure, disputes over the content of international law (like disputes over the legitimacy of each killing in a primitive feud) become a predictable consequence of the system's structure. As the world is now organized, international law almost requires conflict concerning the substantive provisions relating to a given dispute, and

---

[31] On the character of international law and its sources, see James L. Brierly, *The Law of Nations* (4th edn., London 1949), 1–91, 229–36; Percy E. Corbett, *Law and Society in the Relations of States* (New York 1951), 3–52; and Morton A. Kaplan and Nicholas de B. Katzenbach, *The Political Foundations of International Law* (New York 1961), chap. 9. Some observers of international relations, following John Austin's legal theory, have doubted that a system without a single sovereign authority could have "true" law. For a criticism of this application of Austin's view, see Maine, *International Law*, 47–51.

[32] William Foltz has pointed out to me that there is also a parallel "reverse double standard" in both primitive and international systems; weak and unimportant groups are often permitted actions which major groups would not commit (or which would be strongly criticized if committed). Many primitive systems allow inferior lineages or castes wider latitude in many forms of conduct (dishonesty, petty thievery, public defamation, etc.) than is permitted major lineages or castes. As long as the stability of the system or the vital interests of a major group are not threatened, such behavior may be a useful safety valve. The behavior of so-called "nonaligned" states in the UN General Assembly offers an obvious parallel.

warfare is a legal means of bargaining prior to the conclusion of more or less temporary settlements.[33]

One peculiar characteristic of laws in a stateless political system is thus the legitimization of dispute concerning the application of legal rights to particular circumstances. While it is usual in this context to emphasize the relationship of force to law (by pointing out that "might makes right" in anarchy), the frequency and necessity of disputes over the substance of rights have another consequence: the primacy of political rivalry. Within a society with a government, men whose interests conflict must channel their demands through a specific institutional structure, ultimately recognizing (in principle) the legitimacy of political attitudes which have been sanctioned by governmental decision.[34]

In international politics, this relatively terminal character of intrastate political decisions is often lacking; the policies of one's rivals need not be legitimized even by victory in warfare. In a sense, therefore, might does *not* make right in international politics (as, indeed, the French insisted after 1871 and the Germans after 1918). Like primitive feuds, international disputes are only temporarily settled; a settlement which precludes the possibility of further conflict is rare.[35] This means that political differences, and the interests upon which these differences are based, are often more visible in world politics than in intra-state politics. Conflicting demands for the satisfaction of the desires of one's own group—politics and rivalry—are therefore the prime factors in international relations.[36]

---

[33] From the point of view of a systematic anaysis, law need not be a "good." Indeed, law need not produce peaceful "order," though as civilized men we infer from our political experience that this *should* be so. Hence authorities on international law often feel compelled to go beyond mere restatements of accepted legal principles; the international law texts, long an important method of codifying customary international law, are frequently animated by a desire for reform. Cf. Maine, *International Law*, Lectures 1, xii, *et passim*. Unlike the sphere of domestic politics, in which relativism sometimes seems tenable to scholars, international law and politics are difficult to treat in a wholly positivist fashion without thereby accepting as justifiable a condition of legal self-help and war which civilized men tend to reject as barbarous, if not unjust. Hence world politics is perhaps *the* area in which it is most evident that satisfactory political theory cannot divorce objectivity (and especially freedom from partisanship) from the quest for standards of justice.

[34] But note that, even in domestic politics, the legitimacy of government decisions may be challenged by those who are willing to be "bellicose." Cf. Bertrand de Jouvenel, *The Pure Theory of Politics* (New Haven 1963), 180ff.

[35] For the prerequisites for these rare cases, see the study cited in note 31. Note the function of "marriage" (between representatives of rival kinship groups in primitive societies and between ruling families in the earlier periods of the modern state system) as a means of formalizing such a settlement.

[36] Cf. the "principle of political primacy" emphasized by Robert E. Osgood, *Limited War* (Chicago 1957), 13–15.

This primacy of political conflict in world affairs is especially important because of a further similarity between primitive and international politics. Just as some stateless primitive societies are differentiated into spatial "zones" of increasing opposition, so the world can be divided into areas which are politically "far" from each other.[37] Here again, a characteristic of world politics which often appears to be *sui generis* can be understood more broadly in the context of a comparison between primitive and international politics.

SOME DIFFERENCES BETWEEN PRIMITIVE AND INTERNATIONAL POLITICAL SYSTEMS

In arguing that stateless primitive political systems resemble the international political system in many ways, the search for analogies should not obscure the massive differences which must have been only too easily noticed by the reader. By specifying some of these differences, however, it will be possible to distinguish those aspects in which world politics is unique from those that are due to the absence of a formally constituted world government. In particular, there are two general differences between primitive and international politics which will make it easier to see the limits of the structural similarity between the two. It will be necessary to consider, first, the role of political culture, and second, the impact of change.

Although it is usually assumed that the beliefs, manners, and customs of nonliterate peoples are homogeneous, many primitive societies are composed of heterogeneous ethnic stocks; indeed, such heterogeneity is particularly important, for it appears to be related to the emergence of governmental institutions, at least among many African peoples.[38] Nonetheless, there is a marked tendency toward cultural homogeneity in primitive stateless societies, since most individuals accept without question the established way of life.[39] Although the application of traditional rules to specific cases may be and frequently is disputed, the relative stability of culture limits the kinds of change occurring in most primitive systems.[40]

---

[37] "Blocs" and regional systems are, of course, ready examples. On the relationship between the global system and regional systems in international politics, see George Liska, *Nations of Alliance* (Baltimore 1962), 19–20, 22–24, 259–62.

[38] See Schapera, *Government and Politics,* 124–25; and Mair, *Primitive Government,* chap. 5.

[39] Cf. Fortes and Evans-Pritchard, *African Political Systems,* 9–10.

[40] Hence there may be disputes concerning the power and influence of opposed groups, but these conflicts are rarely ideological in character.

In contrast, the international political system currently includes radically different political cultures. As Almond has shown, national political systems which face the task of integrating different political cultures are subject to strains that are absent in more homogeneous societies: *a fortiori*, this problem is even greater in a system which permits many antagonistic political cultures to organize themselves into autonomous nation-states.[41] In general, therefore, it could be argued that self-help and structural decentralization tend to produce a greater degree of instability in world politics than in most primitive stateless societies.[42]

An additional feature compounds this problem. The historical development of Western civilization, as it has increased man's control over nature and spread the effects of modern science throughout the world, has produced particularly sharp differences between political cultures, at the same time that it has brought these cultures into closer contact than was possible before the advent of modern technology. And, simultaneously with this intensification of the contact between different cultures, it has become apparent that technologically advanced societies are capable of what seems to be virtually infinite material progress, so that the most powerful nations can continuously increase their technological superiority over "backward" or "underdeveloped" states.

The main consequence of the interaction of modern, scientific technology upon cultural differences has been extraordinarily rapid change in world politics, of which the great increase in the number of nation-states is but the most superficial index.[43] The stateless structure of a primitive political system may be tolerably stable, despite the reliance upon self-help in legal enforcement; a similar structure, in the changing context of international politics, may well lead to chaos. Even in a primitive world, the contact of a more "advanced" people with a society without governmental institutions has often produced a rapid domination of the latter by the former.[44] It is all the more to be expected, therefore, that

---

[41] See Almond, "Comparative Political Systems," 400–2. Cf. the importance of the nationality problem in the USSR.

[42] Note, however, that many primitive societies are not as stable and unchanging as is often believed. E.g., see Southall, *Alur Society*, 224–27, 236, *et passim;* and J. A. Barnes, *Politics in a Changing Society* (London 1954), chap. 2.

[43] On the distinction between "stable" and "revolutionary" international systems, see Hoffmann, "International Systems and International Law," 208–11. Hoffmann suggests that three variables determine the stability or instability of an international system: (1) "the basic structure of the world," (2) "the technology of conflict," and (3) "the units' purposes" (*ibid.*, 207–8). In the present essay, emphasis is placed on the first of these variables—see below, section VII.

[44] Southall, *Alur Society*, 229–34.

the present structure of the international system is essentially transitional, and that quite considerable changes must be expected in the next century.

9. WORLD IN REVOLUTION

Robert Strausz-Hupé

THE COLLAPSE of empires, population growth, the disintegration of old cultures, shifts in the balance of power, new weapons—these things have almost always led to revolution and war. Out of conflict there then emerged a universal order in the image and under the domination of one power. Once again the establishment of such a universal order is the sole alternative to chaos. The great question remains—in the image of what power will a universal order prevail?

The term revolution implies profound, rapid change. An old order dissolves, the new emerges. New rulers replace old ones. Men sense the quickening tempo of events, accept, or try to reject the break with the past. And the transition is marked by violence. These were the characteristics of the French and Russian revolutions. Both produced international as well as national revolutions. The two World Wars were revolutionary.

It is easy to identify these milestones of modern revolution. It is more difficult to relate them to a general development, what can be called a systemic revolution, which, in different ways, occurs in all countries, affects all men, and lasts indefinitely. Cycles of history, completed long ago, afford a better insight into this systemic world revolution than specific recent upheavals. One such vast, prolonged cycle transformed the ancient world. It started with the Peloponnesian War and reached its

From *The Saturday Evening Post* (August 15, 1959), 64ff. Reprinted by permission of the author.

ROBERT STRAUSZ-HUPÉ (1903–   ) Professor of Political Science and Director, Foreign Policy Research Institute, University of Pennsylvania. Co-author of *Building the Atlantic World,* (New York: Harper, 1963); *A Forward Strategy for America,* (New York Harper, 1961); *Protracted Conflict,* (New York Harper, 1959); *International Relations,* (New York: Praeger, 1956). Author of *Power and Community,* (New York: Praeger, 1956).

climax in the Roman civil wars which pitted first Pompey against Caesar, then Caesar's heirs against one another. Its focal stages were Athens and Rome, but it was confined to no one city or country. It raged through the entire Mediterranean region—the universe of the ancients. When it had run its course of four centuries, one state had supplanted the sovereignties of many separate states. A new order had been established, not only for Rome and Athens, for Italy and Greece, but for all the Mediterranean peoples. Similarly, the slow decline of the Roman Empire was a revolution that transcended any one clearly identifiable civilization. The evolving system bore little resemblance to the Roman political and moral values. Those the new order submerged. The Renaissance and Reformation in turn recast Europe. The emergent system of nation-states marked a break with feudalism as decisive as that which loosened the Roman imperial grip from the ancient world.

The present generation faces a bewildering and unprecedented paradox. Unlimited resources lie within our reach. We stand at the threshold of a rich universal civilization. Yet our survival is in doubt. So terrible is this dilemma, so pressing the demands of the hour, that we incline to mistake each bend of the road for a historic turning point. In reality our plight is but the current episode of a long epic, whose outcome no man can foretell. We may surmise, however, that destiny has placed us in the midst of a revolutionary epoch, comparable to those which accompanied the passing of the city-state, Roman imperialism and the breakdown of European feudalism.

During each of these systemic revolutions, states fought each other. But international war was also civil war, for the disturbance of the system affected all the parts, erasing the distinctions between civil and external, national and international. Each upheaval followed a pattern, baffling to the participants, but meaningful to posterity. The pattern of systemic revolution is woven from the actions of masses of men who may neither understand nor necessarily desire the end result. Thus, to those who had fought in the First World War nothing seemed settled. The world had not been made safer for democracy; the power of Germany had not been broken; and the quarrels among the victors made certain that the great war to end all wars would be followed by a greater war. And it now appears that World War II produced results that few men who fought in it thought it would produce. At the end of a war fought for the liberation of Europe, half of Europe exchanged the yoke of the Nazis for that of the Communists. German and Japanese imperialism had been defeated—only to smooth the path for the more ambitious and insidious imperialism of the Soviets and Communist China. The war settled once and for all, the fate of the nation-state—the two emergent super-powers, the United States and the Soviet Union, now dwarfed a congeries of so-called independent nations actually more or less dependent on them. Historic design exists, but not consciously or rationally. No man or group of men controls it. For those caught in its meshes, this remains an un-fathomable riddle.

A paradoxical feature of the systemic revolution has been the decline of the nation-state system in the West, side by side with the rise of the new states in Asia and Africa, each stridently affirming the prerogatives of national sovereignty. In the West, the creative force of nationalism has long been exhausted. It arose from the secularization of European society beginning with the Renaissance and achieved its apotheosis in the French Revolution and the French nation-state. The idea of the nation-state, a French idea, swept Europe. It triggered countermovements that defeated Napoleon's empire and culminated in the unification of Germany and Italy. At the beginning of this century nationalism shattered the last surviving forms of dynastic integration—the empires of the Hapsburgs, the Romanovs and the Ottoman sultans, and spawned the small nation-states of Central and Eastern Europe. The peacemakers of 1919 wrote the concept of national self-determination into the grand settlement of World War I and thus unwittingly put the finishing touches to what has been called the "modern state system." From its inception the arrangement proved neither systematic nor modern. The forces of nationalism turned destructively upon themselves and confounded those trying to establish peaceful order without frustrating national aspirations.

10. NATIONALISM

Hans Kohn

N ATIONALISM as we understand it is not older than the second half of the eighteenth century. Its first great manifestation was the French Revolution, which gave the new movement an increased dynamic force. Nationalism had become manifest, however, at the end of the eighteenth century almost simultaneously in a number of widely separated European

From *The Idea of Nationalism* by Hans Kohn (New York: Macmillan Company: 1960) pp. 3–24. Reprinted by permission of The Macmillan Company. Copyright 1944 by Hans Kohn.

HANS KOHN (1891–   ) Professor Emeritus of History, City College of New York. Visiting Professor, University of Texas, University of Berlin. His other books include *Prologue to Nation-States: France and Germany, 1789–1815*, (Princeton: D. Van Nostrand Company, 1967); *Political Ideologies of the Twentieth Century*, (New York: Harper and Row, 1966); *Reflections on Modern History: The Historians and Human Responsibility*, (Princeton: D. Van Nostrand Company, 1963).

countries. Its time in the evolution of mankind had arrived, and although the French Revolution was one of the most powerful factors in its intensification and spread, this did not mark the date of its birth. Like all historical movements, nationalism has its roots deep in the past. The conditions which made its emergence possible had matured for centuries before they converged at its formation. These political, economic, and intellectual developments took a long time for their growth, and proceeded at a different pace in the various countries. It is impossible to grade them according to their importance or to make one dependent upon another. All are closely interconnected, each reacting upon the others; and although their growth can be traced separately, their effects and consequences cannot be separated otherwise than in the analysis of the scholar; in life, they are indissolubly intertwined.

Nationalism is inconceivable without the ideas of popular sovereignty preceding—without a complete revision of the position of ruler and ruled, of classes and castes. The aspect of the universe and of society had to be secularized with the help of a new natural science and of natural law as understood by Grotius and Locke. The traditionalism of economic life had to be broken by the rise of the third estate, which was to turn the attention away from the royal courts and their civilization to the life, language, and arts of the people. This new class found itself less bound by tradition than the nobility or clergy; it represented a new force striving for new things; it was ready to break with the past, flouting tradition in its opinion even more than it did in reality. In its rise, it claimed to represent not only a new class and its interests, but the whole people. Where the third estate became powerful in the eighteenth century—as in Great Britain, in France, and in the United States—nationalism found its expression predominantly, but never exclusively, in political and economic changes. Where, on the other hand, the third estate was still weak and only in a budding stage at the beginning of the nineteenth century, as in Germany, Italy, and among the Slavonic peoples, nationalism found its expression predominantly in the cultural field. Among these peoples, at the beginning it was not so much the nation-state as the *Volksgeist* and its manifestations in literature and folklore, in the mother tongue, and in history, which became the center of the attention of nationalism. With the growing strength of the third estate, with the political and cultural awakening of the masses, in the course of the nineteenth century, this cultural nationalism soon turned into the desire for the formation of a nation-state.

The growth of nationalism is the process of integration of the masses of the people into a common political form. Nationalism therefore presupposes the existence, in fact or as an ideal, of a centralized form of government over a large and distinct territory. This form was created by the absolute monarchs, who were the pacemakers of modern nationalism; the French Revolution inherited and continued the centralizing tendencies of the kings, but at the same time it filled the central organization with a new spirit and gave it a power of cohesion unknown before. Nationalism is unthinkable before the emergence of the modern state in the period from the sixteenth to the eighteenth century. Nationalism accepted this form, but changed it by animating it with a new feeling of life and with a new religious fervor.

For its composite texture, nationalism used in its growth some of the oldest and most primitive feelings of man, found throughout history as important factors in the formation of social groups. There is a natural tendency in man—and by "natural tendency" we mean a tendency which, having been produced by social circumstances from time practically immemorial, appears to us as natural—to love his birthplace or the place of his childhood sojourn, its surroundings, its climate, the contours of hills and valleys, of rivers and trees. We are all subject to the immense power of habitude, and even if in a later stage of development we are attracted by the unknown and by change, we delight to come back and to be at rest in the reassuring sight of the familiar. Man has an easily understandable preference for his own language as the only one which he thoroughly understands and in which he feels at home. He prefers native customs and native food to alien ones, which appear to him unintelligible and indigestible. Should he travel, he will return to his chair and his table with a feeling of relaxation and will be elated by the joy of finding himself again at home, away from the strain of a sojourn in foreign lands and contact with foreign peoples.

Small wonder that he will take pride in his native characteristics, and that he will easily believe in their superiority. As they are the only ones in which civilized people like himself can apparently feel at home, are they not the only ones fit for human beings? On the other hand, contact with alien men and alien customs, which appear to him strange, unfamiliar, and therefore threatening, will arouse in him a distrust of everything foreign. This feeling of strangeness will again develop in him sentiments of superiority, and sometimes even of open hostility. The more primitive men are, the stronger will be their distrust of strangers, and therefore the greater the intensity of their group feeling. Rudyard Kipling, in his poem "The Stranger," forcefully expressed this general feeling:

> The Stranger within my gate,
> He may be true or kind,
> But he does not talk my talk—
> I cannot feel his mind.
> I see the face and the eyes and the mouth,
> But not the soul behind.

> The men of my own stock
> They may do ill or well,
> But they tell the lies I am wonted to,
> They are used to the lies I tell;
> And we do not need interpreters
> When we go to buy and sell.

> The Stranger within my gates,
> He may be evil or good,
> But I cannot tell what powers control—
> What reasons sway his mood;
> Nor when the Gods of his far-off land
> May repossess his blood.

These feelings have always existed. They do not form nationalism; they correspond to certain facts—territory, language, common descent—which we also find in nationalism. But here they are entirely transformed, charged with new and different emotions, and embedded in a broader context. They are the natural elements out of which nationalism is formed; but nationalism is not a natural phenomenon, not a product of "eternal" or "natural" laws; it is a product of the growth of social and intellectual factors at a certain stage of history. Some feeling of nationality, it may be said, existed before the birth of modern nationalism—a feeling varying in strength and in frequency from time to time: at some epochs almost completely extinguished, at others more or less clearly discernible. But it was largely unconscious and inarticulate. It did not influence the thought and actions of men in a deep and all-pervading way. It found a clear expression only occasionally in individuals, and in groups only at times of stress or provocation. It did not determine their aims or actions permanently or in the long run. It was no purposeful will welding together all the individuals into a unity of emotions, thoughts, and actions.

Before the age of nationalism, the masses very rarely became conscious of the fact that the same language was spoken over a large territory. In fact, it was not the same language; several dialects existed side by side, sometimes incomprehensible to the man of a neighboring province. The spoken language was accepted as a natural fact. It was in no way regarded as a political or cultural factor, still less as an object of political or cultural struggle. During the Middle Ages, people deduced from the Bible that the diversity of languages was the result of the sinfulness of man, and God's punishment for the building of the Tower of Babel. Consciousness of language was aroused only at times of expeditions and travel or in frontier districts. There, the alien character of the group speaking the alien language was felt, and many national groups were first recognized as different and named by those of alien tongue. The Greek word *barbaros* (which meant "strange" or "foreign," and in consequence "rude" and "ignorant") probably had its source in the idea of stammering or inability to speak in a comprehensible way—a word akin to the Sanskrit expression *barbara,* which meant "stammering" or "non-Aryan." The Slavs called the Germans with whom they came into contact *niemci,* "the mutes," people who cannot make themselves understood. A man speaking an incomprehensible tongue seemed outside the pale of civilization. But language was accepted by the Slavs and by other peoples as a natural fact, not as a cultural inheritance. The language in which the treasures of civilization were inherited and trans-ferred—in medieval Europe as well as in Islam, in India as well as in China—was generally not the language spoken by the people: it was a learned language accessible only to the educated class. Even if it was not a language of different origin, it was generally so archaic and so rich in many purely literary, classical associations that it was understood only by a small minority.

.   .   .

2

Nationalism is first and foremost a state of mind, an act of conscious-ness, which since the French Revolution has become more and more common to mankind. The mental life of man is as much dominated by an ego-consciousness as it is by a group-consciousness. Both are complex states of mind at which we arrive through experiences of differentiation and opposition, of the ego and the surrounding world, of the we-group and those outside the group. The collective or group consciousness can center around entirely different groups, of which some have a more permanent character—the family, the class, the clan, the caste, the vil-lage, the sect, the religion, etc.—whereas others are of a more or less passing character—schoolmates, a football team, or passengers on a ship. In each case, varying with its permanence, this group-consciousness will strive towards creating homogeneity within the group, a conformity and like-mindedness which will lead to and facilitate concerted common action. In that sense, we may speak of a group-mind and a group-action. We may speak of a Catholic mind and a Catholic action, of an English mind and an English action; but we may also speak of a rural mind or an urban mind, and of the action of rural or urban groups. All these groups develop their own character. The character of an occupational group, such as peasants, soldiers, civil servants, may be as clearly defined and stable as any character of a national group, or even more so. Each group creates its own symbols and social conventions, is dominated by social traditions, which find their expression in the public opinion of the group.

Group-consciousness is never exclusive. Men find themselves members of different groups at the same time. With the growth of the complexity of civilization, the number of groups of which men find themselves a part generally increases. These groups are not fixed. They have changing limits, and they are of changing importance. Within these pluralistic, and sometimes conflicting, kinds of group-consciousness there is generally one which is recognized by man as the supreme and most important, to which therefore, in the case of conflict of group-loyalties, he owes supreme loyalty. He identifies himself with the group and its existence, frequently not only for the span of his life, but for the continuity of his existence beyond this span. This feeling of solidarity between the individual and the group may go, at certain times, as far as complete submergence of the individual in the group. The whole education of the members of the group is directed to a common mental preparedness for common attitudes and common actions.

In different periods of history, and in different civilizations, we find different groups to which this supreme loyalty is given. The modern period of history, starting with the French Revolution, is characterized by the fact that in this period, and in this period alone, the nation demands the supreme loyalty of man, that all men, not only certain individuals or classes, are drawn into this common loyalty, and that all civilizations (which up to this modern period followed their own, and frequently widely different ways) are now dominated more and more by this one supreme group-consciousness, nationalism.

It is a fact often commented upon that this growth of nationalism and of national sectionalisms happened at the very time when international relations, trade, and communications were developing as never before; that local languages were raised to the dignity of literary and cultural languages just at the time when it seemed most desirable to efface all differences of language by the spread of world languages. This view overlooks the fact that that very growth of nationalism all over the earth, with its awakening of the masses to participation in political and cultural life, prepared the way for the closer cultural contacts of all the civilizations of mankind (now for the first time brought into a common denominator), at the same time separating and uniting them.

Nationalism as a group-consciousness is therefore a psychological and a sociological fact, but any psychological or sociological explanation is insufficient. An American psychologist defined a nation as "a group of individuals that feels itself one, is ready within limits to sacrifice the individual for the group advantage, that prospers as a whole, that has groups of emotions experienced as a whole, each of whom rejoices with the advancement and suffers with the losses of the group. . . . Nationality is a mental state or community in behavior." This definition is valid, as far as it goes, not only for the nation, but for any other supreme group to which man owes loyalty, and with which he identifies himself. It is therefore not sufficient to distinguish the national group from other groups of similar importance and permanence.

Nationalities are the product of the historical development of society. They are not identical with clans, tribes, or folk-groups—bodies of men united by actual or supposed common descent or by a common habitat. Ethnographic groups like these existed throughout history, from earliest times on, yet they do not form nationalities; they are nothing but "ethnographic material," out of which under certain circumstances a nationality might arise. Even if a nationality arises, it may disappear again, absorbed into a larger or new nationality. Nationalities are products of the living forces of history, and therefore always fluctuating, never rigid. Nationalities are groups of very recent origin and therefore are of the utmost complexity. They defy exact definition. Nationality is an historical and a political concept, and the words "nation" and "nationality" have undergone many changes in meaning. It is only in recent history that man has begun to regard nationality as the center of his political and cultural activity and life. Nationality is therefore nothing absolute and it is a great mistake, responsible for most of the extremities of today to make it an absolute, an objective *a priori,* the source of all political and cultural life.

Nationality has been raised to an absolute by two fictitious concepts which have been accepted as having real substance. One holds that blood or race is the basis of nationality, and that it exists eternally and carries with it an unchangeable inheritance; the other sees the *Volksgeist* as an ever-welling source of nationality and all its manifestations. These theories offer no real explanation of the rise and the role of nationality: they refer us to mythical pre-historical pseudo-realities. Rather, they must be taken as characteristic elements of thought in the age of nationalism, and are subject themselves to analysis by the historian of nationalism.

3

Nationalities come into existence only when certain objective bonds delimit a social group. A nationality generally has several of these attributes; very few have all of them. The most usual of them are common descent, language, territory, political entity, customs and traditions, and religion. A short discussion will suffice to show that none of them is essential to the existence or definition of nationality.

Common descent seemed of great importance to primitive man, for whom birth was as great a mystery as death, and therefore was surrounded by legends and superstitions. Modern nationalities, however, are mixtures of different, and sometimes even very distant, races. The great migratory movements of history and the mobility of modern life have led everywhere to an intermingling, so that few if any nationalities can at present claim anything approaching common descent.

The importance of language for the formation and life of a nationality was stressed by Herder and Fichte. But there are many nationalities who have no language of their own—like the Swiss, who speak four different languages, or the Latin American nationalities, all of whom speak Spanish or Portuguese. The English-speaking nations (also the Spanish-speaking) are partly of similar descent; they speak the same language, and had until quite recently the same historical background, and also traditions and customs very much akin to each other; yet they represent different nationalities with frequently conflicting aspirations. Another example of the comparative irrelevance of objective criteria for the formation and continued existence of separate nationalities is to be found in Norway and Denmark, where the people are of common racial stock and speak almost the same language. Nevertheless, they consider themselves as two nationalities, and the Norwegians set up their own language only as the result of having become a nationality.

Customs and traditions were first stressed in their importance for nationality by Rousseau. Each nation undoubtedly has its customs, traditions, and institutions; but these often vary greatly from locality to locality, and, on the other hand, tend in our times to become standardized all over the world, or at least over large areas. Customs and manners nowadays often change with great rapidity.

Religion was the great dominating force before the rise of nationalism in modern times. This is true in Western as well as Eastern Christianity, in Islam and in India. The dividing limes were not drawn according to nationalities, but according to religious civilizations. Therefore the rise of nationalities and of nationalism was accompanied by transformations in the religious attitude of man, and in many ways the growth of nationalities has been helped or hindered by the influence of religion. Religious differences sometimes divided and weakened nationalities, and even helped to create new nationalities, as in the case of the Catholic Croats and the Orthodox Serbs. On the other hand, national churches have frequently been an important element in helping to arouse nationalism; and when conflicting nationalities were of different religions often played a large part in the defense mechanism of the weaker nationality, as Catholicism did in Ireland and in Prussian Poland.

The most important outward factor in the formation of nationalities is a common territory, or rather, the state. Political frontiers tend to establish nationalities. Many new nationalities, like the Canadian, developed entirely because they formed a political and geogaphic entity. Generally we may say, for reasons which will be considered later, that statehood or nationhood (in the sense of common citizenship under one territorial government) is a constitutive element in the life of a nationality. The condition of statehood need not be present when a nationality originates; but in such a case (as with the Czechs in the late eighteenth century) it is always the memory of a past state and the aspiration toward statehood that characterizes nationalities in the period of nationalism.

Although some of these objective factors are of great importance for the formation of nationalities, the most essential element is a living and active corporate will. Nationality is formed by the decision to form a nationality. Thus the French nationality was born of the enthusiastic manifestation of will in 1789. A French nation, the population of the French kingdom, existed before, as did some of the objective conditions necessary for the foundation of a nationality. But only the newly aroused consciousness and will made these elements active and effective, fused them into a source of immense centripetal power, and gave them a new importance and meaning. The English and the American nationalities were constituted by "covenants," by free acts of will, and the French Revolution evolved the plebiscite, as a result of which membership in a nationality was determined, not by objective characteristics, but by subjective declaration. The foundation of the Swiss nationality was dramatized by Friedrich Schiller in his *Wilhelm Tell* according to legendary tradition into the famous oath on the Rutli, "Wir wollen sein ein einig Volk von Brudern." This mythical declaration, "We wish to be one single nation of brothers," was uttered at the birth of every nationality, whether this birth happened, after a long pregnancy, in the enthusiasm of a revolutionary period, or whether the awakening of the masses required many years of ceaseless propaganda. Nationalities as "ethnographic material," as "pragmatic" and accidental factors in history, existed for a very long time; but only through the awakening of national consciousness have they become volitional and "absolute" factors in history. The extensive use of the word "nationality" must not blind us to the fact that the lack of this voluntaristic element makes what are sometimes called nationalities of the period before the rise of modern nationalism fundamentally different from nationalities of the present time. To base nationality upon "objective" factors like race implies a return to primitive tribalism. In modern times it has been the power of an idea, not the call of blood, that has constituted and molded nationalities.

Nationalities are created out of ethnographic and political elements when nationalism breathes life into the form built by preceding centuries. Thus nationalism and nationality are closely interrelated. Nationalism is a state of mind, permeating the large majority of a people and claiming to permeate all its members; it recognizes the nation-state as the ideal form of political organization and the nationality as the source of all creative cultural energy and of economic well-being. The supreme loyalty of man is therefore due to his nationality, as his own life is supposedly rooted in and made possible by its welfare. A short discussion of the components of this definition will help to clarify the issues involved.

A state of mind of the large majority of the people: Even before the age of nationalism, we find individuals who profess sentiments akin to nationalism. But these sentiments are confined to individuals; the masses never feel their own life—culturally, politically, or economically—dependent upon the fate of the national group. Periods of oppression or danger from the outside may arouse a feeling of nationalism in the masses, as it happened in Greece during the Persian wars or in France in the Hundred Years' War. But these sentiments pass quickly. As a rule, wars before the French Revolution did not arouse a deep national sentiment. In religious and dynastic wars, Germans fought against Germans and Italians against Italians, without any realization of the "fratricidal" nature of the act. Soldiers and civilians entered the service of "foreign" rulers and served them often with a loyalty and faithfulness which proved the absence of any national sentiment.

The nation-state as the ideal form of political organization: That political boundaries should coincide with ethnographic or linguistic frontiers is a demand of recent times. Formerly, the city or the fief or a multilingual state held together by dynastic ties was the accepted form of political organization and frequently was regarded as the "natural" or ideal form. At other periods the educated classes as well as the masses believed in the ideal of a universal world-state, although on account of the technical and geographic conditions this ideal never approached realization.

The nationality as the source of cultural life: During most of historical time, religion was regarded as the true source of cultural life. Man was thought to become creative by his profound immersion in religious tradition and by his abandonment in the divine fountainhead of all being. At other times, man's education was steeped in the civilization of a class which spread beyond all national boundaries, like the civilization of knighthood in medieval Europe or of the French court in the seventeenth and eighteenth centuries. During and after the Renaissance, man's education was rooted in the soil of classical civilization. Education and learning, the formation of man's mind and character, were not bound by any national limits.

The nationality as a source of economic well-being: This phase of nationalism, as well as the political, was prepared by the period of absolute monarchy, with its mercantilism. But mercantilism never became more than a scheme imposed from above, trying to achieve a national unity which it in reality never approached; continuing in many ways the medieval confusion and disruption of economic life and leaving provinces, cities, and villages as centers of production. The purpose of mercantilism was to strengthen the state and its power in international politics. The system following mercantilism, in the period of *laissez faire*, had as its aim the promotion of individual welfare. Economic nationalism brought about a neo-mercantilism, filling with life, as had been the case with the centralized state, the form erected by the monarchs. It is a much younger development than political or cultural nationalism, and it holds that the well-being of the individual can be achieved and secured only by the economic power of the nation. The close political and cultural identification of the individual with his nationality, which took place at the end of the eighteenth and the beginning of the nineteenth century, extended to the economic field only during the latter part of the nineteenth century.

The supreme loyalty due to the nationality: The Austrian Monarchy was generally accepted as long as man's supreme loyalty was due to the legitimate king; its existence became precarious with the shift of loyalty from the dynasty to the nationality. Only a very few centuries ago, man's loyalty was due to his church or religion; a heretic put himself beyond the pale of society as a "traitor" to his nation does today. The fixation of man's supreme loyalty upon his nationality marks the beginning of the age of nationalism.

4

Nationalism is a state of mind. The process of history can be analyzed as a succession of changes in communal psychology, in the attitude of man toward all manifestations of individual and social life. Such factors as language, territory, traditions—such sentiments as attachment to the native soil, the *Heimat,* and to one's kin and kind—assume different positions in the scale of values as communal psychology changes. Nationalism is an idea, and idée-force, which fills man's brain and heart with new thoughts and new sentiments, and drives him to translate his consciousness into deeds of organized action. Nationality is therefore not only a group held together and animated by common consciousness; but it is also a group seeking to find its expression in what it regards as the highest form of organized activity, a sovereign state. As long as a nationality is not able to attain this consummation, it satisfies itself with some form of autonomy or pre-state organization, which, however, always tends at a given moment, the moment of "liberation," to develop into a sovereign state. Nationalism demands the nation-state; the creation of the nation-state strengthens nationalism. Here, as elsewhere in history, we find a continuous interdependence and interaction.

"Nationality is a state of mind corresponding to a political fact," or striving to correspond to a political fact. This definition reflects the genesis of nationalism and of modern nationality, which was born in the fusion of a certain state of mind with a given political form. The state of mind, the idea of nationalism, imbued the form with a new content and meaning; the form provided the idea with implements for the organized expression of its manifestations and aspirations. Both the idea and the form of nationalism were developed before the age of nationalism. The idea goes back to the ancient Hebrews and Greeks, and was revived in Europe at the time of the Renaissance and the Reformation. During the period of the Renaissance, the literati rediscovered Greco-Roman patriotism; but this new attitude never penetrated to the masses, and its secularism was soon swept away by the retheologization of Europe through the Reformation and Counter-Reformation. But the Reformation, especially in its Calvinistic form, revived the nationalism of the Old Testament. Under the favorable circumstances which had developed in England, a new national consciousness of the English as the godly people penetrated the whole nation in the revolution of the seventeenth century. Meanwhile in Western Europe a new political power—that of the absolute kings—had developed a new political form, the modern centralized sovereign state; and this became the political form into which, during the French Revolution, the idea of nationalism was infused, filling it with a consciousness in which all citizens could share, and making possible the political and cultural integration of the masses into the nation. With the advent of nationalism, the masses were no longer in the nation, but of the nation. They identified themselves with the nation, civilization with national civilization, their life and survival with the life and survival of the nationality. Nationalism thenceforward dominated the impulses and. attitudes of the masses, and at the same time served as the justification for the authority of the state and the legitimation of its use of force, both against its own citizens and against other states.

Sovereignty has a twofold significance. One aspect deals with the relations of the state to its citizens, the other with the relations between states. Similarly, the sentiment of nationalism is double-faced. Intranationally, it leads to a lively sympathy with all fellow members within the nationality; internationally, it finds its expression in indifference to or distrust and hate of fellow men outside the national orbit. In intranational relations, men are guided not only by supposedly permanent common interests, but also by sentiments of sympathy, devotion, and even self-sacrifice. In international relations, they are guided by the supposed lack of permanent common interests among different states, and by sentiments which vary from complete indifference to the most bitter antipathy, and are subject to swift changes within that range. Nationality, which is nothing but a fragment of humanity, tends to set itself up as the whole. Generally this ultimate conclusion is not drawn, because ideas predating the age of nationalism continue to exercise their influence. These ideas form the essence of Western civilization—of Christianity as well as of enlightened rationalism: the faith in the oneness of humanity and the ultimate value of the individual. Only fascism, the uncompromising enemy of Western civilization, has pushed nationalism to its very limit, to a totalitarian nationalism, in which humanity and the individual disappear and nothing remains but the nationality, which has become the one and the whole.

5

Important periods of history are characterized by the circumference within which the sympathy of man extends. These limits are neither fixed nor permanent, and changes in them are accompanied by great crises in history. In the Middle Ages, the people of the Ile de France felt a violent antipathy and contempt for the people of Aquitaine or of Burgundy. A very short time ago, a similar feeling existed in Egypt between the Mohammedans and the native Christians, the Copts. In ancient times, the Athenians hated and despised the Spartans. Almost unscalable barriers separated members of rival religious sects within a community. In China, until very recently, the family set the limit of sympathy, and very little if any loyalty and devotion were left for the nation or larger social group.

Beginning with the nineteenth century in the Western world, and with the twentieth century in the Orient, the circumference was set by the nationality. These changes involved in many cases the establishment of new dividing lines. This grouping of men into new forms of organization, their integration around new symbols, gained a momentum unknown in former days. The rapid growth of population, the spread of education, the increased influence of the masses, the new techniques developed for information and propaganda, gave the new feeling of nationality a permanent intensity which soon made it appear as the expression of something "natural," of something which had always existed and would always exist. But the circumference of sympathy need not remain forever drawn as it is today. With the transformation of social and economic life, with the growing interdependence of all nationalities on a shrinking earth, with a new direction to education, the circumference may widen to include supranational areas of common interest and common sympathy.

Such an extension of solidarity, should it come, will arise only as the result of a struggle of unprecedented dimensions. For nationalism represents "vested interests," not only political and economic but also intellectual and emotional, of an intensity and extent shown by no previous idea. In the face of the omnipotence of nationality, humanity seems a distant idea, a pale theory or a poetic dream, through which the red blood of life does not pulsate. And so it is. But at one time in history the French or the German nation was also nothing more than a distant idea. Historical forces, amid great struggles and convulsions lasting for a long time, brought these ideas to life. An organization of mankind was a Utopia in the eighteenth century; the stage of development of state and economy, of technique and communication, was then in no way adequate to the task. It is different today. At present, nationalism—at its beginning a great inspiration, widening and deepening the understanding of man, the feeling of solidarity, the autonomous dignity of the masses—seems unable to cope, politically and emotionally, with the new situation. Once it increased individual liberty and happiness; now it undermines them and subjects them to the exigencies of its continued existence, which seems no longer justified. Once it was a great force of life, spurring on the evolution of mankind; now it may become a dead weight upon the march of humanity.

Neither the German nor the French nation is an entity predestined by nature, any more than the American nation is. They all, as well as the national consciousness which animates them, were formed by historical forces. The growth of the German national consciousness, the formation of the German nation state, encountered innumerable difficulties, and was again and again in danger of being wrecked on the cliffs of political vested interests, of the inertia of venerable and cherished traditions and of ingrained sectionalism and provincialism. The pioneers of nationalism often were driven to despair of achieving their goal. But nationalism, filling the hearts of men with great hopes of a new freedom and of better and more humane relations between peoples, was victorious. This has changed. "Political nationalism under present conditions conflicts with the main trends of human affairs, which is away from isolation towards interdependence. Its aim is not service and cooperation, but exclusiveness and monopoly." The individual liberty of man has to be organized today on a supranational basis. Democracy and industrialism, the two forces which rose simultaneously with nationalism and spread with it over the world, have both today outgrown the national connection.

But the "Thirty Years' War" of our century has shown how firmly nationalism is entrenched at present. The nation-state is more deep-rooted in the emotions of the masses than any previous political organization. The growth of nationalism has influenced historiography and the philosophy of history, and each nation has developed its own interpretation of history which not only makes it feel itself different from all other nationalities but gives to this difference a fundamental, and even metaphysical, meaning. The nationality feels that it has been chosen for some special mission, and that the realization of this mission is essential to the march of history, and even to the salvation of mankind. By the identification of nation and state, the modern basis of which was prepared by Rousseau, the cultural and emotional life of the masses has become closely integrated with the political life. Any change in the principles of political organization will therefore encounter the strongest resistance, which, against considerations of the rational and universal good, will appeal to deep-rooted traditions.

Sociologists have pointed out the intimate relation between nationalist and religious movements. Both have an inspirational and sometimes revivalist character. "Both of them are fundamentally cultural movements with incidental political consequences." These consequences, however, are not incidental; rather, they have been conditioned by the stages of historical development. At a given time in history, religion, essentially a spiritual movement, had very fundamental and substantial political implications. It molded and dominated politics and society. At present, the same is true of nationalism. When interminable and ferocious religious wars threatened to destroy human happiness and civilization, the movement of Enlightenment, the wave of rationalism which started about 1680 and dominated the eighteenth century, led to the depolitization of religion. In this process, religion did not lose its true dignity; it remained one of the great spiritual forces, comforting and exalting the human soul. But it lost the element of coercion which had been so "natural" to it for many centuries; its connection with the state, with political authority, was severed; religion retreated into the intimacy and spontaneity of the individual conscience. The process of the depolitization of religion was slow. Two centuries from "The Bloudy Tenent of Persecution for Cause of Conscience Discussed in a Conference Between Truth and Peace," which Roger Williams published in 1644, had to elapse before, at least in Western Europe, its cause won general acceptance. A similar depolitization of nationality is conceivable. It may lose its connection with political organization, it may remain an intimate and moving sentiment. If and when that day arrives, however, the age of nationalism, in the sense in which it is considered here, will be past.

11. NATIONALISM IN UNDERDEVELOPED COUNTRIES

John H. Kautsky

THE CONCEPT of nationalism had taken its meaning from the "national" consciousness which began to grow in France with the Revolution and from the movements that completely changed the map of Central and Eastern Europe during the following century and a half. Nationalism may be defined from this European experience as an ideology and a movement striving to unite all people who speak a single language, and who share the various cultural characteristics transmitted by that language, in a single independent state and in loyalty to a single government conducted in the people's language. A looser and less meaningful connotation of the word nationalism has also been widespread, which would seem to define it merely as the loyalty and emotional attachment of a population, regardless of its language, to an existing government and state. In this sense, one can refer to Soviet, Swiss, Belgian, and American nationalism, though all of these countries include inhabitants of different language and cultural backgrounds and the languages spoken by at least some of them are also the languages of other countries.

When we now turn to a consideration of what is generally referred to as nationalism in the underdeveloped areas, it becomes clear immediately that we are confronted with a phenomenon quite different from European nationalism. While it might therefore have been preferable to avoid the use of the term with reference to underdeveloped countries altogether, this would be futile in view of its adoption on all sides. We can only hope that the use of a single term to designate the two phenomena will not obscure the differences between them, that an easy assumption that the "nationalism" of Europe will not obstruct recognition of the quite different forces producing it.

From *Political Change in Underdeveloped Countries: Nationalism and Communism,* by John H. Kautsky (New York: 1966) pp. 32–38; 45–49. Reprinted by permission of John Wiley and Sons, Inc. Footnotes have been renumbered to appear in consecutive order.

JOHN H. KAUTSKY (1922–   ) Professor of Political Science, Washington University. His other books include *Moscow and the Communist Political Change in Underdeveloped Countries,* (New York: Wiley, 1962); *Moscow and the Communist Party of India: A Study in the Postwar Evolution of International Communist Strategy,* (Cambridge: Massachusetts Institute of Technology Press, 1956).

Neither of the two definitions of nationalism we derived from European experience can account for the nationalism of underdeveloped areas. It seeks to create new independent states and governments where there were none before. This is clearly a nationalism different from one that may be defined as loyalty to an already existing state and government (although, once independent states do exist, this kind of nationalism may well emerge in underdeveloped countries, too). However, the nationalism that did create new states in Europe also proves to be irrelevant for the explanation of nationalism in underdeveloped countries, for in Europe the language or nationality factor was, as we saw, a key element in its growth. Only the American, Latin American, and Irish independence movements, for which the language factor was not responsible, may offer some fruitful parallels to present-day nationalism in underdeveloped countries. The independence movements in the Western Hemisphere, however, were directed against colonial powers that were then little more advanced industrially than their colonies. They differ, therefore, in significant respects from current anticolonial nationalism. Ireland, on the other hand, an agrarian country with a distinct culture, confronted highly industrialized Britain, and did, indeed, develop a nationalism akin to that of other underdeveloped countries, though it is located in Western Europe.

Being economically backward, the underdeveloped countries have not yet been subject (or were not until very recently) to the economic and political integration that created the pressure for the adoption of a single language in large areas of Europe. Nor, as we have seen, can there be in non-industrialized societies sufficiently widespread participation in politics to provide any large proportion of the population with the loyalty to "their" government that was essential to the growth of European nationalism. Typically, the more backward a country is economically, the more languages or dialects are spoken in a given area or by a given number of people. There are some striking exceptions to this generalization. Notable are the use of Arabic over a vast area, resulting from conquests which (like the earlier Roman ones) became sufficiently permanent to lead to gradual, voluntary adoption of the language of the conqueror by the conquered, the somewhat similar spread of Spanish and Portuguese in Latin America, and of Russian across northern Asia. Yet, even in these areas, many groups speak languages other than the major ones to this day, and the major ones themselves are frequently subdivided into various dialects.

In most underdeveloped countries, the existence of numerous languages inhibits communication among the population. Thus, the Chinese do not, in effect, speak a single Chinese language, but several mutually incomprehensible dialects.[1] Even more clearly, there is no such thing as a single Indian or Indonesian language. Some ten or twelve major languages and hundreds of minor tongues and local dialects are spoken in India. Some thirty languages are spoken in the Republic of Indonesia, many of them totally unrelated to each other. In territories in which commerce and communications are not even so highly developed as in these three major Asian countries and which have not, like these countries, been united under a single government for centuries, many more languages may be in use. Thus, in Nigeria a population of approximately 34,000,000 speaks roughly 250 different languages, a situation that is not unusual in much of Africa and among the tribes in the interior of Southeast Asia and Latin America. In Australian-ruled Papua and New Guinea, perhaps the most backward area in the world, 1,750,000 natives speak 500 different languages and dialects, no one language being used by more than 50,000 and some by only 300.

In spite of the fact that most underdeveloped countries are inhabited by numerous "nationalities," i.e., language and culture groups, their nationalists have virtually nowhere sought to change the boundaries of their new states to conform to language lines. Apart from boundary changes due to the creation of Pakistan and of Israel, which were not chiefly motivated by language considerations, and the splitting of Korea and Vietnam into Communist—and non-Communist-governed halves, there have been only two significant boundary changes in the formerly colonial world: the somewhat tenuous linking of Egypt and Syria in the United Arab Republic and the unification of British and Italian Somaliland.[2] In each of these two cases, some, but not all, of the people speaking a single language were brought under a single government. Each of the unions, however, has been talked of as the nucleus of a future larger unification movement based on language. These exceptions apart, it is striking that existing boundaries have remained intact as colony after colony has become independent in recent years and already independent countries, too, have undergone nationalist revolutions. Countries including many language and culture groups, like most African and Asian ones, have not split up and those taking in only part of a single language

---

[1] The Chinese merely share a single system of writing which, being ideographic, is not bound to any particular language, and is, at any rate, not available to the great bulk of the population. Their intellectuals can communicate in a single language, the Peking dialect of Mandarin Chinese, which serves roughly the same function as Latin in medieval Europe.

[2] As this essay goes to the printer (October 1961), an army coup in Syria is severing that country's ties with Egypt. On the domestic and international politics of the Somali area, see Leo Silberman, "Change and Conflict in the Horn of Africa," Foreign Affairs, XXXVII, No. 4 (July 1959), 649–659.

group, like the Arab ones in the Near East and North Africa, have, with the two exceptions noted, not united. The colonial boundaries which have thus persisted beyond the attainment of political independence, like the boundaries of older independent underdeveloped countries, were in virtually all cases drawn without any regard to language or cultural divisions among the natives. They chiefly reflected the political and economic requirements of the colonial powers, or of earlier conquerors, as in China, Turkey, and Latin America. Whatever it may be, then, nationalism in underdeveloped countries—if it does not aim at changing these boundaries—cannot be a movement seeking to unite all people speaking a particular language under a single independent government.[3]

Only after nationalism has been produced, chiefly by other factors, is an attempt sometimes made by Western-trained intellectuals to introduce the language and cultural element into it. The artificial resurrection of the Irish language may be a case in point. So is the pan-Arab movement insofar as it is not a mere tool of the nationalist movements of individual Arab states. The continuing failure of Arab unification would seem to indicate that these nationalist movements are in any case a good deal more powerful than pan-Arabism. More significant is the attempt of the Chinese Communist regime, itself a continuation of earlier Kuomintang policy, to impose a single language (that of the Peking region) and a simplified system of writing on all of China, a policy required, and facilitated, by the rapid economic and political integration of that area. Similar in nature, though not in the methods used to attain it, is the goal of the Indian government to spread the use of Hindi to all of India.

Though pursued with more awareness and greater speed, the Chinese and Indian policies (and similar ones in Indonesia) correspond roughly to those of the French kings, who integrated the population of their territory in terms of the language spoken at the seat of government Just as French absolutism thereby laid the basis for the later language-based nationalism, so such a nationalism may arise in underdeveloped countries if and when most of their population speaks a single language.[4] However,

---

[3] On the relationship of nationalism to existing colonial boundaries, see Rupert Emerson, "Nationalism and Political Development," *The Journal of Politics,* XXII, No. 1 (February 1960), 3–28, an article offering many insights into the nature of nationalism in underdeveloped countries. See also William Bascom, "Obstacles to Self-Government," *The Annals of the American Academy of Political and Social Science,* vol. 306 (July 1956), 62–70; C. E. Carrington, "Frontiers in Africa," *International Affairs,* XXXVI, No. 4 (October 1960), 424–439; and E. R. Leach, "The Frontiers of 'Burma'," *Comparative Studies in Society and History,* III, No. 1 (October 1960), 49–67.

[4] Turkish nationalism under Kemal to some extent assumed this form when the Ottoman Empire was reduced to its Turkish-speaking provinces by its defeat in World War I.

in India there has arisen a counter-movement to the policy of language integration demanding that provincial boundaries be redrawn along linguistic lines to provide greater autonomy for the various major language groups. This may roughly correspond to the nationalism of some of the nationalities in the Austro-Hungarian and other multi-language empires of Europe. It remains to be seen whether the central government of India will, like the French kings, succeed in uniting its country around a single language or whether, as in Austria-Hungary, some of the other languages are too firmly established (at least among the literate and particularly the intellectuals) to be easily uprooted, leading India to disintegration.[5]

Even in India and China, as well as in Ireland and the Arab countries, the desire to make all people under one government speak one language (or to give a new autonomous government to those speaking one language) was not among the original motivations underlying the nationalist movement. In most underdeveloped countries no such desire has to this day appeared at all. If the origins of nationalism have nothing to do with nationality, i.e., with a common language and culture, nor with loyalty to an existing independent government, for there is none, then what is nationalism?

Nationalism in underdeveloped countries appears to have in common with European nationalism the desire of people to be rid of alien rulers and to have their own government, and it is probably for this reason that it has been labeled nationalism. In fact, the matter is not so simple, even if we leave aside the point made at greater length earlier, that in underdeveloped countries, until modernization progresses, most people have no desires with reference to the central government at all, and they do not play any active role in politics. Apart from that, the words "alien" and "own" as just used, however, assume what is yet to be proved, that there is a collectivity of people, somehow defined by a common element other than a language, who share "their" nationalism. Why does a community in the South of India regard a prime minister from the North more as their "own" ruler than a viceroy from Britain? Why does one tribe in the Congo think of a government dominated by another tribe as less "alien" than a government of Belgians? In terms of language differences, these questions cannot be answered.

In some underdeveloped countries, notably Moslem ones, a religion and other cultural characteristics shared by all the natives regardless of their

---

[5] On this problem, see Selig S. Harrison, "The Challenge to Indian Nationalism," *Foreign Affairs*, XXXIV, No. 4 (July 1956), 620–639, and the same author's *India: The Most Dangerous Decades* (Princeton, N.J.: Princeton University Press, 1960).

language, but different from those of their colonial rulers, may have been a common element around which their nationalism could have grown. But in many underdeveloped countries there are caste, religious and cultural differences among the natives who nevertheless produced a single nationalist movement. And not infrequently, such movements are led by Christian natives who share their religion with their colonial rulers, whom they oppose, rather than with the great majority of the natives whom they claim to represent.

A more important element of unity setting the nationalists apart from their colonial rulers may be race, i.e., physical (as distinguished from cultural) characteristics. Some undeveloped countries are inhabited by people of more than one race, however, and yet, in the Sudan, a European remains more "alien" to an Arab than a Negro, in Bolivia a "North-American" is more alien to a white nationalist than an Indian, in Cuba the "Yanqui" is regarded by nationalists as the enemy of both whites and Negroes. Sometimes certain unity among the natives has been created by Europeans or Americans who set themselves apart by discriminatory practices directed against all natives or "colored" people regardless of their particular race. The racial factor, then, is undoubtedly an important element in an explanation of nationalist unity in some underdeveloped countries, particularly where all natives are of a single non-white race and where it appears as a reaction to racial discrimination by whites. But not everywhere is this the case. There is no clear racial distinction between the European and the native inhabitants of North Africa nor is there between the English and the Irish or between some Americans and some Mexicans or Cubans.

. . .

The key role of the intellectuals in the politics of underdeveloped countries is largely due to their paradoxical position of being a product of modernization before modernization has reached or become widespread in their own country.[6] In the universities, the intellectuals absorb the professional knowledge and skills needed by an industrial civilization; they became students of the humanities and social sciences qualified to teach

---

[6] The leading role of the intellectuals is excellently stressed in Hugh Seton-Watson, "Twentieth Century Revolutions," *The Political Quarterly*, XXII, No. 3 (July-September 1951), 251–265, an article all the more valuable for relating, as we shall try to do, developments in Russia and Southern Europe to those in the present underdeveloped countries. See also Martin L. Kilson, Jr., "Nationalism and Social Classes in British West Africa," The Journal of Politics, XX, No. 2 (May 1958), 368–387.

in universities, and they became lawyers and doctors, administrators and journalists, and increasingly also scientists and engineers. When they return from the universities, whether abroad or not, the intellectuals find, all too often for their taste, that in their old societies their newly acquired skills and knowledge are out of place. Not only is there as yet little need—though it is often rapidly growing—for engineers and scientists where there is little industry, but professors will find few advanced students and lawyers will find few clients in a society still operating largely through simple face-to-face contacts. Although there is plenty of sickness, most patients might prefer the traditional herb-doctor or medicine man to the trained physician and, in any case, could not pay him. Few administrators are needed where the sphere of government activity is still very limited and fewer still where all higher posts are occupied by representatives of a colonial power. Where the bulk of the population is illiterate journalists are confined to writing for their few fellow intellectuals. As a result, intellectuals in underdeveloped countries are frequently unemployed or underemployed, especially since, for all their "industrial" education, they are likely to have retained the aristocratic attitude that manual labor is demeaning and hence will refuse to do other than intellectual work.

During their studies, the intellectuals are likely to acquire more than new knowledge. They also absorb the values of an industrial civilization, above all the notion that continuing material improvement of the life of the mass of the population through continuing technological progress and popular participation in government is both possible and desirable, and they become admirers of the political systems and ideologies embodying these values, whether they be American liberalism, Western European democratic socialism or Soviet Communism. On their return, they discover that these values, too, are inappropriate to the old society. Continuous and cumulative technological progress, which is so typical of an industrial system, is absent from purely agrarian economies. Until industrialization (and changes in agricultural techniques resulting from industrialization) are introduced, a belief in any substantial improvement in the standard of living of the mass of the population is, in fact, unrealistic. At the same time, advocacy, based on such a belief, of ideals of democracy, equality, and social justice, which arose out of an industrial environment, is subversive to the existing order of government by the native aristocracy and the foreign colonial power and is therefore not likely to endear the intellectuals to these powerful forces.

To the extent, then, that a native intellectual has substituted for the values of his traditional society those of an industrial one—a process which need by no means be complete in each case—he becomes an alien, a displaced person, in his own society. What could be more natural for him than to want to change that society to accord with his new needs and values, in short, to industrialize and modernize it? A number of motivations intermingle to produce the intellectuals' drive for rapid modernization. Most obviously, there is their desire for gainful and satisfying employment for an opportunity to use the knowledge and to practice the skills they have acquired. But beyond this relatively narrow motive, there may be the more or less clear realization that only through industrialization can an eventual end be put to the poverty prevalent in underdeveloped countries, that only rapid industrialization can solve the problem posed by increasing populations, and that only industrialization can produce the "better" society at home which the intellectuals have come to admire abroad.

The peasant's typical response to overpopulation and his consequent hunger for land (if he is sufficiently politically conscious and organizable to respond effectively at all) is the demand for land reform. The intellectuals echo and support that demand, for one thing, because it is in accord with their new ideas of justice and equality. These ideas also make it desirable for them to become the leaders of a mass movement, of "the people." Since most of the people are peasants, they are inclined to seek peasant support, and advocacy of land reform is the most obvious way of mobilizing such support. Intellectuals may favor land reform also because a higher standard of living for the peasantry would create a better market for, and thus further the growth of, native industry. Finally, they press for land reform not because of anything it will do *for* the peasants, but because of what it will do *to* the aristocracy. The latter is the intellectuals' only powerful domestic enemy, and land reform strikes at the very root of its economic and social position.

However, where overpopulation is greatest, as in China, redistribution of land by itself is no longer an adequate solution to the problem, because there is simply not enough arable land to go around. Thus there is underemployment among the peasantry, which in turn tends to depress the wages of labor in the cities. Sooner or later only industrialization can satisfy the "rising expectations" in underdeveloped countries, which are, first and foremost, the expectations of the intellectuals, though they have spread them to the poorer strata accessible to them in the rural and especially in the urban areas. Only through industrialization can the intellectuals hope to realize their various dreams of democracy, equality, and social justice, of liberalism, socialism, or Communism in their own countries.

As the only ones in their societies who can even visualize a new, and, to them, a better order, the intellectuals naturally think of themselves as the leaders of the future society and of the transition to it. Thus a more narrowly political motivation is added to the others underlying their desire for modernization. Modernization serves to undermine and ultimately do away with the leadership of the old aristocratic ruling strata, and replace it with that of the intellectuals. Similarly, industrialization is the only road to the economic independence and military strength that can eventually provide freedom from colonial domination for their "country," that is, their government, which means more power for its new leaders, the intellectuals. Their anti-colonial nationalism thus makes the intellectuals desire industrialization.

It is equally true, however, that it is their desire to industrialize that makes the intellectuals nationalists. They see colonialism as opposed to industrialization, in part because the colonial power does not want industries in the colony to compete with its own industries for the colonial supply of raw materials or for the colonial market, and more generally because, as we have seen, modernization in the colony constitutes a threat to colonialism. Hence colonialism is regarded as an obstacle in the intellectuals' path to modernization as well as in their path to power. This helps explain the apparent paradox of intellectuals in underdeveloped countries who were trained in the West and came to admire it and yet turn against the West in their policies. They do so exactly because they admire it and at the same time see the West as denying them, through colonialism, the opportunity to make their own country more like the West.[7] To the intellectuals in underdeveloped countries nationalism and modernization have become inextricably intertwined as means and ends. Each has become an essential aspect of the other.

In Western Europe, during the process of industrialization, the intellectuals played an important role in developing the ideology of liberalism, but industrialization itself was accomplished by industrial capitalists. In underdeveloped countries, the intellectuals, in effect, play the roles of both groups. A native class of industrial capitalists is virtually or completely absent, and sufficient wealth for the development of industry is not available in private hands—or, if available in the hands of aristocrats, is (for reasons to be indicated later) not likely to be invested in industry. Under these circumstances, the government appears to be the only possible major domestic source of capital, and the intellectuals—if they want to industrialize their country—must wrest control of it from the native aristocracy and the colonial administrators who oppose industrialization. This need to control their government in order to industrial-

---

[7] The intellectuals' ambiguous attitudes are well discussed and documented in Mary Matossian, "Ideologies of Delayed Industrialization: Some Tensions and Ambiguities," . . . Her attempt to generalize about a large number of ideologies of nationalism in underdeveloped countries is most suggestive, though the inclusion of Shintoism, Fascism, and Nazism can, for reasons indicated later in this essay, be accepted only with some reservations. The ambivalence of the nationalist intellectuals toward the West is also noted by Rupert Emerson, "Paradoxes of Asian Nationalism," *The Far Eastern Quarterly*, XIII, No. 2 (February 1954), 131–142.

ize provides another reason both for the intellectuals' anti-colonial nationalism and for the appeal of various "socialist" ideas, whether Communist or not, to them. Thus, Nehru and U Nu, Nkrumah and Touré, Castro and many other nationalist intellectuals regard themselves as "socialists".

Through the dominance of the intellectuals in the nationalist movements, which we will have to analyze next, it is their peculiar form of nationalism, which looks at steel mills both as symbols of anti-colonialism and as its instruments, that has become characteristic of nationalism in underdeveloped countries. To borrow some phrases from Marx's prophecies about capitalism, nowhere are the "internal contradictions" of colonialism, its dual nature as a modernizing and a conservative force in the underdeveloped countries,[8] clearer than in its relation to the intellectuals. It produces the intellectuals and yet by its very existence it frustrates them and hence arouses their opposition. In them, it has thus produced "its own gravediggers," it has sown "the seeds of its own destruction."

---

[8] On the effects on nationalism, both before and after the attainment of independence, of this dual character of colonialism, see S. N. Eisenstadt, "Sociological Aspects of Political Development in Underdeveloped Countries," *Economic Development and Cultural Change*, V, No. 4 (July 1957), 289–307.

SE TION TWO: Power and the International System

12. THE CONCEPT OF POWER IN THE STUDY OF INTERNATIONAL RELATIONS

K. J. Holsti

H ANS MORGENTHAU [*Politics Among Nations,* New York: Alfred A. Knopf, 1960] is the foremost advocate of the concept of power as the theoretical core of international politics. In his view, all politics is a struggle for power. He derives this dictum from the assumption that the desire to dominate is "a constitutive element of all human associations." Thus, regardless of the goals and objectives of government, the immediate aim of all state action is to obtain and to increase power. Since by definition all states seek to maximize their power, international politics can be conceived of and analyzed as a struggle between independent units seeking to dominate others.

Professor Morgenthau unfortunately fails to submit the concept of power to further examination so that some ambiguity remains.[1] He implies, for example, that power is also a major goal of policy or even a

From *Background: Journal of the International Studies Association,* VII, No. 4, (February 1964), 179–192. Reprinted by permission of the author and the publisher.

K. J. HOLSTI (1935–   ) Associate Professor of Political Science, University of British Columbia. Author of *International Politics: A Framework for Analysis,* (Englewood Cliffs, New Jersey: Prentice-Hall, Inc., 1967). Co-author of *Enemies in Politics,* (Chicago: Rand McNally, 1967).

[1] Other noteworthy proponents of the "power" theory of international relations are Thorsten V. Kalijarvi [*Modern World Politics,* New York: Thomas Y. Crowell, 1953] and Robert Strausz-Hupé and Stefan Possony [*International Relations,* New York: McGraw-Hill, 1950].

determining motive of any political action. Elsewhere, however, he suggests that power is a relationship and a means to an end. Because of this ambiguity, we do not know what the concept explains or fails to explain in international politics. Does the term "struggle for power" shed light on the many processes that go on within an international system? The word "struggle" certainly does not tell us much about the relations between Norway and Sweden or between Canada and the United States. Does the term "power," defined as the immediate goal of all governments, explain the major external objectives of Nicaragua or Chad or Switzerland?

In contrast to the "struggle for power" concept is the "anti-power theory" of international relations. The proponents of this theory (including Woodrow Wilson) claim that there is a distinction between "power politics" and some other kind of politics. Not pessimists regarding human nature, they assume that man is essentially tolerant and pacific and that the human community is united through many bonds. Statesmen, they claim, have a choice between practicing "power politics" and conducting foreign relations by some other means. Wilson and others made the further assumption that there is a correlation between a nation's social and political institutions and the way it conducts its foreign relations. To them, autocracies which did not consult "the people" usually engaged in deception, duplicity, and saber-rattling. Democracies, on the other hand, displayed tolerance, morality, and justice, and sought only peace and stability. In the new order which they envisaged for the post World War I period, negotiations would replace threats of war, and world-wide consensus on the desirability of peace would sustain democratic statesmen. In other words, power politics was synonymous with autocracy. But how democratic governments were supposed to achieve their objectives is left unexplained.[2] This view is also of limited use because it is mostly prescriptive: it enunciates how international processes *should* be carried on, but it fails to help us understand what actually occurs.

A third view of power is found in past and contemporary texts on international relations. Authors present the student with a brief and formal definition of power, often equating power with the physical assets a nation possesses. Most texts, in fact, concentrate on the analysis of these assets (often called the "elements of national power") without discussing the actual relations between governments and the techniques by

---

[2] There is room for disagreement on this characterization of the Wilsonian theory of power. Wilson was obviously aware of the role of power as military force and as public opinion. His concept of collective security, where all peaceful nations would band together to enforce the peace, implies that democracies no less than autocracies, should use force when necessary.

which these assets are brought to bear on the pursuit of national objectives.

Should we not, however, define power in a way which best clarifies what we observe and what we wish to know? A definition should suggest areas of inquiry and reality, though no definition is likely to account for the totality of the subject. Thus, one definition of the concept may be useful for describing and analyzing social relations within a political party or within a family, but it may not be useful for studying international relations. Let us first describe an *act* which we conceive to be central to the process of international politics; that is, the act or acts that A commits toward B so that B pursues a course of behavior in accordance with A's wishes. The act can be illustrated as follows:

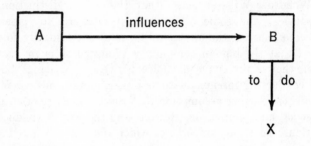

A seeks to influence B because it has established certain goals which cannot be achieved (it is perceived) unless B (and perhaps many other actors as well) does X. If this is an important act in international political processes, we can see that it contains several elements:

1. Influence (an aspect of power) is essentially a *means* to an end. Some governments or statesmen may seek influence for its own sake, but for most it is instrumental, just like money. They use it primarily for other goals, which may include prestige, territory, souls, raw materials, security, or alliances.

2. The act also implies a base of capabilities which the actor uses or mobilizes to use in his efforts to influence the behavior of B. A capability is any physical or mental object or quality available as an instrument of inducement. The concept of capability may be illustrated in the following example. Suppose an armed man walks into a bank and asks the clerk to give him all her money. The clerk observes clearly that the man has no weapons and refuses to comply with his order. The man has sought to influence the behavior of the clerk, but has failed. The next time, however, he walks in armed with a pistol and threatens to shoot if the clerk does not give him the money. This time, the clerk complies. In this instance the man has mobilized certain resources or capabilities (the gun) and has succeeded in influencing the clerk to do as he wished. The gun, just like a nation's military forces, *is not synonymous with the act of*

influencing, but it is the instrument that was used to induce the clerk to change her behavior to comply with the robber's objectives.

3. The act of influencing B obviously involves a *relationship* between A and B, though as we will see later, the relationship may not even involve communication. If the relationship covers any period of time, we can also say that it is a *process.*

4. If A can get B to do something, but B cannot get A to do a similar thing, then we can say that A has more power than B *vis à vis* that action. Power, therefore, is also a *quantity.* But as a quantity it is only meaningful when compared to the power of others. Power is therefore relative. To summarize, then, power may be viewed from several aspects: it is a means, it is based on capabilities, it is a relationship, and a process, and it can also be a quantity.

But for purposes of analyzing international politics, we can break down the concept of power into three separate elements: power is (1) the act (process, relationship) of influencing other factors; (2) it includes the capabilities used to make the wielding of influence successful; and (3) the responses to the act. The three elements must be kept distinct.[3] However, since this definition may seem too abstract, we can define the concept also in the more operational terms of policymakers. In formulating policy and the strategy to achieve certain goals, they would explicitly or implicitly ask the four following questions:

1. Given our goals, what do we wish B to do or not to do? (X)
2. How shall we get B to do or not to do X? (implies a relationship and process)
3. What capabilities are at our disposal so that we can induce B to do or not to do X?
4. What is B's probable response to our attempts to influence its behavior?

Before discussing the problem of capabilities and responses we have to fill out our model of the influence act to account for the many patterns of behavior that may be involved in an international relationship. First, as J. David Singer ["Inter-Nation Influence: A Formal Model," *American Political Science Review,* 57 (1963), 420–30.] points out, the exercise of influence implies more than merely A's ability to *change* the behavior of B. Influence may also be seen where A attempts to get B to *continue* a course of action or policy which is useful to, or in the interests of, A. The exercise of influence does not always cease, therefore, after B does X. It

---

[3] The recent texts of John Stoessinger [*The Might of Nations: World Politics in our Time,* New York: Random House, 1961.] and Charles Schleicher [*International Relations: Cooperation and Conflict,* Englewood Cliffs, New Jersey: Prentice-Hall, 1962.] distinguish between the act and the capabilities involved in the act.

is often a continuing process of reinforcing B's behavior. Nevertheless, power is "situational" to the extent that it is exercised within a framework of goals.[4]

Second, it is almost impossible to find a situation where B does not also have some influence over A. Our model has suggested that influence is exercised only in one direction, by A over B. In reality, however, influence is multilateral. State A, for example, would seldom seek a particular goal unless it had been influenced in a particular direction by the actions of other states in the system. At a minimum, there is the problem of feedback in any relationship: if B complies with A's wishes and does X, that behavior may subsequently prompt A to change its behavior, perhaps in the interest of B. Suppose, for example, that state A, after making threats, persuades B to lower its tariffs on the goods of state A. This would seem to be influence travelling only in one direction. But where state B does lower its tariffs, that action may prompt state A to reward state B in some manner. The phenomenon of feedback may be illustrated as follows:

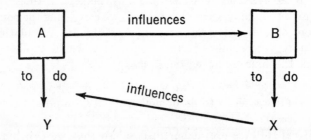

Third, the number of times a state becomes involved in acts of influence depends upon the general level of involvement of that particular actor in the system. The first requisite for attempting to wield influence is a perception that somehow state B (or any other) is related to the achievement of state A's goals and that there is, or will be, some kind of relationship of interdependence. If the relationship covers only inconsequential matters, few acts of influence may be necessary; but the greater the involvement of an actor in the system, the greater the necessity to wield influence over other actors. For example, except for limited trade relations, there is little perception of interdependence between Iceland and Uganda, hence little need for the government of Iceland to attempt to influence the domestic or external policies of the African country.

Fourth, there is the type of relationship which includes what Herbert

---

[4] State A might also wish state B to do w, y, and z, which may be incompatible with the achievement of X.

Simon ["Notes on the Observations and Measurement of Political Power," *The Journal of Politics*, 15 (1953), 500–517] has called "anticipated reaction." This is the situation, frequently found in international relations, where A might wish B to do X, but does not try to influence B for fear that B will do Y instead, which is an unfavorable response from A's point of view. In a hypothetical situation, the government of India might wish to obtain arms from the United States to build up its own defenses, but it does not request such arms because it fears that the United States would insist on certain conditions for the sale of arms which might compromise India's neutrality. This "anticipated reaction" may also be multilateral, where A wishes B to do X, but will not try to get B to do it because it fears that C, a third actor, will do Y, which is unfavorable to A's interests. India wants to purchase American arms, but does not seek to influence the United States to sell them for fear that Pakistan (C) will then build up its own armaments and thus start an arms race. In this situation, Pakistan (C) has influence over the actions of the Indian government even though it has not deliberately sought to influence India on this particular matter or even communicated its position in any way. The Indian government has imply perceived that there is a relatively high probability that if it seeks to influence the United States, Pakistan will react in a manner that is contrary to India's interests.

Fifth, power and influence may be. measured quite objectively by scholars and statesmen, but what is important in international relations is the *perceptions* of influence and capabilities that are held by policymakers. The reason that governments invest millions of dollars for the gathering of intelligence is to develop or have available a relatively accurate picture of other states' capabilities and intentions. Where there is a great discrepancy between perceptions and reality, the results to a country's foreign policy may be disastrous. To take our example of the bank robber again, suppose that the man held a harmless toy pistol and threatened the clerk. The clerk perceived the gun to be real and hence complied with his demand. In this case the robber's influence was far greater than the "objective" character of his capabilities, and the distorted perception by the clerk led her to act in a manner that was unfavorable to her and her employers.

Finally, as our original model suggests, A may try to influence B *not to do* X. Sometimes this is called "negative" power, where A acts in a manner to *prevent* a certain action it deems undesirable to its interests. This is a very typical relationship and process in international politics. By signing the Munich treaty, for example, the British and French governments hoped to prevent Germany from invading Czechoslovakia: the Soviet government by using a variety of instruments of foreign policy, has sought to prevent West Germany from obtaining nuclear weapons; by organizing the Marshall Plan and NATO, the United States sought to prevent the growth of communism in western Europe and/or a Soviet military invasion of this area.

CAPABILITIES

The second element of the concept of power consists of those capabilities that are mobilized in support of the act of influencing. It is difficult to understand how much influence an actor is likely to wield unless we also have some knowledge of the capabilities that are involved.[5] Nevertheless, it should be acknowledged that social scientists do not understand all the reasons why some actors—whether people, groups, governments, or states—wield influence successfully, while others do not.

It is clear that in political relationships not everyone possesses equal influence. We frequently use the terms "great powers" and "small powers" as a shorthand way of suggesting that some actors make commitments abroad and have the capacity to meet them that others lack. The distinction between the "great powers" and the "small powers" is usually based on some rough estimation of tangible and intangible factors which we have called capabilities. In domestic politics it is possible to construct a lengthy list of those capabilities and attributes which seemingly permit some to wield influence over large numbers of people and over important public decisions. Robert A. Dahl [*Who Governs?* New Haven: Yale University Press, (1961)] lists such tangibles as money, wealth, information, time, political allies, official position, and control over jobs, and such intangibles as personality and leadership qualities. But not everyone who possesses these capabilities can command the obedience or influence the behavior of other people. What is crucial in relating capabilities to influence, according to Dahl, is that the person *mobilize these capabilities for his political purposes,* and that he possess skill in mobilizing them. A person who uses his wealth, time, information, friends, and personality for political purposes will likely be able to influence others on public issues. A person, on the other hand, who possesses the same capabilities but uses them to invent a new mousetrap is not likely to be important in politics.

The same propositions also hold true in international politics. Capabilities may also be tangible or intangible. We can predict that a country in possession of a high Gross National Product, a high level of industrial development, sophisticated weapons systems, and a large population will have more influence and prestige in the system than a state with a primitive economy, small population, and old-fashioned armaments. And yet, the intangibles are also important. In addition to the physical resources

---

[5] We might assess influence for historical situations solely on the basis of whether A got B to do X, without having knowledge of either A's or B's capabilities.

of a state, such factors as leadership and national morale have to be assessed. We could not, for example, arrive at an estimation of India's influence in world politics unless we regarded the prestige and stature of its leadership abroad.

Moreover, the amount of influence a state wields over others can be related, as in domestic politics, to the capabilities that are *mobilized* in support of foreign policy objectives. Or, to put this proposition in another way, we can argue that a capability does not itself determine the uses to which it will be put. Nuclear power can be used to provide electricity or depends less on their quality and quantity than on the external objectives to coerce and perhaps to destroy other nations. The use of capabilities depends less on their quality than on the external objectives that a government formulates for itself.

However, the *variety* of foreign policy instruments available to a nation for influencing others is partly a function of the quantity and quality of capabilities. What a government will seek to do, and how it attempts to do it will depend at least partially on the resources it finds available. A country such as Thailand which possesses relatively few and underdeveloped resources cannot, even if it desired, construct nuclear weapons with which to intimidate others, or establish a world-wide propaganda network, or dispense several billion dollars annually of foreign aid to try to influence other countries. And in other international systems, such as in the ancient Hindu interstate system, the level of technology limited the number of capabilities that could be used for external purposes. Kautilya suggested in the *Arthasastra* that only seven elements made up the capability of the state: the excellence (quality) of the king and the ministers, and the quality and quantity of the territory, fortresses, treasury, army, and allies [Narandra Nathaniel Law, *Interstate Relations in Ancient India*, London: Luzac, 1920; U. N. Ghoshal, "The System of Inter-State Relations and Foreign Policy in the Early Arthasastra Stage," *India Antiqua*, E. J. Brill, 1947]. In general, advanced industrial societies are able to mobilize a wide variety of capabilities in support of their external objectives. We can conclude, therefore, that how states *use* their capabilities depends on their external objectives, but the choice of objectives and the instruments to achieve those objectives are limited or influenced by the quality and quantity of available capabilities.

THE MEASUREMENT OF CAPABILITIES

For many years students of international politics have made meticulous comparisons of the mobilized and potential capabilities of various nations. Comparative data relating to the production of iron ore, coal, hydroelectricity, economic growth rates, educational levels, population growth rates, military resources, transportation systems, and sources of raw materials are presented as indicators of a nation's power. Unfortunately, few have acknowledged that in making these comparisons they are not measuring a state's power or influence, but only its base. Our previous discussion would suggest that such measurements and assessments are not particularly useful unless they are related to the foreign policy objectives of the various states. Capability is always the capability to do something; its assessment, therefore, is most meaningful when carried on within a framework of certain goals and foreign policy objectives.

The deduction of actual influence from the quantity and quality of potential and mobilized capabilities may, in some cases, give an approximation of reality, but historically there have been too many discrepancies between the basis of power and the amount of influence to warrant adopting this practice as a useful approach to international relations. One could have assumed, for example, on the basis of a comparative study of technological and educational level, and general standard of living in the 1920's and 1930's that the United States would have been one of the most influential actors in the international system. A careful comparison of certain resources, called by Frank H. Simonds and Brooks Emeny [*The Great Powers in World Politics*, New York: The American Book Company, (1939)] the "great essentials," revealed the United States to be in an enviable position. In the period 1925 to 1930, it was the only major country in the world that produced from its own resources adequate supplies of food, power, iron, machinery, chemicals, coal, iron ore, and petroleum. If actual influence had been deduced from the quantities of "great essentials" possessed by the major actors the following ranking of states would have resulted: (1) United States, (2) Germany, (3) Great Britain, (4) France, (5) Russia, (6) Italy, (7) Japan. However, the diplomatic history of the world from 1925 to 1930 would suggest that there was little correlation between the capabilities of these countries and their actual influence. If we measure influence by the impact these actors made on the system and by the responses they could invoke when they sought to change the behavior of other states, we would find for this period quite a different ranking, such as the following: (1) France, (2) Great Britain, (3) Italy, (4) Germany, (5) Russia, (6) Japan, (7) United States.

Other historical discrepancies can also be cited. How, for example, can we explain the ability of the French after their defeat in the Napoleonic wars to become, within a short period of time, one of the most influential members in the Concert of Europe? More recently, how could such figures as Dr. Castro, Colonel Nasser and Marshal Tito successfully defy the pressure of the great powers? The answer to these questions lies not solely in the physical capabilities of states, but partly in the personalities and diplomacy of political leaders, the reactions of the major powers, and other special circumstances. Hence, the ability of A to change the behavior of B is enhanced if it possesses physical capabilities which it can use in the influence act; but B is by no means defenseless because it fails to own a large army, raw materials, and money for foreign aid. Persuasiveness is often related to such intangibles as personality, perceptions, friendships, traditions, and customs, all of which are almost impossible to measure accurately.

The discrepancy between physical capabilities and actual influence can also be related to credibility. A nuclear capability, for example, is often thought to increase radically the diplomatic influence of those who develop it. Yet, the important aspect of a nuclear capability is not its possession, but the willingness to use it if necessary. Other actors must know that the capability is not of mere symbolic significance. Thus, a leader like Dr. Castro possesses a particular psychological advantage over the United States (hence, influence) because he knows that in almost all circumstances the American government would not use strategic nuclear weapons against his country. He has, therefore, effectively broken through the significance of the American nuclear capability as far as Cuban-American relations are concerned.

Finally, discrepancies between actors' physical capabilities and their actual influence can be traced to the habit of analyzing capabilities only in terms of a single state. The wielding of influence in modern international politics is, however, seldom a bilateral process. In a system where all states perceive some involvement and relationship with all other actors, governments seek to use the capabilities and diplomatic influence of other actors by forming diplomatic or military coalitions. Indeed, modern diplomacy is largely concerned with eliciting support of friends and neutrals, presumably because widespread diplomatic support for an actor's policies increases the legitimacy of those objections, thereby increasing the influence of the actor. "Small" states in particular can increase their influence if they can gain commitments of support from other members of the system.[6] physical capabilities and actual influence, how do we proceed to measure influence? Assessment of physical capabilities may be adequate for rough estimations of influence or war potential and in some circumstances it may suffice to rely on reputations of power. But for precise knowledge, we have to refer to the actual processes of international politics and not to charts or indices of raw materials. We can best measure influence, according to Robert A. Dahl ["The Concept of Power," *Behavioral Science*, 2 (1957) 201–15], by studying the

---

[6] This is one reason why international conflicts seldom remain confined to the original disputants. Recognizing the dangers of increasing the numbers of parties to a dispute, the United Nations has sought to "isolate" conflicts as much as possible.

responses of those who are in the influence relationship. If A can get B to do X, but C cannot get B to do the same thing, then in reference to that particular action, A has more influence. Or, if B does X despite the protestations of A, then we can assume that A, in this circumstance, did not enjoy much influence over B. It is meaningless to argue that the Soviet Union is more powerful than the United States unless we cite how, for what purposes, and in relation to whom, the Soviet Union and the United States are exerting influence. We may conclude, then, that capabilities themselves do not always lead to the successful wielding of influence and that other variables have to be considered as well. In general, influence varies with (1) the type of goals an actor pursues, (2) the quality and quantity of capabilities (including allies and intangibles) at its disposal, (3) the skill in mobilizing these capabilities in support of the goals, and (4) the credibility of threats and rewards.

HOW INFLUENCE IS EXERCISED

Social scientists have noted several fundamental techniques that individuals and groups use to influence each other. In a political system which contains no one legitimate center of authority (such as a government, or a father in a family) that can command the members of the group or society, bargaining has to be used among the sovereign entities. A. F. K. Organski [*World Politics,* New York: Alfred Knopf, 1958], Charles Schleicher [*op. cit.,* (1962)], and Quincy Wright ["The Nature of Conflict," *The Western Political Quarterly,* 4 (1951), 193–209] suggest four typical bargaining techniques in international politics[7]: persuasion, offering rewards, threatening punishments, and the use of force. These categories are very useful for analyzing the wielding of influence in the system, but they can be expanded and refined to account for slightly different forms of behavior. Recalling that A seeks one of three courses of conduct from B (e.g., B to do X in the future, B not to do X in the future, and B to continue doing X) it may use six different tactics.

1. *Persuasion.* Persuasion may include threats, rewards and actual punishments, but we will mean here those situations in which an actor simply initiates or discusses a proposal or situation with another and elicits a favorable response without explicitly holding out the possibility of rewards or punishments. We cannot assume that the exercise

---

[7] Francois de Callieres, a renowned French diplomat of the eighteenth century, also suggested these techniques when he wrote: "Every Christian prince must take as his chief maxim not to employ arms to support or vindicate his rights until he has employed and exhausted the way of reason and persuasion. It is to his interest also, to add to reason and persuasion the influence of benefits conferred, which indeed is one of the surest ways to make his own power secure, and to increase it." *On the Manner of Negotiating with Princes,* trans. by A. F. Whyte, p. 7 (1919).

of influence is always *against* the wishes of others and that there are only two possible outcomes of the act, one favoring A, the other favoring B. For example, state A asks B to support it at a coming international conference on the control of narcotics. State B might not originally have any particular interest in the conference or its outcome, but decides, on the basis of A's initiative, that something positive might be gained not only by supporting A's proposals, but also by attending the conference. In this case there might also be the expectation of gaining some type of reward in the future, but not necessarily from A.

2. *The offer of rewards.* This is the situation where A promises to do something favorable to B if B complies with the wishes of A. Rewards may be of almost any type in international relations. To gain the diplomatic support of B at the narcotics conference, A may offer to increase foreign aid payments, to lower tariffs on goods imported from B, to support B at a later conference on communications facilities, or it may promise to remove a previous punishment. The latter tactic is used often by Soviet negotiators. After having created an unfavorable situation, they promise to remove it in return for some concessions by their opponents.

3. *The granting of rewards.* In some instances, the credibility of an actor is not very high and state B, before complying with A's wishes, may insist that A actually give the reward in advance. Frequently in armistice negotiations neither side will unilaterally take steps to demilitarize an area or to demobilize troops until the other shows evidence of complying with the agreements. One of the clichés of cold war diplomacy holds that deeds, not words, are required for the granting of rewards and concessions.

4. *The threat of punishment.* Threats of punishment may be further subdivided into two types:

   a) positive threats, where, for example, state A threatens to increase tariffs, to cut off diplomatic relations, to institute a boycott or embargo against trade with B, or to use force.

   b) threats of deprivation, where A threatens to withdraw foreign aid or in other ways to withhold rewards or other advantages that it already grants to B.

5. *The infliction of non-violent punishment.* In this situation, threats are carried out in the hope of altering B's behavior which, in most cases, could not be altered by other means. The problem with this tactic is that it usually results in reciprocal measures by the other side, thus inflicting damage on both, though not necessarily bringing about a desired state of affairs. If, for example, A threatens to increase its military capabilities if B does X and then proceeds to implement the threat, it is not often that B will comply with A's wishes because it,

too, can increase its military capabilities easily enough. In this type of a situation, then, both sides indulge in the application of punishments which may escalate into more serious form unless the conflict is resolved.

6. *Force.* In previous eras when governments did not possess the variety of foreign policy instruments that are available today, they had to rely frequently in the bargaining process upon the use of force. Force and violence were not only the most efficient tactics, but in many cases they were the only means possible for influencing. Today, the situation is different. As technological levels rise, other means of inducement become available and can serve as substitutes for force.[8]

PATTERNS OF INFLUENCE IN THE INTERNATIONAL SYSTEM

Most governments at one time or another use all of these techniques for influencing others, but probably over ninety per cent of all relations between states are based on simple persuasion and deal with relatively unimportant technical matters. Since such interactions seldom make the headlines, however, we often assume that more relations between states involve the making or carrying out of threats. But whether a government is communicating with another over an unimportant technical matter or over a subject of great consequence, it is likely to use a particular type of tactic in its attempts to influence, depending on the general climate of relations between those two governments. Allies, for example, seldom threaten each other with force or even make blatant threats of punishment. Similarly, governments which disagree over a wide range of policy objectives are more likely to resort to threats and to the imposition of punishments. We can suggest, therefore, that just as there are observable patterns of relations between states in terms of their foreign policy strategies (alliances, isolation, neutrality, etc.), there are also general patterns of relations between actors with reference to the methods used to influence each other. The methods of exerting influence between Great Britain and the United States are *typically* those of persuasion and rewards, while the methods of exerting influence between the Soviet Union and the United States in the early post World War II era were typically those of threatening and inflicting punishments of various types. Since such typical patterns exist, we can then construct rough typologies of international relationships as identified by the typical techniques used in the act of influence.

---

[8] Presumably, therefore, disarmament and arms control would become more feasible because other instruments of policy can be used in the influence act. In previous eras, to disarm would have led to the collapse of the most important—if not only—capability that could be mobilized for foreign policy purposes.

1. *Relations of consensus.* Relations of consensus would be typical between actors that had few disagreements over foreign policy objectives, and/or had a very low level of interaction and involvement in each other's affairs. An example of the former would be Anglo-American relations, and of the latter, the relations between Thailand and Bolivia. In the relations of consensus, moreover, influence is exercised primarily by the technique of persuasion and through the subtle offering of rewards. Finally, since violence as a form of punishment is almost inconceivable between two countries, the military capabilities of neither actor are organized, mobilized, and "targeted" toward the other.

2. *Relations of overt manipulation.* Here, there may be some disagreement or conflict over foreign policy objectives, or state A might undertake some domestic policy which was disapproved by state B, such as a form of racial discrimination. Since there is some conflict, there will also be at least a modest degree of involvement between the two actors, or a perception that A and B are in some kind of a relationship of interdependence. The techniques used to influence will include, if normal persuasion fails, (a) offers of rewards, (b) the granting of rewards, (c) threats to withhold rewards (e.g., not to give foreign aid in the future), or (d) threats of non-violent punishment, including, for example, the raising of tariffs against B's products. Militarily, in relations of overt manipulation there is still no mobilization or targeting of military capabilities toward state B. Examples of overt manipulation would include the relations between China and the Soviet Union, 1960-1963, and the relations between France and the United States during this same period.

3. *Relations of coercion.* In relations of coercion, there are fundamental disagreements over foreign policy objectives. Almost all actions that A takes externally are perceived by B to be a threat to its own interests. Involvement is, therefore, high. A seeks to influence B's behavior typically by (a) threatening punishments, (b) by inflicting non-violent punishments and under extreme provocation, (c) by the selective and limited use of force as, for example, in a peace-time blockade. Military capabilities, finally, are likely to be targeted towards each other. Examples would include the Soviet Union and the western coalition for most of the period since 1947, Cuba and the United States between 1960 and 1963, Nazi Germany and Czechoslovakia between 1937 and 1939 and Egypt and Israel since 1948.

4. *Relations of force.* Here there is almost total disagreement on foreign policy objectives and the areas of consensus are limited to a few necessities such as communications. The degree of involvement is obviously extremely high. The typical form of exercising influence is through the infliction of violent punishment, though in some instances rewards (e.g., peace offers) might be offered. National capabilities are mobilized

primarily with a view to conducting the policy of punishment. However the quantity of military capabilities that is used will vary with the geographic and force-level boundaries which the disputants place on the conflict.

Though most relations between states could be placed in one of the previous categories, it should also be apparent that under changing circumstances, governments are required to resort to techniques of influence toward others that they would normally avoid. However, the cold war represents a curious phenomenon in the history of international politics because in the relations between east and west *all* of the techniques of influence are being used simultaneously. There are several areas of policy where consensus exists between the Soviet Union and the leaders of the west and where agreements—either in treaties or through "understandings"—can be reached without making threats or imposing punishments.[9] There are also areas of great controversy where the antagonists commit military capabilities and seek to influence each other's behavior most of the time by making threats and carrying out various forms of punishment.

SELECTED BIBLIOGRAPHY

PART II

The Nature of the International System

Ash, Maurice A., "An Analysis of Power with Special Reference to International Politics." *World Politics*. January 1951.

Carr, E. H., *Nationalism and After*. New York: Macmillan, 1945.

De Jouvenal, Bertrand, *On Power*. Boston: Beacon Press, 1962.

Deutsch, Karl W., and J. David Singer, "Multipolar Power Systems and International Stability." *World Politics*. April 1964.

---

[9] Areas of agreement between the Soviet Union and the west which have resulted either in treaties or "understandings" would include the cessation of nuclear tests, the demilitarization of the Antarctic and, possibly, outer space, the renouncing of nuclear war as an instrument of policy, and efforts to prevent the spread of nuclear weapons.

Deutsch, Karl W., and William J. Foltz (eds.), *Nation Building*. New York: Atherton Press, 1963.

Deutsch, Karl W., *Nationalism and Social Communication*. New York: John Wiley and Sons, Inc., 1953.

———, "The Growth of Nations: Some Recurrent Patterns in Political and Social Integration." *World Politics*, January 1953.

Emerson, Rupert, *From Empire to Nation*. Boston: Beacon Press, 1960.

Jones, Stephen B., "The Power Inventory and National Strategy," *World Politics*, July 1954.

Kaplan, Morton A., *System and Process in International Politics*. New York: John Wiley and Sons, 1957.

Knorr, Klaus and Sidney Verba (eds.), *The International System: Theoretical Essays*. Princeton: Princeton University Press, 1961.

Kohn, Hans, *American Nationalism: An Interpretative Essay*. New York: Macmillan, 1957.

———, *Nationalism: Its Meaning and History*. Princeton: Van Nostrand, 1955.

———, *Pan Slavism: Its History and Ideology*. Notre Dame: University of Notre Dame Press, 1953.

———, *Prophets and Peoples: Studies in Nineteenth Century Nationalism*. New York: Macmillan, 1946.

———, *The Age of Nationalism: The First Era of Global History*. New York: Harper and Brothers, 1962.

———, *The Mind of Germany: The Education of a Nation*. New York: Charles Scribner's Sons, 1960.

Palmer, Norman C., and Howard C. Perkins, *International Relations*. Boston: Houghton-Mifflin, 1957.

Rosecrance, Richard N., *Action and Reaction in World Politics: International Systems in Perspective*. Boston: Little, Brown and Company, 1963.

Schwarzenberger, Georg, *Power Politics*. New York: Praeger, 1964.

Snyder, Louis L. (ed.), *The Dynamics of Nationalism*. Princeton: Van Nostrand, 1964.

Spiro, Herbert J., *World Politics: The Global System*. Homewood: Dorsey Press, 1966.

Strausz-Hupé, Robert and Stefan T. Possony, *International Relations*. New York: McGraw-Hill, 1954.

Strausz-Hupé, Robert, *Power and Community*. New York: Praeger, 1956.

Part III

Conflict and Military Potential

STUDENTS OF International Relations, since its beginnings as a field of study, have had as a major concern the study of the causes of conflict. Some theories of conflict are based upon economics as a determinant of international violence. Undoubtedly the most celebrated economic theory of conflict is found in Lenin's work on imperialism. According to Lenin, under capitalism, domestic markets become saturated, and capitalists engage in a life and death struggle in order to obtain control of overseas markets. Writing during World War I, Lenin saw the war as the result of conflict among capitalist states for overseas colonies, with their raw materials, abundant labor supply, and markets for exports. Thus Lenin's theory of imperialism constitutes not only an important communist theory of conflict, but also a communist theory of international relations.

In an examination of economic theories of conflict, Lionel Robbins acknowledges that historically economic motives have played an important role in certain kinds of international conflict. In some periods, merchants with economic interests in colonial markets have influenced the conduct of governmental policy. National units have expanded their territorial boundaries in order to gain access to factors of production. However, Robbins concludes that, on balance, economic considerations have not been a primary determinant of conflict. According to Robbins, colonial expansion, which Lenin links to conflict, represented a response to factors other than the strictly economic. In fact, in most cases the expenditures for colonial territories far outweighed the economic gain to the colonial country. Robbins suggests that European expansion into colonial areas was undertaken by one country in order to prevent other countries from expanding into a given region.

After examining historical cases, Quincy Wright draws in Selection 15 several general conclusions about the causes of war. He contends that wars are the result of "changing relations of technological, psychic, social, and intellectual variables. There is no single cause of war." He suggests, however, that historically wars have increased both in frequency and severity in times of rapid technological and cultural change. What he terms "political lag" is a major cause of war in contemporary civilization, since political and legal changes have not kept pace with technological and cultural changes.

Especially since World War II, there has been a proliferation of literature on military strategy. Although for the most part such writings have been focused on nuclear strategy, there is a growing literature on limited and guerrilla warfare. This voluminous new literature represents but the latest addition to writings on military strategy. Of great importance to the student of strategic affairs are the writings of Karl von Clausewitz. Writing in the early nineteenth century, Clausewitz saw war as but one means toward the achievement of political objectives, the "continuation of political intercourse, with a mixture of other means." Put in contemporary terms, war is but one of the many techniques available to national units in the demand-response relationships in which they are engaged in the international system.

As a result of the exponential increase in destructive capabilities from developments in military technology, the importance of Clausewitz's dictum about war has increased. In fact, implicit in writings on nuclear warfare is the notion that there are few political objectives for which nations would be prepared to use nuclear weapons. Hence at the nuclear level there is a form of international stability between the United States and the Soviet Union. If such stability exists, it is based upon the deterrent capabilities of each superpower. Each possesses sufficient nuclear forces to deter, or prevent, the other from attacking, since in the event of nuclear war both superpowers, their leaders are convinced, would be destroyed, or at least heavily devastated. According to J. David Singer, deterrence is a strategy of threatened punishment in which a state will reap either destruction or reward, i.e., the absence of punishment.

The United States more than any other nation has attempted not only to develop theories of nuclear strategy, but to evolve official strategic doctrine reflective of prevailing technologies and U.S. security interests. An examination of the history of the U.S. State Department's official strategic doctrine since World War II reveals a changing emphasis upon nuclear as opposed to conventional forces in an effort to develop the appropriate mix of weapons systems. In Selection 17, William R. Kintner presents an account of the evolution of U.S. doctrine and examines theories of massive retaliation, counterforce, and damage limiting strategies.

Of considerable concern to students of military strategy is the impact of new weapons upon the international system. Under what circumstances does the acquisition of additional offensive or defensive capabilities by one power constitute a destablizing influence upon the international system? What is the impact upon the international system of the building of an offensive weapon such as an intercontinental ballistic missile which can carry many warheads, or the creation of a defensive weapon such as an antiballistic missile system? According to Richard Whalen, the international strategic environment is highly dynamic in nature. Advanced technologies make it likely that one side or the other will attempt to accelerate its development of offensive and defensive weapons capabilities. Whalen compares and contrasts American and Soviet weapons developments, and draws conclusions about the potential impact upon the international environment of the acquisition of major new weapons systems by one superpower or the other. This discussion is illustrative of the implications of major advances in technology for the international system. (See Part IV.) To what extent will changes in technology widen the gap between the United States and the Soviet Union, on the one hand, and the smaller national units of Western Europe, on the other?

A nuclear war has never been fought, and with the Hiroshima and Nagasaki experiences behind it, the world may even have entered the post-nuclear age. However, there are not only historical, but also contemporary, examples of limited war. In the postwar period, Morton Halperin suggests, there have been several examples of limited war. In such war, there is general agreement among the participants over limitations on some or all of the following: targets, weapons systems, and political objectives. According to Halperin, with the advent of nuclear weapons, it is possible to envisage a "limited" conflict approximating in size World War II without its escalation to a general nuclear war. Thus the concept of limited war includes conflicts of varying intensity, whose common characteristic is the existence of agreement among the participants about limitations.

Historically there are many examples of guerrilla warfare. (The term guerrilla derives from the struggle of Spanish partisans against French forces occupying Spain during the Napoleonic wars.) Paradoxically, in an age of spectacular new military technologies, guerrilla warfare, with its emphasis upon relatively unsophisticated weapons systems, has gained new importance. Perhaps because of the effectiveness of deterrence at the nuclear level, conflicts have been fought, and will continue to be fought, at the levels of limited and guerrilla warfare.

Much of the twentieth century has been a period of revolutionary upheaval, with new nation-states replacing colonial systems, and governments of existing nation-states being overthrown by revolutionary forces. In such circumstances, the strategy of guerrilla warfare has seemed to be peculiarly suited to the needs of those seeking to overthrow the existing order. In national units where the gap psychologically, politically, economically and militarily between the central government and the hinterland is great, there is potential for guerrilla warfare. Thus the reduction in the incidence of guerrilla warfare is related in no small measure to the development of political systems in which governmental control and support are broadly based.

Mao Tse-tung, the greatest twentieth-century theorist and practitioner of guerrilla warfare, outlines its strategic framework. In much the same fashion of Clausewitz, Mao posits the existence of a close relationship between war, in this case, guerrilla operations, and political objectives. This relationship Mao explores in his analysis of the strategy of guerrilla warfare.

SECTION ONE: The Causes of War

13. IMPERIALISM

V. I. Lenin

MONOPOLIST captalist combines—cartels, syndicates, trusts—divide among themselves first of all, the whole internal market of a country, and impose their control, more or less completely, upon the industry of that country. But under capitalism the home market is inevitably bound up with the foreign market. Capitalism long ago created a world market. As the export of capital increased, and as the foreign and colonial relations and the "spheres of influence" of the big monopolist combines expanded, things "naturally" gravitated towards an international agreement among these combines, and towards the formation of international cartels.

. . .

. . . International cartels show to what point capitalist monopolies have developed, and they *reveal the object* of the struggle between the various capitalist groups. This last circumstance is the most important; it alone shows us the historico-economic significance of events; for the *forms* of the struggle may and do constantly change in accordance with

From *Imperialism: The Highest Stage of Capitalism* by V. I. Lenin (New York: 1939), pp. 68; 74–75; 81–82; 88–89; 118–119. Reprinted by permission of International Publishers Co., Inc. Copyright © 1939. Footnotes have been renumbered to appear in consecutive order.

VLADIMIR I. LENIN (1870–1924) Leader of Bolshevik group, Russian Communist Party, which seized power during the Russian Revolution. Chairman of the Council of People's Commission Union of Soviet Socialist Republics. Author of *The State and Revolution,* (New York: International Publishers, 1932); *What is to be Done?* (New York: International Publishers, 1929); *Collected Works,* (New York: International Publishers, 1927–1945).

varying, relatively particular, and temporary causes, but the *essence* of the struggle, its class *content, cannot* change while classes exist.

· · ·

Colonial policy and imperialism existed before this latest stage of capitalism, and even before capitalism. Rome, founded on slavery, pursued a colonial policy and achieved imperialism. But "general" arguments about imperialism, which ignore, or put into the background the fundamental difference of social-economic systems, inevitably degenerate into absolutely empty banalities, or into grandiloquent comparisons like "Greater Rome and Greater Britain."[1] Even the colonial policy of capitalism in its *previous* stages is essentially different from the colonial policy of finance capital.

The principal feature of modern capitalism is the domination of monopolist combines of the big capitalists. These monopolies are most firmly established when *all* the sources of raw materials are controlled by the one group. And we have seen with what zeal the international capitalist combines exert every effort to make it impossible for their rivals to compete with them; for example, by buying up mineral lands, oil fields, etc. Colonial possession alone gives complete guarantee of success to the monopolies against all the risks of the struggle with competitors, including the risk that the latter will defend themselves by means of a law establishing a state monopoly. The more capitalism is developed, the more the need for raw materials is felt, the more bitter competition becomes, and the more feverishly the hunt for raw materials proceeds throughout the whole world, the more desperate becomes the struggle for the acquisition of colonies.

· · ·

CHAPTER VII

. . . Imperialism emerged as the development and direct continuation of the fundamental attributes of capitalism in general. But capitalism only became capitalist imperialism at a definite and very high stage of its development, when certain of its fundamental attributes began to be transformed into their opposites, when the features of a period of transition from capitalism to a higher social and economic system began to take shape and reveal themselves all along the line. Economically, the main thing in this process is the substitution of capitalist monopolies for capitalist free competition. Free competition is the fundamental attribute of capitalism, and of commodity production generally. Monopoly is exactly

---

[1] A reference to the book by C. P. Lucas, *Greater Rome and Greater Britain,* Oxford 1912, or the Earl of Cromer's *Ancient and Modern Imperialism,* London, 1910.

the opposite of free competition; but we have seen the latter being transformed into monopoly before our very eyes, creating large-scale industry and eliminating small industry, replacing large-scale industry by still larger-scale industry, finally leading to such a concentration of production and capital that monopoly has been and is the result: cartels, syndicates and trusts, and merging with them, the capital of a dozen or so banks manipulating thousands of millions. At the same time monopoly, which has grown out of free competition, does not abolish the latter, but exists over it and alongside of it, and thereby gives rise to a number of very acute, intense antagonisms, friction and conflicts. Monopoly is the transition from capitalism to a higher system.

If it were necessary to give the briefest possible definition of imperialism we should have to say that imperialism is the monopoly stage of capitalism. Such a definition would include what is most important, for, on the one hand, finance capital is the bank capital of a few big monopolist banks, merged with the capital of the monopolist combines of manufacturers; and, on the other hand, the division of the world is the transition from a colonial policy which has extended without hinderance to territories unoccupied by any capitalist power, to a colonial policy of monopolistic possession of the territory of the world which has been completely divided up.

But very brief definitions, although convenient, for they sum up the main points, are nevertheless inadequate, because very important features of the phenomenon that has to be defined have to be especially deduced. And so, without forgetting the conditional and relative value of all definitions, which can never include all the concatenations of a phenomenon in its complete development, we must give a definition of imperialism that will embrace the following five essential features:

1) The concentration of production and capital developed to such a high stage that it created monopolies which play a decisive role in economic life.

2) The merging of bank capital with industrial capital, and the creation, on the basis of this "finance capital," of a financial oligarchy."

3) The export of capital, which has become extremely important, as distinguished from the export of commodities.

4) The formation of international capitalist monopolies which share the world among themselves.

5) The territorial division of the whole world among the greatest capitalist powers is completed.

Imperialism is capitalism in that stage of development in which the dominance of monopolies and finance capital has established itself; in which the export of capital has acquired pronounced importance; in which the division of the world among the international trusts has begun;

in which the division of all territories of the globe among the great capitalist powers has been completed.

. . .

. . . Let us consider India, Indo-China and China. It is known that these three colonial and semi-colonial countries, inhabited by six to seven hundred million human beings, are subjected to the exploitation of the finance capital of several imperialist states: Great Britain, France, Japan, the U.S.A., etc. We will assume that these imperialist countries form alliances against one another in order to protect and extend their possessions, their interests and their "spheres of influence" in these Asiatic states; these alliances will be "inter-imperialist," or "ultra-imperialist" alliances. We will assume that all the imperialist countries conclude an alliance for the "peaceful" division of these parts of Asia; this alliance would be an alliance of "internationally united finance capital." As a matter of fact, alliances of this kind have been made in the twentieth century, notably with regard to China. We ask, is it "conceivable," assuming that the capitalist system remains intact—and this is precisely the assumption that Kautsky does make—that such alliances would be more than temporary, that they would eliminate friction, conflicts and struggle in all and every possible form?

This question need only be stated clearly enough to make it impossible for any other reply to be given than that in the negative; for there can be no other conceivable basis under capitalism for the division of spheres of influence, of interests, of colonies, etc., than a calculation of the *strength* of the participants in the division, their general economic, financial, military strength, etc. And the strength of these participants in the division does not change to an equal degree, for under capitalism the development of different undertakings, trusts, branches of industry, or countries cannot be *even*. Half a century ago, Germany was a miserable, insignificant country, as far as its capitalist strength was concerned, compared with the strength of England at that time. Japan was similarly insignificant compared with Russia. Is it "conceivable" that in ten or twenty years' time the relative strength of the imperialist powers will have remained *un*changed? Absolutely inconceivable.

Therefore, in the realities of the capitalist system, and not in the banal philistine fantasies of English parsons, or of the German "Marxist," Kautsky, "inter-imperialist" or "ultra-imperialist" alliances, no matter what form they may assume, whether of one imperialist coalition against another, or of a general alliance embracing *all* the imperialist powers, are *inevitably* nothing more than a "truce" in periods between wars. Peaceful alliances prepare the ground for wars, and in their turn grow out of wars; the one is the condition for the other, giving rise to alternating forms of peaceful and non-peaceful struggle out of *one and the same* basis of imperialist connections and the relations between world economics and world politics.

14. THE ECONOMIC CAUSES OF WAR

Lionel Robbins

NATIONAL POWER AND ECONOMIC FACTORS

L ET US START from the most obvious phenomena of international rela- tions—diplomatic manœuvres, ententes, alliances, war. It is easy to see that, in their most general aspect, all these can be conceived as part of a perpetual struggle for power—a struggle either to conserve power or to increase it. Whatever view we may hold concerning the ultimate *raison d'être* of power, we can all agree that, in the day-to-day conduct of international relations, it is in terms of efforts to achieve this proximate end that most of the activities of the agents immediately concerned can probably be most realistically summarized. There is no need to marshal detailed evidence. The whole body of diplomatic literature—state papers, ambassadors' dispatches, general staff memoranda—are couched in a language of which this is, so to speak, the permanent implicit major premise. Our object is to conserve (or increase) our power. Such and such an action will affect our power in such and such a way. This action is therefore to be commended (or rejected).

It should be clear that, in such considerations, economic factors are almost necessarily involved. The attainment of military power in the narrowest sense involves the control of scarce resources. The attainment of any kind of power, save perhaps the power of the spirit, is similarly conditioned. This is so whatever the social system of the state in question.

From *The Economic Causes of War* by Lionel Robbins (London: 1939–New York: Howard Fertig, Inc., 1968) pp. 60–65; 80–85. Reprinted by permission. Footnotes have been renumbered to appear in consecutive order.

SIR LIONEL C. ROBBINS (1898–   ) Chairman, *The Financial Times* (London). Formerly Professor of Economics, London School of Economics and Political Science. His other books include *The University in the Modern World*, (New York: St. Martin's Press, 1966); *Bentham in the Twentieth Century*, (London: Athlone Press, 1965); *Politics and Economics: Papers in Political Economy*, (New York: St. Martin's Press, 1963).

Under socialism, as much as under capitalism, national power rests on economic factors.

Thus national power involves command of raw materials. If raw materials essential for the prosecution of war or for the general functioning of the economic system are situated in territories liable to be inaccessible in time of war, national power is substantially limited. It is all very well to argue that, *given peace,* the raw material problem is only a matter of tariffs and other barriers to trade; and that, *given an absence of restriction,* it does not exist at all. This is true enough. But the fact is that peace is not given and an absence of restriction cannot be assumed. The given fact of the world situation, as we have known it hitherto, is not peace but war and the danger of war; and, if raw material supplies are in the hands of powers with whom the state is likely to be at war, or from whose territories it may be cut off, then the preservation of national power must necessarily involve concern with the securing of adequate provisions.[1] This, of course, is the main explanation of the continual preoccupation of certain modern powers, with the ownership or control of territories in which oil is situated. To the eye sophisticated by Marxian theory it seems to appear that the various manœuvres in this respect have been inspired solely by sinister interest. But this is most improbable. We do not know with any certainty how much sinister interest has been operative here; the material for sound judgment is not available. It is quite possible that there may have been most substantial rake-offs in particular cases. But, having regard to the importance of oil in naval and aerial warfare, to suppose that independent socialist states having to take account of the danger of war, would have manœuvred very differently, is to lack all sense of proportion.

In the same way, considerations of national power involve concern with command over communications. To safeguard supplies and to facilitate naval and military operations, ownership by the citizens of the state of certain important canals or railways may be regarded as fundamental. We have seen already, in the case of the Bagdad railway, how considerations of this sort resulted in impediments being placed on the agreement of financial syndicates. In spite of the not infrequent operation of sinister interest in this region, it is probable that similar considerations have played a large part in determining the long-run tendencies of United States policy in Central America.[2] Less obvious, but no less important in

---

[1] It is no accident that it is the powers who have most consciously regarded war as a permanent and justifiable instrument of national policy, who have always insisted that the raw material problem is not merely a problem of trade restrictions and monetary policy. The silence of the so-called permanently neutral states on this point is a most significant contrast.

[2] See ANGELL, *Foreign Economic Policy of the United States, passim.*

this respect, is the role of other types of foreign investments. It is a great source of strength in war, and hence in diplomacy involving appeal to war, to have available extensive supplies of realizable foreign assets. The enormous strength of Great Britain in the Great War of 1914–18 owed much to the foreign investments of her citizens. To have an international money market within the borders of the state may have technical advantages of no small importance in the conduct of war and diplomacy. We have seen how such powers were exploited by France and Germany in the balance-of-power struggle between 1870 and 1914. Moreover, particular types of foreign assets may provide apt instruments for exercising particular kinds of diplomatic control and pressure. Disraeli's investment in Suez Canal shares is a classical instance of this kind;[3] and the great solicitude of British policy for Egyptian investments in general is probably to be explained in a similar manner.

All this is so important, if we are to understand what goes on in the foreground of diplomatic consciousness, that Mr. R. G. Hawtrey has been led to argue that it is futile to attempt to disentangle economic from other causes. "The distinction between economic and political causes is an unreal one," he says. "Every conflict is one of power and power depends on resources." [4] Power in Mr. Hawtrey's view is something ultimate; he even goes so far as to deny the possibility of interpreting the wars of nationalism in terms other than those of the struggle for power.

Now, as we have seen already, there is a plane of analysis on which power may very well be regarded as the objective most clearly aimed at. No one can study the detailed literature of diplomatic intercourse without coming to feel that, for many of the participants involved, the mere preservation or increase of power has become the only objective. The diplomatic game acquires a sort of independent status; and the wider

---

[3] It is often said that the whole episode of British intervention in Egypt was dictated by the interests of British Bondholders; and advocates of a more or less Marxian interpretation of diplomacy (e.g. H. N. BRAILSFORD, *The War of Steel and Gold*) seem to regard the whole Egyptian episode as a classic case of aggressive economic imperialism. This is very unplausible. Nobody would wish to deny that some part was played by regard for the interests of investors. But it is very doubtful whether a succession of both liberal and conservative cabinets would have maintained a position of such extreme diplomatic embarrassment if it had not been for the overriding strategic considerations involved. The idea of Mr. Gladstone as the agent of Rothschilds and Barings can only be regarded as comic. On the history of the occupation of Egypt, probably the most solid and reliable account is to be found in LANGER, *European Alliances and Alignments,* chap. viii.

[4] *The Economic Aspects of Sovereignty,* p. 120. I hope that my disagreement with Mr. Hawtrey on this particular point will not be thought to indicate an undervaluation of this brilliant and illuminating essay which must be a stimulus to all who read it.

forces involved may themselves be deflected by the skill, the mistakes or the idiosyncrasies of the participants. How much of the history of the world has been determined by influences of this sort is a question about which wise men may well differ. But no one who has attentively studied the facts will be inclined to minimize their significance. There is a real profundity in Mr. Hawtrey's remark that the principal cause of war is war itself. In the absence of the rule of law in international relations, a situation is created in which the maintenance or increase of power in the military sense is an almost inevitable objective of the conduct of independent governments.

Nevertheless, it is surely too drastic a simplification to regard the desire for power as being always a final objective. The foreign ministers and ambassadors who are the immediate agents in the detailed manœuvres of international relations, may from day to day think only in such undifferentiated terms; but the leaders of opinion, the representatives of various interests, not to mention the introspective citizen, will certainly from time to time conceive the issues in terms of something more ultimate. Power as such may indeed be an ultimate attraction; we must never underestimate the extent of sheer irrationality which is operative in these large affairs. In the case of a monomaniac like Hitler, it is obviously the governing consideration. But sometimes, at least, somebody will pause to ask what it is all about. Somebody will indicate the further objectives for the realization of which national power is essential. It is indeed extraordinarily difficult to get a right sense of proportion here. But it is surely wrong to suppose that such ultimate objectives are not often very important. And it is surely wrong to argue that, because the achievement of any kind of objective involves the use of scarce resources, it is impossible to distinguish between the economic motive, which is concerned with the enhancement of command of resources in general, and other motives which are more specific in character.

. . .

HISTORICAL OBSERVATIONS: ENGLAND AND GERMANY

Here surely we have the outlines of a theory which affords a much more plausible explanation of the economic causes of the diplomatic struggles of the modern period than any other we have yet examined. Whether or not foreign ministers and ambassadors often thought in these terms, here, if they reflected, there was a permanent justification for maintaining and increasing national power. It was a justification, too, which could vindicate insistence on petty points which in themselves involved no grave economic injury. If, by a series of small losses, the general standing of the nation were weakened, then there was danger of the "catastrophe" so often vaguely alluded to, the substantial loss of prestige and influence which might carry with it the danger of exclusion and impoverishment. So long as other powers practised exclusion, so long there was danger of substantial damage from alterations of national boundaries. It is unlikely that the rationale of policy was frequently stated in these particular terms; public apologia were more apt to rely on the more grandiose imagery of power. But if a cross-examiner had pressed sufficiently persistently the naïve question "Why do we want to maintain our power?" it is probable that, sooner or later, such an explanation would have been forthcoming.

It is an explanation furthermore which, better than any other, fits the facts of the scramble for colonies. During the period in which this took place Great Britain was the only great power which did not practise a policy of commercial restriction. The British colonial empire was run on free trade principles. But the other powers pursued other policies. It followed therefore that, for any one power, if any of the others, save great Britain, "got there first," there was a loss of potential markets; and of course there was always the danger, more feared at that time than was necessary, that British policy might turn restrictionist. Hence there was a real national interest in expansion; an interest, be it noted, not confined to the propertied classes. Working people, equally with capitalists, stood to lose from the narrowing of potential markets.[5] With the recrudescence of protectionism in the seventies, the division of the world's surface between the different nations, which in the period of Cobdenism had seemed likely to become a matter of smaller and smaller importance, once more became a matter of real concern to responsible national leaders.

This is plain enough in the history of British colonial expansion. Undoubtedly, from time to time, particular annexations were supported by particular groups of interests. But the main object of the policy of successive governments was to prevent a curtailment of the market. Committed, as they were, to the principles of free trade, they had no desire to exclude other people. But they had every reason to fear that, if other people were in first, they themselves would be found shut out.[6] Even an historian, so obviously unsympathetic to the British position as Professor Langer, admits this. "With the setting aside of large parts of the unclaimed world as French and German Colonies," he says, "there was an obvious danger that the British Market would be steadily restricted. Hence the emergence and sudden flowering of the movement for expansion. The English

---

[5] Indeed they stood to lose more, for capital was more mobile than labour.

[6] Probably the most instructive episode here is the struggle regarding China. The British were only very reluctantly converted to the principle of 'spheres of influence'. But they continually used their diplomatic machinery to press for the policy of the open door.

felt that they had to take over large blocks of territory if only to prevent them falling into the hands of exclusive rivals." [7] And again, "It was the embarkation of France, Germany and other countries on the course of Empire that brought the British to the conviction that only political control could adequately safeguard markets." [8]

Even in the case of Germany, this explanation probably fits the facts more often than any other. It is true that owing to the cartel policy which was fostered by the German government, there was a contact between certain groups of German industrialists and the German government probably closer than existed in any other country; and it is possible that some at least of the German expansion was initiated in such circles—not, be it noted, the circles of high finance. It is true, moreover, that the writings of the ruling school of German economists went far to justify a policy of aggressive trade expansion. But although these had some influence at the time, it is probable that the main lines of Bismarckian policy were dictated by defensive considerations. The change in Bismarck's attitude to the colonial question coincided with the general return to protectionism, of which of course he was so largely the architect; and, taking into account what we know of the man and his conception of his mission, it is plausible to argue that the hypothesis that he was fearful of exclusion does less injustice to the facts than the hypothesis of more active aggressiveness. The aggressive economic philosophy had more influence on Bismarck's successors and on their military and naval staffs than it had on the Iron Chancellor. But for the full fruition of such

---

[7] *The Diplomacy of Imperialism,* p. 75.

[8] Ibid., p. 95. After these eminently sensible pronouncements it is something of a shock to find that, in his summing up of the whole period, at the end of the book, Professor Langer says that the Germans 'with some justice felt that John Bull, already bloated with colonial spoils, wanted the whole world *for his private preserve'* (p. 794, my italics). Private preserve is precisely the term which cannot be applied to a free trade empire. Whatever we may say about British in general—and the present writer has never been a silent critic of its obvious deficiencies—we must surely admit that until the introduction of the notorious Ottawa system, British trade policy was immune from the charge of sectional exclusiveness. Professor Langer goes on to say that 'it would be hopeless to try to understand the Anglo-German problem without taking account of this clash of economic forces'. It is perhaps hopeless to expect that students of diplomacy will try to understand economic theory. But before committing himself to so weighty a pronouncement, it would surely have been well for the foremost diplomatic historian of our day to have considered a little further the testimony of Prince Lichnowsky. 'England', said this candid man, 'would no more have drawn the sword against us on account of our Navy alone than she would have done so on account of our trade, which is supposed to have called forth envy and finally the war . . . The theory of England's trade envy of which there has been so much talk, is based upon faulty judgment'. *Auf dem Wege zum Abgrund* I, pp. 116–118.

teaching we have had to wait for the practice of the Third Reich. Fear of exclusion was probably the dominating motive of the earlier period.

In the years since the Great War of 1914–18, such fears have been increasingly justified. Beside the gigantic restrictionist apparatus of the "post-war" period, the earlier tariff walls are mere pigmies. If the statesmen of the times of our fathers had reason to fear the exclusiveness of their neighbours, justification for such fears has been afforded to us in double measure. It is no accident that this age affords a classic example of an expansionist war designed to relieve such restrictions. Whatever we may think of the justice of the Japanese attack on China, there can be no doubt of its connection with the restriction of the Japanese market. In 1929, with the advent of the Great Depression, the market for Japanese silk in the United States and elsewhere collapsed. Now silk was the chief item of Japanese export. The collapse was a major catastrophe. It was only to be expected, therefore, that the Japanese would turn as rapidly as possible to other forms of export. This they did; and immediately the markets elsewhere were effectively closed against them. In Ceylon, for instance, in one year the import of a certain kind of Japanese cloth was reduced to one-tenth of its former dimensions. The connection between such events and the invasion of China is so obvious as to need no elaboration.

It is not only restrictions on trade which have become more menacing in the most recent period; there has emerged also a type of policy from which the earlier period was almost entirely free, the policy of restriction of migration. In the years before the Great War it was possible to travel from one end of Europe to the other without a passport; and the enterprising youth of the more congested areas had no difficulty in transferring their efforts to areas offering greater scope. We have changed all that nowadays. The political exile crouches in ditches between frontiers and the youth of impoverished Europe, denied access to the open spaces, dons a shirt and prepares for the wars. The present generation of Englishmen, to whom the obligation to carry a passport has rapidly become part of the natural order of things, have never paid much attention to the effects of the stoppage of migration. But there can be little doubt that, in a world perspective, it has been one of the most potent factors making for conflict. It is very difficult to take seriously the complaints of dictators who impede emigration and encourage the birth rate. But their subjects nevertheless have a real and legitimate grievance.

It would be a great mistake, however, to regard the tensions of this period as springing merely from fear of economic exclusion. Enough has been said earlier to make it clear that there is no intention here to ascribe the spiritual disease, the collective schizophrenia of Europe, to purely economic factors. But it is worth noting that, with the rise of the totalitarian systems, the aggressive economic motive has become more and more in evidence. In the Nazi literature, the desire for expansion is not merely a desire to escape the effects of other peoples' restrictions; it is much more a desire positively to exploit subject races and to dominate the world. We are no longer moving within the intellectual limits of the assumptions of nineteenth-century diplomacy. In the ideology of pre-war Europe, the exploitation of even the most backward people by non-reciprocal trade restrictions was becoming slightly discredited. In the practice of totalitarian Germany, not only is the concept of subject peoples enlarged to include, for instance, Czechs and Jews, but the admissibility of forced labour, that is the virtual restoration of slavery, is also taken more or less for granted. The economic motives of the powers who became involved in the catastrophe of the Great War of 1914–18, were the motives of distrustful and irascible but, for the most part, fairly civilized men. The economic motives of the totalitarian powers are the motives of barbarian hordes.

15. THE CAUSES OF WAR

Quincy Wright

W^ARS ARISE because of the changing relations of numerous variables —technological psychic, social, and intellectual. There is no single cause of war. Peace is an equilibrium among many forces. Change in any particular force, trend, movement, or policy may at one time make for war, but under other conditions a similar change may make for peace. A state may at one time promote peace by armament, at another time by disarmament; at one time by insistence on its rights, at another time by a spirit of conciliation. To estimate the probability of war at any time involves, therefore, an appraisal of the effect of current changes upon the complex of intergroup relationships throughout the world. Certain relationships, however, have been of outstanding importance. Political lag deserves attention as an outstanding cause of war in contemporary civilization.

Reprinted from *A Study of War* by Quincy Wright by permission of The University of Chicago Press, copyright © 1965, pp. 1284–1288. Footnotes have been renumbered to appear in consecutive order.

QUINCY WRIGHT—See biographical note, page 6.

POLITICAL LAG

There appears to be a general tendency for change in procedures of political and legal adjustment to lag behind economic and cultural changes arising from intergroup contacts. The violent consequences of this lag can be observed in primitive and historic societies,[1] but its importance has increased in modern times. The expansion of contacts and the acceleration of change resulting from modern technology has disturbed existing power localizations and has accentuated the cultural opposition inherent in social organization. World-government has not developed sufficiently to adjust by peaceful procedures the conflict situations which have arisen. Certain influences of this political lag upon the severity and frequency of wars will be considered in the following paragraphs.

War tends to increase in severity and to decrease in frequency as the area of political and legal adjustment (the state) expands geographically unless that area becomes as broad as the area of continuous economic, social, and cultural contact (the civilization). In the modern period peoples in all sections of the world have come into continuous contact with one another. While states have tended to grow during this period, thus extending the areas of adjustment, none of them has acquired world-wide jurisdiction. Their growth in size has increased the likelihood that conflicts will be adjusted, but it has also increased the severity of the consequences of unadjusted conflicts. Fallible human government is certain to make occasional mistakes in policy, especially when, because of lack of universality, it must deal with conflicts regulated not by law but by negotiation functioning within an unstable balance of power among a few large units. Such errors have led to war.

War tends to increase both in frequency and in severity in times of rapid technological and cultural change because adjustment, which al-

---

[1] . . . Sociologists have used the term "cultural lag" to refer to the differential rates of change in different aspects of a culture . . . and have emphasized especially the lag of social or adaptive changes behind technological changes and the social disorganization which results (see W. F. Ogburn and M. F. Nimkoff, *Sociology* [Boston, 1940], pp. 865, 884 ff.). Political lag may be considered a lag in the change of certain aspects of intergroup distance behind change in other such aspects, but it can also be considered an instance of cultural lag. Contacts between groups of different culture result in interchange of objects, procedures, and ideas, many of which are new in the receiving group and have the same effect as inventions or technological changes. The socially disorganizing effect is likely, however, to be attributed to the sending state, resulting in an international conflict situation. Since precedures of international adjustment lag behind the need for them, such conflicts may become aggravated and sentimentalized into war. See W. F. Ogburn, *Social Change* (New York, 1922), p. 247.

ways involves habituation, is a function of time. The shorter the time within which such adjustments have to be made, the greater the probability that they will prove inadequate and that violence will result. War can, therefore, be attributed either to the intelligence of man manifested in his inventions which increase the number of contacts and the speed of change or to the unintelligence of man which retards his perception of the instruments of regulation and adjustment necessary to prevent these contacts and changes from generating serious conflicts. Peace might be kept by retarding progress so that there will be time for gradual adjustment by natural processes of accommodation and assimilation, or peace might be kept by accelerating progress through planned adjustments and new controls. Actually both methods have been tried, the latter especially within the state and the former especially in international relations.[2]

Sovereignty in the political sense is the effort of a society to free itself from external controls in order to facilitate changes in its law and government which it considers necessary to meet changing economic and social conditions. The very efficiency of sovereignty within the state, however, decreases the efficiency of regulation in international relations. By eliminating tensions within the state, external tensions are augmented. International relations become a "state of nature." War therefore among states claiming sovereignty tends to be related primarily to the balance of power among them.

Behind this equilibrium are others, disturbances in any one of which may cause war. These include such fundamental oppositions as the ambivalent tendency of human nature to love and to hate the same object and the ambivalent tendency of social organization to integrate and to differentiate at the same time. They also include less fundamental oppositions such as the tendency within international law to develop a world-order and to support national sovereignty and the tendency of international politics to generate foreign policies of both intervention and isolation. Elimination of such oppositions is not to be anticipated, and their continuance in some form is probably an essential condition of human progress. Peace, consequently, has to do not with the elimination of oppositions but with the modification of the method of adjusting them.

With an appreciation of the complexity of the factors involved in the causation of war and of the significance of historic contingency in estimating their influence, caution is justified in anticipating results from analytical formulations of the problem. An effort will, however, be made to draw together some of the conclusions arrived at in the historical and analytical parts of this study.

---

[2] . . . Ogburn and Nimkoff (*op. cit.*, p. 889) point out that it is usually more difficult to retard the leading than to accelerate the lagging element.

Warfare cannot exist unless similar but distinct groups come into contact. Its frequency and its intensity are dependent upon the characteristics of the groups and are roughly proportionate to the rapidity with which these contacts develop so long as the groups remain distinct and self-determining. However, when these contacts have passed a critical point of intensity, sympathetic feelings and symbolic identifications tend to develop among individuals of different groups sufficiently to permit the functioning of intergroup social, political, and legal institutions, adjusting conflicts and broadening the area of peace. The smoothness of this process is greatly influenced by the policies pursued by groups and the degree of the consistency of these policies with one another.

It is in the relation of political groups to one another and to their members and in the relation of group policies to one another and to the world-order that the explanation of war is to be found. War may be explained sociologically by its function in identifying and preserving political groups, psychologically by the conflict of human drives with one another and with social requirements, technologically by its utility as a means to group ends, and legally by inadequacies and inconsistencies in the law and procedure of the whole within which it occurs.

SOCIOLOGICAL FUNCTIONS OF WAR

Animal warfare is explained by the theory of natural selection. The behavior pattern of hostility has contributed to the survival of certain biological species, and consequently that behavior has survived. In the survival of other species other factors have played a more important role. The peaceful herbivores have on the whole been more successful in the struggle for existence than have the predators and parasites.

Among primitive peoples before contact with civilization warfare contributed to the solidarity of the group and to the survival of certain forms of culture. When population increased, migrations or new means of communication accelerated external contacts. The war-like tribes tended to survive and expand; furthermore, the personality traits of courage and obedience which developed among the members of these tribes equipped them for civilization.

Among peoples of the historic civilizations war tended both to the survival and to the destruction of states and civilizations. Its influence depended upon the stage of the civilization and the type of military technique developed. Civilized states tended to fight for economic and political ends in the early stages of the civilization, with the effect of expanding and integrating the civilization. As the size and interdependence of political units increased, political and economic ends became less tangible, and cultural patterns and ideal objectives assumed greater importance. Aggressive war tended to become a less suitable instrument for conserving these elements of the civilization. Consequently, defensive strategies and peaceful sentiments developed, but in none of the historic civilizations were they universally accepted. War tended toward a destructive stalemate, disintegrating the civilization and rendering it vulnerable to the attack of external barbarians of younger civilization but not its cultural and intellectual inhibitions.

In the modern period the war pattern has been an important element in the creation, integration, expansion, and survival of states. World-civilization has, however, distributed a singularly destructive war technique to all nations, with the consequence that the utility of war as an instrument of integration and expansion has declined. The balance of power has tended to a condition such that efforts to break it by violence have increasingly menaced the whole civilization, and yet this balance has become so complex and incalculable that such efforts have continued to be made.

SECTION TWO: The Nature of War

16. WHAT IS WAR?

General Karl von Clausewitz

WAR IS NOTHING but a duel on an extensive scale. If we would conceive as a unit the countless number of duels which make up a
War, we shall do so best by supposing to ourselves two wrestlers. Each
strives by physical force to compel the other to submit to his will: each
endeavours to throw his adversary, and thus render him incapable of
further resistance.

*War is therefore an act of violence intended to compel our opponents
to fulfill our will.*

Violence arms itself with the inventions of Art and Science in order to
contend against violence. Self-imposed restrictions, almost imperceptible
and hardly worth mentioning, termed usages of International Law, accompany it without essentially impairing its power. Violence, that is to
say, physical force (for there is no moral force without the conception of
States and Law), is therefore the *means;* the compulsory submission of
the enemy to our will is the ultimate *object*. In order to attain this object
fully, the enemy must be disarmed, and disarmament becomes therefore
the immediate object of hostilities in theory. It takes the place of the final
object, and puts it aside as something we can eliminate from our calculations.

.   .   .

The War of a community—of whole Nations, and particularly of
civilised Nations—always starts from a political condition and is called
forth by a political motive. It is, therefore, a political act. Now if it was a

---

From *On War* by General Karl von Clausewitz (London: 1911) Volume 1, pp. 1,
22–23; Volume 3, pp. 121–122. Reprinted by permission of Barnes and Noble, Inc.,
and Routledge and Kegan Paul, Ltd.

KARL VON CLAUSEWITZ (1780–1831) Prussian Chief of Staff and Director of the
General War Academy, Berlin. He also wrote *The Campaign of 1812 in Russia*, (London: J. Murray, 1843).

perfect, unrestrained, and absolute expression of force, as we had to deduce it from its mere conception, then the moment it is called forth by policy it would step into the place of policy, and as something quite independent of it would set it aside, and only follow its own laws, just as a mine at the moment of explosion cannot be guided into any other direction than that which has been given to it by preparatory arrangements. This is how the thing has really been viewed hitherto, whenever a want of harmony between policy and the conduct of a War has led to theoretical distinctions of the kind. But it is not so, and the idea is radically false. War in the real world, as we have already seen, is not an extreme thing which expends itself at one single discharge; it is the operation of powers which do not develop themselves completely in the same manner and in the same measure, but which at one time expand sufficiently to overcome the resistance opposed by inertia or friction, while at another they are too weak to produce an effect; it is therefore, in a certain measure, a pulsation of violent force more or less vehement, consequently making its discharges and exhausting its powers more or less quickly—in other words, conducting more or less quickly to the aim, but always lasting long enough to admit of influence being exerted on it in its course, so as to give it this or that direction, in short, to be subject to the will of a guiding intelligence. Now, if we reflect that War has its root in a political object, then naturally this original motive which called it into existence should also continue the first and highest consideration in its conduct. Still, the political object is no despotic lawgiver on that account; it must accommodate itself to the nature of the means, and though changes in these means may involve modification in the political objective, the latter always retains a prior right to consideration. Policy, therefore, is interwoven with the whole action of War, and must exercise a continuous influence upon it, as far as the nature of the forces liberated by it will permit.

.   .   .

War as an Instrument of Policy

.   .   .

We know, certainly, that War is only called forth through the political intercourse of Governments and Nations; but in general it is supposed that such intercourse is broken off by War, and that a totally different state of things ensues, subject to no laws but its own.

We maintain, on the contrary, that War is nothing but a continuation of political intercourse, with a mixture of other means. We say mixed with other means in order thereby to maintain at the same time that this political intercourse does not cease by the War itself, is not changed into something quite different, but that, in its essense, it continues to exist, whatever may be the form of the means which it uses, and that the chief lines on which the events of the War progress, and to which they are attached, are only the general features of policy which run all through the War until peace takes place. And how can we conceive it to be otherwise? Does the cessation of diplomatic notes stop the political relations between different Nations and Governments? Is not War merely another kind of writing and language for political thoughts? It has certainly a grammar of its own, but its logic is not peculiar to itself.

Accordingly, War can never be separated from political intercourse, and if, in the consideration of the matter, this is done in any way, all the threads of the different relations are, to a certain extent, broken, and we have before us a senseless thing without an object.

17. THE NUCLEAR THRUST: FROM ALAMOGORDO TO CUBA

William R. Kintner

THE NUCLEAR AGE began on a Manhattan Project test stand at Alamogordo, New Mexico, in July, 1945, and the first two-sided contest was waged and won by the United States in the 1962 Cuban missile crisis. The thinking and the preparations leading to this bloodless[1] and novel but crucial confrontation comprise one of the shortest and most turbulent chapters of military history.

The advent of nuclear bombs threw an entirely new element into the military equation. Patterns of strategic thought were rendered obsolete almost overnight. Comprehending the significance of the nuclear weapon, the United States, and subsequently the Soviet Union, slowly began to

From *Peace and the Strategy Conflict* by William R. Kintner (New York: 1967) pp. 22–26; 32–42; 45–47. Reprinted by permission of Frederick A. Praeger, Inc. Footnotes have been renumbered to appear in consecutive order.

WILLIAM R. KINTNER (1915–   ) Professor of Political Science, Deputy Director, Foreign Policy Research Institute, University of Pennsylvania. His other books include *The Nuclear Revolution in Soviet Military Affairs,* (Norman: University of Oklahoma Press, 1968), co-editor; *Building the Atlantic World,* (New York: Harper, 1963); *A Forward Strategy for America,* (New York: Harper, 1961).

[1] Major R. Anderson, Jr., who was shot down by Soviet missiles while flying a U-2 reconnaissance plane over Cuba, was the only casualty of this conflict.

formulate strategic concepts in keeping with the new era; but the task of the United States was made even more difficult by the Soviet Union's postwar challenge to U.S. power. The strategic revolution had been spurred by the arrival of nuclear weapons, and strategic decisions had to be made for (and in spite of) a politically uncertain future.

THE TRUMAN YEARS

At the end of World War II, the United States demobilized its armed forces and acted as though the world was indeed at peace. But in late 1946 and early 1947, the United States began responding to the challenge of Soviet thrusts in Iran, Greece, Czechoslovakia, and Berlin.

At that time, the relatively small and poorly equipped Strategic Air Command (SAC) was the United States' prime instrument for containing Communist aggression. As long as the Soviet Union had neither strategic air power nor nuclear explosives, SAC's mission was clear and simple: to deter the Soviet Union from a land invasion of Europe by threatening a retaliatory nuclear strike against the Soviet Union itself.

The Soviet atomic explosion in the fall of 1949 ended U.S. atomic monopoly and foreshadowed a revision of U.S. strategic concepts.

In response to Communist aggression in South Korea, the United States increased its military outlay and helped to organize the defense efforts of its non-Communist allies. The defense budget rose from $15 billion in 1950 to $51 billion in 1952. In addition to increasing conventional forces, these funds allowed the Strategic Air Command to grow into a full-fledged fighting force.

In 1951, to convince the Soviets that the United States would fight if Western Europe were attacked, President Truman committed U.S. ground forces to the North Atlantic Treaty Organization, which had been formed by the allies in 1949 as a mutual defense alliance. Despite its atomic advantage, the United States began to plan for a conventional defense of Western Europe; and in Korea, combined units of the U.S. Army, Navy, and Air Force, armed with conventional weapons, were fighting a World War II type of war. Although superior U.S. strategic air power was never directly employed, its effect was to limit the Korean War and to keep the Soviets out of Western Europe.

THE U.S.S.R. ENTERS THE NUCLEAR AGE

Although by 1945, Soviet prestige as a world power had attained hitherto unknown heights, the Soviets were still militarily and economically weak in comparison with the United States. The Soviet Union ended World War II with essentially one basic force, the Red Army. During the war, the role of the Soviet Air Force remained subordinate to that of the Army, and the Soviet Navy was negligible. Soviet industry had been severely damaged, and probably 20 million Russian people had perished in World War II. The Soviet leaders knew that among the great powers, the United States alone not only survived unscathed but also possessed the weapons of the future—atomic bombs. Until the Soviets achieved equal capabilities,[2] they publicly disparaged the military value of atomic weapons.

In the history of the Soviet armed forces, an institutional bias for defense has been a persistent element. A prime task of Soviet forces since the Allied intervention in Russia in 1918 has been the preservation of Communism within the U.S.S.R. Thus, before the Soviet Union obtained a nuclear capability, it developed an air defense system designed to cope with nuclear attack by U.S. long-range bombers. Hundreds of captured German experts on early-warning radar were pressed into service by Stalin; and by 1950, the Soviets deployed a warning net from the Baltic to the Pacific. The development of jet interceptors kept pace with the Soviet warning system; by 1950, the Soviets had a 2,000-aircraft interceptor force. Billions of rubles were spent on surface-to-air missiles (SAM's), which replaced antiaircraft artillery and supplemented the interceptors.

Despite a traditional defense orientation (seen today in the emphasis on both active and passive defense), neither Russian military tradition nor Soviet military doctrine ever ignored the value of taking the offensive to achieve victory. Parallel with Soviet efforts for active and passive defense and before the Soviets possessed nuclear weapons, great strides were taken to obtain long-range delivery systems. Apparently, the Soviets were embarking on a broad and varied program of their own in the field of rockets and missiles. In April, 1944, a leading specialist in nuclear weapons and long-range missiles, Major General G. I. Pokrovski, published the first Soviet article on long-range missiles.[3] In 1946, A. A. Blagonravov, who was both a military officer and an academician, was named President of the Academy of Artillery Sciences, an institute that was to play an important role in developing ICBM's and space rockets.[4] As in the case of defensive weapons, the Soviets made use of captured German technicians for developing offensive weaponry. Meanwhile, Soviet interest in nuclear weapons and missile warfare amounted to almost an obsession.[5]

In 1947, our whole budget for research and development in the intercontinental field was eliminated for reasons of economy. In 1946

---

[2] See Marshall Shulman, *Stalin's Foreign Policy Reappraised* (Cambridge: Harvard University Press, 1963), Chapter 2, "Moscow in the Spring of 1949."

[3] *Science and Technology in Contemporary War*, trans. by Raymond L. Garthoff (New York: Praeger, 1959), pp. vi–vii.

[4] U.S. Congress, Senate Committee on Aeronautical and Space Sciences, *Soviet Space Programs: Organizations, Plans, Goals, and International Implications*, 87th Cong., 2nd Sess., 1962, p. 64.

[5] S. N. Koslov, M. V. Smirnov, I. S. Boz, and P. A. Sidorov, *O sovietskoi voennoi nauke* (*On Soviet Military Science*) (Moscow: Voenizdat, 1954), p. 249.

the Soviet budget for research and development in these categories was trebled. It reconstituted its research bodies for jet engines, for swept-wing aircraft design, for nuclear explosives, for rocket propulsion. The whole basis for a shift in the balance of power, as the Soviet leaders saw it, was laid in the period at the end of the war; and beginning immediately thereafter, the Soviets turned on an intense concentration of resources in these categories in order to shorten their period of vulnerability as much as possible. The Soviets' expectation was that when these things began to bear fruit, a shift in the balance of power would result.[6]

Under Stalin, early Soviet moves toward obtaining the best that modern postwar technology had to offer were not, however, hand in hand with a basic reformulation of Soviet military doctrine. A number of retrospective Soviet accounts of the postwar development of Soviet military theory make clear that in the period before meaningful numbers of modern weapons were acquired, Soviet thinking was directed toward using new weaponry within the framework of past methods of warfare.[7] Critical nuclear-age problems such as surprise attack and the decisive initial period of a modern war bred new views that were confronting the old outlook. The lag was not unnatural; for from the first Soviet atomic test in the fall of 1949 until the Soviet acquisition of the hydrogen bomb in 1953, quantities of nuclear weapons and numbers of long-range bombers were very small.

Stalin's insistence that Soviet military thinking focus on elaborating the significance for warfare of his "permanently operating factors" was another reason for discrepancy between technology and military doctrine in his time. These "factors" dealt with stability of the rear, morale of the army, quantity and quality of divisions, armament of the army, and organizational ability of army commanders. Originally formulated in 1942, these factors of warfare were, in part, an outgrowth of Soviet experience in World War II. The subsequent emphasis given these principles represented an *ex post facto* rationalization for the kind of war conducted by the U.S.S.R. under Stalin's guidance.

. . .

THE MISSILE REVOLUTION

The so-called missile gap in the latter years of the Eisenhower Administration had been sired by questionable information, inadequate analy-

---

[6] Philip E. Mosely and Marshall Shulman, *The Changing Soviet Challenge* (Racine, Wisc.: The Johnson Foundation, 1964).

[7] Colonel I. Korotkov, "The Development of Soviet Military Theory in the Postwar Years," *Voennoi-istoricheskii zhurnal* (*Military-Historical Journal*), April, 1964, p. 43. This account is one of the most candid and critical treatments of the subject to appear in Soviet literature to date.

sis, and bad politics; and we now know that the Soviet missile force was not superior in either quantity or accuracy. The Soviets had built a large force of some 700 to 800 intermediate missiles that could strike Western Europe—a missile preponderance over NATO that still exists. They were ahead in some aspects of medium- and long-range-missile development, and in this sense, there was indeed a missile gap; but an intercontinental-missile gap never existed. The Soviets did not exploit their developmental advantage in booster thrust and did not procure large quantities of expensive, vulnerable, and inaccurate ICBM's. In view of the uncertainty of the strategic situation, President Eisenhower had placed part of SAC on airborne alert and energetically (though without fanfare) launched a crash missile-production program.

Regardless of the confusion surrounding the missile gap, Soviet development of the ICBM drastically and irrevocably altered the strategic balance—far more so than Soviet long-range bombers had. Under the pressure of growing Soviet strategic capabilities, the United States began to develop a command and control system that could survive a nuclear attack. If the command facilities of the Strategic Air Command could be destroyed by a few Soviet missiles, the President, as Commander in Chief, might not be able to communicate the "go" code to U.S. forces in case of war. Constitutionally, the decision of going to war or attacking the Soviet Union could not be left to subordinate commanders; and if the President's survival and his ability to communicate with American commanders could not be assured, there was a real possibility that under attack, the United States might never launch its retaliatory force (or what was left of it after the enemy's strike). During the later years of the Eisenhower Administration, measures were taken to provide sufficiently invulnerable command capabilities. Since then, the National Command and Control System has been further improved.

By 1960, U.S. military strategy was in a state of flux. Voices of dissent grew more strident both within and outside the Eisenhower Administration, and from this opposition developed the strategic concepts that initially guided the military program of the Kennedy Administration.[8]

THE VOCABULARY OF NUCLEAR STRATEGY

Since the period when massive retaliation was in vogue, nuclear strategy has become subtler and more complex, and the vocabulary used to describe nuclear confrontation has become a language of its own.[9] To

---

[8] See General Maxwell Taylor's criticism of the massive-retaliation strategy in his *The Uncertain Trumpet* (New York: Harper & Brothers, 1960), which had a profound effect on President Kennedy and, later, on President Johnson.

[9] One of the most articulate contributors to the Western glossary on nuclear warfare has been Herman Kahn. See Herman Kahn, *On Escalation: Scenarios and*

understand the issues and nuances of the Kennedy-McNamara strategic doctrine, one must first understand the semantics of nuclear war.

Terms describing various strategies are used to convey a general attitude toward nuclear conflict rather than to depict the complex reality of a given strategic posture or nuclear confrontation. The U.S. strategic posture has never fitted precisely into these or other descriptive molds, nor is it ever likely to for several reasons. Strategies have overlapping boundaries. Furthermore, there are always weapons around from an earlier strategic era that, for political and economic reasons are difficult to discard abruptly even though they do not fit the prevailing strategy. None of these strategies could be used in warfare with strict adherence to its presumed distinctions. The execution for example of a *finite-deterrence* (FD) strategy, which hypothetically includes only cities as targets, would also destroy military forces located in urban areas. Likewise, some damage to cities would result from a *counterforce* (CF) exchange, which, in theory, would be directed only toward enemy strategic forces. Shorthand terms, however, permit orderly distinctions between alternative force levels, targeting concepts, and even strategic intent.

Long before nuclear weapons, heavy bombers, and ballistic missiles were introduced, the Italian General, Giulio Douhet foresaw, almost prophetically, how total war could one day be waged by means of strategic bombing, with ground and naval forces playing a defensive, holding role. For many years, technology lagged behind Douhet's vision. With the development of the atomic bomb and then, and more importantly, the thermonuclear bomb, the defeat of an enemy without the need for ground combat became possible.

In the early days of the Cold War—the period of U.S. monopoly of not only the atomic bomb but also strategic air power—most U.S. political leaders assumed that the complete solution to problems of national security had been found. As long as the United States constituted an invulnerable Western base from which an aggressor could be struck a devastating blow, it was unnecessary to build up ground forces for waging long-drawn-out wars like World Wars I and II. The enemy would instead be deterred from aggressive war by the very magnitude of the inevitable retribution.

When the Soviets developed atomic and nuclear weapons, as well as intercontinental aircraft and missile systems, Western strategists realized that it might become impossible to attack the enemy's forces so effectively as to annul his ability to retaliate. The array of opposing forces might be such that neither side could afford to initiate attack against the

---

Metaphors (New York: Praeger, 1965), Appendix, "Relevant Concepts and Language for the Discussion of Escalation," pp. 275–300.

other without risking enormous damage to its own social and industrial structures.

As armies came to depend more and more on the full resources of the country, war progressively became more total. Industry became a target because troops depended on vast quantities of munitions and other implements of war. Before the airplane was developed, factories could not be directly attacked, so attempts were made to blockade the flow of raw materials or to seize areas that were producing war material. The airplane made it possible to reach over enemy defenses and attack the heartland of a nation. Thus, with the introduction of the airplane, three classes of targets emerged: enemy forces, industry, and population—the latter two comprising *value targets*. If, however, strategic bombing missions could destroy the enemy force in a matter of hours, why proceed to bomb his industries and his population? With its air force destroyed, a nation would lie helpless before an opponent. Yet, the strategists of the nuclear age only gradually perceived this theoretically simple point. Consequently, for some years, targets for nuclear war remained the same as the World War II targets. For example, the concept of bonus damage persisted for some time in strategic war planning: *bonus damage* or *collateral damage* is a result of bombing a military target so that nearby towns and industries are simultaneously destroyed. To an unprecedented degree, thermonuclear bombs made it possible to strike civilian targets in the proximity of the intended military objective; but the conditions of nuclear war made destruction of such targets both unnecessary and undesirable. For a long period of time, however, U.S. targeting doctrine remained tied to the concept of bonus damage.

Western military strategists now recognize that it is not necessary to maximize damage by extending it to nonmilitary targets. On the contrary, the more desirable objective may be to limit damage to hostile populations by a judicious combination of high-delivery accuracy and low-yield weapons. The logical use of nuclear weapons leads to a military strategy that pits armed force against armed force rather than against civilians. Yet, paradoxically, the civilian populations now play a key role as potential hostages, for in a nuclear war the fate of a civilian population is the final bargaining issue. Even though strategic military forces rather than people are the operational targets of nuclear war, the very life of a nation is still threatened. In "escalating" a limited conflict, not only military forces and supplies but also industrial and population centers could become targets.

ALTERNATIVES TO TOTAL WAR.

As the strategic nuclear capability of the Soviet Union grew, the potential disaster of a general war came to be appreciated. Belatedly, the West, seeking alternatives to total war, sought a doctrine of war that would relate nuclear arms to the values they were supposed to defend.

When the Kennedy Administration assumed power, the two most commonly advocated strategies for U.S. strategic nuclear force were finite deterrence and counterforce.

By 1960, spasm war was no longer regarded as the only possible nuclear confrontation with an adversary. Moreover, an all-out disarming attack on the enemy's strategic forces was no longer considered feasible, since, as a practical matter, it was impossible to prevent some retaliatory attack. For this reason, an attempted *disarming strike*—a strike directed at all strategic weapons to compel *unconditional surrender*—was no longer a suitable strategy for the thermonuclear era.

Both finite deterrence and counterforce provide alternatives for dealing with the basic attribute of nuclear weapons—the ability to inflict almost unlimited damage. The counterforce concept is intended to lessen nuclear damage by inducing the enemy not to strike our cities because we would not strike his. The enemy would be assured that we would hit his cities if he attacked ours; that we could reduce his offensive striking power (and hence the damage he could do) by attacking his offensive forces that had not yet been launched; that we could defeat the attack that had been launched by means of active defense measures; and that we could minimize the destructiveness of his weapons that reached target by using our fallout shelters and blast shelters. In essence, this strategy focused on the destruction of enemy offensive forces rather than cities, so that ultimately the surviving populations would be the final bargaining issue.

Finite deterrence rejects the counterforce concept that nuclear wars can be fought in a controlled fashion, that a country's industry and population might be spared, and that damage can be held to acceptable limits. The goal of finite deterrence is to make nuclear war so catastrophic as to be unthinkable, and its purpose is to deter any nuclear attack on the United States by fact of a U.S. capability to destroy the enemy's cities in retaliation. In effect, this strategy would force each opposing state to offer the other its respective population and economy as hostage. The posture makes only limited provision for active air defense; it does not seek an antimissile system; it provides for only minimal civil defense. This strategy is also called *basic deterrence,* a felicitously descriptive name that conveys the key idea; it is a strategic posture that can deter attack on only this country and cannot offer protection to U.S. allies. In other words, by making the possibility of a first strike totally incredible, it repudiates the extension of U.S. deterrent capability, or "nuclear umbrella," to the NATO countries or other allies.

SECOND-STRIKE FORCES

As the Soviet Union gained the capability of launching a nuclear attack against the U.S. mainland, it became necessary for the United States to develop a *second-strike force*—a force capable of absorbing the enemy's blow and then striking back. Confusion then arose between first-strike *strategy* and first-strike *weapons*. First-strike weapons are delivery systems that could not survive an enemy attack and hence could be used only for a first strike, that is, for attacking the enemy before he is able to land his blow. When the Soviets acquired ICBM's, the United States faced a radically altered strategic situation, one in which the possibilities of a pre-emptive attack by either side became too great for comfort. At this point, the Soviet strategic force was as vulnerable as the U.S. force, both of which were comprised of bombers located on unprotected fields and vulnerable first-generation ICBM's. The danger of accidental war was considerably heightened by the instability of a tense international situation in which either side, anxiously aware of the vulnerability of its entire force, could launch a pre-emptive attack. The need for a second-strike force was clear.

Fundamentally, second-strike forces are to some degree invulnerable. *Invulnerability* can be acquired through a variety of means: (1) *dispersal of forces* from a few sites to many sites—for example, SAC bombers were dispersed from seventeen bases to sixty-one bases; (2) acquisition of *warning systems*—for example, the Ballistic Missile Early Warning System (BMEWS) was added to the already existing Distant Early Warning (DEW) line, which served to deter bomber attacks; (3) *mobility* and *concealment*—for example, the development of Polaris missile-firing submarines; and (4) *hardening*—for example, the placing of missiles in concrete silos for protection against the effects of nuclear warheads. Bombers, like missiles, were protected by a combination of warning and dispersal (permitting the bombers to take off before the enemy warheads exploded) and mobility.

Invulnerability, though, is never absolute. It depends not only on the measures taken to protect one's own forces but also on the kind and number of offensive weapons the enemy builds. A weapons system that is highly invulnerable today, such as Polaris, may become vulnerable if a break-through—for example, in antisubmarine warfare (ASW)—should occur.

No single hardened missile site is invulnerable, but the combination of the number of missiles and the hardening of the missile sites safeguards the whole force against destruction in an initial attack. Also, the degree of protection given to each missile site may compel the enemy to employ more than one missile in attacking it; on the other hand, improved accuracy and higher-yield warheads will reduce the number of missiles required to destroy a given target. For hardened missile sites, invulnerability may be lost by 1975.

An invulnerable, hardened, fixed-site command and control system may be difficult if not impossible, to build, man, and operate because of practical limitations. Since they are complex and costly, command sites cannot be dispersed by the hundreds as can missile sites. Thus the *exchange ratio*—the cost to the enemy of destroying a military command center in relation to the cost to the defender of adding an alternative command center—would be highly favorable to the enemy. For missile sites, the exchange ratio favors the defender as long as it is more than 1:1—that is, if it takes more than one attacking missile to destroy a single defending missile. If, for example, the missile exchange ratio is 5:1, an aggressor must build five missiles for every one that the defender adds to his force. In the case of command and control sites, however, a 5:1 ratio would be highly favorable to the attacker, since the cost of building five missiles is far less than the cost of adding another command site.

A second-strike force need not be inconsistent with a first-strke strategy. Invulnerable weapons systems, which constitute a second-strike force, could be launched in a first strike; however, the invulnerability of a second-strike force may inhibit its use in a first strike. The key concept is *credibility*.[10] Any weapon can be used in a first strike, but the question is: How credible is a threat to do so? In the days when the Soviets did not have the capability to retaliate against the United States, the U.S. threat was entirely credible. Now a nuclear strike in response to Soviet aggression in Europe could lead to terrible damage to the United States. Hence the U.S. nuclear guarantee to Europe seems less credible.

Ironically, the U.S. first-strike threat remained credible as long as the United States had only a vulnerable force; for with such a vulnerability, the United States could not afford to sit out a Soviet attack on Europe. We would have had to attack to keep our own force from being destroyed on its home base. Similarly, the Soviets could not attack Europe without first attacking the United States for fear that the United States in turn would have to attack them. Mutually vulnerable systems, despite their advantages for deterrence, posed excessive dangers of war by accident or miscalculation; whereas secure second-strike forces removed the necessity for a virtually automatic U.S. nuclear strike against the Soviet Union in the event of aggression against NATO. The United States, secure in its ability to ride out a Soviet attack, would be able to assess a threatening situation. Paradoxically, as the invulnerability of the U.S. force increased, the credibility of the U.S. nuclear guarantee to NATO declined.

A first-strike threat could, however, be made by a nation possessing a credible first-strike force—a force that possesses one of the merits of a

---

10 This question was reviewed in Herman Kahn's defense of a credible first-strike strategy. By adding the term "credible" to "first strike," Kahn attempted to deal with the problem of a U.S. first-strike strategy in reaction to a Soviet attack on Europe, in a situation in which the United States was vulnerable to a missile attack. See *On Thermonuclear War* (Princeton, N.J.: Princeton University Press, 1961), pp. 27–36.

second-strike force, namely, invulnerability. The primary purpose of a credible first-strike force is not to initiate war but to warn the adversary that he cannot attack Western Europe, for example, without running an unacceptable risk of U.S. retaliation. The expectation is that, faced with the necessity of attacking the United States, the Soviets would be deterred from major aggression in Europe.

The invulnerability of a second-strike force does not rule out the threat of an enemy's first strike against it; however, the term "second-strike force" can be, and often is, understood to rule out its credibility as a first-strike strategy. The force need not be—and this is the key to many strategic disputes—merely an invulnerable one, but logically it should be incapable of striking first. This would be the case if an invulnerable missile force had low accuracy and weapon yield—too low to strike first and successfully or even to issue a credible first-strike threat.[11]

PARITY, STABILITY, AND STALEMATE

A situation in which both sides have armed themselves only with vulnerable weapons, which are therefore suitable only for a first-strike strategy, is inherently unstable and accident-prone—like a Western gun duel in which the faster draw wins. Yet, when both sides possess invulnerable offensive forces and neither can rationally contemplate an attack given the retaliatory power of the other, a *stalemate* exists. According to many experts, the objective of U.S. second-strike forces should be the achievement of stalemate by such a margin of superiority that potential enemy would realize that by attacking he would worsen his relative position rather than improve it.

In a strict sense, a condition of *parity* exists if two forces are approximately equal, although it is often asserted that parity exists even though the forces of the two great nuclear powers are quite unequal. In the latter sense, parity refers to a situation in which the party with the larger arsenal cannot afford to attack because the other side, though weaker, still is able to retaliate with a countervalue attack. Parity in the sense of equality of strategic forces is sometimes advocated as the U.S. goal in lieu of strategic superiority.

Opposing views on a strategic posture for the United States reflect a basic disagreement on the meaning of *nuclear stalemate*. According to one school of thought, nuclear stalemate renders nuclear weapons useless for any positive political purpose; consequently, their negative role—deterring nuclear attack—could just as well be played by *nuclear disarmament*. Since nuclear forces impose a burden on national economies and since nuclear war might be triggered by accident or miscalculation,

---

[11] The French *force de frappe* fits this description.

nuclear disarmament is a more rational course of action. But since unresolved political issues bar the road to total nuclear disarmament for the near future, it is proposed that *arms control* measures either lead step by step toward disarmament or take the place of disarmament. Arms control can be accomplished by numerous methods, all of which have in common the objective of either reducing the risk of nuclear war or mitigating its effects.

THE KENNEDY PHASE

New strategic concepts for nuclear weapons began to be articulated during the late 1950's, and in the spring of 1961 President Kennedy called for new U.S. strategy and tactics to meet the continuing Soviet challenge. Early in his administration, President Kennedy announced the broad outlines of his military strategy:

> The primary purpose of our arms is peace, not war—to make certain that they will never have to be used—to deter all wars, general or limited, nuclear or conventional, large or small—to convince all aggressors that any attack would be futile—to provide backing for diplomatic settlement of disputes—to insure the adequacy of our bargaining power for an end to the arms race. . . . Our military policy must be sufficiently flexible and under control to be consistent with our efforts to explore all possibilities and to take every step to lessen tensions, to obtain peaceful solutions and to secure arms limitations.[12]

President Kennedy intended to achieve a wider range of strategic options primarily by increasing U.S. general-purpose forces and by increasing the invulnerability of our bombers and missiles. Doctrinally, Kennedy pioneered the concept of a deliberate, selective, flexible, controlled response to be prepared for any type of warfare at whatever level and to force on the adversary the onus of striking the first nuclear blow. A flexible response necessitated not only conventional forces capable of meeting limited aggression but also, and most crucially, second-strike nuclear forces capable of fighting a controlled nuclear war. The Eisenhower nuclear control system had tied virtually all the U.S. strategic forces together under "one button," leaving the President with the single option of pushing or not pushing. The Kennedy-McNamara combination was designed to give the President a series of options on his "nuclear console" as well as a range of nonnuclear options, thus avoiding an "all or nothing" dilemma.

An inherent part of the selective-response doctrine was a rapid build-

---

[12] U.S. President, *Recommendations Relating to Our Defense Budget,* U.S. House Document No. 123 (Washington: Government Printing Office, 1961), p. 2. The concepts in this document were developed in the Pentagon under McNamara's aegis and were accepted *in toto* by President Kennedy.

up of conventional "below-the-threshold" forces, for without additional means to cope with limited conflicts, the new flexible strategy would be useless. A substantial increase in funds was consequently allotted for conventional armaments and forces. Concurrently, emphasis was placed on special forces for aiding nations subjected to Communist "wars of national liberation," and the number of personnel authorized for these activities was increased. Although conventional forces that are sufficient for meeting a range of contingencies are essential for Free World defense, these forces were never intended to be a substitute for a credible nuclear deterrent.

The policy developed by the Kennedy and Johnson administrations for strategic nuclear weaponry differed essentially from that of their predecessors. Rather than a missile gap, as had been touted during the 1960 Presidential campaign, the United States possessed nuclear superiority and a considerable lead in strategic delivery vehicles (primarily the manned bomber) on the day Secretary McNamara arrived in the Pentagon. Revised intelligence estimates, based on some new data, led to a changed assessment of the United States—Soviet strategic balance. Secretary McNamara nevertheless decided to increase the U.S. missile capability and to convert strategic retaliatory forces to second-strike forces, which entailed hardening the delivery systems and otherwise making the force invulnerable to an enemy first strike. To carry out these decisions, Secretary McNamara stepped up the production of first-generation Minuteman missiles and increased the number of nuclear bombers on fifteen-minute alert.

The Kennedy Administration took steps to assure civilian control over the military commanders of U.S. strategic forces. Constitutional provisions for civilian control of military forces have never been questioned; but in 1961, civilian control halted at the same point as did military control, namely, before the giving of the "go" orders. By his own authority, the SAC commander could put his force on alert and, if he concluded that an enemy attack was under way, could order his aircraft to fly to the positive control point. But without a direct order from the President (or a lawfully designated successor), he could not command his force to attack the enemy. When a Soviet surprise missile attack on the United States became a possibility, appropriate civilian authorities had to be endowed with means for surviving the initial attack and for commanding a controlled nuclear war; thus, a *national control system* became the capstone of the U.S. military posture.

· · ·

THE SEARCH FOR OPTIONS

In 1961, Secretary of Defense McNamara, a major force in reorienting U.S. nuclear strategy in the years just before and after the Cuban missile crisis, began to seek new doctrine with which to govern U.S. strategic nuclear forces. Massive retaliation with its specter of spasm war was categorically rejected, but some consideration was given to the concept of finite deterrence, which was developed in the late 1950's. According to that strategy, anything beyond a capability to destroy a certain portion of enemy society would be considered "overkill" and would therefore be undesirable and unnecessary. Finite deterrence, which could not be used as a credible threat against the U.S.S.R., would provide minimal military support for U.S. allies and would have little usefulness in meeting crises. In the event of a Soviet attack, the United States, incapable of waging a controlled attack on the enemy's forces, would have no alternative except countervalue retaliation and thus would undoubtedly assure a similar retaliatory response from the enemy.

The United States sought an incentive for the Soviets to avoid targeting our cities in the event of nuclear war. A two-pronged concept of nuclear strategic war gradually emerged that would provide for: (1) retaliation against a large-scale Soviet attack, if American cities were avoided, using systems and command and control that would permit a deliberate, selective, and controlled option; and (2) a carefully controlled, discriminating response against a small-scale, ambiguous, or accidental attack. Furthermore, the use of conventional forces for NATO's initial defense was stressed repeatedly by U.S. authorities.

These innovations of the Kennedy and Johnson administrations signified a major reappraisal of the role of strategic weapons in supporting U.S. foreign policy—a role subsequently centering around two major alternative strategies. Counterforce reached its high point by mid-1962; the other strategy, *damage limiting*, gradually evolved after the Cuban missile crisis. The difference between these and other possible strategies is one of intent, degree, and emphasis. Counterforce hews to the classic military doctrine that the proper objective of military action is the destruction of the enemy's armed forces. It may be defined as the neutralization of hostile military actions against the United States through: (1) direct attack against enemy strategic bases and missiles sites; (2) in-flight destruction of launched hostile aircraft, missiles, and space vehicles; and (3) the blocking, interdiction, or destruction of hostile surface or undersea forces.

Secretary McNamara expressed the reasons for his initial attraction to the counterforce concept in a speech at Ann Arbor, Michigan, in June, 1962:[13]

By building into our forces a flexible capability, we at least eliminate the prospect that we could strike back in only one way, namely,

---

[13] Robert S. McNamara, commencement speech, University of Michigan, Ann Arbor, Michigan, June 16, 1962, cited in Department of Defense news release No. 980–62.

against the entire Soviet target system including their cities. Such a prospect would give the Soviet Union no incentive to withhold attack against our cities in a first strike.

He explicitly espoused the counterforce option:

> If, despite all our efforts, nuclear war should occur, our best hope lies in conducting a centrally controlled campaign against all of the enemy's vital nuclear capabilities, while retaining reserve forces, all centrally controlled.

Yet, McNamara gave two substantially different reasons for seeking a counterforce targeting strategy. On the one hand, he stated:

> The United States has come to the conclusion that to the extent feasible, basic military strategy in a possible nuclear war should be approached in much the same way that the more conventional military operations have been regarded in the past. That is to say, principal military objectives in the event of a nuclear war stemming from a major attack on the Alliance should be the destruction of the enemy's military forces, not of his civilian population.

On the other hand, he declared:

> [It is] possible for us to retain . . . reserve striking power to destroy an enemy society if driven to it. In other words, we are giving a possible opponent the strongest imaginable incentive to refrain from striking our own cities.

By introducing his thought, the Secretary suggested that the threat of a massive retaliatory attack could be used to deter an enemy's nuclear attack on U.S. cities—an objective quite different from the goal of a pure counterforce strategy: to disarm.

A U.S. counterforce posture also offered a powerful argument against proliferating national nuclear forces, particularly the French force. In returning to the more traditional view of warfare, in which battle is waged against enemy armed forces rather than population, McNamara cited the fact that small national nuclear forces could not wage such a war against a major power like the Soviet Union. Moreover, the existence of small national nuclear forces within the Western Alliance would make it impossible for the United States to wage a controlled counterforce campaign in the event of Soviet aggression against Europe.

It subsequently became clear that strategy could take various forms either of counterforce or of the strategy known as damage limiting. Objections were quickly raised against the nascent counterforce doctrine. For one thing, a counterforce attack could not be easily distinguished from a countervalue attack if very high-yield warheads were used. This problem would be aggravated if some counterforce targets were located in urban complexes, as many Soviet targets were believed to be. At the time of the Cuban missile crisis, the United States fortuitously possessed superior nuclear delivery systems capable of both countervalue and counterforce targeting. Most of these forces were available because of the weapons decisions previously made by the Eisenhower Administration, and President Kennedy exploited these inherited capabilities to bring about the Soviet missile withdrawal.

18. DETERRENCE AND ITS CAPABILITY REQUIREMENTS

J. David Singer

IT SHOULD BE immediately evident that a strategy of deterrence is but a particular form of influencing by discouragement; more specifically it is a strategy of threatened punishment or threatened denial, and proceeds from the premise that the anticipated but conditional destruction or denial of a player's values will discourage certain forms of behavior.[1] Conversely, it is assumed that encouragement can be offered by promised rewards, or even by the absence of punishment.

. . .

CAPABILITY REQUIREMENTS: DESTRUCTION LEVELS[2]

There would appear to be four major elements influencing the deterrent effectiveness of destruction levels: nuclear stockpiles available to the

From *Deterrence, Arms Control and Disarmament* by J. David Singer (Columbus: 1962) pp. 21–22; 30–38. Reprinted by permission of the author and the Ohio State University Press. Footnotes have been renumbered to appear in consecutive order.

J. DAVID SINGER (1925–   ) Professor of Political Science and Research Political Scientist, Mental Health Research Institute, University of Michigan. His other books include *Quantitative International Politics*, (New York: Free Press, 1968), editor; *Human Behavior and International Politics*, (Chicago: Rand McNally, 1965) editor; *Financing International Organization; The United Nations Budget Process*, (The Hague: M. Nijhoff, 1961).

[1] One of the few analyses of strategy to explicitly reflect any awareness of this range of alternate influence techniques is Glenn H. Snyder, *Deterrence by Denial Punishment* (Princeton, N.J.: Center of International Studies, 1958). See also the same author's *Deterrence and Defense* (Princeton, N.J.: Princeton University Press, 1961), the most serious *empirical* effort to date to apply game theory to military strategy.

[2] This analysis of capability requirements is heavily indebted to the germinal studies by William W. Kaufmann, *The Requirements of Deterrence* (Princeton, N. J.: Center of International Studies, 1954); and Morton A. Kaplan, "The Calculus of Nuclear Deterrence," *World Politics*, XI (October, 1958), 20–43.

deterrer (potential retaliator), destruction levels acceptable to the deteree (potential attacker), and the passive and active defenses available to the attacker as he braces for the retaliatory blow. Let us discuss each in turn.

Retaliator's Nuclear Stockpiles

Perhaps the most dramatic and obvious factor is the total destructive force available to the deterrer. We shall start with this seemingly overwhelming quantity and then go on to examine the elements that begin to erode its impressiveness. As of the early 1960's, it is estimated that in nuclear bombs and warheads, ranging in size from low kiloton to multimegaton, the United States (with or without Britain and France) possesses a stockpile whose total yield could thoroughly obliterate, several times over, all relevant and vulnerable targets in the Soviet Union or its allies.[3] Such a destruction capability has often been referred to as "overkill," but as we shall see in a moment, this may not always be an accurate characterization.

Attacker's Level of Acceptable Destruction

The second variable in our destruction-level equation is the degree of destructiveness which the potential aggressor is willing to accept in exchange for whatever destruction he is able to carry out.[4] This quantity is, of course, a function of more than just an educated guess as to how many casualties could be suffered without the total collapse of his nation. If he has a large population, much of which is not economically or militarily essential, he may be willing to accept personnel losses up to perhaps 75 per cent. Or if he has only just begun an industrialization program and he offers very few such targets, he may well find obliteration of his transport facilities a tolerable price to pay for certain types of "gain." Another

---

[3] The warheads used against Hiroshima and Nagasaki were each of about twenty kilotons yield: that is, they were equivalent in destructiveness to the effect of 20,000 tons of conventional high explosive. The term "megaton" is used to express millions of tons of high-explosive equivalent. A detailed analysis of the destructive power of a one-megaton warhead may be found in the testimony of Frank Shelton in *Joint Committee on Atomic Energy* (Special Subcommittee on Radiation), *Hearings* . . . , June 22, 1959, pp. 15–42. See also Samuel Glasstone (ed.), *The Effects of Nuclear Weapons* (Washington, D.C.: Atomic Energy Commission, 1957). One recent estimate made by Congressman Alger of the House Ways and Means Committee, sets the total stockpile at about 35,000 megatons, almost half of which is available for immediate retaliation (*New York Times,* November 11, 1961).

[4] As I apologized earlier for the use of obvious anthropomorphizations, I must here express the hope that the reader will not object to my personification of states. The use or *he* saves many words and eliminates many distracting qualifications. It is understood throughout that the writer has in mind a rather complex decision-making apparatus at or near the apex of the various national governments.

factor in the acceptability of retaliatory destruction is the nature of the national and elite value systems. In societies long-accustomed to recurrent decimation by disease, hunger, revolution, guerrilla war, or government terrorism, wholesale human slaughter may not be viewed by either the public or the elite as morally undesirable.[5] Some societies may see periodic population losses as inherent in the cosmic order, and some may even see them as a desirable way of eliminating the "unfit" or the "surplus." A final factor in the acceptability calculus is the political system. If it is of a highly authoritarian and centralized nature and the population is well controlled, the elites may in effect compel even a non-revolutionary or well-industrialized nation to accept astronomical human and material casualties. Thus it seems clear that tolerable destruction is a function of many factors, and that the acceptable level will range widely from one nation to another or within one nation over a period of time.[6]

ATTACKER'S PASSIVE DEFENSE

A third variable in the physical-capability equation revolves about the aggressor's capacity to reduce his losses by passive means. If he institutes a comprehensive civil defense, evacuation, and underground production program, the total damage a given nuclear megatonnage will do is appreciably diminished. There is, of course, considerable debate as to how effective such programs can be in reducing human and material losses. It has been argued that the warning times will soon be so short as to preclude evacuation of cities or retreat into shelters between the moment of warning and the moment of warhead impact, even for the side which strikes first. Roughly speaking, the intercontinental ballistic missile can travel between most Soviet launch sites and American targets (or vice versa) in slightly under thirty minutes. It is unlikely that the radar tracking stations now in operation would detect these missiles until they were about ten minutes from their destination, and the logistic problems of moving even a few hundred people out of a building and into a near-by shelter in so short a time seem insuperable to most critics of civil defense. Moreover, the expense and effort of building shelters capable of with-

---

[5] Raising the level of destruction that one finds tolerable produces one result that has been largely ignored: As side A's elite gradually comes to accent (publicly) an increased estimated loss, side B must, if he sees himself as the deterrer, raise his destructive capability so as to represent a sufficiently menacing threat of reprisal to deter A.

[6] For some optimistic calculations concerning the amount of destruction that the United States could withstand and still "continue" as a society, see Herman Kahn, *On Thermonuclear War* (Princeton, N.J.: Princeton University Press, 1960), pp. 74–94. One of my criticisms of this study is that it contributes to the rising level of acceptable destruction mentioned in the previous note.

standing the percussion impact of multimegaton air or ground bursts are usually seen as prohibitive on both sides. In addition, there is the question of remaining alive within a shelter for the weeks that must elapse before it is comparatively safe to emerge. Moreover, the wholesale moving of industry underground or of dispersing it is seen to be so costly and dysfunctional that it is rejected by many. Despite these criticisms, however, there is no doubt that a passive defense system against nuclear attack would reduce somewhat the number of non-military casualties and the amount of destruction sustained.[7]

ATTACKER'S ACTIVE DEFENSE

The fourth major variable involved in our calculation of the destructive levels needed to deter is that of active defense. The aggressor may reduce the impact of the retaliatory blow he receives not only by protecting or dispersing his people and plants (as well as his military installations) but also by actually throwing up an umbrella which reduces the quality of megatonnage which reaches him. At this writing, with both sides still relying heavily (but to a rapidly declining degree) upon manned bombers to deliver the parcels of nuclear retribution, the number of such bombers shot down en route or over their targets by fighter planes or antiaircraft fire could reduce significantly the destruction the aggressor must accept. Even at extreme altitudes and speeds (50,000 feet, and 1,200 miles per hour for the B-58 medium jet bomber), the problem of interception is not great, and most estimates anticipate that the Soviet Union could probably destroy approximately one-half of any retaliatory bomber fleet directed toward its industrial or population centers, and perhaps more if the attack was concentrated on Soviet military installations.[8] The survival figure is, of course, a function of such elements as the number and type of bombers employed, their flight pattern, and the target's dispersal and the readiness of the defenders. Furthermore, such technological elements as our use of the stand-off air-to-ground missile,[9] the

---

[7] For a discussion of the requirements of a relatively effective civil defense program under present technological conditions, see Kahn, *op. cit.*, appendixes iii and iv. This program is based on Kahn *et al.*, "Some Specific Suggestions for Obtaining Early Non-Military Defense Capabilities and Initiating Long-Range Programs" (Santa Monica: Rand Corporation Research Memorandum RM–2206–RC). . . .

[8] Air Force Chief of Staff Thomas D. White argues, on the other hand, that as (and if) the B-70 long-range bomber becomes operational, "it makes all of his . . . air defenses against the air-breathing threat obsolete." House Committee on Appropriations, *Department of Defense Appropriations for 1961, Hearings* . . . , Part 2, p. 313.

[9] One reason for our retention of the "obsolete" B-52 is that it would be used to carry the 500-mile Hound Dog air-breathing missiles to within the range of its targets, fire them, and then turn away—perhaps without ever encountering anti-

speed, maneuverability, altitude, and defensive fire power of our planes, the rapidity with which the Soviets or Chinese ground-to-air missiles, their progress with small and compact nuclear warheads, and the effectiveness of their detection and fire-control tracking and plotting equipment, will all affect the attrition rate.

This description might lead one to conclude that the attacker-turned-defender enjoys such an edge over the retaliatory aircraft that he may (as long as the deterrer is without a massive missile force) be in a position to strike with little fear of retribution. This, however, is not the case.[10] Even if only a fraction of the retaliatory fleet were to penetrate the aggressor's defenses, the amount of destruction power it would bring is still many times greater than all the destruction rendered by the saturation bombing raids made by both sides during World War II. Stated more graphically: A single bomber can easily deliver a ten-megaton warhead whose surface blast could decimate almost everything above ground within a range of seven miles from ground zero. The point is, then, that no matter how effective his defense is, until it approaches 100 per cent, the original attacker must accept tremendously high levels of retributive destruction.

Now all of the above refers to the capability of manned bombers, launched from ground bases in North America, Europe, Africa, and Asia, and from aircraft carriers in the Atlantic, the Pacific, the Mediterranean, and the Indian Ocean; it also assumes that the victim of our hypothetical attack is the United States, and although this makes the entire discussion more credible, it should be borne in mind that a model that would be more realistic from the Soviet point of view might well have the Russians in the role of retaliator.

Let us now modify some of these assumptions, particularly those concerning the nature of the delivery system by which the victim of the postulated attack delivers his retaliatory payload. As this is being written, both the Soviets and ourselves are deeply immersed in making

---

aircraft-missile or conventional fire. Furthermore, because its radar reflection is, to quote General White, "almost zero . . . as against the aircraft," it is much less likely to be intercepted. A successor, or supplement, to Hound Dog will be the 1,000-mile mach 5 (roughly five times the speed of sound, which is 600 miles per hour at sea level) Sky Bolt ballistic missile.

[10] One might also wonder, if this were the case, how the attacker—even with the advantage of surprise—could expect to do much damage in the first place. For some detailed quantitative calculations of force-damage levels in a nuclear exchange, using pure and mixed systems respectively, see John B. Phelps, Raymond Foye, and Daniel Howland, *Some Calculations on Counterforce Strategies in a General Nuclear War,* and Raymond Foye and John B. Phelps, *Counterforce Calculations: Attack and Retaliation with Mixed Weapons Systems* (Columbus, O.: Mershon National Security Program, 1959).

the great transition from manned bombers to ballistic missiles; and among the results of this transition will be a dramatic increase in the difficulties of active defense. Later in this chapter we shall discuss the problem of dealing with these delivery systems prior to their launching, but our concern here is with the problem of a defense against them after they have been launched, and, more particularly, after they have begun their downward path toward the attacker's territory. Very briefly, there is at present no operational and effective anti-ICBM system available to either side. Because of inadequate warning time, their great speed, and the height from which they descend, ballistic missiles present a nearly insoluble problem to the defender in the early and middle 1960's. It is perfectly safe to assume that by the end of the decade some important developments in antimissile warfare will have appeared, but for the present there is no defense against them. Thus, if the attacker is unable to destroy them on the ground during his initial strike, devastating retribution is nearly inevitable.

What are some of the techniques by which the calculating attacker may in time hope to achieve some immunity from the price he must now be prepared to pay? The most promising one, technologically, is the antimissile missile. Both sides are working feverishly on such a device, and we, at least, have had some experimental successes with a very crude version of this defensive weapon.[11] This type of missile is launched from near the expected impact area on an upward trajectory which is, hopefully, the reciprocal of the attacking (or retaliating, in this case) missile's path. If the defender can acquire adequate warning time, launch his antimissile weapon soon enough, and plot the incoming path accurately, there is a fair chance that the two will collide at an altitude and distance great enough to spare the defender any (or most) of the fallout, heat, and blast from the resulting detonation. One refinement might be to equip the antimissile missile with a proximity or ground-controlled warhead which could, even if a perfect hit is impossible, go off close enough to the incoming weapon to produce the desired detonation. Better still, it might be so equipped that it could produce, not a detonation, but a fission of fusion process rapid enough to destroy the missile, yet slow enough to eliminate any serious fallout;[12] the closer the incoming warhead is to the

---

[11] According to the Soviet Defense Minister, Rodion Y. Malinovsky, the Russians, too, are progressing in this field. His statement to the Twenty-second Party Congress was: "I must report to you especially that the problem of destroying missiles in flight has been successfully solved." (*New York Times,* October 24, 1961.)

[12] This is an application of the neutron-flux principle. See the brief comments in Arnold Wolfers *et al., Developments in Military Technology and Their Impact on U. S. Strategy and Foreign Policy,* prepared for the Senate Foreign Relations Committee (Washington, D. C., 1959), pp. 68–69. See also Eugene Sanger, "The Photon

target, the more imperative it is to avoid detonation. Another modification might be the installation of a self-regulated homing or ground-controlled guidance system, so that the interceptor, even if launched on an erroneous course, might be directed toward the missile as the distance between the two diminishes.

However, before one assumes that it is merely a matter of a year or so before the "bugs" are removed from these interceptor systems and the antimissile weapon is an effective reality, two points must be emphasized. First, the technical difficulties are great, and the most optimistic estimate of the time required for a U.S.-owned system to become operational is five to ten years, at least in regard to the anti-ICBM.[13] Second, and of greater long-range significance, is the fact that no matter how effective the defense against a single descending missile may become, it is nearly impossible to design a defending system capable of intercepting all the missiles in a barrage. And, as in the case of a manned bomber attack, only a few have to get through with megaton payloads in order to inflict incredible damage.[14]

A closely related problem for the calculating attacker is to determine the sort of antimissile defense pattern to install in order to diminish the weight of the retaliatory blow. If he establishes an "area" defense, he may achieve greater flexibility in assigning interceptors to incoming missiles, but certain points in that area will inevitably be hit by a concentrated barrage. On the other hand, if he chooses a "point" defense, he may be able to intercept all or most of a first wave aimed at a given point (cities, air bases, missile sites, factories, rail terminals, harbors, manpower concentrations, staging sites, etc.) but at the expense of leaving a great many other points undefended; that is, unless he has unlimited

---

Rocket and the Weapon Beam," *New Scientist,* VI (September 10, 1959), 383–84. There is also the possibility that the final arming switches—which usually close while in flight—could be paralyzed, preventing any nuclear detonation at all. Also worth noting are the Laser and Haser projects, directed toward the development of so powerful and concentrated a beam of light energy that it could destroy or deflect on incoming ICBM. Equally incredible, but not to be dismissed, is the technique of throwing up a cloud of fine, hard particles which would roughen the nose-cone, generating enough additional head to cause the missile to burn up on re-entering the atmosphere. According to a writer in the Polish weekly *Polityka,* the U.S.S.R. may U.S.S.R. may be working on the latter technique (*New York Times,* February 18, 1962).

[13] Although no significant numbers are yet operational, the United States has had some success with the Nike-Hercules, Nike-Zeus, Honest John, and Corporal anti-IRBM's at altitudes up to 10,000 feet and closing speeds up to mach 7.

[14] To cope with any sort of saturation attack (or counterattack) requires that data be processed quickly and that target information be relayed rapidly from detection equipment to active-defense equipment. The SAGE system developed by the United States is only the first step toward solving the problem involved.

resources and ample time to convert these resources into a multitude of point defense or interceptor systems. (Naturally, the choice of a defense or interceptor system will depend heavily on his estimate of the adversary's doctrine. If he perceives it to be a counter-force one, he will seek to protect his missile sites, air bases, and military installations; if a counter-city or counter-economy doctrine, then these latter points will more likely be ringed with antimissile systems.) [15]

These then, are the four major variables which determine whether the deterrer-turned-retaliator has the warhead and bomb capability to inflict sufficient damage on the attacker so that the latter is convinced that the price of attack is too high: the retaliator's stockpile, the attacker's level of acceptable damage, the attacker's passive defense, and the attacker's active defense. As suggested at the beginning of this section, however, this set of variables still provides only half of the picture. Not only must the would-be deterrer have an adequate level of destructive force available to reach the attacker's territory, but he must also have the delivery systems with which to carry these destructive payloads from his own bases to the territory of the potential enemy.

---

[15] A "counter-force" doctrine implies that the retaliator will strike at the attacker's missile sites, airfields, and other military installations. A "counter-city" or "counter-economy" doctrine implies that he will strike at the population or industrial centers of the attacker. The alert reader may question the sense of retaliating against sites whose missiles and planes may have already departed; this and other problems raised by a counter-force doctrine will be explored in the next chapter. If one or both sides sees himself as the retaliator rather than as the aggressor, the picture is further complicated; this, too, will be covered subsequently.

19. THE SHIFTING EQUATION OF NUCLEAR DEFENSE

Richard J. Whalen

O N HIS DESK in the Kremlin, Nikita Khrushchev used to keep a laser-scarred piece of steel, a reminder to himself and visitors of the potential for Soviet superiority in advanced military technology. He often dreamed aloud of the terrible wonders of the future, as when he said in 1960: "The armament which is being created and which is to be found in the folders of the scientists and designers is truly unbelievable." In his bold Cuban missile adventure, Khrushchev impatiently ran ahead of his strategic weaponry, and the retreat from the brink led to his overthrow. But the promise symbolized by the prized piece of steel also fascinates his dour, methodical successors. Under their more efficient management, Soviet scientists, engineers, and technicians are turning ideas into hardware at an accelerating rate. The current swift buildup of Soviet strategic offensive and defensive systems reflects Moscow's evident determination to forge ahead in a new technological arms race.

The U.S., preoccupied with Vietnam and anxious to preserve the hope of détente, has made a studied effort so far not to over-react. Addressing the Russians early this year, President Johnson spoke of the common "duty" to slow down the race and warned that a renewed arms spiral "would impose on our peoples, and on all mankind, an additional waste of resources with no gain in security to either side." He proposed negotiations to halt the Soviet deployment of antiballistic-missile (ABM) defenses, receiving in return Soviet Premier Aleksei Kosygin's unenthusiastic consent "to discuss the problem of averting a new arms race, both in offensive and defensive weapons." While negotiations have not even begun, Soviet ICBM and antiballistic-missile deployments are continuing.

The one-sidedness of concern is increasingly apparent and puts U.S. leaders under rising pressure. Secretary of Defense Robert McNamara, overriding for the second time the unanimous recommendation of the Joint Chiefs of Staff, has further deferred the crucial decision on whether

From *Fortune* (June 1, 1967) 85–87; 175–178; 183. Reprinted by permission of the author and the publisher.

RICHARD J. WHALEN (1936–   ) Writer-in-residence, Center for Strategic Studies, Georgetown University. Author of *A City Destroying Itself*, (New York: W. Morrow, 1965); *The Founding Father*, (New York: New American Library, 1964).

to begin production of the U.S.'s own Nike-X antiballistic-missile system. McNamara argued his position at length before Congress last January, and later circulated a confidential memorandum among his staff, the military, and defense contractors, urging the widest possibe dissemination of the message contained in his Congressional Posture Statement.

"The foundation of our security," McNamara declared in his statement, "is the deterrence of a Soviet nuclear attack. We believe such an attack can be prevented if it is understood by the Soviets that we possess strategic nuclear forces so powerful as to be capable of absorbing a Soviet first strike and surviving with sufficient strength to impose unacceptable damage on them." McNamara conceded that the kind and amount of damage the U.S. would have to be able to inflict to provide this deterrent "cannot be answered precisely," but he ventured the "reasonable" assumption that the destruction of one-fifth to one-fourth of the Soviet Union's population and one-half to two-thirds of its industrial capacity "would certainly represent intolerable punishment." The U.S. ability to inflict such punishment, regardless of Soviet defensive countermeasures, is the key to the deterrence philosophy of "Assured Destruction."

But McNamara went further in his remarkable document, which may deserve a place among the most important state papers of our time. The Secretary gave the Russians cost-effectiveness advice on their own best defense interests. "If our assumption that the Soviets are also striving to achieve an Assured Destruction capability is correct, and I am convinced that it is," said McNamara, "then in all probability all we would accomplish by deploying ABM systems against one another would be to increase greatly our respective defense expenditures, without any gain in real security for either side." This line of reasoning was clearly intended to reinforce the President's plea to the Soviet leaders for negotiations on arms limitation. But it fell on some ears in Washington, particularly those of well-informed members of Congress, as disturbing evidence of the amount of faith that U.S. defense policy was putting into a hypothetical equation under rapidly shifting circumstances.

THE UNEASY ENVIRONMENT OF SURPRISE

The experts who read the intelligence reports on Soviet activity are aware, as the public is not, that the enormous U.S. advantage in weaponry and technology of the 1950's and early 1960's is steadily being narrowed. Not only has the Soviet Union run harder; the U.S., wishing to avoid leading an arms race, has also deliberately limited production and deferred deployment of major new offensive and defensive weapon systems. The Russians, in effect, have been told: "We won't build it if you won't." The appealing notion has prevailed that weapon technology stands on a "plateau." As former White House scientific adviser

Jerome B. Wiesner declared in 1963, the "scientific military revolution" has "stabilized."

The limited nuclear test-ban treaty, which ushered in the present period of search for a détente, has been widely interpreted as a joint U.S.-Soviet admission that further arms competition was pointless. A "stalemate psychology" has spread, which takes for granted and even discounts the military superiority the U.S. has enjoyed throughout the trials of the cold war. Reductions have been made in "soft" first-strike weapons such as bombers, and the U.S. missile deterrent force, after rising rapidly throughout the early Sixties, is now leveling off. It consists of 1,000 Minutemen, 54 Titan II's (to be phased out in 1970), 656 missiles aboard 41 Polaris submarines (about half of which are on station at any given moment), and 680 strategic bombers, which will be cut back to 465 in 1972. From a peak of $11.2 billion in fiscal 1962, U.S. outlays for strategic forces declined to a low of $6.8 billion in fiscal 1966 and stood at $7.1 billion in fiscal 1967.

The relatively stable level of R. and D. spending over this period conceals a significant shift in emphasis, away from innovation and toward refinement of existing weapon systems. The U.S. has chosen not to maintain the initiative, while the U.S.S.R. has visibly bent every effort toward seizing it.

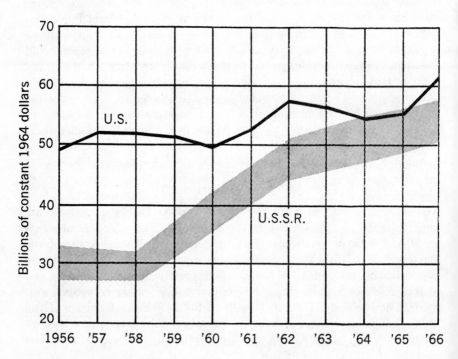

Now a new era is opening in which the U.S. and the U.S.S.R. can be expected to possess increasingly comparable military technology. Far from being an omen of "stability," that elusive nirvana of the thermonuclear age, the environment of near parity promises to be extremely unpredictable and therefore marked by much apprehension. The U.S., to be sure, has carefully hedged against foreseeable Soviet capabilities; over the past few year, for example, more than $1 billion has been spent to prepare advanced warheads and sophisticated penetration aids to defeat the newly installed Soviet ABM defenses. However, this kind of hedging leaves the U.S. vulnerable to surprise in the form of an unforeseen or successfully concealed weapon advance on the Soviet side.

In a congressional hearing more than a year ago, General John P. McConnell, Air Force Chief of Staff, warned: "We know . . . the Soviets today are engaged in a massive program of research and development in military weapons systems of all types. In a program of such great scope, the possibility of technological surprises or dramatic breakthroughs cannot be overlooked, particularly when such surprises could ease the margin of strategic superiority which we currently enjoy." In spite of improved U.S. satellite surveillance, the Russians have simultaneously improved their skill in the arts of concealment, and they are now capable of deploying weapons that the West has never seen tested.

Close observers of the unfolding Soviet R. and D. enterprise worry because the adversary has a dynamic view of military capability and strategy, as contrasted with the static conception of technology and strategy implicit in the U.S. posture. Deterrence depends not only on existing forces; it also depends on the adversary's state of mind. The very rationality of Soviet leaders, which the U.S. relies upon to restrain attack, could find in advancing technology the incentive to consider the gamble of a first strike. A veteran analyst of the nuclear balance observes: "Never has fundamental strategy been so sensitive to a few—a *very* few—technical parameters."

The intentions of the uncommunicative Soviet leaders are a mystery, perhaps even to themselves, but it requires a minimum of theorizing to grasp the point of what they are currently doing. They are altering the existing balance of strategic forces that favors the U.S., and they are doing it at a pace that startles the most knowledgeable American students of Soviet military capability. Just two years ago McNamara said the Soviet leaders "have decided that they have lost the quantitative race, and they are not seeking to engage us in that contest." Now Pentagon authorities are no longer sure. In contrast to the earlier false alarms of the bomber and missile "gaps," based on projections of potential that went unfulfilled, the present rate of confirmed Soviet hardware deployment is forcing upward revisions of Russia's potential.

"Now We See the Threat"

Soviet production of intercontinental missiles has surged ahead, from an annual rate of 30 to 40 in 1962 to 110 to 120 last year, and this rate appears to be accelerating. Since Khrushchev backed down in the missile confrontation of the fall of 1962—and the date is relevant because of the long lead times involved—the operational Soviet ICBM force based on land and sea has grown from fewer than 75 to an officially estimated 470 (as of October, 1966) and a likely current figure of close to 600. By mid-1968, according to informed estimates, land- and sea-based Soviet ICBM's could leap to between 800 and 900, or more than half the U.S. force. And there is no reason to assume the Soviets will halt there.

The rapid growth in numbers, however, is less significant than the *qualitative* improvements, apparent and suspected, between the first and second generation of Soviet ICBM's. Two new missiles—the SS-9 and the SS-11—have been identified as entering the operational inventory in dispersed and hardened silos. The SS-9 is a large three-stage missile propelled by storable liquid fuel, which is not necessarily a sign of inferiority when compared to solid-fueled U.S. missiles. Storable liquid and demi-liquid fuels provide greater thrust than solids. The SS-9 is roughly comparable in size to the U.S. solid-fuel Titan II, but it carries a warhead twice as heavy, estimated at over twenty megatons. The SS-11 is a small single-stage missile, propelled by either solid or storable liquid fuel. It resembles the early Minuteman in range and ability to carry a similar one-megaton warhead.

The Russians, well ahead of the buildup schedule assumed until recently by American defense planners, are fast approaching a critical point in the development of their ICBM force. If their missiles are equipped with the advanced warheads and the more accurate guidance systems known to be within their technical ability, their force could quickly become a real threat to the hardened Minuteman missiles that are the backbone of the U.S. deterrent. In designing the U.S. deterrent forces, Pentagon planners have weighed the alternatives open to an aggressor: a strike against our cities; a "counterforce" strike against our retaliatory missile sites; or a combination strike aimed at some key population centers and some portion of the land-based ICBM's. The U.S. has sought to deny an aggressor the "counterforce" option by building and deploying a thousand Minutemen, presumably a large enough number of targets to be safely beyond the productive and economic capacity of the Russians. This estimate of their capabilities has now been rudely shaken.

"As recently as a year ago," says a high-ranking officer in the

Pentagon, "we didn't think the Soviets could get a counterforce capability. Now we see the threat." It could materialize by the mid-1970's.

THE "NEW MATH" OF MIRV

The U.S. itself has discovered how to use a single ICBM launcher to carry several individually propelled warheads, which can be guided accurately to different targets hundreds of miles apart. The multiple individually guided reentry vehicle, known as MIRV, could revolutionize nuclear strategy if the Soviet capability should match our own.

The strong side of Secretary McNamara's philosophy of deterrence is apparent in the improvement of U.S. striking power. The entire front end of new missiles is being redesigned. The land-based Minuteman III, scheduled to replace the Minuteman I, and the submarine-launched Poseidon, the successor of the Polaris A-3, will be equipped with MIRV, decoys, and penetration aids. When they are in place within the next three years, McNamara declares that these formidable missiles will surely be capable of penetrating the Soviet anti-missile defenses currently being deployed. And so they doubtless will—*if* they are ever fired in anger.

By preparing to meet a changing offensive threat *and* defensive capability with an improved offense only, however, McNamara displays the weak side of his strategic philosophy. The development of MIRV in missiles means that a new way of calculating striking power is needed, and therefore a new way of appraising the U.S. deterrent. The long-vaunted U.S. lead in ICBM boosters, currently estimated at three to one, no longer provides the reassurance it once did, and Pentagon officials now quietly downgrade such rough numerical comparisons. As McNamara himself said in his Posture Statement, "It is not the number of missiles which is important, but rather the character of the payloads they carry; the missile is simply the delivery vehicle."

He did *not* add that, with all the additional payload weight resulting from multiple warheads and penetration aids, the thrust of the delivery vehicle also becomes a critical factor—and in the case of the U.S. at the present, a sharply limiting factor. Except for the relative handful of Titan II's, which are scheduled to be phased out, the lift capacity of U.S. missiles averages about one megaton for each booster. Soviet boosters, in contrast, can carry an average warhead load of more than seven megatons. If these missiles are, in addition, capable of being fitted with multiple warheads, the U.S. booster advantage of three to one over the Russians could quickly become a fiction. The new SS-9 could be fitted, at least in theory, with ten or more individually guided warheads. In one fashion or another, MIRV introduces a new kind of missile math—a relatively inexpensive means for the U.S.S.R. swiftly to achieve parity or better with the U.S. in terms of deliverable megatonnage. They are known to have *tested* the components of a multiple-warhead system. Therefore, U.S. watchers on the outside, peering through the cracks in a closed society, are anxiously anticipating an operational capability because of the short lead time involved. As little as eighteen months could separate our discovery of a MIRV development program and the operational deployment of Soviet missiles carrying multiple warheads. Those who would know whether such a development program has been detected are quite properly silent.

THE IMPLICIT AND EXPLICIT THREAT

The memory of the nonexistent ICBM "gap" debated during the 1960 presidential campaign may prompt a certain skepticism toward the potential new danger implicit in a Soviet resort to multiple warheads. This time, however, the Soviet missiles that might be fitted with such warheads *already* exist; the numbers *are* growing rapidly; and the new missile math suggests the advantages of their going the route of MIRV if they can. The kind of targeting problem that the U.S. poses for Soviet war planners provides the logic for traveling that route. The major U.S. cities, in which population and industry are concentrated, have long been the presumed targets of a relatively few Soviet ICBM's fitted with high-yield warheads. So long as an ICBM could deliver only one warhead to one target, the small Soviet missile force was believed to be checkmated by the sheer number of U.S. Minuteman and Titan missiles in their dispersed and hardened silos. But the problem of multiple targets could be brought temptingly near "solution," however Soviet planners may define it, through the use of multiple warheads on their growing missile force.

Until last year MIRV was considered so secret that even members of the congressional defense committees had not heard about it in executive session. Reports of multiple-warhead contracts were published in the technical press late last year, and discussion began in earnest last November when McNamara announced the accelerated program to produce and deploy the Poseidon in the Polaris fleet. Oddly enough, within four months after MIRV came into public view, it was abruptly covered up again by the Secretary's order. No longer a secret, it has become an unword scarcely ever uttered in the Pentagon. "It's ridiculous, this trying to stuff the genie back in the bottle," comments a dissenting official. "Apparently we're concerned that the Soviets might be alerted to their own capability. It's part of trying not to be provocative."

THE MOVE TO ABM

The mounting uncertainties facing decision makers in the White House and the Pentagon center on the Soviet construction of extensive new ABM defenses. Reconnaissance satellites and monitoring radars alerted the Joint Chiefs of Staff to this activity in 1965. In January, 1966, Mc-Namara secretly briefed the members of the congressional defense committees, and last November he publicly disclosed that the U.S. had "considerable evidence" of the Soviet ABM deployments without being specific about their nature and location. However, he declared: "I think it is important that we assume [the Soviet ABM system] is effective, and, of course, that will be the assumption on which we base the development and deployment of our own ICBM's." This prudent assumption leaves unanswered the urgent question: *how* effective are the Soviet defenses?

The U.S. possesses a good deal of intelligence data, but it does not support definitive judgments. If experience counts for anything, as it surely does in this esoteric realm of weaponry, the U.S.S.R.'s capabilities should be taken very seriously. It is known that the Russians, heeding their doctrinal imperative of balance between offensive and defensive military forces, began concurrent development of missiles and anti-missiles as early as 1948. By the early 1960's they had built what was apparently the prototype of a defense system aimed against medium- and intermediate-range missiles, and they deployed it at Leningrad. U.S. intelligence rates this system capable of handling as many as five targets simultaneously, but it was regarded as ineffective against ICBM's. In a rare secret session of the Senate in April, 1963, Senator Strom Thurmond, of South Carolina, a member of the Armed Services Committee, warned that Russia had an operational ABM system, and he urged that the U.S. proceed at once with the Nike-Zeus, then ready to go into production. Soon afterward, the U.S. turned to the improved Nike-X system (see "Countdown for Nike-X," FORTUNE, November, 1965).

The Zeus ABM system, which grew out of the Nike-Hercules anti-aircraft defenses deployed in 1958, had a limited range and "kill radius," and its effectiveness against a large-scale attack was doubtful. The successor Nike-X (the X stood for "unknown") exploited major breakthroughs in radar technology, which greatly increased the number of targets the system could handle; and it also supplemented the Zeus missile with a new high-acceleration interceptor, Sprint, which was designed to provide last-ditch defense against ICBM's that got past Zeus. Even with the improvements, however, the Nike-X remained a "point" defense intended to protect a single target by engaging incoming ICBM's in a "bullet-to-bullet" duel in the atmosphere. An "area defense," which would protect several targets at once, would be much more effective, but this kind of ABM requires a long-range missile equipped with a large warhead that can intercept ICBM's above the atmosphere. In 1965 the U.S. began development of such a missile, named the Spartan, which will replace Zeus in the Nike-X system. But by this time the Russians had abandoned the Leningrad ABM and were well along in the development of more advanced concepts.

Incomplete and often contradictory information currently available on the Soviet antiballistic-missile defenses has caused some divergence of opinion within the U.S. intelligence community. There is no question that an "area defense" system has been deployed in the vicinity of Moscow. The command center, containing radar scanners and computers, is a multi-level structure built entirely underground. A large phased-array radar is located northwest of the city, and it is integrated with small tracking radars at several points.

THE TALLINN ABM SYSTEM

A quite different type of installation has appeared in an arc extending several hundred miles along the northwestern border of the country, and this is the focus of disagreement within the U.S. Known as the "Tallinn line" after the Estonian city where one of the defensive sites has been detected, this deployment has been subject to various interpretations: as an advanced anti-aircraft system, another type of ABM, or perhaps a combination of both. Existing Soviet SAM-2's and SAM-3's would seem to provide ample defense against aircraft, particularly in view of the declining U.S. reliance on bombers. Moreover, the line sits athwart the principal "threat corridor" of land-based missiles launched over the North Pole from the U.S. It is the unanimous judgment of the Joint Chiefs of Staff that the Tallinn line is an anti-missile system, but McNamara so far remains publicly unpersuaded.

In addition to the Moscow and Tallinn deployments, informed sources report a great deal of activity elsewhere in the Soviet Union at existing anti-aircraft installations and new sites as well. Some of these sites are in the South and may represent the early stages of defenses directed against Polaris missiles launched from U.S. submarines on station in the Mediterranean. Other sites spotted east of the Ural Mountains face Red China. The small tracking radars along the Tallinn line apparently are tied together with the phased-array radar at Moscow. As evidence of such links accumulates, the likely scope of Soviet ABM plans expands, confirming McNamara's statement to Congress last January: ". . . we must, for the time being, plan our forces on the assumption that they will have deployed some sort of an ABM system around their major cities by the early 1970's." Not only the cities, of course, would be defended, but also military installations, particularly hardened offensive missile silos within a vast territory.

MEETING MIRV IN MID-COURSE

Debate continues inside the Pentagon concerning the characteristics of the antiballistic missile (or missiles) that the Russians are deploying. In

November, 1963, a missile was shown in a Moscow parade for which the Russians claimed an ABM capability. Western officials, who code-named the missile Griffon, were skeptical, and inclined toward the belief that it was primarily intended for interception of supersonic aircraft and their air-to-surface missiles; but they did not rule out the possibility that it had been developed originally to counter the medium-range Thor, Jupiter, and Polaris A-1. Griffon was not credited with an exoatmospheric (above the atmosphere) range, though some observers, reflecting now on the pace of subsequent Soviet advances, believe it should have been. An advanced model of Griffon, in fact, may be deployed on the Tallinn line; or the ABM missile there may be one the West has never seen.

The missile used in the Moscow ABM system was first shown a year later than Griffon, in 1964, when tractors dragged it through Red Square coyly concealed in its protective canister. Given the unglamorous code name Galosh, it is believed to be a solid-fueled, long-range interceptor carrying a high-yield warhead. Estimates of Galosh's range cluster around a few hundred miles, comparable to the Spartan missile the U.S. is now developing. But a minority opinion maintains it could have a much longer range, perhaps as much as 2,000 miles.

This minority view begins with the fact that the best anti-ballistic-missile system the U.S. has been able to devise uses *two* missiles and several types of radar. It is suggested that Galosh, the only missile deployed at Moscow, may combine the long range of Spartan with the high acceleration of Sprint, the companion short-range interceptor of the Nike-X system. If this is the case, or if the missile used in the Tallinn line has such a performance capability, the Soviet Union could engage incoming ICBM's far away from their territory and above the atmosphere where fallout would not be a problem—in mid-course of the missiles' trajectory, before multiple warheads and penetration aids could separate. An effective mid-course ABM would provide a formidable defense against multiple warheads.

An experienced defense scientist cautions against overdrawing Soviet capabilities from scant information ("generalizing from the heel of the dinosaur"), but he adds: "If you're honest, you can't say flatly that the Soviets *can't* do what some people say they are doing. We just don't know."

WEAPONRY IN THE VOID

Easily the most important area of uncertain knowledge, and one where secrets and doubts are kept most carefully guarded, concerns the effects of high-yield nuclear explosions in the thin upper atmosphere and above. This is the environment in which our own and Soviet ABM missiles would function. Questions about the precise "kill mechanism" of an ABM have aroused intense speculation and prompted official reassurance,

with the result that the known facts often get lost in a welter of alarming
or comforting words. . . .

. . .

The effects of nuclear weapons vary principally with their design and
yield and the altitude at which they are exploded. (Other factors, including the time of day a weapon is exploded, also play a significant role.)
The predominant effects of weapons designed to be detonated *in* the
atmosphere are blast and heat; weapons for use *above* the atmosphere are
designed to maximize the release of energy in the form of radiation, the
most useful effect in this environment. Witnesses who testified during the
test-ban hearings generally assumed that the U.S. held a marked lead in
the technology of smaller-yield (one megaton and below) weapons while
the Russians were well ahead in the very-high-yield (twenty megaton
and above) range.

The advantage in the intermediate range (one to twenty megatons)
was open to debate, but there was no arguing the fact that the Russians,
during their massive 1961–62 test series that broke the *de facto* moratorium, had exploded many more weapons than the U.S. in this intermediate
range both in the atmosphere and above, providing them with the opportunity to learn more and apply their knowledge. The Soviet tests clearly
had been planned years in advance. Among their seventy-one shots were
proof tests, weapon-system tests, effects tests, and tests with missiles and
radar. The Russians, obviously extending their ABM technology, on two
occasions during the tests launched an ICBM, intercepted it with a
nuclear blast, and then fired a *second* missile, presumably to determine
whether its warhead was affected by the radiation resulting from the
prior explosion. They also studied the blackout effects of the blasts on
their radar.

Thoughts About an Umbrella

Such sophisticated Soviet tests could not have been matched at the
time by the U.S. In the summer of 1958 the U.S. had detonated its first
high-altitude explosions, code-named "Teak" and "Orange." These
megaton-range explosions produced astonishing results that clearly her-
alded the dawn of a new era in weapon effects. Communication links in
the Central Pacific were blacked out for several hours, and satellites
detected charged particles trapped in the earth's magnetic field. In the
Argus series that quickly followed, the U.S. exploded three kiloton bursts,
which disrupted shortwave radio and radar and again produced man-
made belts of charged particles. The creation of these belts suggested, at
least in theory, the possibility of a transient "shield" or "umbrella"
ABM defense, provided the particles could be created in sufficient density. However, U.S. scientists concluded that the belts formed by the
Argus shots were too weak to injure a warhead passing through them at

five miles per second. Even so, the U.S. at least discovered that the obvious ABM problems of early warning, discrimination, and precision tracking could be greatly compounded by the mysterious effects of high-altitude nuclear explosions.

Following the Soviet tests, the U.S. staged a hastily prepared and politically restricted series in 1962–63, which provided valuable data but also disclosed great gaps in our scientific knowledge. Dr. Edward Teller, testifying on the test-ban treaty, revealed that the U.S. had not even completed theoretical studies of some of the high-yield effects the Russians had actually tested. Impressed by recurrent descriptions of the "void" in U.S. nuclear technology, the Senate Preparedness Subcommittee concluded that the treaty "will affect adversely the future quality of this Nation's arms, and . . . will result in serious, and perhaps formidable, military and technical disadvantages."

With the signing of the treaty banning atmospheric testing, the U.S. put its ingenuity to work underground and discovered that more could be learned there than its experts had believed. Under a top-priority program, the Atomic Energy Commission has been staging low-yield, directional explosions in deep, instrument-crammed tunnels from which the air has been pumped to simulate as nearly as possible the vacuum of space. But the apprehensions brought to light almost four years ago in the test-ban hearings have scarcely been buried. At bottom, the present controversy over the Soviet ABM capability revolves around whether these half-forgotten fears of technological surprise are now being realized.

Recent uninformed speculation has suggested the possibility that the Russians, by exploding very-high-yield weapons above the atmosphere at the proper altitude and latitude, might be able to create dense belts of charged particles and so establish a "shield" type of ABM defense. U.S. scientists, extrapolating from data provided by tests of much-smaller-yield explosions, are reported to have erred by a factor of 1,000 in estimating the number of such particles that would be caused by a 100-megaton blast. The AEC isn't saying what its latest calculations have disclosed, but a high-ranking AEC official emphatically declares: "Right now, we don't see how the effects of any radiation belt could be made to persist." An impressive body of scientific opinion, within and outside the government, says there is no technical foundation for theorizing about what a Pentagon R. and D. official calls the "ping," or residual umbrella defense. Before the man-made radiation belts could achieve a particle density lethal to warheads the earth's magnetic field would prove, too weak to support them, and the umbrella would "leak."

THE ANTI-MISSILE THAT GOES "ZAPP!"

The improbability of a "shield" form of defense does not rule out other possible defense using radiation effects. Quite the contrary; the

U.S. intends to use such effects in the improved Nike-X system now under development. The Spartan missile carrying a warhead of more than one megaton will rely upon what is believed to be the most efficient anti-missile defense above the atmosphere—the so-called "zapp effect," that is, the tremendous surge of thermal or "hot" Xrays produced by a high-yield explosion. As Dr. Foster has explained to the Senate Armed Services Committee: "Nuclear explosives have a very small surface area to them . . . When they release [their] energy, they get very, very hot. A small surface that has to release enormous energies in a very short time cannot do so without getting so hot that it radiates its energy away. This radiation [is] . . . of such a temperature that it is in the Xray region."

As much as 75 percent of the total energy of the detonated ABM warhead would escape in the form of such Xrays and flash over thousands of miles in the near-vacuum of space. Within the much smaller "kill radius," which would vary with the yield and design of the warhead and the altitude at which it was exploded, the thermal Xrays would deposit their immense energy within any unshielded object, such as a missile warhead, causing its components to explode internally. An ABM system using the Xray effect can provide an "area defense" covering thousands of square miles with relatively few installations. Moreover, the requirements for guidance accuracy are greatly reduced, a factor worth bearing in mind when the Soviet radars are described as somewhat "crude."

The U.S. takes the Xray threat from Soviet ABM defenses seriously enough to be engaged in costly modification of missiles whose components are vulnerable. For example, the fine gold wires (which readily absorb X-rays) are being replaced in the guidance computer circuitry of the Minuteman II, and the change is being incorporated into the design of Poseidon and Minuteman III. Because reflective coatings used to protect a missile nose cone from the heat of re-entry are ineffective against thermal Xrays, new hardening techniques and shielding materials are being sought. The test ban makes it impossible to expose such materials to actual thermal Xrays and underground explosions are no substitute, so experimenters are using newly created electron beams of comparable energy—beams capable of depositing energies inside a test material a thousand times greater than the pulse from the most powerful production laser.

U.S. missiles have been modified more than once to counteract an unforeseen or newly arising hazard. During the test-ban hearings, many military officers, nuclear scientists, and informed Senators dared not give publicly a major reason for their opposition to the treaty. They feared that the Russians, through their high-yield testing, had discovered a kind of "ultimate ABM," and might be able to use nuclear-weapon effects to turn much of the U.S. missile force into a Maginot Line. An offensive first strike would simultaneously achieve a defensive objective, not only destroying American cities with blast and heat, but also creating electromagnetic pulse (EMP) effects extending well beyond the radius of destruction that might deactivate the electronic systems of missiles in their silos. The U.S. has since revised the electrical circuits in the Minuteman silos, and has modified and shielded missiles, warheads, computers, and guidance systems to protect them against electromagnetic pulse. These counter-measures, of course, can be only as effective as our grasp of such phenomena.

GROWING DOUBTS, BRAVE CERTAINTIES

Last fall, an etxraordinary study known as "Strat-X" (for "Strategic Exercise") was launched by Secretary McNamara's order to lay out the full range of alternatives for improving the posture of U.S. offensive forces through the mid-1970's. Strat-X will evaluate offensive missile and warhead designs in terms of different sea and land basing options, and it will weigh the resulting force "mixes" against various levels of threat from the Soviet Union and Red China. In this study the Nike-X is being considered only for the defense of U.S. offensive missile forces—not cities. This shift of emphasis is striking because up to this point the whole debate about Nike-X has concentrated on its use in city defense. This new turn in the thinking of key officials is a clear indication of the changing Soviet threat. A preliminary report will go to the Secretary in a few weeks and a final report is due in September. Little has been said about this highly secret study, and an official in the Office of Defense Research and Engineering tersely summarizes the objective of Strat-X: "more survivable payload." Another high defense official, concerned about appearances, confides: "From the outside, it may look as though we're not sure of the deterrent. That's not so. We *are* sure."

The determined air of confidence in the upper reaches of the Pentagon does credit to earnest men performing difficult tasks. What worries informed observers on the outside is the apparent assumption that the U.S. can safely confine itself to reacting within familiar parameters to a changing threat. The perils of losing the initiative are coming plainly into view. In a recent speech Dr. Harold Agnew, the forty-six-year-old head of the weapon division at the AEC's Los Alamos Scientific Laboratory, said the "apparent drift in national policy on the concept of balance of power and stability is resulting in a stifling of innovation." Because U.S. scientists are authorized to build or consider only those systems that respond to a clearly defined threat, "We are continually in danger of coming up with answers to threats which have changed." The prevailing official attitude of certainty may not take account of a steadily widening range of uncertainty.

The Ultimate Unbalancing Factor

It is Secretary McNamara's firmly held conviction that the possession of secure "second-strike" (retaliatory) missile forces by both the U.S. and the Soviet Union creates a stable condition of mutual deterrence. As he told a British television interviewer earlier this year, ". . . technically it's a relationship that's very difficult for either of us to move out of unless the other simply fails to act in a rational fashion." By deploying antiballistic-missile defenses, the Russians, according to McNamara's logic, are behaving irrationally. The U.S. has reacted by making preparations to upgrade its offensive missile forces to the point where the effect of the Soviet defenses will be negated and the prospect of "Assured Destruction" by a U.S. second strike will be maintained. However, the hoped-for maintenance of stability depends not only on the U.S.'s estimate of the situation, but also on the Soviet Union's, and the Russians are clearly moved by their own judgments and not McNamara's. Their belief that they have upset the U.S. deterrent would be, as McNamara himself has declared, "the ultimate unbalancing factor."

In the radically altered strategic circumstances that may lie just ahead, the Russians could begin to doubt the U.S.'s capacity and willingness to inflict unacceptable damage upon them. As General Earle G. Wheeler, Chairman of the Joint Chiefs of Staff, testified earlier this year: "Should the Soviets come to believe that their ballistic-missile defense, coupled with a nuclear attack on the United States, would limit damage to the Soviet Union to a level acceptable to them, *whatever that level is* [italics FORTUNE's], our forces would no longer deter, and the first principle of our security policy is gone."

It should always be remembered that the vast U.S. deterrent force exists solely to influence Soviet behavior. If it ever must be used, deterrence has failed and catastrophe looms. The threat of its use was a rational instrument of national policy during the days of overwhelming U.S. preponderance under Eisenhower and Dulles, and even as recently as the Kennedy Administration's eyeball-to-eyeball confrontation with Khrushchev. Now, however, such a U.S. threat made in the face of the Soviet offensive buildup would amount to an irrational summons to mutual suicide. The Russians soon may be able to use *their* deterrent to inhibit the U.S. and gain for themselves greater freedom of maneuver. Short of an all-out Soviet attack, it is difficult to imagine a provocation sufficiently extreme to warrant U.S. resort to the means of assured self-destruction.

Though the emerging second-strike capability on both sides may satisfy the definition of "stability" favored by McNamara and the Pentagon's defense intellectuals, this symmetry of opposing offensive forces is upset by the Soviet commitment to ABM defenses. Add to this the possible first-strike, counterforce use of the proliferating Soviet ICBM's and "stability" vanishes. Though offensive capabilities may match up neatly, intentions and therefore uncertainties do not. The deterrent equation is in danger of becoming unbalanced by the one-sided shift of uncertainty to the U.S. side.

U.S. behavior is already being influenced by the Soviet deterrent. The likely failure of the diplomatic attempt to talk the Russians out of their "worthless" ABM defenses has forced the U.S. into offsetting offensive steps involving major spending—e.g., the $3.3-billion accelerated development and deployment of Poseidon. And the anticipated Soviet counterforce capability is shifting all serious discussion of deploying Nike-X—at least within McNamara's sphere—from defense of cities to defense of "super-hardened" Minuteman silos.

WOULD THE PRESIDENT PUSH THE BUTTON?

If present trends are allowed to continue and U.S.-Soviet forces grow more asymmetrical, the situation by the mid-1970's could become menacing. An ABM defense lends itself superbly to bluffing and blackmail. The mere existence of Soviet defenses would exert psychological influence on both sides. It is easy to imagine a suddenly belligerent Soviet attitude toward Western Europe. Would the undefended U.S. react strongly if the defended U.S.S.R. appeared willing to risk war? It is possible to imagine a threat aimed directly at the U.S. itself, perhaps even the execution of the threat by the obliteration of a selected city. Would the President choose automatically to avenge the limited number of dead Americans by ordering a response certain to end civilized life in this country? Soviet planners, as they "war game" with the forces of the 1970's, surely ask themselves such questions.

The U.S. must soon recognize that a gradual but almost certainly irreversible change is occurring in the nature of deterrence. The Assured Destruction concept, founded on the superiority of the offense in modern warfare, has been challenged by technology and its application to defense. The technology of missile defense is now advancing more rapidly than the technology of offense. The relative costs and effectiveness of ballistic-missile defense are measured within the Pentagon through the "cost-exchange ratio." A few years ago, the high cost and ineffectiveness of defense were officially expressed in a cost-exchange ratio of between 10:1 and 100:1—that is, every $100 spent on defense could be offset by spending from $1 to $10 on increased offense. Now, however, by Secretary McNamara's own reckoning, the ratio is between 4:1 and 1:1, or parity. Of course, such numerical comparisons take no account of the relative burdens imposed on the U.S. and Soviet economies by higher arms spending. If the technological trend continues over the next decade, defense could gain a margin of superiority.

The improving prospects for defense are welcomed by the Russians, as their respected military commentator, Major General Nikolai Talensky, has written: "The creation of an effective anti-missile missile system enables the state to make its defenses dependent chiefly on its own capabilities, not only on mutual deterrence, that is, on the good will of the other side." More is involved here than a Soviet state of mind that Secretary McNamara dismisses as "an absolute religious fanaticism on the subject of defense." Another Soviet military strategist has emphasized the balanced nature of the emerging Soviet offensive-defensive deterrent: "It must be remembered that victory in war is determined not merely by the character of weapons but by the *relationships of forces* of the combatant sides."

In future psycho-political conflict, which uses weapons as manipulative symbols, the decisive advantage could lie with the side that possesses defenses. Even though these may be ineffective, the undefended side cannot determine this without exposing itself to mortal risk. A situation in which *both* sides had defenses would balance uncertainties and might well produce greater stability than the previous state of anxious nakedness.

The case for a prompt U.S. commitment to a limited deployment of Nike-X is compelling. Though Secretary McNamara argues that an anti-ballistic-missile defense would not reduce American casualties "in any meaningful sense," a Nike-X system might save thirty to fifty million lives and as General Wheeler testified, this would be "meaningful, we believe, in every sense." There is little time to act if the President in the mid-1970's, whoever he may be, is to have available a full range of policy alternatives. Clearly the effect of the present policy is to foreclose options for the future President.

From the moment of a decision to proceed, five to seven years would be required to deploy Nike-X around twenty-five major cities and key defense installations. Lieutenant General Austin Betts, Chief of R. and D. for the Army, who has overseen the development of Nike-X, believes the "optimum" moment has arrived for a decision to begin production. Further delay could mean the breakup of contractor teams and the onset of obsolescence in important components.

THE SYSTEM THAT'S READY

An argument can be made that it is better to postpone deployment of Nike-X if further R. and D. could produce a more advanced ABM—and it probably can. But Nike-X is the only defense system that can be deployed by the mid-1970's. Secretary McNamara's projected cost of $40 billion for a full-scale deployment of Nike-X includes such "damage limiting" measures as interceptor aircraft and shelters. However, this forbidding figure would be spent over ten years. Senator Russell describes it as "a sort of congressional deterrent." Beyond the question of how many billions of dollars are involved lies the uncertainty about the performance of Nike-X systems in a nuclear environment. These questions cannot be resolved entirely in the laboratory. A decision to go ahead might stir demands for a resumption of nuclear testing, which would surely arouse a world outcry.

But every objection to the limited deployment of Nike-X can be met with soundly based apprehensions about the grave risks of *not* having at least a measure of defense in the next decade. A light attack ("thin") defense has been estimated to cost perhaps $4 billion and could be modified or superseded by new technology. Such a defense would serve several purposes: it would at once restore strategic balance and reassure the Russians that the U.S. is not obsessed with the offense and tempted to strike first; it would cope with the accidental firing of a missile; it would counter the threat expected from Red China until well into the late 1970's; and it could help check the recent estrangement from our European and Asian allies by enhancing the credibility of our promise to defend them. Should the Soviet threat become more extreme, NATO might be rebuilt around a sharing of defensive nuclear weapons.

Perhaps most significant of all, the deployment of a limited Nike-X defense system, combined with the vigorous pursuit of an improved ABM, would signal the Soviet Union that the U.S. has not, after all, misunderstood the dynamic force of technology. The American will to lead the technological race and to maintain superiority is the most enduring deterrent.

20. LIMITED WAR

Morton H. Halperin

WHEN THE UNITED STATES and the Soviet Union have clashed on local military battlefields, they have used far less than all of their military power. They have exercised what Bernard Brodie* has called "a deliberate hobbling of a tremendous power that is already mobilized and that must in any case be maintained at a very high pitch of effectiveness for the sake only of inducing the enemy to hobble himself." On a number of occasions in the postwar period the United States and the Soviet Union have clashed directly or by proxy in local areas and have employed force or the threat of force. In Cuba in 1962, in Laos and Vietnam throughout the postwar period, in the Taiwan Straits in 1955 and 1958, in Korea in 1950–1953, in China in 1946–1949, in Lebanon in 1958, in Greece in 1946–1949, and in Berlin in 1948 and in 1958–1962, force or the threat of force has been used in local areas. Each of these was a "local war" (or potential local war), that is, a war in which the United States and the Soviet Union saw themselves on opposing sides but in which the homelands of the two major powers did not come under attack.

Not every war in the postwar period has been a "local war." The Arab-Israeli War of 1948 was one of the largest postwar incidents of violence in which the Soviet Union and the United States never lined up on opposite sides. In other cases Soviet-American opposition has played only a small role in the conflict. In the Suez crisis of 1956, for example, it was only when the Soviet Union made missile threats against Britain and France, and the United States made counterthreats against the Soviet Union, that the crisis became a potential local war. The Congo crisis of the early 1960's, on the whole, has not involved any East-West clash except for the short period when the United States was supporting

---

From *Limited War in the Nuclear Age* by Morton H. Halperin (New York: 1965) pp. 1–15. Reprinted by permission of the author and John Wiley & Sons, Inc.

MORTON H. HALPERIN (1938–   ) Special Assistant to Assistant Secretary of Defense, International Security Affairs, U.S. Department of Defense; Assistant Professor of Government, Harvard University. His other books include *Sino-Soviet Relations and Arms Control,* (Cambridge: Massachusetts Institute of Technology Press, 1967; *China and Nuclear Proliferation,* (Chicago: University of Chicago Center for Policy Study, 1966); Limited W *Strategy and Arms Control,* (New York: Twentieth Century Fund, 1961), co-author.

* Bernard Brodie is a Senior Staff Member of the Rand Corporation and a lecturer at the University of California. His is the author of *Escalation and the Nuclear Options,* (Princeton: Princeton University Press, 1966) and *A Guide to Naval Strategy* (5th edition), (New York: Praeger, 1965). [Editor's Note.]

Kasavubu and the Soviet Union was backing Lumumba. Similarly the Sino-Indian border dispute for a long time was not a "local war" but became one in November 1962 when the United States began to supply military aid to the Indians.

. . .

Because the United States and the Soviet Union have a capability to destroy very large parts of each other's homelands, they share an interest in restraining their mutual destruction in the event of war. It is sometimes argued that this condition makes war obsolete in the sense that we will never have another major war. Demonstrating the necessity for a condition, however, does not demonstrate its possibility, not to say its probability. Even for a number of years prior to the atomic age, it has not been in the interest of a major power to go to war in most situations. Though the development of thermonuclear weapons and intercontinental missiles makes the disutility of warfare even clearer, it by no means eliminates the possibility of war. If war does come the major powers have shared and will continue to share an interest in trying to limit the use of force to something short of the all-out use of their military power in an effort to destroy each other. The existence of thermonuclear weapons and the lack of any mechanism for guaranteeing the absence of war makes it necessary to take seriously the problem of how war, once it erupts, can be kept limited.

The Sino-Soviet threat to the United States makes it even more imperative that the United States develop an understanding of and an ability to engage in limited war. The Sino-Soviet bloc has demonstrated an understanding of the techniques of various forms of local warfare (including guerrilla warfare) as well as a willingness to exploit the use and the threat of force to advance its international objectives. The experience of the postwar period suggests that the United States will continue to be faced with the local use of violence by the Soviet Union, China, and other Communist states and indigenous Communist forces.

Both major powers have shown a willingness to use force and the threat of force when they have felt it necessary to secure vital objectives. In engaging in the local use of force, either directly or by supporting indigenous groups, the major powers have been concerned with avoiding "explosion"—the sudden transformation of a local war into a central war by the unleashing of strategic nuclear forces. In fighting a local war the major powers have been and will be trying to prevent an explosion, but they will also be making a series of decisions about when and how to expand, contract, or conclude a local military encounter. During a local war both sides will be continually assessing the likelihood of an explosion and the question of whether or not they ought to unleash their strategic forces. They will also be assessing the likelihood and desirability of "expansion"—a gradual increase in the level of military force employed.

These two processes, "explosion" and "expansion," are frequently discussed together as "escalation." However it is important to keep the two processes separate. The considerations that go into the decision to begin a central war would be very different from the considerations that have gone and will go into decisions to expand a local war. These latter decisions will be influenced by a number of factors, including the foreign-policy objectives of the two sides, their estimate of the risk of central war, their images of the role of force, and their domestic political objectives. Each of these factors will be discussed to show how it influences the decisions of the major powers during a local war.

FOREIGN-POLICY OBJECTIVES

The United States and the Soviet Union will have three levels of foreign-policy objectives that will influence their conduct in a local war: basic foreign-policy objectives, political-effects objectives, and battlefield objectives. The desire to avoid central war, which may be viewed as an additional foreign-policy objective, is discussed in the following section.

The basic foreign-policy objectives of the two sides provide the framework in which decisions about the use of particular tools, including local violence, are made. One basic objective of the Soviet Union is to expand the area of Communist control and to reduce Western influence throughout the world. In the long run the Soviet leaders may envision the total Communization of the world. To what extent this long-run objective influences Soviet policy is a matter of much dispute, but there seems to be little doubt of the Soviet leaders' desire to increase Russian influence and decrease Western influence throughout the world. The United States, on the other hand, whatever hopes its leaders may have for an ultimate transformation of Communist society, is committed to seeking to stop the growth of the area under the control of Communist regimes. The Soviet Union, has an incentive to use as much force as is necessary to accomplish this objective, and the United States has an incentive to use whatever amount of force is sufficient to hold the area being attacked. Other pressures, however, will lead the major powers to temper their military efforts to expand their area of influence or to prevent the expansion of the influence of the other major power by force. Within these constraints the leaders of the Soviet Union and the United States will be guided by the political effect they hope to gain by supporting the use of force.

POLITICAL-EFFECTS OBJECTIVES

When the major powers participate in a local war it is because of the expected political effects of doing so and not because of the direct pay-off from battlefield success. Neither the United States nor the Soviet Union, for example, has any interest in the small Quemoy and Matsu islands off the coast of China. Nor is the precise parallel that divides North Korea from South Korea something that in itself is worth fighting a war over. It is rather the political consequences of losing or gaining territory that are the major concern of the two sides in committing their forces, their matériel, or their prestige in a local war.

Perhaps the most important political-effects objective with which each side has been and will be concerned in a local war is the message which its conduct will give to its main enemies. The estimates which the leaders of the United States and the Soviet Union have about each other's willingness to use force or the threat of force to secure objectives will be influenced by the conduct of the major powers at any time at which they clash on a local battlefield. In deciding, for example, to prevent the Soviets from establishing a missile base in Cuba, the United States was at least partly motivated by the feeling that it was important to demonstrate to Soviet Premier Nikita Khrushchev that the United States was prepared to use force and risk a nuclear war in order to secure its objectives. The United States acted to convince Khrushchev that the Kennedy Administration was not too "liberal" to fight when it felt its rights were threatened.

Another major political-effects objective in a local war is to demonstrate, to other countries in the area, which way the tide is running. The manner in which the United States responds to Communist aggression in Indochina, for example, affects the orientation of Thailand, the Philippines, and other Asian nations. Our willingness to support the Chinese Nationalist Government in the Taiwan Straits has been seen by at least some of our Asian allies as a test of our willingness to support them under pressure. In the same sense the Korean War may be seen partly as a fight over the orientation of Japan.

Though the ramifications of the outcome of a local war are likely to be felt most keenly in the immediate geographic area of the battle, the implications may also be world-wide. If, for example, the Russians have been restraining the Chinese in the Taiwan Straits for fear of active American intervention, they are likely to be more ready to approve of a Chinese military move if the Western position has collapsed in Berlin. Alternatively, Chinese Communist success in the Taiwan Straits might well embolden the Russians in Central Europe. Soviet success in establishing a missile base in Cuba might have led America's NATO allies to believe that the United States would not defend Berlin.

Even when the battlefield itself may have some intrinsic value, as in the case of Berlin, the political-effects objectives of the two sides will still be more important. It has been clear to at least some Western leaders, since the renewed Soviet effort to change the status of Berlin dating from 1958, that the real Russian objective concerned Germany, the NATO alliance, and the consolidation of Soviet control in Eastern Europe. If the United States uses force over Berlin it will be clearly fighting to maintain the Western orientation of Germany and the cohesion of the NATO alliance as well as to defend the freedom of the West Berliners.

The United States is interested in defending an abstract principle of international conduct—that international boundaries cannot be changed by the use of force. This was a major consideration in dealing with the 1958 Chinese Communist attempt to seize Quemoy. Although the American government may at times have been willing to cede the offshore islands, it has not been prepared to give them up if this would weaken the principle of no change of boundaries by the use of force. In some situations even when there is no clear violation of international law the United States wants to demonstrate its willingness to commit military forces and matériel, to "act tough" when necessary to defend its allies. In some situations, as in the case of covert aggression in South Vietnam, for example, the United States has had to act to secure this objective in the face of less clear-cut violations of international law. From the Sino-Soviet point of view the aim is to convince nations that the West is not prepared to defend them against either overt or covert aggression and that the wave of the future is international Communism.

These political-effects objectives of the two sides produce pressures to intervene in local-war situations and to expand the level of military effort. However there are other political-effects objectives which tend to work in the other direction.

In contrast to a period of central war when attention will be focused almost exclusively on political and military implications of the "battlefield" encounter and its effects, during a local war the attention of policy makers on both sides will be divided between the particular local encounter and other aspects of the international political struggle. There will continue to be other points of contact and dispute between the two sides. Some of these may be other local wars or situations of potential local war, in which the political-effects objectives will be those tending toward expansion, but at other points of contact one or both sides may be trying to come to accommodation. Each side will be conscious of the possible impact of a local war on its efforts to reach accommodation in other geographic areas or on other problems. In 1954, for example, the Sino-Soviet bloc was about to launch a peace offensive which would have been embarrassed by the continuation or expansion of the war in Indochina. Similarly in 1958 when East and West were beginning to clash over Berlin, they were at the same time attempting to negotiate a treaty to ban nuclear tests. The successful conclusion of these negotiations would have been highly unlikely in the event of armed conflict on the European continent.

Another major restraint on the fighting of a local war will be the reluctance of the major powers to commit resources that may be required to deal with other areas of potential violence or to deter central war. In committing troops to Lebanon in 1958, for example, the United States was faced with the fact that it was thereby reducing its ability to deal with possible violence in the Taiwan Straits; and in 1962 American moves in Southeast Asia must have been restrained by the consciousness of the need to maintain an ability to deter or fight on the European continent. With both sides aware of the possibility of simultaneous or future clashes in other geographic areas, neither will be disposed to commit resources to one local conflict at the risk of dangerously exposing itself at other points. The degree to which this consideration restrains local war depends, of course, on the magnitude of the military action and on the size of the local-war forces of the two sides.

Although the desire to convince other allies that the United States is prepared to defend them produces pressures to use force sufficient to defend the local areas, this objective also generates pressures to use only that force which does not destroy the area being defended. For example, if the United States defended Taiwan by engaging in a nuclear duel with the Sino-Soviet bloc and if this led to the total destruction of Taiwan, it would hardly encourage other nations to seek American defense support. Similarly the initiation of local military action to defend Berlin might cause such devastation in Central Europe as to lead to the disintegration of the Atlantic alliance. To show an ability to restrain the use of violence may be as important as demonstrating a willingness to use violence.

For similar reasons the United States may find it necessary to try to maintain in power the government which was in control at the beginning of the crisis and which called for American support. If the outcome of a local-war situation in which American intervention is invited is always or frequently a change of government, a group in power may seek an accommodation with its enemies rather than accept American support.

The Sino-Soviet bloc on the other hand has an incentive to increase the destruction in a local war fought outside the Communist bloc, in order to demonstrate the lack of utility of American military aid. It also has an interest in a change in government, particularly if the change is from a strongly pro-Western to a neutral government. The Soviet leadership may also be seeking to demonstrate in dealing with a local-war situation that it is prepared to act vigorously to expand the area under Communist control and that it is not unduly afraid of Western counteraction. In its competition with the Chinese for the support of Communist revolutionary groups, the Soviet leadership may feel compelled to expand its intervention to prove to other Communist groups that Russia is prepared to support them when they are close to a seizure of power.

To some extent the policymakers themselves of the major powers will be conscious of the political effects of local war, but in addition both their allies and the neutral nations will continually bombard them with advice, suggestions, and other forms of pressure. Again these pressures may be to expand the war in particular ways or to contract it or to bring it to an end. For example, the United States has received conflicting advice from its SEATO allies as to its policy in dealing with military action in Vietnam and Laos. Beginning in 1954 the British, later joined by the French, have continually opposed proposals for the intervention of SEATO or American forces into the internal wars in Laos and Vietnam. On the other hand, the Thais, the Filipinos, and the Pakistanis have frequently urged a more active intervention by the United States into these situations. More extensive action by the United States in support of the Chinese Nationalists has been opposed by America's European allies.

The ability of allied countries to influence American policy in a local-war situation will in part depend on their general relationship with the United States. The British have exercised a major influence on American local-war policy during the entire postwar period beginning with their transfer to the United States of primary responsibility for aiding the suppression of the Greek Communist rebellion. On the other hand, the extent of the influence of any particular allied country will be affected by whether or not it is actively engaged in the combat. Allied pressure seems to have been most effective in the Korean War when a number of nations joined the United States by committing forces, albeit token ones, in the defense of South Korea. Allied pressure was least important in the 1962 Cuban crisis when the United States was prepared to act alone. The Soviet Union may find that the influence of its Chinese or even North Vietnamese allies increases as they make greater contributions to joint efforts. Though Chinese influence in the present period probably tends toward the use of force, this was not the case in 1956 when the Chinese seem to have counseled restraint on the Soviets in Poland.

TERRITORIAL OBJECTIVES

Since the battlefield itself is likely to be of little intrinsic importance, territorial objectives in a local war will be determined by the nature of the perceived political effects of different outcomes. Some battlefields such as Western Europe, however, will have significant intrinsic value, and in some cases the loss of a particular area will make it more difficult, for tactical military reasons, to defend nearby areas. A Communist takeover in Laos might, for example, make it harder for the United States to defend South Vietnam and Thailand.

As long as the United States and the Soviet Union confine a war to the territories of other countries, they cannot demand or expect the unconditional surrender of the other major power. However, their objectives may be very extreme, including the ceding of large amounts of territory and the unconditional surrender of the local government; or they may be extremely limited, involving a return to the *status quo ante* or even less. At least at some times, and perhaps at all times, during a local war, both sides will have at least implicitly formulated war-termination conditions, that is, battlefield conditions which if accepted by the other side will lead them to terminate the local conflict. However these war-termination conditions may fluctuate during the war through a range of possible territorial objectives. The territorial objectives, as they are determined by political-effects objectives and other pressures to be discussed hereafter, will be the most immediate determinant of the decision to expand a local war. A side with relatively limited territorial objectives is less likely to find it necessary to expand the scope of its military operations. As each side recognizes the relatively limited objectives of the other, the danger of *explosion* into central war will be substantially reduced. However, even minor objectives may produce pressures to *expand* the war if one or both sides find that their limited objectives cannot be obtained at the level at which the battle is being fought, or if the objectives of the two sides are incompatible.

In addition to the extent of territorial objectives of the two sides, another crucial factor will be whether or not the objectives are specific, concrete, and clearly stated. Although some commentators have suggested that specific objectives clearly stated are more likely to lead both sides to contract rather than to expand a local war, this is not necessarily the case. Certainly if the specific battlefield objectives of the two sides were clearly incompatible, there would be strong pressures toward the expansion of the war. The United States in particular might find it more difficult to compromise if it had clearly stated its territorial objectives than if it had not spelled out its objectives in advance, and if they were in fact flexible. Flexible and moderate battlefield objectives of the two sides are likely to be most conducive to the stabilization, contraction, and termination of a local war. On the other hand, extreme war-termination conditions which expand with success on the battlefield are likely to lead to the expansion of a local war.

The fluctuation of war-termination conditions in a local war will stem in part from the difficulty of assessing the relationship between political-effects objectives and territorial objectives. For example, the United States is not really sure what the impact of a withdrawal from the Chinese Nationalist-held offshore islands would be on its foreign-policy objectives. During the Korean War, the political effect of the stopping of the war at the thirty-eighth parallel clearly would have been different from what it was when it finally occurred if the United States had stopped of its own volition after routing the North Korean army. And no one can really be sure as to the difference in political effect of stopping at the thirty-eighth parallel as opposed to moving to the narrow neck, or seeking to capture all of North Korea. This difficulty of clearly correlating political-effects objectives with territorial objectives is likely in general to be a pressure to expand the local war. When in doubt as to their ability to secure their objectives with particular war-termination conditions, the leaders of a major power may play it safe by expanding their war-termination conditions. Territorial objectives will also fluctuate with military success or failure. The American decision to unite Korea by force stemmed directly from the defeat of the North Korean army. The importance given to defending Taiwan is the result of Communist control of the Chinese mainland. Military success and defeat, and changes in the loyalty of indigenous groups drastically alter the range of possible battlefield objectives.

The role of foreign-policy objectives in influencing the decision to expand or contract a local war, then, may be summarized as follows: unconditional surrender of the other major power is incompatible with local warfare. Neither of the major powers will be seeking in a single local war to implement all of its foreign-policy objectives. The major objectives of the two sides in a local war will be their political-effects objectives, particularly those centering around the legitimacy of the use of force and the need to convince enemies that they will be opposed and allies that they will be supported. Territorial objectives and the war-termination conditions will be shaped largely by the general political-effects objectives although the relationship between the two will not always be clear.

RISK OF CENTRAL WAR

The desire to avoid central war exercises a major influence on decision makers during a local war. Though this desire is one of the foreign-policy objectives of each side, it is sufficiently critical to require separate consideration. Almost all analysts agree that the fighting of a local war increases the possibility of central war, but it is impossible to determine precisely the extent to which any local war in fact increases the danger of central war. One can, however, envision several ways in which a local war might lead to central war. These include expansion which seems most likely to occur in an important region such as Europe and in a nuclear war. There is also the possibility of an explosion which may occur for one of two reasons. Central war which results from explosion may be an "inadvertent war" that occurs although neither side wants it. It may be the result of pressures to strike first in the event of war which become aggravated as the local war goes on. However central war might also be "deliberate war" resulting from the decision of the losing side in a local war to initiate a strategic strike rather than accept defeat on the local battlefield. If the losing side in a local war considers the area under contest to be of vital significance to it and if it feels that it can win a central war, it might unleash its strategic forces rather than accept local defeat.

It is impossible to make a general assessment in the abstract of the probability that a local war will cause a central war. Certainly there is a widespread belief shared by many decision makers that local wars are dangerous because of the likelihood that they will spark a nuclear holocaust. Whether this danger is as great as decision makers think is less important in this context than the recognition that decision makers will be motivated in the conduct of a local war by their perception of the danger of a central war taking place.

The image which decision makers have of the danger of central war will be determined partly at least by their image of the nature of the strategic balance. In fact, in discussing local wars in any historical period, it is important to specify the nature of the strategic balance, and in particular the image which decision makers have of the balance and their beliefs about how this balance should influence their own and their opponents' behavior in a local-war situation.

Two kinds of questions about the nature of the strategic balance are relevant: How stable is the balance? Is one side more likely than the other to initiate and to win a central war?

The danger of an inadvertent war is greatest in a period in which one or both sides have a strong incentive to strike first if war should occur. In this situation, because strategic forces themselves are vulnerable to destruction by the opponent's strategic forces, one or both sides may see that it is vitally important to be first or at least a close second should there be an explosion into central war. Such a situation might imply two different outcomes of a strategic exchange. The side going first might escape all retaliatory damage. On the other hand, the side going first might suffer significantly less damage than the opposing side and end up winning the war. It appeared to most public military commentators in 1962 that in the late 1950's and early 1960's the United States was in such a position that if it struck first it would probably win and might not suffer extensive damage. On the other hand, in retrospect, it appears in 1962 that the Soviets have never been in that position, although the damage that they might suffer now in the event of central war would undoubtedly be less if they struck first than if they waited for the first blow from the United States.

In this situation, in which the opponents must be sensitive to the possibility of an explosion into central war and to the importance of responding quickly to such an attack, both sides will be constantly concerned with the danger of explosion during a local war. Should a local war occur in a period of strategic instability, both of the major powers will probably seek to minimize their stake in the war so that no outcome will appear to affect their basic relationship in ways that make the danger of an explosion more likely. During such a period, the direct use of combat forces of the major-power countries may seem so risky as to be untenable in almost all local-war situations. With both sides alert to the danger of inducing a preemptive attack, the local war is likely to remain in low key while both sides refrain from expansionist actions such as the introduction of nuclear weapons or the crossing of an international border which will heighten the tension and the expectation that an explosion is imminent. This does not mean that there will be no use of military force, but rather that if one side decides that it must initiate war, it may decide that the only prudent thing to do is to initiate central war or very low-level, ambiguous violence.

Though both sides are likely to feel that it is extremely important to avoid the kind of head-on clash that makes both believe that central war is more likely, the Soviets and the Chinese might find an unstable strategic situation a particularly appropriate one for the kind of ambiguous military actions for which they, in general, seem to have a preference. The optimum strategy for this sort of strategic situation is one which creates for the opponent the alternative of instituting major war or yielding.

While producing powerful incentives for both sides to be cautious, an unstable strategic balance is also likely to provide profitable payoffs for a side willing to take risks. Faced with a *fait accompli*, the defending side is likely to be inhibited from joining the battle in a situation of unstable deterrence. Thus, if local military action does not lead to preemption, it also is not likely to lead to intervention. An unstable strategic balance, then, is likely to reduce the danger of local war and central war by expansion if both sides act cautiously. If both sides try to use an unstable situation as an opportunity to make daring gains, hoping that the other side will be paralyzed by the threat of thermonuclear war, then such a situation may prove to be very dangerous with the world constantly teetering on the brink of preemptive central war.

On the other hand, the initiation of fairly large local war may be one way of signaling to the other side that one does not believe that the strategic balance is unstable, and that one does not believe that there is any danger of preemption. For example, the United States might believe that the Soviet strategic forces cannot be as vulnerable as the Administration thinks they are, if the Soviets are prepared to unleash a fairly large local war.

Beginning about 1957 both sides seemed to have begun to take seriously the possibility of a successful preemptive first strike. Without necessarily having been preoccupied with this danger of preemption, the leaders of the major powers seem to have had and continue to have an appreciation of the possibility of explosion. Among the many other determinants of decision on whether to expand local wars, this general perception of the danger of central war was probably an important factor in keeping down the level of local violence during the past several years.

If and when the strategic balance becomes more stable, that is, when both sides have strategic forces so well protected that there is no perceived advantage in striking first, the effect of the strategic balance will change.

As Glenn Snyder and Thomas Schelling have pointed out, both sides are more likely to run risks in a local war when they are complacent about the stability of the strategic balance. What will count is the perception that each side has of the likelihood of an explosion. Even if strategic forces are well protected, the leaders of the major powers may continue to believe that the danger of an inadvertent war of one kind or another is still so great that they cannot afford to underestimate this risk in dealing with a local-war situation; they may also believe that the cost of a central war is so great that expansion of a local war must always be carried out with caution because the gains of success in a local war are not worth a large risk of causing an explosion.

Nevertheless it is possible that by the late 1960's we will be in a situation where both sides perceive a very small risk of a local war exploding into central war. The pressure against the expansion of local war may thus be alleviated to such a point that very large local wars involving the territory of a number of states, the armies of the major powers, and the use of nuclear weapons will not be impossible. It is conceivable that a war of the size of World War II would be fought without its expanding or exploding into central war. Certainly a major restraint against wars of the size of Korea will be eliminated when the pressure against expansion, stemming from the fear of an explosion, has been greatly reduced. This very lack of pressure against the expansion of a local war might, unless other pressures intervened, lead to a war which very slowly and gradually expanded to the point where it became a central war. One might imagine, for example, a war on the European continent becoming larger and larger until it led to strategic attacks on the Soviet homeland which were followed by attacks on the United States. In such a war, however, the major powers might still observe a number of important limits including not attacking cities.

Not only is the major powers' perception of the likelihood of central war important, but so also is their perception of what a central war might look like, and specifically, the possibility of one side or the other winning.

Certainly, during the 1950's and, according to recent statements by

American defense officials, into the 1960's as well, the United States has had a preponderance of strategic force. Should a war occur, then, the United States could probably expect to win, although the amount of damage that it would suffer in such a war has steadily been increasing. Sometime in the late 1950's the American strategic position vis-à-vis the Soviet Union switched from that of total predominance to relative superiority. Prior to this time, although the Soviets could perhaps have made significant gains in local areas including Western Europe, they could not have inflicted any damage of significance on the United States. At the present time while the United States still apparently has strategic superiority, the Soviets might be able to inflict major damage on the United States even in the event of an American first strike. At present we are in a period in which there remains a premium on striking first and in which there continues to be an American predominance of strategic forces such that the United States is likely to win any central war. In this situation there is strong pressure on the Soviet Union not to expand the level of violence in a local war and not to initiate any kind of local war, particularly one involving a crossing of international boundaries, which might create a substantial danger of explosion. On the other hand, although the United States need not fear losing a central war, American policymakers place a high utility on the avoidance of the damage which would be likely to be inflicted on the United States and Western Europe in such a war. Thus, even given American superiority, the fear of central war will still operate on both sides, albeit perhaps unequally, to generate pressure to contract or end a local war. The relative caution on both sides in dealing with the Laos conflict and in maneuvering over Berlin very likely reflects in part their fear of an explosion into central war.

No matter how stable the strategic balance becomes and regardless of the relative inferiority of one side or the other, the fear of an explosion into central war will exercise major pressures on decision makers on both sides in any local-war situation. These pressures will always be toward the contraction or ending of the war although they will considerably lessen if and when both sides become convinced that the strategic balance is extremely insensitive to pressures from a local-war situation.

21. WHAT IS GUERRILLA WARFARE?

Mao Tse-tung

I N A WAR of revolutionary character, guerrilla operations are a necessary part. This is particularly true in a war waged for the emancipation of a people who inhabit a vast nation. China is such a nation, a nation whose techniques are undeveloped and whose communications are poor. She finds herself confronted with a strong and victorious Japanese imperialism. Under these circumstances, the development of the type of guerrilla warfare characterized by the quality of mass is both necessary and natural. This warfare must be developed to an unprecedented degree and it must coordinate with the operations of our regular armies. If we fail to do this, we will find it difficult to defeat the enemy.

These guerrilla operations must not be considered as an independent form of warfare. They are but one step in the total war, one aspect of the revolutionary struggle. They are the inevitable result of the clash between oppressor and oppressed when the latter reach the limits of their endurance. In our case, these hostilities began at a time when the people were unable to endure any more from the Japanese imperialists. . . .

Guerrilla warfare has qualities and objectives peculiar to itself. It is a weapon that a nation inferior in arms and military equipment may employ against a more powerful aggressor nation. When the invader pierces deep into the heart of the weaker country and occupies her territory in a cruel and oppressive manner, there is no doubt that conditions of terrain, climate, and society in general offer obstacles to his progress and may be used to advantage by those who oppose him. In guerrilla warfare, we turn these advantages to the purpose of resisting and defeating the enemy.

During the progress of hostilities, guerrillas gradually develop into orthodox forces that operate in conjunction with other units of the regular army. Thus the regularly organized troops, those guerrillas who have attained that status, and those who have not reached that level of development combine to form the military power of a national revolu-

From *On Guerrilla Warfare* by Mao Tse-tung. Translated by Samuel T. Griffith (New York: 1961), pp. 41–47; 51–56; 77–81; 82–87. Reprinted by permission of Frederick A. Praeger, Inc. and Cassell and Co., Ltd.

MAO TSE-TUNG (1893–) Chairman of the Politburo, Communist Party of China. His other books include *Selected Military Writings,* (Peking: Foreign Language Press, 1966); *An Analysis of the Classes in Chinese Society,* (Peking: Foreign Language Press, 1956): *On Coalition Government,* (Peking: Foreign Language Press, 1955).

tionary war. There can be no doubt that the ultimate result of this will be victory.

Both in its development and in its method of application, guerrilla warfare has certain distinctive characteristics. We first discuss the relationship of guerrilla warfare to national policy. Because ours is the resistance of a semicolonial country against an imperialism, our hostilities must have a clearly defined political goal and firmly established political responsibilities. Our basic policy is the creation of a national united anti-Japanese front. This policy we pursue in order to gain our political goal, which is the complete emancipation of the Chinese people. There are certain fundamental steps necessary in the realization of this policy, to wit:

1. Arousing and organizing the people.
2. Achieving internal unification politically.
3. Establishing bases.
4. Equipping forces.
5. Recovering national strength.
6. Destroying enemy's national strength.
7. Regaining lost territories.

There is no reason to consider guerrilla warfare separately from national policy. On the contrary, it must be organized and conducted in complete accord with national anti-Japanese policy. It is only those who misinterpret guerrilla action who say, as does Jen Ch'i Shan, "The question of guerrilla hostilities is purely a military matter and not a political one." Those who maintain this simple point of view have lost sight of the political goal and the political effects of guerrilla action. Such a simple point of view will cause the people to lose confidence and will result in our defeat.

What is the relationship of guerrilla warfare to the people? Without a political goal, guerrilla warfare must fail, as it must if its political objectives do not coincide with the aspirations of the people and their sympathy, cooperation, and assistance cannot be gained. The essence of guerrilla warfare is thus revolutionary in character. On the other hand, in a war of counterrevolutionary nature, there is no place for guerrilla hostilities. Because guerrilla warfare basically derives from the masses and is supported by them, it can neither exist nor flourish if it separates itself from their sympathies and cooperation. There are those who do not comprehend guerrilla action, and who therefore do not understand the distinguishing qualities of a people's guerrilla war, who say: "Only regular troops can carry on guerrilla operations." There are others who, because they do not believe in the ultimate success of guerrilla action, mistakenly say: "Guerrilla warfare is an insignificant and highly specialized type of operation in which there is no place for the masses of the people" (Jen Ch'i Shan). Then there are those who ridicule the masses and undermine resistance by wildly asserting that the people have no understanding of the war of resistance (Yeh Ch'ing, for one). The moment that this war of resistance dissociates itself from the masses of the people is the precise moment that it dissociates itself from hope of ultimate victory over the Japanese.

What is the organization for guerrilla warfare? Though all guerrilla bands that spring from the masses of the people suffer from lack of organization at the time of their formation, they all have in common a basic quality that makes organization possible. All guerrilla units must have political and military leadership. This is true regardless of the source or size of such units. Such units may originate locally, in the masses of the people; they may be formed from an admixture of regular troops with groups of the people, or they may consist of regular army units intact. And mere quantity does not affect this matter. Such units may consist of a squad of a few men, a battalion of several hundred men, or a regiment of several thousand men.

All these must have leaders who are unyielding in their policies—resolute, loyal, sincere, and robust. These men must be well educated in revolutionary technique, self-confident, able to establish severe discipline, and able to cope with counterpropaganda. In short, these leaders must be models for the people. As the war progresses, such leaders will gradually overcome the lack of discipline, which at first prevails; they will establish discipline in their forces, strengthening them and increasing their combat efficiency. Thus eventual victory will be attained.

Unorganized guerrilla warfare cannot contribute to victory and those who attack the movement as a combination of banditry and anarchism do not understand the nature of guerrilla action. They say: "This movement is a haven for disappointed militarists, vagabonds and bandits" (Jen Ch'i Shan), hoping thus to bring the movement into disrepute. We do not deny that there are corrupt guerrillas, nor that there are people who under the guise of guerrillas indulge in unlawful activities. Neither do we deny that the movement has at the present time symptoms of a lack of organization, symptoms that might indeed be serious were we to judge guerrilla warfare solely by the corrupt and temporary phenomena we have mentioned. We should study the corrupt phenomena and attempt to eradicate them in order to encourage guerrilla warfare, and to increase its military efficiency. "This is hard work, there is no help for it, and the problem cannot be solved immediately. The whole people must try to reform themselves during the course of the war. We must educate them and reform them in the light of past experience. Evil does not exist in guerrilla warfare but only in the unorganized and undisciplined activities that are anarchism," said Lenin, in *On Guerrilla Warfare*.[1]

What is basic guerrilla strategy? Guerrilla strategy must be based primarily on alertness, mobility, and attack. It must be adjusted to the enemy situation, the terrain, the existing lines of communication, the relative strengths, the weather, and the situation of the people.

In guerrilla warfare, select the tactic of seeming to come from the east and attacking from the west; avoid the solid, attack the hollow; attack; withdraw; deliver a lightning blow, seek a lightning decision. When guerrillas engage a stronger enemy, they withdraw when he advances; harass him when he stops; strike him when he is weary; pursue him when he withdraws. In guerrilla strategy, the enemy's rear, flanks, and other vulnerable spots are his vital points, and there he must be harassed, attacked, dispersed, exhausted and annihilated. Only in this way can guerrillas carry out their mission of independent guerrilla action and coordination with the effort of the regular armies. But, in spite of the most complete preparation, there can be no victory if mistakes are made in the matter of command. Guerrilla warfare based on the principles we have mentioned and carried on over a vast extent of territory in which communications are inconvenient will contribute tremendously towards ultimate defeat of the Japanese and consequent emancipation of the Chinese people.

A careful distinction must be made between two types of guerrilla warfare. The fact that revolutionary guerrilla warfare is based on the masses of the people does not in itself mean that the organization of guerrilla units is impossible in a war of counterrevolutionary character. As examples of the former type we may cite Red guerrilla hostilities during the Russian Revolution; those of the Reds in China; of the Abyssinians against the Italians for the past three years; those of the last seven years in Manchuria, and the vast anti-Japanese guerrilla war that is carried on in China today. All these struggles have been carried on in the interests of the whole people or the greater part of them; all had a broad basis in the national manpower, and all have been in accord with the laws of historical development. They have existed and will continue to exist, flourish, and develop as long as they are not contrary to national policy.

The second type of guerrilla warfare directly contradicts the law of historical development. Of this type, we may cite the examples furnished

---

[1] Presumably, Mao refers here to the essay that has been translated into English under the title "Partisan Warfare." See *Orbis,* II (Summer, 1958), No. 2, 194–208.—S.B.G.

by the White Russian guerrilla units organized by Denikin and Kolchak; those organized by the Japanese; those organized by the Italians in Abyssinia; those supported by the puppet governments in Manchuria and Mongolia, and those that will be organized here by Chinese traitors. All such have oppressed the masses and have been contrary to the true interests of the people. They must be firmly opposed. They are easy to destroy because they lack a broad foundation in the people.

.   .   .

The general features of orthodox hostilities, that is, the war of position and the war of movement, differ fundamentally from guerrilla warfare. There are other readily apparent differences such as those in organization, armament, equipment, supply, tactics, command; in conception of the terms "front" and "rear"; in the matter of military responsibilities.

When considered from the point of view of total numbers, guerrilla units are many; as individual combat units, they may vary in size from the smallest, of several score or several hundred men, to the battalion or the regiment, of several thousand. This is not the case in regularly organized units. A primary feature of guerrilla operations is their dependence upon the people themselves to organize battalions and other units. As a result of this, organization depends largely upon local circumstances. In the case of guerrilla groups, the standard of equipment is of a low order, and they must depend for their sustenance primarily upon what the locality affords.

The strategy of guerrilla warfare is manifestly unlike that employed in orthodox operations, as the basic tactic of the former is constant activity and movement. There is is nothing comparable to the fixed, passive defense that characterizes orthodox war. In guerrilla warfare, the transformation of a moving situation into a positional defensive situation never arises. The general features of reconnaisance, partial deployment, general deployment, and development of the attack that are usual in mobile warfare are not common in guerrilla war.

There are differences also in the matter of leadership and command. In guerrilla warfare, small units acting independently play the principal role, and there must be no excessive interference with their activities. In orthodox warfare, particularly in a moving situation, a certain degree of initiative is accorded subordinates, but in principle, command is centralized. This is done because all units and all supporting arms in all districts must coordinate to the highest degree. In the case of guerrilla warfare, this is not only undesirable but impossible. Only adjacent guerrilla units can coordinate their activities to any degree. Strategically, their activities can be roughly correlated with those of the regular forces, and tactically, they must cooperate with adjacent units of the regular army. But there are no strictures on the extent of guerrilla activity nor is it primarily characterized by the quality of cooperation of many units.

When we discuss the terms "front" and "rear," it must be remembered, that while guerrillas do have bases, their primary field of activity is in the enemy's rear areas. They themselves have no rear. Because an orthodox army has rear installations (except in some special cases as during the 10,000-mile[2] march of the Red Army or as in the case of certain units operating in Shansi Province), it cannot operate as guerrillas can.

As to the matter of military responsibilities, those of the guerrillas are to exterminate small forces of the enemy; to harass and weaken large forces; to attack enemy lines of communication; to establish bases capable of supporting independent operations in the enemy's rear; to force the enemy to disperse his strength; and to coordinate all these activities with those of the regular armies on distant battle fronts.

. . .

While it is improper to confuse orthodox with guerrilla operations, it is equally improper to consider that there is a chasm between the two. While differences do exist, similarities appear under certain conditions, and this fact must be appreciated if we wish to establish clearly the relationship between the two. If we consider both types of warfare as a single subject, or if we confuse guerrilla warfare with the mobile operations of orthodox war, we fall into this error: We exaggerate the function of guerrillas and minimize that of the regular armies. If we agree with Chang Tso Hua, who says, "Guerrilla warfare is the primary war strategy of a people seeking to emancipate itself," or with Kao Kang, who believes that "Guerrilla strategy is the only strategy possible for an oppressed people," we are exaggerating the importance of guerrilla hostilities. What these zealous friends I have just quoted do not realize is this: If we do not fit guerrilla operations into their proper niche, we cannot promote them realistically. Then, not only would those who oppose us take advantage of our varying opinions to turn them to their own uses to undermine us, but guerrillas would be led to assume responsibilities they could not successfully discharge and that should properly be carried out by orthodox forces. In the meantime, the important guerrilla function of coordinating activities with the regular forces would be neglected.

Furthermore, if the theory that guerrilla warfare is our only strategy were actually applied, the regular forces would be weakened, we would be

---

[2] It has been estimated that the Reds actually marched about 6,000 miles. See Introduction, Chapter II.—S.B.G.

divided in purpose, and guerrilla hostilities would decline. If we say, "Let us transform the regular forces into guerrillas," and do not place our first reliance on a victory to be gained by the regular armies over the enemy, we may certainly expect to see as a result the failure of the anti-Japanese war of resistance. The concept that guerrilla warfare is an end in itself and that guerrilla activities can be divorced from those of the regular forces is incorrect. If we assume that guerrilla warfare does not progress from beginning to end beyond its elementary forms, we have failed to recognize the fact that guerrilla hostilities can, under specific conditions, develop and assume orthodox characteristics. An opinion that admits the existence of guerrilla war, but isolates it, is one that does not properly estimate the potentialities of such war.

Equally dangerous is the concept that condemns guerrilla war on the ground that war has no other aspects than the purely orthodox. This opinion is often expressed by those who have seen the corrupt phenomena of some guerrilla regimes, observed their lack of discipline, and have seen them used as a screen behind which certain persons have indulged in bribery and other corrupt practices. These people will not admit the fundamental necessity for guerrilla bands that spring from the armed people. They say, "Only the regular forces are capable of conducting guerrilla operations." This theory is a mistaken one and would lead to the abolition of the people's guerrilla war.

A proper conception of the relationship that exists between guerrilla effort and that of the regular forces is essential. We believe it can be stated this way: "Guerrilla operations during the anti-Japanese war may for a certain time and temporarily become its paramount feature, particularly insofar as the enemy's rear is concerned. However, if we view the war as a whole, there can be no doubt that our regular forces are of primary importance, because it is they who are alone capable of producing the decision. Guerrilla warfare assists them in producing this favorable decision. Orthodox forces may under certain conditions operate as guerrillas, and the latter may, under certain conditions, develop to the status of the former. However, both guerrilla forces and regular forces have their own respective development and their proper combinations."

THE METHOD OF ORGANIZING GUERRILLA REGIMES

Many of those who decide to participate in guerrilla activities do not know the methods of organization. For such people, as well as for students who have no knowledge of military affairs, the matter of organization is a problem that requires solution. Even among those who have military knowledge, there are some who know nothing of guerrilla regimes because they are lacking in that particular type of experience. The subject of the organization of such regimes is not confined to the organization of specific units but includes all guerrilla activities within the area where the regime functions.

As an example of such organization, we may take a geographical area in the enemy's rear. This area may comprise many counties. It must be subdivided and individual companies or battalions formed to accord with the subdivisions. To this "military area," a military commander and political commissioners are appointed. Under these, the necessary officers, both military and political, are appointed. In the military headquarters, there will be the staff, the aides, the supply officers, and the medical personnel. These are controlled by the chief of staff, who acts in accordance with orders from the commander. In the political headquarters, there are bureaus of propaganda organization, people's mass movements, and miscellaneous affairs. Control of these is vested in the political chairmen.

The military areas are subdivided into smaller districts in accordance with local geography, the enemy situation locally, and the state of guerrilla development. Each of these smaller divisions within the area is a district, each of which may consist of from two to six counties. To each district, a military commander and several political commissioners are appointed. Under their direction, military and political headquarters are organized. Tasks are assigned in accordance with the number of guerrilla troops available. Although the names of the officers in the "district" correspond to those in the larger "area," the number of functionaries assigned in the former case should be reduced to the least possible. In order to unify control, to handle guerrilla troops that come from different sources, and to harmonize military operations and local political affairs, a committee of from seven to nine members should be organized in each area and district. This committee, the members of which are selected by the troops and the local political officers, should function as a forum for the discussion of both military and political matters.

All the people in an area should arm themselves and be organized into two groups. One of these groups is a combat group, the other a self-defense unit with but limited military quality. Regular combatant guerrillas are organized into one of three general types of unit. The first of these is the small unit, the platoon or company. In each county, three to six units may be organized. The second type is the battalion of from two to four companies. One such unit should be organized in each county. While the unit fundamentally belongs to the country in which it was organized, it may operate in other counties. While in areas other than its own, it must operate in conjunction with local units in order to take advantage of their manpower, their knowledge of local terrain and local customs, and their information of the enemy.

The third type is the guerrilla regiment, which consists of from two to four of the above-mentioned battalion units. If sufficient manpower is available, a guerrilla brigade of from two to four regiments may be formed.

Each of the units has its own peculiarities of organization. A squad, the smallest unit, has a strength of from nine to eleven men, including the leader and the assistant leader. Its arms may be from two to five Western-style rifles, with the remaining men armed with rifles of local manufacture, bird guns, spears, or big swords. Two to four such squads form a platoon. This, too, has a leader and an assistant leader, and when acting independently, it is assigned a political officer to carry on political propaganda work. The platoon may have about ten rifles, with the remainder of its weapons being bird guns, lances, and big swords. Two to four of such units form a company, which, like the platoon, has a leader, an assistant leader, and a political officer. All these units are under the direct supervision of the military commanders of the areas in which they operate.

The battalion unit must be more thoroughly organized and better equipped than the smaller units. Its discipline and its personnel should be superior. If a battalion is formed from company units, it should not deprive subordinate units entirely of their manpower and their arms. If, in a small area, there is a peace-preservation corps, a branch of the militia, or police regular guerrilla units should not be dispersed over it.

The guerrilla unit next in size to the battalion is the regiment. This must be under more severe discipline than the battalion. In an independent guerrilla regiment, there may be ten men per squad, three squads per platoon, three platoons per company, three companies per battalion, and three battalions to the regiment. Two of such regiments form a brigade. Each of these units has a commander, a vice-commander, and a political officer.

.   .   .

All these units from the lowest to the highest are combatant guerrilla units and receive their supplies from the central government. . . .

All the people of both sexes from the ages of sixteen to forty-five must be organized into anti-Japanese self-defense units, the basis of which is voluntary service. As a first step, they must procure arms, then they must be given both military and political training. Their responsibilities are: local sentry duties, securing information of the enemy, arresting traitors, and preventing the dissemination of enemy propaganda. When the enemy launches a guerrilla-suppression drive, these units, armed with what weapons there are, are assigned to certain areas to deceive, hinder, and harass him. Thus, the self-defense units assist the combatant guerrillas. They have other functions. They furnish stretcher-bearers to transport the wounded, carriers to take food to the troops, and comfort missions to provide the troops with tea and rice. If a locality can organize such a self-defense unit as we have described, the traitors cannot hide nor can bandits and robbers disturb the peace of the people. Thus the people will continue to assist the guerrillas and supply manpower to our regular armies. "The organization of self-defense units is a transitional step in the development of universal conscription. Such units are reservoirs of manpower for the orthodox forces."

. . .

EQUIPMENT OF GUERRILLAS

In regard to the problem of guerrilla equipment, it must be understood that guerrillas are lightly armed attack groups, which require simple equipment. The standard of equipment is based upon the nature of duties assigned; the equipment of low-class guerrilla units is not as good as that of higher-class units. For example, those who are assigned the task of destroying railroads are better-equipped than those who do not have that task. The equipment of guerrillas cannot be based on what the guerrillas want, or even what they need, but must be based on what is available for their use. Equipment cannot be furnished immediately but must be acquired gradually. These are points to be kept in mind.

The question of equipment includes the collection, supply, distribution, and replacement of weapons, ammunition, blankets, communication materials, transport, and facilities for propaganda work. The supply of weapons and ammunition is most difficult, particularly at the time the unit is established, but this problem can always be solved eventually. Guerrilla bands that originate in the people are furnished with revolvers, pistols, bird guns, spears, big swords, and land mines and mortars of local manufacture. Other elementary weapons are added and as many new-type rifles as are available are distributed. After a period of resistance, it is possible to increase the supply of equipment by capturing it from the enemy. In this respect, the transport companies are the easiest to equip, for in any successful attack, we will capture the enemy's transport.

An armory should be established in each guerrilla district for the manufacture and repair of rifles and for the production of cartridges, hand grenades, and bayonets. Guerrillas must not depend too much on an armory. The enemy is the principal source of their supply.

For destruction of railway trackage, bridges, and stations in enemy-controlled territory, it is necessary to gather together demolition materials. Troops must be trained in the preparation and use of demolitions, and a demolition unit must be organized in each regiment.

As for minimum clothing requirements, these are that each man shall have at least two summer-weight uniforms, one suit of winter clothing, two hats, a pair of wrap puttees, and a blanket. Each man must have a haversack or a bag for food. In the north, each man must have an overcoat. In acquiring this clothing, we cannot depend on captures made from the enemy, for it is forbidden for captors to take clothing from their prisoners. In order to maintain high morale in guerrilla forces, all the clothing and equipment mentioned should be furnished by the representatives of the government stationed in each guerrilla district. These men may confiscate clothing from traitors or ask contributions from those best able to afford them. In subordinate groups, uniforms are unnecessary.

. . .

In the guerrilla army in general, and at bases in particular, there must be a high standard of medical equipment. Besides the services of the doctors, medicines must be procured. Although guerrillas can depend on the enemy for some portion of their medical supplies, they must, in general, depend upon contributions. If Western medicines are not available, local medicines must be made to suffice.

The problem of transport is more vital in North China than in the south, for in the south all that are necessary are mules and horses. Small guerrilla units need no animals, but regiments and brigades will find them necessary. Commanders and staffs of units from companies up should be furnished a riding animal each. At times, two officers will have to share a horse. Officers whose duties are of minor nature do not have to be mounted.

Propaganda materials are very important. Every large guerrilla unit should have a printing press and a mimeograph stone. They must also have paper on which to print propaganda leaflets and notices. They must be supplied with chalk and large brushes. In guerrilla areas, there should be a printing press or a lead-type press.

For the purpose of printing training instructions, this material is of the greatest importance.

In addition to the equipment listed above, it is necessary to have field glasses, compasses, and military maps. An accomplished guerrilla group will acquire these things.

Because of the proved importance of guerrilla hostilities in the anti-Japanese war, the headquarters of the Nationalist Government and the commanding officers of the various war zones should do their best to supply the guerrillas with what they actually need and are unable to get for themselves. However, it must be repeated that guerrilla equipment will in the main depend on the efforts of the guerrillas themselves. If they depend on higher officers too much, the psychological effect will be to weaken the guerrilla spirit of resistance.

ELEMENTS OF THE GUERRILLA ARMY

The term "element" as used in the title to this section refers to the personnel, both officers and men, of the guerrilla army. Since each guerrilla group fights in a protracted war, its officers must be brave and positive men whose entire loyalty is dedicated to the cause of emancipation of the people. An officer should have the following qualities: great powers of endurance so that in spite of any hardship he sets an example to his men and is a model for them; he must be able to mix easily with the people; his spirit and that of the men must be one in strengthening the policy of resistance to the Japanese. If he wishes to gain victories, he must study tactics. A guerrilla group with officers of this caliber would be unbeatable. I do not mean that every guerrilla group can have, at its inception, officers of such qualities. The officers must be men naturally endowed with good qualities which can be developed during the course of campaigning. The most important natural quality is that of complete loyalty to the idea of people's emancipation. If this is present, the others will develop; if it is not present, nothing can be done. When officers are first selected from a group, it is this quality that should receive particular attention. The officers in a group should be inhabitants of the locality in which the group is organized, as this will facilitate relations between them and the local civilians. In addition, officers so chosen would be familiar with conditions. If in any locality there are not enough men of sufficiently high qualifications to become officers, an effort must be made to train and educate the people so these qualities may be developed and the potential officer material increased. There can be no disagreements between officers native to one place and those from other localities.

A guerrilla group ought to operate on the principle that only volunteers are acceptable for service. It is a mistake to impress people into service. As long as a person is willing to fight, his social condition or position is no consideration, but only men who are courageous and determined can bear the hardships of guerrilla campaigning in a protracted war.

A soldier who habitually breaks regulations must be dismissed from the army. Vagabonds and vicious people must not be accepted for service. The opium habit must be forbidden, and a soldier who cannot break himself of the habit should be dismissed. Victory in guerrilla war is conditioned upon keeping the membership pure and clean.

It is a fact that during the war the enemy may take advantage of certain people who are lacking in conscience and patriotism and induce them to join the guerrillas for the purpose of betraying them. Officers must, therefore, continually educate the soldiers and inculcate patriotism in them. This will prevent the success of traitors. The traitors who are in the ranks must be discovered and expelled, and punishment and expulsion meted out to those who have been influenced by them. In all such cases, the officers should summon the soldiers and relate the facts to them, thus arousing their hatred and detestation for traitors. This procedure will serve as well as a warning to the other soldiers. If an officer is discovered to be a traitor, some prudence must be used in the punishment adjudged. However, the work of eliminating traitors in the army begins with their elimination from among the people.

Chinese soldiers who have served under puppet governments and bandits who have been converted should be welcomed as individuals or as groups. They should be well treated and repatriated. But care should be used during their reorientation to distinguish those whose idea is to fight the Japanese from those who may be present for other reasons.

SELECTED BIBLIOGRAPHY

PART III

Conflict and Military Potential

Aron, Raymond, *On War*. New York: Doubleday Anchor Books, 1959.

———, *The Century of Total War*. Boston: Beacon Press, 1956.

Bergman, Jules, "If Zeus Fails, Can Sprint Save Us?" *New York Times Magazine*. March 20, 1966.

Berkowitz, Morton and P. G. Bock, *American National Security: A Reader in Theory and Practice*. New York: The Free Press, 1965.

Boehm, George, "Countdown for Nike-X," *Fortune*. November 1965.

Boulding, Kenneth E., *Conflict and Defense: A General Theory*. New York: Harper and Row, 1962.

Brody, Bernard, *Strategy in the Missile Age*. Princeton: Princeton University Press, 1959.

Coser, Lewis A., *The Functions of Social Conflict*. New York: The Free Press, 1964.

Deitchman, Seymour J., *Limited War and American Defense Policy*. Cambridge: The MIT Press, 1964.

Dyson, Freeman J., "Defense Against Ballistic Missiles." *Bulletin of the Atomic Scientists*. June 1964.

Eckstein, Harry (ed.), *Internal War*. New York: Free Press, 1964.

Etzioni, Amitai, *Winning without War*. New York: Doubleday, 1964.

Fisher, Roger (ed.), *International Conflict and Behavioral Science*. New York: Basic Books, Inc., 1964.

Gallois, Pierre, *The Balance of Terror.* Boston: Houghton Mifflin Company, 1961.

Gareau, Frederick H. (ed.), *The Balance of Power and Nuclear Deterrence.* Boston: Houghton Mifflin Company, 1962.

Ginsburgh, Robert N., *U.S. Military Strategy in the Sixties.* New York: W. W. Norton and Company, 1965.

Hahn, Walter F., and John C. Neff (eds.), *American Strategy for the Nuclear Age.* New York: Doubleday, 1960.

Kahn, Herman, *On Escalation: Scenarios and Metaphors.* New York: Praeger, 1965.

——, *On Thermonuclear War.* Princeton: Princeton University Press, 1960.

Kaufman, William, *The McNamara Strategy.* New York: Harper and Row, 1964.

Kintner, William R., and Stefan T. Possony, "Strategic Asymmetries," *ORBIS.* Spring 1965.

Kissinger, Henry A., *Nuclear Weapons and Foreign Policy.* New York: Harper and Brothers, 1957.

—— (ed.), *Problems of National Strategy.* New York: Praeger, 1965.

Knorr, Klaus and Thornton Read, *Limited Strategic War.* New York: Praeger, 1962.

Levine, Robert A., *The Arms Debate.* Cambridge: Harvard University Press, 1963.

Lorenz, Konrad, *On Aggression.* New York: Harcourt, Brace and World, 1963.

McNeil, Elton (ed.), *The Nature of Human Conflict.* Englewood Cliffs: Prentice-Hall, 1965.

Morgenstern, Oskar, *The Question of National Defense.* New York: Vintage Books, 1961.

Norman, Floyd, "Nike-X: To Deploy or Not to Deploy," *Army.* March 1967.

Osgood, Charles E., *An Alternative to War or Surrender.* Urbana: University of Illinois Press, 1962.

Osgood, Robert E., *Limited War.* Chicago: University of Chicago Press, 1957.

Paret, Peter and John W. Shy, *Guerrillas in the 1960's.* New York: Praeger, 1962.

Richardson, Lewis F., *Arms and Insecurity: A Mathematical Study of the Causes and Origins of War.* Pittsburgh: Boxwood Press, 1960.

Rock, Vincent P., *A Strategy of Interdependence*. New York: Charles Scribner's Sons, 1964.

Schelling, Thomas C., *The Strategy of Conflict*. New York: Oxford University Press, 1963.

Snyder, Glenn H., *Deterrence and Defense: Toward a Theory of National Security*. Princeton: Princeton University Press, 1961.

Sokolovskii, V. D. (ed.), *Soviet Military Strategy*. Translated by Thomas Wolfe, Herbert S. Dinerstein, and Leon Goure. Englewood Cliffs: Prentice-Hall, 1963.

Strausz-Hupé, Robert, William R. Kintner, Alvin J. Cottrell, and James E. Dougherty, *Protracted Conflict*. New York: Harper and Brothers, 1959.

Strausz-Hupé, Robert, William R. Kintner, and Stefan T. Possony, *A Forward Strategy for America*. New York: Harper and Brothers, 1961.

Tanham, George K., *Communist Revolutionary Warfare: The Vietminh in Indochina*. New York: Praeger, 1961.

Tarr, David W., *American Strategy in the Nuclear Age*. New York: Macmillan, 1966.

Taylor, General Maxwell P., *The Uncertain Trumpet*. New York: Harper and Brothers, 1960.

Thayer, Charles W., *Guerrilla*. New York: Harper and Row, 1963.

"The ABM Debate," Parts One and Two, *Bulletin of the Atomic Scientists*. May, June 1967.

Waltz, Kenneth, *Man, the State and War*. New York: Columbia University Press, 1959.

Wiesner, Jerome, and Herbert F. York, "The Test Ban." *Scientific American*. October 1964.

Zawodny, J. K., "Guerrilla and Sabotage: Organization Operations, Motivations, Escalation." *The Annals of the American Academy of Political and Social Science*. May 1962.

Part IV

Technology and the
International System

TECHNOLOGY, or applied science, has had a major impact upon the international system and upon political relationships in general. Since the Industrial Revolution of the eighteenth century, changes in technology have narrowed distances and vastly increased the coercive and destructive capabilities available to man. As a result of advances in technology, the volume of transactions—movement of persons, trade, and messages—has increased dramatically. With greater ease and speed than ever before, people, goods, and messages can move from one part of the globe to another. Depending upon the meaning attached to them, the effect of such greatly increased transactions is either to increase the prospects for a more peaceful world, or to contribute to a growth in international tensions.

Technology has made available to national units greater capabilities for affecting the behavior of other national units. In many cases, technology has contributed to the cohesiveness of national units, for modern communication has narrowed the distance which historically separated the central government from the population living in the hinterland. But technology has had the effect, according to John von Neumann, of outmoding many of the political units into which mankind is organized.

The crisis that technology produces for the national unit is most evident in Western Europe. Over the past generation, the cost of research and development has risen astronomically. At the same time, the opportunities for exploiting science and technology have grown enormously. There the national units are inadequate to maximize the potential inherent in advanced science and technology. In many fields, according to William Kintner and Robert Pfaltzgraff, the cost of research and development is beyond the means of individual West European national units. In comparison with the United States and the Soviet Union, West European countries spend less, both in relative and absolute terms, for research and development. European national units are not large enough to permit the necessary level of mass production which would lower the unit cost of certain products based upon advanced technology. As a result, in such fields as aircraft, space exploration, and electronics, there is a widening gap—sometimes called the Atlantic technological imbalance—between the United States and Western Europe.

As in the past, technology may spread from its point of origin to peoples around the world. Other nations can duplicate existing technologies at less cost than the pioneering nation spends to develop them. Nevertheless, the cost of producing new technology may continue to increase, so that no nation, not even the United States or the Soviet Union, will have adequate resources for the full exploitation of the potentials inherent in science and technology.

22. CAN WE SURVIVE TECHNOLOGY?

John von Neumann

"THE GREAT GLOBE itself" is in a rapidly maturing crisis—a crisis attributable to the fact that the environment in which technological progress must occur has become both undersized and underorganized. To define the crisis with any accuracy, and to explore possibilities of dealing with it, we must not only look at relevant facts, but also engage in some speculation. The process will illuminate some potential technological developments of the next quarter-century.

In the first half of this century the accelerating industrial revolution encountered an absolute limitation—not on technological progress as such but on an essential safety factor. This safety factor, which had permitted the industrial revolution to roll on from the mid-eighteenth to the early twentieth century, was essentially a matter of geographical and political *Lebensraum:* an ever broader geographical scope for technological activities, combined with an ever broader political integration of the world. Within this expanding framework it was possible to accommodate the major tensions created by technological progress.

Now this safety mechanism is being sharply inhibited; literally and figuratively, we are running out of room. At long last, we begin to feel the effects of the finite, actual size of the earth in a critical way.

Thus the crisis does not arise from accidental events or human errors. It is inherent in technology's relation to geography on the one hand and to political organization on the other. The crisis was developing visibly in the 1940's, and some phases can be traced back to 1914. In the years between now and 1980 the crisis will probably develop far beyond all earlier patterns. When or how it will end—or to what state of affairs it will yield—nobody can say.

From *Fortune* (June 1955), 106–108; 151–152. Reprinted by permission of the publisher.

JOHN VON NEUMANN (1903–   ) Member of U.S. Atomic Energy Commission, 1954–1957; Member of Institute for Advanced Study, Princeton University, 1933–1954. Author of *The Computer and the Brain,* (New Haven: Yale University Press, 1958). Co-author of *The Theory of Games and Economic Behavior,* (Princeton: Princeton University Press, 1944).

In all its stages the industrial revolution consisted of making available more and cheaper energy, and more and easier controls of human actions and reactions, and more and faster communications. Each development increased the effectiveness of the other two. All three factors increased the speed of performing large-scale operations—industrial, mercantile, political, and migratory. But throughout the development, increased speed did not so much shorten time requirements of processes as extend the areas of of the earth affected by them. The reason is clear. Since most *time* scales are fixed by human reaction times, habits, and other physiological and psychological factors, the effect of the increased speed of technological processes was to enlarge the *size* of units—political, organizational, economic, and cultural—affected by technological operations. That is, instead of performing the same operations as before in less time, now larger-scale operations were performed in the same time. This important evolution has a natural limit, that of the earth's actual size. The limit is now being reached, or at least closely approached.

Indications of this appeared early and with dramatic force in the military sphere. By 1940 even the larger countries of continental Western Europe were inadequate as military units. Only Russia could sustain a major military reverse without collapsing. Since 1945, improved aeronautics and communications alone might have sufficed to make any geographical unit, including Russia, inadequate in a future war. The advent of nuclear weapons merely climaxes the development. Now the effectiveness of offensive weapons is such as to stultify all plausible defensive time scales. As early as World War I, it was observed that the admiral commanding the battle fleet could "lose the British Empire in one afternoon." Yet navies of that epoch were relatively stable entities, tolerably safe against technological surprises. Today there is every reason to fear that even minor inventions and feints in the field of nuclear weapons can be decisive in less time than would be required to devise specific countermeasures. Soon existing nations will be as unstable in war as a nation the size of Manhattan Island would have been in a contest fought with the weapons of 1900.

Such military instability has already found its political expression. Two superpowers, the U.S. and U.S.S.R., represent such enormous destructive potentials as to afford little chance of a purely passive equilibrium. Other countries, including possible "neutrals," are militarily defenseless in the ordinary sense. At best they will acquire destructive capabilities of their own, as Britain is now doing. Consequently, the "concert of powers"—or its equivalent international organization—rests on a basis much more fragile than ever before. The situation is further embroiled by the newly achieved political effectiveness of non-European nationalisms.

These factors would "normally"—that is, in any recent century— have led to war. Will they lead to war before 1980? Or soon thereafter? It would be presumptuous to try to answer such a question firmly. In any case, the present and the near future are both dangerous. While the immediate problem is to cope with the actual danger, it is also essential to envisage how the problem is going to evolve in the 1955–80 period, even assuming that all will go reasonably well for the moment. This does not mean belittling immediate problems of weaponry, of U.S.—U.S.S.R. tensions, of the evolution and revolutions of Asia. These first things must come first. But we must be ready for the follow-up, lest possible immediate successes prove futile. We must think beyond the present forms of problems to those of later decades.

Technological evolution is still accelerating. Technologies are always constructive and beneficial, directly or indirectly. Yet their consequences tend to increase instability—a point that will get closer attention after we have had a look at certain aspects of continuing technological evolution.

First of all, there is a rapidly expanding supply of energy. It is generally agreed that even conventional, chemical fuel—coal or oil—will be available in increased quantity in the next two decades. Increasing demand tends to keep fuel prices high, yet improvements in methods of generation seem to bring the price of power down. There is little doubt that the most significant event affecting energy is the advent of nuclear power. Its only available controlled source today is the nuclear-fission reactor. Reactor techniques appear to be approaching a condition in which they will be competitive with conventional (chemical) power sources within the U.S.; however, because of generally higher fuel prices abroad, they could already be more than competitive in many important foreign areas. Yet reactor technology is but a decade and a half old, during most of which period effort has been directed primarily not toward power but toward plutonium production. Given a decade of really large-scale industrial effort, the economic characteristics of reactors will undoubtedly surpass those of the present by far.

Moreover, it is not a law of nature that all controlled release of nuclear energy should be tied to fission reactions as it has been thus far. It is true that nuclear energy appears to be the primary source of practically all energy now visible in nature. Furthermore, it is not surprising that the first break into the intranuclear domain occurred at the unstable "high end" of the system of nuclei (that is, by fission). Yet fission is not nature's normal way of releasing nuclear energy. In the long run, systematic industrial exploitation of nuclear energy may shift reliance onto other and still more abundant modes. Again, reactors have been bound thus far to the traditional heat-steam-generator-electricity cycle, just as automobiles were at first constructed to look like buggies. It is likely that we shall gradually develop procedures more naturally and effectively adjusted to the new source of energy, abandoning the conventional kinks and detours inherited from chemical-fuel processes. Consequently, a few decades hence energy may be free—just like the unmetered air—with coal and oil used mainly as raw materials for organic chemical synthesis, to which, as experience has shown, their properties are best suited.

It is worth emphasizing that the main trend will be systematic exploration of nuclear reactions—that is, the transmutation of elements, or alchemy rather than chemistry. The main point in developing the industrial use of nuclear processes is to make them suitable for large-scale exploitation on the relatively small site that is the earth or, rather, any plausible terrestrial industrial establishment. Nature has, of course, been operating nuclear processes all along, well and massively, but her "natural" sites for this industry are entire stars. There is reason to believe that the minimum space requirements for her way of operating are the minimum sizes of stars. Forced by the limitations of our real estate, we must in this respect do much better than nature. That this may not be impossible has been demonstrated in the somewhat extreme and unnatural instance of fission, that remarkable breakthrough of the past decade.

What massive transmutation of elements will do to technology in general is hard to imagine, but the effects will be radical indeed. This can already be sensed in related fields. The general revolution clearly under way in the military sphere, and its already realized special aspect, the terrible possibilities of mass destruction, should not be viewed as typical of what the nuclear revolution stands for. Yet they may well be typical of how deeply that revolution will transform whatever it touches. And the revolution will probably touch most things technological.

Also likely to evolve fast—and quite apart from nuclear evolution—is automation. Interesting analyses of recent developments in this field, and of near-future potentialities, have appeared in the last few years. Automatic control, of course, is as old as the industrial revolution, for the decisive new feature of Watt's steam engine was its automatic valve control, including speed control by a "governor." In our century, however, small electric amplifying and switching devices put automation on an entirely new footing. This development began with the electromechanical (telephone) relay, continued and unfolded with the vacuum tube, and appears to accelerate with various solid-state devices (semi-conductor crystals, ferromagnetic cores, etc.). The last decade or two has also witnessed an increasing ability to control and "discipline" large numbers of such devices within one machine. Even in an airplane the number of vacuum tubes now approaches or exceeds a thousand. Other machines, containing up to 10,000 vacuum tubes, up to five times more crystals, and possibly more than 100,000 cores, now operate faultlessly over long periods, performing many millions of regulated, preplanned actions per second, with an expectation of only a few errors per day or week.

Many such machines have been built to perform complicated scientific and engineering calculations and large-scale accounting and logistical surveys. There is no doubt that they will be used for elaborate industrial process control, logistical, economic, and other planning, and many other purposes heretofore lying entirely outside the compass of quantitative and automatic control and preplanning. Thanks to simplified forms of automatic or semi-automatic control, the efficiency of some important branches of industry has increased considerably during recent decades. It is therefore to be expected that the considerably elaborated newer forms, now becoming increasingly available, will effect much more along these lines.

Fundamentally, improvements in control are really improvements in communicating information within an organization or mechanism. The sum total of progress in this sphere is explosive. Improvements in communication in its direct, physical sense—transportation—while less dramatic, have been considerable and steady. If nuclear developments make energy unrestrictedly available, transportation developments are likely to accelerate even more. But even "normal" progress in sea, land, and air media is extremely important. Just such "normal" progress molded the world's economic development, producing the present global ideas in politics and economics.

Let us now consider a thoroughly "abnormal" industry and its potentialities—that is, an industry as yet without a place in any list of major activities: the control of weather or, to use a more ambitious but justified term, climate. One phase of this activity that has received a good deal of public attention is "rain making." The present technique assumes extensive rain clouds, and forces precipitation by applying small amounts of chemical agents. While it is not easy to evaluate the significance of the efforts made thus far, the evidence seems to indicate that the aim is an attainable one.

But weather control and climate control are really much broader than rain making. All major weather phenomena, as well as climate as such, are ultimately controlled by the solar energy that falls on the earth. To modify the amount of solar energy is, of course, beyond human power. But what really matters is not the amount that hits the earth, but the fraction retained by the earth, since that reflected back into space is no more useful than if it had never arrived. Now, the amount absorbed by the solid earth, the sea, or the atmosphere seems to be subject to delicate influences. True, none of these has so far been substantially controlled by human will, but there are strong indications of control possibilities.

The carbon dioxide released into the atmosphere by industry's burning of coal and oil—more than half of it during the last generation—may have changed the atmosphere's composition sufficiently to account for a general warming of the world by about one degree Fahrenheit. The volcano Krakatao erupted in 1883 and released an amount of energy by no means exorbitant. Had the dust of the eruption stayed in the stratosphere for fifteen years, reflecting sunlight away from the earth, it might have sufficed to lower the world's temperature by six degrees (in fact, it stayed for about three years, and five such eruptions would probably have achieved the result mentioned). This would have been a substantial cooling; the last Ice Age, when half of North America and all of northern and western Europe were under an ice cap like that of Greenland or Antarctica, was only fifteen degrees colder than the present age. On the other hand, another fifteen degrees of warming would probably melt the ice of Greenland and Antarctica and produce worldwide tropical to semitropical climate.

Furthermore, it is known that the persistence of large ice fields is due to the fact that ice both reflects sunlight energy and radiates away terrestrial energy at an even higher rate than ordinary soil. Microscopic layers of colored matter spread on an icy surface, or in the atmosphere above one, could inhibit the reflection-radiation process, melt the ice, and change the local climate. Measures that would effect such changes are technically possible, and the amount of investment required would be only of the order of magnitude that sufficed to develop rail systems and other major industries. The main difficulty lies in predicting in detail the effects of any such drastic intervention. But our knowledge of the dynamics and the controlling processes in the atmosphere is rapidly approaching a level that would permit such prediction. Probably intervention in atmospheric and climatic matters will come in a few decades, and will unfold on a scale difficult to imagine at present.

What could be done, of course, is no index to what should be done; to make a new ice age in order to annoy others, or a new tropical, "interglacial" age in order to please everybody, is not necessarily a rational program. In fact, to evaluate the ultimate consequences of either a general cooling or a general heating would be a complex matter. Changes would affect the level of the seas, and hence the habitability of the continental coastal shelves; the evaporation of the seas, and hence general precipitation and glaciation levels; and so on. What would be harmful and what beneficial—and to which regions of the earth—is not immediately obvious. But there is little doubt that one *could* carry out analyses needed to predict results, intervene on any desired scale, and ultimately achieve rather fantastic effects. The climate of specific regions and levels of precipitation might be altered. For example, temporary disturbances—including invasions of cold (polar) air that constitute the typical winter of the middle latitudes, and tropical storms (hurricanes)— might be corrected or at least depressed.

There is no need to detail what such things would mean to agriculture or, indeed, to all phases of human, animal, and plant ecology. What power over our environment, over all nature, is implied!

Such actions would be more directly and truly worldwide than recent or, presumably, future wars, or than the economy at any time. Extensive human intervention would deeply affect the atmosphere's general circulation, which depends on the earth's rotation and intensive solar heating of the tropics. Measures in the arctic may control the weather in temperate regions, or measures in one temperate region critically affect another, one-quarter around the globe. All this will merge each nation's affairs with those of every other, more thoroughly than the threat of a nuclear or any other war may already have done.

The problems created by the combination of the presently possible forms of nuclear warfare and the rather unusually unstable international situation are formidable and not to be solved easily. Those of the next decades are likely to be similarly vexing, "only more so." The U.S.- U.S.S.R. tension is bad, but when other nations begin to make felt their full offensive potential weight, things will not become simpler.

Present awful possibilities of nuclear warfare may give way to others even more awful. After global climate control becomes possible, perhaps all our present involvements will seem simple. We should not deceive ourselves: once such possibilities become actual, they will be exploited. It will, therefore, be necessary to develop suitable new political forms and procedures. All experience shows that even smaller technological changes than those now in the cards profoundly transform political and social relationships. Experience also shows that these transformations are not *a priori* predictable and that most contemporary "first guesses" concerning them are wrong. For all these reasons, one should take neither present difficulties nor presently proposed reforms too seriously.

The one solid fact is that the difficulties are due to an evolution that, while useful and constructive, is also dangerous. Can we produce the required adjustments with the necessary speed? The most hopeful answer is that the human species has been subjected to similar tests before and seems to have a congenital ability to come through, after varying amounts of trouble. To ask in advance for a complete recipe would be unreasonable. We can specify only the human qualities required: patience, flexibility, intelligence.

23. THE PROSPECTS
FOR WESTERN SCIENCE AND TECHNOLOGY

William R. Kintner and Robert L. Pfaltzgraff, Jr.

TECHNOLOGY is transforming relations among nations. The changes induced by the technological revolution affect not only the economic well-being of peoples everywhere but drastically transform strategic relationships in the international system. However, not all nations have benefited equally from the forward thrust of technology during the last generation, nor have they reaped, in equal measure, the fruits of technological advance.

Since the end of the Second World War, the most important technological advances have been scored either by the United States or the Soviet Union. The nations of Western Europe, which prior to the war led in both scientific inquiry and advanced military technology, have not participated fully in the technological revolution of the past twenty years. The relative decline of European technology lies at the root of much of the strategic controversy which cleaves the Atlantic Alliance. Since Western Europe has been unable through its own technological efforts to provide for its defense, the United States has assumed this task.

There is a complex relationship between science and technology, on the one hand, and defense and economic change on the other. U.S. technological developments in atomic engineering, electronics and space are pushing American industry ahead so rapidly that Europe faces the risk of falling even farther behind the United States in certain key sectors of advanced technology. Yet the major advances in U.S. technology over the last decade have resulted, to a considerable extent, from the energetic application on a very large scale of basic scientific ideas first developed in Europe. Basic science in the United States—the source of future tech-

---

From *ORBIS,* a quarterly journal of world affairs published by the Foreign Policy Research Institute of the University of Pennsylvania (Fall 1965), 565–578. Reprinted by permission of the authors and the Trustees of the University of Pennsylvania. Footnotes have been renumbered to appear in consecutive order.

WILLIAM R. KINTNER—See biographical note, page 173.

ROBERT L. PFALTZGRAFF, JR. (1934–   ) Assistant Professor of Political Science and Research Associate, Foreign Policy Research Institute, University of Pennsylvania. Author of *The Atlantic Community: A Complex Imbalance,* (Princeton: Van Nostrand, 1969), *Britain Faces Europe,* 1957–1967, (Philadelphia: University of Pennsylvania Press, 1969).

nologies—is by no means so advanced or so clearly superior as U.S. engineering and industrial techniques. Many of the technologies in which the United States leads the world—nucleonics, electronics and space—rest upon European scientific achievements.

The quality of U.S. technology may depend in the future, as it has in the past, upon our ability to draw upon scientific advances elsewhere. The history of knowledge, as well as the strength of basic science which European universities and research institutes have displayed, attest to the potential contribution of other countries to technological innovation. By assuring the best possible qualitative standards in science through collaboration at the international level, the United States could assure the Free World a technological lead for the indefinite future.

The necessity for such a definition of the national interest is underlined by a consideration of scientific and technological advances in the Soviet Union. The improvements which the Soviet Union has registered in scientific training in recent years can be expected to reveal themselves in technological advances over the next generation, as the graduates of Soviet technical schools during the last decade reach their most productive years. While qualitative differences may exist between certain categories of Soviet and Western scientists and engineers, it appears that only when the educational efforts of the United States and Western Europe in the physical sciences are more closely combined will the potential advantage of the Soviets in this sector diminish. Greater Western collaboration may become essential if the peoples of the North Atlantic area are to remain in the forefront of the scientific and technological revolution of our age.

The United States thus faces the problem of assuring a scientific base which, at the very least, will permit this country to maintain its existing position in technology. Western Europe, if it does not achieve a higher level of technological proficiency, will be unable over the next decade to assume a greater part of the burden of its own defense than it presently bears. In part, the United States might assist Western Europe to acquire or develop much of the advanced technology necessary for its defense as well as for its industrial future. In return, the United States might take steps to assure that advances in European science would become immediately available to U.S. technology. Clearly there exists, by virtue of expertise to be found on both sides of the Atlantic, a community of interest in science and technology.

The problem of technological collaboration has yet another dimension. Some Europeans, in recent years, have become concerned with what they perceive to be the U.S. technological-industrial domination of the Atlantic Alliance. Europeans have become resentful of what sometimes appears to be the overzealous efforts of U.S. firms to press NATO allies to purchase U.S. weapons systems, even when European firms may have developed what they believe is a superior product.[1] Therefore, the problem of technological collaboration is related, in part, to the development of policies in NATO which will enable European member countries to secure what they consider to be a more equitable share of defense contracts.

EUROPE AND THE TECHNOLOGICAL REVOLUTION

Many of the great technological advances of the United States over the last thirty years are the product of European basic research transplanted to this country. European scientists played a decisive part in the harnessing of nuclear energy and in the development of capabilities for space exploration. In fact, the United States has been traditionally to a great extent the consumer rather than the producer of the insights provided by pure scientific research.

Yet it appears that Western Europe is deficient, in comparison with the United States and the Soviet Union, in the allocation of resources to technological research and development. The disparity between U.S. and European efforts in technology may account in part for the inability of Western Europe to rival the superpowers. A comparison between European and U.S. expenditures for scientific research (see Table I) illustrates the disparities between the capability of European countries and the United States to engage in technological innovation.

No European country devotes to research and development (R&D) a percentage of national income comparable to that of the United States. The total expenditures of the United Kingdom, France and West Germany, taken together, fall far short of the U.S. figures. Even though costs in Western Europe may be lower, the total European effort for technological research and development is considerably less than that of the United States. Considered either singly or as part of the total West European expenditure for technology, European programs lag far behind those of their major ally. Moreover, Europe remains deficient in comparison with the United States in the granting of patents and licenses, one indication of technological innovation.

In sheer numbers, if not in quality, Europe remains behind the United States and the Soviet Union in school enrollment. In 1963, for example, the United States granted approximately 465,000 undergraduate degrees in the natural sciences and engineering. Universities in Belgium, France, the German Federal Republic, Italy, the Netherlands and the United Kingdom together awarded an estimated 100,000 degrees in the same

---

[1] See, for example, *The Observer,* July 18, 1965, p. 6.

TABLE I

EXPENDITURES ON INDUSTRIAL AND SCIENTIFIC RESEARCH
IN MAJOR NORTH ATLANTIC COUNTRIES

	Total Expenditure*		Government Expenditure*	
	Millions of dollars	Per cent of national income	Millions of dollars	Per cent of budget
United States	14,039	3.3	9,218	11.3
United Kingdom	1,775	2.8	1,078	6.2
West Germany	966	1.6	529	4.7
France	700	1.5	546	3.6

*The figures are from 1961, the latest year for which comparable figures are available.

Source: *EFTA Reporter*, April 5, 1965.

year.[2] Although European countries will probably have narrowed this gap by 1970, the number of persons enrolled in universities in Europe as candidates for degrees in science is likely to remain well below comparable enrollment in the United States.

Beyond the problem of producing trained personnel in sufficient numbers, some European countries have suffered an exodus of scientists and engineers attracted to the United States by higher salaries, superior laboratory facilities and greater opportunities for scientific achievement and personal advancement. The so-called brain drain has caused considerable concern especially in Britain, for Britain's economic future depends to a large extent upon its ability to utilize advanced technology to sustain competitive export industries.

Since 1947 U.S. government expenditures for R&D have risen from $0.7 billion to $14.7 billion in 1963. The government now accounts for two-thirds of the nation's total annual expenditure on scientific research.[3] U.S. defense expenditures in 1965 are expected to exceed $52 billion, and will represent about 8.2 per cent of this country's Gross National Product. Most West European countries devote a considerably lower percentage of their GNP to defense and to R&D for defense-related technology. If Western Europe, including the Six and Britain, were to raise its level of defense spending to 10 per cent of its total GNP of approximately $340 billion at 1964 rates, European expenditures for defense would begin to approach those of the United States and the Soviet Union.[4]

· · ·

---

[2] Organization for Economic Cooperation and Development, *Resources of Scientific and Technical Personnel in the OECD Area* (Paris: OECD, 1963), pp. 214–215.

[3] See Edward T. Chase, "Politics and Technology," *Yale Review*, March 1963, p. 333.

[4] The Soviet Union, it is estimated, spends about 20 per cent of its annual GNP on defense or about $50 billion, i.e., roughly the same amount as the United States. See Timothy Sosnovy, "The Soviet Military Budget," *Foreign Affairs*, April 1964, pp. 487–494, for further information on Soviet defense spending.

GOVERNMENT AND CORPORATE SPONSORSHIP OF TECHNOLOGICAL INNOVATION

Thanks to the heavy government investment in research and development and the large markets for advanced products, the United States appears to enjoy an advantage in the exploitation of the potential inherent in modern science. Since government-sponsored research and the development of advanced technology are closely related industries in which major scientific breakthroughs are most prevalent, they will maintain a competitive advantage over their foreign counterparts less abundantly supplied with government funds. This problem, for example, confronts the electronics industries of several European countries. European firms have found it difficult to penetrate markets for computers even in their own countries. Although British scientists played a major part in the development of the computer, one U.S. firm, International Business Machines, supplies 80 per cent of the world market. The remainder is controlled largely by two other U.S. producers, Radio Corporation of America and General Electric. U.S. firms have even secured a large measure of control over those European companies which produce computers. Only one European computer manufacturer remains beyond U.S. control: International Computer and Tabulator (ICT) of Great Britain, which has received substantial support from the British government. Nevertheless, ICT supplies less than one-half of the British market, while IBM alone accounts for 40 per cent of the sales of computers in Britain. Other European computer manufacturers are now controlled totally or in part by U.S. corporations.[5] President de Gaulle is said to have agreed reluctantly to permit General Electric to acquire half ownership of Machines Bull in order to enable France to benefit from the infusion of U.S. computer technology. Such companies are in fact international in their personnel, programs of research and scope of operations, although their policies are influenced, if not controlled, by U.S. industry.

The technical lead attained by U.S. companies, which can rely upon a larger domestic market, poses serious problems for European producers of computers and other items derived from advanced technologies. Because of the necessity for large capital investment in R&D, together with constant modernization of production facilities, European firms with smaller markets than their U.S. counterparts find considerable difficulty in competing with them in many fields of advanced technology.

The ability to exploit existing scientific data, although not necessarily to produce new ideas or techniques, appears to lie with those countries able to support large corporate enterprises either through government

---

[5] See *The Economist,* September 26, 1964, pp. 1251–1253.

subsidization or vast markets, or both. Standardization and concentration among firms, it appears, have been furthered in the United States more than in Europe. For example, in the field of avionics the United States has two firms which develop and build interceptor fire control radars; there are four such companies in Western Europe. Four U.S. firms build ground surveillance radar for air defense and traffic control; Western Europe has eight suppliers of this product.[6] Such a division of effort appears to reduce the opportunities for specialization in R&D and to limit the capabilities of European firms for large-scale production.

It is difficult to assess the relationship between the size of a firm and its ability to develop new technologies. Large firms appear to enjoy certain advantages in the application of science, including the funds necessary to employ scientific and technical personnel and to build well-equipped laboratories. Much of the R&D effort of corporate enterprise is undertaken by large firms: of all firms in the United States undertaking R&D, only 16 per cent of medium-sized firms (1,000–5,000 employees) conducted any basic research, while among firms employing more than 5,000 people the figure was 47 per cent.[7]

Whatever the limitations of smaller economic units, the United States does not lead other industrialized nations in every sector of technology. Perhaps because the United States has devoted a major portion of its efforts to the development of those technologies where the gap between U.S. and European achievements is most marked, in certain other fields it now lags behind its competitors in Western Europe and Japan. For example, the United States has not developed the new technologies for shipbuilding which enable other nations to compete successfully in world markets. The funds spent in the United States on research for naval design for cargo carriers and other kinds of merchant shipping are minute by comparison with the investment in R&D for air transportation and space exploration. In the building and operation of high-speed intra- and inter-urban transportation systems, the United States might benefit from

---

[6] See Philip J. Klass. "European Defense Efforts Mold Future of Avionics," *Aviation Week and Space Technology,* June 25, 1965, p. 109.

[7] OECD, *Ministers Talk Science* (Paris: 1965), p. 103. According to the General Manager, Defense Electronics Division, General Electric Company, one of the largest U.S. corporations: "For large companies like General Electric, a broad technological base is essential. Tomorrow's products and services will be coming from research carried out today, and any major industrial organization, to compete effectively, must be willing to devote a healthy effort to new technology and reasonable risk-taking. An example of this situation is the fact that half of General Electric's $5 billion worth of business today is estimated to come from new products introduced since World War II." Gerald A. Hoyt, "Industrial Strength and National Security: The Management of Change," *The General Electric Forum,* July-September 1965, p. 23.

techniques pioneered abroad.[8] Thus the U.S. economy might gain new technologies in a variety of important fields in a program of technological collaboration and perhaps specialization with other industrialized countries.

EDUCATION AND TECHNOLOGY

The national educational system is vital to the efforts of any country to achieve major advances in science and technology. In educational institutions scientists and technicians are trained and basic research is conducted. It is perhaps impossible, regardless of expenditures for scientific education, to assure the emergence of talented persons such as those responsible for the major breakthroughs in nuclear energy, electronics and medicine. Nevertheless, the development of new technologies may be impossible without the training of large numbers of scientists, engineers, technicians and managers, as well as the investment of large sums of money—all of which have marked the technological efforts of the United States and, to an even greater extent over the last generation, of the Soviet Union. In the last two decades, the United States has impressively increased governmental funds available for university scientific research. Whereas in 1955 governmental grants to universities for R&D totaled $300 million, by 1963 such funds had risen to $1.2 billion. It is anticipated that by 1970 this figure will reach $2.5 billion.[9] Beyond their impact on technological innovation, such inflows of capital have served to increase considerably the number of students and faculty engaged in research in American universities.

Great disparities exist between U.S. and comparable European government programs to support scientific studies in universities. Nevertheless, European governments have made major efforts in recent years to remedy the serious deficiency of technical training in their educational systems. Since World War II, there has been a rising enrollment at all levels of education in Europe, especially in technical and professional programs. Technical studies now occupy a place of importance. In greater numbers than ever before, European students are being trained as engineers, draftsmen, scientists, technicians, and in the other skills essential in a modern industrialized society. European governments are making great efforts to adapt their educational systems to an age of science and technology. The Netherlands government, for example, is planning to create new technical universities; France has built fourteen more colleges

---

[8] Seymour Melman, "Behind the Mask of Success," *Saturday Review*, July 31, 1965, pp. 9–10 ff. Melman contends that the United States, by concentrating its efforts on the development of military technologies, is allowing "entire industries" devoted to nondefense-oriented production "to fall into disrepair."

[9] " 'Uncle Sam' Big Man on Campus," *Business Week*, November 2, 1963, p. 90.

of science; and the British government has given special emphasis to science in the new universities established in the United Kingdom since the Second World War, as well as in the older universities.

In certain European countries, notably Great Britain, occupations related to the applied sciences do not yet attract sufficient numbers of youths to fill the growing demand for engineers, technicians and managers. British education in the applied sciences and business administration still lags behind the needs of the 1960's. According to the Robbins Report, studies leading to careers in pure science not only attract greater numbers of students, but also persons of "better quality" than does technology. The Robbins Report recommended the creation of five special Institutions for Scientific and Technological Education and Research. In other colleges, it was recommended, "a new system for degrees should be established, covering business studies, languages and other subjects as well as science and technology." [10]

INTEGRATION OF EUROPEAN TECHNOLOGICAL EFFORTS

Were Western Europe to aspire to a technological and military structure comparable to that of the United States and the Soviet Union it would be necessary to increase substantially the numbers of persons trained in scientific and technological skills. Furthermore, it might be necessary to achieve a high level of political, military and economic integration in Western Europe. Only a central authority might be capable of allocating efficiently the massive expenditures necessary for research and the development and production of advanced weapons systems, as well as technologies with peacetime applications. In all likelihood, the organization directing a centralized effort for R&D would have to be endowed with the power of taxation. The substantial funds required would have to come, at least in part, from a source other than national parliaments, for such expenditures must be planned and sustained over a period of several years. Thus the creation of an integrated European defense effort might be dependent upon the building of integrated institutions possessing considerably greater supranational authority than is to be found in the existing European Communities.

European countries have already initiated efforts to achieve a measure of technological collaboration within Europe. Programs in space are illustrative of the new kinds of technological collaboration which have been developed in recent years. According to the Convention and Protocol

---

[10] *Higher Education.* Report of the Committee appointed by the Prime Minister under the chairmanship of Lord Robbins 1961–63. Cmnd. 2154 (London: HMSO, 1965), pp. 126–146.

of the European Space Research Organization (ESRO), ten European countries have agreed "to establish European collaboration, exclusively for peaceful purposes, in the fields of space research." [11] Founded in 1962, ESRO will include centers for the design, development and construction of rocket nose cones, satellites and space probes; a space data center for the analysis of the problems of estimating and analyzing orbits; telemetry and telecommand stations, and launching sites. For the first three years of its existence, ESRO was granted a budget of $78 million. Expenditures for the second three-year period were expected to total $122 million. ESRO itself was not empowered by its members to undertake such projects as the placing of manned satellites into orbit. Instead it planned to launch sounding rockets, to place small satellites (about 100 kgs.) into orbit, and eventually to put into orbit around the earth an astronomical observatory, and around the moon a planetary observatory. ESRO was designed to enable national groups of scientists to collaborate in the preparation of rocket nose cones containing several different experiments, in the testing of rocket components and payloads, in experimenting with heavy satellites, and in the recording and analysis of data.

In 1962, the year of ESRO's formation, the European Space Vehicle Launcher Development Organization (ELDO) was established in London.[12] Its purpose, according to its Convention, was to enable its member governments to "cooperate in the development of space vehicle launchers and to study their scientific and commercial application." The negotiations for ELDO resulted from a British proposal, in the Council of Europe in September 1960, for European collaboration in the development of the Blue Streak rocket, originally designed as a British strategic missile, as the launching vehicle for a joint European satellite. Britain was to contribute the first stage of the rocket, France the second, and Germany the third. Italy was given the task of building the first series of experimental satellite test vehicles. Belgium was to provide down-range ground guidance stations. The Netherlands agreed to furnish long-range telemetry links, and Australia was to make available its Woomera launching site for firings. The first satellite is not scheduled to be launched until 1967.

Both ESRO and ELDO have experienced difficulties in achieving the necessary coordination of effort among participant nations, especially in meeting production deadlines. Moreover, the cost of launching a European satellite appears to be substantially in excess of original budget allocations. It is reported that the launching of ELDO's first rocket will

---

11 ESRO's members include Belgium, Denmark, France, Germany, Italy, the Netherlands, Spain, Sweden, Switzerland and the United Kingdom.

12 The members of ELDO include Australia, Belgium, France, the German Federal Republic, Italy, the Netherlands and the United Kingdom.

require at least $100 million more than the original allocation of $200 million.[13] ELDO was given by its member governments a budget of $196 million for its initial five-year program. This multinational scientific project came up for critical review when its costs seemed likely to exceed original estimates, yet its expenditures are small in comparison with those of the United States.

The countries of Western Europe, with their comparatively meagre efforts, can hardly hope to narrow the gap which separates them from the United States in technology without a substantially greater investment than they have been willing to make thus far. The cost of research and development is growing. Consequently, there is an even greater likelihood in the future that smaller national political units will be excluded from participation in many advanced technological fields. The smallness of domestic markets raises the unit costs of production in military and industrial goods. Only a unified Europe, it appears, could afford the outlays of capital necessary to purchase U.S. technological skills and, subsequently, to engage in a European R&D effort designed to narrow appreciably the Atlantic technological gap.

SELECTED BIBLIOGRAPHY

Part IV

Technology and the International System

Calmann, John, "European Co-operation in Defense Technology: The Political Aspect." *Defense, Technology and the Western Alliance*, No. 1 (April 1967). London: Institute for Strategic Studies, 1967.

Deutsch, Karl W., "The Impact of Science and Technology on International Politics." *Daedalus*. Fall 1959.

Dupré, J. Stefan, and Sanford A. Lakoff, *Science and the Nation: Policy and Politics*. Englewood Cliffs: Prentice-Hall, Inc., 1962.

Freeman, C., and A. Young, *The Research and Development Effort in Western Europe, North America, and the Soviet Union*. Paris: Organization for Economic Cooperation and Development, 1965.

---

[13] See *Christian Science Monitor*, June 1, 1965.

Gilpin, Robert, *American Scientists and Nuclear Weapons Policy*. Princeton: Princeton University Press, 1962.

Goldsen, Joseph M. (ed.), *Outer Space in World Politics*. New York: Praeger, 1963.

Hall, J., "Atoms for Peace, or War," *Foreign Affairs*. July 1965.

Haskins, C. P., "Technology, Science and American Foreign Policy." *Foreign Affairs*. January 1962.

Haskins, Caryl P., *The Scientific Revolution and World Politics*. New York: Harper and Row, 1964.

Hogg, Q. M., *Science and Politics*. New York: Atheneum Press, 1964.

Jacobson, Harold K., and Eric Stein, *Diplomats, Scientists, and Politicians*. Ann Arbor: University of Michigan Press, 1966.

Mesthene, Emmanuel G. (ed.), *Ministers Talk about Science*. Paris: Organization for Economic Cooperation and Development, 1965.

Pfaltzgraff, Robert L., Jr., "The Atlantic Technological Imbalance," *The New Republic*. January 23, 1967.

Price, Don K., *Government and Science: Their Dynamic Relation in American Democracy*. New York: Oxford University Press, 1954.

Quinn, James Brian, "Technological Competition: Europe vs. U.S." *Atlantic Community Quarterly*. Winter 1966–1967.

Skolnikoff, Eugene B., *Science, Technology, and American Foreign Policy*. Cambridge: MIT Press, 1967.

Snow, C. P., *The Two Cultures and the Scientific Revolution*. New York: Cambridge University Press, 1959.

Sprout, Harold and Margaret, "Geopolitical Hypotheses in Technological Perspective," *World Politics*. January 1963.

Van Dyke, Vernon, *Pride and Power: The Rationale of the Space Program*. Urbana: University of Illinois Press, 1964.

Wiesner, Jerome B., *Where Science and Politics Meet*. New York: McGraw-Hill, 1965.

Wohlstetter, Albert, "Scientists, Seers and Strategy." *Foreign Affairs*. April 1963.

Wright, Christopher and Robert Gilpin (eds.), *Scientists and National Policy-making*. New York: Columbia University Press, 1964.

Part V

Economics and the International System

THE DEVELOPMENT of advanced technology has altered the significance of national economic capabilities. Only those national units with vast and advanced economies can provide the base needed to exploit fully the potential of science and technology for military and non-military purposes.

Although practically all warfare is essentially economic in character, since it is designed to damage or destroy an opponent's economic base, it is necessary to distinguish more clearly the idea of economic warfare. Economic warfare may be defined as nonviolent operations designed specifically to weaken an enemy's economic base and thus to undermine his political position, or to strengthen a friendly country's economic position. Economic warfare constitutes one of the forms which the demand-response relationships may assume. (See Part II.)

Robert Strausz-Hupé and Stefan Possony examine the major economic instruments available to national units. In their demand-response relationships, national units may make use of foreign investments as a means of economic penetration and seek to exploit the dependence of another nation upon certain vital forms of trade. National units have made use of blockade, controls against certain types of trade with an opponent, pre-emptive buying, stockpiling, and subsidies designed to influence the international behavior of another government.

Of the many economic instruments since World War II, none has received greater emphasis than foreign aid, used extensively by both the United States and the Soviet Union. According to

Lucian Pye, these two nations base their foreign aid programs upon widely differing assumptions. In the case of the United States, it is assumed that great social change can result from a small aid program; that the changes induced by aid will be beneficial both to the recipient country and the United States; and that populations in national units receiving aid will respond with a new emphasis upon economic modernization and self-improvement. In contrast, Pye suggests that the Soviets hold the following kinds of assumptions about foreign aid: that social change is costly, that people resist change, that large-scale aid cannot induce immediate, or even long-range, transformation in the economic and social structure of recipient countries. Given such limitations, in the Soviet Union aid programs there is greater emphasis upon the attainment of immediate political objectives than is the case with the U.S. foreign assistance. Moreover, implicit in Soviet foreign aid is the assumption that Western political influence in recipient countries can be reduced by lessening the economic dependence of African, Asian, and Latin American countries upon the United States.

24. ECONOMICS AS A WEAPON

Robert Strausz-Hupé and Stefan T. Possony

NATIONAL SECURITY is the foremost obligation of any government. Hence each government regulates its economic life in view of its defense requirements. The purpose of such regulatory policies is to strengthen a nation's own economy and to weaken the economy of prospective opponents. By strengthening is meant not only the securing of all raw materials which might become necessary in case of war, but also the acquisition of finished products, weapons, ammunition, technological know-how, financial support and the establishment of an international network of economic auxiliaries, while at the same time denying all these advantages to the opponent. The economic weapons also can be used for the acquisition of political friends and the development of alliances.

It is quite true that international trade, if unobstructed, flourishes spontaneously and that this spontaneous growth would strengthen the economic posture of all trading nations. Yet the play of the free market may make a nation rich in consumers' goods while depriving it of those items which are indispensable in wartime. A free-trade organization is the logical economic structure of a world at peace. In periods of conflict, however, trade must be controlled, at least partially, in order to maximize a nation's military power.

Similarly, the sale of commodities in a peaceful world is highly advantageous for a nation's living standard. Yet when a prospective opponent wants to buy commodities in order to strengthen his war potential, economic logic must be displaced by military logic. For ex-

From *International Relations* by Robert Strausz-Hupé and Stefan Possony (New York: 1954) pp. 509; 516–517; 519–520; 522–523; 526; 528; 530–532; 534. Copyright 1954 by McGraw-Hill, Inc. Used by permission of McGraw-Hill Book Company. Footnotes have been renumbered to appear in consecutive order.

ROBERT STRAUSZ-HUPÉ—See biographical note, page 107.

STEFAN T. POSSONY (1913–   ) Director of International Studies, the Hoover Institute, Stanford University. His other books include *Lenin, A Reader*, (Chicago: H. Regnery Company, 1966), editor; *The Geography of Intellect*, (Chicago: H. Regnery Company, 1963), co-author; *A Forward Strategy for America*, (New York: Harper, 1961), co-author.

ample, Japan bought in the United States large quantities of scrap iron. Normally the sale of scrap iron would have been highly advantageous to the United States. Yet Japan used American scrap iron to build up its war machine. Hence the United States ultimately was compelled to embargo the sale of scrap iron.

One of the most important means of economic warfare consists in attacks on the opponent's financial strength for the purpose of diminishing the exchange value of his currency. These attacks can take the form of withdrawals of credits, dumping of large amounts of currency in order to compel the target country to pay in gold, manipulation of international currency exchanges, and sometimes simply psychological means which undermine confidence in the victim's financial honesty or economic strength.

. . .

ECONOMIC PENETRATION

Nations may acquire economic interests in a given country and through economic pressure determine its policy. Such a policy can be most successfully applied against smaller and underdeveloped states. Foreign economic interest thus manipulated the politics of the Near East. But even in a large country foreign-owned firms can exert pressure on the government, as the history of Russia before 1914 and of Germany between 1919 and 1930 shows. For that matter, in the late 19th century British capital was influential in the United States, and prior to the First World War German capital played a minor, though by no means negligible, role in shaping the course of American foreign policy.

British capital in Argentina often oriented the country's policy toward British interests. The economic penetration of Austria, Czechoslovakia, and Hungary by German industrial firms and banks during the 1930's created powerful pro-German factions and prepared the eventual annexation of these countries. The technique is not a new one; the various "charter companies" organized by west European countries in the 17th and 18th centuries initiated the conquests of immense territories in the Orient—the trade preceded the flag.[1] Today, Soviet-controlled "joint stock companies" are instruments of Soviet political domination of Hungary and Rumania.

Investments in foreign countries play a great role in the use of

---

[1] The personnel of such charter companies was often trained by economists of the highest achievement. Malthus, for example, taught the cadets of the East India Company for more than thirty years; see James Bonar, "The Malthusiad: Fantasia Economia," in *Economic Essays: Contributed in Honor of John Bates Clark,* edited by Jacob H. Hollander, New York, Macmillan, 1927, p. 237.

economics as a weapon. These investments serve subversive, political, financial, technological, and industrial purposes. Foreign investments can be made openly in the name of the true owner, whose nationality would be admitted, or ownership can be camouflaged. For example, a German firm may own openly a firm in the United States, or it may possess a large amount of stock in an American firm. If open ownership is not advisable, the German firm may set up a holding company which ostensibly is of Swiss nationality, as did the I.G. Farben when it founded the so-called I.G. Chemie Basel. This company took over all the foreign investments of the German I.G. Farben which, in turn, did *not* "own" even one share of I. G. Chemie Basel.[2] Control was maintained through private and personal commitments. Or again a German firm would send a few associates to the United States where they would found a company, in due time become American citizens, and thus end up with an "American" business enterprise. Or finally, a German firm would finance American friends to establish themselves in business without ever assuming legal title to the property.

Foreign investments can be exploited for subversive purposes and may serve the attainment of three objectives: (1) propaganda which would be paid for by the proceeds from the investment; (2) espionage which, among other methods, could be accomplished through the firms obtaining classified orders; and (3) economic sabotage which could take various forms, including slowdowns of output, stimulation of strikes, defective production, etc.[3]

. . .

CARTELS AND MONOPOLIES

Perhaps no topic of international economics is as important and as hotly debated by the experts as is the question of international cartels. Very little is known about their actual operations and in particular about their connections with individual governments. In most cases it is probably safe to say that cartels operate in order to maximize profits. Yet sometimes their activities appear to further deliberately the political objectives of governments. In other cases, governments take political advantage of the economic situation created by the cartels.

Statistically speaking, there were in 1939 somewhat less than 200 international cartels, with about one-third of international trade under some form of marketing control. About 75 per cent of these cartels pro-

---

[2] Hearings before the Special Committee Investigating the Munitions Industry, U.S. Senate, 74th Cong., 2d Sess., part 12, Government Printing Office, 1937, p. 2888.

[3] For examples, see Yuan-li Wu, *Economic Warfare*, New York, Prentice-Hall, 1952, pp. 166*f*.

vided for the division of international markets, while 44 per cent provided for licensing and mutual use of patents.[4]

There are two characteristics of cartels which are of great military and political consequence. First, firms which are members of an international cartel usually pool their patents and inform each other of technical procedures. Therefore firms participating in international cartels can procure intelligence about the economic, technological, and military preparations of foreign countries. For example, I.G. Farben supplied the German *Wehrmacht* with information about British chemical factories.[5]

Second, cartel agreements entail the reduction of output in various areas and sometimes lead to the discontinuance of production. A country which is the base of an international cartel can thus acquire important patents and, at the same time, inhibit the production of military matériel in hostile countries. While such a procedure may be somewhat difficult to apply in democratic countries, it has been used effectively by countries operating under dictatorial controls. The Nazis succeeded in deriving great technical advantages from various German-controlled cartels; when it was their turn to live up to agreements entered into by these cartels with foreign firms, they hid behind the excuse of officially imposed restrictions and *ad hoc* legislation. In this fashion, they obtained foreign patents but refused to disclose their own by the simple device of classifying them as military secrets. They also insisted upon limitations of output, but themselves produced as much as they chose, sometimes by keeping the production secret, sometimes by paying the penalties prescribed in the cartel agreement. Generally speaking, the Germans were most successful in this tactic with respect to the production of aluminum, the output of which they were able to curtail in the Western countries.[6] Maximizing their own production, they gained a very considerable advantage in aircraft production. Similarly they gained a head start in the manufacture of medical drugs.

Perhaps one of the most interesting episodes in the international competition for supremacy in the technological field prior to and during the First World War was the capture by Germany of the lead in the manufacture of dyes. The German chemical industry took advantage of the in-

---

[4] *Ibid.*, p. 172. The number of national cartels is far greater. In Germany it rose from 385 in 1905 to about 2,500 in 1925.

[5] See *Trials of War Criminals before the Military Tribunals,* Government Printing Office, 1953, Vol. VII, "The Farben Case," pp. 676*ff*.

[6] A somewhat different view is taken by Louis Marlio, *The Aluminum Cartel,* Washington, Brookings, 1947, pp. 95*ff*.; see also Erwin Hexner, *International Cartels,* Chapel Hill, The University of North Carolina Press, 1946, pp. 133*ff*.; also Wendell Berge, *Cartels: Challenge to a Free World,* Washington, Public Affairs Press, 1944, p. 222.

vention of the Englishman Perkin who showed how coal tars could be transformed into aniline dyes, and whose discoveries were not put to use by his countrymen. The German chemical industry had grown by leaps and bounds during the last third of the 19th century. Soon the world market for dye and derivative products was virtually under German control. The growth of competitive chemical industries abroad was deliberately stifled by patent manipulation, price cutting, cartel output agreements, buying up of installations, refusal of delivery of intermediate products, and similar practices.[7] While chemical factories were built in the United States, Britain, and France, the Germans either gained partial control or diverted them to the production of finished goods so that they were dependent on German imports for their requirements of so-called "intermediates" or semifinished products, sold to them at very high prices.

. . .

EXPLOITATION OF STRATEGIC ECONOMIC POSITION

Economic power based on the seller's or the buyer's monopoly (monopsony) wields great and, at times, decisive political influence. The War between the States deprived the world of most of its cotton supply, an event which both belligerents exploited to gain military and diplomatic advantages; if the North had not deprived the South of its export outlet, it might have lost the war. In 1905, the Austrians waged a "pig war" against Serbia.[8] Pigs were that little country's most important article of exportation, and Austria was practically its only customer. Since political relations between the two states were strained, the Austrian government hit upon the heroic device of stopping the importation of Serbian pigs. This measure was intended to create such economic dislocation in Serbia that the stricken country would be ultimately compelled to comply with Austrian demands. The Serbs, disappointing Austrian expectations, succeeded in reorienting their exports. Serbia, however, had suffered great economic damage, a circumstance which contributed to the radicalization of Serbian domestic politics and, indirectly, by aggravating Austro-Serbian antagonism, to the outbreak of the First World War.

Under modern conditions, rice-exporting countries like Burma and Thailand could exert considerable pressure on India or Japan, since both

---

[7] Victor Lefebure, *The Riddle of the Rhine: Chemical Strategy in Peace and War*, New York, Chemical Foundation, 1923, Preface and Introduction by Marshals Foch and Wilson, p. 146; see also Hearings . . . Munitions Industry, part 11, pp. 2560*ff*.

[8] See Sidney Bradshaw Fay, *The Origins of the World War*, 2d ed., New York, Macmillan, 1931, Vol. I, p. 359.

of the latter countries are heavily dependent on the importation of rice. Similarly, Russia has used her dominant position in manganese to obtain advantages from the United States. Improper use by Malaya of its tin resources could have vast repercussions on the preservation of food and thus affect practically the entire world.

. . .

ECONOMIC WARFARE

Economic warfare is an integral part of war. In one way or another, it has been waged at all times and in all climes. Many wars serve predominantly economic purposes. The nomads must conquer territory to live. In a society based on slave labor, the supply of the labor force must be maintained by war. The time-honored strategy of the attack upon the enemy's supplies and food reserves, destruction of crops, stealing or killing of cattle, plunder, and pillage—all these thrusts against the fabric of a people's wealth and economic warfare.

Economic motives are among the most potent causes of war. To give a lesser known but highly illustrative example, a memorandum written by an unknown French official in 1747 explains why British control of America would make Britain unconquerable, since America would furnish Britain gold and silver as well as trading outlets and thus the material resources required for the construction of a large navy. The memorandum concludes: "The balance of money in the hands of the British entails the balance of power. They would be the masters of the sea through their navy, and the masters of the land through their wealth. They would draw the means from America to dictate the law to Europe." Sainte-Croix, 18th-century historian of the British navy, explained the reason why the logic of the situation compelled France to support American independence:[9]

> If she were to possess an immense and fertile country whose population doubles every twenty years, what high degree of power would England reach? What counterweight of force would be necessary to oppose against her? Was not the independence of the universe menaced? By taking the side of the Anglo-Americans, France helped general welfare as well as her own safety.

BLOCKADE AND CONTRABAND

In modern times, the most telling weapon of economic warfare is naval blockade, i.e., the halting of a country's maritime imports and exports of

---

[9] Quoted from Bertrand de Jouvenel, *Napoléon et l'économie dirigée: le blocus continental,* Brussels, Éditions de la Toison d'Or, 1942, pp. 22–23.

vital commodities. The purpose of naval blockade was defined as early as 1601 by Queen Elizabeth. Seizing upon Spain's dependence on overseas trade, she said: "The stopping, hindrance and impeading of all commerce and traffick with him [Philip II] in his territories of Spain and Portugal will quickly in likelihood give an end to these bloodie unnatural warres which disturb the generall peace and quiet of all these parts of Christendome." [10]

.   .   .

MODERN NAVAL BLOCKADE

During the First World War the naval blockade of Britain against the Central Powers caused decisive shortages in oil and foodstuffs.[11] German strategy during the Second World War, adapted to the lessons of the first, was directed at defeating the naval blockade which Britain again, by automatic reflex as it were, imposed upon her adversary. The pursuit of that objective forced Germany to adopt an economy of substitutes and stockpiles, led to expansion into the Balkans and Scandinavia, and finally to German attack on Russia.

Naval blockade involves a highly complicated technique and a nice sense of discrimination between essentials and nonessentials. It is impractical to throw a line of ships around the blockaded country, seeking thereby to prevent the passage of every ship. Blockade runners will often break through the blockading patrols. Neutral states must be permitted a minimum of trade. A continental country always has access to supplies via land routes. None can be completely blockaded from the sea. Naval blockade must, therefore, be supplemented by measures designed to prohibit the reexport from neutral countries of sea-borne supplies, and to reduce the sales to the enemy of commodities originating in adjacent neutral states.

In the 19th century a distinction was evolved between absolute and conditional contraband. The distinction was not always clear, but in 1909 an international agreement on the meaning of the term was reached: absolute contraband consisted of every type of *war* material, while conditional contraband comprised goods needed for the civilian population but which, under certain conditions, could be used for military purposes; if there was evidence of such a use, they could be confiscated. During the subsequent wars, which were contests between the industrial

---

[10] David L. Gordon and Royden Dangerfield, *The Hidden Weapon: The Story of Economic Warfare*, New York, Harper, 1947, p. 1.

[11] See M. W. W. P. Consett, *The Triumph of Unarmed Forces 1914–1918*, London, Williams & Norgate, 1923.

capacities of the belligerents, this separation lost its validity, simply because virtually every important commodity must now be used for war production. The distinction was all but abandoned during the Second World War.

It made its reappearance during the Korean War when most trading nations, with Britain in front, sold to China commodities which allegedly were not of military significance. During the Cold War in Europe East-West trade in "civilian" goods also was continued without letup. These trading arrangements were criticized widely because, in modern times, there are barely any commodities which directly or indirectly cannot be put to military use or be used to enhance a nation's warmaking capacity. Undoubtedly, medicines and low-octane gasoline shipped to China were not unwelcome to the Chinese armies fighting in Korea against the very nations which traded with them.

. . .

PREEMPTION

Hand in hand with rationing went "preemption." [12] This euphemistic term means simply the purchase of a goods produced in a neutral country in order to forestall its delivery into hostile hands, lest it increase the enemy's war potential. Country A prevents country B from buying a product by buying itself that product regardless of price and regardless of whether it can be put to use or not. During the First World War the Germans bought several chemicals in the United States which the Allies were trying to secure for the production of explosives and gases. When preemption proved impossible, German agents resorted to sabotage as, for example, in the famous Black Tom case when they blew up ammunition ships lying in New York Harbor.

During the Second World War, the Iberian Peninsula was the principal theater of preemptive warfare; the bone of contention was the mineral wealth of Spain and Portugal. Copper and iron mines were largely in British possession, and therefore no great difficulty was encountered by the Allies in repelling German buyers of these metals—a good example of the military importance of capital holdings abroad. Yet the wolframite (tungsten) mines in Spain and Portugal were not owned by Allied nationals; some of them were actually in German hands. The flow of wolframite extracted from these mines to Germany was not altogether halted, though the control exercised through navicert reduced it. The Allies acquired some mines. Nevertheless, it became necessary to buy the

---

[12] See Geoffrey Crowther, *Ways and Means of War*, New York, Oxford, 1940, p. 58. See also Wu, *op. cit.*, pp. 83*ff*.

output of the remaining mines. As the Allies bought the ores, prices rose disproportionately. The total cost of the operation ultimately reached fantastically high figures. Nevertheless, the Germans were deprived of great quantities of this vitally needed alloy and forced to reduce drastically the production of tungsten steel, thus lowering the quality of their ammunition. Similar operations were carried out with Turkish chromium and, at the beginning of the war, with Yugoslav copper and bauxite. In the case of Swedish ball bearings an entire yearly output of the principal factories was bought and purchases of future output guaranteed.

The method of preemption also can be employed effectively in the field of technology. For this purpose patent laws can be used. For example, the exploitation, though not the purchase, of a patent can be denied to foreign nationals. The Soviet for many years systematically acquired knowledge about patents issued in industrialized countries, but they denied similar information about their own patents to foreign nationals and, in fact, have failed to publish any information about Russian inventions.[13]

. . .

STOCKPILING

To defend themselves against blockade and preemptive buying, nations often resort to the stockpiling of vital commodities. In previous times stockpiling extended mostly to raw materials, but under the threat of modern air war there is a tendency to stockpile machine tools and finished products, including weapons. Stockpiling must be undertaken in peacetime, or during the very first weeks of a war before blockade arrangements have been completed.

The difficulties of an adequate stockpiling program are very great. Most

---

[13] On German methods in this area see *Trials of War Criminals before the Military Tribunals*, Vol. VII, "The Farben Case," pp. 1273–1295. See particularly Farben memorandum of January 25, 1940 (*i.e.*, after the outbreak of World War II), which reads: "There are agreements and arrangements between the German production companies (I.G. Farbenindustrie A.G. and Ruhrchemie) and the large oil companies such as Standard Oil, Shell, et cetera, with regard to mineral oil. Among other things, these agreements provide for the exchange of know-how with regard to mineral oil between the parties to the contract. This exchange of know-how, which is still being handled in the usual way by the neutral countries abroad even now and which is transmitted to us via Holland and Italy, first gives us an insight into the development work and production plans of the companies and/or their respective countries, and at the same time informs us about the progress of technical developments with regard to oil. . . . Up to now, we have carried out this exchange in such a way that from our side we have only sent reports . . . which contained only such technical data as concerned facts which are known or out of date according to the latest developments."

of the commodities needed are in short supply. This leads, first, to a considerable increase in the price of the commodity and therefore to economic dislocation affecting all nations habitually buying the particular commodity. Second, it leads to an overexpansion of production facilities. Once the stockpiling program has been completed, inevitable retrenchment must be paid for by unemployment and financial loss. Third, if the threat of war has receded and the government decides to release its stockpiles, prices will fall. Necessary though stockpiling may be, it is a dislocating factor in world economy. This became obvious shortly after the outbreak of the Korean War, when the acceleration of the American stockpiling program produced repercussions all over Europe. One method to reduce the adverse effects of stockpiling is to fix prices by international agreements; another is to carry out the program over a long period of time, taking advantage of drops in prices and periods of overproduction as they occur in the economic cycle. But if large purchases have to be made rapidly, and if there is no time to arrive at intergovernmental agreements, grave disturbances are inevitable.

Economic Subsidies

Economic warfare in wartime includes "supply programs." Unlike activities designed to *deny* supplies to certain countries, these programs serve to *support* neutrals which are to be influenced. At the beginning of the Second World War, the Allies maintained trade with Italy, a token demonstration of the profitability of neutrality. Vichy-controlled North Africa was supplied with sugar in order to keep the natives well disposed toward the Allies and facilitate continued control by the French. In addition, North Africa was supplied with all kinds of materials, including fuel, in order to increase French power of resistance against German pressure. Food was delivered to France and Greece to stave off famine among a friendly population. If Turkey could have been abundantly provisioned with military materials, she might have entered the war at a strategically opportune moment; as it was, Turkey was inadequately equipped for waging war against as formidable an enemy as Germany.

The Anglo-Saxon powers also helped to confirm Spain in her neutrality by providing her with foodstuffs and oil—positive economic warfare, as it were.[14] The German high command credited this policy with keeping Spain "nonbelligerent." Yet a similar policy against Japan failed; American scrap and oil shipped to Japan, in order to insure Japanese neutrality, actually made possible Japanese aggression. Russia's strategy to supply Germany with raw materials, foodstuffs, and oil failed and redounded to Russia's own detriment.[15]

---

[14] See Sir Samuel Hoare, *Complacent Dictator,* New York, Knopf, 1947, *passim.*
[15] See *Nazi-Soviet Relations,* pp. 85, 119, 196, 199, and 339.

During World War II lend-lease operations contributed great to Allied victory. The assertion has been rashly made that lend-lease was a historically unique operation. Economic subsidy is a time-honored means of war, employed whenever a rich state sought to induce poorer states to fight its battles or to replenish its effectives with troops from abroad. Subventions always played an important role in coalition warfare. During the 17th and 18th centuries they were used on a large scale, chiefly by Britain, Holland, and France. Countries such as Prussia waxed powerful because they had been liberally subsidized; between 1674 and 1688, the Grand Elector received almost 900,000 thalers, while his successor Frederick I amassed 14 million. During the Seven Years' War, Frederick the Great received altogether 27 million thalers from Britain. While direct subventions fell into disrepute during the 19th century, credits were given by the Western powers to smaller European countries and Russia, and by the United States to England and France. Since some of these debts remained unpaid, they must be considered as subsidies in fact, though not in name.

25. SOVIET AND AMERICAN STYLES IN FOREIGN AID

Lucian W. Pye

E conomic aid and technical assistance are essentially American innovations in the realm of foreign affairs. In the classical nation-state system, allies did on occasion assist each other with credits, and wealthier states frequently used economic means to influence poorer and weaker nations. However, foreign aid in the modern sense is clearly the product of American decisions. Indeed, some might say that foreign aid reflects

From *ORBIS*, a quarterly journal of world affairs published by the Foreign Policy Research Institute of the University of Pennsylvania (Summer 1960), 159-173. Reprinted by permission of the Trustees of the University of Pennsylvania.

Lucian W. Pye (1921–   ) Professor of Political Science, Massachusetts Institute of Technology. Author of *Spirit of Chinese Politics*, (Cambridge: Massachusetts Institute of Technology Press, 1968); *Southeast Asia's Political Systems*, (New York: Prentice-Hall, 1967); *Aspects of Political Development*, (Boston: Little, Brown, 1966). Co-author of *Political Culture and Political Development*, (Princeton: Princeton University Press, 1965).

accurately the peculiar genius of the American people, for it combines an opportunity for expressing idealism and generosity with an eminently practical device for advancing our enlightened self-interest. Be this as it may, the fact remains that during the immediate post-war period we had a monopoly in this field that was only slightly less complete than our monopoly of atomic weapons.

It is therefore quite understandable that we should have felt deeply uneasy when the Soviet Union turned to ruble diplomacy and a campaign of economic aid to the uncommitted areas. When the Soviets, shortly after breaking our atomic monopoly, announced their intentions to provide massive amounts of economic assistance to the less developed areas, we were assailed by a host of doubts. Had we used our period of monopoly to full advantage? Were we aware of the full potentialities of this unique instrument of foreign policy? Are not the Soviets likely to be more skilled in utilizing foreign aid for their self-interest? We were prone to discount our years of experience, and to feel that advantage lay with the Soviets as late-comers who would surely profit from our early mistakes. We even began to wonder whether in this form of competition the Soviet system might have some inherent advantages: could they not allocate resources, particularly human resources, in a more efficient manner; were they not free to engage in long range planning? Certainly they would never have to be embarrassed by Congressional scrutiny and public discussions of the behavior and integrity of foreign governments. In this state of mind it was easy for us to imagine countries which had steadfastly withstood all our efforts at friendship becoming the easy victims of Soviet blandishments.

II

In part, our sense of uneasiness came from the novelty of the Soviet actions, and in part it stemmed from our tendency to picture the Soviets as being unaffected by the difficulties and handicaps that have been most frustrating for us. However, there seems to be a far deeper source for our anxiety, for Soviet policies have brought into question the most fundamental assumptions and the most sophisticated lines of reasoning behind our total foreign aid effort. Soviet foreign economic policy has challenged not just our superficial views about techniques, but our most advanced theories about the political significance of economic aid. For, according to these theories we should welcome Soviet contributions to economic growth in the underdeveloped areas as promoting our interests. To rephrase Lenin, the Soviets would be acting as "the grave diggers of communism." If this is not so, then our theories must be inaccurate and our actions premised on fallacious notion.

During the last decade considerable thought has gone into all aspects of foreign aid, and if we survey the dominant American opinion, as expressed in Congressional hearings, administration statements and the general literature on the subject, we find a remarkably widespread consensus on the nature and purpose of our economic aid programs. Hence it is possible to speak of an American doctrine on the subject; and it is this doctrine, based upon our best judgments and an elaborate and subtle set of reasons, which has been challenged by the new Soviet campaigns. What we may refer to as American doctrine on foreign aid reflects in part well recognized aspects of American character. It involves much more though, for it is strongly informed by economic theories and a vision of the social system.

Briefly, American doctrine holds that foreign aid is a long term proposition which works to our advantage by creating and supporting a process of social change in which a steadily increasing gross national product will in time provide the essential basis for a stable political process. It is improper, and indeed naïve, to expect an immediate return on our aid. We should not seek to buy friendships or influence the short range policies of recipient countries. Our concern is with the evolution of the under developed countries into modern nation-states.

In our view, foreign aid can serve a broad range of functions by helping to give the newly independent countries a sense of focus and constructive purpose for their sentiments of nationalism. If the leaders of underdeveloped countries commit themselves to serious programs of economic development, then their restless people will be able to channel their ambitions in constructive directions. People who are losing the fatalism of custom and tradition will be able to find a realistic basis for their hopes of a better life.

American doctrine has thus conceived of foreign aid as providing not just the physical basis but also the psychological atmosphere necessary for the establishment of a more stable world. By giving purpose, direction and hope to those who want to be a part of the modern world, foreign aid should reduce irrational tendencies, weaken the appeals of communism, and strengthen democratic institutions. Thus according to our most sophisticated views we can, and we should, ignore day-to-day political considerations in favor of aid programs based upon advanced economic theories. The reason why we can confidently follow this initially economic approach to our political objectives lies in the peculiar nature of economic growth. Our theories suggest to us that once stagnant economies have been given the necessary push from the outside then they can, in a short time, reach a stage in which they will be able to continue to grow without added external aid; once the snowball has been started down the hill it can gain momentum even as it grows in size.

Finally, the logic of our doctrines holds that since economic growth is an impersonal phenomenon it is only the quantity and not the source of capital that is important. Economic resources are politically neutral.

Therefore, if we have the courage to follow our doctrines wherever they may lead us, we cannot escape the conclusion that Soviet aid should have the effect of speeding up precisely the course of events American aid is designed to facilitate.[1] Presumably Soviet thinking does not bring the Soviets to the same conclusions about the nature and potentialities of foreign aid. We cannot avoid a sense of uneasiness as we ask whether it is our doctrine or the Soviets' that comes the closest to reality.

It is appropriate that there should be at this time numerous attempts to reappraise the functions of foreign aid. The old issue of whether there should be foreign aid programs is dead; we will not give up a major instrument of foreign policy at this stage. The problem is to gain a keener appreciation of the nature of foreign aid and particularly its potentialities and its limitations for foreign policy.

III

It is in the spirit of such a quest for understanding that we may take note of some of the basic differences in the American and Soviet approaches to foreign aid. Indeed, an analysis of operational styles in economic assistance programs can provide an interesting basis for examining fundamental assumptions about politics, society, and history. This is because any strategy of economic aid must reflect notions about the character of human society, the nature of change and progress, the significance of human effort in consciously controlling history, the relationship of the economic and political spheres, and other similar fundamental issues about man and society.

As a point of departure we may observe that there appears to be considerable difference between American and Soviet assumptions about the costs and difficulties of inducing and accelerating social change. The American approach is essentially optimistic, for it is premised on the belief that great changes can be expected from relatively small expenditures of energy. Foreign aid is understood to be only the marginal investment of outside effort necessary to push transitional societies into self-sustained and nearly automatic growth. A small input can produce a disproportionately large output because of the operations of the "multiplier effect" in the economy. The problem is only that of locating the particular "lever" or "button" that must be pushed to set off the expected chain reactions. We are often prepared to expend prodigious

---

[1] For an analysis of why Soviet aid might contribute to the realization of American national interests see: Charles Wolf, Jr., "Soviet Economic Aid in Southeast Asia: Threat or Windfall," *World Politics,* Vol. X (October 1957), pp. 91–101.

amounts of energy to locate the trigger, but the expectation is always that when the right thing is done the ultimate effects will be far greater than the initial measures. Indeed, if massive amounts of aid have produced only slight change, then we tend to be suspicious about whether the program is being wisely administered.

In contrast, the Soviets tend to the view that social change is a terrible and brutally costly process in which massive assaults on the existing order are necessary to produce modest changes. In their thinking huge inputs are necessary to bring about significant change. Products of a revolutionary experience and committed to an ideology of struggle, the Soviets have few illusions about the costs of altering the structure of a society. Certainly most Russians are acutely aware that all social changes in the Soviet Union have been extremely demanding and painful.

Only recently has explicit communist doctrine accepted the point of view that parliamentary democracy and popular elections can be the vehicle of historically significant changes. However, in spite of Khrushchev's pronouncement on the possibilities of gaining power through legal means, which has given respectability to the communist parties of the underdeveloped regions, the basic Soviet feeling still seems to be that no efforts short of revolution can bring fundamental changes. Since the Soviets are impressed only with such fundamental changes, they cannot avoid discounting the significance of all non-communist programs of social change. The path to the next stage in history is always a difficult one and only those who are prepared to struggle and suffer can follow it. Indeed, all who would influence the course of history, whether they be the early bourgeoisie who produced the first industrial revolutions in Europe, or the present-day "vanguards of the proletariat" in Russia and China, have had to be willing to engage in heroic struggle. In the Soviet mind the processes of social change are comparable to war; the old order must be "overpowered," "stormed" and "assaulted."

A second distinction between American and Soviet thinking, consistent with these first two sets of assumptions, is related to the question of the popularity of social change. In the American picture of the underdeveloped regions, the people are anxious for change and impatient with any deterrent to progress. In the American view, it is not inconsistent to depict the people of the underdeveloped countries as engrossed in a "revolution of rising expectations" and yet to spend considerable sums on techniques and programs to stimulate, prod and encourage these very same people into giving up their old ways and taking greater interest in the prospects for change. People may be ignorant of the possibilities for self-improvement, but once shown new ways they are certain to accept them eagerly and to reject their old and inefficient ways. It is this assumption which gives us such confidence in the demonstrational effects of pilot projects. A few well-run model enterprises should have incalculable influence on all who see or hear about them.

Also, since we have little appreciation for why people may not be continually enthusiastic for change, we tend to be discouraged by examples of back-sliding. In our thinking there is very little room for the notion that traditional modes of life can be comfortable while change and progress are painful. We are too much the products of acculturation ourselves to hold such views; we know the value of becoming Americanized but not the costs.

In the Soviet mode of thinking, people are seen as stubbornly resisting all forms of change. The problem of stimulating change is more than just the firm grip of tradition, for people, even when presented with the opportunity to improve their lot, are generally too lazy and slovenly to alter their habits. If the masses are not constantly prodded they are certain to slip back into their old practices. Such students of Bolshevik behavior as Nathan Leites and Merle Fainsod have noted the anxieties of Russian communists about relaxing, for the alternative to determined effort is disintegration and the aimless ways of the peasant. The theme that ran through the entire early history of the radical movement among Russian intellectuals was that of frustration and exasperation at the Russian peasant for not showing greater interest in improving his lot. In the Soviet view today, any attempt at modernizing is certain to be only a superficial effort if it is not driven on by the select few who understand the problems of revolution. Thus in spite of reference to "revolutionary tides," and "intensified contradictions" which bring about "popular demands," the basic Soviet feeling is that ceaseless struggle is necessary to create the new in a world in which people tend to resist change tenaciously.

If we turn next to the problem of planning social development, we find that Americans and Soviets differ on time perspectives and the relationship of the short run and the long run. Our feeling is clearly that the long run is all important, and considerations of the short run are a constant source of danger that threaten the realization of our ultimate objectives. We are firmly convinced that a great hazard is that administrators will be overpowered by the demands of their day-to-day problems and lose sight of their long run objectives. The demands of the immediate world are frustrating and exasperating and can absorb all of one's energies and time.

Conversely, we tend to feel that while the long run is all important it does not of its own accord demand our attention. At the same time we seem to believe that it should be relatively easy to "solve" long-term problems if only we could escape from the day-to-day pressures. The assumption is that a little thought can go a long way in producing understanding of long-range issues. A pause from our daily tasks should be enough to give us the time to grasp completely the configuration of the future. Our suspicion is always that others, and particularly our enemies, are somehow able to avoid the demands of the present and follow more long-run considerations.

The Soviet tradition, in contrast, is that the long run is predetermined by the "laws of history" and all attention and energies should be directed to the problems immediately at hand. A basic Bolshevik attitude is that people are all too likely to idle their time away with heated but futile discussions of the distant future. Some students of Russian affairs see the Bolsheviks as standing in sharp opposition to the propensities of earlier Russian intellectuals for engaging in endless speculation and agonizing soul searching about ultimate questions. For the new Russian man nothing can come of such activities, and progress can only follow from a complete commitment to the pressing problems of the moment. Effective action is, in fact, short-run action. The true revolutionary takes pride in not wasting time or energy in thinking about the long term; instead he throws himself completely into day-to-day problems.

The Soviets thus see danger in the seductive appeal of philosophical reflection and safety in the concrete and the immediate. Their suspicions are exactly the opposite of ours. They tend to believe that their enemies are better able to focus their energies on immediate issues while they fear that those who profess to champion revolution will have their eyes fixed too much on the long run and will thus be ineffectual.

This brings us to what is possibly the most critical difference in underlying assumptions of the American and Soviet doctrines on foreign aid: the difference in the predictability of social change. Oddly enough, even though we are not as given to explicit theories about the nature of society as the Soviets are, we do seem to hold in our minds a considerably more complicated, more subtle, and more integrated picture of human society. This is particularly so when we consider economic matters. The nature of society is such that a change in one realm is certain to bring about changes in all others. Since all phases of life are interrelated, it should be possible in our view to predict the indirect consequences of any policy. We are quite prepared to accept the suggestion that the secondary and tertiary effects of a policy action can be readily charted through a series of chain reactions. Indeed, we accept so completely the possibility of such predictions that we have no difficulty with the idea that it is unnecessary to concentrate our efforts directly on our most desired objectives. Such objectives can often best be realized by an indirect approach.

It is this view of the interrelated nature of the social system which convinces us that changes in the economic sphere will have predictable consequences in the political realm. Although the pattern of cause and effect may be extremely complicated, we are fairly certain that it must run its course throughout the society. We even take at times the position that very delicate and fine adjustments can be made through indirect manipulations of facets of the society, for we readily appreciate the importance of such control mechanisms as we have in our monetary and fiscal policies.

The Soviets, in spite of a formal ideology that pretends to a scientific explanation of human society, act as though they are far less confident about the possibilities of predicting the indirect consequences of policy actions. They generally take a more direct and frontal approach to the problem of directing social change. Since massive attacks on a society are necessary to produce even limited changes, it is impossible to expect much of the indirect consequences of specific policies.

The Soviets, of course, are informed by their Marxist doctrines that economic relationships determine the nature of the political sphere. It might be assumed that this would make them more sensitive than we to the possibilities of making marginal changes in the economic sphere in order to influence the course of political development. It seems, however, that in practice the Russian believes only revolutionary changes in the economic order will produce significant political change, that is, change equivalent to the stages of history recognized by Marxism. Short of such fundamental changes in the structure of society, there is little possibility of subtle and indirect manipulation of the social order. Instead, economic power can be, and often is, directly employed as political power; the capitalists employ their financial power to "suppress" and "crush down" the workers, and thus the struggle is a direct one.

In the final analysis, the Soviets act as though it were impossible to predict the indirect effects of any action, and therefore it is absolutely essential to gain complete and direct control of events. Since the day-to-day workings of the social order cannot be predicted, all effort must be directed to controlling and commanding important developments. This feeling about the unpredictability of the immediate future and their views about the importance of the short run tend to reinforce each other in the Soviet mind and produce the conviction that there is an absolute need to "control" all events.[2]

In contrast, we are far more prepared to remove ourselves several steps from even those developments that we feel to be highly important. We are the ones who see wisdom in dams and in agriculture in the underdeveloped regions which will have long-run effects and only indirectly influence the course of political development. The Soviets tend to invest in those activities which are likely to have a direct and immediate effect

---

[2] Nathan Leites in his *Study of Bolshevism* (Glencoe, 1953) has placed this need to "control" others at the center of his interpretation of Bolshevik behavior.

on people's political views: sports stadiums, hotels, pavement for streets, factories and other enterprises which are likely to be highly visible in the recipient country. Our feelings about the importance of the indirect effects of any policy are such that we welcome cooperative arrangements with recipient governments under which we may have little direct administrative control. In contrast, the Soviets, even when the project is a "gift," as in Burma, insist on retaining all administrative controls during the planning and building stages.

This brings us to a final distinction in the American and Soviet approaches toward foreign aid, namely attitudes toward the autonomy and interrelatedness of specialized bodies of knowledge about human society. It seems that in spite of our mental image of the interrelatedness of all facets of society, we generally act as though each of the spheres into which we arbitrarily divide society has its own "laws" which should be acknowledged and respected. We accept the idea that there are different perspectives for viewing human behavior which generally correspond to the separate academic disciplines. Thus we have the economic and the sociological, the psychological and the political approaches, each one of which is assumed to have its own body of "laws." Consequently, we assume that programs can be guided by "economic," "technical," or "administrative'" principles and hence they can be essentially a-political in character. We can sincerely see our foreign aid efforts as inherently "non-political," and we fully expect other countries to recognize this to be the case.

At the same time, we do have the view that the indirect consequences of our economic policies can be felt in the political realm. We seem to push the possibility of contradiction out of mind by assuming that in the final analysis there must be a basic harmony among the various bodies of knowledge and perspectives for viewing society. What is good sense according to economic theory must also be good politically. It is inconceivable to us that there can be fundamental conflicts in the outcomes of the various approaches or disciplines. We also seem to believe that if we act according to the best knowledge of any particular field we will also be acting in the best interest of the United States. There is not only a basic harmony of the spheres of knowledge, but this harmony extends to the American national interest.

We also, of course, hold that the specialized knowledge of any "technician" can be the servant of any political master, and thus the specialist must be given guidance in matters of value, and he must accept the direction of the "broker" in values, the politician. Thus the economist, like the soldier and all other specialists, will acknowledge that the ultimate choices in policy must come from the political authorities. In practice, however, all specialists tend to feel that they are qualified experts in the realm of values and are capable of judging the national interest. Indeed, most of the various experts tend to see their specialties as being peculiarly important to the national interest. Although the conflict of specialists is endemic in our system of government, we still preserve our faith in the inherent harmony of all knowledge by attributing such conflicts to faults in personality, to ambition, and to the evils of "playing politics."

The Soviets seem to avoid these problems by assuming all specialized bodies of knowledge to be subservient to political considerations, for any form of knowledge can be used to political advantage. The unity of society is, for the Soviets, the all-pervasive character of politics. There are no such things as "a-political" acts in international affairs. Therefore, there is no point in pretending that foreign aid is not influenced by political ambitions.

The Soviets generally act as though explicit political considerations provide the only basis for ensuring the harmony of the various special fields of knowledge. Indeed, in the Soviet mind, knowledge cannot be neutral; instead there are, for example, "bourgeois" economic theories, and communist theories. All must bow to the logic of politics.

It may be helpful to summarize the differences we have been noting by presenting them in the form of a paradigm.

American	Soviet
1. Great social change can come from marginal investments. Possibility of small input resulting in large output because of "multiplier effect."	1. Social change is extremely costly; big investments of effort yield slight changes.
2. Change is progress and it is popular.	2. Change is progress but people resist it.
3. People will "naturally" work for self-improvement.	3. People will "naturally" slip back into lazy ways.
4. The long run is all important, but short run considerations tend to absorb all one's time and energies.	4. The long run is predetermined, but people tend to waste their time and energies in idle speculation about the distant future. Need is for people to channel their energies into the short run.
5. One's enemies and competitors have the advantage of being able to reflect on the long run.	5. One's enemies and competitors have the advantage of being able to direct effectively all their attention to immediate problems.
6. All aspects of society are interrelated; secondary and tertiary effects important because of our mechanistic vision of society.	6. Secondary and tertiary effects unimportant; necessity for a frontal assault in achieving all objectives because indirect manipulations ineffectual.
7. Indirect effects of policy predictable and hence direct controls not necessary.	7. Limited possibility for predicting immediate effects of policies, and hence need for constant control.
8. Different bodies of knowledge have their own "laws" and hence possible to have "a-political" policies.	8. All specialized knowledge the servant of political considerations and hence no action can be "a-political."

IV

It would seem from these observations that the Soviets consider economic aid to be a considerably more blunt and limited instrument of policy than we do. It is, of course, impossible to state with confidence what are the Soviet expectations about foreign aid. From their behavior, however, we can draw conclusions which all point to a more directly political use of aid than is our practice.

Fundamentally, the Soviets seem to expect their economic aid to create relationships which will provide in time the basis for direct political influence. Such a direct link between the economic and the political spheres has always seemed most "natural" to the Soviet mind. For example, in their theories of imperialism the search for new markets and new sources of raw materials under capitalism led inevitably to political controls and colonial regimes. In their own case, they certainly see foreign aid as a device for gaining respectability for communism and for neutralizing Western influences. By economic aid they can present themselves as a major power capable of assisting weak nations. Above all else, the Soviets seem quite prepared to conceive of foreign aid as simply a method for gaining entry into a foreign society so as to carry out other activities ranging from espionage to the cultivation of friendships. In fact, the Soviets are quite frank in stating that they are ready to use their aid to win friends and strengthen "fraternal bonds"; nowhere in Soviet propaganda is there a counterpart to the American disclaimer of employing foreign aid for "merely" winning friends.

The Soviet approach is thus quite direct and uncomplicated. But what about the question we posed at the beginning: could it be that by concentrating on the short-run potentialities of foreign aid they are in part working for long-range developments which would favor democracy and harm communism? Are the Soviets so myopic that they cannot see that they may be helping us to realize our objectives? Presumably the Soviets are not disturbed by this possibility, because in their view foreign aid activities are far too marginal a force to produce significant change in the social order.

If we turn to communist doctrines on the underdeveloped regions, we find quite explicit interpretations of all non-communist attempts at economic development. Briefly, in their view, all such government-directed programs represent nothing more than "bureaucratic capitalism," which is not to be confused with socialism since it lacks a strong class base. Those involved in developing these countries, in the communist way of thinking, are mainly the intelligentsia, and other technicians and administrators who are members of the petty bourgeois class and thus are thought to be unstable, vacillating and indecisive in political activities. Petty bourgeois leaders may act in opportunistic fashions, but they are extremely ineffectual and easy victims of outside manipulations. Above all else, they do not have strong roots in their societies for they are not members of the historically significant classes, the proletariat and the big bourgeoisie. The sum effect of their attempts at economic development will thus be little more than the creation of projects which will be mainly of interest to administrators and technicians who have limited political sophistication. Those involved in the building of "bureaucratic capitalism" are supposed to lose touch with the masses even as they achieve greater successes in their enterprises.

This suggests, when shorn of its communist jargon, that the Soviets do not expect the development programs which were initiated by the Nehrus and the Nassers, the U Nus and the Sukarnos, to yield significant changes. Rather the Soviets count on these leaders isolating themselves even farther from the masses of their peoples because they are focusing their energies on mere administrative problems.

In the meantime, the communists contribute aid to these programs for the opportunities they provide for advancing the direct political influence of communism. The key to their approach is their belief that structural changes in society are extremely difficult to achieve while political relations involving the question of who controls whom are all important and all pervasive. The argument that revolutionaries can advance their cause even while appearing to support those committed to bourgeois institutions, which Lenin advanced in *"Left-Wing" Communism: An Infantile Disorder*, still seems to govern Soviet calculations. Indeed, their attitude toward foreign aid is analogous to the classic communist belief that it is advantageous to support the demands of labor unions for higher wages because the agitational returns are certain to outweigh any danger of a better paid working class adopting bourgeois sentiments.

V

In appraising the two approaches to foreign aid, it becomes apparent that the thread of consistency in the Soviet style is the extraordinary degree to which they have been uninhibitedly political. Out of the logic of politics they have been able to realize a coherence between ends and means, between goals and techniques. We, on the other hand, in denying the sovereignty of politics, find ourselves without an explicit method for dealing rigorously with the relationships between goals and techniques. We have built up our doctrines as though little attention need be given to the links between our practices and the end values we seek, or between economic aid and our other instruments of policy.

Our difficulty seems to arise, in part, from an uneasiness about the propriety of discussing openly the relationship between our values and the available means for influencing events. We are disturbed by our traditional uncertainties about the concept of manipulation in human affairs. A further complication is our feeling that in speaking across the gap in technology between our society and the underdeveloped countries, it is improper and indelicate to discuss values and objectives. Instead, we behave as though the situation calls for innocent discussions about impersonal and technical matters.

By putting off to the side the crucial problem of how to relate our objectives and our practices to each other, we have allowed the center of the stage to be taken over by supposedly technical economic considerations. As a consequence we have made techniques into the molders of doctrine rather than treating them as the servants of doctrine. We have built our ideology by pushing beyond the realm of its relevance the analytical reasoning of economics. In so moving from technique to doctrine we have been easily captivated by a false sense of realism.

This approach has also made it hard to avoid exaggerating the importance of techniques. We have, for example, been prone to suspect that our primary weaknesses must be in the application and administration of our aid programs. This is the theme which made the novel, *The Ugly American,* both plausible and popular to Americans. The truth is that a survey of our total operations would reveal that we are far more skilled in operational techniques than the Soviets. Indeed, our problems would not be greatly relieved by mere improvements in the application of aid.

The Soviets have not demonstrated either great skill in administering their programs or a deep understanding of the processes of change in the underdeveloped countries. They have, however, a focus for relating all their activities, and thus in a perverse fashion they have been able to treat the processes of domestic change in transitional societies as a part of a larger process of change, that of creating a new world order. Soviet policies have thus appeared to be sensitive to two levels of revolutionary change; namely, the breaking up of traditional domestic societies, and the reshaping of the international systems after the stresses of two world wars. Thus, in working single-mindedly for their political goals, the Soviets have been able to offer the peoples of the newly emergent countries the vision of not only a new society at home, but also a place in a new international community.

In time the Soviets will no doubt become more technically competent in the field of foreign aid. They will then be in a much stronger position to order the world in their own image. Our current advantage will then disappear unless we are able to resolve, in the meantime, the basic problem of placing our aid programs into the larger context of our efforts to create a satisfactory world system. If we come to see this instrument as a more integral part of our total relations with a developing world, we may have less grandiose and dogmatic expectations. We might then value it more highly for the wide range of contributions it can make to the political development of the world.

SELECTED BIBLIOGRAPHY

PART V

Economics and the International System

Brockway, Thomas, *Battles without Bullets: The Story of Economic Warfare*. New York: Foreign Policy Association, 1939.

Gordon, David L., and Royden Dangerfield, *The Hidden Weapon*. New York: Harper and Brothers, 1947.

Hitch, Charles J., and Roland N. McKean, *The Economics of Defense in the Nuclear Age*. Cambridge: Harvard University Press, 1960.

Lauterbach, Albert K., *Economics in Uniform*. Princeton: Princeton University Press, 1943.

Mason, Edward S., *Foreign Aid and Foreign Policy*. New York: Harper and Row, 1964.

Moon, Parker Thomas, *Imperialism and World Politics*. New York: Macmillan, 1927.

Morgenthau, Hans J., "The Economics of Foreign Policy," *Challenge*. February 1959.

Schlesinger, James R., *The Political Economy of National Security*. New York: Praeger, 1960.

————, "Strategic Leverage from Aid and Trade." In David Abshire and Richard V. Allen, *National Security*. New York: Praeger, 1963.

Schurr, Sam H., and Jacob Morschak, *Economic Aspects of Atomic Power*. Princeton: Princeton University Press, 1950.

Wit, Daniel, "A New Strategy for Foreign Economic Aid," *Orbis*. Winter 1964.

Part VI

Man-Milieu Relationships

I N ALL MAJOR APPROACHES to the study of International Relations, relationships between man and his environment are accorded a place of considerable importance. Utopian theorists, it was suggested in Part I, held that if man was corrupted by his environment, he could nevertheless be improved if new international norms and institutions could be developed; in short, if the international environment could be changed. The Realist approach posited the existence of an environment which was essentially unchangeable. Environmental factors, especially geography, conditioned international behavior. In behavioral approaches as well, scholarly activity is often directed to an examination of interaction between man and his environment.

Some students of International Relations have posited the existence of relationships between geography and political behavior. According to Harold and Margaret Sprout, environmental factors can affect human activities to the extent that they are perceived and taken into account by the actors in a given setting. It is in this way only that "environmental factors can be said to influence, condition, or otherwise affect human values and preferences, moods and attitudes, choices and decisions." Geography is said not only to influence political behavior, but to favor some national units more than others.

Nicholas Spykman maintained that the geo-political significance of the Old and New Worlds is defined by the power potential and internal distribution of forces in each sphere. He saw the Eurasian continent as more self-sufficient than the American, and predicted future alignments which have since become realities. As a "realist," Spykman contended that international relations were characterized

by a struggle for power. That nation which dominated the vast
Eurasian land mass would possess the industrial, technological, natural, and human resources to achieve world rule. The objective of
United States policy should be to prevent the domination of Eurasia
by assuring the preservation of a balance of power there. Thus,
Spykman, writing during the early stages of World War II, when
there were demands for the unconditional surrender of enemy powers, argued for a policy designed to curb, but not to destroy Germany
and Japan, both of which would prove important components of a
postwar Eurasian balance of power.

In two world wars, the United States fought to prevent the
domination of the Eurasian land mass by a nation, or combination
of nations, hostile to the United States. In the postwar period, the
U.S. commitment to the defense of Western Europe, as well as other
regions on the Eurasian perimeter, has issued from similar considerations. Thus, U.S. policymakers have often operated on the
basis of geo-political concepts.

26. GEOGRAPHY AND FOREIGN POLICY

Nicholas J. Spykman

THE TERRITORY of the United States is located on the northern land mass of the Western Hemisphere between Canada and Mexico. Our state is unique in that its base is of continental dimensions and fronts on two oceans. It represents an immense area in the temperate zone with large sections of fertile soil and a rich endowment of mineral resources. The national economy, in which a highly developed industrial structure supplements an extensive agriculture of great productivity, sustains a high standard of living for about 135 million people. No other country in the Western Hemisphere has a war potential equal to our own. Our power position is one of unquestioned hegemony over a large part of the New World. We are far stronger than our neighbors to the north and south, we dominate completely the American Mediterranean, and we are able to exert effective pressure on the northern part of South America. The remoteness of the economic and political centers of the A.B.C. countries has given them a relative degree of independence and they represent the only region in the hemisphere where our strength could not be exerted with ease.

The Western Hemisphere is surrounded by the Old World across three ocean fronts, the Pacific, the Arctic, and the Atlantic, and, because the earth is a globe, the same applies in reverse, the New World also surrounds the Old. It is the power potential of these two worlds and the internal distribution of forces in each sphere that define the geo-political significance of this geographic fact. The Old World is 2½ times as large as the New World and contains 7 times the population. It is true that, at present, industrial productivity is almost equally divided, but, in terms of relative self-sufficiency, the Eurasian Continent with the related con-

From *America's Strategy in World Politics* by Nicholas J. Spykman, pp. 447–450; 465–470. Copyright, 1942, by Harcourt, Brace & World, Inc. and reprinted with their permission.

NICHOLAS J. SPYKMAN (1893–1943) Formerly Chairman, Department of International Relations and Director, Institute of International Studies, Yale University. His other books include *The Geography of the Peace*, (New York: Harcourt, Brace and Company, 1944); *The Social Theory of Georg Simmel*, (Chicago: University of Chicago Press, 1925).

tinents of Africa and Australia is in a much stronger position. If the three land masses of the Old World can be brought under the control of a few states and so organized that large unbalanced forces are available for pressure across the ocean fronts, the Americas will be politically and strategically encircled. There is no war potential of any size in any of the southern continents and South America can, therefore, offer the United States no compensation for the loss of the balance of power in Europe and Asia.

It is true that the Western Hemisphere is separated from the Old World by large bodies of water, but oceans do not isolate. Since the Renaissance and the development of modern navigation, they have been not barriers but highways. The world has become a single field of forces. Because power is effective in inverse ratio to the distance from its source, widely separated regions can function as relatively autonomous power zones, but no area in the world can be completely independent of the others. Only if the available military forces within a zone balance each other out, will the area be inert and unable to influence other regions, but in that case the explanation lies in the power equilibrium, not in the geographic distance. If power is free, unbalanced, unabsorbed, it can be used in distant regions.

Originally, the center of military and political power was in Europe and it was the European balance that was reflected in other sections of the world. Later, relatively autonomous power zones emerged in the Western Hemisphere and in the Far East, but they have all continued to influence each other. The New World, notwithstanding its insular character, has not been an isolated sphere in which political forces found their natural balance without interference from outside. On the contrary, European power relations have influenced the political life of the people of this hemisphere from the beginning of their history. The growth and expansion of the United States has been challenged by every great power in Europe except Italy. We achieved our position of hegemony only because the states of that continent were never able to combine against us and because preoccupation with the balance of power at home prevented them from ever detaching more than a small part of their strength for action across the Atlantic.

Since the states of the Western Hemisphere have achieved their independence, there has never been a time in which the transatlantic and transpacific regions have been in the hands of a single state or a single coalition of states. Balanced power in Europe and Asia has been characteristic of most of the period of our growth. But four times in our history there has been a threat of encirclement and of destruction of the balance of power across the oceans. The first threat was the appeal of France to the Holy Alliance for co-operation in the reconquest of the Spanish colonies. Our reply was the Monroe Doctrine. The second threat came in 1917 when the defeat of Russia, the demoralization of the French army, and the success of the submarine campaign suggested that Germany might win the First World War. Japan was using the golden opportunity presented by European withdrawal from Asia to make herself the dominant power in the Far East. Our answer to the danger in Europe was full participation in the war. The completeness of the victory made the existing British-Japanese Alliance a minor danger to our security. In terms of geography, the agreement did mean encirclement and both partners had come out of the war with greatly increased naval strength, practically unbalanced in their respective spheres. We, therefore, made the termination of their alliance the condition of our participation in disarmament in 1921.

The fourth threat has emerged since 1940 and this time it is in a form more serious than ever before. The German-Japanese Alliance, signed in that year, provided for co-operation against the Western Hemisphere. By the fall of 1941, Germany had conquered most of Europe; Japan most of the coastal regions of the Far East. Only Great Britain and Russia in Europe and China and the Dutch East Indies in Asia stood between them and the complete conquest of the Old World. Victory would have meant for Germany the realization of her dream of a great Euro-African sphere controlled from Berlin. Victory would have meant for Japan the transformation of her island state into a unit of continental dimensions. For the New World, such a situation would have meant encirclement by two gigantic empires controlling huge war potentials.

HEMISPHERE DEFENSE?

In the face of this contingency, what was the correct policy for the United States to pursue? Public debate followed the traditional pattern of intervention versus isolation. Those interventionists who were impressed with the importance of power relations, contended that the first line of defense was of necessity the preservation of a balance of power in Europe and Asia. Those isolationists who were impressed with oceanic distances, felt convinced that we could disengage ourselves from the power struggles across the oceans and rely on hemisphere defense.

During the progress of the war, the interventionist position found wider and wider acceptance and the policy of the United States became one of increasing support to the Allies. The American people were spared the necessity of deciding on the last step, the transition from Lend-Lease Aid to full belligerency. The German-Japanese Alliance decided to strike before our war industries went into full production and large quantities of material became available for our allies. We are now full participants in the Second World War and our opponents have begun their attack on the outposts of the Western Hemisphere before their victory in the Old World is complete.

Isolation versus intervention is no longer a debate over war participation but the two geo-political theories which these attitudes represent will continue to influence our thinking about the principles of grand strategy that should guide us in the conduct of the war and in the formulation of the conditions of peace. There is still a danger that the erroneous ideas regarding the nature of the Western Hemisphere inherent in the isolationist position may tempt people to urge a defensive strategy in the belief that the New World could survive a German-Japanese victory abroad.

.   .   .

THE UNITED STATES AND EUROPE

The post-war policy of the United States will have to operate in a world of power politics under conditions very similar to those that prevailed before the outbreak of the conflict. It should be guided by a political strategy which demands the preservation of a balance of power in Europe and in Asia, and by the consideration that territorial security and peaceful change are more likely to be achieved if the individual states in the different power zones do not differ too widely in their relative strength.

.   .   .

The greatest difficulty will be that of balancing Germany and Russia. In case of Allied victory, the Soviet Union will come out of the war as one of the great industrial nations of the world with an enormous war potential. Germany, unless destroyed, will continue to represent an impressive military strength as demonstrated in the First and Second World Wars. The easiest solution would be to give them a common frontier. But if this should prove impossible, then the political unit between them should be a great eastern European federation from the Baltic to the Mediterranean, not a series of small buffer states. More troublesome is going to be the problem of Holland and Belgium, the old buffer states that have ceased to perform their protective function and that can neither shield Great Britain from bombing nor France from invasion under conditions of modern warfare. It is possible to conceive of several different combinations in addition to an eastern European federation, such as a British-Scandinavian group around the North Sea and the Baltic, and a Latin group around the Mediterranean. The Versailles settlement sacrificed economic and power considerations to the exclusive demands of the principle of self-determination with the result that the whole power structure came to rest on two weak crutches, a disarmed Germany and a nonfortified Rhineland. The new peace will not only have to correct the Balkanization of Europe, which was introduced after the First World

War, but it will also have to achieve the integration of other states into a few large units.

. . .

THE UNITED STATES AND ASIA

The United States has been interested in the preservation of a balance of power in the Far East primarily for the protection of her position as an Asiatic power. But even if she were to withdraw from Asia and grant independence to the Philippines, she would still remain interested in the power relations of the transpacific zone. The Asiatic Mediterranean is perhaps the most important single source of strategic raw materials for the United States, and its control by a single power would endanger the basis of our military strength. The Far East was the last area to become an autonomous power zone and it is still inferior to both Europe and the United States as a source of political power. Advanced technology will however sooner or later translate the inherent power potential of the region into actual military strength, and, when that occurs, its relative importance compared to the two other zones will increase. The preservation of a balance will then be necessary not only because of our interest in strategic raw materials but also because of what unbalanced power in this region could do to the rest of the world.

The end of the Second World War will also find in existence in the Far East a number of independent units: Russia, China, and perhaps Japan; Great Britain, the Dutch East Indies, Australia, and New Zealand. The problem of building out of these units a balanced power structure in terms of states of approximately equal strength is going to be even more difficult than in Europe, and the main difficulty of the post-war period will be not Japan but China. The power potential of the former Celestial Kingdom is infinitely greater than that of the Land of the Cherry Blossom and once that power potential begins to express itself in actual military strength, the position of a defeated Japan as a small off-shore island near the Asiatic mainland is going to be very uncomfortable. When long-range bombing squadrons can operate from the tip of the Shan-tung peninsula as well as from Vladivostok, fire insurance rates in the Japanese paper cities will undoubtedly go up.

A modern, vitalized, and militarized China of 450 million people is going to be a threat not only to Japan, but also to the position of the Western Powers in the Asiatic Mediterranean. China will be a continental power of huge dimensions in control of a large section of the littoral of that middle sea. Her geographic position will be similar to that of the United States in regard to the American Mediterranean. When China becomes strong, her present economic penetration in that region will undoubtedly take on political overtones. It is quite possible to envisage the day when this body of water will be controlled not by British, American, or Japanese sea power but by Chinese air power.

It will be difficult to find public support in the United States for a Far Eastern policy based on these realities of power politics. It is true that intervention in Far Eastern affairs is traditionally much more acceptable than intervention in Europe, but this tradition is also tied up with a pro-Chinese and anti-Japanese orientation which the war itself will greatly intensify. Public opinion will probably continue to see Japan as the great danger, long after the balance has shifted in favor of China and it has become necessary to pursue in the Far East the same policy that we have pursued in regard to Europe. Twice in one generation we have come to the aid of Great Britain in order that the small off-shore island might not have to face a single gigantic military state in control of the opposite coast of the mainland. If the balance of power in the Far East is to be preserved in the future as well as in the present, the United States will have to adopt a similar protective policy toward Japan.

27. THE ECOLOGICAL PERSPECTIVE

Harold and Margaret Sprout

. . . So far as we can determine, environmental factors (both non-human and social) can affect human activities in *only two ways*. Such factors can be perceived, reacted to, and taken into account by the human individual or individuals under consideration. In this way, *and in this way only*, . . . environmental factors can be said to "influence," or to "condition," or otherwise to "affect" human values and preferences, moods and attitudes, choices and decisions. On the other hand, the rela-

From *The Ecological Perspective on Human Affairs* by Harold and Margaret Sprout, pp. 11–15. Copyright 1965 by the Princeton University Press, and reprinted with their permission. Footnotes have been renumbered to appear in consecutive order.

HAROLD SPROUT (1901–   ) Henry Grier Bryant Professor of Geography and International Relations, Princeton University. Co-author with Margaret Sprout of *An Ecological Paradigm for the Study of International Politics*, (Princeton: Center for International Studies, 1968); *The Ecological Perspective on Human Affairs with Special Reference to International Politics*, (Princeton: Princeton University Press, 1965); *Foundations of National Power*, (Princeton: Van Nostrand, 1951).

tion of environmental factors to performance and accomplishment (that is, to the operational outcomes or results of decisions and undertakings) may present an additional dimension. In the latter context, environmental factors may be conceived as a sort of matrix, or encompassing channel, metaphorically speaking, which limits the execution of undertakings. Such limitations on performance, accomplishment, outcome, or operational result may not—often do not—derive from or depend upon the environed individual's perception or other psychological behavior. In many instances, environmental limitations on outcome or performance may be effective even though the limiting factors were not perceived and reacted to in the process of reaching a decision and initiating a course of action.

The American debacle at Pearl Harbor is a historic example of this central thesis. The American commanders there made their defensive preparations for hostilities which they believed to be imminent. But they remained in ignorance of the approaching Japanese fleet. The environment as they perceived it contained no hostile fleet. Hence that fleet's presence was not reacted to in any way; that is to say, it had no effect whatever on the decisions of the American commanders prior to the moment of attack on that December morning in 1941. Yet the Japanese fleet was indubitably an ingredient of the environment in which the decisions of the American commanders were executed; and their ignorance of its presence did not prevent it from affecting decisively the operational outcome that occurred.

. . .

While our discussion of ecological perspective, concepts, and theories is set specifically in the context of international politics, much of the illustrative material . . . is drawn from other fields, in particular from the field of human geography. This is appropriate for two reasons: (1) because geographic dimensions—identified by such terms as location, distance, space, distribution, and configuration—are nearly always significant in discussions of political undertakings and the operational results thereof; and (2) because geographers have given much attention to certain aspects of environmental relationships.

Perhaps we should insert here a few paragraphs that may seem to most geographers to be an elaboration of the obvious, but which may not be quite so obvious to many others. There is some tendency (probably diminishing, and discernible mainly among those relatively unfamiliar with modern geographic concepts) to think of geography as a subject that pertains chiefly to the physical earth. There can be no doubt that geographers are concerned with the physical conformation of the earth's surface: with the layout of lands and seas, the distribution of mineral rocks upon and beneath the surface, the patterns of vegetation and weather, the distribution of subhuman organisms that subsist upon the earth and on each other. All these phenomena exhibit geographic quality, in the sense that geographic science "is concerned with the arrangement of things on the face of the earth, and with the associations of things that give character to particular places." [1]

Applying this test, geographic quality also attaches to many kinds of phenomena besides the physical earth and subhuman organisms. People are geographic objects, in the sense that they are areally distributed in social groups of many kinds and sizes. The same holds for the physical structures—cultivated fields, planted forests, buildings, roads, and many other tangible structures—that human hands have superimposed upon the earth's surface, changing and often obliterating the primordial landscape. Geographic patterns are also observable in many kinds of human processes: for example, farming, manufacturing, commerce, recreation, governing; likewise, in many other intangibles of human behavior: values and norms, attitudes and preferences, customs and habits, as well as institutions and other more formal patterns. Geographic quality, in short, attaches to any phenomena—human as well as nonhuman, intangible as well as tangible—that exhibit areal dimensions and variations upon or in relation to the earth's surface.

This concept of geographic quality is central to the ecological perspective and to any scheme for analysis of ecological relationships. This is so because systematic analysis confirms the common-sense observation that the distribution and arrangement of phenomena upon the earth's surface are always, or nearly always, related significantly to what people undertake and to what they accomplish. The ecological perspective and ecological theories bring the dimensions of location, distance, space, distribution, and configuration sharply into focus in many social contexts, not least in the context of politics in general and of international politics in particular.

Every political community (though not necessarily every political organization) rests upon a geographic base. Territory is universally recognized to be one of the essential attributes of statehood. Probably the geographic exhibits most familiar to the most people are the maps that delineate the boundaries and differentiate the territories of national and subnational political communities.

The territory of each political community differs from all the rest—in location, in size and shape, in distance from the others, in arable land and climate and other so-called natural resources. Each differs from the rest in numbers of people, in their level and variety of knowledge and skills,

---

[1] P. E. James et al., American Geography: Inventory and Prospect, Syracuse University Press, 1954, p. 4.

in their mechanical equipment and stage of economic development, in their form of government, and in many other respects. All these phenomena, nonhuman and human, are unevenly distributed among the communities that comprise the society of nations. In most (if possibly not quite all) transactions among nations (and the same holds for relations among individuals and groups within national communities), at least some of the geographic dimensions noted above are certain to be significantly related to what is undertaken and also to what is accomplished.

This is conspicuously the case with transactions which exhibit some element of conflict of purpose or interest among the interacting persons, groups, or organized communities—transactions that exhibit political quality in the narrower sense of that term. Political demands and responses thereto are projected through space from one point to another upon the earth's surface. All the techniques of statecraft, domestic as well as international, involve expenditures of energy and consumption of other resources. This is obviously the case with respect to military operations and the administration of public order. But it is likewise the case in varying degrees with respect to nonsubversive public relations and propaganda, subversive conspiracy and internal war, economic and technical assistance, diplomacy and conference, and all the variants and combinations of these modes of operation. In any period of history, the results of international statecraft exhibit more or less clearly discernible patterns of coercion and submission, and influence and deference, patterns reflected in political terms with strong geographic connotations: such as balance of power, bipolarity, political orbit, satellite, bloc, coalition, alliance, the Monroe Doctrine, the Atlantic Community, the Near East, and many others.

SELECTED BIBLIOGRAPHY

PART VI

Man-Milieu Relationships

Bowman, Isaiah, *Geography in Relation to the Social Sciences.* New York: Charles Scribner's Sons, 1934.

Cohen, Saul B., *Geography and Politics in a Divided World.* New York: Random House, 1963.

Dorpalen, Andreas, *The World of General Havshofer*. New York: Farrar and Reinhart, 1942.

Gottmann, Jean, "Geography and International Relations," *World Politics*. January 1961.

Gyorgy, Andrew, *Geopolitics*. Berkeley: University of California Press, 1944.

Huntington, Ellsworth, *World Powers and Evolution*. New Haven: Yale University Press, 1919.

Jugan, Arthur B., "Mackinder and His Critics Reconsidered." *Journal of Politics*. May 1962.

Kruszweski, Charles, "The Pivot of History." *Foreign Affairs*. April 1954.

Mackinder, H. J., *Democratic Ideals and Reality*. New York: Henry Holt and Company, 1942.

——, "The Round World and the Winning of the Peace." *Foreign Affairs*. July 1943.

Mahan, Alfred Thayer, *The Influence of Sea Power upon History, 1660–1783*. Boston: Little, Brown and Company, 1890.

Sprout, Harold and Margaret, "Environmental Factors in the Study of International Politics," *Journal of Conflict Resolution*. December 1957.

Spykman, Nicholas J., *The Geography of Peace*. New York: Harcourt, 1944.

Strausz-Hupé, Robert, *Geopolitics*. New York: G. P. Putnam's Sons, 1942.

——, *The Balance of Tomorrow*. New York: G. P. Putnam's Sons, 1945.

Weigert, H. W., "Mackinder's Heartland," *The American Scholar*. Winter 1945–46.

Part VII

National Character and Transnational Images

PEOPLE HOLD images both of themselves and other people. In the international system peoples hold images both of themselves as a nation and of other nations. Because such images may affect political behavior, and, thus foreign policy, many students of International Relations have attempted to describe and analyze the images which nations hold about themselves and other national units. Moreover, there is a considerable literature about national character which, as Harold and Margaret Sprout suggest, may be defined as "patterns of thinking, feeling, and doing which appear to be quite widely prevalent within the country in question."

Although many studies are impressionistic in nature, the Sprouts present a framework for the study of national character. By devising methods with which to ascertain and study such phenomena as national myths and traditions, patterns of morale and discipline, attitudes toward the allocation of resources, and commitments to certain goals, it might be possible to gain a more precise understanding of the phenomenon called national character, as well as the form which it assumes in individual national units.

According to Gabriel Almond, the American national character conditions popular and elite attitudes toward foreign policy. Almond finds a tendency toward wide fluctuations of mood between withdrawal-intervention, optimism-pessimism, tolerance-intolerance, idealism-cynicism, and superiority-inferiority. Such moods affect not only the American outlook toward other peoples, but influence U.S. foreign policy.

Peoples may hold images about the national character, and the international behavior and foreign policy goals of other peoples. According to Urie Bronfenbrenner, the Soviet image of the United States bears a remarkable resemblance to the U.S. image of the Soviet Union. In U.S.–Soviet reciprocal images Bronfenbrenner notes the operation of a "phenomenon well known to psychologists— the tendency to assimilate new perceptions to old, and unconsciously to distort what one sees in such a way as to minimize a clash with previous expectations." Unconsciously, both sides are said to distort what they report to their peoples in such a way as to conform to previous information and ideas. The result, according to Bronfenbrenner, is "serious distortions in the reciprocal images of the Soviet Union and the United States." Whether or not Bronfenbrenner is justified in believing the U.S. and Soviet reciprocal images to be equally distorted, his work is illustrative as an effort to study the interaction of images and their effect upon the behavior of national units in the international system.

28. A FUNCTIONAL APPROACH TO NATIONAL CHARACTER

Harold and Margaret Sprout

I MPRESSIONISTIC IMAGES of national character may reflect keen observation and shrewd intuition. But such impressions, as Leighton* says, are just as apt to reflect sheer bias and almost limitless capacity of people for self-deception about their own behavior and the behavior of other nationalities.

Impressionistic images, we repeat, have influenced policy-makers in the past. It would be unrealistic to suppose that such notions will not be just as influential in the future. But pure impressionism is an insecure basis upon which to build national policies or to estimate the international capabilities of nations. It would be highly desirable to put thinking about national character on a more trustworthy basis. One step in this direction is to establish an explicit frame of concepts within which to compare the behavioral patterns of different nations.

One can go about this task in various ways. Table 16.2 suggests one possible scheme for classifying those facets of national character which may be regarded as having special relevance in the context of international politics. Running through the categories of patterns identified in the table, one will find *normative* aspects (notions of what is right, proper, desirable, and vice versa), *cognitive* or *existential* aspects (notions of how things actually are in the real world), and *affective* aspects (emotional reactions or feelings—friendliness, hostility, fear, etc.).

A given pattern may be primarily normative: for example, notions as to what goals one's government should be trying to achieve. Or a pattern may be primarily affective: for example, feelings of distrust towards certain nations. Normative, cognitive, and affective aspects may also be associated in the same pattern, as, for example, in the rather widespread

From *Foundations of International Politics* by Harold and Margaret Sprout (Princeton: 1962) pp. 500–503. Reprinted by permission of the Van Nostrand Company, Inc.

HAROLD AND MARGARET SPROUT—See biographical note, page 296.

* Alexander H. Leighton, American psychologist, author of *Human Relations in a Changing World,* (New York: E. P. Dutton, 1949, 1st edition). [Editor's note.]

American attitude towards China in the late 1940's, compounded of a generally kindly feeling towards Chinese, abhorrence of Communism, and expectation that somehow the anti-Communist forces in China would in the end prevail. The same three aspects are associated, to cite another example, in the rather prevalent American attitude towards female physicians: the notion that it is improper for female physicians to practice on adult male patients, the notion that female physicians are generally less competent than male physicians, and the reluctance of most men to consult female physicians no matter how competent they may be.

Finally, no matter how national behavioral patterns are classified, it should always be kept in mind that one is classifying personal images that are deemed to be more or less characteristic or typical (that is, prevalent) within a given national community; and that different observers, with different preconceptions and viewpoints, may reach different conclusions, sometimes startlingly different conclusions, regarding the behavioral characteristics of their own and other national communities. In short, one can systematize, and make them more explicit, but one cannot eliminate the factor of subjective personal judgment. Now, with these points in mind, let us examine Table 16.2.

Most of the categories of Table 16.2 are self-explanatory, but a few comments and illustrations on them may be helpful. Attitudes towards authority, obedience, and loyalty (A.1.a) and towards service to the state and those who serve the state (A.1.b) should cast light on the measure of a nation's political solidarity and on its government's ability to command both loyal and dedicated service from its citizens—factors of manifest relevance in any calculation of a nation's international capabilities.

National myths and traditions (A.1.c) always contribute something to an understanding of current conceptions of national interest, purpose, and destiny (A.1.d). These, in turn, provide valuable indicators regarding the specific objectives and strategies to be expected from the governments under consideration. How, for example, could one make sense out of the United States government's refusal, throughout the 1950's, to accept the irreversibility of the Communist Revolution in China, without some knowledge of historic American myths and traditional American policies with regard to China? Very few Americans have visited China. But for several generations China was the scene of dedicated service by Christian missionaries of many faiths. American merchants never sold great quantities of goods in China. But the myth persisted that this most populous country was potentially the world's greatest market. When European imperialists moved in on the moribund Chinese empire in the waning years of the nineteenth century, the official voice of America was raised in protest. From that time on there was close to consensus among Americans who thought about foreign affairs at all that it was the duty of the United States to protect the political and territorial integrity of

TABLE 16.2

SELECTED INGREDIENTS OF NATIONAL CHARACTER

A. Behavioral patterns pertaining primarily to citizens' attitudes toward and relations with the national community of which they are members:
1. Attitudes toward and relations with the community as a whole:
   a. Attitudes toward authority, obedience, loyalty, and the moral limits thereof
   b. Attitudes toward service to the state and toward those who serve the state
   c. Ideas, myths, and traditions regarding the nation's past
   d. Conceptions of national interest, purpose, and destiny
   e. Conceptions of and degree of commitment to intranation social goals
   f. Morale, discipline, and behavior under stress
   g. Other patterns
2. Attitudes toward and relations with fellow members of the national community:
   a. Attitudes regarding role allocation: who should and should not do what
   b. Attitudes toward and relations with persons regarded as social equals, social inferiors, and social superiors
   c. Tolerance of values and attitudes antagonistic to one's own
   d. Other patterns
B. Behavioral patterns pertaining primarily to attitudes toward and relations with other national-states and the citizens thereof:
1. Attitudes toward and opinions regarding other nation-states conceived as entities:
   a. Images regarding states identified as allies or potential allies
   b. Images regarding states identified as enemies or potential enemies
   c. Images regarding other states
2. Attitudes toward and opinions regarding other nationalities:
   a. Images regarding nationalities toward which orientation is predominantly friendly and/or favorable
   b. Images regarding nationalities toward which orientation is predominantly hostile and/or unfavorable
   c. Other images
3. Attitudes toward and relations with individual foreign persons:
   a. Patterns that prevail within our country
   b. Patterns that prevail when in foreigner's country

China until such time as a responsible and democratic Chinese government could assume effective responsibility for the country's future. The Communist victory was repugnant to everything Americans had stood for in China since the turn of the century, and the repugnance was heightened by the rather widely prevalent American fear and hatred of Communism.

Commitment to particular intranation social goals (A.1.*e*) relates to public demands and expectations which may significantly limit the efforts and resources which politicians will venture to allocate for military defense, foreign aid, or other international projects. In the middle 1950's, for example, the British people had lived with austerity for some fifteen years—rationing, high taxes, and other policies that cramped the individual consumer's ability to purchase goods and services. During the same period, the British people had become accustomed to a range of publicly financed welfare services—of which the National Health Service became the symbol. By the mid-1950's public demands for an end to austerity and public expectations regarding the welfare services set highly inelastic limits on the proportion of the GNP which it was politically expedient to allocate to national defense—with consequent serious deterioration of the military establishment.

Patterns of morale, discipline, and especially behavior under stress (A.1.f) focus on the vitally important issue of how a national community is likely to react, not only to austerity and adversity, but especially to overwhelming disaster. For obvious reasons this aspect of national character obtrudes into any thorough examination of national capability, these days. Estimates of casualties in the initial hours or days of a full-scale nuclear war might run as high as 30 to 50 percent or more of a nation's civilian population. Buildings would be smashed; fires would become conflagrations; water systems would be wrecked; food and water would become contaminated; hospitals would be destroyed or rendered unusable by fallout. Transport would be so crippled as to render all but impossible any large-scale evacuation of survivors to safer places (if any).

How would the survivors of such a catastrophe behave? Would their routines and habits break down completely? At what point would a society cease to be a going concern, and become a hysterical mob? And (the sixty-four dollar question) are there grounds for believing that nations would react differently in such a catastrophe?

Official thinking and planning in the United States (and probably in some other countries as well) appears to rest upon optimistic assumptions regarding the nation's ability to carry on and recover from extreme catastrophe. Such optimism is frequently rationalized by reference to civilian behavior under bombing in World War II. That evidence, as we have emphasized already, has limited relevance because of the enormous rise in firepower since 1945.

29. THE MIRROR IMAGE IN SOVIET-AMERICAN RELATIONS

Urie Bronfenbrenner

LET US THEN briefly examine the common features in the American and Soviet view of each other's societies. For the Russian's image I drew mainly not on official government pronouncements but on what was said to me by Soviet citizens in the course of our conversations. Five major themes stand out.

1. *They* are the aggressors.

The American view: Russia is the warmonger bent on imposing its system on the rest of the world. Witness Czechoslovakia, Berlin, Hungary, and now Cuba and the Congo. The Soviet Union consistently blocks Western proposals for disarmament by refusing necessary inspection controls.

The Soviet view: America is the warmonger bent on imposing its power on the rest of the world and on the Soviet Union itself. Witness American intervention in 1918, Western encirclement after World War II with American troops and bases on every border of the USSR (West Germany, Norway, Turkey, Korea, Japan), intransigence over proposals to make Berlin a free city, intervention in Korea, Taiwan, Lebanon, Guatemala, Cuba. America has repeatedly rejected Soviet disarmament proposals while demanding the right to inspect within Soviet territory—finally attempting to take the right by force through deep penetration of Soviet air space.

2. Their government exploits and deludes the people.

The American view: Convinced communists, who form but a small proportion of Russia's population, control the government and exploit the society and its resources in their own interest. To justify their power and expansionist policies they have to perpetuate a war atmosphere and a fear of Western aggression. Russian elections are a travesty since only one party appears on the ballot. The Russian people are kept from knowing the truth through a controlled radio and press and conformity is insured through stringent economic and political sanctions against deviant individuals or groups.

From *The Journal of Social Issues* XVII, No. 3, 46–51. Reprinted by permission of the author and the publisher.

URIE BRONFENBRENNER (1917–   ) Professor of Child Development and Family Relationships, Cornell University. Co-author of *Talent and Society,* (Princeton: Van Nostrand, 1967). Author of *Measurement of Sociometric Status, Structure and Development,* (New York: Beacon House, 1945).

The Soviet view: A capitalistic-militaristic clique controls the American government, the nation's economic resources, and its media of communication. This group exploits the society and its resources. It is in their economic and political interest to maintain a war atmosphere and engage in militaristic expansion. Voting in America is a farce since candidates for both parties are selected by the same powerful interests leaving nothing to choose between. The American people are kept from knowing the truth through a controlled radio and press and through economic and political sanctions against liberal elements.

3. *The mass of their people are not really sympathetic to the regime.*

The American view: In spite of the propoganda, the Soviet people are not really behind their government. Their praise of the government and the party is largely perfunctory, a necessary concession for getting along. They do not trust their own sources of information and have learned to read between the lines. Most of them would prefer to live under our system of government if they only could.

The Soviet view: Unlike their government, the bulk of the American people want peace. Thus, the majority disapproved of American aggression in Korea, the support of Chiang Kai Shek, and, above all, of the sending of U2. But of course they could do nothing since their welfare is completely under the control of the ruling financier-militaristic clique. If the American people were allowed to become acquainted with communism as it exists in the USSR, they would unquestionably choose it as their form of government. ("You Americans are such a nice people; it is a pity you have such a terrible government.")

4. *They* cannot be trusted.

The American view: The Soviets do not keep promises and they do not mean what they say. Thus while they claim to have discontinued all nuclear testing, they are probably carrying out secret underground explosions in order to gain an advantage over us. Their talk of peace is but a propaganda maneuver. Everything they do is to be viewed with suspicion since it is all part of a single coordinated scheme to further aggressive communist aims.

The Soviet view: The Americans do not keep promises and they do not mean what they say. Thus they insist on inspection only so that they can look at Soviet defenses; they have no real intention of disarming. Everything the Americans do is to be viewed with suspicion (e.g., they take advantage of Soviet hospitality by sending in spies as tourists).

5. *Their* policy verges on madness.

The American view: Soviet demands on such crucial problems as disarmament, Berlin, and unification are completely unrealistic. Disarmament without adequate inspection is meaningless, a "free Berlin" would be equivalent to a Soviet Berlin, and a united Germany without free elections is an impossibility. In pursuit of their irresponsible policies the Soviets do not hesitate to run the risk of war itself. Thus it is only due to the restraint and coordinated action of the Western alliance that Soviet provocations over Berlin did not precipitate World War III.

The Soviet view: The American position on such crucial problems as disarmament, East Germany, and China is completely unrealistic. They demand to know our secrets before they disarm; in Germany they insist on a policy which risks the resurgence of a fascist Reich; and as for China, they try to act as if it did not exist while at the same time supporting an aggressive puppet regime just off the Chinese mainland. And in pursuit of their irresponsible policies, the Americans do not hesitate to run the risk of war itself. Were it not for Soviet prudence and restraint, the sending of U2 deep into Russian territory could easily have precipitated World War III.

It is easy to recognize the gross distortions in the Soviet views summarized above. But it is our own outlook completely realistic? Are we correct, for example, in thinking that the mass of the Soviet people would really prefer our way of life and are unenthusiastic about their own? Certainly the tone and tenor of my conversations with Soviet citizens hardly support this belief.

But, you may ask, why is it that other Western observers do not report the enthusiasm and commitment which I encountered?

I asked this very question of newspaper men and embassy officials in Moscow. Their answers were revealing. Thus one reporter replied somewhat dryly, "Sure, I know, but when a communist acts like a communist, it isn't news. If I want to be sure that it will be printed back home, I have to write about what's wrong with the system, not its successes." Others voiced an opinion expressed most clearly by representatives at our embassy. When I reported to them the gist of my Soviet conversations, they were grateful but skeptical: "Professor, you underestimate the effect of the police state. When these people talk to a stranger, especially an American, they *have* to say the right thing."

The argument is persuasive, and comforting to hear. But perhaps these very features should arouse our critical judgment. Indeed, it is instructive to view this argument against the background of its predecessor voiced by the newspaperman. To put it bluntly, what he was saying was that he could be sure of getting published only the material that the *American people wanted to hear*. But notice that the second argument also fulfills this objective, and it does so in a much more satisfactory and sophisticated way. The realization that "Soviet citizens *have* to say the right thing" enables the Western observer not only to discount most of what he hears, but even to interpret it as evidence in direct support of the West's accepted picture of the Soviet Union as a police state.

It should be clear that I am in no sense here suggesting that Western reporters and embassy officials deliberately misrepresent what they know to be the facts. Rather I am but calling attention to the operation, in a specific and critical context, of a phenomenon well known to psychologists—the tendency to assimilate new perceptions to old, and unconsciously to distort what one sees in such a way as to minimize a clash with previous expectations. In recent years, a number of leading social psychologists, notably Heider (1958), Festinger (1957), and Osgood (1960), have emphasized that this "strain toward consistency" is especially powerful in the sphere of social relations—that is, in our perceptions of the motives, attitudes, and actions of other persons or groups. Specifically, we strive to keep our views of other human beings compatible with each other. In the face of complex social reality, such consistency is typically accomplished by obliterating distinctions and organizing the world in terms of artificially-simplified frames of reference. One of the simplest of these, and hence one of the most inviting, is the dichotomy of good and bad. Hence we often perceive others, be they individuals, groups, or even whole societies, as simply "good" or "bad." Once this fateful decision is made, the rest is easy, for the "good" person or group can have only desirable social characteristics and the "bad" can have only reprehensible traits. And once such evaluative stability of social perception is established, it is extremely difficult to alter. Contradictory stimuli arouse only anxiety and resistance. When confronted with a desirable characteristic of something already known to be "bad," the observer will either just not "see" it, or will reorganize his perception of it so that it can be perceived as "bad." Finally, this tendency to regress to simple categories of perception is especially strong under conditions of emotional stress and external threat. Witness our readiness in times of war to exalt the virtues of our own side and to see the enemy as thoroughly evil.

Still one other social psychological phenomenon has direct relevance for the present discussion. I refer to a process demonstrated most dramatically and comprehensively in the experiments of Solomon Asch (1956), and known thereby as the "Asch phenomenon." In these experiments, the subject finds himself in a group of six or eight of his peers all of whom are asked to make comparative judgments of certain stimuli presented to them, for example, identifying the longer of two lines. At first the task seems simple enough; the subject hears others make their judgments and then makes his own. In the beginning he is usually in agreement, but then gradually he notices that more and more often his judgments differ from those of the rest of the group. Actually, the experiment is rigged. All the other group members have been instructed to give false responses on a predetermined schedule. In any event, the effect on our subject is dramatic. At first he is puzzled, then upset. Soon he begins to have serious doubts about his own judgment, and in an appreciable number of cases, he begins to "see" the stimuli as they are described by his fellows.

What I am suggesting, of course, is that the Asch phenomenon operates even more forcefully outside the laboratory where the game of social perception is being played for keeps. *Specifically, I am proposing that the mechanisms here described contribute substantially to producing and maintaining serious distortions in the reciprocal images of the Soviet Union and the United States.*

My suggestion springs from more than abstract theoretical inference. I call attention to the possible operation of the Asch phenomenon in the Soviet-American context for a very concrete reason: I had the distressing experience of being its victim. While in the Soviet Union I deliberately sought to minimize association with other Westerners and to spend as much time as I could with Soviet citizens. This was not easy to do. It was no pleasant experience to hear one's own country severely criticized and to be constantly out-debated in the bargain. I looked forward to the next chance meeting with a fellow Westerner so that I could get much-needed moral support and enjoy an evening's invective at the expense of Intourist and the "worker's paradise." But though I occasionally yielded to temptation, for the most part I kept true to my resolve and spent many hours in a completely Soviet environment. It was difficult, but interesting. I liked many of the people I met. Some of them apparently liked me. Though mistaken, they were obviously sincere. They wanted me to agree with them. The days went on, and strange things began to happen. I remember picking up a Soviet newspaper which featured an account of American activities in the Near East. "Oh, what are they doing now!" I asked myself, and stopped short; for I had thought in terms of "they," and it was my own country. Or I would become aware that I had been nodding to the points being made by my Soviet companion where before I had always taken issue. In short, when all around me saw the world in one way, I too found myself wanting to believe and belong.

And once I crossed the Soviet border on my way home, the process began to reverse itself. The more I talked with fellow Westerners, especially fellow Americans, the more I began to doubt the validity of my original impressions. "What would you expect them to say to an American?" my friends would ask. "How do you know that the person talking to you was not a trained agitator?" "Did you ever catch sight of them following you?" I never did. Perhaps I was naive. But, then, recently I reread a letter written to a friend during the last week of my stay. "I feel it is important," it begins, "to try to write to you in detail while I am still in it, for just as I could never have conceived of what I am now experiencing, so, I suspect, it will seem unreal and intangible once I am back in the West." The rest of the letter, and others like it, contain the record of the experiences reported in this account.

In sum, I take my stand on the view that there *is* a mirror image in Soviet and American perceptions of each other and that this image represents serious distortions by *both* parties of realities on either side.

30. AMERICAN CHARACTER AND FOREIGN POLICY

Gabriel Almond

. . . I T IS POSSIBLE to distinguish those "traits" which are referred to frequently in the literature over a period of many decades. The fact that successive generations of observers tend to reach similar conclusions suggests a greater credibility. In addition, some propositions seem to have an inherent plausibility, as tending to agree with informal observation, while others convey the impression of gifted, if untrustworthy, fantasy or theoretical presuppositions which have focused attention on particular phenomena regardless of their connection or representativeness. In the systematic inventory which follows we have made an effort to include only those observations which have continually recurred and those which seem to have an inherent plausibility, recognizing that the criterion of "plausibility" is a purely subjective one.

GENERAL VALUE ORIENTATION

The characteristic American value orientation would appear to consist of the following interrelated traits.

a. The degree of atomization in the United States is perhaps greater than in any other culture. The American is primarily concerned with "private" values, as distinguished from social-group, political, or religious-moral values. His concern with private, worldly success is his most

From *The American People and Foreign Policy* by Gabriel A. Almond, pp. 47–65; 137–148; 226–244. Copyright, 1950, by Harcourt, Brace & World, Inc. and reprinted with their permission.

GABRIEL A. ALMOND (1911–   ) Director of Political Science Dept., Stanford University. His other books include *Comparative Politics: A Developmental Approach*, (Boston: Little, Brown, 1966), co-author; *The Civic Culture*, (Princeton: Princeton University Press, 1963); *The Politics of the Developing Areas*, (Princeton: Princeton University Press, 1960).

absorbing aim. In this regard it may be suggested by way of hypothesis that in other cultures there is a greater stress on corporate loyalties and values and a greater personal involvement with political issues or with other-worldly religious values.

b. The "attachment" of the American to his private values is characterized by an extreme degree of competitiveness. He views himself and his family as in a state of competition with other individuals and families for success and achievement. American culture tends to be atomistic rather than corporate, and the pressure of movement "upward," toward achievement, is intense. Here again a hypothesis might be proposed that in other cultures individual competition for success tends to be more localized within specific classes or regions, tends to be subordinated to, or assimilated in, political competition, and tends to be muted by religious conceptions of life.

c. The American views himself and his family as in a state of competition with other individuals and families for values which are largely "material" in character. What he appears to want are the material evidences of success—money, position, and the consumer-goods of the moment. While the stress is toward money, or what money can buy, the important thing is not the money itself, but the sense of accomplishment or fulfillment which it gives. This sense of accomplishment rests on matching and exceeding the material standard of community and social class; it requires external approval and conformity. Because of the stress in the American value system on having what others want, and because of the great emphasis on the elaboration of material culture, the American tends to be caught up in an endless race for constantly changing goals—the "newest" in housing, the "latest" in locomotion, the most "fashionable" in dress and appearance. This love of innovation, improvement, and change tends to be confined to the material culture. Attitudes toward human and social relations tend to be more conservative. By way of hypothetical comparison it may be said that in other cultures the criteria of accomplishment are more stable. Religious salvation and political resentment provide greater consolation for the poor and the failures. The material culture tends to be hemmed in by tradition. The criteria of achievement have a more stable subjective basis in the sense of craftsmanship, esthetic and intellectual subtlety, and the fulfillment of social and religious routines.

d. There are certain derivative elements of this general value orientation which call for comment. First, intense individualistic competitiveness, in which the primary aim is to get more of what other people want, produces diffuse hostile tension and general apprehension and anxiety, which pervades every aspect of the culture including the competing unit itself, the family. The fear of failure and the apprehension over the hostility which is involved in one's relations with other persons produce on the one hand an extraordinary need for affection and reassurance, and on the other, an extraordinary tendency to resort to physiological and spiritual narcosis. In other words, as a consequence of being impelled by cultural pressure toward relationships in which one is aggressively pitted against others, the resulting unease and apprehension is characteristically mitigated by demands for external response, attention, and warmth, or by resort to escapism. Thus an excessive concern with sexuality, an excessive resort to alcohol, and, what is a uniquely American form of narcosis of the soul—the widespread addiction to highly stimulating mass entertainment, the radio, movies, comics, and the like—provide culturally legitimate modes of discharging hostility and allaying anxiety.

Thus, by way of summary, the value orientation of the American tends to be atomistic rather than corporate, worldly rather than unworldly, highly mobile rather than traditional, compulsive rather than relaxed, and externally directed rather than autonomous. Needless to say, these are presented as hypothetical tendencies, which are supported only by an inadequate and quite heterogeneous body of evidence.

VALUE EXPECTATIONS

The American is an optimist as to ends and an improviser as to means. The riches of his heritage and the mobility of his social order have produced a generally euphoric tendency, that is, the expectation that one can by effort and good will achieve or approximate one's goals. This overt optimism is so compulsive an element in the American culture that factors which threaten it, such as failure, old age, and death, are pressed from the focus of attention and handled in perfunctory ways.[1] This belief that "things can be done" is coupled with a faith in common sense and "know-how" with regard to means. The American has a double approach to complex reasoning and theory. He has great respect for systematic thinking and planning in relation to technological and organizational problems. But even this type of intellectualism is brought down to earth by referring to it as "know-how." Know-how implies both the possession of formal technical knowledge and the capacity to improvise and overcome obstacles on the basis of a "feel" for the problem or the situation. In complicated questions of social and public policy there is a genuine distrust of complex and subtle reasoning and a preference for an earthy "common sense." Thus, in these important areas his compulsive optimism, his anti-intellectualism, and his simple rationalism leave the

---

[1] See the comment on this point by Wolfenstein and Leites in C. and F. Kluckhohn, "American Culture: Generalized Orientation and Class Patterns" in *Conflicts of Power in Modern Culture,* Seventh Symposium of Conference on Science, Philosophy and Religion, Harper, 1947, p. 109.

American vulnerable to deflation and pessimism when his expectations are thwarted and when threats and dangers are not effectively warded off by improvisations. This vulnerability is, to be sure, balanced by a certain flexibility and experimentalism, a willingness to try new approaches. If Americans typically avoid the rigidity of dogma in dealing with new problems, they also typically fail to reap the advantages of thoughtful policy-planning. What is involved here is not so much a net loss, but rather the failure to realize the net gain that would result from a greater intellectual discipline.

ATTITUDES TOWARD AUTHORITY AND MORALITY

The American tends to "cut authority down to his own size." He has a respect for achievement and a toleration of order-enforcing agencies, but a distrust of arbitrary or traditional authority. This attitude toward authority also carries over into the field of tradition and custom. Certainly the urban American, and many of the rural ones as well, are not seriously limited by traditional methods of doing things. They are iconoclasts with respect to earlier aspects of culture, and conformists in relation to the most recent value changes. They reject what was done in the past, and they conform to the new things that are being done *now*. But again this iconoclasm is especially noticeable in the sphere of material culture. A greater conservatism obtains in relation to social and political matters. This social and political conservatism is not unique to Americans. What seems to be unique is this combination of mobility of material values and fundamentalism with regard to social and political values.

Similar trends are observable in American attitudes toward moral norms. The norms of Christianity still constitute an important theme in contemporary American culture. Since these moral standards are in obvious and continual rivalry with the competitive ethic, Americans tend to suffer from ambivalence and conflicts in determining what is "proper." Under normal circumstances this conflict does not appear to have a seriously laming effect. It tends to be disposed of by adding a moral coloration to actions which are really motivated by expediency, and an expediential coloration to actions which are motivated by moral and humanitarian values. These tendencies are related to a rather widespread naïve belief in the compatibility of morality and expediency.[2] While this ambivalence is a factor which generally affects American behavior, there is also a characteristic pendulum movement between the two ethics. Thus, if generous actions, motivated by moral and humanitarian considerations, are accepted without gratitude, are misinterpreted, or are unrequited, a

---

[2] *Ibid.*, p. 111.

"cynical" rejection of humanitarianism may follow, resulting from the humiliation at having been "played for a sucker." To yield to humanitarian impulses in the "market place" or to moderate one's own demands in the light of "Christian" considerations, to give without the expectation of receiving, to suffer injury without retaliation—these are impulses which have a partial validity; but it is dangerous to give way to them since they dull the edge of competitiveness, confuse and retard the forward course of action.

MOOD VERSUS POLICY

Since Americans tend to exhaust their emotional and intellectual energies in private pursuits, the typical approach to problems of public policy is perfunctory. Where public policy impinges directly on their interest, as in questions of local improvements, taxation, or social security policy, they are more likely to develop views and opinions resting on some kind of intellectual structure. But on questions of a more remote nature, such as foreign policy, they tend to react in more undifferentiated ways, with formless and plastic moods which undergo frequent alteration in response to change in events. The characteristic response to questions of foreign policy is one of indifference. A foreign policy crisis, short of the immediate threat of war, may transform indifference to vague apprehension, to fatalism, to anger; but the reaction is still a mood, a superficial and fluctuating response. To some extent American political apathy is a consequence of the compulsive absorption of energy in private competitiveness. To inform oneself on public issues, to form policies on the basis of careful thought-taking, is hardly a task that is beyond the intellectual competence of a large proportion of the population. The intellectual demands of business life are in some respects as complicated as those of foreign policy. But the American has a powerful cultural incentive to develop policies and strategies relating to his business and professional career, and little incentive, if any, to develop strategies for foreign policy.

The orientation of most Americans toward foreign policy is one of mood, and mood is essentially an unstable phenomenon. But this instability is not arbitrary and unpredictable. American moods are affected by two variables: (1) changes in the domestic and foreign political-economic situation involving the presence or absence of threat in varying degrees, (2) the characterological predispositions of the population. Our knowledge of American character tendencies, meager as it may be, makes it possible to suggest potential movements of opinion and mood which may have significant effects on foreign policy.

WITHDRAWAL-INTERVENTION

Given the intense involvement of most Americans with private interests and pursuits, the normal attitude toward a relatively stable world political situation is one of comparative indifference and withdrawal. This was the case throughout the greater part of the nineteenth century, in the period between World War I and II, and as we shall show in a later chapter, in the period immediately following World War II. The existence of this cyclical withdrawal-intervention problem suggests at least two serious dangers for foreign policy decision-making: (1) possible over-reactions to threat; (2) possible overreactions to temporary equilibria in world politics. Under ordinary circumstances American emotion and action are directed with considerable pressure in the normal orbits of private competition. However, when threats from abroad become grave and immediate, Americans tend to break out of their private orbits, and tremendous energies become available for foreign policy. Thus, we see the explosions of American energy in World Wars I and II when, after periods of indifference and withdrawal, exceptional feats of swift mobilization were achieved. There is some evidence to suggest that the Russian threat may, if carelessly handled, produce dangerous overreactions. Thus the press conference of Secretary of State Marshall in the spring of 1947, in which he urged the American people to "keep calm," produced what amounted to a war scare. The volatility and potential explosiveness of American opinion must be constantly kept in mind if panic reactions to threat are to be avoided.

The danger of overreaction to threat is only one aspect of this withdrawal-intervention tendency of American opinion. Equally serious is the prospect of overreaction to temporary stabilizations in the world crisis. Because of the superficial character of American attitudes toward world politics, American opinion tends to react to the external aspects of situations. A temporary Russian tactical withdrawal may produce strong tendencies toward demobilization and the reassertion of the primacy of private and domestic values. The pull of "privatism" in America creates a strong inclination to self-deception. And while this is less characteristic of the informed and policy-making levels, it undoubtedly plays an important role here as well. The great American demobilization of 1945, both in the military establishment and in the civilian bureaucracy, and the hasty dismantling of war agencies and controls reflected the overhelming eagerness to withdraw to private values and normal conditions. This movement was not based on a sober evaluation of the foreign situation and what this might require in military and political terms, but was a response to the overwhelming urge to have done with alarms and external interruptions and get back to the essential and important values.

MOOD-SIMPLIFICATION

Closely connected with the withdrawal-intervention pattern is a tendency which has to do with characteristic changes in the internal structure of American foreign policy moods. It has already been pointed out that under conditions of political equilibrium American attitudes toward world politics tend to be formless and lacking in intellectual structure. We define policy, as distinguished from mood, as consisting of a relatively stable intellectual structure including (1) explicit assumptions as to the values involved in domestic or international political conflict, (2) explicit evaluations of the relative costs and efficiency of alternative means of maximizing the value position of one's own country or political group. From the point of view of this criterion, American attitudes tend to range from unstructured moods in periods of equilibrium to simplification in periods of crisis. So long as there is no immediate, sharply defined threat, the attitude is vague and indefinite—e.g., apathetic, mildly apprehensive, euphoric, skeptical. When the crisis becomes sharpened American responses become more specific. Here American distrust of intellectualism and subtlety, the faith in "common sense," and the belief in simple answers lead to oversimplications of the threat and the methods of coping with it.

While these tendencies are more characteristic of the "uninformed" general run of the population, they affect policymakers as well. Thus during World War II, the Roosevelt shift from "Dr. New Deal" to "Dr. Win-the-War" reflected this need at the very highest level of policymaking to reduce the issues to simplified proportion. The "unconditional surrender" policy was a similarly oversimplified resolution of the moral and political problems of the war.[3] The journalists and writers who directed American propaganda efforts in World War II solved their complex policy problems by the slogan of "the strategy of truth," which left to the lower-level, competitive policy-making process practically all of the important decisions of propaganda policy during the war. The policy of "non-fraternization" with Germans which was imposed on the American army of occupation similarly was understandable as a gratification of a need for moral simplism, but it bore only a slight relation to the complex and uncomfortable realities on which it was imposed. The entire sequence of American policies toward Germany had this character of mixed moral-expediential improvisations. At first these improvisations were motivated primarily by anti-German reactions; more recently the tendency is toward more pro-German improvisations. At the present time this tendency to over-simplify seems to be taking the form of reducing all the problems of world politics to a simple "East-West" conflict. There is considerable pressure to take as an ally any country or movement which is anti-Communist and anti-Russian.

---

[3] See among others Wallace Carroll's book on American propaganda policy during the war, *Persuade or Perish*, Houghton Mifflin, 1948. Apparently Roosevelt had in mind Grant's rather benevolent treatment of Lee at the time of the Southern surrender. But Roosevelt apparently never got around to explaining this to top advisers and administrators. Robert Sherwood in *Roosevelt and Hopkins* (Harper, 1948, pp. 696 ff.) makes the same point in detail.

It would, of course, be an exaggeration to attribute the same degree of "simplism" to policy-makers as might be expected of the "man in the street." But there can be little doubt that the process of foreign policy-making is strongly influenced by this common-sense, improvisation tendency. Faith in policy-planning (which means in simple terms, taking the "long view," acquiring sufficient reliable information on which sound policy can be based, weighing and balancing the potential value of military, political, diplomatic, and psychological means in relation to proposed courses of action) has hardly taken root in the American policy-making process.

OPTIMISM-PESSIMISM

The problem of shifts in mood from euphoric to dysphoric expectations is clearly related to those aspects of American opinion already described. The involvement in private concerns, coupled with an optimistic faith in good will, common sense, and simple answers, renders the American public vulnerable to failure. This reaction tends to result from the frustration of successive improvisations, none of which have been adapted to the complex character of the problem. Under these circumstances there are two possible dangers: (1) withdrawal reactions: (2) hasty measures motivated by irritation and impatience. The development of American attitudes toward Russia since the end of the war is an excellent illustration of this problem. During the war and in the period immediately following its termination there was a widely shared belief among Americans and among American policy-makers that the Russian problem could be readily solved by good will and the "man-to-man" approach. The continued thwarting of American overtures and concessions to the Russians now seems to have produced an attitude of hopeless pessimism. Pessimism certainly seems to be justifiable on the basis of the facts, but the negativism which has resulted may possibly constitute a danger if negotiation and bargaining with the Russians in principle is interdicted. The objective problem would seem to be one of choosing the time, the occasion, and the conditions when negotiation might lead to advantage. There is a similar danger of excessive pessimism in relation to potential allies. Perhaps there is a tendency toward a premature "writing off" of peoples whose social and political structures are unstable, countries which don't react with "American speed" to American proposals or which are not ready to commit themselves to the American "side" in as wholehearted a fashion as we might desire.

TOLERANCE-INTOLERANCE

The point has already been made that the American attitude toward authority, toward moral and ideological norms, contains conflicting elements. On the one hand, the American is not hemmed in by the mores and morals of "the horse and buggy days," and at the same time he is a conformist, a value-imitator. He is ready to try new things and new methods, but not if they make him look "different" or "peculiar." The truth of the matter would seem to be that, while he has loosened himself from the bonds of earlier moral standards and beliefs, he has not replaced these guides for conduct with any other set of principles. The autonomous conscience of Puritanism has been replaced by the "radar-directed" conduct of the "marketer."[4] He tends to take his judgments as to what is right and wrong, proper and improper, from the changing culture as it impinges on him through the various social institutions and media of communication. This makes for a certain flexibility in attitudes toward other cultures and ideologies. But the flexibility is negative rather than positive. That is, the American has moved away from older moral and traditional norms without acquiring new bases of judgment. His toleration of difference therefore is unstable, and there is a substratum of ideological fundamentalism which frequently breaks through the surface and has an important impact on foreign policy. Thus in our efforts to stabilize the weakened and chaotic areas of Western Europe we have been prepared to go a long way in aiding "Socialist Great Britain" and the left-inclined powers of Western Europe. But there is a continual sabotage of this tolerance, frequent efforts at ideological imperialism, even occasional interferences at the administrative level, which are motivated by ideological fundamentalism.

In general, this intolerance of difference is more clearly expressed in periods of normalcy. Thus, even though the possibility appears to be remote, the prospect of a recrudescence of isolationism cannot be excluded. A tactical cessation of Russian pressure might produce just this kind of demobilization and withdrawal reaction and the reassertion of older principles of conduct. This is not to say that such a reaction would be decisive so far as policy is concerned; but it is a prospect which sound policy-planning should anticipate.

IDEALISM-CYNICISM

In still another respect American moral predispositions may have consequences for foreign policy. The annoyance and irritation of the peoples of foreign countries over American self-righteousness is, on the whole, a relatively minor source of difficulty. Americans would appear to be happiest when they can cloak an action motivated by self-interest with an aura of New Testament selflessness, when an action which is "good business," or "good security" can be made to "look good" too. Similarly there is resistance among Americans over the straightforward

---

[4] D. Riesman and N. Glazer, "Character Types and Political Apathy," *Research Project in Mass Communications,* Yale University, May 26, 1948, p. 9.

expression of conscience-motivated behavior. What is "good" has to be represented as satisfying the criteria of self-interest. They are happiest when they can allay the Christian conscience at the same time that they satisfy self-interested criteria. In this regard the peoples of foreign countries are well protected, perhaps overprotected, by their own cynicism.

But there are a number of respects in which this moral dualism may produce more serious problems for the policy-maker. There would appear to be a certain cyclical trend in American moral attitudes. The great wave of idealism in the first world war gave way to the cynicism about foreign countries of the 1920's. The friendliness for our British and French allies of World War I gave way to bitterness over their defaults on their indebtedness. A little more than a decade ago the little country of Finland had a place at the very center of the American heart because she had kept up her payments on her war debts, while the European powers which had defaulted, and on the fate of which our security rested, were prevented from borrowing money in the American capital market. The chiliastic faith in the reasonableness of the Russians has now been supplanted by deep resentment over their base ingratitude.

American generosity and humanitarianism is a tentative phenomenon. Along with impulses toward good will and generosity, there is a deep-seated suspicion that smart people don't act that way, that "only suckers are a soft touch." In this connection a recent study which appeared in a popular magazine is of considerable interest.[5] This investigation, claiming to have been based on "reliable sampling procedures," reflected a degree of religious piety among Americans considerably greater than had previously been estimated. Of greatest interest was its description of American attitudes toward ethics. It would appear that almost half of the sample was sharply aware of the conflict between what was "right" and the demands of secular life. A somewhat smaller proportion considered that religion influenced their activities in business, political and social life. Considerably more than half felt that their conduct toward neighbors was governed by the golden rule; but more than 80 per cent felt that their neighbors fell considerably short of the golden rule in their conduct toward their fellow men.

Quite aside from the question of the full reliability of a study asking such "loaded" and personal questions, there seems to be confirmation here for the proposition regarding the moral dualism in the American character. The aspiration to conform to Christian ethical ideals is clearly present among most members of the culture, but there would appear to be

---

[5] Lincoln Barnett, "God and the American People." *Ladies' Home Journal*, November, 1948, pp. 37 ff.

a strong apprehension that such standards of conduct are inapplicable because the outside world does not behave that way. Hence any impulse toward ethically motivated generosity is impaired not only by the feeling that it will go unrequited, but that one's neighbors will ridicule it or attribute it to some concealed, self-interested motive.

It would appear to be a reasonable speculation from the foregoing findings that any action involving the giving or loaning of American wealth to foreign peoples, even though it be motivated by calculations of self-interest, activates this fear that "only a sucker is a soft touch." Under conditions of threat, such as those of the present, these doubts and suspicions about "giving things away" have been kept within manageable proportions. But in a period of temporary stabilization when the superficial aspect of the foreign situation encourages withdrawal reactions, these feelings may play a role of some significance.

SUPERIORITY-INFERIORITY

In a sense America is a nation of parvenus. A historically unique rate of immigration, social, and geographic mobility has produced a people which has not had an opportunity to "set," to acquire the security and stability which come from familiar ties, associations, rights, and obligations. It is perhaps not accidental that in the vulgarization of psychoanalytic hypotheses in America in the last decades one of the first to acquire popular currency was the "superiority-inferiority" complex. In more stably stratified societies the individual tends to have a greater sense of "location," a broader and deeper identification with his social surroundings. He has not *made* his own identity, while in America a large proportion of each generation is *self-made*. Being self-made produces a certain buoyancy, a sense of mastery, but it leaves the individual somewhat doubtful as to his social legitimacy. This sense of insecurity and uncertainty may add a strident note to American claims for recognition. This may explain the stereotype of the American abroad, confronted with complex and ancient cultures, taking alcoholic refuge in assertions of American moral, political, and technical virtue. It may also account for a feeling in the United States that American diplomats are no match for the wiliness and cunning of Old World negotiators. In other words, Americans typically overreact in their self-evaluations. They over- and underestimate their skills and virtues, just as they over- and under-estimate the skills and virtues of other cultures and nations.

It is perhaps this quality among Americans—and among the American elites—which strongly militates against a balanced and empathic appreciation of cultural and national differences so essential to the development of an effective diplomacy. One may entertain the hypothesis that Americans tend to judge other nations and cultures according to a strictly American scoreboard, on the basis of which America is bound to win. It is difficult for Americans to accept a humane conception of cultural and national differences. Somehow, other cultural values must be transmuted into an American currency so that it becomes possible in a competition of national cultures to rate the United States as the "best all-round culture of the year."

There is a noticeable sensitivity among Americans on the score of cultural and intellectual inferiority. Only recently the American press cited the throngs of visitors to art museums exhibiting the Habsburg collection of paintings as effectively refuting European claims of American cultural inferiority. Feelings of crudeness and inferiority are not only expressed in the form of direct refutation by citing such evidence as the above; they also are frequently expressed in the tendency to equate esthetic and intellectual subtlety with lack of manliness—artists and intellectuals are "queers."

This superiority-inferiority ambivalence may manifest itself in policy-making in a number of ways. It may take the direct and perhaps more typical form of cultural arrogance—assertions of the superiority of the American way in politics, in economics, in social relations, in morality, or in the physical amenities of life. In this case the psychological mechanism involved is a reaction-formation; unconscious feelings of inferiority lead to the assertion of superiority. Or it may take the form of an admisssion of inferiority and an attribution of superiority to other cultures or elite groups. In either case there is an alienation from the real character and potentialities of the self. One either becomes an ideal and non-existent American—a *persona* American—or one rejects one's Americanism entirely and attempts to "pass," for example, into English or French culture. These formulations, of course, state the problem in the extreme for purposes of clarity.

These reactions have a selective appeal among the various elite groups. Thus American artists, writers, and intellectuals have historically tended to manifest inferiority feelings in the form of imitativeness, or in expatriation. It has been asserted that members of the American foreign service have tended to assimilate themselves too readily to foreign cultures and aristocratic "sets," perhaps at the expense of their American perspective. The tendency for American families of wealth and prestige to ape the English and Continental aristocracies is too well known to call for detailed comment. All of these groups have in common the quality of having differentiated themselves from the American pattern through extraordinary wealth, through artistic or intellectual deviation, or through long residence abroad. The more "representative" American—the Congressman for example—tends to manifest the simpler form of cultural arrogance.

Either inferiority or superiority feelings in relation to other cultures may have a negative effect on the national interest. Cultural arrogance may alienate other peoples, impair confidence in the United States among actual and potential allies, or aid in some measure in the mobilization of hostile sentiment among neutrals and potential enemies. Cultural subservience, particularly if manifested by American diplomats and negotiators, may result in real and unnecessary sacrifices of the national interest.

The hypothesis may also be advanced that there is a certain periodicity of national moods of confidence and lack of confidence. These have perhaps been associated in the United States with the fluctuations of the business cycle. One may speculate that not least among the catastrophic foreign policy consequences of a serious depression in the United States would be an impairment of national self-confidence, a sudden welling to the surface of underlying doubt, which might result in a weakening of foreign policy resolution, a feeling of being overextended, a need for contraction, for consolidation, for withdrawal.

SELECTED BIBLIOGRAPHY

Part VII

National Character and Transnational Images

Barghoorn, Frederick C., *The Soviet Image of the United States: A Study in Distortion.* New York: Harcourt Brace, 1950.

Benedict, Ruth, *The Chrysanthemum and the Sword.* Boston: Houghton Mifflin Company, 1946.

Blanchard, W. H., "National Myth, National Character, and National Policy: A Psychological Study of the U-2 Incident." *Journal of Conflict Resolution.* June 1962.

Buchanan, W., and Hadley Cantril, *How Nations See Each Other.* Urbana: University of Illinois Press, 1953.

Duijker, H. C. J., and N. H. Frijda, *National Character and National Stereotypes.* Amsterdam: North-Holland Publishing Company, 1960.

Goser, Geoffrey, *The American People: A Study in National Character.* (Revised Edition). New York: Norton, 1964.

Hertz, F., *Nationality in History and Politics: A Study of the Psychology and Sociology of National Sentiment and Character.* New York: Oxford, 1944.

Holsti, O. R., "The Belief System and National Images: A Case Study." *Journal of Conflict Resolution,* September 1962.

Honigmann, J. J., *Culture and Personality.* New York: Harper and Brothers, 1954.

Joseph, Franz M. (ed.), *As Others See Us: The United States through Foreign Eyes.* Princeton: Princeton University Press, 1959.

Kelman, Herbert C. (ed.), *International Behavior: A Social-Psychological Analysis.* New York: Holt, Rinehart and Winston, 1965.

Klinebert, Otto, *The Human Dimension in International Relations.* New York: Holt, Rinehart and Winston, 1964.

Kluckholn, Clyde, *Mirror for Man.* Greenwich, Connecticut: Fawcett, 1960.

Lasswell, Harold, *Psychopathology and Politics.* Chicago: University of Chicago Press, 1930.

———, *World Politics and Personal Insecurity.* New York: McGraw-Hill, 1935.

Mead, Margaret, *Soviet Attitudes Toward Authority: An Interdisciplinary Approach to Problems of Soviet Character.* New York: McGraw-Hill, 1951.

Nicolson, Sir Harold, *National Character and National Policy.* Nottingham: University College Press, 1938.

Platt, W., *National Character in Action: Intelligence Factors in Foreign Relations.* New Brunswick: Rutgers University Press, 1961.

Singer, J. David (ed.), *Human Behavior and International Politics: Contributions from Social Psychological Science.* Chicago: Rand McNally and Company, 1965.

Stanton, H. H., and S. E. Perry (eds.), *Personality and Political Crisis: New Perspectives from Social Science and Psychiatry for the Study of War and Politics.* Glencoe: The Free Press, 1951.

Strausz-Hupé, Robert, *The Zone of Indifference.* New York: G. P. Putnam's Sons, 1952.

Part VIII

Propaganda and
Psychological Warfare

THROUGHOUT HISTORY, governments as well as individuals have
sought to influence the behavioral patterns of other governments and peoples. Propaganda may be defined as a technique that
employs the spoken or written word to spread an idea designed to
influence behavior. Like propaganda, psychological warfare is designed to mold the behavior of governments or individuals. The
term psychological warfare has come into use as more sophisticated
techniques for remolding human thought have become available.
The development of psychology as a field of study has contributed
to the use of truth serums, thought control groups or "brainwash-
ing," and conditioning techniques described by J. A. C. Brown in
Selection 32.

Propaganda and psychological warfare may be used against essentially two broad target groups. They may be employed by a
government against its own population or against the population
of some other national unit. It is generally more difficult to make
effective use of propaganda and psychological warfare against the
population of another country than against one's own people. To a
greater extent, the populations of other national units are subjected
to countervailing influences from which they cannot easily be
isolated. Both within national units and the international system,
advances of technology, especially communications, as well as
literacy, have enhanced the potential audience for propaganda and
psychological warfare. In the international system there is interaction in which governments utilize propaganda and psychological
warfare in their demand-response relationships.

In one way or another, all governments make use of propaganda and psychological warfare. According to Jacques Ellul, the participation of the masses of the population in political affairs has increased the importance of propaganda. If a government is to assure popular compliance with its policies, it must make use of propaganda to influence world public opinion.

Propaganda and psychological warfare may be applied against small groups or entire populations. Brown describes the use of truth drugs and thought control groups, in which a few individuals meet to discuss political writings, to confess past errors, and to receive indoctrination. The constant repetition of a series of themes, together with their application in group discussions to the analysis of personal and political problems, is part of the process of thought reform. Moreover, Brown discusses the use of conditioning techniques developed by Pavlov in his experiments with dogs. It is suggested that states of emotional stress, anxiety and breakdown similar to those which Pavlov produced in dogs can be developed in human beings. Whatever the implications of Pavlov's experimentation, which received support from the Soviet government, the techniques for thought remolding available to modern governments have increased dramatically.

31. PROPAGANDA

Jacques Ellul

PROPAGANDA IS NEEDED in the exercise of power for the simple reason that the masses have come to participate in political affairs. Let us not call this democracy; this is only one aspect of it. To begin with, there is the concrete reality of masses. In a sparsely populated country, politics can be made by small groups, separated from each other and from the masses, which will not form a public opinion and are remote from the centers of power. The nearness of the masses to the seats of power is very important. Pericles and Tiberius were well aware of it, as were Louis XIV and Napoleon: they installed themselves in the countryside, far from the crowds, in order to govern in peace outside the reach of the pressure of the masses, which, even without clearly wanting to, affect the conditions of power by their mere proximity. This simple fact explains why politics can no longer be the game of princes and diplomats, and why palace revolutions have been replaced by popular revolutions.

Nowadays the ruler can no longer detach himself from the masses and conduct a more or less secret policy; he no longer has an ivory tower; and everywhere he is confronted with this multiple presence. He cannot escape the mass simply because of the present population density—the mass is everywhere. Moreover, as a result of the modern means of transportation, the government is not only in constant contact with the population of the capital, but also with the entire country. In their relations with the governing powers, there is hardly any difference now between the population of the capital and that of the countryside. This physical proximity is itself a political factor. Moreover, the mass knows its rulers through the press, radio, and TV—the Chief of State is in contact with the people. He can no longer prevent people from knowing a

From *Propaganda: The Formation of Men's Attitudes* by Jacques Ellul (New York: 1965), pp. 121–126; 242–250. © Copyright 1964 by Alfred A. Knopf, Inc. Reprinted by permission. Footnotes have been renumbered to appear in consecutive order.

JACQUES ELLUL (1912–   ) Professor of History and Contemporary Sociology, University of Bordeaux. His other books include *The Political Illusion,* (New York: Alfred A. Knopf, 1967); *The Technological Society,* (New York: Alfred A. Knopf, 1964).

certain number of political facts. This development is not the result of some applied doctrine; it is not because democratic doctrine demands the masses' participation in public power that this relationship between mass and government has developed. It is a simple fact, and the inevitable result of demographic changes. Hence, if the ruler wants to play the game by himself and follow secret policies, he must present a decoy to the masses. He cannot escape the mass; but he can draw between himself and that mass an invisible curtain, a screen, on which the mass will see projected the mirage of some politics, while the real politics are being made behind it.

Except for this subterfuge, the government is in fact under the control of the people—not juridical control, but the kind of control that stems from the simple fact that the people are interested in politics and try to keep up with and understand governmental action, as well as make their opinions known. For, after all, the masses are interested in politics.[1] This, too, is new. Even those who do not read the papers carefully are appalled at the thought of censorship, particularly when they feel that the government wants to hide something or leave them in the dark. Nowadays the masses are accustomed to making political judgments; as the result of the democratic process they are accustomed to be consulted on political alternatives and to receive political information. This may only be a habit, but it is deeply ingrained by now; to try to reverse it would immediately provoke feelings of frustration and cries of injustice. That the masses are interested in politics, whether deeply or superficially, is a fact. Besides, one very simple reason explains this: today, as never before in history, small number of soldiers and a negligible piece of territory; today every-political decisions affect everybody. In the old days, a war affected a body is a soldier, and the entire population and the whole territory of a nation are involved. Therefore, everybody wants to have his say on the subject of war and peace.

Similarly, taxes have increased at least tenfold since the seventeenth century, and those who pay them naturally want some control over their use. The sacrifices demanded by political life keep increasing and affect everybody; therefore everybody wants to participate in this game, which affects him directly. Because the State's decisions will affect me, I intend to influence them. As a result, governments can no longer govern without the masses—without their influence, presence, knowledge, and pressure. But how, then, can they govern?

---

[1] Democracy rests on the conviction that the citizen can choose the right man and the right policy. Because this is not exactly the case, the crowd is propagandized in order to make it participate. Under such conditions, how could the mass not be convinced that it is deeply concerned?

The rule of public opinion is regarded as a simple and natural fact. The government is regarded as the product of this opinion, from which it draws its strength. It expresses public opinion. To quote Napoleon's famous words: "Power is based on opinion. What is a government not supported by opinion? Nothing." Theoretically, democracy is political expression of mass opinion. Most people consider it simple to translate this opinion into action, and consider it legitimate that the government should bend to the popular will. Unfortunately, in reality all this is much less clear and not so simple. More and more we know, for example, that public opinion does not express itself at the polls and is a long way from expressing itself clearly in political trends. We know, too, that public opinion is very unstable, fluctuating, never settled. Furthermore, this opinion is irrational and develops in unforeseeable fashion. It is by no means composed of a majority of rational decisions in the face of political problems, as some simplistic vision would have it. The majority vote is by no means the real public opinion. Its basically irrational character greatly reduces its power to rule in a democracy. Democracy is based on the concept that man is rational and capable of seeing clearly what is in his own interest, but the study of public opinion suggests this is a highly doubtful proposition. And the bearer of public opinion is generally a mass man, psychologically speaking, which makes him quite unsuited to properly exercise his right of citizenship.

This leads us to the following consideration: On the one hand, the government can no longer operate outside the pressure of the masses and public opinion; on the other hand, public opinion does not express itself in the democratic form of government. To be sure, the government must know and constantly probe public opinion.[2] The modern State must constantly undertake press and opinion surveys and sound out public opinion in a variety of other ways. But the fundamental question is: Does the State then obey and express and follow that opinion? Our unequivocal answer is that even in a democratic State it does not. Such obeisance by the State to public opinion is impossible—first, because of the very nature of public opinion, and second, because of the nature of modern political activities.

Public opinion is so variable and fluctuating that government could

---

[2] The Soviet Union, despite its authoritarian character and the absence of opinion surveys, makes just as much effort to keep informed of public opinion—through agitators (who inform the government on the people's state of mind) and through letters to the press. The government does not consult opinion in order to obey it, however, but to know at what level it exists and to determine what propaganda action is needed to win it over. The Party must neither anticipate public opinion nor lag behind it. To determine the State's rhythm of action, it must know the masses' state of mind.

never base a course of action on it; no sooner would government begin to pursue certain aims favored in an opinion poll, than opinion would turn against it. To the degree that opinion changes are rapid, policy changes would have to be equally rapid; to the extent that opinion is irrational, political action would have to be equally irrational. And as public opinion, ultimately, is always "the opinion of incompetents," political decisions would therefore be surrendered to them.

Aside from the near-impossibility of simply following public opinion, the government has certain functions—particularly those of a technical nature—entirely outside such opinion. With regard to an enterprise that involves billions and lasts for years, it is not a question of following opinion—either at its inception, when opinion has not yet crystalized, or later, when the enterprise has gone too far to turn back. In such matters as French oil policy in the Sahara or electrification in the Soviet Union, public opinion can play no role whatever. The same holds true even where enterprises are being nationalized, regardless of an apparent socialist opinion. In many instances, political decisions must be made to suit new problems emerging precisely from the new political configurations in our age, and such problems do not fit the stereotypes and patterns of established public opinion. Nor can public opinion crystalize overnight—and the government cannot postpone actions and decisions until vague images and myths eventually coalesce into opinion. In the present world of politics, action must at all times be the forerunner of opinion. Even where public opinion is already formed, it can be disastrous to follow it. Recent studies have shown the catastrophic role of public opinion in matters of foreign policy. The masses are incapable of resolving the conflict between morality and State policy, or of conceiving a long-term foreign policy. They push the government toward a disastrous foreign policy, as in Franklin Roosevelt's policy toward the Soviet Union, or Johnson's push-button policy. The greatest danger in connection with foreign policy is that of public opinion manifesting itself in the shape of crisis, in an explosion. Obviously, public opinion knows little about foreign affairs and cares less; torn by contradictory desires, divided on principal questions, it permits the government to conduct whatever foreign policy it deems best. But all at once, for a variety of reasons, opinion converges on one point, temperatures rise, men become excited and assert themselves (for example, on the question of German rearmament). And should this opinion be followed? To the same extent that opinion expresses itself sporadically, that it wells up in fits and starts, it runs counter to the necessary continuity of foreign policy and tends to overturn previous agreements and existing alliances. Because such opinion is intermittent and fragmentary, the government could not follow it even if it wanted to.

Ergo: even in a democracy, a government that is honest, serious, benevolent, and respects the voter *cannot follow* public opinion. But it *cannot escape* it either. The masses are there; they are interested in politics. The government cannot act without them. So, what can it do?

Only one solution is possible: as the government cannot follow opinion, opinion must follow the government. One must convince this present, ponderous, impassioned mass that the government's decisions are legitimate and good and that its foreign policy is correct. The democratic State, precisely because it believes in the expression of public opinion and does not gag it, must channel and shape that opinion if it wants to be realistic and not follow an ideological dream. The Gordian knot cannot be cut any other way. Of course, the political parties already have the role of adjusting public opinion to that of the government. Numerous studies have shown that political parties often do not agree with that opinion, that the voters—and even party members—frequently do not know their parties' doctrines, and that people belong to parties for reasons other than ideological ones. But the parties channel free-floating opinion into existing formulas, polarizing it on opposites that do not necessarily correspond to the original tenets of such opinion. Because parties are so rigid, because they deal with only a part of any question, and because they are purely politically motivated, they distort public opinion and prevent it from forming naturally. But even beyond party influence, which is already propaganda influence, government action exists in and by itself.

.   .   .

EFFECTS OF INTERNATIONAL PROPAGANDA

In the domain of external politics and the propaganda that is directed toward the outside, there is practically no more private propaganda or any diversity of propagandas. Even parties indentured to a foreign government, and thus making propaganda different from that of their own national government, direct their propaganda to the interior. But what character does this unique form of propaganda (directed to the outside) take, and what repercussions has it on a democracy that conducts it? Can it be that it really exists in the domain of information?

We have abundant proof nowadays that straight information addressed to a foreign country is entirely useless.[3] Where the problem is to overcome national antipathies (which exist even between friendly nations), allegiance to a different government, to a different psychological and historical world, and finally to an opposite propaganda, it is fruitless to expect anything from straight information: the bare fact (the truth) can accomplish nothing against such barriers. Facts are not believed. Other than in exceptional cases (military occupation and so on), people

---

[3] We are talking here primarily of propaganda directed at the Communist countries.

believe their own government over a foreign government. The latter's facts are not believed. In fact, propaganda can penetrate the consciousness of the masses of a foreign country only through the myth. It cannot operate with simple arguments pro and con. It does not address itself to already existing feelings, but must create an image to act as a motive force. This image must have an emotional character that leads to the allegiance of the entire being, without thought. That is, it must be a myth.

But then democracy takes a path that needs watching. First of all, it begins to play a game that drives man from the conscious and rational into the arms of irrational and "obscure forces"; but we already know that in this game the believer is not the master, and that forces thus unleashed are rarely brought under control again. To put it differently: mythical democratic propaganda in no way prepares its listeners for democracy, but strengthens their totalitarian tendencies, providing at best a different direction for those tendencies. We will have to come back to this. But above all we must ask ourselves what myth the democracies should use. From experience we have seen that the democracies have used the myths of Peace, of Freedom, of Justice, and so on.

All that has now been used, and is all the more unacceptable because everybody uses these words. But the myth used by propaganda must be specific: the myth of Blood and Soil was remarkable. What specific myths are left for democracy? Either subjects that cannot possibly form the content of a myth, such as well-being or the right to vote, or democracy itself.

Contrary to what one may think, the myth of democracy is far from exhausted and can still furnish good propaganda material. The fact that Communist authoritarian regimes also have chosen democracy as the springboard of propaganda tends to prove its propagandistic value. And to the extent that democracy is presented, constructed, and organized as a myth, it can be a good subject of propaganda. Propaganda appeals to belief: it rebuilds the drive toward the lost paradise and uses man's fundamental fear. Only from this aspect does democratic propaganda have some chance of penetration into non-democratic foreign countries. But one must then consider the consequences.

The first consequence is that any operation that transforms democracy into a myth transforms the democratic ideal. Democracy was not meant to be a myth. The question arose early—in 1791 in France. And we know what, shortly after, Jacobinism made of French democracy. We must understand this: Jacobinism saved the country. It claimed to have saved the Republic, but it is clear that it only saved the Jacobin regime by destroying all that was democratic. We cannot analyze here at length the influence of the myth on the abolition of democracy during 1793–5. Let us merely say that democracy cannot be an object of faith, of belief: it is expression of opinions. There is a fundamental difference between regimes based on opinion and regimes based on belief.

To make a myth of democracy is to present the opposite of democracy. One must clearly realize that the use of ancient myths and the creation of new ones is a regression toward primitive mentality, regardless of material progress. The evocation of mystical feelings is a rejection of democratic feelings. Considerable problems arise in the United States because of such diverse myths as, for example, the Ku Klux Klan, the American Legion, or Father Divine. These are anti-democratic, but they are localized, only partial, and private. The matter becomes infinitely more serious when the myth becomes public, generalized, and official, when what is an anti-mystique becomes a mystique.

Of course, we have said that such democratic propaganda is created for external use. People already subjected to totalitarian propaganda can be reached only by the myth, and even that does not change their behavior or mentality; it simply enters into the existing mold and creates new beliefs there. But looking at things this way implies two consequences.

First, we accept the fact that such external democratic propaganda should be a *weapon*, that we are dealing here with psychological warfare, and that we adjust ourselves to the enemy's train of thought; and that, proceeding from there, the people that we subject to our propaganda are not those whom we want to see become democratic but whom we want to defeat. If we actually work on such a nation with the help of the myth, we confirm it in a state of mind, in a behavior, and in a concept of life that is anti-democratic: we do not prepare it to become a democratic nation, for on the one hand we reinforce or continue the methods of its own authoritarian government; and on the other, we cannot give the people, by such means, the desire to adhere to something else in another way. We are simply asking for the same *kind* of acceptance of something else, of another form of government. Is this sufficient to make people switch allegiance? That is the democratic propaganda problem in Germany and Japan.

In the second place, such methods imply that we consider democracy an abstraction; for if we think that to cast different ideas in the mold of propaganda is sufficient to change the nature of propaganda, we make a mere theory or idea of democracy. Propaganda, whatever its content, tends to create a particular psychology and a determined behavior. Superficially there can be differences, but they are illusory. To say, for example, that Fascist propaganda, whose subject was the State, and Nazi propaganda, whose subject was the race, were different from each other because of their difference in content, is to become a victim of unreal and academic distinctions. But "the democratic idea" when promulgated by means that lead to non-democratic behavior only hardens the totalitarian man in his mold.

This does not take into account that this democratic veneer and the myth of democracy as a propaganda subject are very fragile. It is, in fact, one of propaganda's essential laws that its objects always adjust themselves to its forms. In this, as in so many other domains of the modern world, the means impose their own laws. To put it differently: the objects of propaganda tend to become totalitarian because propaganda itself is totalitarian. This is exactly what I said when I spoke of the necessity to turn democracy into a myth.

Thus, such propaganda can be effective as a weapon of war, but we must realize when using it that we simultaneously destroy the possibility of building true democracy.

I have said that such propaganda was for external use, that the myth was directed to the outside. But it is not certain that one can impose such a limitation. When a government builds up the democratic image in this fashion, it cannot isolate the external and internal domains from each other. Therefore the people of the country making such propaganda must also become convinced of the excellence of this image. They must not merely know it, but also follow it. This, incidentally, sets a limit to the degree to which propaganda can lie; a democratic government cannot present to the outside world a radically inexact and mendacious picture of its policies, as can a totalitarian government.

But one must qualify this thought in two ways: on the one hand a democratic nation is itself more or less in the grip of propaganda and goes along with the idealistic image of its government because of national pride; on the other, even authoritarian governments are aware that in propaganda the truth pays, as I have said: this explains the final form of propaganda adopted by Goebbels in 1944.

From there on, the myth created for external use becomes known at home and has repercussions there; even if one does not try to influence people by making propaganda abroad, they will react indirectly. Therefore, the repercussions on a democratic population of the myth developed by its government for external use must be analyzed; these repercussions will lead primarily to the establishment of unanimity.

This is a primary and very simple consequence. A myth (an image evoking belief) can stand no dilution, no half-measures, no contradictions. One believes it or does not. The democratic myth must display this same form, incisive and coherent; it is of the same nature as other myths. In order for the myth to be effective abroad, it must not be contradicted at home. No other voice must arise at home that would reach the foreign propaganda target and destroy the myth.

Can anyone believe that it was possible to make effective propaganda, for example, toward Algeria, when it was immediately contradicted at home? How could the Algerians—or any other foreigners—take seriously a promise made by General de Gaulle in the name of France when the press immediately declared that one part of France was in disagreement with it?[4]

This will lead to the elimination of any opposition that would show that the people are not unanimously behind the democracy embodied by the government. Such opposition can completely destroy all effectiveness of democratic propaganda. Besides, such propaganda is made by a government supported by a majority. The minority, though also democratic, will tend to be against such propaganda merely because it comes from the government (we saw this in France after 1945). From there on, though in accord with the idea of democracy, this minority will show itself hostile to the democratic myth. Then the government, if it wants its propaganda to be effective, will be forced to reduce the possibility of the minority's expressing itself—*i.e.*, to interfere with one of democracy's essential characteristics; we are already used to this from wartime, as with censorship. Here we are face to face with the fact discussed above: propaganda is by itself a state of war; it demands the exclusion of opposite trends and minorities—not total and official perhaps, but at least partial and indirect exclusion.

If we pursue this train of thought, another factor emerges: for the myth to have real weight, it must rest on popular belief. To put it differently: one cannot simply project a myth to the outside even by the powerful modern material means; such an image will have no force unless it is already believed. The myth is contagious because beliefs are contagious. It is indispensable, therefore, that democratic people also believe the democratic myth. Conversely, it is not useful that the government itself should follow suit; but the government must be sure that its propaganda abroad is identical with its propaganda at home, and understand that its foreign propaganda will be strong only if it is believed at home. (The United States understood this perfectly between 1942 and 1945.) And the more the myth will appear to be the expression of belief of the entire nation, the more effective it will be. It thus presumes unanimity.

We have seen how all propaganda develops the cult of personality. This is particularly true in a democracy. There one exalts the individual, who refuses to be anonymous, rejects the "mass," and eschews mechanization. He wants a human regime where men are human beings. He needs a government whose leaders are human beings. And propaganda must show them to him as such. It must create these personalities. To be sure, the object at this level is not idolatry, but idolatry cannot fail to follow if the propaganda is done well. Whether such idolatry is given to a man in uniform bursting with decorations, or a man in work shirt and

---

[4] This non-coherence, leading to the ineffectuality of the myth, was the cause—among many others—of years of unsuccessful negotiations.

cap, or a man wearing a business suit and soft hat makes no difference; those are simple adaptations of propaganda to the feelings of the masses. The democratic masses will reject the uniform, but idolize the soft hat if it is well presented. There can be no propaganda without a personality, a political chief. Clemenceau, Daladier, De Gaulle, Churchill, Roosevelt, MacArthur are obvious examples. And even more, Khrushchev, who, after having denounced the cult of personality, slipped into the same role, differently, but with the same ease and obeying the same necessity. The nation's unanimity is necessary. This unanimity is embodied in one personality, in whom everyone finds himself, in whom everyone hopes and projects himself, and for whom everything is possible and permissible.

This need for unanimity is accepted by some of those who have studied the problem of propaganda in democracy. It has been claimed that this unanimity indicates the transition from an old form of democracy to a new one: "massive and progressive democracy." In other words, a democracy of allegiance; a system in which all will share the same conviction. This would not be a centrifugal conviction, *i.e.*, one expressing itself in diverse forms and admitting the possibility of extreme divergences. It would be a centripetal conviction with which everything would be measured by the same yardstick; democracy would express itself in a single voice, going further than just forms—all the way to rites and liturgies. It would, on the other hand, be a democracy of participation in which the citizen would be wholly engaged; his complete life, his movements would be integrated into a given social system. And one of the authors gives as an example the Nuremberg Party Congress! What a strange example of democracy.

It is true that only such a unanimous and unitary society can produce propaganda that can be effectively carried beyond the borders. But we must ask ourselves whether such a society is still democratic. What is this democracy that no longer includes minorities and opposition? As long as democracy is merely the interplay of parties, there can be opposition; but when we hear of a massive democracy, with grandiose ceremonies in which the people participate at the prompting of the State, that signifies, first of all, a confusion between the government and the State, and indicates further that anyone who does not participate is not merely in opposition, but excludes himself from the national community expressing itself in this participation. It is a truly extraordinary transformation of the democratic structure, because there can no longer be any respect for the minority opposition to the State—an opposition that, lacking the means of propaganda—or at least any means that can compete with those of the State—can no longer make its voice heard.

The minority is heard even less because the effects of the myth, inflated by propaganda, are always the same and always antidemocratic. Anyone who participates in such a socio-political body and is imbued with the truth of the myth, necessarily becomes sectarian. Repeated so many times, being driven in so many different forms into the propagandee's subconscious, this truth, transmitted by propaganda, becomes for every participant an absolute truth, which cannot be discussed without lies and distortion. Democratic peoples are not exempt from what is vaguely called "psychoses." But such propaganda, if it is effective, predisposes people to—or even causes—these psychoses.

If the people do not believe in the myth, it cannot serve to combat totalitarian propaganda; but if the people do believe in it, they are victims of these myths, which, though democratic on the surface, have all the traits of all other myths, particularly the impossibility, in the eyes of believers, of being questioned. But this tends to eliminate all opposing truth, which is immediately called "error." Once democracy becomes the object of propaganda, it also becomes as totalitarian, authoritarian, and exclusive as dictatorship.

The enthusiasm and exaltation of a people who cling to a myth necessarily lead to intransigence and sectarianism. The myth of democracy arose, for example, during the period of the Convention; there we had forms of massive democracy, with great ceremonies and efforts at unanimity. But was that still democracy? Are there not also changes in the mores of the United States when everything is called un-American that is not strict conformism? This term, *un-American,* so imprecise for the French, is in the United States precise to the extent that it is a result of the belief in the myth. To provoke such belief and launch a people on the road to such exaltation, without which propaganda cannot exist, really means to give a people feelings and reflexes incompatible with life in a democracy.

This is really the ultimate problem: democracy is not just a certain form of political organization or simply an ideology—it is, first of all, a certain view of life and a form of behavior. If democracy were only a form of political organization, there would be no problem; propaganda could adjust to it. This is the institutional argument: propaganda is democratic because there is no unitary State centralized by propaganda. If, then, we were merely in the presence of an ideology, there still would be no problem: propaganda can transmit any ideology (subject to the qualifications made above) and, therefore, also the democratic ideology, for example. But if democracy is a way of life, composed of tolerance, respect, degree, choice, diversity, and so on, all propaganda that acts on behavior and feelings and transforms them in depth turns man into someone who can no longer support democracy because he no longer follows democratic behavior.

Yet propaganda cannot "create" democratic behavior by the pro-

mulgation of a myth—which is the only way of making propaganda on
the outside, but which modifies the behavior of the people at home. We
shall find the same problem in examining certain effects of domestic
propaganda.

32. TECHNIQUES OF PERSUASION

J. A. C. Brown

. . . $\mathbf{P}$SYCHOTHERAPY is directed towards the modification or change of
faulty attitudes and is a somewhat elastic term which includes
anything from mere suggestion with or without hypnosis, where the intention is simply to increase the patient's confidence and so enable him
to face his problems, to analytic psychotherapy, where the intention is to
break down old attitudes and allow them to be replaced by new ones more
close to reality.

Psychoanalysis, the method of therapy devised by Freud, is the most
thoroughgoing of these analytic procedures and also, unfortunately, the
most prolonged, necessitating fifty-five minutes every day for five days a
week over a period of two or more years. During these sessions the
patient lies on a couch and is asked to talk at random, saying whatever
comes into his head no matter what its nature, and in due course the free
association leads to the basic sources of conflict which are, of course,
unconscious. The patient has come to the analyst with various symptoms
such as irrational fears or phobias, attacks of uncontrollable anxiety,
insomnia, and the like, but these are regarded as being the result of
underlying conflicts which arise basically from defects in inter-personal
relations. The aim of analysis is to bring such conflicts into consciousness
so that they can be dealt with at the rational level in a practical manner.
In this process the patient's attitude towards the analyst, the transfer-
ence, plays a leading part; for it is this attitude which, as it were, forms a

From *Techniques of Persuasion* by J. A. C. Brown (London: 1963), pp. 198–201;
205–208; 214–219. Reprinted by permission of Penguin Books, Ltd.

J. A. C. BROWN (1911–1965) Formerly Deputy Director, Institute of Social Psy-
chology, London. His other books include *Freud and the Post-Freudians*, (London:
Cassell, 1961); *The Social Psychology of Industry*, (Baltimore: Penguin Books, 1958);
The Evolution of Society, (London: Watts, 1947).

representative sample of his faulty attitudes towards significant figures in his early life when the basic conflicts arose. The analyst points out the irrational nature of these attitudes, previously not fully realized by the patient, and the early problems are acted out in relation to the analyst and in this way finally lose their compulsive nature. Since complete psychoanalysis is out of reach to most people for practical reasons of time, money, and general suitability of the method in a given case, attempts have been made to shorten analysis which have for the most part been in one or other of two directions: either an attempt is made to reach the conflicts in the unconscious by means of short cuts such as the use of drugs or hypnosis, or the interpretation of the analyst is active—i.e., knowing on the basis of his knowledge of psychopathology and the general clinical picture what the patient's conflicts are, he will force them upon the patient's attention without waiting for them to appear gradually in free association. Such methods are quite satisfactory when the onset of the neurosis is relatively recent and in direct response to some fairly severe provocation from the environment, or in cases which are monosymptomatic as when the most obvious problem is a single phobia. In fact, they approximate to those used by Freud in the early days of the movement, when a symptom was regarded as the tombstone marking the spot where a traumatic memory lay repressed. Later evidence, however, made it clear that neurosis is a disorder of the total personality even if on cursory examination only a single symptom can be observed, and it is generally accepted that removing a symptom in this way is not in itself tantamount to cure any more than suppressing a troublesome cough is a cure for bronchitis. However, in an otherwise good personality it may be regarded as a satisfactory result, especially if the environmental stress was severe and is unlikely to be met with again. For this reason such short methods are specially useful in battle neurosis where a terrifying memory has been repressed with resultant symptom-formation. In such cases, the patient is given an injection of Pentothal (thiopentone sodium), sodium amytal, or scopolamine which makes him drowsy enough for repression to be relaxed and the memory is brought into consciousness, producing great emotional upset whilst the traumatic incident is relived. This emotional crisis is known as abreaction and is therapeutic to the degree that the patient is able to accept the rejected material and integrate it into his ego as part of past history. It is then no longer an undigested mass causing symptoms by reason of repression, but a formerly traumatic memory which has been made a part of consciously-recalled experience and integrated into the rest of the patient's awareness. Similar results may be obtained by the use of ether anaesthesia or hypnosis and the same methods are frequently employed in everyday practice to make a patient aware of his or her problems when they have been partly or wholly repressed. By these means the period of analysis is

greatly shortened, although the best results are obtained, as already indicated, in people of previous good personality who have been under
considerable environmental stress.

Drugs employed in this way are, of course, what are popularly known
as 'truth drugs', and it is necessary to consider how far they are, or can
be, employed for other than therapeutic reasons. Can they be used, for
example, to extract the truth from unwilling prisoners, whether political
or otherwise? All the evidence suggests the contrary. Can they be used, on
the other hand, to cause prisoners to make false confessions, as was
frequently suggested during the Soviet purges of the nineteen-thirties?
Certainly they cannot. The so-called 'truth drugs' are simply ordinary
anaesthetics most of which have been in use for many years (ether, widely
believed to be the most effective of all in psychiatry, is actually the
oldest, dating back to 1847) and in sub-anaesthetic doses they produce
much the same effect as amounts of alcohol sufficient to lead to drunkenness. That is to say, they relax conscious control and enable the individual to speak without his usual censorship coming into action. Their
use is based on the ancient, if not entirely true, saying: '*In vino veritas*.'
Fortunately or unfortunately, as everyone knows, drunkenness does not
necessarily cause everyone to tell the objective truth in terms of external
reality, otherwise we should not so frequently be exposed to the drunk-
ard's fantasies of how badly he is treated at home and how he was
instrumental in winning the last war, or the war before the last. What the
good psychologist learns is a great deal of truth not about objective
happenings but about the character of the individual himself. This suits
the psychiatrist very well, for in the sense that matters to him everything
his patient says is 'true' in so far as it reveals his real attitudes to life.
When, in his early years, Freud listened to his patients' accounts of how
they had been sexually seduced in childhood by near relatives and subsequently found that these happenings were fabricated and had never
really happened in the vast majority of cases, he was at first perplexed.
But finally he came to realize that the important thing was not whether
or not they had happened but rather that the patient felt as if they
had.

But this kind of 'truth' is of no use at all to the political investigator
who wants to catch his prisoner out and, unfortunately for him, no drug
exists which can compel an unwilling victim to tell the truth. The evidence given under the influence of 'truth drugs' is admitted in certain
American courts of law provided the accused is willing to undergo the
test, but it is well-known that people can lie just as effectively under the
influence of a drug as without it and, even when his censorship is relaxed,
a prisoner who is on his guard is able to stick to his original story. He
may, indeed, have got to the stage where he largely believes it himself.
Patients are more susceptible to the influence of such drugs because they

are usually ready to cooperate with the psychiatrist in order to lose their symptoms; but even in these instances objective recall is not always possible. 'Truth drugs' have no magical or inevitable power and the writer well remembers a soldier who, during the last war, was able to maintain for more than two years that he did not know his name, unit, birthplace, or any other facts about his past life, in spite of every thera-peutically permissible attempt to discover them.

. . .

When we speak of masses of people being 'hypnotized' by a powerful orator this must not be understood to imply that they have been hypno-tized in the clinical sense, but, on the other hand, it is true that they are being drawn into a state of increased suggestibility which is one of the features of the hypnotic state. Furthermore, the methods employed by a certain type of orator are very similar to those employed by the hypno-tist and, as Kimball Young has noted: 'Direct suggestion, abetted by rhythm, monotony, stagesettings, and appeals to deep, though uncon-scious, attitudes and ideas, may well induce emotional states not unlike those found in hypnosis.' The most obvious changes which take place in the susceptible individual when he becomes a member of a crowd are heightened emotionality, heightened suggestibility with decreased self-criticism and intellectual alertness, diminished sense of responsibility or loss of the usual social controls, and a sense of power and anonymity. These changes take place and are brought about by the same stimuli no matter what the basic purpose of this type of crowd and are as common to the political agitator and his public as to the evangelist appealing to sinners—to John Wesley as much as to Hitler. Nor is it only the tub-thumping evangelist who employs them; for what is the function of the semi-darkness, the monotonous chanting, the incense, the rhythmic re-sponses, the religious pictures and stained glass windows of the more orthodox religions, if not to increase the suggestibility of the congrega-tion? Such phenomena together with their causes are discussed more fully in the following chapter, and here it is sufficient to note their exis-tence.

Small groups produce effects upon their members which, whilst in some respects similar to those seen in crowds, in other ways are strikingly different, and these effects are put to therapeutic use in what is known as group psychotherapy or group analysis. It is not easy to describe briefly the processes at work in group psychotherapy, partly because various methods are employed, from the 'Freudian' type of group in which the members are given no specific instructions but told simply to say what-ever comes into their minds, to the group which is really very little different from group instruction in its approach. Partly, too, authorities would differ in emphasis as to what actual processes go on in group psychotherapy. For our present purposes it is sufficient to say that neurotics or psychopaths who are treated by this method are people who are basically in rebellion against society, the neurotic by reason of unconscious anti-social impulses, the psychopath by reason of quite conscious ones which, however, are not entirely understood by him. In the simplest type of group psychotherapy the members openly discuss their personal problems (i.e. those matters which, by reason of the guilt attached to them, separate them from society) and also such subjects as their views of other members. Since the fundamental defect in these abnormal conditions is a defect in inter-personal relationships acquired in childhood it is obvious that this type of discussion is valuable in two special ways: the member is able in a permissive atmosphere to express his sense of guilt, which, in effect, is pardoned by the group as the representative of society, and he is enabled to see as in a mirror what are his characteristic faulty attitudes to others as he could not to the same extent in discussion with a single individual. Group attitudes are much more potent than individual ones because, by accepting membership of the group and becoming integrated into it, the person comes to accept its norms, since that is in part what group membership means.

In group psychotherapy the individual confesses his 'sins' and is 'pardoned', becomes integrated emotionally with a social body, thus accepting the norms it painfully works out for itself, and discovers in interaction with others a revelation of himself. All these are useful therapeutic results in those who have hitherto felt cut off from society. But they are employed in other fields too. For example, it has been found in industry that incentive wage plans offering bonuses to individual workers often do more harm than good, whereas group incentives in which the bonus is based upon the work of the whole team are likely to be effective, and even more so when the workers' groups are allowed to discuss plans together and set their own targets of production. The reason for this is that a target which has been set by the members of the group themselves becomes 'ego-involved' for each individual—it is *his* decision he is fulfilling, and the decision of the group with which he identifies himself instead of 'theirs' in the shape of management. But identification with the group naturally results in some flattening out of each member's individual characteristics to approximate towards those approved by the group and this is obviously a desirable end from the point of view of totalitarian social systems, especially when there is added to this the practice of group confession of political 'errors' or moral failings.

Such groups are a regular feature of Communism on the one hand and certain religious movements such as Moral Rearmament on the other. One of the duties of Communist party members as recalled in the revised Party Statutes adopted by the Nineteenth Congress of 1952 in the Soviet Union is 'to develop self-criticism and criticism from below, to expose and eliminate shortcomings in work, and to fight against a show of well-being and against being carried away by success in work'. Criticism in this context means the duty of every party member to bring to the notice of the authorities anything which seems calculated to weaken the régime, and it therefore ranges from denouncing individuals to complaints as to how a factory or collective farm is being run. It must be remembered, however, that such complaints and denunciations must remain within the bounds of accepted doctrine and that a measure may be criticized only until a clear decision has been reached by higher authority, after which criticism is no longer permissible. So although in theory the party member is encouraged to criticize, unwelcome remarks may well be condemned as implying an attack on the established order. How this was regarded prior to the Twentieth Congress is revealed in a cartoon in *Krokodil* showing a large cat addressing a frightened mouse with the words: 'Well! You have made your complaint. And now, what is your defence?' Self-criticism, on the other hand, means the public confession of short-comings at all levels of the party organization and although its ostensible purpose is efficiency, there can be no doubt that it assists the Party in keeping under constant scrutiny the motives and behaviour of everyone who holds a responsible position. In addition it symbolizes the complete obedience of every individual to the collective will of the party, so that the good Communist must be prepared to confess even when his sole offence was carrying out a policy, now rejected, with which he was entrusted by the very members who are now criticizing him. Thus the public disavowal by leaders of their policies, or by artists, composers, writers, and scientists of their work, commonly takes the form of a self-criticism even although it is also a recantation imposed by higher authority.

. . .

In the Communist countries Freudian theory is regarded as 'reactionary' and the theories upon which their psychiatric practice is based are those of I. P. Pavlov, the great Russian physiologist and contemporary of Freud who died in 1936. As many writers have been concerned to show, Pavlov's work with dogs sheds a flood of light not only upon the problems of mental illness but also upon the stress reactions of war and the allegedly extraordinary results obtained by the practitioners of brain-washing and 'thought reform'. On the other hand, there is not the slightest evidence that the Russians or Chinese have made deliberate use of Pavlovian theory in this way or that those who carry out such practices have any special knowledge concerning this or any other branch of psychology. Many authoritative papers have made it clear that 'thought reform' is neither mysterious nor even new, and it contains nothing for which the histories of the countries concerned do not furnish ample precedent. Nor, although some would assert the contrary view, does Pavlovian theory at any important point contradict the views of Freud; what it does do is to provide additional evidence at the physiological level of many psychopathological mechanisms. Such concepts as conditioning, fixation, inhibition, repression, regression to more primitive behaviour in response to stress, and the root of neurosis in conflict are common to both theories.

So far as practice is concerned there is no reason to suppose that psychiatric treatment in the Communist countries is in any way superior to the more eclectic methods employed in the West and, in fact, all the new methods described here from the new psychotrophic drugs to E.C.T. and leucotomy were developed by non-Communist nations. A reading of contemporary Russian psychiatric literature reveals a depressingly doctrinaire approach and a concern with theories long discarded elsewhere, such as the assumption that schizophrenia is caused by autointoxication, found to be baseless in Britain and the U.S.A. more than thirty years ago after thorough trials. This is not said in order to discredit the Soviet Union, but simply to show the improbability that Soviet psychiatrists have any access to information not available in the West.

As is well known, Pavlov was extremely critical of the Soviet régime, but his fame and the credit which was reflected on his country by his researches protected him and he was allowed to carry on his work in Leningrad with the active cooperation of the Soviet government. His basic discovery, made in 1901, and of immense importance to psychology, was the conditioned reflex, demonstrated in the following way: if each time a dog is given food a bell is rung simultaneously, the dog becomes 'conditioned' to the sound of the bell and in time salivates on hearing it even though it is unaccompanied by food. Not only sounds, but light, smell, or touch stimuli may condition dogs to salivate when no food is present. The conditioned reflex results if the stimulus occurs before or simultaneously with the original unconditioned stimulus (food). Thus if the bell is habitually sounded two minutes before food is given, the dog inhibits salivation until two minutes after hearing the bell. Moreover, a conditioned reflex can be extinguished as well as established by constantly ringing the bell without presenting food, when salivation is soon inhibited. After being extinguished the conditioned reflex can be brought back in two ways: by spontaneous recovery after a lapse of time, or by reinforcement—that is, by again presenting food with the bell. The degree of response in each experiment can be accurately measured by bringing one salivary duct on to the surface of the cheek so that the number of drops of saliva can be counted.

Pavlov's next step was to investigate the effect of stress upon these established brain patterns, but he shortly discovered that all dogs did not respond alike to stress and that there appeared to be four basic inherited temperaments in the animals which he equated with those (mentioned elsewhere) first described by Hippocrates in ancient Greece. The first was the 'strong excitatory' type which corresponded to Hippocrates' 'choleric' temperament; the second or 'lively' type corresponded to Hippocrates' 'sanguine' temperament. Both these types tended to respond to stress situations with increased excitement and aggression, although, whereas the former might become completely uncontrolled, the latter responded in a more purposeful and controlled way. The other two types met stress situations with passive or inhibitatory responses rather than with excitement and aggression. The 'calm imperturbable type' or 'phlegmatic type' of Hippocrates lived up to its name, whereas the 'weak inhibitory type' or 'melancholic type' as Hippocrates described it was reduced by severe stress to a state of brain inhibition and 'fear paralysis'. However, all four types when subjected to more stress than they could deal with ended up in a state of inhibition, which Pavlov regarded as a protective mechanism when the brain was disturbed beyond endurance. The 'weak inhibitory' dog broke down before the others and in response to lighter stresses. Thus the final pattern of behaviour in dogs, and as we now know in man, depends both upon inherited temperament and the degree of stress to which they are exposed.

Pavlov then began to investigate the effect of stress on conditioned behaviour patterns when the dog's nervous system was 'transmarginally' stimulated by stresses beyond its adaptive capacity. These were of four main types.

In the first, a dog which had developed a conditioned reflex to salivate in response to a light electric shock applied to one leg which was the signal for food would be subjected to a gradual increase in the strength of the current. When the shock became more than its system could bear, the dog broke down.

Secondly, a breakdown could be brought about by conditioning a dog to expect food at a fixed time after applying the stimulus, and then increasing the waiting period. Pavlov found that the dog's nervous system broke down when it was subjected to long periods of protracted inhibition as the result of waiting under stress. Some, of course, broke down more readily than others.

The third method of inducing breakdown was to alternate positive and negative stimuli thus inducing a state of confusion. If a dog had been conditional to respond to one stimulus with salivation because it was associated with food and not to respond to another when food was not given then, if positive and negative stimuli were given one after the other, breakdown occurred. Similar effects might be produced by feeding a dog when a white circle was exposed and not feeding it when an ellipse was shown; if the ellipse was then approximated more and more closely to a circular shape, breakdown happened when the dog could no longer distinguish between the two.

Finally, breakdown occurred when a dog was subjected to long periods of fatiguing work, fevers, and other forms of debilitating circumstance. Even when the three other methods failed to produce much effect in the more stable type of dog, it was found that when they were repeated after castration or an infection of the intestines breakdown inevitably occurred. An interesting observation was that when, after such interference, new behaviour patterns had developed their stability depended upon the type of dog. Thus new patterns of a neurotic nature could be fairly readily removed in the 'weak inhibitory' animal by small doses of bromides whereas in the 'calm imperturbable' or 'lively' types of animal the new patterns were likely to persist with the same tenacity as the original ones. The more difficult it was to change a pattern of behaviour, the more stable was the new pattern once it had been brought about.

There appeared to be three distinct and progressive stages of 'transmarginal' inhibition which made their appearance in the course of Pavlov's experiments: (1) the so-called 'equivalent' phase when the dog responded by producing the same amount of saliva, no matter what the strength of the stimulus; (2) the 'paradoxical' phase when weak stimuli actually produced more active responses than stronger ones, which only increased the protective inhibition; (3) the 'ultra-paradoxical' phase when positive stimuli came to be reacted to as negative ones and vice versa; behaviour during this phase became precisely the opposite of that previously learned. Pavlov also found that transmarginal inhibition led to increased suggestibility in dogs similar to the hypnotic state in human beings so that when one area of the brain was stimulated the rest of the cortex might become inhibited as a result, and conversely when a localized area was inhibited the remainder might be in a state of excitation. He showed too that when one small area in a dog's brain reached what he called a 'state of pathological inertia and excitation' there might develop a stereotyping of certain movements, of the nature of nervous tics in human beings.

Now all these states experimentally produced in dogs correspond to similar conditions found in human mental illness or under the stress of war or political indoctrination, and, it is alleged, the same sort of stimuli are capable of bringing them about. Thus, prolonged periods of waiting, especially when it is not known when the expected event is about to happen, are known to produce great anxiety in certain types of people, and the debilitation produced by undernourishment or illness plays a large part both in political indoctrination and in the phenomena of religious conversion where fasting is often used as a deliberate spiritual technique to induce change. We also know that (like the dog in the 'equivalent' phase of transmarginal inhibition) many mentally ill people reach a stage in which all happenings are received alike without either the natural joy or sorrow normally appropriate to the occasion. Examples have already been given of the apparent reversal of normal patterns of behaviour under stress as in the conversion of Saul to Christianity, and in some cases of schizophrenia negative stimuli are said to become positive and positive ones negative (as in the 'ultra-paradoxical' phase of brain activity): e.g., the sight or touch of a chamberpot is a strongly positive conditioned response to the desire to urinate or defecate from childhood onwards, whereas clothes, beds, and floors are negatively charged in this respect, but the schizophrenic may appear to reverse this order of events and soil his bed or clothing whilst ignoring the bedpan provided. The observation that, when one part of the brain is in a state of excitation, other areas are inhibited forms a basis for what Freud described as 'dissociation' where a traumatic event may lead to loss of sensation or paralysis in some parts of the body and, on the other hand, the converse state of affairs in which a small area of inhibition leads to generalized excitability or anxiety fits in well with Freud's description of the anxiety which may accompany a repressed memory. Pavlov's dogs' occasional repetitive movements when one area reached a state of 'pathological inertia and excitation' has already been noted as similar in nature to the development of nervous tics in human beings, but when a similar condition occurs in the field of thought obsessive ideas may be the result when the individual is unable to get certain fixed thoughts or words out of his mind. If, to employ Pavlovian terms, these occur at the paradoxical or ultra-paradoxical phases of brain activity the obsessive ideas may be the very reverse of those natural to the individual: the fond mother will have thoughts that she may injure or even kill her child and the excessively puritanical character may be unable to stop ruminating on obscene events or phrases. Also, the induction of states of hyper-suggestibility under stress is well-documented in the tendency of frightened or excited people in the absence of accurate information to accept the most incredible statements as literal truth. Hence the phenomenon of absurd rumours, particularly in wartime.

SELECTED BIBLIOGRAPHY

PART VIII

Propaganda and Psychological Warfare

Barghoorn, Frederick C., *The Soviet Image of the U.S.: A Study in Distortion.* New York: Harcourt, Brace and World, 1950.

Bartlett, F. C., *Political Propaganda.* London: Cambridge University Press, 1940.

Carter, J. F., *Power and Persuasion*. New York: Duell, Sloan and Pearce, 1960.

Christenson, Peo M., and Robert O. McWilliams, *Voice of the People, Readings in Public Opinion and Propaganda*. New York: McGraw-Hill, 1962.

Daugherty, William E., *A Psychological Warfare Casebook*. Baltimore: Johns Hopkins Press, 1958.

Dyer, M., *The Weapon on the Wall: Rethinking Psychological Warfare*. Baltimore: Johns Hopkins Press, 1959.

Eckhardt, William, "War Propaganda, Welfare Values, and Political Ideologies." *Journal of Conflict Resolution*. September 1965.

Holt, Robert T., and Robert Van De Velde, *Strategic Psychological Operations and Foreign Policy*. Chicago: University of Chicago Press, 1960.

Hunter, Edward, *Brain-washing in Red China*. New York: Vanguard, 1951.

Katz, Daniel, Dorwin Cartwright, Samuel Eldersveld, and Alfred McClung Lee, (eds.), *Public Opinion and Propaganda*. New York: Holt, Rinehart and Winston, 1962.

Lerner, Daniel (ed.), *Propaganda in War and Crisis*. New York: George W. Stewart, 1951.

Linebarger, Paul M., *Psychological Warfare*. Washington: Infantry Journal Press, 1948.

Martin, L. John, *International Propaganda: Its Legal and Diplomatic Control*. Minneapolis: University of Minnesota Press, 1958.

Merton, Robert K., *Mass Persuasion*. New York: Harper, 1946.

Mills, Harriet C., "Thought Reform: Ideological Remolding in China," *Atlantic Monthly*. December 1959.

Qualter, T. H., *Propaganda and Psychological Warfare*. New York: Random House, 1962.

Reisky de Dubinic, Vladimir, *Communist Propaganda Methods*. New York: Praeger, 1961.

Whitaker, U. G. (ed.), *Propaganda and International Relations*. San Francisco: Chandler Publishing Company, 1960.

Part IX

The Management of Power

I F STUDENTS of International Relations have devoted considerable
attention to the phenomenon of power, they have also produced
an abundance of literature on the management of power in the
international system. The techniques for the management of power
include (1) institutions such as international organization and
world government, (2) the development of procedures for the resolution of problems among nations, and (3) the conclusion of agreements, formal or tacit, for the balance of power, a reduction of
levels of armaments, and the formation of alliances.

Diplomacy provides the oldest procedure for the resolution of
problems among nations. In discussions about diplomacy, a distinction is often drawn between the "old" and the "new" diplomacy.
The old diplomacy was characterized by secrecy and was largely
divorced from public opinion. Although the diplomat was a reporter
of events, he was often a policymaker, since he could not communicate instantaneously with his home government. In several
ways, diplomacy was considered important to the operation of the
international system. It provided a technique for the adjustment
of international differences. Moreover, according to many writers,
the diplomat as a reporter of events was crucial to the functioning
of another technique for the management of power, namely, the
balance of power. By reporting on changes in the capabilities of the
national unit to which he was assigned, the diplomat supposedly
contributed to an ongoing effort to preserve a balance of power
among the principal participants of the international system.

Harold Nicolson describes the decline of the "old" diplomacy and
its replacement by the "new" diplomacy. Secret diplomacy was held
to have been a principal cause for the outbreak of World War I. The

rise in importance of public opinion contributed to an unwillingness to tolerate secrecy in diplomacy. At least in the West, international relations, to an unprecedented extent, became democra-
tized. The increased speed of communications is said to have
reduced the function of the diplomat as a policymaker and to have
contributed to the rise of the policymaker as diplomat. Contrasting
the role of the diplomat before and after World War I, Nicolson
concludes: "Before the war, the continental Powers allowed their
foreign policy to be framed, as well as conducted, by professional
diplomatists. After the war, Great Britain, and other countries,
allowed their foreign policy to be conducted, as well as framed, by
professional politicians."

Realists in the study of International Relations have called for
a return to a form of diplomacy which embodies at least some of the
features of the "old" diplomacy. In particular, summit diplomacy
is illustrative of the problems of the "new" diplomacy. In summit
conferences, the chief policymaker, namely the President, becomes
a diplomat, and thus performs a function for which by training and
temperament he is likely to be unsuited. Summit conferences take
place in an atmosphere of intense publicity. The expectation of
major results can lead to frustration in the period following a
summit conference. Hence, to not a few writers, the summit conference is illustrative of the "new" diplomacy at its worst.

Although the role of the diplomat today differs from the function
which he performed before World War I, diplomacy remains crucial
to the management of power in the international system. To be
sure, the role of the diplomat as policymaker has diminished as a
result of the growth of communications. Yet his tasks have increased in complexity because of the need to maintain contact in
the country to which he is accredited with a variety of groups which
historically were unimportant to the political process. Although
communications have been speeded, the information to be reported
and analyzed has grown enormously. By his selection of information
to be reported, the diplomat becomes in effect a policymaker, for
the formulation of foreign policy is related to the data available.
Formally, the ambassador presides today over a diplomatic establishment far more complex than ever before in history. Thus in
order to understand the operation of the international system one
must visualize a continuing stream of diplomatic interaction, with
messages passing from one government to another through their

accredited representatives. In fact, much of the interaction which takes place within the international system relates to diplomacy.

According to Schelling there is a process of bargaining which continues even after the failure of diplomacy to prevent national units from resorting to armed conflict. War itself is a bargaining process about such issues as the rules for the conduct of conflict, including the treatment of civilian population, the exclusion of certain regions from the list of targets, the kinds of weapons systems to be employed. There is a bargaining process about reductions in the level of conflict, or even its termination. Often by their actions rather than as a result of formal agreement, participants may "signal" their intentions to each other. Thus they are engaged in an interactive process.

In the second category of techniques for the management of power delineated at the outset are agreements, usually formally worked out among national units for balance of power, alliances, or arms control. However, such arrangements may result from tacit undertakings among the major participants.

Balance of power is widely assumed to be one of the oldest and most enduring techniques for the management of power. Especially in the decade after World War I, however, balance of power was in disrepute, especially in Utopian thought on international relations. Secret agreements for the establishment of opposing alliance systems, and hence balances of power, were assumed to have contributed to the outbreak of war. Among Realists, however, the balance of power regained a measure of its lost stature. Realist emphasis upon balance of power accorded with the Realist assumption about the nature of man. If man was evil and power-seeking it was appropriate to devise techniques for the management of power in which one man, or group of men, whether within the national unit or in the international system, would be balanced against another.

According to Sir Eyre Crowe, the balance of power represented one of the most enduring, and most important, principles of British foreign policy. In the most succinct and celebrated statement of this position, Crowe maintained that Britain sought to prevent the domination of Europe by any one power by joining the side of the weaker coalition to oppose the stronger. Spykman, it will be recalled, suggested in Part VI that for geopolitical reasons, that national unit which dominated the Eurasian land mass would place itself in the position of potential ruler of the world. The conception of balance of power, contained in his memorandum, Crowe suggests, has informed British foreign policy.

Although balance of power is one of the most widely used techniques for the management of power in international relations, it is fraught with semantic ambiguity. A review of the extensive literature on balance of power reveals the use of this term to describe such widely differing phenomena as an equilibrium between national units, a preponderance of power in the hands of one national unit, or simply a prevailing distribution of power among members of the international system. According to Ernst Haas, the absence of conceptual clarity has limited the utility of the term balance of power. Given its ambiguities, the student must make an effort to ascertain the meaning, or meanings, of the term balance of power as used by different authors, or even the same author.

Historically, alliance systems and the balance of power have been closely related. Often the international system consisted of opposing alliances of nation-states in what was termed a balance of power. Alternatively, weaker national units formed alliances in order to oppose a more powerful national unit.

As Liska suggests, alliances are seldom durable. Within the international system, nations shift from one alliance to another in response to perceived national interest. For example, erstwhile allies may conclude a separate peace with the country against which they once formed an alliance. Since alliances are usually formed in an environment of actual or potential conflict, with the termination of conflict, or the decline in perception of threat, an alliance system loses its *raison d'etre* and is beset with disintegrative tendencies.

In addition to the existence of formal treaties of alliance, national units engage in other activities which may be indicative of alignment. According to Henry Teune and Sig Synnestvedt, it is possible to establish several objective, quantitative indicators of alignment. Votes in international organizations such as the United Nations, patterns of diplomatic recognition, visits by heads of state and other ranking officials, and military and economic agreements provide measures of alignment. By examining such indicators over time, it might be possible to ascertain shifts in alignment within the international system.

With the use of such indicators, the student of International Relations could group nations according to categories of alignment or non-alignment. As Khalid Babaa and Cecil Crabb suggest, there is considerable confusion about the concept of non-alignment. Although there are different kinds of non-alignment, this concept is used to describe nations allied neither with the United States nor the Soviet Union. With the use of quantitative indicators such as those described above, new insights into the meaning of alignment and non-alignment, as well as the extent of a country's alignment, might be gained.

Especially in the twentieth century, disarmament and arms control have come to occupy an important place in the list of techniques for the management of power in the international system. According to Hedley Bull, disarmament may be defined as the reduction or abolition of armaments. Disarmament may be undertaken by one nation, or by many nations at a given time. Disarmament may be localized, that is, confined to a specific geographic region or weapons system; it may be comprehensive or partial; it may be controlled or uncontrolled. According to Bull's definition, arms control, in contrast to disarmament, may be defined as the exercise of restraint by a national unit upon armaments policy. If a nation places limitations upon the levels of armaments, their character, deployment, or use, it is engaged in one form or another of arms control. In Bull's definition, a decision by the United States or the Soviet Union to reduce the numbers of intercontinental ballistic missiles in its arsenal, or to make cuts in military manpower would constitute disarmament. A decision by the United States or the Soviet Union not to develop some new weapons system, or not to deploy an existing weapons system, would represent a form of arms control.

The relationship between armed conflict and arms races has long preoccupied students of International Relations. Do arms races produce conflict, or do they stem from, and reflect, underlying political disputes? Bull contends that arms races issue from, and are kept alive by, political disputes, and subside with the resolution of basic differences between nations. Although disarmament and arms control agreements may contribute to an easing of tensions between nations desiring to improve relations, they are often expensive, especially if they rely upon elaborate systems of inspection in order to detect violations. Bull contends that the objective of disarmament and arms control should be to promote international security. From this premise he argues that reductions in the quantities of forces or weapons, or restrictions in military expenditures, do not necessarily contribute to international stability, and may even lead to instability in the international system. Instead, he states a preference for controls on armaments in such a way as to contribute to equilibrium in the international system.

In the arms control literature and in international negotiations, the proliferation of nuclear weapons to previously non-nuclear countries has been a topic of great concern. According to Leonard Beaton and John Maddox, the proliferation of nuclear weapons "carries the great danger of turning local wars into nuclear ones." Implicit in this argument is the contention that the national units which might gain access to nuclear weapons would be less restrained in their use than are the superpowers, and might even draw the United States and the Soviet Union into a nuclear conflict. According to James Dougherty, the risk of nuclear war would not necessarily rise as additional nations obtained nuclear weapons although admittedly a "world of twenty nuclear powers might be more unstable than a world of only 5-6." An agreement to halt the proliferation of nuclear weapons places great burdens upon both the nuclear and the non-nuclear countries. In return for signing a non-proliferation treaty, non-nuclear countries such as India seek guarantees from nuclear states that they will come to their defense in the event of attack from a nuclear power such as China. The effect of a non-proliferation treaty is to increase the dependence of non-nuclear states upon nuclear powers, and to extend the military commitments of nuclear powers such as the United States.

A third major category of techniques for the management of power includes the development of institutions at the international level. Students of International Relations have sought to develop an understanding of those factors which lead peoples to form political institutions. Philip Jacob and Henry Teune ask if such factors as geographic proximity, homogeneity, high levels of transactions, knowledge about each other, functional interest, or previous integrative experience contribute to an integrative process.

Karl Deutsch attempts to develop an understanding of similarities in the process of nation-building in order to develop a theory of integration based upon the data of history. Deutsch and his associates found that the national units which they studied were built around core areas of superior economic growth and administrative capabilities, that peoples within regions in the process of integration engaged in a wide range of mutual transactions and developed broadened links of social communication. In presenting these and other findings, the authors set forth tentative theories about the building of nations, and thus contribute to our knowledge about nationalism (see Part II). Their findings, it is suggested, may have relevance to conditions essential to the building of political communities at the international level. To what extent, it is appropriate to ask, does the international system have characteristics similar to those of other kinds of political systems, such as those described by Deutsch and his associates, or by Masters in Part II.

There is an abundance of literature on international relations in which authors state their arguments for the creation of a world government. Similarly, there is no dearth of literature which contains authors' critiques of proposals for world government. In this literature can be found, explicitly or implicitly, many of the Utopian or Realist assumptions about international relations (see Part I). In a survey of literature, Inis Claude summarizes the arguments set forth by proponents of world government: that the nation-state is no longer able to provide protection for its people, that modern man may doom himself to extinction unless he joins a new global organization, that through enforceable world law the prospects for the peaceful settlement of international disputes can be enhanced, that fear of nuclear annihilation may bridge differences in ideology and culture and thus provide a consensus upon which to build new international institutions.

In response to such arguments, critics set forth several contentions. It is suggested that governments, although they may be created by force, must rest at least upon some level of consensus. No national unit possesses the resources to impose political institutions upon the rest of mankind. Whatever their fear of annihilation, the peoples of the world have developed little, if any consensus about the form which institutions at the international level should assume. Should they be based upon an American federalist model, or a Soviet model? Even if such agreement existed, would it be possible to achieve accord as to who would control such institutions? *Quis custodiet ipsos?* (Who watches the custodians?)

World government proponents, Claude suggests, place perhaps too much emphasis upon a positivist conception of law, namely, that law is obeyed because of the enforcement procedures available to the community. Instead, critics of world government proposals have contended, law is obeyed essentially because the community as a whole accepts it as corresponding to its conception of justice. Even in such political systems as the United States, it becomes difficult, if not impossible, to enforce laws which do not have the consent of at least a large number of the population. In the international system a considerable body of international law is obeyed, even without elaborate enforcement procedures, because it rests upon a broadly based consensus. Thus Claude directs attention to possible similarities between conditions in the international system and national political systems. Even at the level of the national unit, conditions of civil conflict sometimes resemble conditions prevailing in the model of the international system described by many authors. Yet it is the differences between national political systems and the international system which have contributed to the emergence of International Relations as a field of study and rendered difficult if not impossible, the development of more effective institutions and techniques for the management of power at the international level.

SECTION ONE: Diplomacy and Bargaining

33. THE "OLD" AND THE "NEW" DIPLOMACY

Harold Nicolson

DEFINITION

(a) The best definitions of diplomacy have been furnished by Martens, Cussy, and Sir Ernest Satow. Martens defined it as 'The science of the external relations, or foreign affairs, of States, and, in a more limited sense, the science, or art, of negotiation'. Cussy defined it as 'The sum of the knowledge and the principles necessary for the good conduct of public affairs between States'. Satow defined it as 'The application of intelligence and tact to the conduct of official relations between the Governments of independent States'.

(b) These definitions, although fully descriptive of monarchic and oligarchic diplomacy, do not provide democratic diplomacy with that sharp differentiation which it needs between 'foreign policy' and 'the methods by which that policy is executed'.

Such a differentiation is essential if democratic diplomacy is to benefit by, and not merely to break with, the experience of the past. Policy and negotiation should henceforward be regarded as two wholly separate things.

From *Curzon: The Last Phase* by Harold Nicolson (New York: 1934), pp. 385–387; 391–404. Reprinted by permission of Harcourt, Brace and World, Inc. and Curtis Brown Ltd.

SIR HAROLD NICOLSON (1886–1968) Member of Parliament, 1935–1945; Member of British Diplomatic Service, 1909–1929. His other books include *Kings, Courts, and Monarchy,* (New York: Simon and Schuster, 1962); *Evolution of Diplomatic Method,* (New York: Macmillan, 1962); *Evolution of Diplomatic Method,* (New York: Macmillan, 1954); *The Congress of Vienna,* (London: Constable, 1946).

(c) This differentiation was blurred, not only in pre-war, but also in post-war, diplomacy.

Before the war, the continental Powers allowed their foreign policy to be framed, as well as conducted, by professional diplomatists. After the war, Great Britain, and other countries, allowed their foreign policy to be conducted, as well as framed, by professional politicians.

Each of these methods is equally dangerous. Diplomatists should seldom be allowed to frame policy. Politicians should seldom be allowed to conduct negotiation. Policy should be subjected to democratic control: the execution of that policy should be left to trained experts.

(d) The necessity of defining what we mean by this term 'diplomacy' is therefore a primary necessity.

If the electorate are ever to rise to the standard of their sovereign responsibility in foreign affairs, they should be taught, before they discuss diplomacy, to ask themselves two questions, namely: 'Are we discussing foreign policy? or are we discussing negotiation?'

(e) Much value, in my opinion, will result from this habit of definition. Once public opinion acquires the practice of differentiating between 'policy' and 'negotiation' it will be less inclined to use the word 'diplomacy' to express both.

Policy should never be, and need never be, secret. No system should ever again be tolerated which can commit men and women, without their knowledge or consent, to obligations which will entail upon them, either a breach of national good-faith, or the sacrifice of their property and lives. It should be established that no international obligation need ever be regarded as valid, unless it has been communicated to, discussed and approved by, the sovereign democracy. In other words, no treaty need ever be operative until it has been ratified by the parliament representing the will of the democracies whose interests are pledged by that treaty.

Once this principle is firmly embedded in the practice and conscience of mankind, there will be less hesitation in entrusting to trained experts the confidential conduct of negotiation. This hesitation derives, almost wholly, from the absence of any axiomatic differentiation between 'foreign policy' and 'the means or methods by which that policy is executed'.

.   .   .

DANGERS OF DEMOCRATIC POLICY

The essential defect of democratic policy can be defined in one word, namely 'irresponsibility'. Under a monarchic or oligarchic system the 'sovereign' who enters into a contract with some foreign State feels himself personally 'responsible' for the execution of that contract. For a monarch or a governing class to repudiate a formal treaty was regarded as a dishonourable thing to do, and would have aroused much criticism both at home and abroad. Now, however, that the people are 'sovereign', this sense of individual or corporate responsibility no longer exists. The people are in no sense aware of their own sovereignty in foreign affairs and have therefore no sense of responsibility in regard to treaties or conventions entered into with other Powers, even when they have themselves, through their elected representatives, approved of those treaties. They are honestly under the impression that their own word has not been pledged and that they are therefore fully entitled to repudiate engagements which they may subsequently feel to be onerous or inconvenient. A state of mind is thus created which (to take an obvious instance) allows a popular newspaper publicly to preach the repudiation of the Locarno Treaties, not on the ground that these treaties were unconstitutionally concluded, but on the ground that their application at the present moment would prove inconvenient and unpopular.

Clearly, if such a state of mind is permitted to continue uncriticised and unchecked, there can be no hope for the future of democratic foreign policy. The foundations of policy, as of diplomacy, are reliability, and under a system of popular repudiation of all national engagements which may eventually prove to be onerous, not even the elements of reliability can exist. Compared with this basic defect in democratic foreign policy, all other dangers are insignificant. Not until the people and the press realise their own sovereignty will they be ready to assume their own responsibility. The period which must inevitably elapse between the fact of popular sovereignty in foreign affairs, and the realisation of that fact by the people themselves; in other words the zone of uncertainty which will have to be traversed before we leave the present quicksands of unconscious public irresponsibility and reach the firm ground of conscious public responsibility, constitute the period or zone of greatest danger. Until that zone has successfully been traversed, no sense of international security can possibly be fostered. The essence of the whole problem is how the danger period is to pass without either disturbance or disintegration. The statesmen of the post-war period have endeavoured to create an artificial sense of security by multiplying security pacts. Yet until the world is convinced that these pacts are regarded by the sovereign democracies as involving their own responsibility they merely serve to inflate the currency of international contract and thereby to diminish certainty rather than to increase confidence.

It will take one, or perhaps two, generations of wise education to create in the several democracies a responsible state of mind. Once that state of mind has been created, we may indeed hope for peace on earth. For the moment all we can hope to do is to guard against those secondary or subsidiary dangers which will menace democratic foreign policy and democratic diplomacy during the transition period.

I should define these dangers as follows:

(1) *The failure to differentiate* between 'policy' and 'negotiation' and the use of the term 'diplomacy' as applying to both. This danger has already been examined.

(2) *The tendency to identify* with 'the old diplomacy' the more realistic traditions of British foreign policy and the consequent under-estimation, in such matters, of the continuity of public instinct and tradition.

(3) *Subjectivity*, manifesting itself either in dumb inertia or in patriotic excitement. A tendency to excuse these emotional extremes by attributing public lethargy or neurosis to the machinations, ignorance, malignity, class-privilege, or stupidity of those responsible for foreign policy and its execution. In extreme forms this subjectivity leads either to (*a*) jingoism or (*b*) defeatism. Each of these democratic sensations is equally dangerous.

(4) *The time-lag* between informed opinion and popular feeling. This requires to be dealt with in greater detail.

Although the essential instincts of our democracy in regard to foreign affairs are continuous, stable and shared by a large majority, yet their momentary feelings on the subject are intermittent, variable and diverse. It is possible, I feel, to estimate with approximate certainty what policy the majority of the electorate will in the end desire; yet it is often impossible to elicit this majority approval at the moment when it is most needed.

An unfortunate factor in all representative systems is that the temporary emotions of certain sections of the electorate or the press are apt to manifest themselves in the shape of 'opinions' on the part of certain sections of the House of Commons. These 'opinions' obstruct and impede national policy at times when that policy ought to be formulated in the most categorical and immediate form.

Sir Edward Grey, for instance, ought to have been able in July 1914 to state the 'Peace' and 'Balance of Power' doctrines in such drastic terms as would have discouraged Russia from mobilization and Germany from attacking France or Belgium.

In 1919, again, Mr. Lloyd George should have been able to expound the same doctrines in such a manner as to make it clear to France that Great Britain would not permit her to reduce Germany to ruin.

In both these cases, public opinion would in the end have approved such categorical statements; at the moment, however, public opinion would not have been prepared to accord approval. On each occasion, and with disastrous consequences, the opportunity was missed.

(5) *Imprecision.* The essence of a good foreign policy is certitude. An uncertain policy is always bad.

On the other hand, parliamentary and press opposition is less likely to concentrate against an elastic foreign policy than against one which is precise. It is thus a grave temptation for a Foreign Minister under the democratic system to prefer an idealistic formula, which raises only intellectual criticism, to a concrete formula which is open to popular attack. This temptation is one which should be resisted. Not merely does it promote in Foreign Secretaries a habit of complacent, unctuous and empty rectitude, but it diminishes the credit of international contract.

The Kellogg Pact, for instance, either meant a new heaven and a new earth, or it meant very little. Few people, apart from Mr. Kellogg himself, regarded it as a new revelation; its main effect was to discredit previous instruments, such as the Covenant, which had also endeavoured, though with greater precision, to provide for the pacific settlement of international disputes.

(6) *Hypocrisy.* Democratic foreign policy indulges in the (at present) sentimental fiction that relations between states can be conducted upon the same moral basis as those between individuals. As an ideal, this is a theory which I thoroughly endorse. Yet as a description of existing relations I can regard it only as a false description. Relations between individuals are ultimately governed by law. Relations between States are not governed by law. There can be no real analogy between the ethical values of an organised, and those of an anarchical, society.

Democratic diplomacy endeavours to conceal this awkward fact, and to hide the realities of force under the appearance of consent. For the downright lies of the fifteenth century system it has substituted a technique of self-righteous half-truths. It thus destroys confidence, and confidence, after certitude, is the most important element of good foreign policy.

(7) *Unreality.* Democratic foreign policy—proceeding again from a fallacious identification between states and individuals—pays lip-service to the doctrine of equality among nations.

This exposes it to that miasma of unreality which clouds all its actions. Nicaragua is not the equal of the United States, nor is San Domingo the equal of France. To advance the theory of such equality is to advance something which is senseless and unreal.

By this also are certitude and confidence diminished.

It is not, however, general certainty only which is embarrassed by this egalitarian fallacy, it is also the constructive authority of the British Empire which is damaged by this wholly unproductive fiction. Our physical power may be an unknown quantity: it may, at any given crisis, be either tiny or immense: our moral influence, on the other hand, should become a known and continuous factor in international affairs. In all essential issues, the British Dominions and even the United States *think* the same; although they *feel* in shapes of disconcerting difference. Our potential influence is immeasurable; our actual influence is intermittent; the proportions of power represented by the English-speaking world are

overwhelming; the identity of theory shared in that world is, to all who
have become accustomed to European psychology, very striking. I should
like to see British democracy think more of democracy and less of policy.
It is in our democratic consanguinity with our Dominions, as also with
the United States, and not in any sentimental belief in egalitarianism,
that we shall find our authority. I believe in authority, even as I believe
in power. And I should wish to see democratic authority exercised with
moderation, and without either arrogance or fear. It is the timidity of
democratic policy which verges so frequently upon the selfish and the
inert.

DANGERS OF DEMOCRATIC DIPLOMACY

In spite of the dangers noted above, democratic foreign policy is unquestionably less dangerous than any other form of foreign policy.
Democratic diplomacy, on the other hand, is, owing to its disturbing
inefficiency, very dangerous indeed.

By 'democratic diplomacy' I mean the execution of foreign policy,
either by politicians themselves, or through the medium of untrained
negotiators whom they have selected from among their own supporters or
personal friends.

The failure to differentiate between 'policy' and 'negotiation' has led
to the fallacy that all important negotiation should be carried out, not by
persons possessing experience and detachment, but by persons possessing
a mandate from the people. In its extreme form this fallacy has led to
'Diplomacy by Conference'—perhaps the most unfortunate diplomatic
method ever conceived.

(1) *Diplomacy by Conference.* Obviously there are occasions when
international agreement can only be achieved by oral discussion between
plenipotentiaries. There are occasions, also, when the issues are so vital
and immediate that 'policy' as well as 'negotiation' is involved. On
such occasions the negotiators must be identical with the framers of
policy, and the resultant congresses and conferences must be attended by
the Prime Ministers or Foreign Secretaries of the several Powers.

It should be established, however, that such occasions are exceptional
and dangerous. Such conferences should be entered into only after careful
preparation, on the basis of a programme elaborated and accepted in
advance, against a background of acute public criticism and with full
realisation that many months of discussion will be required. The subjects
for debate should moreover be rigidly curtailed to those requiring a
decision of policy, and all secondary issues, entailing negotiation only,
should be left in expert hands.

In the four years immediately following the war these principles were
discarded. Innumerable conferences were held without adequate preparation, with no precise programme and within a time limit of three or four

days. The subjects discussed were diverse, intricate and suitable only for expert negotiation. The meetings took place in an atmosphere of extreme publicity and uncritical popular expectation. The resultant conclusions, inevitably, were inconclusive, intangible, specious, superficial, and unreal. Compare the expert handling of such conferences as those of Washington, Lausanne and Brussels with the hurried histrionics of Genoa or Cannes.

'Diplomacy by Conference' is to-day so discredited that it may be thought that there is no danger of its revival as a method of international negotiation. The frame of mind which allowed of that method is still, however, a very general frame of mind. It is caused by uncertainty regarding the frontier between democratic control of policy and expert conduct of negotiation. That frontier can only be properly delimitated if we have a clear conception of the dangers of amateurishness on the one hand, and of professionalism on the other.

(2) *The politician as negotiator.* It has already been stated that on exceptional occasions, or in dealing with vital issues of policy, the politician must himself negotiate. I should wish, however, to summarise some of the dangers to which, on such occasions, he is exposed.

(a) *Public opinion.* A politician suffers from the essential disadvantage of being a politician. In other words his position and his future career are dependent upon popular approval. He is acutely sensitive to transitory 'opinions' in the House of Commons, his party, or the press. He is apt to reject what he knows to be reasonable because he also knows that it will be difficult to explain; conversely, he is tempted (as Orlando was tempted in the Fiume controversy) to fabricate by propaganda an artificial popular approval in order to strengthen his diplomatic position.

The professional, on the other hand, places ultimate national interest above immediate popular applause.

(b) *Ignorance.* By this I do not mean an ignorance of foreign facts, but an ignorance of foreign psychology. It mattered nothing at all that Mr. Lloyd George should never have heard of Teschen; it mattered very much indeed that he should treat the French or the Germans as he would treat an English trades-union delegation. Those schoolboy levities which might put a Lancashire Labour leader at his ease were regarded by M. Briand as disconcerting; those rhetorical questions, those revivalist dithyrambs which, to the Mayor of Llanberis would appear as usual forms of human speech, were interpreted by Dr. Rathenau or M. Gounaris as signifying either invective or encouragement. Frequent and serious were the misunderstandings which therefrom resulted.

(c) *Vanity.* A British politician, unaccustomed to negotiation with foreign statesmen, is prone to disturbances of vanity. The fact that his general culture, as his knowledge of foreign languages, is generally below the level of that possessed by those with whom he is negotiating gives him a sense of inferiority to which he reacts in unfortunate ways. Either he will air his schoolboy French to the distress of his audience and the confusion of business, or else he will be truculently insular. Upon weaker minds the mere fact of being, although abroad, a centre of public interest, the lavish hospitality of foreign Governments, the actual salutes of people dressed in foreign uniforms, have a most disintegrating effect. Affability, gratitude and general silliness result.

Such subjective forms of vanity are perhaps less dangerous than its more objective manifestations. A Prime Minister, for instance, who is conscious of a firm majority at home, is apt to acquire an autocratic habit of mind. Not only is he irritated by the fact that he cannot compel foreign statesmen to obey his behests, but he resents, and thus endeavours to ignore, those circumstances which he is unable to influence as well as those areas of knowledge which he can never hope to possess. A tendency develops in him to deny the existence of those circumstances and that knowledge and to soar above them on the light wings of obscurantism and improvisation. Sir Charles Mallet in his *Lloyd George: a Study* (page 156) has well described the effect of this particular manifestation of human vanity. 'Unvarying self-assurance', he writes, 'tempered by an ever-varying opportunism is perhaps the most dangerous equipment that statesmanship can have.'

Democratic diplomacy is very apt to acquire this equipment.

(d) *Controversy*. A mind trained in parliamentary or forensic debate is apt to assume that a conference is a form of controversy. Such people start from the assumption that the interests of foreign countries are necessarily opposed. They tend to envisage negotiation in the form of a debate rather than in the form of a consultation. They thus endeavour to 'score points'. At many a Conference I have seen a whole hour wasted in purely artificial dialectics. The politician is always conscious of an audience; the trained negotiator is conscious only of the negotiation in hand. The reason why lawyers have always made the worst diplomatists is that their argumentative faculties are too much on the alert. Negotiation should never degenerate into an argument; it should be kept always on the level of a discussion.

(e) *Overwork*. The politician, again, is always pressed for time. It thus results that negotiation is seldom pursued to a precise conclusion, but is suspended halfway upon the first landing offered for compromise. This time-pressure, again, leads to impatience. The politician as negotiator is unwilling to listen to information which may tempt him to alter his own opinion and thus necessitate further discussion. Similarly he is prone to reject all suggestions, however admirable, which might entail further study or delay. Time-pressure, in every case, is accompanied by overwork: the results are expedients, half-solutions, evasion of essentials, improvisations, and imprecision.

Such are the major disabilities from which even the noblest politician, when he becomes a diplomatist, is apt to suffer.

DANGERS OF PROFESSIONAL DIPLOMACY

The virtues of professional diplomacy are implicit in the above catalogue of the vices of its opposite. The professional diplomatist is indifferent to public applause, has devoted some thirty years to the study of foreign psychology, is unaffected by vanity, dislikes controversy, eschews all forms of publicity, and is not subject to acute time-pressure or overwork. In addition, as a trained expert in a common science working with other experts, he is intent upon producing a piece of work which will satisfy his own professional standards. All that he cares for is the approbation of those whose judgment is worth having. He is completely indifferent to the opinion of those whose judgment is not worth having. This specialised vanity impels him to prefer competent to incompetent work, real achievement to achievements which have only the appearance of reality.

Yet he, also, has his dangers.

(*a*) *Professionalism.* A man who has spent some thirty years in the diplomatic service acquires, inevitably, an international frame of mind. More specifically he comes to have a masonic feeling for other diplomatists. On occasions he may lack a proper degree of reverence for politicians, or even Press magnates, and an unwarranted contempt for, and suspicion of, their ways and means. In extreme cases he may feel, even, that public and parliamentary opinion is foolish and ill-informed.

Upon himself the effect of these prejudices is seldom serious. Being a civil servant he has been trained to loyalty and obedience, nor would he (I am discussing only British diplomatists) dream of acting contrary to the wishes of the Government in power, and therefore of his democratic sovereign. His prejudices are of negative rather than of positive disadvantage. His experience of democracy in so many lands and in such different forms may induce in him a mood of scepticism. This absence of belief will be interpreted by those politicians with whom he comes into contact as an attitude of superiority. Suspicion and misprisal will result.

(*b*) *Lethargy.* The professional diplomatist is apt to lack initiative. Important problems, in his opinion, settle themselves; unimportant problems are unimportant. He has seen so much damage done by well-meaning officiousness; he has seen so little damage done by letting well alone. His whole training has tended to convince him that good diplomacy is a slow and cautious business, and he looks with exaggerated suspicion upon all dynamic innovations. For him reality is relative and never absolute: he believes in gradations, in grey zones; he is always impatient of those who think enthusiastically in terms of black or white. Lethargy of judgment descends upon him, a slightly contemptuous disbelief in all forms of human certainty. He is thus more prone to analysis than to synthesis, more ready to indicate doubts than to produce dynamic assurances, more inclined to deny than to affirm. This propensity proves very irritating to the politician anxious to score a rapid popular success.

(c) *Narrowness.* The professional diplomatist suffers also from certain limitations of outlook. He observes widely, but he does not observe deeply. He is inclined to attach to superficial events greater importance than he attaches to underlying causes. He is more interested in overt political symptoms than in obscure social or economic diseases. He is well aware that his judgment, if it is to be of any real value to his Government, must be 'sound': he tends therefore to allow the more imaginative and original sections of his brain to atrophy. True it is that a brilliant diplomatist is a grave public menace; the consciousness of this fact is apt to induce our professional diplomatists to attach exclusive importance to not being brilliant. This, certainly, is a fault on the right side. Our diplomatic service is without question (and no foreigner would deny it) the best in the world. Yet upon the casual observer it may produce a false impression of conservatism and mental rigidity.

(d) *Timidity.* This quality should, perhaps, have been cited in the category of virtues and not in the category of defects. The British diplomatist is in fact as frightened of 'causing trouble' as the British naval officer is frightened of sinking his ship. Inevitably, the Foreign Office prefer diplomatists who say soothing and optimistic things to diplomatists who tell home truths in defiant language. Smugness, rather than outspoken realism, is apt to colour many diplomatic reports. A certain narcotic quality thus pervades the information which they supply.

Yet this is but a venial sin.

34. ON NEGOTIATIONS

Henry A. Kissinger

THE INTRACTABILITY OF DIPLOMACY

A s ARMAMENTS have multiplied and the risks of conflict have become increasingly catastrophic, the demands for a "new approach" to end tensions have grown ever more insistent. No country, it is said, has any alternative except to seek to attain its aims by negotiations. The Cold War must be ended in order to spare mankind the horrors of a hot war: "The stark and inescapable fact is that today we cannot defend our society by war since total war is total destruction and if war is used as an instrument of policy eventually we will have total war," wrote Lester Pearson. "We prepare for war like precocious giants and for peace like retarded pigmies."[1]

There is no doubt that the avoidance of war must be a primary goal of all responsible statesmen. The desirability of maintaining peace cannot be the subject of either intellectual or partisan political controversy in the free world. The only reasonable issue is how best to achieve this objective.

And here there is reason for serious concern. A welter of slogans fills the air. "Relaxation of tensions," "flexibility," "new approaches," "negotiable proposals," are variously put forth as remedies to the impasse of the Cold War. But the programs to give these phrases meaning have proved much more difficult to define. The impression has been created that the missing ingredient has been a "willingness to negotiate." While this criticism is correct for some periods, particularly John Foster Dulles' incumbency as Secretary of State, it is not a just comment when applied to the entire post-war era. Hardly a year has passed without at least some negotiation with the Communist countries. There have been six Foreign Ministers' Conferences and three summit meetings.

From *The Necessity for Choice* by Henry A. Kissinger (New York: 1961) pp. 169–175; 181–182; 185–189; 191. Copyright © 1960, 1961 by Henry A. Kissinger. Reprinted by permission of Harper and Row, Publishers, and Chatto and Windus, Ltd. Footnotes have been renumbered to appear in consecutive order.

HENRY A. KISSINGER (1923–   ) Professor of Government, Harvard University. His other books include *The Troubled Partnership: A Reappraisal of the Atlantic Alliance,* (New York: McGraw-Hill, 1965), author; *Problems of National Security,* (New York: Praeger, 1965), editor; *Nuclear Weapons and Foreign Policy,* (New York: Harper, 1957), author.

[1] Lester Pearson, Speech at Oslo, Dec. 11, 1957, quoted in the *New York Times,* Dec. 12, 1957.

Periods of intransigence have alternated with spasmodic efforts to settle all problems at one fell swoop. The abortive summit meeting of 1960 proved that tensions have sometimes been increased as much by the manner in which diplomacy has been conducted as by the refusal to negotiate. The Cold War has been perpetuated not only by the abdication of diplomacy but also by its emptiness and sterility.

What, then, has made the conduct of diplomacy so difficult? Why have tensions continued whether we negotiated or failed to negotiate? There are four basic causes: (1) the destructiveness of modern weapons, (2) the polarization of power in the contemporary period, (3) the nature of the conflict, (4) national attitudes peculiar to the West and particularly to the United States.

It is not an accident that the diplomatic stalemate has become more intractable as weapons have grown more destructive. Rather than facilitating settlement, the increasing horror of war has made the process of negotiation more difficult. Historically, negotiators have rarely relied exclusively on the persuasiveness of the argument. A country's bargaining position has traditionally depended not only on the logic of its proposals but also on the penalties it could exact for the other side's failure to agree. An abortive conference rarely returned matters to the starting point. Rather, diplomacy having failed, other pressures were brought into play. Even at the Congress of Vienna, long considered the model diplomatic conference, the settlement which maintained the peace of Europe for a century was not achieved without the threat of war.

As the risks of war have become more cataclysmic, the result has not been a universal reconciliation but a perpetuation of all disputes. Much as we may deplore it, most major historical changes have been brought about to a greater or lesser degree by the threat or the use of force. Our age faces the paradoxical problem that because the violence of war has grown out of all proportion to the objectives to be achieved, no issue has been resolved. We cannot have war. But we have had to learn painfully that peace is something more than the absence of war. Solving the problem of peaceful change is essential; but we must be careful not to deny its complexity.

The intractability of diplomacy has been magnified by the polarization of power in the post-war period. As long as the international system was composed of many states of approximately equal strength, subtlety of maneuver could to some extent substitute for physical strength. As long as no nation was strong enough to eliminate all the others, shifting coalitions could be used for exerting pressure or marshaling support. They served in a sense as substitutes for physical conflict. In the classical periods of cabinet diplomacy in the eighteenth and nineteenth centuries, a country's diplomatic flexibility and bargaining position depended on its availability as a partner to as many other countries as possible. As a result, no relationship was considered permanent and no conflict was pushed to its ultimate conclusion. Disputes were limited by the tacit agreement that the maintenance of the existing system was more important than any particular disagreement. Wars occurred, but they did not involve risking the national survival and were settled in relation to specific, limited issues.

Whenever the number of sovereign states was reduced, diplomacy became more rigid. When a unified Germany and Italy emerged in the nineteenth century, they replaced a host of smaller principalities. This reflected the dominant currents of nationalism. But from the point of view of diplomatic flexibility, some of the "play" was taken out of the conduct of foreign policy. To the extent that the available diplomatic options diminished, the temptation to achieve security by mobilizing a country's physical strength increased. The armaments race prior to World War I was as much the result as the cause of the inflexibility of diplomacy. France and Germany were in fundamental conflict. And neither state could organize an overwhelming coalition. As a result, power had to substitute for diplomatic dexterity and the period prior to World War I witnessed a continuous increase of the standing armies.

World War I accelerated the polarization of power. By the end of World War II only two major countries remained—major in the sense of having some prospect of assuring their security by their own resources. But a two-power world is inherently unstable. Any relative weakening of one side is tantamount to an absolute strengthening of the other. Every issue seems to involve life and death. Diplomacy turns rigid, for no state can negotiate about what it considers to be the requirements of its survival. In a two-power world these requirements are likely to appear mutually incompatible. The area where diplomacy is most necessary will then appear most "unnegotiable."

The inherent tensions of a two-power world are compounded by the clash of opposing ideologies. For over a generation now the Communist leaders have proclaimed their devotion to the overthrow of the capitalist world. They have insisted that the economic system of their opponents was based on exploitation and war. They have never wavered from asserting the inevitability or the crucial importance of their triumph. To be sure, periods of peaceful coexistence have alternated with belligerence, particularly since the advent of Mr. Khrushchev. But one of the principal Communist justifications for a *détente* can hardly prove very reassuring to the free world; peace is advocated not for its own sake but because the West is said to have grown so weak that it will go to perdition without a last convulsive upheaval. At the height of the spirit of Camp David, Khrushchev said: "The capitalist world is shaking under the blows of the

Socialist camp. What shakes it even more than the rockets is the attitude of our workers towards their work. . . . We have the will to win."[2]

Negotiations with Communist leaders are complicated by one of the key aspects of Leninist theory: the belief in the predominance of "objective" factors. One of the proudest claims of the Communist leaders is that in Marxist-Leninist theory they possess a tool enabling them to distinguish appearance from reality. "True" reality consists not of what statesmen say but of the productive processes—the social and economic structure—of their country. Statesmen, particularly capitalist statesmen, are powerless to alter the main outlines of the policy their system imposes on them. Since everything depends on a correct understanding of these "objective factors" and the relation of forces they imply, "good will" and "good faith" are meaningless abstractions. One of the chief functions of traditional diplomacy—to persuade the opposite party of one's view point—becomes extremely difficult when verbal declarations are discounted from the outset. Khrushchev said in 1959: "History teaches us that conferences reflect in their decisions an established balance of forces resulting from victory or capitulation in war or similar circumstances."[3]

Much of the diplomatic stalemate has therefore little to do with lack of good will or ingenuity on the part of the statesmen. Without an agreement on general principles, negotiations become extremely difficult. What will seem most obvious to one party will appear most elusive to the other. When there is no penalty for failing to agree and when at the same time the balance of power is so tenuous, it is no accident that the existing dividing lines are so rigidly maintained. For the *status quo* has at least the advantage of familiarity while any change involves the possibility of catastrophe. At the same time, since these dividing lines are contested, protracted tension is nearly inevitable.

This impasse has led either to long periods in which diplomacy has for all practical purposes abdicated its role; or else it has produced a form of negotiations which has almost seemed to revel in *not* coming to grips with the issues dividing the world. The reference which is often made to the coexistence achieved by Mohammedanism and Christianity or by Protestantism and Catholicism is not fully relevant to the contemporary problem. In both cases, coexistence was the result of protracted, often ruinous, warfare—the very contingency diplomacy is now asked to prevent. We must be aware that the factors that intensify the desire to resolve the impasse of the Cold War may also make a creative response more difficult.

---

[2] *New York Times,* Dec. 3, 1959.

[3] Speech at Leipzig, March 7, 1959, quoted in *Foreign Radio Broadcasts: Daily Report,* No. 62, 1959, BB 16.

These obstacles to serious negotiations are magnified by Western, and in particular American, attitudes towards negotiating with the Communists. A *status quo* power always has difficulty in coming to grips with a revolutionary period. Since everything it considers "normal" is tied up with the existing order, it usually recognizes too late that another state means to overthrow the international system. This is a problem especially if a revolutionary state presents each demand as a specific, limited objective which in itself may seem quite reasonable. If it alternates pressure with campaigns for peaceful coexistence, it may give rise to the belief that only one more concession stands in the way of the era of good feeling which is so passionately desired. All the instincts of a *status quo* power tempt it to gear its policy to the expectation of a fundamental change of heart of its opponent—in the direction of what seems obviously "natural" to it.

Were it not for this difficulty of understanding, no revolution would ever have succeeded. A revolutionary movement always starts from a position of inferior strength. It owes its survival to the reluctance of its declared victims to accept its professions at face value. It owes its success to the psychological advantage which single-minded purpose confers over opponents who refuse to believe that some states or groups may prefer victory to peace. The ambiguity of the Soviet challenge results in part from the skill of the Soviet leadership. But it is magnified by the tendency of the free world to choose the interpretation of Soviet motivations which best fits its own preconceptions. Neither Lenin's writings, nor Stalin's utterances, nor Mao's published works, nor Khrushchev's declarations has availed against the conviction of the West that a basic change in Communist society and aims was imminent and that a problem deferred was a problem solved.

It is only to posterity that revolutionary movements appear unambiguous. However weak it may be at the beginning, a revolutionary state is often able to substitute psychological strength for physical power. It can use the very enormity of its goals to defeat an opponent who cannot come to grips with a policy of unlimited objectives.

The United States has had particular difficulty in this respect. From the moment in our national history when we focused our attention primarily on domestic development, we met very few obstacles that were really insuperable. We were almost uniquely blessed with the kind of environment in which the problems that were presented—those at least that we really wanted to solve—were difficult but manageable. Almost from our colonial infancy we have been trained to measure a man, a government, or an era by the degree of energy with which contemporary problems have been attacked—and hence by the success in finding a final, definite solution. If problems were not solved, this was because not enough energy or enough resolution had been applied. The leadership or the government was clearly at fault. A better government or a better man would have mastered the situation. Better men and a better government, when we provide them, *will* solve all issues *in our time*.

As a result, we are not comfortable with seemingly insoluble problems. There must be *some* way to achieve peace if only the correct method is utilized. Many of the erratic tendencies in American policy are traceable to our impatience. The lack of persistence, the oscillation between rigid adherence to the *status quo* and desire for novelty for its own sake show our discomfort when faced with protracted deadlock. We grow restless when good will goes unrewarded and when proposals have to be maintained over a long period of time.

When reality clashes with its anticipated form, frustration is the inevitable consequence. We have, therefore, been torn between adopting a pose of indignation and seeking to solve all problems at one fell swoop. We have been at times reluctant, indeed seemingly afraid, to negotiate. We have also acted as if all our difficulties could be removed by personal rapport among the statesmen. Periods of overconcern with military security have alternated with periods when we saw in a changed Soviet tone an approach to an end of tensions.

The quest for good will in the abstract has been as demoralizing and as fruitless as the insistence that negotiations are inherently useless. The abortive summit meeting in Paris is as certain a symptom of the perils of a purely formal conciliatoriness as Secretary Dulles' rigidity was a symptom of a largely mechanical intransigence. It is, therefore, necessary to examine Western, and particularly American, attitudes towards negotiations in more detail.

· · ·

THE RELIANCE ON PERSONALITIES: THE PROBLEM OF SUMMIT MEETINGS

The temptation to conduct personal diplomacy derives from the notion of peace prevalent in both the United States and Great Britain. If peace is the "normal" relation among states, it follows that tensions must be caused by shortsightedness or misunderstanding and that they can be removed by a change of heart of the leading statesmen. President Eisenhower, before embarking on an unprecedented round of visits to foreign capitals, was at pains to insist that his purpose was to "clear" the atmosphere rather than to negotiate. If peace ultimately depends on personalities, abstract good will may well seem more important than a concrete program. Indeed, the attempt to achieve specific settlements can appear as an obstacle rather than as an aid to peace. "Our many post-war conferences," said President Eisenhower in 1955, prior to the Geneva summit conference, "have been characterized too much by attention to detail, by an effort apparently to work on specific problems rather than to establish the spirit and the attitude in which we shall approach them." [4]

Within two years of assuming office, President Eisenhower, whose party had charged its opponents with being soft towards Communism, found himself engaged in a summit meeting which called forth a flood of self-congratulatory comment, both in America and abroad. After a decade of Soviet intransigence, the press was almost unanimous in its assertion that Soviet policy had been mellowed by the personal charm of one man. "No one would want to underestimate the change in the Russian attitude," said the *New York Herald Tribune.* "Without that, nothing would have been possible. . . . But it remains President Eisenhower's achievement that he comprehended the change, that he seized the opening and turned it to the advantage of world peace." [5] "Mr. Eisenhower had done even better than defeat an enemy in battle as had been his assignment a decade ago," read an editorial in the *New York Times.* "He had done something to prevent battles from happening. . . . The occasion was, in fact, made for Mr. Eisenhower. Other men might have played strength against strength. It was Mr. Eisenhower's gift to draw others into the circle of his good will and to modify the attitudes if not the policies of the little band of visitors from the other side of the Elbe." [6]

The conviction was widespread on both sides of the Atlantic that the Cold War had been due largely to personal distrust. Since this had been removed at Geneva, an era of peace was beginning: "It is indeed an intense sense of relief which unites President Eisenhower with President [sic] Bulganin. Neither ever conceived that his own country would launch war. But each giant was quite convinced that the other giant was capable of doing so. It was this conviction which created the climate of cold war and precipitated the rearmament race. *The cold war was suddenly called off at Geneva because both sides recognized that these suspicions were entirely unfounded.*" [7] [Emphasis added.]

．　　．　　．

When the summit conference of 1960 collapsed before it had even started, a shudder of apprehension went through the world. A chance for peace seemed to have been lost. But what really imperiled peace was our self-righteousness and evasion of responsibility. After all, the prelude to the Paris summit conference had given little cause for the hopes attached to it. At first, we found ourselves maneuvered into the position of seeming to fear meeting the Soviet leaders face-to-face. By insisting on "progress"

---

[4] *New York Times,* July 16, 1955.

[5] *New York Herald Tribune,* Editorial, July 21, 1955.

[6] *New York Times,* Editorial, July 25, 1955.

[7] "Problems of the Garden-Party Peace," *New Statesman and Nation,* Aug. 13, 1955.

at a lower level before he would agree to a conference of heads of state, President Eisenhower only brought about the preposterous situation where he finally claimed that Mr. Khrushchev's ambiguous postponement of an unprovoked threat and his willingness to go to the summit were in themselves an indication of progress. These vacillations were hardly calculated to motivate the Soviet leaders to approach the summit conference with responsibility.

Moreover, many of the arguments advanced on behalf of summit diplomacy were fatuous in the extreme. It was urged that only the heads of state could settle the really intractable disputes. No subordinate, it was said, would dare to abandon the rigid positions of the Cold War. In the Soviet Union, in particular, only Mr. Khrushchev was in a position to make really fundamental decisions. And the mere fact that a summit meeting was in prospect was thought to place constraints on Soviet intransigence. A series of summit meetings, according to this line of argument, could not fail to relieve tensions.

Many of these contentions were open to serious doubt even before the collapse of the Paris Conference. It is trivial to pretend that problems of the complexity of those which have rent the world for a decade and a half can be solved in a few days by harassed men meeting in the full light of publicity. It cannot be in the interest of the democracies to adopt a style of diplomacy which places such a premium on the authority of a few leaders. Mr. Khrushchev may be the supreme ruler in the Soviet Union and the only one with sufficient power to make binding agreements. It does not follow that the democracies can coexist with a dictatorship only by imitating its method of operation.

The notion that a series of summit meetings might induce Mr. Khrushchev to forget his demands on Berlin did not do justice to the intelligence of the Soviet dictator. Surely it bordered on the frivolous to suggest that Mr. Khrushchev could be induced to table his demands without noticing it, as it were. This view, moreover, took no account of Mr. Khrushchev's domestic position. Even assuming that he is the most "conciliatory" Soviet leader, he could hardly be expected to tell his colleagues in the Kremlin that the privilege of meeting Western leaders periodically seemed to him more important than specific gains. Indeed, personal diplomacy of the type preceding the Paris summit meeting may force a Soviet leader either to press for some tangible gain or into outbursts of intransigence to prove his ideological toughness to his colleagues. Far from being the most moderate policy, it is the most risky one.

In any case, it soon became apparent that whatever the benefits of high-level meetings for the Soviet Union, these could be realized without any concrete concessions and indeed without a summit conference. The "preparatory" meeting between Mr. Khrushchev and the Western heads of state individually still further reduced the already slight chances of the summit meeting. They gave Mr. Khrushchev all the symbolic gains he might have expected from a summit conference and without the need of confronting the Western alliance as a unit. They ensured that nothing of consequence could possibly happen at the summit. If concessions were to be forthcoming, it was certain that Mr. Khrushchev would prefer to make them to the Allies individually than at a summit conference—where they might appear as a response to Western unity.

At the same time, one crucial function of high-level meetings—to inform the heads of state of each other's point of view—had already been accomplished in individual conferences and with a greatly heightened possibility of misunderstanding. It has been argued that Mr. Khrushchev interpreted President Eisenhower's behavior at Camp David as indicating a readiness to make major concessions on Berlin and that part of his rage during the abortive summit conference was due to disappointment in this respect. Whether or not this was in fact the case, the diplomacy leading up to the summit was made to order for this kind of misapprehension. Moreover, since each side had staked a great deal on a presumed expertise in assessing the domestic situation of the other, they were forced into repeated public declarations designed to reassure their own public opinion and—in Khrushchev's case—their own die-hards. This in turn guaranteed that statements of extreme intransigence would alternate with intimations of normality through a year and a half of ambulatory diplomacy which was unable to settle any of the issues or even define them.

Finally, the idea that the imminence of a summit meeting places a constraint upon intransigence is not borne out by the record. In the period preceding the summit, both sides restated their positions in the sharpest possible forms. Mr. Khrushchev in particular delivered a series of extremely menacing speeches. The West, if it wanted to proceed with the summit, thus found itself in the humiliating position of having to explain that no threat had been uttered. These maneuvers were inherent in the nature of personal diplomacy. When heads of state are the principal negotiators, their most effective bargaining device—in some circumstances the only available one—is to stake their prestige in a manner which makes any concession appear as an intolerable loss of face.

The evasion of concreteness, the reliance on personalities, the implication that all problems can be settled with one grand gesture, all these tempt the Soviet leaders to use negotiations to demoralize the West. It is in the Soviet interest to turn all disputes into clashes of personalities. The peoples of the free world cannot be expected to run risks or to make exertions because of a personal dispute. If the only obstacle to peace is the absence of personal rapport among leading statesmen, then all tensions and exertions of a decade and a half have been a frivolous imposition. Whenever the Soviet leaders succeed in giving the impression that all tensions are due to an unfortunate misunderstanding or else to the evil machinations of individuals, they make it that much more difficult for the West to raise later the need for concrete settlements. This is why whenever the Communist leaders have pressed for a relaxation of tensions they have tied the success of it to personalities. Then, whenever the underlying causes of the tension reassert themselves—as they inevitably must if not resolved—the charge can be made that the breakdown is due to the operation of the capitalist system or to the predominant influence of hostile personalities—as is shown by Mr. Khrushchev's vicious attacks on President Eisenhower after the abortive summit conference at Paris. By contrast, it should be the responsibility of our statesmen to make clear that, while we are always ready to negotiate, the negotiation must be serious, detailed and specific.

This is not to say that summit conferences are always to be avoided. It does suggest that we must learn to distinguish form and substance. In assessing the utility of summit meetings, it is essential to weigh the pros and cons without sentimentality.

The advantage of a summit meeting is that the participants possess the authority to settle disputes. The disadvantage is that they cannot be disavowed. A summit conference can make binding decisions more rapidly than any other diplomatic forum. By the same token, the disagreements are liable to be more intractable and the decisions more irrevocable. The possibility of using summit conferences to mark a new departure in the relations of states should not be underestimated. At the same time, it would be foolish to deny the perils of having as principal negotiators the men who make the final decision about the use of hydrogen bombs. Frustration or humiliation may cause them to embark on an irrevocable course. A summit conference may contribute to clarification of the opposing points of view. But this is helpful only if the original tension was caused by misunderstanding. Otherwise, clarifying the opposing points of view may only deepen the schism. In short, the same factors which make for speed of decision also increase the risks of disagreement.

Moreover, when heads of state become the principal negotiators, they may soon find themselves so preoccupied with the process of bargaining that they have little time or energy available for formulating policy.[8] In the ambulatory diplomacy preceding the Paris summit conference, it was an oddity when all heads of state were at home simultaneously. During his last two years in office President Eisenhower was at conferences, preparing for or recuperating from good will visits almost constantly. Such

---

[8] For a brilliant discussion of the problem posed by summit diplomacy for the American presidency see Dean Rusk, "The President," *Foreign Affairs*, April, 1960, pp. 353–369.

a diplomacy may suit a dictatorship or a state which wishes to demoralize its opponents by confusing all issues. It is not conducive to developing constructive long-range policies. It is a useful device to buy time, though at a price which makes it unlikely that the time will be well used.

. . .

When the primary purpose of summit meetings is thought to be the fostering of abstract good will, they become not a forum for negotiations but a substitute for them; not an expression of a policy but a means of obscuring its absence. The constant international travels of heads of government without a clear program or purpose may be less an expression of statesmanship than a symptom of panic.

The real indictment of the diplomacy culminating in the fiasco at Paris, then, is the attitude of trying to get something for nothing, the effort to negotiate without goal or conception. This is what must be remedied. The problem is not to save summit diplomacy by leavening it with the presence of heads of state from the uncommitted areas—as has been suggested.[9] Rather, it is to clarify our program for whatever negotiations may take place at any level. We can negotiate with confidence if we know what we consider a just arrangement. If we lack a sense of direction, diplomacy at any level will be doomed.

---

[9] Denis Healey, "The View from London," *New Leader*, June 13, 1960.

35. NEGOTIATION IN WARFARE

Thomas C. Schelling

TO THINK OF WAR as a bargaining process is uncongenial to some of us. Bargaining with violence smacks of extortion, vicious politics, callous diplomacy, and everything indecent, illegal, or uncivilized. It is bad

---

From *Arms and Influence* by Thomas C. Schelling (New Haven: 1966) pp. 215–220. Reprinted by permission of the Yale University Press.

THOMAS C. SCHELLING (1921–   ) Professor of Economics, Harvard University. His other books include *The Strategy of Conflict*, (Cambridge: Harvard University Press, 1960); *Strategy and Arms Control*, (New York: The Twentieth Century Fund, 1961), co-author; *International Economics*, (Boston: Allyn and Bacon, 1958), author.

enough to kill and to maim, but to do it for gain and not for some transcendent purpose seems even worse. Bargaining also smacks of appeasement, of politics and diplomacy, of accommodation or collaboration with the enemy, of selling out and compromising, of everything weak and irresolute. But to fight a purely destructive war is neither clean nor heroic; it is just purposeless. No one who hates war can eliminate its ugliness by shutting his eyes to the need for responsible direction; coercion is the business of war. And someone who hates mixing politics with war usually wants to glorify an action by ignoring or disguising its purpose. Both points of view deserve sympathy, and in some wars they could be indulged; neither should determine the conduct of a thermonuclear war.

What is the bargaining about? First there is bargaining about the conduct of the war itself. In more narrowly limited wars—the Korean War, or the war in Vietnam, or a hypothetical war confined to Europe or the Middle East—the bargaining about the way the war is to be fought is conspicuous and continual: what weapons are used, what nationalities are involved, what targets are sanctuaries and what are legitimate, what forms participation can take without being counted as "combat," what codes of reprisal or hot pursuit and what treatment of prisoners are to be recognized. The same should be true in the largest war: the treatment of population centers, the deliberate creation or avoidance of fallout, the inclusion or exclusion of particular countries as combatants and targets, the destruction or preservation of each other's government or command centers, demonstrations of strength and resolve, and the treatment of the communications facilities on which explicit bargaining depends, should be within the cognizance of those who command the operations. Part of this bargaining might be explicit, in verbal messages and replies; much of it would be tacit, in the patterns of behavior and reactions to enemy behavior. The tacit bargaining would involve targets conspicuously hit and conspicuously avoided, the character and timing of specific reprisals, demonstrations of strength and resolve and of the accuracy of target intelligence, and anything else that conveys intent to the enemy or structures his expectations about the kind of war it is going to be.

Second, there would be bargaining about the cease-fire, truce, armistice, surrender, disarmament, or whatever it is that brings the war to a close— about the way to halt the war and the military requirements for stopping it. The terms could involve weapons—their number, readiness, location, preservation, or destruction—and the disposition of weapons and actions beyond recall or out of control or unaccounted for, or whose status was in dispute between the two sides. It would involve surveillance and inspection, either to monitor compliance with the armistice or just to establish the facts, to demonstrate strength or weakness, to assign fault or innocence in case of untoward events, and to keep track of third parties' military forces. It could involve understandings about the reassembling or reconstituting of military forces, refueling, readying of missiles on launching pads, repair and maintenance, and all the other steps that would prepare a country either to meet a renewed attack or to launch one. It could involve argument or bargaining about the degree of destruction to people and property on both sides, the equity or justice of what had been done and the need to inflict punishment or to exact submissiveness. It could involve the dismantling or preservation of warning systems, military communications, or air defenses. And it very likely would involve the status of sheltered or unsheltered population in view of their significance as "hostages" against resumption of warfare.

A third subject of bargaining could be the regime within the enemy country itself. At a minimum there might have to be a decision about *whom* to recognize as authority in the enemy country or with whom one would willingly deal. There might be a choice between negotiating with military or civilian authorities; and if the war is as disruptive as can easily be imagined, there may be a problem of "succession" to resolve. There could even be competing regimes in the enemy country—alternative commanders to recognize as the inheritors of control, or alternative political leaders whose acquisition of control depended on whether they could monopolize communications or get themselves recognized as authoritative negotiators. To some extent, either side can determine the regime on the other side by the process of recognition and negotiation itself. This would especially be the case in the decision to negotiate about allied countries—China, or France and Germany—or alternatively to refuse to deal with the primary enemy about allied and satellite affairs and to insist upon dealing separately with the governments of those countries.

A fourth subject for bargaining would be the disposition of any theater in which local or regional war was taking place. This could involve the evacuation or occupation of territory, local surrender of forces, coordinated withdrawals, treatment of the population, use of troops to police the areas, prisoner exchanges, return or transfer of authority to local governments, inspection and surveillance, introduction of occupation authorities, or anything else pertinent to the local termination of warfare.

The tempo and urgency of the big war and its armistice might require ignoring theater affairs in the interest of reaching some armistice. If so, there might be an understanding, implicit or explicit, that the theater war is to be stopped by unilateral actions or by immediately subsequent negotiation. There might conceivably be the expectation that the theater war goes on, risking renewed outbreak of the larger war; and possibly the outcome of the major war would have made the theater war inconsequential or its local outcome a foregone conclusion. A theater war would in any case pose acute problems of synchronization: its tempo would be so slow compared with that of the bigger war that the terms of the theater armistice simply could not be met within the time schedule on which the larger war had to be brought to a close.

Fifth would be the longer term disarmament and inspection arrangements. These might be comprised in the same package with the armistice itself; but stopping a war safely and reliably is different from maintaining safe and reliable military relations thereafter. The first involves conditions to be met at once, before the war is ended or before planes return to base, before relaxation has occurred and before populations have been brought from their shelters. The second involves conditions to be met afterward.

For that reason the armistice might, as in the days of Julius Caesar, involve the surrender of hostages as a pledge for future compliance. What form these might take is hard to foretell; but selective occupation of communication centers, preplaced demolition charges, destruction of particular facilities to make a country dependent on outside aid, or even personal hostages might appear reasonable. The purpose of any of these types of hostages—hostages not taken by force but acquired by negotiation—is to maintain bargaining power that would otherwise too quickly disappear. It is to provide a pledge against future compliance, when one's capacity for sanctions is too short-lived. The principle is important, because there is no necessary correspondence between the duration of one's power to coerce and the time span of the compliance that needs to be enforced.

A sixth subject for negotiation might be the political status of various countries or territories—dissolution of alliances or blocs, dismemberment of countries, and all the other things that wars are usually "about," possibly including economic arrangements and particularly reparations and prohibitions. Some of these might automatically be covered in disposing of a theater war; some would already be covered in deciding on the regime to negotiate with. Some might be settled by default: the war itself would have been so disruptive as to leave certain problems no longer in need of solution, certain issues irrelevant, certain countries unimportant.

Of these six topics for bargaining, the first—conduct of the war—is inherent in the war itself if the war is responsibly conducted. The second—terms of armistice or surrender—is inherent in the process of getting it stopped, even though by default most of the terms might be established through an unnegotiated pause. The third—the regime—is at least somewhat implicit in the process of negotiation; the decision to negotiate involves some choice and recognition. The fourth—disposition of local or regional warfare—might be deferred until after the urgent business of armistice had been settled; but the armistice may remain tentative and precarious until the rest of the fighting is actually stopped.

The same is probably true of the longer-term disarmament arrangements, and of political and economic arrangements.

We are dealing with a process that is inherently frantic, noisy, and disruptive, in an environment of acute uncertainty, conducted by human beings who have never experienced such a crisis before and on an extraordinarily demanding time schedule. We have to suppose that the negotiations would be truncated, incomplete, improvised, and disorderly, with threats, offers, and demands issued disjointedly and inconsistently, subject to misunderstanding about facts as well as intent, and with uncertainty about who has the authority to negotiate and to command. These six topics are therefore not an agenda for negotiation but a series of headings for sorting out the issues that might receive attention. They are an agenda only for thinking in advance about the termination of war, not for negotiation itself.

How soon should the terminal negotiations begin? Preferably, before the war starts. The crisis that precedes the war would be an opportune time to get certain understandings across. Once war became an imminent possibility, governments might take seriously a "strategic dialogue" that could powerfully influence the war itself. In ordinary peacetime the Soviet leaders have tended to disdain the idea of restraint in warfare. Why not? It permits them to ridicule American strategy, to pose the deterrent threat of massive retaliation, and still perhaps to change their minds if they ever have to take war seriously. On the brink of war they would. It may be just before the outbreak that an intense dialogue would occur, shaping expectations about bringing the war to a close, avoiding a contest in city destruction, and keeping communications open.

It is sometimes wondered whether communications could be established mid-course in a major war. The proper question is whether communications should be cut off. There would have been intense communication before the war, and the problem is to maintain it, not to invent it.

SECTION TWO: Balance of Power

36. ENGLAND'S FOREIGN POLICY

Sir Eyre Crowe

THE GENERAL CHARACTER of England's foreign policy is determined by the immutable conditions of her geographical situation on the ocean flank of Europe as an island State with vast oversea colonies and dependencies, whose existence and survival as an independent community are inseparably bound up with the possession of preponderant sea power. The tremendous influence of such preponderance has been described in the classical pages of Captain Mahan. No one now disputes it. Sea power is more potent than land power, because it is as pervading as the element in which it moves and has its being. Its formidable character makes itself felt the more directly that a maritime State is, in the literal sense of the word, the neighbour of every country accessible by sea. It would, therefore, be but natural that the power of a State supreme at sea should inspire universal jealousy and fear, and be ever exposed to the danger of being overthrown by a general combination of the world. Against such a combination no single nation could in the long run stand, least of all a small island kingdom not possessed of the military strength of a people trained to arms, and dependent for its food supply on oversea commerce. The danger can in practice only be averted—and history shows that it has been so averted—on condition that the national policy of the insular and naval State is so directed as to harmonize with the general desires and ideals common to all mankind, and more particularly that it is closely

From *British Documents on the Origins of the War, 1898–1914,* Vol. III, "The Testing of the Entente, 1904–06," edited by G. P. Gooch and Harold Temperley (London: 1929) pp. 402–403. Reprinted by permission of His Majesty's Stationery Office.

SIR EYRE CROWE (1864–1925) Formerly permanent Under-Secretary of State for Foreign Affairs, Foreign Office, Great Britain.

identified with the primary and vital interests of a majority, or as many as possible, of the other nations. Now, the first interest of all countries is the preservation of national independence. It follows that England, more than any other non-insular Power, has a direct and positive interest in the maintenance of the independence of nations, and therefore must be the natural enemy of any country threatening the independence of others, and the natural protector of the weaker communities.

Second only to the ideal of independence, nations have always cherished the right of free intercourse and trade in the world's markets, and in proportion as England champions the principle of the largest measure of general freedom of commerce, she undoubtedly strengthens her hold on the interested friendship of other nations, at least to the extent of making them feel less apprehensive of naval supremacy in the hands of a free trade England than they would in the face of a predominant protectionist Power. This is an aspect of the free trade question which is apt to be overlooked. It has been well said that every country, if it had the option, would, of course, prefer itself to hold the power of supremacy at sea, but that, this choice being excluded, it would rather see England hold that power than any other State.

History shows that the danger threatening the independence of this or that nation has generally arisen, at least in part, out of the momentary predominance of a neighbouring State at once militarily powerful, economically efficient, and ambitious to extend its frontiers or spread its influence, the danger being directly proportionate to the degree of its power and efficiency, and to the spontaneity or "inevitableness" of its ambitions. The only check on the abuse of political predominance derived from such a position has always consisted in the opposition of an equally formidable rival, or of a combination of several countries forming leagues of defence. The equilibrium established by such a grouping of forces is technically known as the balance of power, and it has become almost an historical truism to identify England's secular policy with the maintenance of this balance by throwing her weight now in this scale and now in that, but ever on the side opposed to the political dictatorship of the strongest single State or group at a given time.

If this view of British policy is correct, the opposition into which England must inevitably be driven to any country aspiring to such a dictatorship assumes almost the form of a law of nature, as has indeed been theoretically demonstrated, and illustrated historically, by an eminent writer on English national policy.

By applying this general law to a particular case, the attempt might be made to ascertain whether, at a given time, some powerful and ambitious State is or is not in a position of natural and necessary enmity towards England; and the present position of Germany might, perhaps, be so tested. Any such investigation must take the shape of an inquiry as to

whether Germany is, in fact, aiming at a political hegemony with the
object of promoting purely German schemes of expansion, and establishing a German primacy in the world of international politics at the cost
and to the detriment of other nations.

37. THE BALANCE OF POWER:
PRESCRIPTION, CONCEPT OR PROPAGANDA

Ernst B. Haas

CLASSIFICATION OF VERBAL MEANINGS

. . .

A MONG THE VARIOUS MEANINGS of the term "balance of power," one of
the more common is a mere factual description of the distribution of
political power in the international scene at any one time. But, in another
sense, the term is used to mean a theoretical principle acting as a guide to
foreign policy-making in any and all international situations, so that the
preponderance of any one state may be avoided. Expanding this notion
and assuming that almost all states guide their policies by this principle,
a general system of the balance of power is thought to come about, a
system in which each participating state has a certain role. Such a system
may take the form of two or more power blocs in mutual opposition to
each other and it may exist with or without the benefit of a balancer, i.e.,
a state willing and able to throw its weight on either scale of the balance,
to speak in terms of the classical metaphor, and thus presumably bring
about the diplomatic or military victory of the bloc so supported, or
possibly prevent any change in existing conditions. In addition to these
various shades of theoretical meaning implying some sort of system, the

From *World Politics*, XV, No. 4 (July 1953), 446–477. Reprinted by permission of
the author and the publisher. Footnotes have been renumbered to appear in consecutive order.

ERNST B. HAAS (1924–   ) Professor of Political Science and Associate Director,
Institute for International Studies, University of California, Berkeley. Author of
Beyond the Nation State: Functionalism and International Organization, (Stanford:
Stanford University Press, 1964); *The Uniting of Europe,* (Stanford: Stanford Uni-
versity Press, 1957). Co-author of *The Dynamics of International Relations,* (New
York: McGraw-Hill, 1956).

term "balance of power" has frequently been used to describe the existence of a political equilibrium, i.e., such a distribution of power that each state (or each major state) is the approximate equal of every other. On the other hand, the term is commonly employed to connote the exact opposite of the equilibrium notion; it then comes to be identical with a notion of hegemony. Still other commentators insist on the presence of general historical laws of the balance of power, a notion to which the term "natural law" has been given by some. By this they mean that the search for hegemony by one state will inevitably be met by a coalition of all other states, thus forming a "counterweight" against political preponderance and tending to re-establish the *status quo ante*. And, finally, balance of power very frequently means power politics generally and the establishment of certain military and strategic conditions specifically. Some writers equate the term with peace, others with war. This general differentiation now remains to be supported with apposite illustrative citations.[1]

(1) *Balance meaning "Distribution of Power."* The simplest and most commonly found use of the term "balance of power" occurs in plain descriptive statements. Thus when Bolingbroke wrote that "Our Charles the First was no great politician, and yet he seemed to discern that the balance of power was turning in favor of France, some years before the treaty of Westphalia . . . ,"[2] he was merely saying that the Stuart ruler was noticing that the power of France was increasing as compared to that of Britain. Or, again, Henry Wallace once remarked that Japan's joining the Axis meant

> that the old balance of power upon which the U.S. relied for safety is now gone. Only if we are speedy and efficient in our defense can we keep aggressor nations, or any combination of them, from coming to this country. . . . The old balance of power under which the Monroe

---

[1] It is of some significance that the terminological confusion is not confined to Western writing. Raymond L. Garthoff has shown that even though the Russian political vocabulary has separate expressions for most of the usages cited, in practice loose application creates exactly the same difficulty as in English so far as classification and analysis are concerned. Garthoff concludes that, from an examination of 250 citations using some form of balance of power expression, this summary can be made: 136 instances of balance meaning general "relation of forces," especially in the class struggle; 87 instances meaning a "general distribution" of power; 17 instances of balance meaning "equilibrium"; and 10 instances of balance meaning "preponderance" or hegemony. In discussions of international relations, the Soviet use of the term "balance of power" generally connotes an equilibrium of forces between the "imperialist" and "socialist" worlds, and is therefore associated with short-term policies of peaceful coexistence. "The Concept of the Balance of Power in Soviet Policy-Making," *World Politics*, IV (October 1951), pp. 88–90, 102–3, 108–9.

[2] Bolingbroke, *Works*, Philadelphia, 1841, II, p. 257.

Doctrine was easily defended is gone. We must look to our own defenses, relying on ourselves to repel any aggression.[3]

Balance of power, in usages such as these, means no more than distribution of power. It does not connote any "balancing" of weights at all. When a statesman says that the "balance of power has shifted," he wants to say that his opponent has grown more powerful than was the case previously.

(2) *Balance meaning "Equilibrium."* An imposing array of politicians and political scientists has urged that the term "balance of power" means what it seems to imply to the uninitiated layman: an exact equilibrium of power between two or more contending parties. Wrote Réal de Curban, for instance:

> Speaking generally, the rulers regard Europe as a balance in which the heaviest side subdues the other side and believe that in order to retain Europe in a solid and peaceful condition it is necessary to maintain between the principal parties this point of equilibrium, which, preventing either side of the balance from sinking, proves that they are on an exactly equal level. . . . The House of France and the House of Austria have been regarded as the scales of the balance of Europe. One or the other of these scales have received their support from England and Holland, which acted as the balancers.[4]

His distinguished compatriots, Duplessis-Mornay and Rohan, agreed with this postulation in important seventeenth-century pamphlets on the nature of the balance of power, recommending, by the way, that the Bourbons subdue the Habsburgs in order to achieve this much-vaunted equilibrium.[5] In Germany Konstantin Frantz, in 1859, urged the same definition and denounced the Vienna settlement for not having permitted Prussia and Austria to gain equality of power with the other three major states.[6] This juxtaposition of arguments gives considerable support to Professor Pollard's conclusion that the meaning of equilibrium should be taken with a great deal of reserve:

---

[3] U.P. despatch in *Los Angeles Times,* September 1940, cited in Alfred Vagts, "The Balance of Power: Growth of an Idea," *World Politics,* I (October 1948), p. 86.

[4] Réal de Curban, *La science du gouvernement,* Paris, 1764, VI, pp. 443ff.

[5] Henri de Rohan, *De l'intérest des princes et estats de la Chréstienté;* Duplessis-Mornay, *Sur les moyens de diminuer l'Espagnol;* both cited in A. de Stieglitz, *De l'équilibre politique, du légitimisme et du principe des nationalités,* Paris, 1893–1897, I, pp. 21ff. This work contains brief analyses of all the major pamphlets and treatises on the balance of power before 1800, and an analysis of the opinions of most writers on international law since Grotius.

[6] K. Krantz, *Untersuchungen über das Europäische Gleichgewicht,* cited in K. Jacob, "Die Chimäre des Gleichgewichts," *Archiv für Urkundenforschung,* VI (1918), pp. 359–60.

One has a shrewd suspicion that those who believe in a balance of power, do so because they think it is like a balance at the bank, something better than mere equality, an advantage which they possess. Unconsciously they have both meanings in their minds when they use the phrase. The equality-meaning commends it as propaganda; the advantage is a mental reservation for private use. Statesmen and publicists have sometimes betrayed an uneasy consciousness of the ambiguity and incautiously talked about a just, good, or proper balance of power, admitting thereby that a mere balance was not good enough; and an eighteenth century biographer of Cardinal Wolsey lets the cat out of the bag when he refers to "that grand rule, whereby the counsels of England should always be guided, of preserving the balance of power *in her hands.*" [7]

These formulations of the balance of power as a purely external and international equilibrium between contending states or blocs of states take no account of the possible existence of a similar relationship between contending groups within the state. Such an addition to the theory, however, was furnished by Harold Lasswell.[8] Lasswell speaks of a balancing of power rather than a "balance," since the attempt toward equilibrium can never be a wholly successful one, owing to various non-objective factors which interfere with scientific balancing. Lasswell rounds out the conventional presentation of the search for equilibrium by pointing to the domestic political process as offering a parallel spectacle. Furthermore, he establishes a relationship between the domestic and international balancing processes by describing liaison and support between various societal groups in one state, working with or against certain other groups in the opposing state or in the "balancer" state.

(3) *Balance meaning "Hegemony."* This analysis leads easily to the meaning of balance of power equivalent to hegemony. Examples from the literature are numerous and only two will be given: one from the eighteenth century and one modern. Thus, the Count of Hauterive, a pamphleteer for Napoleon I, argued that the balance of power demanded Napoleon's breaking the Treaty of Campo Formio, to enable France to bring about a confederation of the continent against England and in this way reduce the hegemonial superiority of Britain on the seas and, incidentally, establish the hegemony of France.[9] And Napoleon himself, in December of 1813, expressed his desire for a peace "based on the balance of rights and interests"! [10]

---

[7] A. F. Pollard, "The Balance of Power," *Journal of the British Institute on International Affairs, II* (1923), p. 59 (italics in original).

[8] H. D. Lasswell, *World Politics and Personal Insecurity*, New York, 1935, ch. III.

[9] Hauterive, *De l'état de la France à la fin de l'an VIII*, cited in Stern, *op. cit.*, p. 32.

[10] L. Donnadieu, *Essai sur la théorie d'équilibre*, Paris, 1900, p. 111.

Nicholas Spykman also understood the balance of power as implying a search for hegemony. His thesis—that all states seek a hegemonial position and therefore are in more or less continual conflict with each other—has for its natural corollary that this conflict, if it stops short of total war, has to result in some sort of equilibrium. This, however, can never be stable, because statesmen do not seek "balance" but hegemony:

> The truth of the matter is that states are interested only in a balance which is in their favor. Not an equilibrium, but a generous margin is their objective. There is no real security in being just as strong as a potential enemy; there is security only in being a little stronger. There is no possibility of action if one's strength is fully checked; there is a chance for a positive foreign policy only if there is a margin of force which can be freely used. Whatever the theory and the rationalization, the practical objective is the constant improvement of the state's own relative power position. The balance desired is the one which neutralizes other states, leaving the home state free to be the deciding force and the deciding voice.[11]

Should equilibrium be attained at one point, it would immediately be wiped out by the search for slight superiority.

(4) *Balance meaning "Stability" and "Peace."* A number of analysts have persisted in identifying what they have called the "balance of power" with the kind of idyllic world they desire to establish. They do not mean that the balance of power is a method for realizing peace and stability, but that peace and stability are identical with a balance of power. Typical of this approach is Francis Gould Leckie.[12] Leckie's tome is free from the usual recommendations of balancing the power of state A against state B, with states C and D holding the balance between them. He confines himself to recommending that feudal succession law be abolished and Europe go in for large-scale colonization in Africa and America, thus creating a "stable balance of power." At other times he does, however, lapse into more conventional meanings of the balance—an inconsistency unfortunately found all too frequently in these writings. Similarly, Olof Höijer tends to use the term in this sense, arguing that whenever the powers decided peace was desirable and should be maintained on a given issue—e.g., the London Conference of 1830–1839—a true balance of power existed, though to some analysts it might appear as if here the term "concert" might be more appropriate.[13]

(5) *Balance meaning "Instability" and "War."* Occasionally, by contrast, we find writers using the term "balance of power" as being

---

[11] N. Spykman, *America's Strategy in World Politics*, New York, 1942, pp. 21–25.

[12] F. G. Leckie, *An Historical Research into the Nature of the Balance of Power in Europe*, London, 1817, pp. 4, 242ff., 292, 303, 350ff.

[13] O. Höijer, *La théorie de l'équilibre et le droit des gens*, Paris, 1917, pp. 52–59.

synonymous with the very kind of world conditions they abhor: war, intervention, competition, and instability. Thus the Abbé de Pradt argued that the balance of power means war, while peace is identical with the settling of all issues on their moral, economic, and ethnographic merits.[14] This approach is also typical of that extraordinary eighteenth-century writer, Johann Gottlob Justi, of Cobden and Bright, of the elder Mirabeau, and of Kant, who called the balance of power a *Hirngespinst*.[15] It is true of de Pradt, however, that he tends to identify "balance of power" with power politics generally, a very common identification indeed.

(6) *Balance meaning "Power Politics" generally.* Edmund Waller once exclaimed:

> Heav'n that has plac'd this island to give law,
> To balance Europe and her states to awe.

"Balance" in this jingle comes to mean the exertion of power pure and simple. And as the anonymous author of *The Present State of Europe* (ed. of 1757) stated, "The struggle for the balance of power, in effect, is the struggle for power."[16] Power, politics of pure power, *Realpolitik*, and the balance of power are here merged into one concept, the concept that state survival in a competitive international world demands the use of power uninhibited by moral considerations. Lord Bolingbroke, in his fascinating *Letters on the Study and Use of History*, expressed similar ideas. He argued, in effect, that the concept of the balance of power was simply an eminently practical contrivance by which the states of Europe could determine when to combine in defensive alliances against whichever state seemed to be working for hegemony, to "endanger their liberties," i.e., to absorb them. Since this desire was thought to be inherent in either France or Austria at all times, the balance of power comes to mean any power combination to stop "aggression." [17]

This formulation of the term is commonly expanded to include all the factors making for state power, and especially military installations, military potentials, and strategic positions. State A's position in the balance of power is "good" after the construction of a given line of fortresses, or "bad" if that line is obliterated by boundary changes. The point need not be labored. Use of the term "balance of power" in this

---

14 D. de Pradt, *Du Congrès de Vienne*, Paris, 1815, 1, pp. 67–69, 75ff., 84ff., 95, 104.

15 A. Stern, "Das politische Gleichgewicht," *Archiv für Politik und Geschichte*, IV (1923), pp. 31–34.

16 L. Bucher, "Über politische Kunstausdrücke. II. Politisches Gleichgewicht," *Deutsch Revue*, XII (1887), pp. 336, 338.

17 Bolingbroke, *op. cit.*, pp. 249, 258, 266, 291; W. T. R. Fox, *The Super Powers*, New York, 1944, pp. 161ff.

very commonly employed meaning signifies the over-all power position of states in an international scene dominated by power politics. States are pictured as fighting for power, and only for power—for whatever reasons —and the struggle in or for a balance of power is equivalent to the power political process as a whole. Balance of power here is not to be understood as a refinement of the general process of power politics, but as being identical with it.

(7) *Balance as implying a "Universal Law of History."* John Bassett Moore once wrote that

> What is called the balance of power is merely a manifestation of the primitive instinct of "self-defense," which tends to produce combinations in all human affairs, national as well as international, and which so often manifests itself in aggression. Not only was the Civil War in the United States the result of a contest over the balance of power but the fact is notorious that certain sections of the country have, during past generations, constantly found themselves in general relations of mutual support because of a continuing common interest in a single question.[18]

The point of departure of these usages is again the assumed inevitable and natural struggle among states for preponderance, and the equally natural resistance to such attempts. Given these two considerations, it follows that as long as they continue in force, there is bound to be a "balance" of states seeking aggrandizement and states opposing that search. In Frederick L. Schuman's version of the balance, there is a tendency for all revisionist states to line up against the ones anxious to conserve given treaties, and in Professor Morgenthau's analysis the "imperialistic" states tend to line up against those defending the status quo, producing a balance in the process.[19] It is often inherent in this formulation to consider Europe as a great "confederation" unified by homogeneous morals and religion and tied together by international law. The balance of power struggle, equally, is part of that system and tends toward its preservation by avoiding the hegemony of a single member. And, of course, it is in this formulation that the analogy to the mechanical balance is most frequently found. As Rousseau put it:

> The nations of Europe form among themselves a tacit nation. . . . The actual system of Europe has precisely the degree of solidity which maintains it in a constant state of motion without upsetting it. The balance existing between the power of these diverse members of the European society is more the work of nature than of art. It

---

18 J. B. Moore, *International Law and Some Current Illusions,* New York, 1924, p. 310.

19 H. J. Morgenthau, *Politics Among Nations,* New York, 1948, passim; also F. L. Schuman, *International Politics,* New York, 1941, pp. 281ff.

maintains itself without effort, in such a manner that if it sinks on one side, it reestablishes itself very soon on the other. . . . This system of Europe is maintained by the constant vigilance which observes each disturbance of the balance of power.[20]

Ratzel gave this outlook a geographical orientation by arguing that during the "youth period" of states, a continuous process of expansion and contraction in a given *Raum* takes place, ending in a natural balance between the youthful contenders.[21] Whether in this version or without the benefit of geopolitical notions, the theory is a widely held one, corresponding roughly to what Professor Wright calls the "static balance of power." It was stated in detail by Donnadieu, who claimed that

"Destiny takes along him who consents and draws along him who refuses!" said Rabelais. The balance of power is one of these necessary forces; in other words, it is the expression of a law in the life of nations.[22]

In the hands of Albert Sorel the universal law version of the balance of power underwent further sophistication. In the first place, Sorel made no claim for the "universality" of the principle, but confined its application to the Europe of the *ancien régime*, during which time politics among sovereign rulers was held to be entirely free from ideological determinants. Furthermore, while he treated balance of power policies as "natural" and largely instinctive, he admitted nevertheless that the practice of balancing was the result of reasoned decisions based on the principle of *raison d'état*. Political action is the result of the desire for "power after power," greed and covetousness. Aggrandizement is the policy motive which holds the key to the understanding of international relations. And *raison d'état*

rules in all situations in which one feels oneself strong enough to follow with impunity the policies suggested by it. It inspires the same thoughts in Vienna and in Berlin. Young rulers and future ministers are taught about it. I read in the *Institutions politiques* of Bielfeld: "In whatever situation a state may find itself, the fundamental principle of *raison d'état* remains unchanged. This principle, accepted by all ancient and modern nations, is that the welfare of the people should always be the supreme law." "The great powers," wrote an Austrian diplomat in 1791, "must only conduct themselves in accordance with *raison d'état*. . . . Interest must win all varieties of resentment, however just they may be."

---

[20] J. J. Rousseau, *Extrait du project de paix perpetuelle de M. l'abbé de Saint-Pierre,* cited in Donnadieu, *op. cit.,* pp. 9–10.

[21] F. Ratzel, *Politische Geographie,* Munich, 1903, cited in Kaeber, *op. cit.,* p. 4.

[22] Donnadieu, *op. cit.,* p. xx. See also the description of Sir Eyre Crowe in the famous State Paper of 1907, in which the "universal law" approach predominates.

Something that can be taught to young rulers clearly is not instinctive. Yet Sorel holds that the very excesses of unrestrained and aggressive *raison d'état* doctrines result in their antithesis: moderation, willingness to forego expansion when the prize is small, and a willingness to abide by treaties if no undue sacrifice seems implied. Sorel sums up these restraints in the term "understood interest" (*intérêt bien entendu*), and maintains that if practiced they result in a balance of power:

> The converging of ambitions is the limit to aggrandizement. Since there are no more unclaimed territories in Europe, one state can only enrich itself at the expense of its neighbors. But all the powers agreed in not permitting a single one among them to rise above the others. He who pretends to the role of the lion must see his rivals ally themselves against him. Thus there arises among the great states a sort of society, through common concern: they want to preserve what they possess, gain in proportion to their commitment and forbid each of the associated states to lay down the law to the others.[23]

Balance of power thus comes to mean the instinctive antithesis to the reasoned thesis of *raison d'état*. Unconscious moderation, temporarily, restrains deliberate greed. A general dialectic of power relationships is thus created in which balances of power play a definite part. However, no balance is permanent and is subject to change at a moment's notice. It guarantees neither peace nor law; in fact, it implies war and its own destruction whenever a former counterweight state acquires sufficient power to challenge the very balance which it was called upon to maintain.

(8) *Balance as a "System" and "Guide" to policy-making.* In the formulation of the balance of power as a universal law of history there was an element of instinctive, unconscious, and unplanned behavior which would defy any analysis in terms of conscious human motivations. Statesmen were represented as acting in accordance with the prescriptions of the balance of power as if they were the unconscious pawns of some invisible hand, to borrow a phrase from Adam Smith. In the formulation of the balance of power as a system of political organization and guide to policy-making, emphasis is firmly thrown on conscious and deliberate behavior and decision-making.

What is the balance of power as a system and guide? A few short definitions might suggest tentative answers. Thus, Professor Fay says: "It means such a 'just equilibrium' in power among the members of the family of nations as will prevent any of them from becoming sufficiently strong to enforce its will upon the others."[24] Or, again, in the words of Professor Gooch, the balance of power is

---

[23] A. Sorel, *L'Europe et la Révolution Française*, Paris, 1908, I, pp. 19–20, 30–35.
[24] S. B. Fay, *Encyclopedia of the Social Sciences*, article on the balance of power, I, pp. 395–99.

the determination, partly conscious and partly instinctive, to resist by diplomacy or arms the growth of any European state at once so formidable and so actually or so potentially hostile as to threaten our liberties, the security of our shores, the safety of our commerce, or the integrity of our foreign possessions.[25]

Needless to add, this is a particularly British understanding of the balance of power, underlining once more the difficulty—if not the impossibility—of stating the theory in such terms that all governments could subscribe to it at any one time. Both definitions, however, are in very close agreement with some of the classical statements of the nature of the balance of power, understood as a guide to statesmen on how to prevent any other state from acquiring enough power to threaten their state in any way. Thus Fénelon, a moralist with considerable experience in policy-making, said:

> To hinder one's neighbor from becoming too strong is not to do harm; it is to guarantee one's self and one's neighbor from subjection; in a word it is to work for liberty, tranquility, and public safety. Because the aggrandizement of one nation beyond a certain limit changes the general system of all nations connected with it . . . the excessive aggrandizement of one may mean the ruin and subjection of all the other neighbors. . . . This attention to the maintenance of a kind of equality and equilibrium between neighboring states is what assures peace for all.[26]

Leagues to preserve the balance of power are then advocated by the learned bishop, but he is careful to specify that they may not be used for offensive purposes. Moreover, the balancing process was to assure that no state was eliminated from the map of Europe, no matter how much it might have to be "limited" to assure the security of its neighbors. No less a thinker than David Hume also understood the balance in this sense. He postulated, first, the existence of a multi-state system, dominated by competition and hostility among the members. Statesmen ever since Thucydides, said Hume, have made good policy when they checked in due time, through alliances and coalition wars, the growth of a state potentially able to absorb them all, and made bad policy when they ignored this guiding principle.[27] It is interesting to note in passing that Hume approved of the balance of power as a guide to "good" policy-making while opposing the mercantilist balance of trade theory, whereas most of

---

[25] G. P. Gooch. "European Diplomacy Before the War in the Light of the Archives," *International Affairs,* XVIII (1939), p. 78.

[26] Fay, *op. cit.,* p. 396. Stieglitz is to be counted among those in agreement with the guide-and-system theory.

[27] D. Hume, "On the Balance of Power," *Essays Moral, Political and Literary,* London, 1889, I, pp. 352–53.

the other opponents of mercantilism in his age—e.g., the elder Mirabeau
—attacked the balance of power as well.[28] This, in essence, is the formulation given by the majority of publicists to the theory of the balance of
power, considered only as a conscious guide to policy-making. It is stated
succinctly and incisively by Dupuis:

> The simple instinct of prudence would suffice to suggest the idea of
> the balance of power; the meditations of statesmen and the lessons of
> experience have transformed the instinct into a rule of conduct and
> raised the idea to the dignity of a principle. And in the role of
> political principle, the balance of power does not only have the
> advantage of reminding councils of the prudence confirmed by the
> teachings of the past; it has the merit of opening, during periods of
> crisis, a field for negotiation and if it cannot dictate the solutions of
> the conflict, it can prepare the setting for an alliance.[29]

The guide, therefore, merely tells statesmen to prevent the growth of any
state which, merely because of its power, is potentially able to absorb or
limit their own states. There is a good deal of diplomatic evidence to
support this contention, in that some leaders have actually made their
decision to go to war on just these grounds. The policy of William III in
going to war against France in 1701 is a case in point, as shown by the
King's speech to Parliament. And the text of the treaty of peace with
Spain, of July 18, 1713, gives expression to the same principle once more.[30]
In the anonymous *Free Britain*, attributed to none other than Sir Robert
Walpole himself, it is stated that

> Our liberty and our welfare depend on the greatest possible division
> and on a just balance of power among the princes of Europe: the
> British nation can and must maintain, and if need be, enclose the
> powers within the limits in which they find themselves today. She
> must make alliances with the princes who, for their own preserva-
> tion, are interested in preventing the aggrandizement of others
> intending the eventual attack upon Great Britain.[31]

So much for the guide. How does the balance of power then become a
system? It stands to reason that if all the states of Europe (or the world)

---

[28] For a study of the relationship between balance of trade and balance of power
theories, cf. K. Pribram, "Die Idee des Gleichgewichts in der älteren nationalökono-
mischen Theorie," *Zeitschrift für Volkswirtschaft, Sozialpolitik und Verwaltung,* XVII
(1908), pp. 1–28; see also Felix Gilbert, "The 'New Diplomacy' of the Eighteenth
Century," *World Politics,* IV (October 1951), pp. 1–38.

[29] C. Dupuis, *Le principe d'équilibre et le concert européen,* Paris, 1909, pp. 104–5.

[30] The text of the speech and of the treaty are cited in E. Nys, "La théorie de
l'équilibre européen," *Revue de droit international et de législation comparée,* XXV
(1893), pp. 47–49.

[31] *Ibid.,* pp. 55–56.

were to base their policies on the prescription of the balance of power, a "system" would come about in the sense that the least movement toward hegemony by one would immediately result in the coalition of the other states into an opposing alliance. The ever-present readiness to do just that and the constant vigilance declared necessary to prevent any one state's hegemony would in themselves produce this system of the balance of power. It is at this point that the theory grows more fanciful. The earlier doctrines, based on the guide-and-system idea, contented themselves with the so-called simple balance. The analogy is that of a pair of scales, and the supposition was that there would be only two major states, with their satellites, in the "system." The idea of a strict physical equilibrium—or slight hegemony—would then apply. Later doctrines, however, introduced the notion of the complex balance, or the analogy of the chandelier. More than two states, plus satellites, were postulated, and the necessity for preserving the freedom of all from the lust for dominance by any one was thought to involve the setting into motion of various weights and counterweights on all sides of the chandelier. It is this system which is closely related to the idea of the "balancer," introduced into the theory by British writers during the seventeenth century and a commonplace in the eighteenth. It implied, of course, the existence of powers sufficiently unconcerned by the merits of whatever the issue of the crisis was to be willing to "add their weight" to whichever side was the weaker, and thus prevent the possible victory—and implied hegemony—of the stronger. The balance of power considered as a guide was the reasoning process at the base of the system.[32]

MEANINGS AND THE INTENTIONS OF USERS

The foregoing analysis of verbal applications of the term "balance of power" has resulted in the demonstration of eight more or less distinct meanings and connotations which the term may carry. Of more significance to the application of balance of power terminology in the discussion of international affairs, however, is the use to which these meanings may be put. For just as the emphasis on collective security and Wilsonian liberalism in international relations tends to exclude discussion of the balance of power—either as irrelevant or else as undesirable—for essentially ideological reasons, so can the application of the term by its proponents vary with their ideological, theoretical, and practical preoccupations. An attempt will therefore be made to correlate the application of various usages of the term with the intentions of its users, at least insofar

---

[32] E. de Vattel, *Le doit des gens ou principes de la loi naturelle,* III, pt. 3, pars. 28, 33, 42, 43, 44, 47, 48, 49, 50; Sir R. Phillimore, *Commentaries upon International Law,* London, 1871, I, pp. 468–511. Examples of this usage are found most commonly in the writings of statesmen. They will be cited below.

as these intentions may be ascertained from the context of the writings and statements examined. Four areas of intention can thus be distinguished: a purely descriptive intent; a conscious or unconscious propagandistic intent; an intention of using the term as an analytical concept in the development of a theory of international relations; and an intention of using the term as a guide to foreign policy-making.

BALANCE OF POWER AS DESCRIPTION

Forswearing any theoretical or analytical purpose, writers commonly have recourse to the term "balance of power" in discussing international affairs. Current references to the balance of power by journalists and radio commentators most frequently fall into this category. And in most instances the meaning to be conveyed to the audience merely implies "distribution" of power, rather than "balance" in anything like the literal sense. The citations from Bolingbroke, the reference by C. L. Sulzberger, and the statement of Henry Wallace quoted above all meet these criteria. By using the term "balance of power" these writers were merely describing a particular distribution of power. Their intentions then did not carry them into any more ambitious realm.

On other occasions, however, the descriptive use of the term implies more than a mere distribution of power. It may then come to mean "equilibrium" or even "hegemony" or "preponderance" of power, still without implying more than a descriptive intent. It is quite possible that the political motivations of the particular user may make their entrance at this point. Thus Lisola, writing in the seventeenth century, saw in the balance of power the equilibrium between Habsburg and Bourbon interests. But he used his description to counsel war on France in order to maintain that very equilibrium. Austrian writers again invoked the balance of power principle during the wars of the Polish and Austrian Succession in order to secure allies against France and Prussia, represented as seeking hegemony. During the preceding century, French writers had used the equilibrium connotation of the term to demand war on Austria. And it might be pointed out parenthetically that during the Seven Years' War British officials frowned on the use of balance of power terms to justify British aid to Prussia, since it was Frederick II who had "disturbed the balance" with his attack on Austria.[33] In all these writings and statements the term "balance of power" is used and abused as a descriptive phrase, connoting the existence or non-existence of equilibrium and the actual or threatened hegemony of some state or alliance.

---

[33] For examples, see E. Kaeber, *Die Idee des Europäischen Gleichgewichts in der publizistischen Literatur vom 16. bis zur Mitte des 18. Jahrhunderts*, Berlin, 1906, pp. 44–47.

The same easy transition in meaning from "distribution" to "equilibrium" and finally to "hegemony" can sometimes be detected in contemporary references to the balance of power. These usages are rarely kept in their separate compartments. And, when the users' intentions go beyond that of mere description, clarity of thought and purpose may be seriously jeopardized.

BALANCE OF POWER AS PROPAGANDA AND "IDEOLOGY"

A precise understanding of the verbal meaning of the term "balance of power" becomes especially important when it is used as a propagandistic slogan or as an ideological phrase, in the Mannheimian sense. The meanings of "balance" as being identical with either "peace" or "war" fall into this category. Obviously, while it might be correct to speak of a state of balance or imbalance *implying* or *engendering* either war or peace, the balance as such cannot logically be equated with conditions which might arise as a consequence of the balance, i.e., war or peace. In the cases in which the authors employed it to mean "peace" or "war," "balance of power" then became no more than a convenient catchword to focus individual aspirations into a generally acceptable mold; and there can be no doubt that at certain times the concept of balance was an extremely popular one, whether it was used for policy-making or not. If used in a patently forced manner, the term becomes indistinguishable from plain propaganda. Of this particular usage some striking examples may be cited.

Thus, the anonymous author of the *Relative State of Great Britain in 1813* saw fit to make the phrase cover the total complex of his social, economic, moral, and political predilections:

> The French revolution being founded in the principle of depraving and reversing the human heart and feeling (as the American Republic is built upon frigid indifference and calculation of gain), it is not difficult to perceive how everything which tended to preserve the bond of sacredness of national contracts, and the reciprocity of benefits and engagements—how history, and memory itself, became objects of hatred and jealousy, and organized assault and hostility—and how the balance of power, in particular, opposed and threatened the views of France, which were to ruin and destroy everything, and the views of America to make profit and percentage upon the ruin and destruction of everything. Nor is it easy to pronounce a juster or more happy panegyric upon that system, than what evidently and immediately results from the forced and unnatural coalition of such powers as these (the very worst extremes of democracy and despotism), and the common interest their leaders conceive themselves to have discovered in extinguishing it.

The depraved ideology of France and the United States seemed here to be identified with the upsetting of the balance of power. And the re-estab-

lishment of the balance would be the means to end this deplorable state
of morality:

> For my part, I shall never blush to confess, that I am able to form no
> conception of any security in any peace that shall have no guaran-
> tees—any effectual guarantee, without a distribution and partition of
> force, adjusted by political alliance and combination—of any defense
> or protection for that distribution without a permanent and recog-
> nized system of public law, and a real or reputed balance of power
> amongst the several states it embraces.[34]

This treatment, then, identifies the balance of power with the kind of
world conditions, in their totality, which the author desires. The fact that
domestic, moral, and ideological factors are haphazardly mixed up with
considerations of pure power seems not to have made any difference.

This invocation of the balance of power was no more propagandistic,
however, than the use made of it by Friedrich Wilhelm II in the Declaration of Pillnitz, June 25, 1792, which constituted the manifesto of the
allied monarchs attacking France:

> There was no power interested in maintaining the European balance
> which could be indifferent when the Kingdom of France, which
> formed such a considerable weight in that great balance, was de-
> livered for long periods of time to internal agitation and to the
> horrors of disorder and anarchy, which, so to speak, have nullified
> its political existence.[35]

But the era of the Revolution and the Empire by no means provided
the only examples of this type of application. It enjoyed a renaissance
during World War I. Then F. J. Schmidt, for instance, asserted that
"Germany has the historical call to realize the idea of the balance of
power in all its territorial and maritime consequences." [36] And as detached a scholar as Friedrich Meinecke argued that the peace treaty
should establish a "new balance of power" instead of depriving Germany
of all her conquests.[37] Nor was the invocation of the balance by Louis
XIV much different when he used it to justify the accession of his grand-

---

[34] Anon., *Considerations on the Relative State of Great Britain in 1813*, London,
1813, pp. 3–4.

[35] Cited in Stieglitz, *op. cit.*, I p. 51. See also the facile use of the doctrine made by
Bonald in (1) justifying Napoleonic expansion and (2) asking for a lenient peace
in 1815 (Moulinié, *De Bonald*, Paris, 1915, pp. 390–97).

[36] F. J. Schmidt, in *Preussische Jahrbücher*, CLVIII (1914), pp. 1–15; also H. Oncken,
Das alte und das neue Mitteleuropa, Gotha, 1917, passim.

[37] F. Meinecke, *Probleme des Weltkriegs*, Munich, 1917, p. 134. In his important
Die Idee der Staatsräson in der neueren Geschichte, in which he claims to be analyzing the doctrine and philosophical meaning of the *raison d'état* idea completely
dispassionately, the same argument shows up rather prominently in the last chapter,
dressed up in terms of historical necessity.

son to the throne of Spain, nor Fleury's use of it when he called upon its absolving force to explain France's attack on the Pragmatic Sanction in 1740.[38]

It is apparent that in all these cases the balance of power was invoked in such a way as to serve as the justification for policies not *ipso facto* related to balancing anything. In some instances it was used to cloak ideological conflicts, in others to sanctify the search for hegemony over Europe, and in still others to "justify" the continued strength and size of a defeated state. The significance of this invocation, then, lies not in any theoretical belief, but in the fact that the users of the term felt so convinced of its popularity as to make its conversion into a symbol of proper policy propagandistically profitable.

Propaganda assumes the dishonest use of facts and the distortion of concepts devised on intellectually sincere grounds. It implies conscious and deliberate falsification.[39] Ideology, as defined by Mannheim, however, postulates belief in a set of symbols which, even though they may be "false" objectively, still characterize the total myth system of social groups and are essential to the spiritual cohesion of a ruling group which would lose its sense of control if it were conscious of the "real" state of affairs. It is therefore possible to raise the hypothesis that the balance of power may have served such "ideological" purposes. It may have been used to explain policies in terms of natural laws, in terms of moral rightness, or in terms of historical necessity if the symbol chosen to "put it over" was a sufficiently widely accepted one; indeed, if it was a symbol—even a metaphorical one—which the ruling groups themselves tended to accept. In this sense, the term "balance of power" would not serve a strictly propagandistic purpose, since the element of falsification yields to the element of self-deception.[40]

In a remarkable eighteenth-century essay the whole concept of the balance of power was criticized in these very terms. In his *Die Chimäre*

---

[38] Jacob, *op. cit.*, pp. 349, 351, 354–55.

[39] My conception of propaganda may be expressed in Leonard W. Doob's definition: "Intentional propaganda is a systematic attempt by an interested individual (or individuals) to control the attitudes of groups of individuals through the use of suggestion and, consequently, to control their actions" (*Propaganda,* New York, 1935, p. 89). It is clear that this postulation does not assume that the propagandist himself accepts the material or shares the attitudes he attempts to disseminate. I cannot accept the definition of propaganda offered by Doob in *Public Opinion and Propaganda* (New York, 1948, p. 240), since it seems almost indistinguishable from the more general concept of ideology.

[40] For a masterful analysis of this aspect of the balance of power, see Vagts, *op. cit.*, pp. 88–89, 100ff. I have explored the ideological significance of the concept with respect to European diplomacy in the 1830's in my doctoral dissertation, *Belgium and the Balance of Power,* Columbia University Library.

des Gleichgewichts von Europa, Justi concluded that the balance of
power theory is nothing but the ideological justification adopted by
statesmen eager to hide their real motives, motives usually described by
the term "aggression." As he put it:

> We regard the dependence of a free state upon another and more
> powerful state, the latter trying to prevent the former from adopting
> the proper measures for its happiness, as the greatest misfortune of a
> people, which should be avoided through the system of the balance of
> power. Yet such a coarse idea of universal monarchy which aims at
> reducing all states to provinces of its own state can scarcely ever be
> realized; however, the means proposed to avoid it are far more to be
> feared than the evil itself. If a balance of power were to exist in
> actuality then no slavery would be as hard, since each state would
> oppose every other state. Upon each new domestic arrangement, each
> internal improvement, the other states would be compelled to protest
> and interfere in order to prevent the first state from growing too
> powerful because of its domestic perfection. And the mutual depen-
> dence of such states would be far worse slavery than dependence
> upon one powerful neighbor. One state would object to one feature
> and the second to another feature of the internal improvement, and
> each state would concern itself more with the domestic business of its
> neighbors than with its own perfection.

All this, Justi argues, means that the whole concept is impossible.[41] And
again he urges what he considers the real *raison d'étre* of the usage, thus,
incidentally, coming perilously close to characterizing the balance of
power as a purely propagandistic device:

> When a state which has grown more powerful internally is attacked
> . . . in order to weaken it, such action is motivated least of all by
> the balance of power. This would be a war which is waged by the
> several states against the strong state for specific interests, and the
> rules of the balance of power will only be camouflage under which
> these interests are hidden. . . . States, like private persons, are
> guided by nothing but their private interests, real or imaginary, and
> they are far from being guided by a chimerical balance of power.
> Name one state which has participated in a war contrary to its
> interests or without a specific interest, only to maintain the balance
> of power.[42]

---

[41] J. H. G. von Justi, *Die Chimäre des Gleichgewichts von Europa,* Altona, 1758,
p. 60.

[42] *Ibid.,* p. 65. Albert Sorel's estimate of the invocation of balancing terminology
by statesmen is a similar one. Since he denies that balancing policies are deliberately
chosen by diplomats and since he urges that only the search for unilateral hegemony
motivates policy, he argues in fact that the use of the term by statesmen implies a
disguised hankering for superiority and no more (*op. cit.,* p. 34).

The distinction between the propagandistic and ideological uses is thus a tenuous one. The "camouflage" is ideological only if the actors on the international stage are themselves convinced, to some extent, of the identity of "private interest" with a general need for balancing power *qua* power.

BALANCE OF POWER AS ANALYTICAL CONCEPT

At the opposite pole of the propaganda-oriented application of the term "balance of power" lies the user's intention to employ the term as a tool of analysis. It is in this area of intentions that the term rose to the status of a theory of international relations during the eighteenth and nineteenth centuries, no less than it has in our own era. It is also true, however, that in this area as well as in the other fields of intentions analyzed so far not one but several of the verbal meanings of the term find application. Even as a tool of scholarly analysis the term has been used to mean "power politics," "equilibrium," "hegemony" and, finally, a "universal law" of state conduct.

"The basic principle of the balance of power," wrote Réal de Curban, "is incontestable: the power of one ruler, in the last analysis, is nothing but the ruin and diminution of that of his neighbors, and his power is nothing but the weakness of the others."[43] And in a Hobbesian state of nature which was presupposed to exist among sovereign states no other conclusion seemed possible. This reasoning has led numerous writers to equate the balance of power with power politics or *Realpolitik* generally. The struggle for self-preservation in the state of nature implies the formation of alliances and mutually antagonistic blocs which in turn make negotiations in "good faith" a contradiction in terms. Power politics are the only discernible pattern in which balancing is an inherent process. As such, it is not separate from but identical with competitive power struggles. Consequently, in dispassionate analyses of international affairs the "balance" of power carries no significance other than that usually associated with "power politics," unrefined by any conception of equilibrium or deliberate balancing measures.[44]

Furthermore, the concept of evenly balanced power, or "equilibrium," finds frequent application as a tool of analysis. In the preceding discussion the equilibrium concept found application merely as a descriptive phrase implying no generalized behavior pattern in international relations. In the present context the reverse is true. Lasswell, in speaking of

---

[43] Réal de Curban, *op. cit.,* VI, p. 442.

[44] See, e.g., H. N. Brailsford and G. Lowes Dickinson, as quoted in Georg Schwarzenberger, *Power Politics,* London, 1940, p. 123, and also the author's own comments, which also tend to equate power politics with power balance.

the "balancing process," for instance, assumes that under conditions of expected future violence—domestic as well as international—any increase in the coercion potential of one power unit will lead to a compensatory increase in the competing unit or units. Further increases on the part of one side will always bring corresponding increases on the part of its competitors, so that in effect a rough equality of power potential will always prevail, a factor which may make for either open conflict or induce fear of refraining from hostilities, depending on circumstances, the nature of the elites in question, and the accuracy of intelligence reports concerning the degree of "balancing." The analytical application of the equilibrium-meaning of the balance of power, in short, generalizes the basic assumption of the absence of international consensus and the consequent inherent presence of conflict into a pattern of balancing.

Carrying the equilibrium-meaning one step further results in the application of the balance of power concept as implying the search for hegemony. This application again finds its counterpart in the intentions of detached analysts striving for a generalized understanding of phenomena rather than for description. Spykman, as demonstrated above, clearly sets forth the assumptions of this approach. His argument is that the search for power by sovereign states is an end in itself, since conflict—actual or potential—is the only consistent pattern in relations between state units. While the search for power originally implied the desire for self-preservation, a generalized desire for power-seeking over a long period of time converts this process into an end in itself. On this level, the discussion of the balance of power is identical with power politics generally. As in the case of Lasswell's balancing process, however, the generalized process of competitive power-seeking must result in equilibrium if war is avoided—temporarily. But statesmen, as indicated above, seek a margin of safety in superiority of power and not in equality of power. Hence the search for equilibrium in effect is the search for hegemony, and the balance of power as an analytical concept becomes another term for the simultaneous search for preponderance of power by all the sovereign participants. No wonder Spykman exclaims that

> He who plays the balance of power can have no permanent friends. His devotion can be to no specific state but only to balanced power. The ally of today is the enemy of tomorrow. One of the charms of power politics is that it offers no opportunity to grow weary of one's friends. England's reputation as *perfide Albion* is the inevitable result of her preoccupation with the balance of power.[45]

In this refined analysis, the balance of power comes to be considered as a special case—either in its equilibrium or its hegemony connotation—in

---

[45] Spykman, *op. cit.*, pp. 103–4, 121.

the general pattern of power politics, though Spykman in the passage just cited again tends to use the two terms interchangeably.

The supreme attempt to use the balance of power as an analytical concept arises in the case of those writers who make the balance the essence of a theory of international relations. It is here that the balance attains the quality of a "law of history," as indeed Rousseau and Donnadieu implied by their very choice of words, and many contemporary writers by their emphasis on the "naturalness" of state behavior in accordance with the dictates of balanced power. The universal law connotation of the balance of power presupposes state conduct in no way different from the assumptions of Spykman and Lasswell. But Professors Morgenthau and Schuman, for instance, in giving the balance of power this extended meaning, go beyond the characterization of equilibrium and hegemony. They develop the thesis that it is inherent in the nature of a multi-state system based on sovereignty to engage in mutually hostile policies, for whatever motives. In this process the search for balanced power, the need to form blocs and counterblocs to prevent the feared attainment of hegemony by one or the other of the participants in the conflict is a natural, if not instinctive, choice of policy. A group of revisionist states always lines up against a group of states devoted to the maintenance of the status quo in such a way that approximate balance results. So general is this pattern that it attains the quality of a historical law. And the characteristic feature of this law is that it does not necessarily assume a conscious intention on the part of statesmen to "balance power with power" in a sense which would imply the official acceptance of a balance of power theory by governments. Statesmen, to be sure, may be consciously motivated by balancing notions. But, if they are not, the policies which they would most logically adopt would be those consistent with the balance of power. As Professor Morgenthau indicates, if they fail to do so, they do not make "logical" policy and thereby violate historically proven and generalized modes of conduct. The distinctive feature about the balance of power applied as a tool of analysis, then, is its possible separation from the motivations of governments.

Balance of Power as Prescription

While the analytical application of the term does not imply conscious acceptance of balancing rules by governments, there is a large body of thought—historical and contemporary—which does insist that the balance of power is—or should be—a guiding principle for decision-making on the part of governments. It is this application of the term which makes use of the meaning defined above as "guide-and-system." Once more international relations are pictured, in one version, as being in the Hobbesian state of nature, so that survival dictates the formation of alliances among those states committed to "preserving the balance" against the onslaught of the state(s) allegedly seeking world or regional domination or, as the eighteenth-century writers put it, "universal monarchy." In this sense, the balance is a conscious guide dictating the rules of survival. In another sense, however, the world (or Europe, in the earlier writing) is represented as a "system" of states tied together by mutual interdependence, common institutions, and a common system of law (the law of nations), and the search for hegemony of a single member of this "system" was then represented as an attack upon the whole organic unit.[46] The system was based on the continued independence of all members and their common will to resist the search for hegemony by any one of their number. The balance of power was inherent in the very system itself and also acted as a body of rules dictating the proper policies for preventing the attainment of hegemony, i.e., it acted as a "guide."

That Metternich subscribed in principle and in considerable detail to the theory of the balance of power as a guide to foreign policy-making is beyond any doubt. Consistent with his overall political philosophy of the value of historically sanctioned social and political traditions, of the need for preserving what the historical process had created and for protecting it against the fanaticism and stupidity of misguided men, i.e., the liberals, Metternich considered the balance of power as another of these time-hallowed doctrines, and as an international institution vital to the preservation of the total institutional status quo which he so cherished. As he wrote:

> Politics is the science of the life of the state, on its highest level. Since isolated states no longer exist . . . it is the society of states, this important condition of the contemporary world, which has to be watched carefully. Thus each state, in addition to its particular interests, has certain common interests, either with the totality of the other states or with certain groups among them. The great axioms of political science derive from the understanding of real political interests of all states; the guarantee for their existence rests in these general interests, whereas particular interests . . . only possess a relative and secondary value. History teaches that whenever the particular interests of one state are in contradiction with the general interest and whenever the latter is neglected or misunderstood, this condition . . . is to be regarded as exceptional and pathological. . . . The modern world is characterized, in distinction to the old world, by a tendency of states to approach one another and to enter into the bonds of society in some manner; so that the resulting bond

---

[46] The extreme example of this body of thought is represented by Wolff with his concept of the *civitas maxima* and the role of the balance of power in preventing its destruction (*Ius Gentium Methoda Scientifica Pertractantum*, pars. 642–43, 646, 651, *Classics of International Law*, no. 13, 1934). Also Pufendorf, *Ius Naturae et Gentium*. Book VIII, ch. 6, *ibid.*, no. 17, 1934.

rests on the same foundations as the great society which developed in the shadow of Christianity. This foundation consists of the command of the Book of Books: "Do not do unto others what you would not have others do unto you." Applying this basic rule of all human associations to the state, the result is reciprocity, politically speaking, and its effect is . . . : mutual respect and honest conduct. In the ancient world, politics sought pure isolation and practiced absolute egoism, without any control save common sense. . . . Modern history, however, shows us the application of the principle of solidarity and the balance of power offers us the drama of the unified efforts of several states in restraining the hegemony of a single state and limiting the expansion of its influence, and thus forcing it to return to public law.[47]

This formulation of international relations in general as necessary and close rapport between the states of Europe, which he regarded in the then customary manner as so many atoms in a universe held together by Christian moral rules and the dictates of international law, and of the balance of power as the *ad hoc* regulating mechanism of this system, is in almost all respects identical with the formulation of Ancillon, of Castlereagh, of Brougham, and of Gentz. Thus Ancillon, Prussian court chaplain in the 1820's, tutor to Frederick William IV, and State Secretary for Foreign Affairs from 1832 until 1835, argued:

All forces are similar to the nature of expanding bodies; thus, in the society of large states in which law does not enjoy an external guarantee, we take as our point of departure the possible or even probable misuse of force. What will be the result? Mutual distrust, fear and restlessness, always recurring and always effective. Each state can have no other maxims in its external relations than these: whoever can do us damage through an excessive balance of power in his favor, or through his geographical position, is our natural enemy, but whoever in view of his position and forces is able to harm our enemy, is our natural friend. These simple maxims which the need for self-preservation has given to man, are and have been at all times the anchors on which all of politics rests.[48]

Nor was Castlereagh's understanding of the balance of power much different, even though he indicated that "my real and only object was to

---

[47] Metternich, *Aus Metternichs Nachgelassenen Papieren*, Vienna, 1882, I, pp. 32ff., a section entitled, "Maxims on Which the Actions of My Political Career Have Been Based."

[48] Paul Haake, *J. P. F. Ancillon and Kronprinz Friedrich Wilhelm IV. von Preussen*, Munich, 1920, p. 40. Of Ancillon's own works, see his *Ueber den Geist der Staatsverfassungen und dessen Einfluss auf die Gesetzgebung*, Berlin, 1825, pp. 16–19, 314–14, 317–31, and *Tableau des révolutions du système de l'Europe*, Paris, 1806, IV, pp. 5–19.

create a permanent counterpoise to the power of France in peace as well as in war." The Concert of Europe through its regular conferences was merely to be the consultative mechanism whereby the *ad hoc* balance could be maintained through timely negotiations.[49] However, the likelihood of the guide-and-system version of the balance implying different "rules" for different states is here betrayed.

Gentz's theory of the balance of power was stated in his *Fragmente aus der neusten Geschichte des politischen Gleichgewichts in Europa* (1806), the purpose of which was to give the Austrian and British governments an excuse for unleashing a new war on Napoleon without having been attacked first. Gentz, it might be added, was in the pay of the British cabinet to produce writings of this type. He rejected the arguments that an exact equilibrium is impossible and that power cannot be measured as irrelevant to the system, since all the system requires is eternal vigilance that no state acquires enough power to overawe all of Europe.[50] Also, he thought that the certainty of a strong counterforce being mustered against the hegemony-seeker was a sufficient deterrent and that actual war would usually be unnecessary. And

> Only when one or the other state, with open violence, invented pretexts, or artificially concocted legal titles, undertakes enterprises which, directly or in their inevitable consequences, lead to the enslavement of its weaker neighbors, or to the constant endangering, gradual weakening and eventual demise of its stronger neighbors, only then there will come about a breach of the balance, according to the sound conceptions of the collective interest of a system of states; only then will the several states combine in order to prevent the hegemony of a single state, through a timely contrived counterweight.[51]

Yet Gentz opposed policies of partition and compensation as violating the true conservative character of the theory. Moreover, there could be no such thing as indifference to a given issue, since under the power rules all issues had to be of equal interest to all states in the system.[52] His comments on the right to intervene in the domestic affairs of other states are of the highest interest. Gentz urged that ideological distastes for internal changes elsewhere did not in themselves constitute a ground for balance of power intervention and war. But as soon as such changes had

---

[49] Sir Charles Webster, *British Diplomacy, 1813–1815,* London, 1921, pp. 62, 218; and Castlereagh's memorandum of October 30, 1814, for Alexander I, cited in Angeberg, *Les traités de Vienne,* Paris, 1864, pp. 399–401.

[50] Gentz, *Fragmente aus der neusten Geschichte des politischen Gleichgewichts in Europa,* St. Petersburg, 1806, pp. 1–8.

[51] *Ibid.,* pp. 10–14.

[52] *Ibid.,* ch. II.

the necessary consequence of upsetting the balance of power, i.e., as soon as the new ideology seemed to suggest the search for hegemony, then the right to intervene existed, as in 1793.[53]

The case of Lord Brougham is a fascinating one for the study of the theory of the balance of power. In his essay on "The Balance of Power," written in 1803, he urged that the balance was the only tenable theory of international relations. He defined it in the same terms as Gentz and Ancillon and added:

> Had it not been for that wholesome jealousy of rival neighbors, which modern politicians have learned to cherish, how many conquests and changes of dominion would have taken place, instead of wars, in which some lives were lost, not perhaps the most valuable in the community, and some superfluous millions were squandered! How many fair portions of the globe might have been deluged in blood, instead of some hundreds of sailors fighting harmlessly on the barren plains of the ocean, and some thousands of soldiers carrying on a scientific and regular and quiet system of warfare in countries set apart for the purpose, and resorted to as the arena where the disputes of nations might be determined.

The old argument of the tacit federation of Europe, the common system of law and morals, and the need for the regulating mechanism of the balance to keep one of the "federated" states from absorbing the others is restated in full.[54] The principle, as well as the detailed application of the theory in its guide-and-system form, were stated by the young Brougham in the classical manner, and with unsurpassed and brief lucidity:

> It is not then in the mere plan for forming offensive or defensive alliances; or in the principles of attacking a neighbor in order to weaken his power, before he has betrayed hostile views; or in the policy of defending a rival, in order to stay, in proper time, the progress of a common enemy; it is not in these simple maxims that the modern system consists. These are indeed the elements, the great and leading parts of the theory; they are the maxims dictated by the plainest and coarsest views of political expediency: but they do not form the whole system; nor does the knowledge of them . . . comprehend an acquaintance with the profounder and more subtle parts of modern policy. The grand and distinguishing feature of the balancing theory, is the systematic form to which it reduces those plain and obvious principles of national conduct; the perpetual attention to foreign affairs which it inculcates; the constant watchfulness which it prescribes over every movement in all parts of the system; the subjection in which it tends to place all national passions

---

[53] *Ibid.,* ch. IV.
[54] Brougham, *Works,* London, 1872, VIII, pp. 4–12.

and antipathies to the views of remote expediency; the unceasing care which it dictates of national concerns most remotely situated, and apparently unconnected with ourselves; the general union, which it has effected, of all the European powers in one connecting system—obeying certain laws and actuated, for the most part, by a common principle; in fine, as a consequence of the whole, the right of mutual inspection, now universally recognized among civilized states, in the appointment of public envoys and residents [sic]. This is the balancing theory.[55]

Intervention in domestic developments of other states, of course, is legal if the balance of power is really and truly threatened by these changes. The superiority of the balance to all ideological considerations, so plainly stated here, is especially striking. This principle he repeated in his "General Principles of Foreign Policy" (1843) in most emphatic terms:

But the mere circumstance of our preferring a democratic to an aristocratic or a monarchical to a republican scheme of government, can never afford any good ground for uniting with others who have the same preference, against a community or a league of states, whose views of national polity are of a contrary description.[56]

Hence the Holy Alliance—or the Western bloc against it after 1832—was not consistent with the rules of the balance. Not only is ideological intervention condemned, but Brougham urged that

it is the bounden duty of all rulers to discourage sentiments in their subjects leading to national enmities; and when a popular cry arises against any foreign people, a general clamor for war, there is no more sacred duty on the part of the government than to resist such a clamor and keep the peace in spite of it.[57]

In short, any manifestations of public opinion had to be rigorously excluded from policy-making under balancing rules, a sentiment heard more and more frequently in our present epoch.

Whether the balance of power is regarded merely as a set of rules to be applied to the preservation of the state or whether it is expanded into the defensive mechanism of some "system"—and by analogy the United Nations system might today be considered the successor to the European system postulated by the earlier writers—the rules laid down by Gentz and Brougham remain the same. The statesman who is anxious to preserve his state must have recourse to balancing principles in averting the hegemony of his rival. The perusal of the contemporary literature on this subject confirms this conclusion. George F. Kennan's *American Diplo-*

---

55 *Ibid.*, pp. 12–13, 33–38.
56 *Ibid.*, pp. 70–71, 77, 79–80, 80–83.
57 *Ibid.*, pp. 91–93, 100–2.

macy is merely the latest and best-known example of the continuing importance ascribed to balancing rules in international relations. And the fact that the examples cited concerned statesmen conscious of the balance as a motivating force underlines the possible importance of the concept as prescription.

INTENTIONS AND THEIR SIGNIFICANCE TO A THEORY OF INTERNATIONAL RELATIONS

The breakdown of the "balance of power" phrase into a series of eight distinct verbal meanings has now been categorized into four possible applications which these meanings have found in political literature, and perhaps in diplomacy as well. It is not to be inferred that in these classifications there is one which alone is of general value and applicability to the analysis of international relations. This problem is inherent in the inevitably somewhat arbitrary basis of distinction adopted in the foregoing analysis. It is not claimed, of course, that the term "balance of power," in any of its eight possible connotations, is used as propaganda or description in the intentions of any one writer to the exclusion of other possible intended applications. The four categories here established, in short, cannot be regarded as mutually exclusive even in the intentions of the same writer, analyst, commentator, or statesman.[58] A basic barrier in communication is created by this apparently facile interchangeability of meanings and intentions. A theoretical analysis, therefore, cannot proceed on the basis of identifying one writer with one meaning or one category of intentions. Each meaning and intention must be considered separately in terms of the immediate context, even though meanings and intentions may change as the context changes, either in compliance with the user's overall scheme or in defiance of his thought. Nevertheless, it is clear that not all of these categories are of equal relevance to the effort to construct a theory of international relations. The effort to separate the theoretically meaningful categories from those which, while important in the total context of international relations, are based on inadequate logical or conceptual assumptions is one on which a few general observations must be made.

Thus, the theoretical significance of the descriptive intention may be open to several alternative interpretations. It may well be argued that as long as the distribution of power, in general terms, in terms of equilibrium or lack of equilibrium, i.e., the implied hegemony of one camp, is

---

58 This difficulty may be demonstrated by the perhaps unconscious ease with which some modern writers present a balance of power picture as *description* and then readily switch to a *prescriptive* continuation of their discussion, despite the semantic and logical problems implied in this procedure.

merely discussed with the intention of *describing* an objective state of affairs, there can be no question of theoretical implications. A reference to a "balance" of power in such a context would carry no more general meaning than the application of such terminology to a summary of the number of convention delegates pledged to a given presidential aspirant. And, in fact, it is precisely in such situations that the term is finding a new lease on life.

It can be argued, however, that even the meaning of "distribution" and "equilibrium" in an ordinarily descriptive sense may carry with it theoretical implications. If it is desired to establish the general historical conditions to which the rise of certain institutions can be attributed, for instance, this meaning of "balance" may acquire a theoretical significance beyond the scope indicated above. Thus, it may be suggested that modern international law owes its growth to a "balance" of power—in the sense of "distribution" avoiding "hegemony"—during its crucial decades and that without such a "balance" it could not have developed at all, since the strongest state(s) would have had no interest in its growth.[59] It is in situations such as these that the user's context acquires tremendous significance, since it may well be that in applying the term in this sense what was intended was not description, but analysis or a correlation between the balance as prescription and its historical consequences.

Applications of balance of power terminology for propagandistic or self-deceptive purposes similarly may be interpreted in several ways. *A priori*, such application could not carry with it a significance to a general theory of international relations, since it is used for intellectually dishonest purposes. It is intended for dissimulation, not clarification, and certainly not as a consistent guide to action. Furthermore, the meanings of "balance" subsumed in this category are in themselves open to considerable logical and conceptual doubts. The usage of the term as connoting peace and stability or war and instability, again, is largely descriptive, or else a pure value judgment of no theoretical significance whatever. The fact that some writers have indulged in this loose terminology merely indicates that the term "balance of power" had tended to become a catch-all to accommodate whatever policies writers wanted to recommend. The frankly propagandistic use of the term is thus merely an extreme species of the same genus.

To a general theory of politics based on Mannheimian concepts of ideology, however, even this category might prove to be of relevance. Should the theory be oriented toward the study of value systems— avowed and tacit—and toward the factors of manipulation of external and internal forces, this area of intentions might acquire some impor-

---

[59] I am indebted for this suggestion to Professor Oliver J. Lissitzyn.

tance. What appears to the student of motivations as dishonesty and self-deception might assume far greater causative significance to a student of psychopathology in international relations.

In the area of concept, of course, the balance of power acquires immediate theoretical significance, deservedly or otherwise. It is deliberately chosen as the major support of a widely accepted method of analyzing intergroup relations. But even here some caution with respect to meanings is necessary. Thus, the usage which speaks of the balance of power in terms indistinguishable from power politics generally should not be given separate consideration, since the application of the phrase here is really misplaced in terms of logical consistency as well as of historical tradition. It would be absolutely correct to consider the balance of power as a refinement of a general system of power politics, should one be postulated, as indeed writers such as Dupuis, Donnadieu, Gentz, and Brougham did consider it. But the essential distinction between policies of power for the sake of power—unrefined by any thought of balancing some state's power with some other state's—and the balance of power as defined by Fay, Gooch, and Fénelon should still be maintained. History is full of examples of plain power policies, unqualified by balance notions.

It appears, however, that a theory of international relations which does not insist on the necessity of demonstrating general laws of conduct in terms of actual motivations leaves itself open to attack on grounds of lack of comprehensiveness. And it is this factor which has been responsible for a great deal of the skepticism with which the universal law version of the balance of power as an analytical concept has been treated ever since Justi. The treatment of the balance of power as prescription, in the sense of the guide-and-system connotation, therefore, acquires its theoretical significance in this context. The balancing of power is considered as the primary motivation of governments in this approach and, as Brougham clearly showed, the realization of this motivation assumes the subordination of all other possible policy motivations in international politics, at least insofar as they are inconsistent with the demands of balanced power. To a theory of international relations which relies on demonstrable motivations among policy-makers, therefore, the balance of power as prescription must be a fundamental point of departure.

SECTION THREE: Alliances

38. ALIGNMENTS AND REALIGNMENTS

George Liska

ALLIANCES PERFORM their several functions through movement as much as through being. The main movements are alignment and realignment. The actor making decisions about alignment seeks to maintain or improve his position in the global, regional, or domestic arena. Alignments are always instrumental in structuring the state system, sometimes in transforming it. While "system" denotes interaction of several independent actors, "structure" refers here to the number and configuration of greater and lesser powers and conflicts.

CONFLICTS AND POWERS

When they are sufficiently intense, and security is the chief concern, conflicts are the primary determinants of alignments. Alliances are against, and only derivatively for, someone or something. The sense of community may consolidate alliances; it rarely brings them about. When community feeling is sufficiently strong, it commonly seeks other institutional forms of expression. Cooperation in alliances is in large part the consequence of conflicts with adversaries and may submerge only temporarily the conflicts among allies.

The dynamics of alignment is most apparent when two major core-powers are surrounded by lesser allies. On the face of it, the core-powers have attracted the lesser countries into alliance; in fact, superior power does not attract. The weaker state naturally fears that its identity will be abridged by aligning with a more powerful one; and the strong state, too,

From *Nations in Alliance: The Limits of Interdependence* by George Liska (Baltimore: 1962), pp. 12–24. Reprinted by permission of the Johns Hopkins University Press.

GEORGE LISKA (1922–   ) Professor of Political Science, Johns Hopkins University. His other books include *Alliances and the Third World,* (Baltimore: Johns Hopkins Press, 1968); *Europe Ascendant,* (Baltimore: Johns Hopkins Press, 1964); *The Greater Maghreb: From Independence to Unity?* (Washington: Washington Center for Foreign Policy Research, 1963).

will often shun association with the weak for fear of overextending its commitments and resources. Movement toward alignment sets in only when another state intervenes as a threat. The weaker state rallies then to one stronger power as a reaction against the threat from another strong power. The stronger state assumes the role of a protective ally, interested mainly in keeping the resources of the potential victim out of the adversary's control.

Apparent attraction of greater power is thus a consequence of revulsion; and the addition of a lesser ally's power is often incidental to denying this power to the adversary. For such tendencies and objectives to result in alignment, the lesser state must be accessible to the potential ally directly or at least indirectly. "Indirect" access may mean no more than the stronger power's capacity to exert political or military pressure on the threatening state so as to relieve the latter's pressure against the smaller state.

Geographically conditioned responses to superior power are apt to be modified by cultural, ideological, and economic pulls. Their relative weight in determining alignments varies from case to case. A weaker power will be commonly anxious to seek alignment with geographically remoter powers; the tendency will be only intensified if it has cultural differences with the more powerful neighbor. Among such differences are those dividing Catholic, Westernized Poland from Orthodox, and now Communist, Russia in Europe; and the kind of cultural differences that exist between Latin American states and the United States in the Western Hemisphere. The natural ally of Poland was historically France, while Britain, Germany, and most recently the Soviet Union "attracted" Latin American countries, such as Argentina and Cuba, whenever they revolted against American predominance. Where they exist, ideological affinities among regimes are merely the immediate impetus to such alignments or their consequence. Conversely, cultural affinity can dampen the flight away from superior power, as shown in different attitudes of Canada and Mexico toward the United States and of Bulgaria and Poland toward Russia.

The most direct attraction that stronger states hold for the weaker is probably in response to trade and economic needs. The attraction is only provisional, however, until the resentment of economic dependence and an opportunity to draw on alternative sources and outlets set off a political reaction. At different times, Japan has responded differently to the economic attraction of the West and of China. And even good-neighborly Canada, which has had little reason to shy away from the United States on grounds of national security for some time, has been looking across the Atlantic in reaction against American cultural and economic penetration. Much stronger was the instinct of some of the weaker Central-Eastern European countries pulling away from Germany, and more recently from

Soviet Russia, whenever the main Western powers of the moment were able and willing to supply economic outlets, to keep open politico-military access, and to hinder the local power from employing coercion for the purpose of forestalling permanently the lesser countries' flight into a countervailing alignment.

As a result of various kinds of conflicts which occur on the global, regional, and domestic planes, the interacting system of states tends to be polarized by alliances. The conflicts which primarily determine alignment are not always the dominant ones. A "dominant" conflict is one which would raise the winner or winners to preponderance and might even transform the relevant system's prevailing political culture and structure.

The East-West struggle is not the only globally dominant conflict which polarized the modern state system around two core-powers. Another was the conflict between the Bourbons and the Habsburgs over preponderance in the then "global" European system.

At the peak of the conflict, the rivalry pitting France against Spain and Austria was the dominant one, rather than the religious-ideological contest between Protestantism and Catholicism. The conflict produced religiously mixed alliances, notably in the case of the Franco-Swedish alliance in the Thirty Years' War; and the religiously mixed character of the alliances in turn made it virtually impossible for either of the competing churches to emerge victorious and supervise the reorganization of the state system. A Catholic triumph could have come about only in the unlikely case of France's parting with ascendant Sweden and joining the Habsburg powers in an all-Catholic coalition; and a Protestant victory would have required Sweden to defeat the Catholic powers with the aid of Protestants in the North of Europe—chiefly Denmark, Saxony, and Brandenburg. When free to choose, however, the lesser Protestant powers shunned a Swedish alliance out of a sense of regional rivalry and fear of domination, much as Catholic Bavaria reacted against neighboring, though also Catholic, France.[1]

Communist Yugoslavia's split with the Soviet Union is only a recent

---

[1] A good discussion of the Thirty Years' War may be found in G. Pagès, *La guerre de trente ans* (1939); see also C. V. Wedgwood, *The Thirty Years' War* (1938). On the "diplomatic revolution" I have consulted chiefly R. Waddington, *Louis XIV et le renversement des alliances: préliminaires de la Guerre de Sept Ans 1754-1756* (1896); D. B. Horn, *Sir Charles Hanbury Williams and European Diplomacy 1747-1758* (1930), Part II; Sir R. Lodge, *Great Britain and Prussia in the Eighteenth Century* (1923), Chaps. 3, 4; W. L. Dorn, *Competition for Empire 1740-1763* (1940). On "international system," see M. A. Kaplan, *System and Process in International Politics* (1957), Part I; also L. Binder, "The Middle East as a Subordinate International System," *World Politics* (April, 1958), pp. 408-29.

instance of the pattern. The dominant conflict tends to determine the alignment policy of the major protagonists; within the resulting conditions other states consult their particular regional and domestic interests and tend to downgrade the major powers' ideological concerns as well as their programs for a future order.

When one dominant conflict divides two powers or groups of powers, alliances merely formalize a built-in polarity; they have a more creative role when two major conflicts divide three or more powers. Two such conflicts were gradually supplanting the Bourbon-Habsburg rivalry in European diplomacy of the mid-eighteenth century (whereas a second, North-South, issue was merely being added to the unresolved East-West conflict in the second half of the twentieth century). One was between France and Britain over the balance of trade and empire overseas; another occurred between Austria and Prussia over the balance of power in the Germanic middle of Europe. The two sets of adversaries gravitated spontaneously into opposing alliances of two major powers in both possible combinations. The so-called old system, still rooted in the waning Austro-French enmity, associated France with Prussia and Austria with Britain; following the diplomatic revolution of 1756, Britain aligned with Prussia and France with Austria.

Alliance policy matters most when none of several conflicts is manifestly dominant in a multipolar system of several powers. This was the case in Europe during the period 1815–1870 and, to a diminishing extent, after 1870. The Franco-German conflict was then emerging as a potentially dominant one, owing to the assumption that another German triumph over France would have seriously affected the European balance. Different alliance policies may then forestall a polarization of the state system, retard it, or virtually bring it about.

In an ideal multipolar system, each power should be able to align with any other power, depending on the particular issue. In fact, each state has some alliance handicap in the sense of being unwilling or unable to align with one or more states with which its relations are relatively most hostile. In that respect a multipolar system is but a set of partial, alternately activated bipolarities. If all states have alliance handicaps, alliance making will be impeded for fear that an initial move toward alignment might start polarizing the system into an unpredictable and dangerous configuration. A power may nonetheless set off the chain reaction of alliance making in order to forestall the most dreaded pattern of division of the system. It will do so when it believes its alliance handicap to be greater than that of other states.

The Austro-German alliance of 1879, which initiated the polarization of the state system preceding World War I, can be interpreted in these terms. As a German alliance with France was practically impossible, and French participation in any anti-German coalition certain, Germany apparently had to make sure of Austria-Hungary.[2] The thesis of a necessary alliance with Vienna made the feared Franco-Russian alliance inevitable, when later statesmen in Berlin spurned Bismarck's finesse with Russia, lacked his firmness with Austria, and departed from his noncommittal friendship with Britain. Once Germany severed her tie with Russia and challenged Britain (unattainable as ally) to a naval race, hitherto impossible alignments appeared necessary and, therefore, feasible. France's isolation vanished as Russia began to fear hers and as the splendor went out of Britain's. The progression toward polarization was complete when the necessary alliances became dogmatic ones, their conservation being placed over and above other concerns.

If one takes a different view of the map of conflicts in post–1871 Europe, the first—Austro-German—alliance appears somewhat less necessary. The alliance handicap of Germany was not at all unique or altogether novel. Before 1870, a Franco-Prussian alliance was already highly unlikely; it could occur only on a non-German issue, mainly in Italy, somewhat as a Franco-Austrian alliance could be brought about only on a Near Eastern issue. Moreover, the impossibility of a Franco-German alliance after 1871 constituted a handicap for France, too. The handicap was a lesser one since France was now a defensive power and could hope for assistance against Germany in the interest of the European equilibrium even without prior commitments; but the overall handicap was also a greater one because, unlike Germany, France had other rivalries to worry about. She had a colonial conflict with Great Britain, in particular over Egypt, and an ideological one with Russia over "revolution" and Russian revolutionaries in Paris. France may have been willing to pay a high price for an anti-German coalition; but no one was ready to exact that price before Germany applied pressure to other powers, as it were on France's behalf.

These other powers were not free of handicaps either. Britain had two conflicts, one with France and another with Russia over Asia; and Russia, too, had a second conflict—with Austria-Hungary over the Balkans. Only Germany had a single one. The issue of Alsace-Lorraine was without question the most serious; but conflicts over Egypt, Constantinople, the Balkan principalities, India, and China made other combinations as impractical as a Franco-German alliance was "impossible."

---

[2] The interpretation is essentially Bismarck's. An alternative and possibly supplementary interpretation would stress Germany's interest in stabilizing Austria-Hungary internally. For Bismarck's exchanges on the subject with the Emperor, see *Die Grosse Politik der europäischen Kabinette 1871–1914*, Vol. III, Nos. 455 ff., pp. 26 ff. A recent discussion of the historical background is to be found in W. E. Mosse, *The European Powers and the German Question 1848–1871* (1958).

A dominant conflict affects the global system of a given time in its entirety; but lesser conflicts are often more immediately significant in filling out the complete pattern of alignments. We have noted the way lesser states seek protection against great regional powers. Conflicts among the lesser states themselves may contravene the resulting alignment tendencies, for some of them at least, as local adversaries seek great-power support by aligning on different sides of the larger, dominant conflict.

One great power can rarely have as allies both parties to a local conflict. To be sure, both Greece and Turkey have remained in the Atlantic Alliance despite the conflict over Cyprus, while both Poland and Czechoslovakia are aligned in the Warsaw Pact, despite similar disputes. In the late 1930's, Yugoslavia moved toward Germany for a safeguard against Germany's ally, Italy, when France had failed to serve as a check on both. But such exceptions from the rule merely mean that the free play of alignments has been in abeyance due to the overwhelming challenge or sheer coercion from one power.

Otherwise, the more natural distribution of local rivals will assert itself. Prussia's quest for immunity from Russia by moving toward Russia's ally, Britain, in 1756, only drove Russia to Prussia's enemy, Austria, as part of the so-called diplomatic revolution. And Denmark and Sweden could no more be expected to appear on the same side of a larger conflict in the seventeenth century than Serbia and Bulgaria could before World War I or Czechoslovakia and Hungary before World War II. Following the latter war, non-alignment with an antagonistic bias rather than outright counter-alignment has been an Egypt's or an India's response to the alignment of a local rival in the East-West struggle.

When two or more states in a particular region join different sides of a global conflict, the region itself becomes an integral part of the global system, and the global system itself becomes somewhat more of a unified system by way of local divisions. In the late fifteenth century, competitive alliances of the Italian city-states with barely consolidated France and Spain integrated the previously self-contained Italian system into a larger Western European system; and the system became fully European when a like process subsequently brought in the so-called Northern powers. A genuine world system took shape as local sovereignties and conflicting alignments spread into the Southeast of Europe and on to the Far East, Afro-Asian Middle East, and the Asian and African South. The southern part of the Western Hemisphere may actually be the last region to become more than fitfully a part of world politics in this sense and manner.

A regional system as such can be said to consist of states which are parties to local conflicts that determine alignments within and beyond the region. In addition to local states, a regional system can then comprise outside powers that are "present" as allies on a local issue. Thus the Middle East, notoriously difficult to define in geographic terms, as a regional system consists of local and outside parties to the Arab-Israeli and the inter-Arab conflicts; the United States and the Soviet Union have been more intimately involved in it than Turkey, Pakistan, or, so far, Morocco. And the Middle East as a regional system was most integrally a part of the global system when Iraq pre-empted membership in the West-sponsored Baghdad Pact and a hostile Egypt responded with a tactical alignment with the Soviet Union. Matters were roughly similar in South Asia in regard to the Indian-Pakistani conflict prior to the emergence of the Sino-Indian conflict over frontier regions. This latter conflict between two major powers may develop into a regionally dominant conflict, re-shaping the region's structure and alignment politics, in a way that the Kashmir issue never could.

When analyzed in these terms, domestic systems have much in common with regional ones. As political development progresses, however, a uni-fying national authority tends to make the domestic system separate and distinct from the international one. Factions cease to act directly as "allies" of outside powers; the state alone has a foreign policy. Domestic interest groups can only try to influence the government's foreign policy and act internationally as agents of the sovereign authority, if at all. Only insofar as the central authority does not realize the ideal of foreign policy monopoly, is the domestic system an integral part of the interna-tional system. To a like extent, the domestic system is then defined by parties to internal conflicts—domestic factions and the internally present outside forces capable of influencing local events. The domestic system is fully part of the international system when two or more factions are aligned with outside actors in ways which relate internal and external conflicts. If only one faction so involves itself, the competing groups will seek to neutralize the activist group; if they are not strong enough to do so, they themselves will be forced into countervailing alignments. A coun-try's international alignment may, therefore, be determined by the ruling group's response to internal conflicts and differ from a homogeneous body politic's response to a threat from other more or less proximate and powerful states.

Domestic conflicts influence alignments in various degrees. The At-lantic Alliance was primarily the result of international security con-cerns; internal challenges of local Communist parties merely confirmed the commitment of non-Communist groups to the alliance. The opposite is the case in civil-warlike situations. They tend to revive feudal and tribal patterns of group conflict and invalidate the reason-of-state model in foreign policy making. In 1960, Laos as a domestic system was defined by the conflict between the Pathet Lao and the rightist groups, each allied to one great-power side in the Cold War, with the neutralist government maneuvering between the two groups in an attempt to recover foreign policy monopoly on a compromise basis. At any one time the country's orientation depended on the balance of internal forces, only augmented by external threats and pressures.

The alignment of groups with outside powers can be a strictly tactical one—to gain immediate support—or it may express ideological or ethnic affinities. The Catholic-Huguenot cleavage in France coincided with the conflict of France with Protestant powers, notably England, and aligned the Huguenots with the English. On the other hand, the feudal lords of the Fronde, rebelling against the French monarchy, concluded formal treaties of alliance with autocratic Spain in the name of constitutional liberties. Similarly, just before the French Revolution, the democratic party in the United Provinces was allied to the *ancien régime* against the Dutch monarchical party's alliance with oligarchical England; only the victory of the Orangists restored the United Provinces from a geopolitically unnatural alliance with France to the traditional, protective alliance with Britain.[3]

.   .   .

Lesser actors often seek their advantage in the rivalries among greater powers. When the configuration of power and geography permits choices, the major powers themselves often have to manage regional or domestic conflicts if they are to draw out of them a favorable pattern of global alignment. Like other alliance makers and breakers, the Soviets mediated or sought otherwise to moderate territorial disputes between actual or potential lesser allies—thus between Czechoslovakia and Poland and, more recently, Communist China and nonaligned India—while abetting other territorial conflicts—thus India's with an ally of the West, Pakistan. The eagerness of a major power to pacify will be least when lines of the regional conflict and the global one coincide. Neither of the superpowers was particularly anxious to mitigate the latent dispute between West Germany and Poland over the latter's western frontier; the attitudes would change if and when a settlement could be used to detach the local adversary of one or the other power's lesser ally from the opposing combination without at the same time reducing the ally's interest in *his* alliance with the pacifier. And only when great-power contestants can expect to do no better than divide local rivals between themselves without a net advantage for either—or when local rivals themselves know how to manage their differences without great-power involvement—is there a basis for neutralizing a region or a country as an arena of alignment politics.

---

[3] A. Cobban, *Ambassadors and Secret Agents: The Diplomacy of the First Earl of Malmesbury at the Hague* (1954), *passim.*

39. MEASURING INTERNATIONAL ALIGNMENT

Henry Teune and Sig Synnestvedt

ALIGNMENT, as the term is often used, denotes some aggregative stance of a country with respect to at least one other country. The degree of alignment has to be inferred from a set of acts, including all decisions made by foreign policy officials. The variety of such acts—for example, signing treaties, declaring war, arranging for cultural exchanges—has to be evaluated as to the relative bearing of each upon the general alignment of one nation with another. Ideally, weightings could be developed for clusters of countries, or perhaps for each country. In this study, however, we initially assumed an equal weight for each factor. By assessing how well one indicator relates to others, weights, even if crude, could be estimated.

Several indicators may reveal different aspects of the same alignment factor. The discovery of interrelationships between several presumably valid indicators is one of the ultimate goals of this research. An overall index of alignment might be developed on the basis of the established relationships among the various indicators. When such an index is developed, the degree of alignment can be explained by other variables.

In our preliminary discussions concerning the scope of this project we debated the question as to whether in the mid-1960's the world should be viewed as a bipolar one. Nationalism splits the communist bloc, and Gaullism divides the NATO alliance. New poles of attraction have emerged in Peking and Paris, if not in Belgrade, Cairo, Djakarta, Brasilia and elsewhere. The uncommitted nations appear to have an increasing number of options for alignment. Some of the participants in the project as well as outside consultants argued that the study should take full account of the increasingly multipolar nature of the world. Well taken as was their argument, we decided nonetheless to assume the existence of a two-pole world. This decision seemed warranted by three considerations: First, a multipolar study would have vastly magnified the difficulty of collecting and analyzing the data. Furthermore, there was no assurance that so complex an undertaking would yield any worthwhile

From *ORBIS,* a quarterly journal of world affairs published by the Foreign Policy Research Institute of the University of Pennsylvania (Spring 1965) 175–177; 180–181; 184–189. Reprinted by permission of the Trustees of the University of Pennsylvania. Footnotes have been renumbered to appear in consecutive order.

HENRY TEUNE (1936–   ) Associate Professor of Political Science, Vice Dean, Graduate School of Arts and Sciences, University of Pennsylvania.

SIG SYNNESTVEDT (1925–   ) Associate Professor of History, State University of New York, Brockport.

results. Second, the assumption of the bipolar world seemed justified by the fact that Moscow and Washington have been the two key power centers throughout the history of the Cold War. Third, this study is limited to an epoch that largely antedates the splits in the two blocs.

INDICATORS OF ALIGNMENT

The following variables were developed as candidates for indications of alignment: (1) military alliances, (2) visits by heads of state and of government, (3) important visitors other than heads of state and of government, (4) protests and expulsions of diplomatic personnel, (5) diplomatic recognition of East Germany, (6) total recognition of controversial noncommunist countries, (7) educational and cultural exchanges, (8) U.S. or USSR military presence, (9) anti-U.S. or USSR riots, (10) number of U.S. government or communist bloc technicians, (11) U.S. military aid, 1954–1961, (12) U.S. and USSR economic aid, 1954–1962, (13) voting records in the United Nations on issues on which the U.S. and the USSR took opposite sides, and (14) nonmilitary treaties and agreements with the U.S. and the U.S.S.R.[1]

A set of international alignment indicators of special interest concerned diplomatic recognition patterns toward certain nations. Twelve controversial countries were selected, and inquiries were addressed to the Embassy in Washington or Ministry of Foreign Affairs of these twelve countries in order to ascertain which nations recognized them. The select list was made up of all the split countries, China, Germany, Korea and Vietnam, in addition to Cuba, Yugoslavia, Israel and South Africa. The direction of alignment was determined from the known positions of the governments. The self-identified communist governments were treated as such, and the rest as noncommunists.[2]

. . .

The four sets of indicators which seem best to establish objective measures of alignment are: (1) military commitments, (2) votes in the

---

[1] Other possible international alignment indicators include: (1) Percentage of unions affiliated with international groups other than ICFTU or WFTU. (2) Percentage of unions not affiliated with any international group. (3) U.S. direct private investments. (4) Total trade. (5) Total trade with U.S. and USSR. (6) Total trade with OECD nations. (7) Total trade with Soviet area nations. (8) Professorial exchanges with U.S. and USSR. (9) Student exchanges with U.S. and USSR. (10) Books translated from English. (11) Books translated from Russian. (12) Radio broadcast hours from U.S. and USSR. (13) U.S. propaganda expenditures. (14) Air flights per week from U.S. and USSR. A number of these were taken as raw data and then recorded on a per capita basis or on the basis of a percentage of GNP.

[2] West Germany was recognized by a total of 97 countries and Yugoslavia was not far behind, with recognition extended by 82 nations. There were six communist and six noncommunist controversial countries.

United Nations, (3) diplomatic recognition patterns, and (4) diplomatic visits by heads of state and of government and other important persons. To a lesser extent economic aid indicates alignment, but cultural exchange agreements, treaties signed and anti-U.S. and USSR riots do not clearly support the alignment patterns as judged by the experts. Alignment emerges as largely a political phenomenon. Political decisions pertaining to the military are of first importance. In the second place conscious decisions of political support as expressed by (1) voting in the United Nations, (2) diplomatic recognition, and (3) exchanges of important political figures. Data on the forty countries judged as most closely aligned suggest two distinct categories of alignment indicators: the military and the diplomatic.

Certain other conclusions emerge from the data. For example, the United States engages in a substantial amount of treaty-signing activity. These treaties are signed largely with those countries judged to be aligned with the United States. However, a sizeable number of treaties are signed by the United States with countries aligned with the Soviet Union. The USSR generally signs far fewer treaties than the U.S., but is about as likely to sign treaties with countries judged in the U.S. sphere as with countries in its own sphere. U.S. cultural exchange agreements clearly are not related to the political alignment of the other country; to a lesser extent the same is true for the Soviet Union. Both powers, although showing some preference for the countries aligned with them, maintain a fairly broad rather than selective approach to cultural agreements.

The United States is overtly far more active in foreign affairs, as measured by the indicators used in this study, than is the Soviet Union. It signs more treaties, makes more arrangements for military alliances, stations more troops in foreign countries, receives more visitors from abroad, sends out more economic and military aid, and contends with more riots against its installations overseas. The United States also seems to be more intensely involved with countries closely aligned with it. Further, the evidence suggests that the United States is far less discriminating than the Soviet Union with respect to almost any international activity except treaties. This may be due to the resources at its disposal. If what a country can do to extend its influence in the area of foreign relations is a function of its economic resources, then the United States should be much more active than the Soviet Union. Since the United States has about twice the economic wealth of the Soviet Union, the USSR is proportionately quite active in international activities.

Alignment, perhaps, is a direct function of both the intent and the capability of a major power. Most of the measures of alignment used in this study reflect some type of bilateral activity. How much of this activity is solely (or even primarily) initiated by the United States or the USSR cannot be determined, but evaluating the type of the indicators used here suggests that the two major contenders for world leadership may initiate a disproportionate amount of activity designed to influence international alignment.

. . .

RELATIONSHIPS BETWEEN INDICATORS

. . .

On two of the indicators only U.S. data were available: military aid and government employees stationed in a country. Voting records in the UN were separated—on the basis of whether the votes coincided with the U.S. or USSR position—for purposes of analysis while other indicators, such as visits by heads of state and of government to Washington or Moscow, were combined into a single indicator. Two potential indicators, cultural agreements and number of treaties with the United States and the Soviet Union, did not significantly relate to any other indicators.

Military agreements, unweighted in terms of the amount of commitment they involve, remain a powerful discriminatory indicator of alignments here, as was the case in comparing the indicators with the judgments of experts.

The heavy political investment signified by diplomatic recognition is an important indicator. These data show that the twelve countries, communist and noncommunist, upon which the most intense international debate is focused, do confront political decision-makers in the rest of the world with agonizing choices, which in turn suggest political preferences. The presence of an East German embassy, for instance, indicates a political leaning.

Voting in the United Nations presents a country with important opportunities for publicly stating its political sympathies. The wide range of issues discussed in the UN provides a broad group of questions on which countries can express themselves. Because of the large number of recorded expressions, peculiar circumstances, such as a nation with a special military or geographical importance or a nation with a head of state who likes to travel, will tend to cancel out. This is perhaps the reason why the voting patterns recorded and published by the United Nations are a reliable indication of alignment behavior.

Although the frequency of important official visits furnishes a worthwhile indicator of alignment, visits by heads of state and of government may prove more decisive. The latter, while statistically significant in only four cases resulting in a low ranking among the indicators, nonetheless has two perfect correlations. Present treatment of the data may conceal a hidden strength for this indicator which may be brought out in subsequent refinement.

Certain indicators such as U.S. economic aid and the number of em-

ployees stationed in a country are not closely related to the other indicators of alignment. For example, when the various correlations of U.S.
economic aid are compared to those of military agreements and of votes
in the UN, both apparently valid measures of alignment, it is clear that
the United States does not limit its aid program to those nations disposed
favorably toward its international political position, at least not to the
same extent as the USSR.

.   .   .

FUTURE DIRECTIONS OF RESEARCH

The findings of this preliminary report are admittedly crude. They do
not adequately represent the massive amount of data or statistical expression attempted in the initial analysis, where in addition to a simple
statistical test two expressions of rank order correlation were computed.
The goal here has been to select several indicators which tend to measure
alignment and confirm them by a set of systematic judgments. Out of a
rather large package of indicators, several have been found to be consistently related. The military commitment factor perhaps takes primacy;
the diplomatic is second in value. The sensitivity as an indicator of
voting records in the United Nations was not entirely anticipated.

.   .   .

After more refined measuring devices have been developed, it will be
possible to array countries on the basis of their alignment with the U.S.
and the USSR and to make some projections into the future. An overall
alignment index will enable scholars to make a more accurate assessment
of the impact of a given decision on the general alignment pattern both of
a specific country and of the world.

The important theoretical question, however, is still to be answered.
What explains alignment? It is possible to begin to answer this question
with some of the data accumulated in this research effort. One major
explanatory variable, for example, may be the degree of saliency of the
United States and the Soviet Union in a particular country. The alignment of a country, as represented by the decisions of political leaders is,
it could be argued, a direct function of the saliency or the degree of
psychological penetration by either of the two major powers. Saliency
could be measured by some of the following kinds of data: American and
Russian books translated, professors and students exchanged, number of
hours of radio broadcasts received and amount of money spent on
propaganda.

A second, perhaps less important, explanation may be the degree of
economic dependence of a country on either of the two major powers.
Economic dependence can be measured by trade flows, percentage of total

national product exported, and scheduled air and shipping movements to and from the U.S. and the USSR. Economic needs may condition a nation's decision-makers to commit themselves to one or the other of the major powers on which their economic fortunes depend. In short, perceived economic dependence may issue into political sympathies.

Another general factor that may explain alignments could be the nature of a country's political structure. Do countries that are more democratic have an affinity for the United States in their foreign relations? Do authoritarian regimes find alignment with the Soviet Union to be consistent with their governmental style? Politics has indeed made strange bedfellows in domestic matters. Does the same adage hold for international affairs? The drive of national leaders for political congruity, for legitimization of the form of government that has given them political authority, may inhibit strong alignment with nations having substantially different governmental structures.

Political history may provide another variable for explaining alignments. Past political experience, associated with undesirable consequences, may move countries to shun alignment with either of the major powers. By necessity or preference, the leaders of ex-colonial countries, for example, may have borrowed foreign political forms for domestic use. This imitation, however, may not spill over into foreign policy commitments. Indeed, the contrary may be the case. New nations may find that association with powerful governments raises the image of their past position of political subordination. Such an experience may prompt a conscious international detachment, accomplished by consciously avoiding Western political dominance.

Finally, a further factor that may explain alignment is the degree of confidence a country maintains in its projected course of action. Countries that are strong economically and have some degree of political stability may be more willing to become aligned than countries less sure of themselves and their political and economic structures. A sense of insecurity among a nation's leaders may induce withdrawal from the world of political engagements and avoidance of alignment with either the United States or the Soviet Union.

These propositions need to be analyzed more fully. The data on the number of variables that have been collected and partially analyzed makes it possible to move along many fronts in testing hypotheses of alignment. The data on hand and to be collected will continue to serve as a storehouse of variables for continuing investigation of alignment, a major structural characteristic of the international system.

40. NONALIGNMENT AS A DIPLOMATIC IDEOLOGICAL CREDO

Khalid I. Babaa and Cecil V. Crabb, Jr.

SEMANTIC AND PHILOSOPHICAL CONFUSION

BEFORE IDENTIFYING a number of ideas integral to the concept of non-alignment, we may take note of several factors engendering semantical and philosophical uncertainty and confusion. "Nonalignment," a recent Prime Minister of Ceylon declared, "must always be responsive to changing circumstances" in the external environment. Other spokesmen for the concept, like Marshal Tito of Yugoslavia, have asserted that the idea of nonalignment itself may be rapidly becoming outmoded—as each great cold-war power bloc loses its cohesiveness.[1] Nonalignment is, therefore, an *evolving* concept. Since World War II, its content has been heavily influenced by conditions prevailing in global affairs and by the specific needs of its adherents. If a prevalent desire in the early postwar period was to avoid entanglement in great-power ideological disputes risking nuclear war (as suggested by the term "neutralism"), by the 1960's, nations uncommitted to East or West desired to emphasize certain tangible goals (suggested by "positive neutralism") which they sought to achieve in a period when the East-West conflict had lost some of its more ominous implications.

Complexity and ambiguity also characterize nonalignment because every nation, out of a total of more than fifty espousing it, has its own interpretation of what the doctrine means in theory and in practice. Almost all the broad goals identified with it—keeping free from cold-war commitments, promoting peaceful coexistence, resolving global tensions by negotiations—leave wide scope for interpretation in the light of national and regional aspirations and conditions. Moreover, many issues confronting the international community—like meeting the needs of the

From *The Annals of the American Academy of Political and Social Science* (November 1965), 7–16. Reprinted by permission of the authors and the publisher. Footnotes have been renumbered to appear in consecutive order.

KHALID I. BABAA (1924–   ) Director of the League of Arab States Office, Dallas, Texas. Formerly a member of the Yemen Mission to the United Nations.

CECIL V. CRABB, JR. (1924–   ) Professor of Political Science, Vassar College. Author of *Nations in a Multipoliar World*, (New York: Harper and Row, 1968); *The Elephants in the Grass: A Study of Nonalignment*, (New York: Praeger, 1965); *American Foreign Policy in the Nuclear Age*, (New York: Harper, 1965).

[1] *The New York Times*, September 21, 1963, and March 24, 1964.

developing nations or reforming the United Nations—tend more and more to fall outside the area of active cold-war rivalry.

Uncertainty about the precise connotations of nonalignment is also engendered by the existence of several closely related terms and doctrines, some of which are relatively new and some of which have acquired a traditional meaning under international law and usage. A widespread source of such confusion in the recent period, for example, has been a tendency to equate *juridical neutrality* with neutralism or nonalignment. Contemporary advocates of the neutralist point of view have repeatedly endeavored to distinguish their approach from classical neutrality. This distinction can be made on two levels—the legal plane and the moral-ethical plane.

THE LEGAL PLANE

Under international law, neutrality defines "the legal relationship that exists between states which take no part in the war on the one hand and the belligerents on the other." A state of active war is thus clearly requisite for the existence of juridical neutrality. States not involved in hostilities may assume a neutral position; when they do, they accept certain obligations, and acquire certain rights, recognized under international law.[2] Whatever degree of diplomatic discord, tension, and military or paramilitary conflict is implicit in the Cold War, from the vantage point of international law a condition of outright warfare has not existed among the great powers since 1945, permitting the operation of the rules of neutrality for nations not involved in the conflict.

THE MORAL-ETHICAL PLANE

This leads to a second respect in which neutralism or nonalignment must be distinguished from neutrality: the moral and ethical dimensions of foreign policy. Answering the often-repeated accusation that they were ethically insensitive to the issues at stake in great-power rivalries, advocates of neutralism have asserted (in the words of Prime Minister Nehru in 1949):

The policy India has sought to pursue is not a negative and neutral policy. It is a positive and vital policy that flows from our struggle

---

[2] The rights of neutrals have been internationally recognized by gatherings like the Second Hague Conference in 1907 and spelled out in agreements like the Declaration of London in 1916. For fuller discussion of the conditions required for juridical neutrality, see William W. Bishop, Jr., *International Law: Cases and Materials* (Englewood Cliffs, N.J.: Prentice-Hall, 1953), pp. 651–52.

for freedom. . . . When man's liberty or peace is in danger, we cannot or shall not be neutral; neutrality then would be a betrayal of what we have fought for and stand for.

Again in 1951, Nehru distinguished a position of neutrality from India's effort to "preserve and . . . establish peace on a firm foundation."[3] After some early confusion on the point, the distinction has been grasped by American officials. Replying to perennial complaints in Congress about the coloration of India's neutralism, in 1962 Secretary of State Dean Rusk emphasized that New Delhi's attachment to neutralism applied only to permanent military association with East or West. In the American view, India was not neutral on issues "of importance to us in terms of the general shape of the international community, and what kind of UN we should have and what kind of commitments we should make to law and the processes of law in international relations." A few months later, Rusk observed generally that although there existed "many unaligned states," there were "few neutrals with respect to the Charter [of the United Nations] and, I might add, at moments of crisis we find fewer neutrals than we might have supposed."[4]

NEUTRALIZATION

Closely akin to neutralism or nonalignment is the idea of "neutralization" or *institutionalized neutrality*. One commentator has observed that neutralization occurs when

. . . states proclaim themselves in advance desirous of avoiding participation in any war at any time. These States, if they are favoured with special geographical positions, if they happen to be small enough and not especially attractive to the more rapacious Great Powers, may then be given a status of permanent neutrality or neutralization; that is to say, in terms of power politics they are removed from the arena of conflict.[5]

States may either elect neutralization for themselves or have neutralization imposed upon them by outside powers. Before World War II, for example, Switzerland, Belgium, and Luxembourg were in the former category. Since World War II, the great powers have legally (if not always actually) recognized the neutralization of Austria, Laos, and

---

[3] See Nehru's views, as cited in S. N. Dhar, "Nehru on Nonalignment," *The Indian and Foreign Review*, Vol. 1 (June 15, 1964), p. 34.

[4] See the excerpt from Rusk's speech in *The Asian Recorder*, Vol. 8 (September 24–30, 1962), p. 4802; and *The New York Times*, June 12, 1963.

[5] Michael Brecher, "Neutralism: An Analysis," *International Journal*, Vol. 17 (Summer 1962), p. 224.

Cambodia.[6] In modern history, Switzerland has served as the prototype of a nation embracing permanent or institutionalized neutrality. Besides its nonparticipation in great-power conflicts, Switzerland belongs to no international organizations, including the United Nations. Nor does Switzerland adhere to any military alliances. Yet Switzerland does permit international conferences and diplomatic gatherings (like the disarmament proceedings at Geneva) to take place within its borders. At the same time, the Swiss are anti-Communist and are affiliated ideologically with the Western camp. The case of Austria is quite different. A prolonged cold-war deadlock over the Austrian peace treaty was finally broken in 1955. By its terms, the Soviet military occupation was terminated, upon condition that Austria refrain from entering any great-power alliance system, such as the North Atlantic Treaty Organization (NATO). Like Switzerland, ideologically and politically the Austrian society is oriented toward the West.

DISENGAGEMENT

A variant idea is the *disengagement* of specified countries and regions from the arena of great-power conflict. One scheme for disengagement was suggested by George F. Kennan and supported by a number of European groups, such as spokesmen for the British Labour party. Kennan's plan called for withdrawal of Soviet and American military forces from the center of Europe. The "Rapacki Plan," proposed by Poland's Foreign Minister, is a more or less comparable proposal. Particular countries and regions may also be disengaged from the arena of active great-power conflict. Various schemes have been offered for the *de facto* disengagement of regions in Africa and Latin America from cold-war rivalry, by the creation of "nuclear free zones" in these areas.

Commenting upon proposals contemplating neutralization or disengagement, United Nations Secretary-General U Thant has declared that the value of such schemes

. . . does not lie solely in the creation of buffer states valuable though that is. Neutralization is a form of territorial disarmament, a partial dismantling of the great military machines whose destructive powers have become so terrifying. Each act of neutralization, therefore, is a kind of pilot project for the comprehensive disarmament that alone can rid the world of fear and suspicion.[7]

---

[6] Switzerland was neutralized in 1815, Belgium in 1831, and Luxembourg in 1867. The neutralization of Austria is required by its State Treaty of 1955; the great powers agreed to neutralize Laos and Cambodia in the Geneva Armistice Agreement of 1954.

[7] Secretary-General U Thant, "The Small Nations and the Future of the United Nations," Address delivered at Uppsala University, May 6, 1962, United Nations Press Release S/G/1186, May 6, 1962.

Neutralist nations, a Yugoslav spokesman has emphasized, reject the concept of diplomatic blocs "as a matter of principle." Referring to the Belgrade Conference, Nehru of India said: "I have consistently opposed the formation of a third bloc. Nobody wanted it there and nobody mentioned it there." And Egypt's President Nasser told the Cairo nonaligned conference in 1964 that the breakup of antagonistic cold-war diplomatic blocs must not be followed by the formation of new blocs—"a bloc of the poor and a bloc of the wealthy, a bloc of the advanced nations and a bloc of the developing nations . . . a bloc of whites and a bloc of colored." [8] Such admonitions dealt with another idea often widely misunderstood outside the neutralist zone—the concept of a neutralist or nonaligned "bloc." Neither on ideological nor on purely expediential grounds do nations considering themselves nonaligned accept the existence of such a bloc, or seriously aspire to create one. Nations dedicated to nonalignment are aware that they lack the requisite military and economic power enabling them to compete successfully with the Western and Communist alliance systems. A Yugoslav official has said:

The uncommitted countries are not a bloc of powers. First of all, they have no power. Not only do they not want to, but they cannot build up a third bloc. If they wanted to take part in alliance, they would have to join one or the other side. . . . But, in attempting to influence the course of world affairs, the uncommitted do represent *a group;* their representatives get together from time to time, and there is a permanent cooperation between them.[9]

Reluctance to constitute a bloc, therefore, does not prevent nonaligned nations from exerting their collective influence, or what the Cairo nonaligned conference called their "common wills," in international affairs—chiefly by invoking the force of global public opinion, exerting pressure upon the great powers, relying upon moral suasion, and making their own contribution to the resolution of global issues. Eschewing the idea of a new neutralist bloc, Nehru of India nevertheless urged nonaligned nations to "come closer together" and to "confer together" inside and outside the United Nations.[10] Such consultations, however, had to take place within the dominant neutralist principle, expressed by President Nasser of Egypt to the Belgrade Conference: "We live in a world suffering from the strife

---

[8] See, respectively: Stojan Kobačević, "The U.S.A. and Economic Integration," *Review of International Affairs* (Belgrade), Vol. 13 (January 20, 1962), 15; *The Times of India,* September 12, 1961; Dhar, *op. cit.,* p. 34; "Fifty-seven Heads of State Participate in Second Nonaligned Conference," *Arab News and Views* (Arab Information Center, New York), Vol. X (October 15, 1964), p. 1.

[9] Marko Nikezić, "Why Uncommitted Countries Hold that They Are Not 'Neutral,'" THE ANNALS, Vol. 336 (July 1961), p. 81.

[10] Jawaharlal Nehru, *India's Foreign Policy* (New Delhi: Government of India Ministry of Information and Broadcasting, 1961), pp. 77–78.

between two blocs and we cannot imagine that a third bloc should enter the arena and increase the tension of this strife instead of easing it." [11]

NONALIGNMENT AND NEUTRALISM

Nonalignment and neutralism (with its variant, "positive neutralism") have now gained widest currency as the terms most accurately describing the foreign-policy orientation of nations affiliated with neither the Western or the Communist camp. Nonalignment and neutralism tend to be used synonymously, except when the latter denotes "neutrality" in its legal or ethical connotations. To avoid such connotations, a majority of nations in this group prefers nonalignment as the term best describing its viewpoints and policies toward the great powers.

Although certain fine distinctions might be drawn between these two ideas, the key element in both concepts is a determination by their advocates to exercise maximum diplomatic freedom by avoiding permanent identification with East or West in world affairs. The mentality behind this determination was explained by Burma's Ambassador to the United States, Mr. James Barrington, who observed in 1953:

> With the achievement of our independence we need to be re-assured on every possible occasion that we are regarded as equals, that we will not be taken for granted, and that we will not once again become pawns in the game of power politics which was our lot for decades and centuries while we were the victims of foreign domination.[12]

Or, as President Nkrumah of Ghana once declared:

> We are convinced that by our policy of nonalignment we are able to speak our minds frankly and without fear and favour on issues as they arise. Our policy is not a negative one. Positive neutralism and nonalignment does not mean keeping aloof from burning international issues. On the contrary, it means a positive stand based on our own convictions completely uninfluenced by any of the power blocs.[13]

In practice, the most universal ingredient in the doctrine of nonalignment is refusal to be drawn into great-power military pacts, implying diplomatic identification with, or dependence upon, one of the two cold-war blocs. To countries which lost their freedom as a result of economic

---

[11] *The Conference of Heads of State or Government of Nonaligned Countries* (Belgrade: Government of Yugoslavia, 1961), p. 44.

[12] "Statement by His Excellency Mr. James Barrington, Ambassador of Burma to the United States of America . . . at the International Conference on Asian Problems," November 4, 1953 (Text supplied by Embassy of Burma, Washington, D.C.), p. 7.

[13] Kwame Nkrumah, *I Speak of Freedom* (New York: Frederick A. Praeger, 1961), p. 199.

and military privileges exercised by outsiders, a high Indian official has said, "there is a natural suspicion of any military involvement" with great powers. Or, as the declaration adopted by the nonaligned conference at Cairo in 1964 expressed it: "Maintenance or future establishment of foreign military bases and the stationing of foreign troops on the territories of other countries, *against the expressed will of those countries*," constitutes a "gross violation" of their national sovereignty and "a threat to freedom and international peace." [14]

The governing principle in this injunction, therefore, is that whatever military links are established by neutralist nations with foreign countries must be made *voluntarily*, and not imposed by great powers, on the theory that such nations represent a "power vacuum" or require the "protection" of foreign alliance systems. As with all tenets of neutralist thought, this one leaves ample latitude for interpretation by its adherents. By virtue of its defense treaties with Greece and Turkey, Yugoslavia is linked with NATO; Malaysia and Kenya have maintained intimate defense ties with Great Britain; Cambodia has threatened to invoke the military protection of Communist China to defend itself against South Vietnam and Thailand (nations, in turn, backed militarily by the United States); Tanganyika requested British troops to suppress a military mutiny; several former French dependencies in West Africa (Chad, Gabon, and the Congo Republic, Brazzaville) have leaned heavily upon France in dealing with threats to entrenched political regimes; Cuba precipitated an international crisis by accepting Soviet missiles; and many nonaligned nations accept military aid from one or both cold-war blocs.

POSITIVE NEUTRALISM

In recent years, some nations have increasingly preferred the term "positive neutralism" to describe their diplomatic posture toward cold-war power blocs. This term has a twofold advantage. It makes even clearer the distinction between neutralism and neutrality, and, even more fundamentally, it accentuates certain goals to which these nations are dedicated on the international scene. Construed as a set of positive goals, pursued within a framework of freedom from great-power military and diplomatic commitments, positive neutralism, in the words of an Arab observer, requires its adherents to work "with determination to play an effective role in international affairs." Active neutralist involvement in

---

[14] See the views of Indian Defense Minister Chavan in *India News*, Vol. 3 (June 12, 1964), p. 5; and the "Declaration as Adopted by the Conference of Nonaligned Countries," *Yugoslavia Facts and Views* (Yugoslav Information Center, New York), No. 168 (October 22, 1964), p. 23, italics inserted.

international political decisions "strengthens the chances of peace and lessens tension in the world"; it "transforms the areas of crisis into areas of agreement and interaction." Nonaligned nations, an Indian source has emphasized, have an important part "to play in enlarging the area of freedom in the world, in saving mankind from the menace of a nuclear war, and in promoting international co-operation in the causes of peace and prosperity." [15]

A dynamic conception of nonalignment, in turn, implies several corollaries: (1) deep neutralist concern about international issues, particularly those likely to endanger peace and security; (2) neutralist willingness to "take a stand" on such issues, in contrast to an attitude of isolationism, noninvolvement, or other forms of diplomatic escapism; (3) reasonably distinct neutralist viewpoints and positions on prevailing international questions; (4) neutralist willingness to assume the global and regional responsibilities demanded to facilitate achievement of their goals; and (5) at least minimal co-operation and consensus among neutralist countries in approaching critical international issues engendering hostilities and tensions among nations.

We may conveniently group the leading tenets in the idea of positive neutralism, or nonalignment construed dynamically, into four broad categories of strategies and goals. First, there is the neutralist belief in the necessity for, and possibility of attaining, global peace. United by a conviction that the nuclear weapon is no respecter of nations—that, by the very nature of modern warfare, all societies are involved in the consequences of nuclear annihilation—advocates of nonalignment have insistently demanded that the great powers resolve their political differences by peaceful means. In recurrent global crises—like periodic East-West tensions over Berlin, the Suez crisis of 1956, the Soviet-American confrontation in Cuba in 1962, and the current conflict in Southeast Asia— nonaligned nations have taken the initiative in searching for alternatives to violence in settling international disputes. Certain crisis situations, like the Himalayan dispute between India and Communist China and the turbulence in the Congo, have lent themselves uniquely to neutralist initiatives. [16]

Closely related to the problem of peace is the search for international

---

[15] Clovis Maqsud, "The Story of Arab Positive Neutralism," in Paul F. Power (ed.), *Neutralism and Disengagement* (New York: Charles Scribner's Sons, 1964), p. 18; "The Cairo Declaration," *Indian and Foreign Review,* Vol. 2 (October 15, 1964), p. 3.

[16] The neutralist role in the Himalayan dispute is discussed in detail in Cecil V. Crabb, Jr., "The Testing of Nonalignment," *Western Political Quarterly,* Vol. 17 (September 1964), pp. 533–538.

agreement on arms-control measures. Attachment to positive neutralism
has led its adherents to demand that the quest for disarmament be continued; that the circle of nations represented in disarmament negotiations
be broadened to include neutralist countries; that the great powers
produce fresh proposals designed to break the protracted stalemate; that
they prevent the proliferation of nuclear weapons; that they conclude
agreements like the nuclear-test-ban accord of 1963 and that they
broaden the scope of this agreement to include activities like underground
testing; that they "guarantee" nations lacking atomic weapons (like
India) from nuclear devastation; and that they regard Africa and Latin
America as "nuclear free zones."

PEACEFUL COEXISTENCE

A second category of neutralist goals, directed at what might be called
the "indirect causes" of war and international tension, seeks to improve
the over-all climate of global politics and to provide mechanisms whereby
conflicts among nations may be resolved peacefully. Many of these goals
are embraced under the rubric of "peaceful coexistence." All nations, said
Marshal Tito in 1963, must

> apprehend and recognize the realities of our time—the existence of
> different social systems and the need to establish, between peoples
> and countries with different social systems, relations based on the
> principles of peaceful coexistence. What I have in mind are interna-
> tional relations which, without dramatizing differences, would make
> possible useful cooperation and contacts in all areas where there exist
> common interests.[17]

India, said Prime Minister Nehru, wished "to have the closest contacts"
with all other countries, "because we do . . . firmly believe in the world
coming closer together and ultimately realizing the idea of what is now
being called One World." [18] Or, as a joint communiqué of Ceylon and the
United Arab Republic expressed it in 1963, a conference of nonaligned
nations was being held in Cairo "in the firm conviction and belief that a
better understanding between nations could be created and international
tensions relaxed and eventually resolved by following a policy of nonalignment." [19] In spite of Communist China's attack upon India in 1962,

---

[17] "Address by the President of the Socialist Federal Republic of Yugoslavia, Josip
Broz Tito, to the XVIIIth Session of the General Assembly of the United Nations,
on October 22, 1963," *Yugoslav Facts and Views*, No. 158 (October 31, 1963), p. 2.
[18] Nehru, *Independence and After*, (The Publications Division, Government of
India, 1949), p. 259.
[19] "The Nonaligned Nations," *Indian and Foreign Review*, Vol. 1 (March 1, 1964),
p. 3.

in the neutralist view, peaceful coexistence remains a valid and imperative principle in the conduct of international affairs.[20]

THE UNITED NATIONS

Along with peaceful coexistence, neutralist nations also advocate greater reliance upon the United Nations by members of the international community. A dominant neutralist judgment, expressed by a Malayan source, holds that the United Nations "is now the most effective international body the world has ever seen." Significantly, out of twenty-seven enumerated goals at the Belgrade neutralist conference in 1961, no less than sixteen entailed direct or indirect reliance upon the United Nations. The conference believed, for example, that all "discussions on disarmament should be held under the auspices of the United Nations." [21]

Yet, if nonaligned nations support the United Nations, they are no less convinced that it can be strengthened. Steps must be taken, said a Nigerian official, "to make it impossible for any nation to ignore its authority." Or, as an Indian source lamented, it was "only in the case of small nations" that the United Nations "has been able to function according to its purposes"; unfortunately, "in the face of Great Power conflicts it remains helpless." [22]

Such convictions have prompted neutralist moves to enhance the power of the United Nations General Assembly (where the vote of Senegal and Cambodia counts as much as the vote of the United States and the Soviet Union) and to support a dynamic role in the resolution of global disputes for the Secretary-General, who brings a "United Nations viewpoint" to bear on critical global issues. Neutralist nations have also called for reorganization of the great-power-dominated Security Council, in order

---

20 The neutralist conception of "peaceful coexistence," it is important to note, must be carefully distinguished from the Marxist conception of the same idea, or what might be more accurately called "peaceful competition" or "peaceful struggle" with capitalism. The latter is a diplomatic and military tactic, designed to achieve Marxist goals under certain conditions in the global political environment. The neutralist conception, on the other hand, was expressed in the "Five Principles of Peaceful Coexistence" (or *Panch Shila*), agreed upon between Communist China and India in 1954. These five principles were: mutual respect for each other's territorial integrity and sovereignty; mutual nonaggression; mutual noninterference in each other's internal affairs; equality and mutual benefit; and peaceful coexistence. Cited in Power, *op. cit.,* p. 8.

21 See *The Straits Times* (Singapore), September 19, 1961; and *Documents on American Foreign Relations* (New York: Harper and Row, 1962), pp. 464–473.

22 *The Daily Times* (Lagos, Nigeria), July 28, 1961; *Hindustan Times* (overseas edition), June 30, 1955. Neutralist dissatisfaction with the United Nations of course received its most dramatic manifestation in Indonesia's withdrawal from that body. Considerable sympathy with Indonesia's complaints about the United Nations, however, existed throughout the neutralist community.

that nations outside the zone of cold-war rivalry may exert greater influence upon problems affecting global peace. Conversely, proponents of nonalignment have almost unanimously rejected the Soviet "troika" proposal, designed to reduce the United Nations' effectiveness by incorporating the veto principle into its executive operations. The neutralist attitude toward the United Nations was succinctly expressed by the late Secretary-General Dag Hammarskjöld:

> It is natural for old and well-established countries to see in the UN a limitation on their sovereignty. It is just as natural that a young country, a country emerging on the world stage, should find in the UN an addition to its sovereignty, an added means of speaking to the world.[23]

CULTURAL AND ECONOMIC FACTORS

Under the general heading of promoting international co-operation might also be listed such goals as encouraging cultural contacts among nations, participating in educational programs across national frontiers, and strengthening multilateral trade and financial agreements. Owing in some measure to their own role in attenuating cold-war antagonisms, neutralist nations have increasingly emphasized economic and financial aspects of international relations. Since most nonaligned countries are drawn from the Afro-Arab-Asian world, a dominant concern is the widening gap between industrialized and economically developing societies. In the United Nations and at international conferences devoted to economic problems, therefore, neutralist spokesmen have been in the forefront of those calling for an expansion in foreign assistance to emerging nations, correction of adverse price structures in world trade which penalize nations exporting primary raw materials, reduction of world trade barriers, and price stabilization schemes for major commodities. At the Cairo Conference in 1964, Indian Prime Minister Shastri listed as an urgent goal the "acceleration of economic development through international co-operation."[24]

COLONIALISM AND POLITICAL MODERNIZATION

A third broad group of neutralist objectives relates to enlargement of political freedom and advancement of human welfare. High on the list of urgent neutralist demands is elimination of colonialism. The Afro-Asian

---

[23] Quoted in Swadsh Mehta, "Asian-African Impact in the UN," *Indian and Foreign Review*, Vol. 1 (January 15, 1964), p. 28.

[24] Neutralist viewpoints on the importance of international economic problems are presented in *The Hindu*, June 16, 1964, as quoted in "World Trade Conference," *Indian and Foreign Review*, Vol. 1 (July 1, 1964), p. 24; *India News*, Vol. 3 (October 16, 1964), p. 6.

Conference at Bandung in 1955 called colonialism "an evil which should speedily be brought to an end"; the nonaligned meeting at Cairo a decade later declared it "a basic source of international tension and conflict" and demanded the "unconditional, complete and final abolition of colonialism now." [25]

Neutralist nations are aware that most Western colonial empires have been liquidated and that colonialism in general is a waning force. In their view, however, there remains the danger of "neocolonialism," which may supersede old versions. Certain neutralist states, like Ghana, have been particularly vocal in warning against neocolonialist tendencies, such as the effort to draw unwilling African nations into great-power groupings like the European Common Market.[26]

Linked to the ongoing struggle against colonialism is a companion emphasis upon political modernization in societies still saddled with an *ancien regime*. Toward Yemen, Saudi Arabia, Libya, Ethiopia, or other settings, the neutralist influence has usually been cast in favor of rapid political evolution—and in some instances, revolution—designed to achieve social justice, higher standards of living, and a more democratic political order. A closely related goal is breaking the power of white-dominated political systems in Africa, to permit mass participation in governmental affairs and to compel a new concern for the welfare of disfranchised citizens in South Africa, Southern Rhodesia, and other nations where whites discriminate heavily against nonwhites.

---

[25] "The Final Communiqué of the Asian-African Conference" (Text supplied by the Permanent Mission of the Republic of Indonesia to the United Nations, New York, N.Y.), p. 4; "Declaration as Adopted by the Conference of Nonaligned Countries," *Yugoslavia Facts and Views* (Yugoslav Information Center, New York), No. 168 (October 22, 1964), p. 12.

[26] In 1962, an official Iraqi source stated that neocolonialism entailed "a policy of domination and exploitation of the weak by the strong"; it was not "merely confined to the physical occupation of territories and subjugation of peoples for economic "purposes" but also involved "a policy of indirect domination, and the threat of the use of force, discrimination, and corruption." This kind of colonialism was far from dead. "On the contrary, it survives and generates great trouble and danger." "Iraq's Foreign Policy," *New Iraq* (Baghdad), No. 1 (January 1962), pp. 2–3. Arab states, for example, viewed the American conception of a "power vacuum" in the Middle East as an example of neocolonialism. More recently, Indonesia's antipathy toward Malaysia has also stemmed from a belief that the latter was militarily dependent on Great Britain, and not therefore truly independent. African states, it must be emphasized, were far from united in regard to the Common Market as a neo-colonialist venture. Some, like the Ivory Coast, supported it and desired some kind of affiliation with it.

SECTION FOUR: Arms Control
and Disarmament

41. THE OBJECTIVES OF ARMS CONTROL

Hedley Bull

ARMS RACES are intense competitions between opposed powers or groups of powers, each trying to achieve an advantage in military power by increasing the quantity or improving the quality of its armaments or armed forces.[1] Arms races are not peculiar to the present time or the present century, but are a familiar form of international relationship. Arms races which are qualitative rather than quantitative, which proceed more by the improvement of weapons or forces than by the increase of them, have grown more important with the progress of technology: and what is peculiar to the present grand Soviet-Western arms race is the extent to which its qualitative predominates over its quantitative aspect. However, there have not always been arms races, and they are in no way inherent in international relations, nor even in situations of international political conflict. Where the political tensions between two powers are not acute; where each power can gain an advantage over the other without increasing or improving its armaments, but simply by recruiting allies or depriving its opponent of them; where the economic or demographic resources to increase armaments, or the technological resources to improve them, do not exist, we do not find arms races. The prominent place which the Soviet-Western arms race occupies in international relations at the present time arises from the circumstance that the opportunities available

---

From *The Control of the Arms Race* by Hedley Bull (New York: 1961), pp. 5–8; 25–27; 30–36. Reprinted by permission Frederick A. Praeger, Inc., and G. Weidenfeld & Nicolson, Ltd. Footnotes have been renumbered to appear in consecutive order.

HEDLEY BULL—See biographical note, page 49.

[1] For a pioneering study of arms races see the essay by Samuel P. Huntington: 'Arms Races: Prerequisites and Results', *Public Policy,* Yearbook of the Graduate School of Public Administration (Harvard University 1958).

to each side for increasing its relative military power lie very much more in the exploitation and mobilization of its own military resources, than in the attempt to influence the direction in which the relatively meagre military resources of outside powers are thrown, by concluding favourable alliances or frustrating unfavourable ones. It arises from the circumstance that the balance of military power can at present be affected very much more by armaments policy than by diplomacy.

It is seldom that anything so crude is asserted as that all wars are caused by arms races, but the converse is often stated, that all arms races cause wars: that in the past they have always resulted in war; or even that they lead inevitably to war.

It is true that, within states, armaments tend to create or to shape the will to use them, as well as to give effect to it; and that, between states, arms races tend to sustain or to exacerbate conflicts of policy, as well as to express them. Within each state, the military establishment, called into being by the policy of competitive armament, develops its own momentum: it creates interests and diffuses an ideology favourable to the continuation of the arms race, and generates pressures which will tend to resist any policy of calling it off. In this respect, that they display a will to survive, the armed forces, the armaments industries, the military branches of science and technology and of government, the settled habits of mind of those who think about strategy and defence, are like any great institution involving vast, impersonal organizations and the ambitions and livelihood of masses of men. Apart from these internal pressures of armaments establishments upon policy, it is possible to see in the pressures which each state exerts upon the other, in the action and reaction that constitutes an arms race, a spiralling process in which the moving force is not, or not only, the political will or intention of governments, but their armaments and military capability. One nation's military security can be another's insecurity. One nation's military capability of launching an attack can be interpreted by its opponent as an intention to launch it, or as likely to create such an intention, whether that intention exists or not. Even where neither side has hostile intentions, nor very firmly believes the opponent to have them, military preparations may continue, since they must take into account a range of contingencies, which includes the worse cases. In so far as the competitors in an arms race are responsive to each other's military capabilities rather than to each other's intentions, in so far as they are led, by estimates of each other's capabilities, to make false estimates of each other's intentions, the arms race has a tendency to exacerbate a political conflict, or to preserve it where other circumstances are making towards its alleviation.

But the idea that arms races obey a logic of their own and can only result in war, is false; and perhaps also dangerous. It is false because it conceives the arms race as an autonomous process in which the military factor alone operates. The chief source of this error in recent years has been the belief in the importance of the various armaments competitions among the European powers, and especially the Anglo-German naval race, in contributing to the outbreak of the first world war. Even in this case, the importance of this factor is a matter of controversy. In the case of the origins of the second world war, the autonomous arms race cannot be regarded as having been important. On the contrary, we should say that the military factor which was most important in bringing it about was the failure of Britain, France and the Soviet Union to engage in the arms race with sufficient vigour, their insufficient response to the rearmament of Germany. In general, arms races arise as the result of political conflicts, are kept alive by them, and subside with them. We have only to reflect that there is not and has never been such a thing as a general or universal arms race, a war of all against all in military preparation. The context in which arms races occur is that of a conflict between particular powers or groups of powers, and of military, political, economic and technological circumstances in which an armaments competition is an appropriate form for this conflict to take.

Arms races have not always led to war, but have sometimes come to an end, like the Anglo-French naval races of the last century, and the Anglo-American naval race in this one, when, for one reason or another, the parties lost the will to pursue them. There is no more reason to believe that arms races must end in war than to believe that severe international rivalries, which are not accompanied by arms races, must do so. It is of course the case that wars are made possible by the existence of armaments. But the existence of armaments, and of sovereign powers commanding them and willing to use them, is a feature of international society, whether arms races are in progress or not. What is sometimes meant by those who assert that arms races cause wars is the quite different proposition that armaments cause wars. While armaments are among the conditions which enable wars to take place, they do not in themselves produce war, or provide in themselves a means of distinguishing the conditions of war from the conditions of peace. For all international experience has been accompanied by the existence of armaments, the experience of peace as much as the experience of war. To show why, in a context in which armaments are endemic, wars sometimes occur and sometimes do not; to show why, in this context, arms races sometimes arise, and either persist, subside or end in war, it is necessary to look beyond armaments themselves to the political factors which the doctrine of the autonomous arms race leaves out of account.

.   .   .

We began by asking what disarmament or arms control is for. We have considered the arguments that it promotes international security, that it promotes economic objectives and that it promotes moral objectives. It has been necessary to do this not only to discover what the claims of disarmament and arms control to contribute to such objectives as these are, to discover whether arms control should be pursued at all; but also in order to determine whether there is any conflict among these objectives, and if there is, what is the proper order of priority among them. For if we are indeed to attempt to increase the part played in international relations by disarmament and arms control, we must first of all know what it is we want of them, with regard to which of these objectives we must shape them. It is clearly possible to pursue each of these three objectives at the expense of one or both of the others. There are disarmament policies, for example, that will fill our pockets with gold, but increase the danger of war; and that would be, in consequence, morally wrong. There are disarmament policies shaped by certain moral objectives, such as that of preserving untainted our innocence of war or nuclear war, that might similarly undermine international security.

In my view it is chiefly in relation to the objective of international security that disarmament and arms control should be shaped and judged. By this I do not mean that situations do not arise in which moral or economic considerations override those of security: marginal increases in security may be pursued at exorbitant economical or moral cost. Moral judgments, indeed, should never be overridden or sacrificed: and the singling out of international security as what is most worthy of our attention is itself, in part, a moral judgment. The moral objective, if, as I have suggested, it is not a matter of rigid adherence to specific principles, should not be understood as something separate from, and opposed to, other objectives, but as a dimension in which we view all of them. In treating international security as of chief priority, I mean no more than that the chief relevance of arms control is to the preservation of peace and order, and that this is an objective generally regarded as morally desirable and worth paying for.

It is necessary to define international security more closely.

There is security of, and security from: that which we are concerned to secure, and that from which we are concerned to secure it. What we are concerned to secure is, on the one hand, our particular ways of life: our continued enjoyment of our own political, social, moral and economic habits and institutions; and, on the other hand, our physical survival, our continued existence as human communities of any kind. What we are concerned to secure these things from is, on the one hand, war, which threatens both of them; and, on the other hand, defeat, brought about by war or otherwise, which historically has also threatened both of them, but is more commonly regarded as threatening only the former.

I do not think of security as some future state or condition, some metaphysical plateau which we have not yet reached but towards which we are striving. International security is something we have and have had throughout the history of modern international society, in greater or lesser degree. The promotion of international security is a matter of preserving and extending something with which we are familiar, rather than of manufacturing, out of nothing, some novel device. At the present time it is a matter of restoring, or attempting to recapture, something, for much of it is beyond recapture, of the security of which modern weapons, and the continued existence alongside them of political conflicts bitter enough to promise the use of them, have deprived us; and, in the first instance, a matter of preserving such security as we have now, by arresting or stabilizing its tendency to rapid decline.

Absolute security from war and defeat has never been enjoyed by sovereign states living in a state of nature, and is foreign to all experience of international life. A great deal of public thinking about international relations is, however, absorbed in the pursuit of this fantasy. The solutions and recommendations produced by this kind of thinking are remote from the range of alternatives or spectrum of possible actions from which governments are able to choose. These solutions do not concern the problems with which the world is actually confronted, but concern the arbitrary dismantling or reconstruction of the world, in such a way that these problems would not arise: a reconstruction to be achieved by acts of will, constitutions for world government, declarations, the abolition of war, gestures, research, therapies and cures. They represent, in my view, a corruption of thinking about international relations, and a distraction from its proper concerns. The fact is that we are where we are, and it is from here that we have to begin. There can only be relative security.

The objective of security, as it has been defined, itself disguises awful choices which may have to be made between its different parts. It may be, for example, that certain nations will find themselves in the position of being able to secure their physical survival, their continued existence as organized communities, only by sacrificing their political, social and economic institutions: by the ancient expedient of surrender. The question whether the struggle to preserve political independence should be carried on in the face of the certainty of physical destruction is one which human communities have often faced in the past, and is not especially a product of modern military technology, though the latter does pose it in a peculiarly stark way. Some of the present support for unilateral nuclear disarmament in Great Britain derives from the view that this is the choice with which we are now confronted.[2] I do not believe that this is the position at present: but if it were the position, there is no doubt in my

---

[2] Only some, and perhaps not very much. Most of the supporters do not see any awful choices, but take the view that unilateral disarmament does not involve the surrender of our political independence: persuading themselves either that no one threatens it, or that we can defend ourselves against nuclear bombardment by conventional armaments or passive resistance.

mind that surrender would be the better alternative. It is the view of a fanatic which prefers universal destruction to the acceptance of defeat.[3]

Another awful choice disguised within this objective of security is that between security from all kinds of war, and security from a particular kind of war: nuclear war. If we are specially concerned to increase security against nuclear war, we may find it necessary to maintain military forces and elaborate military doctrines that will diminish our security against other kinds of war. To illustrate: the doctrine that all military policy should be built around the idea of nuclear deterrence, that the only military act of which we should be capable is that of strategic nuclear bombardment, and the only military threat which we should employ is this one—this doctrine promises a world in which the likelihood of war may not be great, but in which any particular war is a catastrophe.

. . .

DISARMAMENT AND THE BALANCE OF POWER

i

The chief objective of arms control is international security. The contribution which arms control can make to international security is limited by the fact that it deals only with the military factor.

However, there is a military factor, and some military situations are more favourable to international security than others. The question with which this chapter is concerned is: if arms control is concerned to foster military situations favourable to international security, what are these? In particular, how far is *disarmament*, or the reduction of armaments, the proper object of arms control? And how far is it the proper object of arms control to promote a stable *balance of power?* The purpose of this analysis is not to provide final answers to these questions; and not, in particular, to demonstrate that the proper object of arms control is to perfect a stable balance or equilibrium of armaments rather than to secure a reduction of armaments. Its purpose is to demonstrate the inadequacy of such prescriptions as 'reduce!' or 'abolish!', and the need to replace them with careful strategic analysis.[4] It is not to be assumed (though cases could conceivably arise in which it could be shown) that the answer to the question, 'what levels and kinds of armaments should arms control systems seek to perpetuate and make legitimate?' is the formula, 'the lowest levels and the most primitive kinds'. The conflict between this

---

[3] The policy of surrender is discussed in Chapter 4, "Arms Control and Unilateral Action" [of *The Control of the Arms Race* by Hedley Bull].

[4] The spirit of these prescriptions is expressed in the title of a recent book: *Assault at Arms*, by Sir Ronald Adam and Charles Judd (Weidenfeld and Nicolson, 1960).

formula, and the doctrine of the balance of power, which is explored in this chapter, indicates only one of the many respects in which it is inadequate. When we consider—as we shall in later chapters in relation to particular arms control proposals—what should be the content of an arms control agreement or system, we must be guided not by any such formula as this, nor by an exclusive concern with the maintenance of the military balance, but by addressing ourselves with determination to the complicated strategic and political calculation demanded by the question: what kinds, levels, deployments or uses of armaments would best promote security?

ii

Disarmament is the reduction or abolition of armaments. The idea that the world is most secure when there is a *minimum* of armaments, the pursuit of the *maximum* disarmament, has been the central assumption of modern negotiations about arms control. The negotiations conducted under the auspices of the League of Nations between 1921 and 1934, and those under the auspices of the United Nations between 1946 and 1957 and in 1960, have had as their chief formal object the promotion of international security by a general reduction of armaments. Even in negotiations which have been concerned with limiting the further growth of armaments, rather than with reducing existing ones (as in the negotiations at the first Hague Conference in 1899, and in those which led to the Washington Naval Treaty of 1922), it was the idea of the desirability of the minimum armaments that provided the starting point. And where arms control negotiations have not been concerned with the quantity of armaments at all, but with regulating or controlling what should be done with them (like the negotiations leading to prohibition of the use of poison gas, those in the abortive East-West conference on surprise attack in November 1958, and the protracted negotiations at Geneva on the banning of nuclear test explosions, these negotiations are regarded as important partly because they may set off a train of events which might result in a general reduction of armaments.

The idea that security is a matter of disarmament has seldom been held without qualification. Article VIII of the Covenant of the League of Nations, on the basis of which the inter-war negotiations were conducted, stated that: 'The members of the League recognize that the maintenance of peace requires the reduction of national armaments to the lowest point *consistent with national safety and the enforcement by common action of international obligations*' (my italics). This qualification provided the basis of the various French plans of the League period, which treated international security as a matter of the establishment of a strong international authority and centralized military force and disarmament as contributing to security only when linked with it. It was often held, moreover, even by nations which did not support plans for a centralized military force, that there were levels beneath which the reduction of armaments would not constitute a contribution to the maintenance of peace, levels determined by the need of members of the League to maintain forces adequate to enable them to contribute effectively to the system of collective security, or pooling of national military forces in defence of the Covenant, to which they were committed. Another qualification which received general assent in principle at the World Disarmament Conference in 1932, and which still has its adherents, is contained in the idea of qualitative disarmament: that 'specifically offensive' weapons undermine security in a way that defensive weapons do not: and that disarmament should not be indiscrimate, but should be especially concerned with reducing or abolishing the former.[5] Moreover, it has usually been recognized in disarmament negotiations that any reductions that are agreed upon should preserve an agreed balance or ratio of power: that the reductions should be so fashioned, and the phases by which they are carried out so ordered, that no nation should be set at what it considers a military disadvantage.

But, by and large, these qualifications have not been seen as detracting from the principle that it is in the reduction of armaments that the contribution of arms control to international security lies. They have rather been seen as qualifications which have to be made so as to bring about the international agreement that can alone set the process of reduction of armaments in motion. Sovereign powers, it has been considered, will not agree to disarm unless they can retain internal security forces, unless a central authority or collective security system will protect them from attack, and unless at all stages in their disarmament there is a balance between their own strength and that of their opponents.

But the idea that security lies in the minimum of armaments cannot be accepted uncritically. In considering this idea, we must examine separately two of the forms it takes: the stronger form, that the abolition of armaments makes war physically impossible; and the weaker form, that the reduction of armaments makes war less likely.

The stronger form is a doctrine which has great popular appeal, because it promises a form of security which is absolute and independent of the continuance of favourable political conditions. It suggests a world in which states cannot make war, even if they want to. It has played an important part in Soviet disarmament policy. Litvinov advocated total disarmament at a meeting of the preparatory commission of the League of Nations Disarmament Conference, on the occasion of the appearance of Soviet delegates at Geneva, in 1927. All armed forces were to be

---

[5] See Philip Noel-Baker, *The Arms Race,* pp. 393–404 (Stevens and Sons, 1958). . . .

disbanded and all armaments destroyed; military expenditure, military
service, war ministers and chiefs of staffs were to be abolished; military
propaganda and military instruction were to be prohibited; and legislation was to be passed in each country making infringement of any of
these provisions a crime against the state. Litvinov contrasted the Soviet
objective of 'total disarmament' with the more modest objective of a
'reduction and limitation of armaments', which was the formula on which
the League of Nations negotiations proceeded. He repeated his proposal
at the World Disarmament Conference in February 1932. The speech he
made on this occasion, and those which followed later in the conference,
were directed towards exposing the hypocrisy of the capitalist powers in
their treatment of the subject of disarmament: the gap between their
professions of intention and their actions; the dilatoriness and humbug of
disarmament proceedings; the passing of problems from committee to
committee; the endless vista of 'preparation'; the adoption now of this
'method', now of that; the swathing of stark realities in a blanket of
diplomatic nicety. His speeches are a brilliant critique of the diplomacy
of disarmament and, indeed, of the most fundamental assumptions on
which all diplomacy rests, and must rest. They contain a clarity of perception, a determination to call a spade a spade, to say what others only
thought, that is extraordinary in the speeches of a foreign minister, and
possible only because he himself was not taking part in diplomacy but in
political warfare, and therefore saw the diplomatic process as an outsider.
In defending his proposal for total disarmament, he advanced two main
arguments. Total disarmament was 'the only way of putting an end to
war',[6] something which the mere reduction and limitation of armaments
could not do. And total disarmament was 'distinguished from all other
plans by its simplicity and by the ease with which it could be carried out
and with which its realization could be controlled'.[7] Total disarmament
by-passed all those 'thorny questions' which prevented agreement on any
lesser measure of disarmament: what armaments were to be abolished and
what not, how far were reductions to be carried out, which would be
reduced first, how was the treaty to provide equal security for all, and so on.

.   .   .

No system of disarmament can abolish the physical capacity to wage
war, and the idea of an absolute security from war emerging from such a
system is an illusion. However, it is at least logically and physically
possible that the art of war might be rendered primitive: by the abolition
of sophisticated weapons and the decay of sophisticated military orga-

---

[6] *League of Nations: Conference for the Reduction and Limitation of Armaments,*
Verbatim Records of Plenary Meetings, Vol. I, p. 82 (Geneva 1932).
[7] *Ibid.,* p. 85.

nization and technique. There may be a great difference between an international society in which sovereign powers are bristling with modern weapons and organized military forces, and one in which they are not: just as there is a great difference between a society in which gentlemen carry swords, and one in which they do not. There is nothing contrary to logic, or nature either, in the idea of an international society not only without such weapons and forces, but with habits, institutions, codes or taboos which could impede the will to utilize the physical capacity for war inherent in it. We should have the imagination and the vision to contemplate the possibility of such a world, to recognize that the political and military structure of the world could be radically different from what it is now. But we should recognize that a world which was radically different from our own in respect of the primitiveness and extent of its national armaments would also be radically different in many other ways. If nations were defenceless, there could hardly be a political order worthy of the name unless there were an armed, central authority: the abolition of national military power appears to entail the concentration of military power in a universal authority. If a universal authority or world government were to be established in any other way than by conquest, and if, once established, it were to maintain itself in any other way than by the constant suppression of dissidence, the bitter political conflicts which now divide the world would have to have subsided. In a world fundamentally different from our own in all these respects, and in other respects, the reduction of national armaments to a primitive level might have a place. But the world in which we now find ourselves is not such as this: nor is it within the power of any political authority or combination of authorities to bring it about by *fiat*. The possession by sovereign powers of armaments and armed forces is not something extraneous to the structure of international society, something whose presence or absence does not affect other of its parts: it is, along with alliances, diplomacy and war, among its most central institutions. It is possible to conceive systems of world politics and political organization from which this institution is absent: but they are systems from which some of the most familiar and persistent landmarks of international experience are also absent; and which, though they might occur, cannot be legislated.

In a world such as our own it seems doubtful whether the reduction of national armaments to a primitive level, even if it could be brought about in isolation from other fundamental changes, would contribute to international security. It would carry within itself no guarantee that arms races would not be resumed. The resumption of an arms race from a primitive level, with its attendant circumstances of unpredictability and surprise, would be likely to lead to extreme instability in the balance of power, and might well produce greater insecurity than that attending a higher quantitative and qualitative level of armaments.

42. THE SPREAD OF NUCLEAR WEAPONS

Leonard Beaton and John Maddox

W HAT ARE THE DANGERS for the world if nuclear weapons do spread
steadily to new countries? It is widely assumed that any further
spread would be a threat to world peace and a disastrous complication
either in balancing terror or enforcing disarmament—the two favourite
prescriptions for peace. Though there is much in this, if only because of
the uncertainties involved, it has suffered from overstatement. The approach to this problem associated with Sir Charles Snow, for example, has
gone so far that the certainty of a great atomic war is already asserted.
This depends on a relation of the chance of accident (spread day by day
over the years) with an assumption that the accidental use of one or two
nuclear weapons would automatically result in a massive nuclear exchange. Since the chance increases with every new power, the period
during which the chance becomes a certainty presumably decreases. Sir
Charles Snow has written[1]: 'Within at the most ten years some of those
bombs are going off. That is a certainty.' Bertrand Russell has concluded
from this that 'if C. P. Snow is right—and there is no reason whatever to
think him wrong—at some day during the next ten years . . . a very
large proportion of our population will be killed outright, and the remainder will die a slow and agonizing death.'[2] This is an extreme statement of the general belief that the more there are of these things and the
more owners they have the more likely they are to be used.

This doctrine is obviously in conflict with the notion that nuclear
weapons are a unique deterrent. Taken to its logical conclusion, it can be
used to demonstrate that the greater the spread of nuclear weapons the
smaller the chance of war. The nuclear shadows which impose caution on
Russians in Berlin or American reconnaissance aircraft would extend to
the dozen minor conflicts between non-nuclear powers. This is the essence

---

From *The Spread of Nuclear Weapons* by Leonard Beaton and John Maddox (New
York: 1962), pp. 201–205. Reprinted by permission of Frederick A. Praeger, Inc., and
Chatto & Windus, Ltd. Footnotes have been renumbered to appear in consecutive
order.

LEONARD BEATON (1929–   ) Consultant, Institute for Strategic Studies, London.
Formerly Naval Correspondent for the *Times* (London) and Defense Correspondent
for the *Guardian*.

JOHN MADDOX (1925–   ) Editor, *Nature,* and Director, Macmillan and Company.
Formerly Science Correspondent, the *Guardian*. Author of *Revolution in Biology,*
(New York: Macmillan, 1963).

[1] *The Moral Un-neutrality of Science,* Monthly Review, February, 1961, p. 156.
[2] *Has Man a Future?,* George Allen & Unwin, p. 108.

of the argument; and it was elaborately expounded in France when the debate on the *force de frappe* was at its height. In its pure form, it is now seldom expressed—though it might be expected to re-emerge with the theorists of any country embarking on nuclear weapons against domestic or world opinion. As with the statistical argument, it contains an element of truth. No doubt conventional conflicts between East and West in Europe would have been more likely in the last 15 years if it had not been for the awesome dominance of nuclear weapons over any use of force. These weapons provided the main incentive to keep the Korean War severely limited. The wary tread of the great powers in the last decade is likely to be a permanent feature of relations between nuclear powers.

The implications of this can, however, be no more than a consolation if nuclear weapons spread widely. Where none of the political coflicts between Russia and the United States are matters of life and death, those between Israel and her Arab neighbours, Pakistan and India, South Africa and black Africa, or Yugoslavia and her Communist neighbours might appear to some of these governments as an issue for which anything must be risked. The threat of mass destruction can be a great controller of tempers in tense situations. But there are likely to be tempers which even this threat cannot control; and, if this happens, the resulting conflict will take on a horror which was only suggested by the sufferings of Hiroshima and Nagasaki. The real danger is the use of nuclear weapons in such conflicts. Where a country (such as Canada or Sweden) seems unlikely to find itself in this position, a nuclear weapons programme is undesirable primarily for the example it sets.

Apart from this direct danger of turning local wars into nuclear wars, there are a number of other reasons why the spread of these weapons cannot be expected to serve the cause of peace and stability. Broadly, there are five serious aspects to this: (1) the instability of the period during which particular countries are known to be developing weapons but have not; (2) the inevitability of imbalance as between rivals as the spread goes on; (3) the possibility that as nuclear forces grow surprise attack may become safe for one side or another; (4) the danger that small powers may obtain the ability to draw great powers into nuclear wars (the notion of catalytic war); (5) the complication of disarmament or arms control negotiations; (6) the general increase in tension which is likely to accompany an increase in the world-wide levels of military power.

The first of these, the gestation period, applies to those countries which do not have a firm guarantee from a major power or who could not be certain that this guarantee would survive if they were building weapons. As long as secrecy is impossible during, at the least, the last two or three years before an operational force exists, a country like Israel or the Federal Republic of Germany might generate an urgent atmosphere

among its rivals. To this extent, a conventional preventive war might become likely more because the simple symmetry of nuclear weapons all round on which the familiar French thesis rests would not be present. Much the same considerations—though now threatening nuclear conflict—apply to the second and third categories of danger. In the second, a country with a good lead might feel obliged to exploit it before the enemy's ability to retaliate became so great as to be unacceptable; in the third, there are likely to be periods in which military planners can see a virtually certain capacity to destroy an enemy's ability to retaliate by a sudden strike. Where countries are very close to one another, tactical warning of air attack becomes negligible and the problem of mounting a counter-force strike is greatly simplified.

While these three dangers seem to apply mainly to possible local conflicts, the issue of catalytic war is more relevant to the alliances. It is generally held that once a war is nuclear the main limitation on it is removed. The ability to trigger a large force becomes a powerful deterrent in the hands of a middle power. Both the British and French nuclear forces have been defended on the ground that they ensure an American nuclear strategy in the defence of Europe. Though this notion has been seriously questioned,[3] it is true enough to inject a new element of uncertainty into the strategic balance between the great powers. The desire to have control over a force large enough to make sure that a country's defence will in fact be nuclear is, as has been shown, a major element in the present official military thinking of Germany. Another aspect of catalytic war has been advanced by some American theorists who have argued that with a wide spread of nuclear weapons unidentifiable attacks might be launched. These might be intended to bring the great powers into a war of mutual destruction while leaving the source of the attacks in a powerful third position. The most skilled creators of war games might have difficulty in showing that a second rate power could get away with such a strike undetected, that the great powers would inevitably respond with massive retaliation on one another, that the third power would not suffer in this process, and that it would end up better off than it was before.[4] Nevertheless, the opportunities for blackmail, especially by a national leader known for his ruthlessness and irresponsibility, are obvious; and there can be little doubt that the spread of nuclear weapons to many states will make these weapons a more immediate fact in the life and policies of many nations.

---

[3] See 'NATO and the N + 1 Problem' by Albert Wohlstetter, *Foreign Affairs*, 1961.

[4] A useful discussion of the whole problem of the spread of weapons with emphasis on this aspect is F. C. Ikle, 'Nth Countries and Disarmament', *Bulletin of Atomic Scientists*, December, 1960.

As for disarmament and arms control, the difficulties of agreement among the nuclear powers might well be increased by larger numbers. While it is true that in many negotiations pressure to agree is put on the major powers by smaller powers, the chances that one or more new nuclear powers might be unwilling to accept a control system or to give up weapons are quite strong. Just as France was unwilling to accept a moratorium on tests during the 1958–61 great power moratorium and would not have conformed to a test ban had it been agreed, it may be expected that any country embarking on nuclear weapons will resist agreements of this kind. Once the bombs have been produced and a period of years has elapsed, a secret stock becomes impossible to check and for every new nuclear power the permanent existence of one more force must be allowed for in a controlled or disarmed world.

Then finally, it is impossible to avoid the general conclusion that the addition of new powers to the list of those already equipped with weapons of mass destruction brings with it fear, uncertainty and a new incentive to military spending in neighbouring countries. Some areas like South America, Africa and the Middle East retain a distinctively non-nuclear character and it seems possible to say this of Asia as long as China has not obtained these weapons.

The spread, then, is undesirable and dangerous. It is also irreversible; once a country has reliable and tested nuclear weapons it has a potentiality which no renunciation can entirely remove. What can be done to limit it? The fact that it is taking place much more slowly than is generally assumed offers opportunities for measures which over a period of years might discourage it. In disarmament discussions it has now become commonplace to say that this is a matter in which the United States and the Soviet Union find themselves in a natural community of interest. Certainly concern with the problem gave powerful support to the British and American entry into negotiations for the abolition of nuclear tests in 1958 and may also have influenced the Soviet Union. It has also been the main reason for the western proposal for a cessation of the production of fissile materials for weapons purposes (the so-called cut-off), for the bilateral and multilateral (IAEA) controls on nuclear sharing and for certain inhibitions on allied technical co-operation. These undoubtedly have had a discouraging effect.

43.   THE NONPROLIFERATION TREATY

James E. Dougherty

S OME YEARS AGO a Soviet mathematician expressed the danger of nuclear
weapons proliferation in the formula $R = N^2$, in which R stood for
the risk of nuclear war and N for the number of nuclear powers. This
formula, which implied a geometric progression in the chance of war with
every increase in the number of nuclear weapon States, ignored certain
political realities—including the kind of governments acquiring control
over nuclear weapons and the character of their foreign policies. Hence if
Sweden and Switzerland were to become nuclear weapon States, the risks
of war would grow (according to this mathematical representation) just
as much as if the acquiring States were North Vietnam and Castro's
Cuba. In this sense, if in no other, the formula was deficient. Nevertheless, in spite of the suggestions that have been made from time to time
that a world of many nuclear powers might be stabler than a world of
few, and that entrance into the nuclear club might compel a militant
power to act with greater responsibility and caution, most arms control
analysts in recent years have taken it for granted that a world of twelve
or fifteen nuclear States would be less stable than a world of three or
four, because it would pose a greater statistical probability of technical
accident, unauthorized use, strategic miscalculation, or uncontrolled escalation from a limited to a general conflict.

Since the conclusion of the Partial Nuclear Test Ban Treaty in 1963, a
nonproliferation treaty has become the principal target of arms control
diplomacy, both within the United Nations General Assembly and in the
Eighteen Nation Disarmament Committee in Geneva.[1] These have been
the salient questions: Can the two superpowers be expected to conclude a

From *Arms Control for the Late Sixties,* edited by James E. Dougherty and John
F. Lehman, Jr. (Princeton: 1967), pp. xxxiv-xxxvi. Reprinted by permission of the
Van Nostrand Co., Inc. Footnotes have been renumbered to appear in consecutive
order.

JAMES E. DOUGHERTY (1923–   ) Executive Vice-President and Professor of Politi-
cal Science, St. Joseph's College, Philadelphia. Pennsylvania; Associate, Foreign
Policy Research Institute, University of Pennsylvania. His other books include *The
Prospects for Arms Control,* (New York: MacFadden, 1965), co-editor; *The Politics
of the Atlantic Alliance,* (New York: Praeger, 1964); *Protracted Conflict,* (New
York: Harper, 1959), co-author.

[1] In 1959, the U.N. General Assembly pointed out that an increase in the number
of nuclear States would aggravate international tensions and compound the difficulty
of reaching arms agreements. Two years later, the Irish Resolution called for a treaty
by which both nuclear and nonnuclear States would pledge restraint. RES/1665

major arms agreement while the conflict in Southeast Asia is in progress? Is a formal treaty necessary, insofar as the five nuclear powers might already be in tacit agreement that it is not in their interest to dilute the currency of nuclear prestige by helping to create other nuclear powers? Should nonnuclear weapon States renounce their option of acquiring a nuclear military capability before they are certain that the nuclear powers will make progress toward disarmament? Can the nuclear powers give credible security guarantees to the nonnuclear weapon countries? How high a price should a superpower pay in respect to the cohesion of its alliance system in order to obtain a treaty?

For several years, the United States has sought to persuade aspirants to nuclear power that the game was not worth the candle, because small deterrents are costly, provocative and accident-prone, lack credibility, become obsolescent quickly and render young nuclear powers vulnerable to attack in their early stages. But in the early 1960's, the French Government remained unimpressed by the arguments advanced by the United States, and it is possible that other States will, in the late 1960's, discern reasons for acquiring nuclear weapons. The arguments of the nuclear advocates can be grouped under three headings. *Militarily,* nuclear weapons provide unprecedented power available in no other form; they alone can deter a nuclear-equipped opponent; they do not necessarily require expensive long-range delivery systems to deter a distant great power; a country might contemplate only their tactical use for defensive purposes against an evenly matched neighbor, to prevent the foe from massing his armies, to interdict him, and to deny him access to avenues of approach, e.g., by detonating atomic mines in mountain passes when an attack seems imminent. *Economically,* nuclear weapons programs undoubtedly siphon off scarce scientific-engineering talent from immediate development purposes, but in the long run they can contribute to the growth of the technological base. Moreover, the initial investment is no longer prohibitive especially for a country which has already developed a civilian reactor program. (It has been estimated that a minimum capability of producing five bombs a year, with a proper testing program but without a sophisticated delivery system, would cost about

---

(XVI), December 5, 1961. For the text of the U.S. draft treaty, see Verbatim Proceedings of the Eighteen Nation Disarmament Committee/152 (ENDC/152), August 17, 1965; also in the *New York Times,* August 18, 1965; *Documents on Disarmament 1965,* U.S. Arms Control and Disarmament Agency Publication 34, December 1966, pp. 347–349 (where ENDC document is misnumbered); for text of Soviet draft treaty, see A/5976, September 24, 1954; *Documents on Disarmament 1965, op. cit.,* pp. 443–446.

$450 million, spread unevenly over a ten-year period.[2]) Eventually, the acquisition of nuclear weapons might permit some savings through the reduction in the size of the conventional armed forces. *Politically,* nuclear weapons provide an ultimate guarantee of a country's independence; insofar as they furnish a State with a nuclear trigger in time of crisis, they foreclose both strong-armed tactics by more powerful States and crisis deals by the superpowers at the expense of that country; they are a source of prestige within an alliance, within the region, and within the world at large, and provide one with a ticket to summit conferences. As for the argument that entrance into the nuclear club renders a country vulnerable in the infant stages, aspirants to Nth power status merely point to the experience of Nos. 2, 3, 4, and 5, for none of whom did mere acquisition, when combined with international strategic restraint, prove to be a *casus belli.* The strength of all the foregoing arguments for is not necessarily greater than that of the arguments against, when both are weighed by an objective logician. But in at least a few of the dozen countries that now produce weapons-grade plutonium, or of the more than twenty that will do so within a few years, the case *for* might prove more attractive than the case *against,* regardless of logic.

Everyone realizes that the proposed nonproliferation treaty would place its major burdens upon the nonnuclear rather than the nuclear powers. It is the former who would be requested to make the greater sacrifice by shutting off an option that might be vital to their security and political interests, while the three likely nuclear signatories would be doing little more than protecting their privileged position. . . . Several of the middle and lesser States keep insisting that there must be an "equality of obligation" in respect to nuclear abstention; they are reluctant to adhere to a treaty that seeks to prevent "horizontal proliferation" to other States while allowing "vertical proliferation" among the members of the "nuclear pentapoly." As indicated previously, some of the neutrals at Geneva have seemed at times to assign a higher priority to the conclusion of a comprehensive test ban (which would impose restraint on the Nuclear Five) than to the conclusion of a nonproliferation treaty.

India undoubtedly wonders whether the international political position of the People's Republic of China will be permanently enhanced as a result of Peking's acquisition of a nuclear missile capability. For many years past, neither neutrals nor aligned middle powers have reacted favorably to the suggestion that nuclear capabilities and the U.N.

---

[2] Leonard Beaton, "Capabilities of Non-Nuclear Powers," in Alastair Buchan, ed., *A World of Nuclear Powers,* for the American Assembly, Englewood Cliffs, N.J.: Prentice-Hall, 1966, p. 32.

Security Council veto might someday be perfectly conjoined, but India has been particularly sensitive on this point. Quite naturally, many Indian policymakers, intellectuals, scientists, and military leaders have been worried about the long-range implications of a nonproliferation treaty. Even some of those who are most opposed to a national decision to exercise the nuclear weapons option (which has not been taken up to the time of this writing) are understandably reluctant to have their government sign a treaty while Peking still shows no interest in adhering even to the partial test ban.

Through the first half of 1967 India continued to serve as principal spokesman for those nonaligned States which suffered misgivings over the proposed treaty. Indian leaders remained apprehensive of Pakistan, guilty in their eyes of rejecting Indian offers to normalize relations in the wake of the Tashkent Agreement. But they were even more suspicious of the long-range threat of Communist China, which supplies arms and guerrilla training aid to Pakistan and seeks to apply protracted political-military pressure along India's borders. India sees trouble ahead if China should seek to demonstrate that her primacy in Asia has not been jeopardized by the internal upheaval known as the "cultural revolution."

Within recent years it has often been suggested that the nuclear States tender security guarantees to nuclear-abstaining States. After the first Chinese nuclear test at Lop Nor in October 1964, President Johnson made this pledge: "The nations that do not seek national nuclear weapons can be sure that, if they need our strong support against some threat of nuclear blackmail, then they will have it." [3] But the precise form in which a guarantee would be given to the nonnuclear powers has remained unclear—whether it be joint or unilateral; whether it would be given to every nonnuclear State or only exposed ones; whether it would come into play only in the event of nuclear aggression or threat thereof, or might be invoked in case of uncontainable conventional attack. The more carefully circumscribed the guarantee, the less willing would nonnuclear weapon countries probably be to trust their future security to it; the more sweeping the pledge, the less prepared would the United States Senate be to ratify it.

---

[3] Radio-Television Address, October 18, 1964. Text in *Documents on Disarmament 1964, op. cit.,* pp. 465–469; quoted on p. 468.

SECTION FIVE: Integration at the International Level

44. THE INTEGRATIVE PROCESS

Philip E. Jacob and Henry Teune

IDENTIFYING INTEGRATIVE FACTORS

E SSENTIAL TO THE DEVELOPMENT of sound research on political integration are reliable methods of identifying and measuring integrative factors. In the following discussion some prevailing hypotheses concerning the ten integrative factors mentioned above are first set forth; indicators of each of these variables are proposed and appraised, and some lines of research to test the hypotheses are explored.

1. PROXIMITY

The hypothesis is that the closer people live together geographically, the more likely are integrative relationships to develop among them; and the closer communities are to each other, the greater the likelihood of their political integration. This hypothesis is usually qualified by recognition of a close relationship to other variables such as homogeneity, interaction or transactions, and mutual knowledge.

There is a noticeable difference between studies of international inte-

---

From *The Integration of Political Communities* edited by Philip E. Jacob and James V. Toscano (Philadelphia: 1964) pp. 16–45. Reprinted by permission of the J. B. Lippincott Company. Footnotes have been renumbered to appear in consecutive order.

PHILIP E. JACOB (1914–   ) Professor of Political Science; Director, International Studies of Values in Politics, University of Pennsylvania. His other books include *The Dynamics of International Organization: The Making of World Order,* (Homewood, Illinois: Dorsey Press, 1965); *Changing Values in College,* (New York: Harper, 1967), co-author.

HENRY TEUNE—See biographical note, page 422.

gration and intergration at the local or metropolitan level in the attention given to proximity. Preoccupation with international regionalism, especially since the Second World War, has led to a kind of rough geopolitical calculation that international integration among nations is facilitated by their regional contiguity. Curiously, this assumption has not been subjected to rigorous testing, and the argument remains largely in the realm of pitting cases against each other to support or refute the proposition of a regional imperative to international association. Against the experience of contiguous "little Europe" is cited the experience of the British Commonwealth or the Organization of American States whose members are widely dispersed. When such reservations are met by refinements of the regionalists' hypothesis, the purely geographic element is in effect qualified by reference to other kinds of proximity.

Regional science intra-nationally, however, has prompted a serious and sophisticated analysis of the proximity factor, although its relationship to political integration has only begun to be explored intensively.[1]

Procedurally there is every reason to move ahead on both the international and intra-national levels to determine the influence of the factor of proximity on political cohesion. With enough cases, it ought to be possible to control other variables sufficiently so that definitive conclusions can be reached about the influence of physical distance, *per se*.

Among indicators used to measure proximity are contiguity, . . . physical distance separating communities from one another, using either boundary to boundary, or center to center; time to travel from one community to another by available transportation (the value of this indicator is that it reflects more realistically the possibility of physical contact between people or communities than does the raw index of distance); cost of transportation; and number of "intervening opportunities" or choice points—such as intersections, traffic lights, shopping centers, etc.—along the way. Distance, in other words, is a function of technology, density of population, or some combination of these indices.

For the moment, we conclude that geography becomes significant only as it engages the motivation of human behavior. Its integrative impact is indirect and must be mediated through other factors.

2. HOMOGENEITY

The problem here is essentially to identify the social boundaries of a community and to see to what extent they correspond to the effective political boundaries. In other words, how much of a difference does it

---

[1] See Walter Isard, *Methods of Regional Analysis* (New York: Technology Press and John Wiley, 1960).

make in holding a group together as a functioning political unit if its members have similar social, economic, or other characteristics?

The hypothesis is that social homogeneity will contribute strongly to the feasibility of political integration and, conversely, that communities whose members are very different from one another will have a very hard time achieving or maintaining political integration. Viewing the problem in inter-community terms, the hypothesis holds that the more that communities are similar, the more successful are attempts to build integrative relationships among them.[2]

The choice of indicators for social homogeneity presents an immediate and large research problem. There are ten different elements that have been used as tests of homogeneity: wealth or income, education, status or class, religion, race, language, ethnic identification, attitudes (a catch-all of different types of dispositional factors such as perceptions, fears, aspirations, loyalties), values, and "character" (which in the sense of social or communal character is taken to be a composite of traits held to distinguish a particular group). Each of these has been applied as a test of homogeneity without much regard to whether similarity or likeness has in fact been associated with a *feeling* of homogeneity—that is, a sense of belonging to the group that shares the particular characteristics.[3]

This has been particularly true in the case of use of economic indicators of homogeneity. Some studies have seemed to take for granted that wealth, income, occupation, and so forth, automatically establish a common social outlook or class affiliation. There is enough empirical evidence, however, to contradict the extreme versions of economic determinism and to call for explicit testing of the degree of interrelationship between economic factors and other elements of social homogeneity.

One approach that can help indicate how people actually feel toward others is to use the well-established concept of "social distance" in measuring attitudes and values. One's readiness to associate with others in a variety of situations is scaled and compared. Similarity in people's expressions of social distance toward one another and toward persons and groups outside their community is taken as evidence of a *feeling* of social homogeneity. If people are wide apart on the social distance scale, one

---

[2] The term "homogeneity" for purposes of empirical research involves the use of statistical measures both of central tendency and dispersion of specific characteristics. For an example of research procedures on homogeneity using socio-economic characteristics, see Eshref Shevky and Wendell Bell, *Social Area Analysis* (Stanford: Stanford University Press, 1955).

[3] See, for instance, the conclusion of Cantril and Buchanan that people within nations feel they have more in common with their fellow nationals than with people of a similar social-economic class in other countries. William Buchanan and Hadley Cantril, *How Nations See Each Other* (Urbana: University of Illinois Press, 1953).

assumes that they are not very homogeneous socially and, hence, according to the integration hypothesis, that political integration among them would be difficult to achieve. The closer the readiness to associate, the stronger the presumption of political cohesion within the community.

If economic indicators are to be used as indicators of homogeneity, it is important to introduce several measures to supplement raw figures of wealth or income level in a social group. We need to know, for instance, not only how equal or unequal people are in their material status but what opportunities they may have to change their situations and to better or worsen themselves. In other words, one wants to have both a measure of dispersion or concentration of wealth and income and a measure of *mobility* among income brackets.[4]

The raw socio-economic indicators of homogeneity need to be supplemented by information concerning the attitude of different groups toward each other, for instance, haves to have-nots and vice versa. The society's homogeneity will be substantially affected even in the case of a large disparity of incomes if the have partners are strongly disposed to assume public responsibilities and, in particular, to be carriers of some of the burdens of the have-nots. Thus, inequality in economic rewards might be offset by readiness to share wealth or at least not to have wealth constitute a social barrier.

This leads the inquiry concerning social homogeneity more strongly toward attitudinal elements. For instance, if we have discovered that a particular group of haves accepts a large measure of social responsibility while others do not, we need to know what motives have persuaded each group to take their differing positions. What "payoffs" do they anticipate, or what norms are influential in one case or the other? It is possible that the more public-spirited attitude, viewed in long-term objectives, might not be an indicator of greater disposition for homogeneity but rather might represent a calculated attempt to prevent greater homogenization resulting from pressures which the intelligent and foresighted haves were clever enough to anticipate and try to forestall.

This vital kind of understanding of motivating hopes and fears in human behavior is fundamental to determining whether homogeneity is deeply grounded and real or merely a surface illusion beneath which people are not really alike at all. From this standpoint attitudinal research seems quite basic in establishing the presence of homogeneity. What is not too clear is whether some kinds of attitudes are more funda-

---

4 The factor of mobility is also relevant to other economic indicators, for instance, in regard to class status, religion, and attitudes. The *fluidity* of a society—the ability of people to cross social lines—may be an important element in increasing the sense of homogeneity.

mental than others when it comes to ascertaining the social boundaries of a community. One is inclined to say that attitudes that reflect fears, fundamental aspirations, loyalties, and values are the critical ones, whereas those that are merely representative of various kinds of information or knowledge are not so.

The use of values as an indicator of homogeneity presents particular difficulties. There has been widespread and fundamental disagreement over what is meant by the term "values." . . . Probably the most important distinction from the standpoint of research on homogeneity is the distinction between values as goals, or preferred events, and values as normative criteria of action representing feelings of obligation, legitimacy, and the like. The distinction is important because goals and norms are fundamentally different kinds of phenomena and hence represent different social characteristics. Each may properly be examined as a human attribute which might have an important effect in establishing the homogeneity or heterogeneity of a social group. The methods of identifying and measuring norms and goals differ because the objects of observation are intrinsically different. Hence research on homogeneity of values must start with a precise definition of the phenomenon under investigation.

A second research problem concerns the identification of *group* values when values are peculiarly the attributes of individuals. There is often a tendency to think of groups or collectivities having a personality or a character of their own which represents something over and beyond the values of the individual members of the community. We can find at this stage no sound empirical foundation for such conceptions and see no way to use them as indicators of homogeneity. The existence of such collective values for groups seems more a matter of subjective impression than of verifiable observation.

On the other hand, if by collective values or value patterns we mean a modal distribution within a community of either goals or normative values, these can be made the object of empirical research. If either goals or norms are widely shared by individual members of the community (as against deviation from these goals or norms by minorities in the community) this might well be the most basic element of likeness or homogeneity. Shared values are close to the springs of motivation; thus if the basic direction of action is similar among the members of a group, one might expect them to constitute a firm and solid unit. Consequently, considerable attention is devoted here to the means of identifying and measuring the distribution of values within and among communities and the determination of the extent to which communities are linked by similarity of the values that prevail among the inhabitants.

In practice, research has moved much further in applying the indicators of wealth, education, class status, and religion, than in examining the impact of attitudes and values. It is important to plan to correct the balance and to conduct at the local level, the national level, and the international level systematic studies which will attempt to plot the map homogeneity of attitudes and values; that is to say, to provide at least rough profiles of the degree to which members of a given community are or differ in the attitudes and values they hold.

Homogeneity should probably not be identified by any single index. The social boundaries of a community should be drawn on the basis of a composite profile of the various indicators previously mentioned. This raises, of course, the difficult question of whether a truly sound composite scale of homogeneity can be derived. At present it seems impossible to determine in more than an arbitrary fashion the proper weights to assign to each element in the total scale, especially in view of the strong probability that their influence will vary with different cultural situations and at different levels of political structure and organization.

Our conclusion is that current research procedures should treat each possible contributing element to homogeneity as a separate variable whose weight as a factor contributing to political integration would be assessed separately. This is particularly necessary if research on political integration is to become comparative across cultural lines and between different systems and levels of political organization.

3. TRANSACTIONS

The influence of *transactions* as a factor of political integration is now the subject of intensive research, partly as a result of developments in the analysis of communications as a field of social behavior. . . . In the most general terms, the hypothesis holds that cohesiveness among individuals and among communities of individuals can be measured by—and is probably promoted by—the extent of mutual relationship or interaction among them.

The range of transactions is, of course, tremendous. As in the case of the factor of homogeneity, it is important to try to determine which of the many forms of transactions may be most critical to the promotion of cohesion. Research has concentrated on three major types of interaction: *communications*—the interchange of messages (mail, telephone, radio, etc.); *trade*—the exchange of goods and services; and *mobility*—the movement of persons (a type of transaction that may be assessed also by frequency of personal contacts).

How much interaction among people is significant? At what point in the spectrum of transactions, from practically no interaction to the most regular and continuous interrelationships, does one decide to identify this factor as worthy of notice? Two approaches have provided useful data for analysis. One is to compare the amount of transactions of a given type among members of a particular community with the amount that is carried on by the membership of the community with the outside world.

This ratio of "domestic" to "foreign" transactions can be ascertained for a community at the lowest or at the highest political level, the term "foreign" referring to all persons outside the given community. The second approach, developed particularly by Deutsch, . . . uses an indifference model to arrive at a figure of expected transactions against which the actual state of transactions can be compared. That is, were there to be no intruding effect of community cohesion, one could calculate how the total body of transactions or particular group of transactions might be expected to be distributed throughout the population. To the extent that transactions exceeded this figure, they would measure the influence of community integration upon the flow of transactions—or conversely, the extent to which transactions could be considered an integrative influence. In either case, the hypothesis would require a demonstration of a close correlation between relative frequency of transaction and the amount of political agreement and corporate activity among the members of a particular community. The question would be whether one could, in effect, superimpose on political boundaries a map of transaction boundaries (representing points at which transactions exceeded either the "expected" rate based on indifference, or the actual rate of transaction outside a given area) and find that these boundaries coincided.

Exchanges or transactions between people in various communities have costs attached to them. Costs of transactions differentially benefit one community over another. Attempts to facilitate transactions, and thus political integration, would probably be resisted by communities whose income depends heavily on inter-community transactions. Switzerland has a large stake in maintaining the nation-state system because it lives largely off international transactions. In much the same way, a local community in New Jersey living off the flow of such transactions as traffic tickets, restaurants, and gasoline stations has a direct interest in opposing reductions in transaction costs resulting from limited access highways, subsidized public transportation, and increased air traffic.

Cost accounting of transactions, then, could explain existing patterns of political integration as well as help predict where greater political integration is likely to occur. A simple scheme for cost accounting transactions between any particular set or group of political communities is presented in Table 1.

If costs of transactions are related to political integration, then the greatest amount of political integration should occur between communities where (1) distance and (2) political boundary factors are negligible, where (3) those who are affected by the changes in costs can participate in decisions relating to costs, and where (4) the benefits of the costs of transactions are rather evenly shared. The use of a particular technique of transaction should be greatest when, after the initial cost of the technique, costs do *not* vary with distance (holding short distances constant) or political boundary and when costs are determined by all those affected thereby and are mutually beneficial.

TABLE 1

TRANSACTION COSTS
FOR A SET OF POLITICAL COMMUNITIES

Technique of Transaction	Changes in Costs as Functions of:			
	1 Distance ($ per mile)	2 Political Boundary ($ per boundary)	3 Distribution of Control of Cost Decisions	4 Distribution of Benefits of Transactions
Communications (movement of messages—mail, telephone, and telegraph, etc.)				
Trade (movement of goods and services)				
Mobility (movement of persons)				

Research on transactions as a factor in integration has been carried farthest in the international field with reference to the analysis of colonial-empire relationships. Its application to the analysis of metropolitan areas is just beginning. . . . What is needed is a large-scale extension of this kind of research, now that its design has been sharpened, to situations at all political levels and involving a variety of cultural contacts.

On the basis of the limited evidence so far produced, it is not at all clear that the hypothesis can be sustained without considerable modification. It is apparent at both the international and local levels that intimacy of transactions does not always lead to political integration. The transactional influences, if indeed they do represent an integrative factor, may be conditioned by other variables; or other variables may need to be present for the transactions to have their integrative impact. Thus, the evidence is conclusive from Deutsch's studies of comunications and trade between colonies and mother countries that transactions far exceeded the expected rate based on indifference; nevertheless, in most of these instances the empires have broken up, indicating that political integration never took hold in the face of both insufficient rewards for at least one party to these transactions and serious lack of homogeneity of values, attitudes, status, wealth, and other factors.

This suggests the great importance in future research of attempts to appraise the interrelationships of transactions with rewards and other variables and to develop estimates of the relative weight of the transactional factors in the total group of pressures and influences.

4. MUTUAL KNOWLEDGE ("COGNITIVE PROXIMITY")

Both attitudinal research and the study of transactions, as well as of the influence of proximity in a geographical sense, have indicated that something more than propinquity is necessary to induce people to work together closely and form a viable political community. Indeed, it is apparent that unless people are aware of each other and know a good deal about one another, they are not likely to enter into social or political partnership. However much alike they may be, in terms of the elements of homogeneity discussed previously, if they don't *know* that they are alike, the effect is lost. People may be next-door neighbors in an apartment house but remain complete strangers. When this occurs they are not inclined to become closely knit members of the same social group or community. The hypothesis here is that mutual knowledge or understanding among people and groups of people is essential to their functioning together effectively as a political community. As a matter of fact, the argument for the integrative influence of all three of the previously discussed factors—proximity, homogeneity, and transactions—rests upon an assumption that they will induce greater mutual acquaintance and understanding which in turn will encourage a community association.

This proposition calls immediately for considerable refinement. First, how much understanding and knowledge and, second, what kind of knowledge may contribute to integration? How much do you need to know about someone else in order to feel inclined to join with him in a community? At the level of political communities, in contrast to more intimate social groups, the evidence suggests that people do not demand close acquaintance as a condition of association. At the international level, loose and informal attachments, including alliances, are formed with virtually no basis of acquaintance across national lines, though it is apparent that more enduring and demanding forms of political integration do not arise among groups that are relative strangers. Thus parochialism, ignorance, and apathy among large populations have often facilitated the creation and maintenance of empires by governing minorities. At the local level, however, some familiarity with the overt behavior patterns of one's neighbors seems to be an element in establishing community. We seem to want to know how people take care of their property, what their church affiliation is, how interested they are in education, and so forth, before we decide to move into their community or encourage them to move into ours.

This familiarity with overt behavior is supplemented by knowledge of certain physical or social characteristics which will enable us to determine whether the persons fit our stereotypes of desirable or undesirable neighbors. In other words, it is not so much knowledge about the specific *individual* which influences integration as it is knowledge about the *type* of person as identified by racial, ethnic, class, and other such group characteristics. Put another way, it is not knowledge *per se* about other people that is significant for political integration but knowledge that links up with a preconceived gallery of stereotypes which each of us holds and uses as a touchstone in determining whether we want to live and work together.[5]

These stereotypes—while strongly persistent—are not immune to change. Actually they may be very volatile. There are repeated demonstrations of people reversing deeply set images of other nations under the impact of new political alignments. A classic illustration is the transformation of widely held American images of Japanese and Germans within a few years after the Second World War and, conversely, of American images of Russians.

This suggests a third qualification. Mutual knowledge will not contribute to integration unless it is accompanied by or linked to experience or memories of experiences which have had a favorable impact. In other words, it depends upon the *quality* of our previous associations whether a fuller understanding of what another person is like will cause us to seek closer association, or on the other hand, to fear him, be contemptuous of him, or simply ignore him. Familiarity in itself seems to have little behavioral influence; it is knowledge which excites an anticipation of reward that exerts an integrative impact.

Finally, it is apparent that *accuracy* of mutual knowledge may have relatively little to do with determining its integrative effect, except to the extent that it enables knowledge to bear up under test and trial. The fundamental requirement is that knowledge will have conveyed *awareness* of others and, second, that it will have aroused favorable or unfavorable *dispositions*.

The object of inquiry, therefore, is not so much the range of mutual knowledge, nor its validity, but the evaluation of this knowledge by the

---

[5] There is now available an excellent comprehensive review and bibliography of research on national stereotypes. See H. C. J. Duijker and N. H. Frijda, *National Character and National Stereotypes*, Vol. 1, "Confluence," (Amsterdam: North-Holland Publishing Co., 1960). See also the important work by Harold Isaacs and other associates of the Massachusetts Institute of Technology Center for International Studies who have developed techniques of interview and survey which effectively establish prevailing patterns of ethnic images. Note also the impressive "Proposal for Cooperative Cross-Cultural Research on Ethnocentrism" by Donald T. Campbell and Robert A. Levine, *Journal of Conflict Resolution*, Vol. 5, No. 1, March, 1961, p. 82. This is an effort supported by Northwestern University's Programs of African Studies, International Relations, and Comparative Politics.

members of the community. The indicators we use should relate, therefore, to ascertaining what people *think* they know about one another rather than what they actually do know and whether they obtain from this knowledge a sense of mutual appreciation or the opposite. Attitudes and images, therefore, are the most productive indicators, and the growing volume of research on stereotypes held by persons of what other people or groups are like is highly relevant.

5. FUNCTIONAL INTEREST

An important influence in the development of political communities may be the convergence of functional interests, that is, the interests to which people are prepared to devote major effort for fulfillment. Such interests might also be defined as actions for which they expect a substantial reward as a result of their efforts (if one assumes a view of human motivation consonant with the stimulus-response theory of learning). The proposition to test is whether the functional interests of the bulk of a community are sufficiently similar so that they will be advanced by the development of common political ties. Conversely, sharp diversity of functional interests within the society might be expected to limit the possibility that any corporate action by the government would be able to convey benefits widely and evenly throughout the society.

If the hypothesis is expressed in inter-community terms, integration would be viewed as dependent on the extent to which the dominant functional interests are shared in each community and thus could be advanced by inter-community agreement or association. By way of illustration, economic interest groups whose prosperity is contingent upon a high external tariff may not be amenable to international economic cooperation which involves a reciprocal lowering of tariffs. Effective economic integration would depend upon whether groups that would benefit in each country from an expansion of trade, or the development of joint investment policies, are more dominant than groups which feel they would not benefit—for instance, farmers who are at a disadvantage in competition with producers in other countries.

In international relations, an illustration of the influence of functional interest as an integrative factor is the alignment of nations in a war for national survival and now, in view of the development of the technology of mass annihilation, the strong pressures for international disarmament agreements for survival.

These converging functional interests, however, may not provide a firm and lasting basis for integration. They often tend to be transitory—people's devotion to particular interests switching as conditions change—and hence functional associations may be simply marriages of convenience.

Analysis of functional interests recalls the issue of homogeneity, raising the question of the extent to which people in the same or different communities share interests. However, considered in political terms, the issue is not so much the identification of *common* interests, as it is the assessment of the influence of *particular* interests in the decision-making process. We want to know not only whether a large number of people have the same stake in a given type of endeavor but what interest groups are politically dominant.

Functional interest analysis should relate to the fancied as well as the real interests of people. Sometimes what people think will contribute to their benefit will not turn out to be beneficial and may even preclude any possibility of their obtaining the benefit they seek. They may see their interest only in the short run and be confounded by long-term developments; or they may accept a statement of some respected leader rather than try satisfying themselves directly that their interest is involved; or they may simply be badly misinformed and think that they are pursuing an interest when they are not. From a short-range action standpoint, and that is of course what concerns us in the analysis of integrative forces, it is the belief that counts most. The reality is significant only indirectly and in the longer run as it serves to reinforce or correct beliefs by facilitating or frustrating action based on those beliefs.

One further point needs to be made concerning functional interest analysis. In the political arena these interests are almost always funneled through *groups*. They represent in a sense embryonic communities or, indeed, may be highly organized and stratified communities operating as social and political forces within the broader political community. Hence, this kind of analysis is primarily concerned with interests as articulated by groups rather than by individuals.

Given these circumstances, appropriate indicators of functional interests are the policies expressed by organized interest groups and actions undertaken by them to advance these policies. One should recognize that these functional interests are by no means limited to economic stakes; they can be developed around a whole range of non-economic goals such as civil rights, education, peace, and civic improvement.

Although there is relatively little difficulty in determining indicators of functional interests, there is no clear solution for the problem of measurement. Mere numbers of people associated with a given functional interest group convey no understanding of their political weight. Political "power" is a highly volatile element, with no reliable indices, despite efforts to measure influence in terms of the subjective judgments of people who are considered by an observer to be influential (the approach taken in studies of community power structure).

Nor is there a good way to measure the *intensity* of the functional interest, that is, the depth of attachment to it of those who share the interest and their readiness to devote themselves to the advancement of their interest. For these reasons research on the influence of functional interest in political integration is handicapped.

An important task that can be undertaken is the identification of interests and interest groups that move the community toward or away from integration. One can also identify those interests that reach beyond a particular community and link up with corresponding interest groups in other communities to form a possible basis for inter-community integration. The studies by Ernst Haas of the functional bases of integration in Western Europe are an excellent pioneer effort in this direction at the international level.[6] Haas closely identifies the degree to which trade unions, business organizations, and other functional groups in the six countries of the European Community share the same objectives and the extent to which they conceive of their interests as being compatible with European integration or to depend on the maintenance of national autonomy.

To some extent the studies of voting behavior both in elections and in legislative activity can provide some measure of the relative political influence of interest groups. This is especially true in countries whose political systems enable major interest groups to dominate particular political parties or blocs—either at national or local levels. One trouble with using voting as a measure of interest group influence, however, is that the vote of an elector or legislator usually reflects a combination of influences and pressures; he is not the minion of a single interest group. In the absence of more adequate instruments, however, the measurement of functional interest by its capacity to command political support is justified, especially in determining its influence as a factor in political integration.

6. COMMUNAL "CHARACTER" OR SOCIAL "MOTIVE"

Some major contributions to the study of social behavior in recent years have reconstructed the concept of social or group character to make it amenable to empirical research. These studies have empirically described modal distributions of attitudes, values, and patterns of overt behavior.

From a motivational standpoint these studies raise the provocative question of whether societies may acquire by cultural inheritance and learning a set of behavioral dispositions so pervasive and compelling that the whole group will tend to act in a distinctive manner. Community behavior will run, so to speak, in grooves which have been carved by the "communal" character. McClelland, for instance, by content analysis of the statistical distribution of relevant symbols in appropriate samples of

---

[6] Ernst Haas, *The Uniting of Europe, op. cit.*

the community's communication stream, has successfully demonstrated differences among societies in the mix of three major motivational sets: an affiliation motive, an achievement motive, and a power motive. In turn, particular combinations of these motives seem to be demonstrably related to certain complexes of social and political action, such as economic development.[7]

Studies of communal character open a new dimension of analysis for students of political integration. If it is established that a community can acquire a collective motivational pattern that strongly influences its behavior on economic enterprise, it may be possible that it will have acquired traits which dispose it toward cohesiveness and integration or, on the other hand, toward anarchy within or belligerence without. Using techniques similar to those developed by McClelland, research should be able to establish profiles of communal character related not only to national entities but to sub-national communities and trans-national groupings. These characterological assessments could be compared with indices of community integration in the same manner that McClelland has linked motivational patterns to economic development.

To our knowledge, sound empirical research on national character has not yet developed evidence of a direct link between communal dispositions or traits and integrative behavior to the point where an integrative syndrome can be identified. Observations of the peculiar patterns of belligerence or cooperativeness, anarchism or responsiveness, of particular societies and national groups have, on the whole, been too impressionistic and scanty to sustain this kind of conclusion at present. This should not preclude an attempt, however, to salvage the concept of national character or communal character and to see whether, with available research techniques, a rough estimate can be made of the integrative force of acquired cultural characteristics or psychological motives of various communities.[8] A point of departure for such research might be to build on McClelland's work and attempt to determine whether there are correlations between the mix of achievement, affiliation, and power motives on the one hand and internal and external community cohesiveness on the other. To put the research problem in hypothesis form, we might take

---

[7] David C. McClelland, *The Achieving Society* (Princeton: Van Nostrand, 1961).

[8] The communal character approach tends to discount the significance of leadership as a determinant of social action, for it generally implies an initiative stemming from the mass of society. To safeguard against the possibility of imputing to communal character an influence which in reality may come from leaders who are in a position to command the following of their society, the analysis of character, or motive, should be conducted in such a way as to permit separate identification of elite patterns, and comparison with the distribution of the motivational patterns through the society as a whole.

McClelland's "affiliation motive" as the aspect of communal character most likely to be associated with integrative or cooperative behavior. We might then suggest that those societies characterized by a high proportion of affiliation motive, in contrast to achievement and power motives, would be both internally cohesive and strongly disposed to cooperate with other communities. The indices of communal character so construed have been specified and scaled with some precision by McClelland. A major set of indicators is to be found in the verbalization of aspirations and beliefs in stories used with children at an early stage of socialization.[9]

Another significant approach to the identification of communal character, this time at the national level, are the studies of aspirations and fears by Hadley Cantril and Lloyd Free using a self-anchoring scale.[10] Employing Cantril's and Free's findings on national differences in hopes and fears, one could establish whether they were significantly correlated with integrative behavior. In other words, do nations that have a generally pessimistic view of the future tend to be less or more cohesive, than those that are more optimistic? Are nations whose aspirations center largely on increases in economic welfare likely to be more cooperative in their international relations than those that are predominantly preoccupied with prestige, physical security, or political independence?

Each of the above sets of studies of what we have called broadly communal character already encompasses enough data so that it should be possible to take their findings as is and, by matching them with measures of both internal and external integrative behavior, conclude whether such characterological features do have significant influence upon the building of cohesive national communities and, further, upon the encouragement of association between nations.

7. STRUCTURAL FRAME

Analysis of the system of decision-making or the power structure within the community introduces a different kind of variable from those previously discussed. The question here is the organization or arrangement of political action, rather than behavioral characteristics of persons or groups. We want to know whether the *system* makes a difference in the amenability of a community to cooperative relationships. If the community is pluralistic, rather than monolithic, if it is organized hierarchically or provides equality in decision-making, if it is socially

---

[9] See McClelland, *op. cit.,* Chapter 5, in which he spells out his typology for content analysis.

[10] This comprehensive program of research, conducted in seventeen countries, is summarized in Hadley Cantril and Lloyd A. Free, "Hopes and Fears for Self and Country: The Self-Anchoring Striving Scale in Cross-Cultural Research" *The American Behavioral Scientist.* Vol. 6, No. 2, Supplement, October, 1962.

stratified or mobile, if its political authority is centralized or dispersed—is the society more or less likely to be internally integrated and more or less disposed to be closely linked to other communities?

While research on social and political structure is voluminous, there has been little attempt to determine whether structural differences carry over into the influencing of community and inter-community cohesion. Prevailing democratic theory holds that consensus or, more explicitly, consent is vital to the growth of a healthy and united political community. Consequently, a political structure that permits wide participation in decision-making should be conducive to cohesion, whereas one that is authoritarian should invite dissidence and in time disintegrate as a result of pent-up frustrations exploding in violence. But this democratic hypothesis has not been systematically tested by applying a reliable measure of the degree of cohesion to communities that have differing forms of government.

In view of the recent evidence from the experience of new and developing countries, the hypothesis might be turned about. A proposition now frequently advanced holds that a structure of highly concentrated political authority, with strict limitations on general participation, particularly on the voicing of dissent, is almost a requisite of national community organization under conditions of threat and social change.

It should be possible to determine whether consistently clear differences in cohesiveness appear in communities at the same political levels which have marked differences in political structure. Thus one might compare a set of local communities in the United States in which political power was tightly held in a few hands with another set where it was widely dispersed with a large amount of public participation in decision-making. A similar comparison might also be undertaken among nations. Both the extent of *internal* cohesion and the disposition toward external cooperation should be examined.

Indicators of political structure would include: the amount of day-to-day decision-making power exercised by top leadership, the degree to which leadership is organized in a strict hierarchy of power, the amount of accountability of policy makers to others, the amount of organized political opposition tolerated, the degree of mobility within the structure of political power, and the amount of political influence exercised upon the leadership group by other segments of the society. A considerable volume of data is available, particularly at the national level, on these points, so that scales of political structure are feasible, enabling countries to be ranked according to some of the dimensions suggested. Correlation with integrative behavior could then be undertaken. It is probable that the analysis of political structure at the local or metropolitan level has also proceeded far enough in the United States and in a few other countries to make possible the same kind of analysis.

In the area of international relations it is hardly possible to test the hypotheses concerning the effect of different structural patterns on integration. International relations, as they are currently conducted, are set within the *single* political frame of reference of the nation-state system: diffused, pluralistic, non-authoritarian, and consensual, with the possible exception of the European Community. International institutions do not have a highly structured pattern of political organization, and they all function within the same over-all system. There are really no situations to contrast. Historically, it is true, there are instances of international association with varying degrees of integration and differing types of political structures—federal, confederal, and unitary. But it is hazardous to reason from such situations to the present state of international affairs because there are so many elements that differ. About all that one might profitably do is to note the extent to which integrative behavior has been able to develop under such pluralistic conditions. To the extent that it has, the democratic hypothesis would be sustained. But in fact, progress toward international integration is so tortured that the hypothesis may well be questioned.

There is another aspect of structural analysis worth exploring: The hypothesis has been advanced that structure results in certain ideological dispositions and that communities with a common or similar political structure have ideological affinities that make it possible for them to integrate more easily. The argument is that countries with democratic political institutions are likely to develop an attachment to these institutions and that this then tends to produce a favorable attitude toward other democracies. Thus, one assumes that the Free World will be able to hold together, and that the North Atlantic Community will become increasingly integrated because a common heritage of political institutions will have engendered devotion to the same set of political ideas. The same argument would hold for communist nations.

A test of this hypothesis would require carefully controlled comparisons of the degree of integration achieved among communities with like political structures in contrast to their relationships with countries whose political institutions differ. It would be vital, of course, to recognize the great differences among institutional arrangements which may be hidden by a common facade of ideological labels. The facts of political organization must be distinguished from the form. How truly similar are the political systems of the United States, France, and West Germany; or, on the other hand, the political systems of the Soviet Union, Yugoslavia, and Poland? Fundamentally, it is a matter of adopting reliable indicators of structural political factors. Sound research would require that we go back to the indicators previously mentioned and look at the informal structure of power to obtain our data, rather than at the formal constitutional arrangements.

8. SOVEREIGNTY-DEPENDENCY STATUS

A major assumption of political theory as applied to the modern state has held that the ultimate mark of a community's political integration is its attainment of a status of "sovereignty." The classic concept of sovereignty holds, first, that within a fully organized society all members of the community are subject to a supreme political authority; and, second, that the community as a political entity is independent of control by any one else. Classic sovereignty implies total *internal* political cohesion and complete *external* autonomy. Sovereignty is synonymous with absolute integration within a community and absolute disintegration among communities.

The classical conception, however, seems to bear little relationship to the realities of modern political communities. Political power within a community is usually dispersed to some degree, even in a nominally sovereign nation-state with an authoritarian system of government. Variations in the amount of concentration or dispersion of power are considerable, but rarely does the structure of power establish the point of extreme concentration called for by the traditional concept of sovereignty.

Sovereignty is also limited externally. A few states exercise a large degree of—but not complete—freedom from outside control. Most are heavily restricted in what they can do by the influence of others, which is often so great that countries are in fact, if not in name, dependent rather than independent.

Conversely, sub-units of sovereign states, such as local governments, may in fact exercise a substantial degree of autonomy in the making of political decisions, or at least certain types of political decisions, even though theoretically they should be totally subservient to the central political powers. Such a situation prevails not only in federally organized countries but also in those where expediency directs that the central government shall leave many decisions to the discretion of lower units.

It is therefore crucial to determine empirically the relationship between political autonomy and political integration, treating each as separate variables and assuming that political communities will vary greatly in the amount of autonomy that they in fact exercise. Sovereignty and dependency represent relatively large or small amounts of autonomy on a continuum of varying political conditions at all levels of government.

The question of sovereignty has an economic dimension as well as a political dimension. A community's autonomy is expressed not only in its control over political decision-making but in the extent to which the allocation of its economic resources may be subject to outside decisions. This aspect, particularly, needs to be observed in societies that are not totalitarian, where the direction of the economic life of the community is not completely under political authority.

. . . Indicators of political autonomy include: (1) the extent to which decisions are subject to review by another political authority; (2) the extent to which discretion is limited by constitutional or contractual commitments which may not be set aside without serious consequences; (3) the scope of the decisions or range of the decisions which are subject to control by the community itself; (4) the percentage of community defense and law enforcement facilities that are shared with other communities; and (5) the percentage and kind of decisions made in one community that are enforceable in another and vice versa (status-of-forces agreements, narcotics control, etc.).

On the economic side, some of the following factors may be used as indicators of sovereignty-dependency: (1) ratios of mutual trade (exports plus imports) to total external trade and to total gross product of each partner; (2) percentage of tax base shared; (3) percentage of gross national product received in forms of loans, grants, or direct aid; (4) percentage of population directly dependent on (employed by or in) other political communities; (5) percentage of vital resources imported (vital in terms of the community's major economic activities).

The significance of political autonomy as an integrative factor may be tested effectively by comparing the degree of sovereignty with the degree of integration prevailing in communities at different political levels. If sovereignty is presumed to solidify a community, then one would expect to discover greater integration on a national basis than within a local community with a much more limited autonomy. If it should appear that there is not a significant difference in the degree of cohesion between a local community and the national community of which it is a dependent part, the sovereignty hypothesis would be seriously discounted.

This is not to suggest that comparisons among communities of the same political level would not be useful. To test the sovereignty hypothesis, great powers possessing a relatively high degree of autonomy could be compared with well-established but less independent smaller countries, such as New Zealand or Denmark, and also with new, small, and recently formed states still heavily dependent for their survival economically, and perhaps politically, on outside assistance or toleration. The question to be answered would be whether those states which were at the dependency end of the scale proved to be any less integrated or cohesive than those that were closer to the sovereignty end.

Another type of study might pinpoint the sovereignty variable while holding many of the other variables relatively constant. Integration within a community could be assessed before—and after—it had achieved political independence. To what extent, for instance, has the achievement of political independence in the new countries of Africa and Asia been accompanied by an increase in community cohesion? If it has not, this would tend to refute the sovereignty hypothesis.

A corresponding study at the local level could be conducted which would examine the degree of integration which prevailed in communities before and after they were granted "home rule" or, conversely, what happened to the cohesiveness of communities which became absorbed in metropolitan or other regional jurisdictions.

As for the influence of sovereignty upon inter-community relations, it is commonly held to be a major hurdle to integration. In the study of international relations it is widely asserted that the more sovereign the state, the less disposed it will be to cooperate with others and in particular the more intensely will it oppose political arrangements that encroach upon its autonomy.

. . .

One problem with the analysis of sovereignty in the ways that have been suggested is that sovereignty may have more influence subjectively as a state of mind than objectively as a condition of autonomy. Some people are extremely sensitive about independence, yet have very little. From the standpoint of political impact, it seems probable that it is the *consciousness* of sovereignty that impels action rather than its actual possession by a political community. If such is the case, one needs a different set of indicators from those that have been suggested. One indicator might be the attention devoted by the members of the community to the issue of sovereignty. Another might be their sensitivity to assumed violations of sovereignty or, indeed, their actual claims that it had been violated or was threatened. The verbalization of community loyalties would be an appropriate index—expressions of "Americanism" for instance—or non-verbal expressions of devotion to the symbols of sovereignty, such as patriotic celebrations. It is possible that one is considering here a variable that is substantively different from actual autonomy; perhaps this is one aspect of social homogeneity. But because it is tied so closely in people's minds to the image or goal of autonomy, it should probably be kept very much in mind whenever the issue is raised concerning the possible influence upon community behavior of the degree of sovereign status which it enjoys.

9. GOVERNMENTAL EFFECTIVENESS

There may be a very close connection between the cohesion of a political community and the effectiveness of its government in meeting demands and expectations of its citizens. . . . Essentially, the hypothesis is that governmental effectiveness is necessary to retain the loyalty of the members of the community, and such loyalty is necessary to maintain internal integration in the community. Governmental ineffectiveness, on the other hand, will engender pressures for new, different, or external forms of integration. Citizens will look outward and pitch their loyalties to new forms of political organization or to other larger units of community.

Such hypotheses require both agreement on what constitutes governmental effectiveness and availability of indicators which can identify governmental effectiveness regardless of cultural or political differences between communities. We believe that governmental effectiveness can be measured uniformly both by objective indices (such as physical survival or increases in gross national product) and by subjective indices (such as feelings of well-being and belief in an ameliorative future). The problem with objective indicators is that they must be shown to correspond to evaluations of the people. This can be done by comparing what people expect of their government with what they think they are getting. Such a measure has the advantage of being "self-anchored" within each community.

While it is clear that this variable may be of vital importance in analyzing the degree of integration in communities that are already politically organized, there is a question as to whether corresponding research can be undertaken on situations, such as international relations, where central governmental institutions do not exist or are rudimentary. Two possible approaches may be considered. First, one could treat international institutions as a form of government, (inter-government) whose effectiveness would be measured in the same way as national or subnational institutions and compared with them. Objectively, the contributions of the United Nations, NATO, or the European Community) to the physical survival and well-being of people could be measured against their failures and frustrations. Subjectively, popular expectations of the United Nations could be compared by means of survey data with their estimates of fulfillment. The second approach would compare the amount of governmental responsibility invested in international institutions with the amount kept strictly within the hands of national or sub-national units of government. Just as within the United States expansion of national government responsibilities has reflected confidence in the government's effectiveness, so an increase in the scope of political actions and economic activities undertaken by international bodies could be a measure of their effectiveness.[11]

---

[11] Care must be taken here to avoid using increases in governmental activities as indicators both of integration and governmental effectiveness.

10. PREVIOUS INTEGRATIVE EXPERIENCE

Some research on international relations, such as the studies of European integration by Haas, suggest that integration may occur more easily if there have been previous integrative experiences. . . . Further research is needed at the international, national, and local levels to determine whether there is a geometrical progression in the building up of political integration, where, after a number of integrative experiences, further integrative acts follow more and more rapidly. A refined spill-over hypothesis would have some basis in learning theory. . . . It would involve the principle of reinforcement. But the reinforcement principle is symmetrical. Integrative experiences, in order to contribute to a generalized habit of integration, must be rewarded. If they are not rewarded or are punished they may encourage habits which lead to disintegration. In this perspective, once having broken the ground of cooperation with someone else or with another community, a person or a community confronted with a situation in any way similar might be expected to follow in the path that has already been tried out.

Lines of research to test this variable of integration at both the international level and the metropolitan are now clear. . . . This is one of the areas in which direct comparison between international and metropolitan experiences should be possible by use of parallel indicators and a common methodological design.

45. SOME ESSENTIAL REQUIREMENTS FOR THE ESTABLISHMENT OF AMALGAMATED SECURITY-COMMUNITIES

Karl W. Deutsch, *et al.*

A NUMBER OF CONDITIONS appear to be essential, so far as our evidence goes, for the success of amalgamated security-communities—that is, for their becoming integrated. None of these conditions, of course, seems to be by itself sufficient for success; and all of them together may not be sufficient either, for it is quite possible that we have overlooked some additional conditions that may also be essential. None the less, it does seem plausible to us that any group of states or territories which fulfilled all the essential conditions for an amalgamated security-community which we have been able to identify, should also be at least on a good part of the way to successful amalgamation.

1. VALUES AND EXPECTATIONS

The first group of essential conditions deals with motivations for political behavior, and in particular with the values and expectations held in the politically relevant strata of the political units concerned. In regard to values, we found in all our cases a compatibility of the main values held by the politically relevant strata of all participating units. Sometimes this was supplemented by a tacit agreement to deprive of political significance any incompatible values that might remain. In this manner the gradual depoliticization of the continuing difference between Protestant and Catholic religious values in the course of the eighteenth century furnished an essential pre-condition for the successful amalgamation of Germany and Switzerland, respectively, in the course of the following century.[1] Examples of a partial depoliticization of conflicting values

---

From *Political Community and the North Atlantic Area* by Karl W. Deutsch, Sidney A. Burrell, Robert A. Kann, Maurice Lee, Jr., Martin Lichterman, Raymond E. Lindgren, Francis L. Loewenheim, Richard W. Van Wagenen. (Princeton: 1957), pp. 46–58. Reprinted by permission of Princeton University Press, Copyright © 1957. Footnotes have been renumbered to appear in consecutive order.

KARL W. DEUTSCH (1912–   ) Professor of Government, Harvard University. His other books include *Arms Control and the Atlantic Alliance: Europe Faces Coming Policy Decisions,* (New York: Wiley, 1967); *The Nerves of Government,* (New York: Free Press of Glencoe, 1963); *France, Germany and the Western Alliance: A Study of Elite Attitudes on European Integration and World Politics,* (New York: Scribner's, 1967), co-author.

[1] For the Swiss solution of the denominational problem, see Hermann Weilenmann, *Pax Helvetica oder die Demokratie der Kleinen Gruppen,* Zurich, Rentsch, 1951, pp. 300–311; Hans Kohn, *Der Schweizerische Nationalgedanke: Eine Studie Zum Thema*

include the partial depoliticization of the slavery issue in the United States between 1775 and 1819, and of the race problem after 1876.[2] Similarly, Germany saw a reduction in the political relevance of the liberal-conservative cleavage after 1866 with the emergence of the National Liberal Party. A similar reduction of political relevance occurred in regard to the conflict of Scottish Presbyterianism with the Episcopal Church in England and Scotland after 1690, and in the further abatement of the Protestant–Catholic issue in Switzerland after the mid-eighteenth century, and further after 1848.

Whether values are "main" values can be determined from the internal politics of the participating units independently from the issue of union— although only, to be sure, within broad margins of error. How important is each value in the domestic politics of the participating units? Acceptance of slavery as a "positive good" had become an essential qualification of candidates for public office in many Southern states in the United States before 1861; this value, important in Southern internal politics, was then also important in the relations between South and North. Conversely, the importance of the distinction between Catholics and Protestants was declining in the domestic politics of nineteenth century Prussia and Bavaria, as well as—more slowly—in the relations between them.

Values were most effective politically when they were not held merely in abstract terms, but when they were incorporated in political institutions and in habits of political behavior which permitted these values to be acted on in such a way as to strengthen people's attachment to them. This connection between values, institutions, and habits we call a "way of life," and it turned out to be crucial. In all our cases of successful amalgamation we found such a distinctive way of life—that is, a set of socially accepted values and of institutional means for their pursuit and attainment, and a set of established or emerging habits of behavior corresponding to them. To be distinctive, such a way of life has to include at least some major social or political values and institutions which are different from those which existed in the area during the recent past, or from those prevailing among important neighbors. In either case, such a way of life usually involved a significant measure of social innovation as against the recent past.

"Nationalismus und Freiheit," Zurich, Verlag der "Neuen Zürcher Zeitung," 1955, pp. 77–78, 88–94; E. Bonjour, H. S. Offler, and G. R. Potter, *A Short History of Switzerland,* Oxford, Clarendon Press, 1952, pp. 272–273, 296–299, etc.

[2] Any survey of American history of the period up to about 1819 reveals how small a part the slavery issue played in politics in the early years of the republic. For the temporary depoliticization of the race problem after 1876 see Paul H. Buck, *The Road to Reunion,* Boston, 1947, pp. 283, 296–297; C. Vann Woodward, *Origins of the New South, 1877–1913,* Baton Rouge, 1951, p. 216.

Putting the matter somewhat differently, we noted in our cases that the partial shift of political habits required in transferring political loyalties from the old, smaller political units, at least in part, to a new and larger political community has only occurred under conditions when also a great number of other political and social habits were in a state of change. Thus we find that the perception of an American people and an American political community, as distinct from the individual thirteen colonies, emerged between 1750 and 1790. This occurred at the same time as the emergence of a distinct American way of life clearly different from that of most of the people of Great Britain or French Canada. This way of life had been developing since the beginnings of colonial settlement in the seventeenth century, but had undergone accelerated change and development in the course of the American Revolution and its aftermath. Another example of this process is the emergence of a distinct way of life of the Swiss people, in contrast to the way of life of the peasants and to a lesser extent of the town dwellers in most of the rest of Europe; here, too, the emergence of this distinctive way of life furnished the social and political background for the gradual emergence of Swiss political community.[3] Similarly, the unifications of Germany and of Italy occurred in the context of a much broader change in political values, institutions, and habits of behavior. These new values were implicit in the modern, liberal nineteenth-century way of life in contrast to the values and institutions of the "old regime" still represented by the policies of the Metternich era.

In regard to expectations, we found that in all our cases amalgamation was preceded by widespread expectations of joint rewards for the participating units, through strong economic ties or gains envisaged for the future. By economic ties, we mean primarily close relations of trade permitting large-scale division of labor and almost always giving rise to vested interests. It was not necessary, however, for such strong economic ties to exist prior to amalgamation. Expectations of rewards were conspicuous in the Anglo–Scottish union of 1707;[4] in the unification of Italy, where the South found itself to some extent disappointed; and in

---

[3] Cf. Leo Weisz, *Die Alten Eidgenossen*, Zurich, Niehaus, 1940, pp. 7–156. Wilhelm Oechsli, *History of Switzerland, 1499–1914,* Cambridge University Press, 1922, pp. 1–7, 17–21. Anton Castell, *Geschichte des Landes Schwyz*, Zurich, *Benziger* Verlag Einsiedelm, 1954, pp. 26–33. Wolfgang von Wartburg, *Geschichte der Schweiz*, Munich, Oldenbourg, 1951, pp. 31–56. Weilenmann, *Die vielsprachige Schweiz*, Basel-Leipzig, Rheim-Verlag, 1925, pp. 20–42, 50–51, 54–57, 60–63, 68; *Pax Helvetica*, pp. 221–284.

[4] One of the more important rewards from the Scottish point of view was participation in trade with England and England's colonies. P. Hume Brown, *History of Scotland*, Cambridge, Eng., 1911, III, 57–58; George S. Pryde, *The Treaty of Union of Scotland and England 1707*, Edinburgh, 1950, 13ff.

the unification of Germany, where such economic expectations were brilliantly fulfilled.

Only a part of such expectation had to be fulfilled. A "down payment" of tangible gains for a substantial part of the supporters of amalgamation soon after the event, if not earlier, seems almost necessary. This was accomplished by the land policies of Jefferson and the fiscal policies of Hamilton in the case of the United States, by Bismarck's "National Liberal" policies in the 1870's,[5] and by Cavour for at least Northern Italy. Somewhat different economic gains may result from the joint or parallel exploitation of some third resource, rather than from trade between one unit and another. Thus, exploitation of Western lands offered joint rewards to members of the American union, apart from the benefits of mutual trade; many Scotsmen, too, in 1707 were more impressed with the prospect of a Scottish share in English overseas markets than in direct trade with England.

Some noneconomic expectations also turned out to be essential. In all our cases of successful amalgamation we found widespread expectations of greater social or political equality, or of greater social or political rights or liberties, among important groups of the politically relevant strata—and often among parts of the underlying populations—in the political units concerned.[6]

2. CAPABILITIES AND COMMUNICATION PROCESSES

Values and expectations not only motivate people to performance, but the results of this performance will in turn make the original values and expectations weaker or stronger. Accordingly, we found a number of essential conditions for amalgamation which were related to the capabilities of the participating units or to the processes of communication occurring among them. The most important of these conditions was an increase in the political and administrative capabilities of the main political units to be amalgamated. Thus the amalgamation of Germany was preceded by a marked increase in the political and administrative capabilities of Prussia from 1806 onward, and by a lesser but still significant increase in the corresponding capabilities of Bavaria and of other

---

[5] Cf. Adalbert Wahl, *Deutsche Geschichte von der Reichsgründung bis zum Ausbruch des Weltkriegs (1871 bis 1914)*, Stuttgart, 1926, I, 61–107; and Johannes Ziekursch, *Politische Geschichte des neuen deutschen Kaiserreiches*, Frankfurt, 1927, II, 279–308.

[6] Hermann Oncken, *Lassalle, Eine politische Biographie*, 4th edn., Stuttgart and Berlin, 1923, pp. 236–237; Erich Eyck, *Der Vereinstag Deutscher Arbeitervereine 1863–1868*, Berlin, 1904; Gustav Mayer, *Johann Baptist von Schweitzer und die Sozialdemokratie*, Jena, 1909; and Eugene N. Anderson, *The Social and Political Conflict in Prussia 1858–1864*, Lincoln, Neb., 1954, pp. 119–175.

German states. Similarly, there were important increases in the capabilities of Piedmont in the course of the last decades preceding Italian unification.[7] In the case of the American colonies, considerable increases in the capabilities of American state governments after 1776, and particularly the adoption of important and effective state constitutions by Pennsylvania, Virginia, Massachusetts, and other states, paved the way for the Articles of Confederation and later for federal union.[8]

Another essential condition for amalgamation, closely related to the increase in capabilities, is the presence of markedly superior economic growth, either as measured against the recent past of the territories to be amalgamated, or against neighboring areas. Such superior economic growth did not have to be present in all participating units prior to amalgamation, but it had to be present at least in the main partner or partners vis-à-vis the rest of the units to be included in the amalgamated security-community. The higher economic growth rates of England, Prussia, and Piedmont, both immediately before and during amalgamation, are conspicuous examples.

Another essential requirement for successful amalgamation was the presence of unbroken links of social communication between the political units concerned, and between the politically relevant strata within them. By such unbroken links we mean social groups and institutions which provide effective channels of communication, both horizontally among the main units of the amalgamated security-community and vertically among the politically relevant strata within them. Such links thus involve always persons and organizations.

Some of the links are horizontal or geographic between different participating units; others involve vertical communications, cutting across classes. An example of geographic links occurred during the course of the Industrial Revolution. The rapid growth of settlement and economic activity in Northern England and Southwestern Scotland deepened the integration of England and Scotland during the century after 1707.[9] Another example would be the rapid growth in population and economic

---

[7] The development of Piedmont is discussed in great detail by Giuseppe Prato in *Fatti e dottrine economiche alla vigilia del 1848: l'Associazione agraria subalpina e Camillo Cavour,* published in *Biblioteca di Storia Italiana recente (1800–1870),* IX, Turin, 1921, pp. 133–484.

[8] Allan Nevins, *The American States During and After the Revolution, 1775–1789,* New York, 1924, 117ff., 621ff.

[9] This, strictly speaking, cannot be documented, since the two areas are not fused industrially even today. They are, however, very close to one another, and there has been an extensive migration back and forth. The term "Geordie" as used to describe a Tyneside Scottish migrant is one indication, however, of the extent of population flow over the border. For evidence of the continuing distinctiveness of the two areas even so late as the early nineteenth century, see John Clapham, *Economic History of Modern Britain,* Cambridge, Eng., 1950, 2nd edn., I, pp. 50–51.

activity in the Middle Atlantic states and in Kentucky, Tennessee, and Ohio which tended to strengthen the links between North and South in the United States during the first decades after 1776. A third example is the role of commerce and transport over St. Gotthard Pass, and of the institutions and organizations related to it, in the consolidation of Switzerland.[10]

An example of a vertical link within Scotland was that between the aristocracy and the middle classes and the people at large, made possible by the ministers and elders of the Scottish Presbyterian Church. In the course of the seventeenth century, the horizontal links of the Scottish Presbyterians to English Protestant sects facilitated Scottish participation in English theological disputes, and this in turn contributed to the acceptance of English (rather than lowland Scots) as the standard language of Scotland.[11] Another example would be the German financial and industrial community that came to link major interests in the Rhineland, Berlin, Darmstadt, Leipzig, and other German centers and states during the 1850's and 1860's.[12]

Another essential condition, related to the preceding one, is the broadening of the political, social, or economic elite, both in regard to its recruitment from broader social strata and to its continuing connections with them.[13] An example of such a broadening of the elite was the

---

[10] See, eg., Hans Nabholz, *Geschichte der Schweiz*, Zurich, Schulthess, 1938, Vol. 1, pp. 105–106, 126, 150–152, 203, etc., Wolfgang von Wartburg, *op cit.*, pp. 32–33, 43, 58, 82, etc., Weilenmann, *Pax Helvetica*, pp. 99–127, 177–181, 197–200, 205–207.

[11] For evidence of the growth of an Anglicized Scottish language during the early seventeenth century see Marjorie A. Bald, "The Anglicisation of Scottish Printing," *Scottish History Review*, XXIII, 1925–1926, pp. 107–115, and "The Pioneers of Anglicised Speech in Scotland," *Scottish History Review*, XXIV, 1926–1927, pp. 179–193.

[12] Cf. the great work of Pierre Benaerts, *Les Origines de la Grand Industrie Allemande*, Paris, 1933, which also indicates the extent to which Austria was increasingly excluded from German economic life. For basic statistical data on this subject see A. Bienengräber, *Statistik des Verkehrs und Verbrauchs im Zollverein für die Jahre 1842–1864*, Berlin, 1868.

[13] An exception must be made here for Germany. In Prussia, in particular, both before and after 1871 there was little, if any, broadening of the political "decision-making" elite; the top offices in the government, the foreign services, the bureaucracy, and the army, continued to be filled with aristocrats; and political considerations continued to govern individual appointments: no Social Democrat or Linksliberaler could hope for a government career, and members of the Catholic Center Party could only if their politics were known to be reliably conservative. Only in some of the South German states, notably Baden and Württemberg, was a somewhat greater political toleration to be found. Cf. Theodor Eschenburg, "Die improvisierte Demokratie der Weimarer Republik von 1919," in *Schweizer Beiträge zur Allgemeinen Geschichte*, IX, 1951, pp. 164–165.

For an important new comparative analysis of the Prussian and Austrian political and military elite in the nineteenth century, see Nikolaus von Preradovich, *Die Führungsschichten in Österreich und Preussen (1804–1918) mit einem Ausblick bis zum Jahre 1945*, Wiesbaden, 1955.

emergence of a new type of political leader among the landowners of Virginia, such as George Washington, who retained the respect of his peers and at the same time also knew, well before the American Revolution,[14] how to gain the votes of poorer farmers and frontiersmen at the county elections in Virginia. Another example might be the shift in leadership in the Prussian elite, during the two decades before 1871, from a noble such as Edwin von Manteuffel, who was unwilling to work with the middle classes, to Bismarck, who retained the respect of his fellow aristocrats but knew how to attract and retain middle-class support.[15]

3. MOBILITY OF PERSONS

Another condition present in all our cases of successful amalgamation was the mobility of persons among the main units, at least in the politically relevant strata. It is quite possible that this condition, too, may be essential for the success of amalgamation. In any event, our cases have persuaded us that the mobility of persons among the main political units of a prospective amalgamated security-community should be given far more serious consideration than has often been the case. Full-scale mobility of persons has followed every successful amalgamated security-community in modern times immediately upon its establishment. Examples of the inter-regional mobility of persons preceding amalgamation are the cases of the American colonies,[16] the German states, and the Anglo-Scottish union. Examples of personal mobility accompanying amalgamation are the unification of Italy, and the union of England and Wales. Taken together with our finding that the free mobility of commodities and money, like other economic ties, was not essential for political amalgamation, our finding of the importance of the mobility of persons suggests that in this field of politics persons may be more important than either goods or money.

4. MULTIPLICITY AND BALANCE OF TRANSACTIONS

We also found that it was not enough for a high level of communications and transactions to exist only on one or two topics, or in one or two respects, among two or more political units if their amalgamation was to be successful. Rather it appeared that successfully amalgamated security-communities require a fairly wide range of different common functions

---

[14] Cf. Charles S. Sydnor, *Gentlemen Freeholders: Political Practices in Washington's Virginia,* Chapel Hill, 1952.

[15] Cf. Gordon A. Craig, *The Politics of the Prussian Army, 1640–1945,* Oxford, 1955, pp. 148–179.

[16] See Michael Kraus, *Intercolonial Aspects of American Culture on the Eve of the American Revolution,* New York, 1928, pp. 42ff., 51, 53, 55, 75–89, 91–102, 146, 160–161, 208.

and services, together with different institutions and organizations to carry them out. Further, they apparently require a multiplicity of ranges of common communications and transactions and their institutional counterparts. Thus the unification of Germany on the political level in 1871 had been prepared by the setting up of common institutions in regard to customs policies, to postal matters, and to the standardization of commercial laws; and beyond the sphere of politics, amalgamation had been prepared by a multiplicity of common institutions in cultural, educational, literary, scientific, and professional affairs.[17] Similarly we find in the American colonies, in the period prior to the Articles of Confederation, a wide range of mutual communications and transactions, as well as of common institutions. The latter included intercolonial church organizations, universities training ministers and physicians, and a postal service, together with ties of travel, migration, friendship, and intermarriage among important elements of the colonial elites.

Two other conditions may well turn out to be essential for the success of amalgamation, but these will have to be investigated further. The first of them is concerned with the balance in the flow of communications and transactions between the political units that are to be amalgamated, and particularly with the balance of rewards between the different participating territories. It is also concerned with the balance of initiatives that originate in these territories or groups of population, and finally with the balance of respect—or of symbols standing for respect—between these partners. In the course of studying cases of successful amalgamation, we found that it was apparently important for each of the participating territories or populations to gain some valued services or opportunities. It also seemed important that each at least sometimes take the initiative in the process, or initiate some particular phase or contribution; and that some major symbol or representative of each territory or population should be accorded explicit respect by the others. Thus it seemed significant to us that in the unification of Wales and England, and of Scotland and England, it was a family of Welsh descent (the Tudors) and the Scottish Stuart dynasty who were elevated to the English throne during important stages of the process; and that in the reunion between North

---

17 On the German postal union see Josef Karl Mayr, "Der deutschöster-reichische Postverein," in *Gesamtdeutsche Vergangenheit. Festgabe für Heinrich Ritter von Srbik*, Munich, 1938, pp. 287–295; on the German commercial code, Rudolph von Delbrück, *Lebenserinnerungen*, Leipzig, 1905, II, 90ff. and 161ff.; and Enno E. Kraehe, "Practical Politics in the German Confederation, Bismarck and the Commercial Code," *Journal of Modern History*, XXV, March 1953, pp. 13–24; on the national significance of the new academic societies see R. Hinton Thomas, *Liberalism, Nationalism, and the German Intellectuals (1822–1847): An analysis of the academic and scientific conferences of the period*, Cambridge, Eng., 1951.

and South in the United States, the name of General Robert E. Lee became a symbol of respect even in the North,[18] and that of Abraham Lincoln even in the South. In the case of the Swiss Confederation the very name of the emerging political community was taken from the small rural canton of Schwyz rather than from the more populous and powerful cantons of Bern or Zurich. Likewise, in the unifications of Germany and Italy it was the strongest participating units, Prussia and Piedmont respectively, that had to accept some of the symbols of the larger unit with which they merged, rather than insist on first place for symbols of their own prestige.

The second condition follows from the preceding one. It was not essential that the flow of rewards, of initiatives, or of respect should balance at any one moment, but it seems essential that they should balance over some period of time. Sometimes this was accomplished by alternating flows or by an interchange of group roles. Territories which received particular prestige, or material benefits, at one time might become sources of benefits for their partners at another; or initiatives might pass from one region to another; or territories whose political elites found themselves ranged with a majority on one political issue might find themselves in a minority on another, without any one particular division between majorities and minorities becoming permanent. Where this was not the case, as in the instance of the permanent minority of Irish Catholics in Protestant Great Britain under the terms of the Anglo–Irish Union, amalgamation eventually failed.[19] In contrast, most political divisions in Switzerland since amalgamation in 1848 have showed every canton, Protestant as well as Catholic, alternating between majority and minority status in accordance with political divisions in terms of agricultural versus industrial cantons, liberal versus conservative, Alpine versus lowland, and the like. This frequent interchange of group roles seems to have aided in the consolidation of the Swiss political community, but further study would be required to say to what extent, if any, this condition was essential in all the other cases of successful amalgamation.

5. MUTUAL PREDICTABILITY OF BEHAVIOR

A final condition that may be essential for the success of amalgamation may be some minimum amount of mutual predictability of behavior. Members of an amalgamated security-community—and, to a lesser extent, of a pluralistic security-community—must be able to expect from

---

[18] Buck, *op. cit.*, pp. 251, 255. However, Lincoln never became as much a national hero to the South as Lee did in the North.

[19] Similarly, the Norwegian fears of a permanent minority status in an amalgamated Norwegian-Swedish union did much to prevent full amalgamation and to destroy eventually even the partial amalgamation that had existed.

one another some dependable interlocking, interchanging, or at least compatible behavior; and they must therefore be able, at least to that extent, to predict one another's actions. Such predictions may be based on mere familiarity. In this way, the Vermonters or English-speaking Canadians may know what to expect of their French-Canadian neighbors and to what extent to rely on them, even though they do not share their folkways and culture and do not know what it feels like to be a French-Canadian. Even so, familiarity may be sufficiently effective to permit the development of an attitude of confidence and trust. (The opposite of such successful predictions of behavior are the characteristic fears of the alleged treacherousness, secretiveness, or unpredictability of "foreigners." Such fear of unpredictable "treachery" seems to be more destructive, as far as the experiences from our cases go, than do any clearcut and realistic expectations of future disagreements. Thus Norwegians and Swedes in the nineteenth century often could predict fairly well the unfavorable response which a given political suggestion from one country would find in the other; but these two peoples, while they failed to maintain even limited amalgamation, did retain sufficient mutual confidence to establish later a successful pluralistic security-community.) While familiarity appears to have contributed successfully to the growth of mutual trust in some of our cases, such as that between Scottish Highlanders and Lowlanders, and later between Scots and Englishmen, or between German, French, and Italian Swiss during much of the eighteenth century, we found in a number of our cases that mutual predictability of behavior was eventually established upon a firmer basis.

This firmer basis was the acquisition of a certain amount of common culture or of common group character or "national character." In this manner, an increasing number of Germans in the German states, of Italians in the Italian principalities, and of Americans in the American colonies, came to feel that they could understand their countrymen in the neighboring political units by expecting them, by and large, to behave much as they themselves would behave in similar situations; that is to say, they came to predict the behavior of their countrymen in neighboring political units on the basis of introspection: by looking into their own minds they could make a fairly good guess as to what their neighbors would do, so they could trust them or at least understand them, to some extent much as they would trust or understand themselves. The extent of mutual predictability of behavior, however, seems to have varied from case to case, and it also seems to have varied with the particular political elites or relevant strata concerned. That some mutual predictability of political behavior is an essential condition for an amalgamated security-community seems clear from our cases; but the extent of such predictability must remain a matter for further research.

46. APPRAISAL OF THE CASE FOR WORLD GOVERNMENT

Inis L. Claude, Jr.

M UCH OF THE LITERATURE pertaining to world government exhibits the qualities usually associated with impassioned advocacy. Typically, the major themes are as follows: The world is in a state of anarchy, which makes war inescapable; the elimination of war has become a dire necessity; this goal cannot be reliably achieved by any means other than world government; the establishment of this fundamentally new system is the necessary and probably sufficient means to world order. If the assurance of a peaceful order *with* world government is less than total, the hope for such an order *without* world government is virtually nil. Thus, world government is presented as a system—the uniquely promising system—for the management of power in international relations.

The theme of anarchy was flatly stated by Albert Einstein: "In relations among nations complete anarchy still prevails. I do not believe that we have made any real progress in this area during the last few thousand years."[1] The characterization of the present-day world as a congeries of fully sovereign states existing in wholly anarchical relationship with each other might be regarded as the product of minds that have not been exercised in any serious way in the study of international relations. In some instances, this is doubtless true. Einstein, for instance, was clearly operating outside his professional sphere when he commented on international relations, and it may well be that he was innocent of any familiarity with the history of international law and organization, or with the imperfect regulatory devices which figure in international politics, or with any of the other factors which would make a prudent scholar

From *Power and International Relations* by Inis L. Claude, Jr. (New York: 1962), pp. 210–223; 267–269; 271. © Copyright 1962 by Random House, Inc. Reprinted by permission. Footnotes have been renumbered to appear in consecutive order.

INIS L. CLAUDE, JR. (1922–   ) Edward R. Stettinius Professor of Government and Member, Center for Advanced Studies, University of Virginia. His other books include *The Changing United Nations*, (New York: Random House, 1967); *Swords into Plowshares: The Problems and Progress of International Organization*, (New York: Random House, 1956); *National Minorities: An International Problem*, (Cambridge: Harvard University Press, 1955).

[1] Otto Nathan, and Heinz Norden, eds., *Einstein on Peace* (New York: Simon and Schuster, 1960), p. 494. Cf. Norman Cousins, *In Place of Folly* (New York: Harper, 1961, pp. 56–57, 111.

hesitant to proclaim that unmitigated anarchy prevails in the twentieth-century world. Only an uninformed man could take it to be a fact that states now claim, or are acknowledged to have, a theoretically complete sovereign right to behave as they please; only an unrealistic observer could take it to be true that any state—much less, every state—possesses sovereignty in the sense that it can determine its own course, unaffected by pressures and inhibitions, necessities and influences, deriving from the international environment. Although Einstein purported to regard anarchy as the cause of the world's precarious situation, it seems likely that he inferred anarchy from his awareness of that situation. He did not establish the fact of anarchy and demonstrate the derivation of the world's troubles from that fact, but he noted the troubles and assumed that their existence indicated a state of anarchy. There is a troublesome circularity in the process of arguing that anarchy causes a global mess while treating the fact of a global mess as the basis for the assertion that anarchy prevails, but it is a process which eliminates the burdensome necessity of examining the aspects of the international system which might be relevant to the question of whether it should be described as anarchic.

In general, however, the assertion that the present condition is one of world anarchy is not to be regarded as the reflection of basic unfamiliarity with the field of international relations. It is typically the product not of ignorance, but of strong conviction. Anarchy is a symbol of peril—the peril of uncontrollable disorder; the claim that the world is anarchic is a way of saving that the world situation is intolerably dangerous. Emphasis upon the theme of anarchy expresses the belief that all the devices which have been introduced into international relations for the purpose of the management of power are fundamentally inadequate to the task; they are mere palliatives, incapable of contributing meaningfully to the ordering of international relations. Thus, champions of world government who cry anarchy frequently do so not in ignorance of existing regulatory factors but in the conviction that those factors are, and are doomed to remain, inconsequential. Anarchy is also the symbol of an insistent denial of the relativity of order in international relations; the either-or proposition, anarchy or world government, is designed to convey a sense of the urgent necessity for discarding reliance on anything short of world government and accepting the prescription for drastic transformation of the international system. The conceptual opposition between anarchy and government suggests the distinctiveness of the world government solution and the exclusiveness of its claim to efficacy. As Einstein put it, "The only real step toward world government is world government itself";[2] short of world government, one finds only varying forms of anarchy.

---

[2] Nathan and Norden, *Einstein on Peace*, p. 443.

As we have noted, a major theme in the literature of advocacy is the proposition that no solution other than the establishment of world government can prevent war. Gilbert McAllister asserts that "War has never been banished from any part of the world except when warring nations have joined together under a common parliament and a common government," and quotes Prime Minister Nehru of India to the effect that "world government must and will come, for there is no other remedy for the world's sickness."[3] This conclusion may be reached by the process of reasoning that in the absence of government we have anarchy, and that anarchy, by definition, implies disorder—persistently in potentiality and recurrently in fact. Alternatively, it may be reached by taking a sweeping glance at history and observing that multistate systems, of either the modern or earlier varieties, have never been free from war and danger of war.

However reached, the conclusion that peace is impossible without world government is a generalization that is not wholly warranted by the available evidence. The international picture is not in fact marked by such a constant and universal "war of every state against every other state" as one might be led to expect by the colorful and extravagantly Hobbesian language employed by some commentators on world politics. The record of international relations is sorry enough, and the present situation dangerous enough, without the unrealistic embroidery of "realistic" analyses which take the image of an international "jungle" too literally. In sober fact, most states coexist in reasonable harmony with most other states, most of the time; the exceptions to this passable state of affairs are vitally important, but they are exceptions nonetheless. Most obviously, states which are widely separated, not involved in intimate interrelationships and not engaged competitively in the pursuit of interests far beyond their own territories, are unlikely to find themselves in strenuous conflict with each other in a world without government. The history of relations between Peru and Belgium, or Cuba and New Zealand, would presumably make rather dull reading; within such combinations as these, the incidence of war, not the maintenance of peace, would require special explanation. In such cases, it is not to be assumed that hostilities will occur unless prevented by the subjection of the states to a common government, but that peace will prevail in the absence of exceptional disruptive factors. More importantly, one should note that settled and highly reliable relationships of a peaceful nature exist in many instances between states that are not significantly isolated from each other. One might consider

---

[3] Gilbert McAllister, ed., *World Government: The Report of the First London Parliamentary Conference, Sept. 24–29, 1951* (London: The Parliamentary Group for World Government, 1952), pp. 7, 8.

the relationships between Canada and the United States, or the United States and Britain, or Britain and Belgium. Within these pairs, we find situations of "peace without government," relationships marked by expectations of non-violence substantially higher than might be found within many national states.

As a British statesman described Anglo-American relations in 1935:

> War between us is, we hope, unthinkable. . . . I can say with confidence, after a Cabinet experience of more than a quarter of a century, that such a possibility has never entered into Great Britain's consideration of her requirements for defense and has never influenced the strength of the forces maintained by her, whether on land or sea.[4]

In the case of Norway and Sweden, Karl W. Deutsch has observed that peaceful relations between them have been more stable during the recent era of their sovereign separateness than in the earlier period of their linkage under a common government.[5] Moreover, Deutsch and his collaborators in an analysis of a number of historical *security-communities* —groupings within which dependable expectations of non-violence are to be found—concluded that the record of those characterized by the retention of political pluralism was generally more favorable than that of those which achieved amalgamation; in short, peace without government tended to be more secure in these cases than peace with government.[6]

These observations are not intended to suggest the general conclusion that anarchy is more productive of peace and order than is government. The fact that happy relationships sometimes develop between independent states does not overshadow the facts that the expectation of war somewhere within the system is endemic in the multistate pattern, that all members of the system are presently endangered by the possibilities of disorder inherent in the international situation, and that no reliable means of controlling or eliminating those possibilities has yet been devised. Proponents of the "no peace without government" line will properly point out that the instances of the formation of pluralistic security-communities are regrettably exceptional, and that we have no evidence that the process by which, say, Anglo-American relationships became dependably peaceful can be put into operation on a universal scale—or even on a Soviet-American scale. Quite so; but it might be retorted that

---

[4] Sir Austen Chamberlain, "Great Britain," in *The Foreign Policy of the Powers*, p. 76.

[5] "Problems and Prospects of Federation," Publications in the Humanities, No. 26 (Cambridge: Massachusetts Institute of Technology, 1958), p. 242.

[6] Karl W. Deutsch *et al.*, *Political Community and the North Atlantic Area* (Princeton: Princeton University Press, 1957), pp. 29–31, 65–69, 163.

the evidence for the peace-keeping efficacy of government is similarly limited. The point is simply that peace without government is a phenomenon which occurs with sufficient frequency to destroy the basis for the dogmatic assertion that human relationships cannot conceivably be ordered except by government. "Never" does not have to be invalidated by "Always"; "Sometimes" will suffice.

The assertion that peace cannot be maintained without world government is but an introduction to the theme that the latter can do the job. World government is necessary because all alternative schemes for producing order are inadequate; it is proper because it represents an adequate approach to the task. Jorge Castaneda puts the case for world government in these terms:

> Who could doubt the perfection of this ideal? History shows that when social units are broadened in order to include formerly uncontrolled and autonomous powers, and authority is centralized—as happened when the modern national state took shape, breaking with the feudal pattern—social relations are stabilized and finally order and domestic peace are achieved within the new social unit.[7]

The certainty that world government could transform chaos into order has never been more confidently expressed than in this passage from Emery Reves:

> We . . . know that, irrespective of the immediate and apparent causes of conflict among warring groups, these causes ceased producing wars and violent conflicts only through the establishment of a legal order, only when the social groups in conflict were subjected to a superior system of law, and that, *in all cases and at all times*, the effect of such a superior system of law has been the cessation of the use of violence among the previously warring groups.[8]

Many advocates of world government argue the case for its efficacy in less absolute, or at any rate more ambiguous, terms. Cousins, for instance, concedes that a world government could not guarantee peace, and describes world law as "not a hope but the *only* hope, the only chance" for the avoidance of war.[9] Einstein made occasional verbal concessions to the possibility of imperfection; at one point, he noted the risk of civil war within a unified global system, and he sometimes confined himself to the assertion that war would be *virtually* impossible.[10] More typically, how-

---

[7] *Mexico and the United Nations* (New York: Manhattan, for El Colegio de Mexico and the Carnegie Endowment for International Peace, 1958), p. 14.

[8] *The Anatomy of Peace* (New York: Harper, 1945), p. 254. Italics mine.

[9] *In Place of Folly*, pp. 90, 118. Italics in original.

[10] Nathan and Norden, *Einstein on Peace*, pp. 439, 487, 617.

ever, he suggested that "the various parts of the federation could not make war on each other," and spoke of "a supranational solution which would make national preparations for war not only unnecessary but impossible." [11] Clearly, Einstein was not plagued by any substantial doubts; with reference to the question of the avoidability of war, he wrote confidently that "There is a very simple answer. If we ourselves have the courage to decide in favor of peace, we will *have* peace." [12]

Einstein's lack of serious concern for the possibility of the failure or inadequacy of world government is fairly typical of the champions of that system. Whether because of honest conviction or the dictates of good salesmanship, they tend to dismiss this possibility as inconsequential, and to concentrate on the positive assertion that world government is the obvious solution to the problem of international disorder. When a writer asserts that "the possibility of major destructive wars cannot be ruled out until the system of sovereign self-determining states has been replaced by some form of world government," [13] he obviously means to be understood as suggesting that this possibility *can* be ruled out when the system has been thus transformed, unless he qualifies his position with a cautious "and perhaps not even then." This brand of caution is seldom a prominent feature of world government thought.

Those who enjoy the blessed assurance that the establishment of a world government would guarantee the elimination of war, or who estimate the possibility of failure as so negligible that prudent men can afford to disregard it, frequently appear to rely upon the dubious logic of a self-fulfilling definition. Government is defined as an institutional scheme characterized by authority to make rules prohibiting disorderly conduct and coercive competence to require conformity to those rules; if such a scheme were put into effect, it would, by definition, be able to prevent disorder. It is small wonder that Einstein could assert that "real security in the world can only come through the creation of a supranational body, a government of the world with powers adequate to preserve the peace." [14] Who can doubt that an institution capable of keeping the peace could keep the peace? In the same vein, a leader of the United World Federalists asserted in 1948 that "There can be no peace within or between nations unless there are both established laws, and the certain knowledge that these laws can be promptly and decisively enforced." [15]

---

[11] *Ibid.*, pp. 418, 487.

[12] *Ibid.*, p. 528. Italics in original.

[13] Geoffrey Sawer in Victor H. Wallace, ed., *Paths to Peace* (Melbourne, Australia: Melbourne University Press, 1959), p. 385.

[14] Nathan and Norden, *op. cit.*, p. 459.

[15] Cord Meyer, Jr., statement reproduced in Johnsen, *Federal World Government*, p. 91.

Reves declares that "Peace is law. It is order. It is government." [16] If government is defined as "that which produces peace," the creation of a world government is unchallengeably a promising method of preventing war.

Much contemporary thought on the problem of preventing war is characterized by this tendency to develop solutions-by-definition. If balance of power is defined as a system which produces equilibrium, and equilibrium is defined as a power configuration which effectively inhibits aggression, the problem seems to have been solved. If collective security is defined as a system which guarantees that a preponderance of power will confront any aggressor, and it is assumed that no state can prevail against such a massing of power, the effectiveness of the system can be regarded as self-evident. The world government school of thought tends to focus on disarmament, law, and enforcement of law, which can be taken to mean that states are rendered incapable of fighting, are forbidden to fight, and are compelled not to fight; if these things are effectively accomplished, there would seem to be little room for doubt that states will not fight.

Government, of course, is not a mere abstract concept, a hypothetical system the merits of which are to be determined by logical derivation from its definition. It is a social institution with which mankind has had considerable experience; it has a long and extensive record of performance, available for examination and evaluation. Advocates of world government are, naturally, aware of this fact, and they do not by any means base their case entirely upon the demonstration that an institution which is by definition capable of keeping order must be judged suitable for that task. In many instances, the argument is explicitly grounded upon a favorable appraisal of the record of government as an order-keeping institution within national societies, followed by the assumption or reasoned contention that government would—or, more modestly, might —function equally well within a globally organized society. In some cases, reference is made to the record of government in general; thus, "An area of government is an area of peace. You are familiar with the keeping of peace in the areas of your city, your state and your nation. A world government is obviously the path to world peace—if government is somehow possible over so great an area." [17] Perhaps more frequently, attention is concentrated upon the federal type of governmental system, with the suggestion that the successes of small-scale federalism could be

---

[16] *The Anatomy of Peace,* p. 150.

[17] Stewart Boal, in the Preface to Everett Lee Millard, *Freedom in a Federal World,* 2nd ed. (New York: Oceana, 1961), p. 9. See also the quotations from Castaneda and Reves, p. 216, above.

duplicated if it were applied on a larger scale: "The task of our generation is to extend to a larger area the basic federal union principles that have already stood the test of time." [18] Not surprisingly, tributes to the efficacy of federalism are usually inspired by a favorable appraisal of the American experience. Everett Lee Millard, for instance, is explicit on this point:

> The formation of a federal union among the American colonies led to their subsequent freedom, peace and prosperity. Therefore, we may reason, a federal union among the world's nations, if it can be made possible, will permit all humanity to thrive in liberty and peace.[19]

Citation of the record of government within national societies as the basis for assurance that a world government could be relied upon to maintain global peace and order is a very dangerous expedient. Aside from the obvious point that macro-government would not necessarily function as effectively as micro-government, the hard fact is that the record does not support the generalization that the establishment of government, within a social unit of whatever dimensions, infallibly brings about a highly dependable state of peace and order.

The ominous phrase *civil war* serves as only the most dramatic symbol of the fallibility of government as an instrument of social order. The student of history and contemporary world politics will discover numerous manifestations of the incapacity of government to guarantee peace; outcroppings of uncontrolled violence are a familiar phenomenon in human societies equipped with governmental mechanisms. Government, indeed, has a very mixed and spotty record in this respect. The glorification of government as a near-panacea for the ill of social disorder may come easily to Americans, whose civil war has faded into a romantic historical memory and who are citizens of one of that small band of happy countries in which domestic order has become a normal and highly dependable expectation. It is likely to seem much less plausible to the unfortunately numerous "peoples whose country is the frequent scene of revolution and domestic violence or suffers the cruel terrors of tyranny; to them 'civil society,' or 'order under government,' if it is experienced at all, possesses most of the objectionable features we attribute to international anarchy." [20] The Latin American region is a notable example of an

---

18 "Publius II" (Owen J. Roberts, John F. Schmidt, and Clarence K. Streit), *The New Federalist* (New York: Harper, 1950), p. 3. This volume looks toward the creation of an Atlantic Union, not a world federation.

19 *Freedom in a Federal World*, p. 43.

20 Arnold Wolfers and Lawrence W. Martin, eds., *The Anglo-American Tradition in Foreign Affairs* (New Haven: Yale University Press, 1956), Introduction, pp. xv–xvi.

area in which government has worked badly as an orderkeeping institution: "In many Latin-American countries military rebellion is a recognized mode of carrying on political conflict." [21] In Bolivia, for instance, it has been estimated that 178 "revolutions or violent, illegal changes of regime" occurred between 1825 and 1952.[22]

Given the elementary facts about the record of government, historical and contemporary, it becomes impossible to conceive how Emery Reves could assert that the establishment of "a superior system of law" has produced, "in all cases and at all times," the elimination of the use of violence among previously discordant groups.[23] It becomes difficult, moreover, to understand the general tendency of champions of world government to minimize the significance of the civil war problem even when they concede its existence.

Henry Usborne states that, in principle, "War is eliminated by merging several states into one." He admits the possibility of civil war, but contends that "this does not affect the argument. Civil war is not inherent in the state; but war is inherent in interstate relations if those relations are based on national sovereignty." [24] Another commentator states the conclusion that "only world government can prevent war in the future. Even this will not exclude the possibility of serious civil war, but civil wars are less probable than international wars." [25]

It must be retorted that while civil war is not inherent in an abstract definition of the governed state, or in an idealized image of the state, it is clearly inherent in the actual operating experience of real states. The historical slate cannot be wiped clear of civil wars by the simple device of asserting that, according to one's definition of the state, they should not have occurred. The judgment that civil wars are relatively improbable is subject to serious challenge. As Philip C. Jessup has observed, "Civil war, revolution, mob violence are more frequent manifestations of man's unruly and still savage will than are wars between states." [26] Moreover, such civil wars as those which have occurred in Spain and China certainly

---

[21] Raymond W. Mack and Richard C. Snyder, "The Analysis of Social Conflict—Toward an Overview and Synthesis," *Journal of Conflict Resolution*, June 1957, Vol. 1, p. 226.

[22] *The New York Times* editorial, Oct. 2, 1958.

[23] Cited above, fn. 8.

[24] "World Federal Government as a Means of Maintaining Peace," in Wallace, *Paths to Peace*, pp. 359, 360.

[25] Excerpt from Harold C. Urey, in Julia E. Johnsen, *Federal World Government* (New York: Wilson, 1948), p. 96.

[26] *A Modern Law of Nations* (New York: Macmillan, 1950), p. 189. Cf. Hans J. Morgenthau, *Scientific Man vs. Power Politics* (Chicago: University of Chicago Press, 1946), p. 49.

deserve a place in any list of the most significant events in world affairs of the last generation.

At the present time, the list of states that an informed student could describe as virtually immune from the threat of large-scale domestic violence is certainly shorter than the list of those in which such disorder must be ranked as an easily conceivable or highly probable occurrence. Moreover, a world government might have a relatively high susceptibility to organized revolt, since it would encompass previously independent states that would undoubtedly retain a considerable capacity to function as bases and organizing centers for dissident movements.[27]

This analysis should not be taken as inviting the conclusion that government is a device of negligible importance in the human quest for social order. Clearly, this is not the case. But, equally, the tactic of creating a government is not tantamount to the waving of a magic wand which dispels the problem of disorderliness. Peace without government is, despite dogmatic denials, sometimes possible; war with government is, despite doctrinaire assurances, always possible. Wars sometimes occur in the absence of government, in the exercise of the freedom from higher social discipline which prevails in that situation. Wars also occur in the presence of government, in protest against and defiance of the central control which is attempted.[28] In short, the concept of world government deserves not to be seized upon as the one and only solution, the obviously effective solution, to the problem of the management of power in international relations, but to be treated as a theoretical approach promising enough to warrant careful consideration.

. . .

One of the lessons of governmental experience is that coercion can seldom be usefully invoked against significant collectivities which exhibit a determination to defend their interests, as they conceive them, against the public authority. The order-keeping function of government is not fulfilled by the winning of a civil war, but by its prevention. If groups cannot be coerced without the disruption of the order which government exists to maintain, it does not follow that the alternative tactic of coercing individuals should be adopted. What follows is rather that the difficult task of ordering group relationships by political means should be attempted.

Clearly, governments are not always able to carry out this task; the

---

[27] See Vernon Van Dyke, *International Politics* (New York: Appleton-Century-Crofts, 1957), p. 421.

[28] See the excerpt from I. Beverly Lake, in Johnsen, *Federal World Government*, p. 217.

incidence of civil wars and analogous disorders testifies to this fact. The establishment of government does not automatically create a social situation in which group conflicts are subject to political accommodation, nor does it necessarily carry with it the development of the institutions and techniques best suited to the exploitation of such adjustment potential as the society may exhibit. But if government does not make order through political adjustment easy or certain, neither does it provide a substitute. Governments maintain social order by presiding over a successful political process, or not at all.

To some degree, this general conception of the operation of government may seem inapplicable to modern totalitarian governments. It is true that totalitarian regimes undertake to atomize their societies, breaking down the collectivities which are deemed likely to challenge the monolithic quality of the state, and to fasten a tyranny of coercion upon their peoples. In some instances, they have succeeded to a degree which is appalling to men who value human freedom, but the evidence suggests that they have never wholly succeeded in this infamous enterprise. Moreover, such regimes are not wholly reliant upon this technique; some trace of political methods of managing social forces always remains in their operations. In any case, advocates of world government are not motivated by the hope of reproducing the totalitarian pattern on a global scale. It would indeed be ironical if men passionately devoted to the rule of law should define their ideal pattern of order-keeping as one which is realized only, or best, in totalitarian systems. The sort of national government which champions of world government propose to emulate is best exemplified by liberal regimes which depend primarily upon processes of political adjustment for maintaining social order.

I would conclude that theorists of world government are not mistaken in their insistence that one should look to domestic governmental experience for clues as to the most promising means for achieving world order, but that they tend to misread the lessons of that experience. In some instances, they treat the domestic problem of crime prevention as comparable to the international problem of war, and draw from national experience the conclusion that the central function of a world government would be to maintain order by enforcing legal restrictions upon individual behavior. In other instances, they note the domestic problem of coping with dissident groups, acknowledge its comparability to the problem of dealing with aggressive states, and suggest that the governmental pattern requires that a central authority be equipped with adequate military force to coerce any possible rebellion within the larger society.

In contrast, I would argue that the prevention of civil war is the function of national government most relevant to the problem of ordering international relations, that governments cannot and do not perform this function by relying primarily upon either police action against individuals or military action against significant segments of their societies, and that governments succeed in this vitally important task only when they are able to operate an effective system of political accommodation.

. . .

In the final analysis, it appears that the theory of world government does not *answer* the question of how the world can be saved from catastrophic international conflict. Rather, it helps us to *restate* the question: How can the world achieve the degree of assurance that inter-group conflicts will be resolved or contained by political rather than violent means that has been achieved in the most effectively governed states? This is a valuable and provocative restatement of the question—but it ought not to be mistaken for a definitive answer.

SELECTED BIBLIOGRAPHY

PART IX

The Management of Power

Barker, C. A. (ed.), *Problems of World Disarmament*. Boston: Houghton Mifflin, 1963.

Bechhoefer, Bernard G., *Postwar Negotiations for Arms Control*. Washington: The Brookings Institution, 1961.

Brennan, Donald G., and George Braziller, *Arms Control, Disarmament, and National Security*. New York: George Braziller, 1961.

Brinton, Crane, *From Many One*. Cambridge: Harvard University Press, 1948.

Buchan, Alastair (ed.), *A World of Nuclear Powers?* Englewood Cliffs: Prentice-Hall, 1966.

Buehrig, Edward H., *Woodrow Wilson and the Balance of Power*. Bloomington: Indiana University Press, 1955.

Carleton, William G., "Ideology or Balance of Power?" *Yale Review*. June 1947.

Clark, Grenville, and Louis B. Sohn, *World Peace through World Law*. Cambridge: Harvard University Press, 1958.

Claude, Inis L., Jr., *Power and International Relations*. New York: Random House, 1962.

Crabb, Cecil V., Jr., *The Elephants and the Grass: A Study of Nonalignment.* New York: Praeger, 1965.

Craig, G. A., and Gilbert Felix, *The Diplomats, 1919–1939.* Princeton: Princeton University Press, 1953.

de Callieres, Francois, *On the Manner of Negotiating with Princes.* Boston: Houghton Mifflin, 1919.

Dennett, R., and J. Johnson (eds.), *Negotiating with the Russians.* Boston: World Peace Foundation, 1951.

Deutsch, Karl W., *Political Community at the International Level.* New York: Doubleday, 1954.

Dinerstein, Herbert S., "The Transformation of Alliance Systems," *American Political Science Review,* September 1965.

Dougherty, James E., *Arms Control and Disarmament: The Critical Issues.* Washington: The Center for Strategic Studies, 1966.

—— (ed.), with John F. Lehman, Jr., *The Prospects for Arms Control.* New York: Macfadden-Bartell, 1965.

Etzioni, Amitai, *Political Unification.* New York: Holt, Rinehart, and Winston, 1965.

Finklestein, Marina and Lawrence S. (eds.), *Collective Security.* San Francisco: Chandler Publishing Company, 1966.

Gardner, Richard N., *In Pursuit of World Order.* New York: Praeger, 1966.

Goodman, Elliot R., *The Soviet Design for a World State.* New York: Columbia University Press, 1960.

Gulick, Edward V., *Europe's Classical Balance of Power.* Ithaca: Cornell University Press, 1955.

Haas, Ernst B., *Beyond the Nation-State.* Stanford: Stanford University Press, 1964.

——, "The Balance of Power as a Guide to Policy-making," *Journal of Politics.* August 1953.

——, *The Uniting of Europe.* Stanford: Stanford University Press, 1957.

——, "The Uniting of Europe and the Uniting of Latin America," *Journal of Common Market Studies.* June 1967.

Hankey, Maurice, *Diplomacy by Conference.* New York: G. P. Putnam, 1946.

Hassell, Arthur, *The Balance of Power, 1715–1789.* New York: Macmillan, 1914.

Herz, John H., *International Politics in the Atomic Age.* New York: Columbia University Press, 1959.

Hume, David, "Of the Balance of Power." In David Hume, *Essays and Treatises on Several Subjects*. Edinburgh: Bell and Bradfute, 1825.

Ikle, Fred Charles, *How Nations Negotiate*. New York: Harper and Row, 1964.

International Political Communities: An Anthology. New York: Doubleday and Company, Inc., 1966.

Kissinger, Henry A., *The Troubled Partnership*. New York: Doubleday, 1966.

Mangone, Gerard J., *The Idea and Practice of World Government*. New York: Columbia University Press, 1951.

Martin, Lawrence W. (ed.), *Neutralism and Non-Alignment*. New York: Praeger, 1962.

McCamy, James L., *Conduct of the New Diplomacy*. New York: Harper and Row, 1964.

Melman, Seymour (ed.), *Inspection for Disarmament*. New York: Columbia University Press, 1958.

Mitrany, David, *A Working Peace System*. Chicago: Quadrangle Books, 1966. London: Royal Institute of International Affairs, 1943.

Nicolson, Harold, "Diplomacy Then and Now," *Foreign Affairs*. October 1961.

——, *The Evolution of Diplomatic Method*. New York: Macmillan, 1955.

Niebuhr, Reinhold, "The Illusion of World Government," *Bulletin of the Atomic Scientists*. October 1949.

Pfaltzgraff, Robert L., Jr., "Alternative Designs for the Atlantic Alliance," ORBIS. Summer 1965.

Polanyi, Karl, *The Great Transformation*. Toronto: Farrar and Rinehart, Inc., 1944.

Power, Paul F. (ed.), *Neutralism and Disengagement*. New York: Charles Scribner's Sons, 1964.

Reinsch, Paul S., *Secret Diplomacy*. New York: Harcourt, Brace, and Company, 1922.

Riker, William H., *The Theory of Political Coalitions*. New Haven: Yale University Press, 1962.

Rossow, Robert, "The Professionalization of the New Diplomacy," *World Politics*, July 1962.

Schelling, Thomas C., and Morton H. Halperin, *Strategy and Arms Control*. New York: The Twentieth Century Fund, 1961.

Schuman, Frederick L., *The Commonwealth of Man*. New York: Knopf, 1952.

Snyder, Glenn H., "Balance of Power in the Missile Age," *Journal of International Affairs*. Vol. 14, No. 1 (1960).

Spanier, John W., and Joseph L. Nogee, *The Politics of Disarmament: A Study of Soviet-American Gamesmanship*. New York, Praeger, 1962.

Strausz-Hupé, Robert, James E. Dougherty, and William R. Kintner, *Building the Atlantic World*. New York: Harper, 1963.

Tannenbaum, Frank, "The Balance of Power in Society," *Political Science Quarterly*. December 1946.

Thayer, Charles, *Diplomat*. New York: Harper and Brothers, 1959.

Thompson, Kenneth W., "The New Diplomacy and the Quest for Peace," *International Organization*. Summer 1965.

Vagts, Alfred, "The Balance of Power: Growth of an Idea," *World Politics*. October 1948.

Wight, Martin, *Power Politics*. London: Royal Institute of International Affairs, 1946.

Wolfers, Arnold *et al.*, *The United States in a Disarmed World*. Baltimore: Johns Hopkins Press, 1966.

Index of Names

Index of Subjects